MEDALLION EDITION · AMERICA READS

QUESTION and FORM in Literature

MEDALLION EDITION · AMERICA READS

PURPOSE in Literature
Edmund J. Farrell
Ruth S. Cohen
L. Jane Christensen
H. Keith Wright

LITERATURE and LIFE
Helen McDonnell
Ruth S. Cohen
Thomas Gage
Alan L. Madsen

ARRANGEMENT in Literature
Edmund J. Farrell
Ouida H. Clapp
James L. Pierce
Raymond J. Rodrigues

QUESTION and FORM in Literature
James E. Miller, Jr.
Roseann Dueñas Gonzalez
Nancy C. Millett

UNITED STATES in Literature
James E. Miller, Jr.
Carlota Cárdenas de Dwyer
Robert Hayden
Russell J. Hogan
Kerry M. Wood

ENGLAND in Literature
Helen McDonnell
Neil E. Nakadate
John Pfordresher
Thomas E. Shoemate

MEDALLION EDITION • AMERICA READS

QUESTION and FORM in Literature

James E. Miller, Jr.
Roseann Dueñas Gonzalez
Nancy C. Millett

Scott, Foresman and Company

Editorial Offices: Glenview, Illinois

Regional Sales Offices: Palo Alto, California • Tucker, Georgia • Glenview, Illinois • Oakland, New Jersey • Dallas, Texas

JAMES E. MILLER, JR. Department Chairman and Professor of English, University of Chicago. Fulbright Lecturer in Naples and Rome, 1958–1959, and in Kyoto, Japan, 1968. Guggenheim Fellow, 1969–1970. President, National Council of Teachers of English, 1970. Chairman, Commission on Literature, NCTE, 1975. Author of *Quests Surd and Absurd: Essays in American Literature; Theory of Fiction: Henry James; Word, Self, Reality: The Rhetoric of Imagination;* and *T. S. Eliot's Personal Wasteland.*

ROSEANN DUEÑAS GONZALEZ Assistant Professor of English and Assistant Director of Freshman English, University of Arizona. Member, National Council of Teachers of English Minority Affairs Advisory Board. Consultant, Tucson School District No. 1, Bilingual Education Project, 1975–1977. Ongoing Consultant, Tucson School District No. 1, Language Arts 7–12. President, Arizona English Teachers Association, 1977–1978. Vice-President, Chicano Teachers of English, 1974–1976. Member of the Conference on College Composition and Communication Executive Board.

NANCY C. MILLETT Associate Professor of Secondary Education and Chairman of the Department of Instructional Services, Wichita State University. Coauthor of *How to Read a Poem* and *How to Read a Short Story.* Author of articles on the teaching of literature and composition. Formerly teacher at the University of Rochester, Rochester, New York; the University of Wichita, Wichita, Kansas; and Wichita High School East.

ISBN: 0-673-12933-0

Copyright © 1982, 1979,
Scott, Foresman and Company, Glenview, Illinois.
All Rights Reserved.
Printed in the United States of America.

12345678910–RRW–9089888786858483828l

Contents

Unit 1

Turnabout

Unit 2

The
Short Story

Unit 3

Modern Drama

Unit 4

Poetry

Unit 5

Greek Drama

Unit 6

Prose Forms

Unit 7

Shakespearean Drama

Unit 8

The Novella

Handbook of Literary Terms

QUESTION and FORM in Literature

UNIT
1

Turnabout

Life is full of twists, turns, zigs, zags, swerves, shifts—and *turnabouts.*
We are often looking ahead when we should be looking behind,
or looking down when we should be looking up. And we are sometimes
gazing into the light when we should be peering into the dark. . . .

See **FORESHADOWING** Handbook of Literary Terms

The Monkey's Paw

W. W. Jacobs

Without, the night was cold and wet, but in the small parlor of Lakesnam Villa the blinds were drawn and the fire burned brightly. Father and son were at chess, the former, who possessed ideas about the game involving radical changes, putting his king into such sharp and unnecessary perils that it even provoked comment from the white-haired old lady knitting placidly by the fire.

"Hark at the wind," said Mr. White, who, having seen a fatal mistake after it was too late, was amiably desirous of preventing his son from seeing it.

"I'm listening," said the latter, grimly surveying the board as he stretched out his hand. "Check."[1]

"I should hardly think that he'd come tonight," said his father, with his hand poised over the board.

"Mate," replied the son.

"That's the worst of living so far out," bawled Mr. White, with sudden and unlooked-for violence; "of all the beastly, slushy, out-of-the-way places to live in, this is the worst. Pathway's a bog, and the road's a torrent. I don't know what people are thinking about. I suppose because only two houses on the road are let, they think it doesn't matter."

"Never mind, dear," said his wife soothingly; "perhaps you'll win the next one."

Mr. White looked up sharply, just in time to intercept a knowing glance between mother and son. The words died away on his lips, and he had a guilty grin in his thin gray beard.

"There he is," said Herbert White, as the gate banged to loudly and heavy footsteps came toward the door.

The old man rose with hospitable haste, and opening the door, was heard condoling with the new arrival. The new arrival also condoled with

From THE LADY OF THE BARGE by W. W. Jacobs. Reprinted by permission of The Society of Authors as the literary representative of the Estate of W. W. Jacobs.

1. **Check,** a call made by a chess player to warn his opponent that the opponent's king piece is in danger and must be moved. When a chess player makes the winning move that will capture his opponent's king, he calls "Mate."

himself, so that Mrs. White said "Tut, tut!" and coughed gently as her husband entered the room, followed by a tall burly man, beady of eye and rubicund of visage.

"Sergeant-Major Morris," he said, introducing him.

The sergeant-major shook hands, and, taking the proffered seat by the fire, watched contentedly while his host got out whiskey and tumblers and stood a small copper kettle on the fire.

At the third glass his eyes got brighter, and he began to talk, the little family circle regarding with eager interest this visitor from distant parts, as he squared his broad shoulders in the chair and spoke of strange scenes and doughty deeds, of wars and plagues and strange peoples.

"Twenty-one years of it," said Mr. White, nodding at his wife and son. "When he went away he was a slip of a youth in the warehouse. Now look at him."

"He don't look to have taken much harm," said Mrs. White politely.

"I'd like to go to India myself," said the old man, "just to look round a bit, you know."

"Better where you are," said the sergeant-major, shaking his head. He put down the empty glass and, sighing softly, shook it again.

"I should like to see those old temples and fakirs and jugglers," said the old man. "What was that you started telling me the other day about a monkey's paw or something, Morris?"

"Nothing," said the soldier hastily. "Leastways, nothing worth hearing."

"Monkey's paw?" said Mrs. White curiously.

"Well, it's just a bit of what you might call magic, perhaps," said the sergeant-major offhandedly.

His three listeners leaned forward eagerly. The visitor absent-mindedly put his empty glass to his lips and then set it down again. His host filled it for him.

"To look at," said the sergeant-major, fumbling in his pocket, "it's just an ordinary little paw, dried to a mummy."

He took something out of his pocket and proffered it. Mrs. White drew back with a grimace, but her son, taking it, examined it curiously.

"And what is there special about it?" inquired Mr. White, as he took it from his son and, having examined it, placed it upon the table.

"It had a spell put on it by an old fakir," said the sergeant-major, "a very holy man. He wanted to show that fate ruled people's lives, and that those who interfered with it did so to their sorrow. He put a spell on it so that three separate men could each have three wishes from it."

His manner was so impressive that his hearers were conscious that their light laughter jarred somewhat.

"Well, why don't you have three, sir?" said Herbert White cleverly.

The soldier regarded him in the way that middle age is wont to regard presumptuous youth. "I have," he said quietly, and his blotchy face whitened.

"And did you really have the three wishes granted?" asked Mrs. White.

"I did," said the sergeant-major, and his glass tapped against his strong teeth.

"And has anybody else wished?" inquired the old lady.

"The first man had his three wishes, yes," was the reply. "I don't know what the first two were, but the third was for death. That's how I got the paw."

His tones were so grave that a hush fell upon the group.

"If you've had your three wishes, it's no good to you now, then, Morris," said the old man at last. "What do you keep it for?"

The soldier shook his head. "Fancy, I suppose," he said slowly. "I did have some idea of selling it, but I don't think I will. It has caused enough mischief already. Besides, people won't buy. They think it's a fairy tale, some of them, and those who do think anything of it want to try it first and pay me afterward."

"If you could have another three wishes," said the old man, eyeing him keenly, "would you have them?"

"I don't know," said the other. "I don't know."

He took the paw, and dangling it between his front finger and thumb, suddenly threw it upon the fire. White, with a slight cry, stooped down and snatched it off.

"Better let it burn," said the soldier solemnly.

"If you don't want it, Morris," said the old man, "give it to me."

"I won't," said his friend doggedly. "I threw it on the fire. If you keep it, don't blame me for what happens. Pitch it on the fire again, like a sensible man."

The other shook his head and examined his new possession closely. "How do you do it?" he inquired.

"Hold it up in your right hand and wish aloud," said the sergeant-major, "but I warn you of the consequences."

"Sounds like the *Arabian Nights*,"[2] said Mrs. White, as she rose and began to set the supper. "Don't you think you might wish for four pairs of hands for me?"

Her husband drew the talisman from his pocket and then all three burst into laughter as the sergeant-major, with a look of alarm on his face, caught him by the arm.

"If you must wish," he said gruffly, "wish for something sensible."

Mr. White dropped it back into his pocket, and placing chairs, motioned his friend to the table. In the business of supper the talisman was partly forgotten, and afterward the three sat listening in an enthralled fashion to a second installment of the soldier's adventures in India.

"If the tale about the monkey's paw is not more truthful than those he has been telling us," said Herbert, as the door closed behind their guest, just in time for him to catch the last train, "we shan't make much out of it."

---

2. *the Arabian Nights,* a collection of old tales from Arabia, Persia, and India, dating from the tenth century.

"Did you give him anything for it, Father?" inquired Mrs. White, regarding her husband closely.

"A trifle," said he, coloring slightly. "He didn't want it, but I made him take it. And he pressed me again to throw it away."

"Likely," said Herbert, with pretended horror. "Why, we're going to be rich, and famous, and happy. Wish to be an emperor, Father, to begin with; then you can't be henpecked."

He darted round the table, pursued by the maligned Mrs. White armed with an antimacassar.

Mr. White took the paw from his pocket and eyed it dubiously. "I don't know what to wish for, and that's a fact," he said slowly. "It seems to me I've got all I want."

"If you only cleared the house,[3] you'd be quite happy, wouldn't you?" said Herbert, with his hand on his shoulder. "Well, wish for two hundred pounds,[4] then; that'll just do it."

His father, smiling shamefacedly at his own credulity, held up the talisman, as his son, with a solemn face somewhat marred by a wink at his mother, sat down at the piano and struck a few impressive chords.

"I wish for two hundred pounds," said the old man distinctly.

A fine crash from the piano greeted the words, interrupted by a shuddering cry from the old man. His wife and son ran toward him.

"It moved," he cried, with a glance of disgust at the object as it lay on the floor. "As I wished it twisted in my hands like a snake."

"Well, I don't see the money," said his son, as he picked it up and placed it on the table, "and I bet I never shall."

"It must have been your fancy, Father," said his wife, regarding him anxiously.

He shook his head. "Never mind, though; there's no harm done, but it gave me a shock all the same."

They sat down by the fire again while the two men finished their pipes. Outside, the wind was higher than ever, and the old man started nervously at the sound of a door banging upstairs. A silence unusual and depressing settled upon all three, which lasted until the old couple rose to retire for the night.

"I expect you'll find the cash tied up in a big bag in the middle of your bed," said Herbert, as he bade them good night, "and something horrible squatting up on top of the wardrobe watching you as you pocket your ill-gotten gains."

In the brightness of the wintry sun next morning as it streamed over the breakfast table Herbert laughed at his fears. There was an air of prosaic wholesomeness about the room which it had lacked on the previous night, and the dirty, shriveled little paw was pitched on the sideboard with a carelessness which betokened no great belief in its virtues.

"I suppose all old soldiers are the same," said Mrs. White. "The idea of our listening to such nonsense! How could wishes be granted in these days? And if they could, how could two hundred pounds hurt you, Father?"

"Might drop on his head from the sky," said the frivolous Herbert.

"Morris said the things happened so naturally," said his father, "that you might if you so wished attribute it to coincidence."

"Well, don't break into the money before I come back," said Herbert, as he rose from the table. "I'm afraid it'll turn you into a mean, avaricious man, and we shall have to disown you."

His mother laughed, and following him to the door, watched him down the road, and returning to the breakfast table, was very happy at the expense of her husband's credulity. All of which did not prevent her from scurrying to the door at the postman's knock, nor prevent her from referring somewhat shortly to retired sergeant-majors of bibulous habits when she found that the post brought a tailor's bill.

"Herbert will have some more of his funny

---

3. **cleared the house,** paid the money that was still owing on the purchase of the house.

4. **two hundred pounds.** At the time of the story, this amount in English money was worth about a thousand dollars.

remarks, I expect, when he comes home," she said as they sat at dinner.

"I dare say," said Mr. White, pouring himself out some beer; "but for all that, the thing moved in my hand; that I'll swear to."

"You thought it did," said the old lady soothingly.

"I say it did," replied the other. "There was no thought about it; I had just—What's the matter?"

His wife made no reply. She was watching the mysterious movements of a man outside, who, peering in an undecided fashion at the house, appeared to be trying to make up his mind to enter. In mental connection with the two hundred pounds, she noticed that the stranger was well dressed and wore a silk hat of glossy newness. Three times he paused at the gate and then walked on again. The fourth time he stood with his hand upon it, and then with sudden resolution flung it open and walked up the path. Mrs. White at the same moment placed her hands behind her and hurriedly unfastening the strings of her apron, put that useful article of apparel beneath the cushion of her chair.

She brought the stranger, who seemed ill at ease, into the room. He gazed furtively at Mrs. White, and listened in a preoccupied fashion as the old lady apologized for the appearance of the room, and her husband's coat, a garment which he usually reserved for the garden. She then waited as patiently as her sex would permit for him to broach his business, but he was at first strangely silent.

"I—was asked to call," he said at last, and stooped and picked a piece of cotton from his trousers. "I come from Maw and Meggins."

The old lady started. "Is anything the matter?" she asked breathlessly. "Has anything happened to Herbert? What is it? What is it?"

Her husband interposed. "There, there, Mother," he said hastily. "Sit down, and don't jump to conclusions. You've not brought bad news, I'm sure, sir," and he eyed the other wistfully.

"I'm sorry——" began the visitor.

"Is he hurt?" demanded the mother.

The visitor bowed in assent. "Badly hurt," he said quietly, "but he is not in any pain."

"Oh, thank God!" said the old woman, clasping her hands. "Thank God for that! Thank——"

She broke off suddenly as the sinister meaning of the assurance dawned upon her and she saw the awful confirmation of her fears in the other's averted face. She caught her breath, and turning to her slower-witted husband, laid her trembling old hand upon his. There was a long silence.

"He was caught in the machinery," said the visitor at length, in a low voice.

"Caught in the machinery," repeated Mr. White, in a dazed fashion, "yes."

He sat staring blankly out of the window, and taking his wife's hand between his own, pressed it as he had been wont to do in their old courting days nearly forty years before.

"He was the only one left to us," he said, turning gently to the visitor. "It is hard."

The other coughed, and rising, walked slowly to the window. "The firm wished me to convey their sincere sympathy with you in your great loss," he said, without looking round. "I beg that you will understand I am only their servant and merely obeying orders."

There was no reply; the old woman's face was white, her eyes staring, and her breath inaudible; on the husband's face was a look such as his friend the sergeant might have carried into his first action.

"I was to say that Maw and Meggins disclaim all responsibility," continued the other. "They admit no liability at all, but in consideration of your son's services they wish to present you with a certain sum as compensation."

Mr. White dropped his wife's hand, and rising to his feet, gazed with a look of horror at his visitor. His dry lips shaped the words, "How much?"

"Two hundred pounds," was the answer.

Unconscious of his wife's shriek, the old man smiled faintly, put out his hands like a sightless man, and dropped, a senseless heap, to the floor.

In the huge new cemetery, some two miles distant, the old people buried their dead, and came back to a house steeped in shadow and silence. It was all over so quickly that at first they could hardly realize it and remained in a state of expectation as though of something else to happen—something else which was to lighten this load, too heavy for old hearts to bear. But the days passed, and expectation gave place to resignation—the hopeless resignation of the old, sometimes miscalled apathy. Sometimes they hardly exchanged a word, for now they had nothing to talk about, and their days were long to weariness.

It was about a week after that that the old man, waking suddenly in the night, stretched out his hand and found himself alone. The room was in darkness, and the sound of subdued weeping came from the window. He raised himself in bed and listened.

"Come back," he said tenderly. "You will be cold."

"It is colder for my son," said the old woman and wept afresh.

The sound of her sobs died away on his ears. The bed was warm, and his eyes heavy with sleep. He dozed fitfully, and then slept until a sudden wild cry from his wife awoke him with a start.

"The monkey's paw!" she cried wildly. "The monkey's paw!"

He started up in alarm. "Where? Where is it? What's the matter?"

She came stumbling across the room toward him. "I want it," she said quietly. "You've not destroyed it?"

"It's in the parlor, on the bracket," he replied, marveling. "Why?"

She cried and laughed together, and bending over, kissed his cheek.

"I only just thought of it," she said hysterically. "Why didn't I think of it before? Why didn't you think of it?"

"Think of what?" he questioned.

"The other two wishes," she replied rapidly. "We've only had one."

"Was not that enough?" he demanded fiercely.

"No," she cried triumphantly; "we'll have one more. Go down and get it quickly, and wish our boy alive again."

The man sat up in bed and flung the bedclothes from his quaking limbs. "You are mad!" he cried, aghast.

"Get it," she panted; "get it quickly, and wish—Oh, my boy, my boy!"

Her husband struck a match and lit the candle. "Get back to bed," he said unsteadily. "You don't know what you are saying."

"We had the first wish granted," said the old woman feverishly; "why not the second?"

"A coincidence," stammered the old man.

"Go and get it and wish," cried the old woman, and dragged him toward the door.

He went down in the darkness, and felt his way to the parlor, and then to the mantelpiece. The talisman was in its place, and a horrible fear that the unspoken wish might bring his mutilated son before him ere he could escape from the room seized upon him, and he caught his breath as he found that he had lost the direction of the door. His brow cold with sweat, he felt his way round the table, and groped along the wall until he found himself in the small passage with the unwholesome thing in his hand.

Even his wife's face seemed changed as he entered the room. It was white and expectant, and to his fears seemed to have an unnatural look upon it. He was afraid of her.

"Wish!" she cried, in a strong voice.

"It is foolish and wicked," he faltered.

"Wish!" repeated his wife.

He raised his hand. "I wish my son alive again."

The talisman fell to the floor, and he regarded

it shudderingly. Then he sank trembling into a chair as the old woman, with burning eyes, walked to the window and raised the blind.

He sat until he was chilled with the cold, glancing occasionally at the figure of the old woman peering through the window. The candle end, which had burnt below the rim of the china candlestick, was throwing pulsating shadows on the ceiling and walls, until, with a flicker larger than the rest, it expired. The old man, with an unspeakable sense of relief at the failure of the talisman, crept back to his bed, and a minute or two afterward the old woman came silently and apathetically beside him.

Neither spoke, but both lay silently listening to the ticking of the clock. A stair creaked, and a squeaky mouse scurried noisily through the wall. The darkness was oppressive, and after lying for some time screwing up his courage, the husband took the box of matches and striking one went downstairs for a candle.

At the foot of the stairs the match went out, and he paused to strike another, and at the same moment a knock, so quiet and stealthy as to be scarcely audible, sounded on the front door.

The matches fell from his hand. He stood motionless, his breath suspended until the knock was repeated. Then he turned and fled swiftly back to his room and closed the door behind him. A third knock sounded through the house.

"What's that?" cried the old woman, starting up.

"A rat," said the old man, in shaking tones—"a rat. It passed me on the stairs."

His wife sat up in bed listening. A loud knock resounded through the house.

"It's Herbert!" she screamed. "It's Herbert!"

She ran to the door, but her husband was before her, and catching her by the arm, held her tightly.

"What are you going to do?" he whispered hoarsely.

"It's my boy; it's Herbert!" she cried, struggling mechanically. "I forgot it was two miles away. What are you holding me for? Let go. I must open the door."

"For heaven's sake don't let it in," cried the old man, trembling.

"You're afraid of your own son," she cried, struggling. "Let me go. I'm coming, Herbert; I'm coming."

There was another knock, and another. The old woman with a sudden wrench broke free and ran from the room. Her husband followed to the landing, and called after her appealingly as she hurried downstairs. He heard the chain rattle back and the bottom bolt drawn slowly and stiffly from the socket. Then the old woman's voice, strained and panting.

"The bolt," she cried loudly. "Come down. I can't reach it."

But her husband was on his hands and knees groping wildly on the floor in search of the paw. If he could only find it before the thing outside got in. A perfect fusillade of knocks reverberated through the house, and he heard the scraping of a chair as his wife put it down in the passage against the door. He heard the creaking of the bolt as it came slowly back, and at the same moment he found the monkey's paw and frantically breathed his third and last wish.

The knocking ceased suddenly, although the echoes of it were still in the house. He heard the chair drawn back and the door opened. A cold wind rushed up the staircase, and a long loud wail of disappointment and misery from his wife gave him courage to run down to her side, and then to the gate beyond. The street lamp flickering opposite shone on a quiet and deserted road.

□□

Discussion

1. (a) Contrast the scene outside the Whites' home with the scene within the living room as the Whites await the sergeant-major's arrival. **(b)** What does the author intend your attitude toward the White family to be?

2. (a) According to the sergeant-major, why did the fakir put a spell on the monkey's paw? **(b)** Do you agree with the fakir's belief? Why or why not?

3. The fact that "The Monkey's Paw" will end tragically is foreshadowed in several ways. Cite specific instances of foreshadowing that occur during the evening of the sergeant-major's visit.

4. (a) What seems to be the Whites' basic purpose in wanting to make a wish on the paw? **(b)** Does the making of the first wish change anyone's attitude toward the paw? Explain your answer.

5. (a) What is Mr. White's third wish? **(b)** Why does he make this third wish? **(c)** Can you think of a third wish which might have ended the story happily? **(d)** Why doesn't the author have Mr. White make such a wish?

W. W. Jacobs 1863 · 1943

Jacobs was born in Wapping, near Tower Bridge, in the ship-docking section of London. There his father was employed as a wharfman, and there Jacobs gathered the raw material for many of his later stories. Educated privately, Jacobs accepted a Civil Service appointment in 1883 and during the next sixteen years served in a department of the General Post Office. In 1896, he published his first book, *Many Cargoes*, which was followed by numerous one-act plays, novels, and short stories. The influence of Jacobs' early life around the docks of London is reflected in many of his book titles, such as *Light Freights*, *Night Watches*, and *Deep Waters*, and in the plots of a number of his short stories.

The Fear

Robert Frost

A lantern light from deeper in the barn
Shone on a man and woman in the door
And threw their lurching shadows on a house
Nearby, all dark in every glossy window.
5 A horse's hoof pawed once the hollow floor,
And the back of the gig they stood beside
Moved in a little. The man grasped a wheel,
The woman spoke out sharply, "Whoa, stand still!—
I saw it just as plain as a white plate,"
10 She said, "as the light on the dashboard ran
Along the bushes at the roadside—a man's face.
You *must* have seen it too."

                              "I didn't see it.
Are you sure——"

               15   —— "Yes, I'm sure!"

                          "—it was a face?"

"Joel, I'll have to look. I can't go in,
I can't, and leave a thing like that unsettled.
Doors locked and curtains drawn will make no difference.
20 I always have felt strange when we came home
To the dark house after so long an absence,
And the key rattled loudly into place
Seemed to warn someone to be getting out
At one door as we entered at another.
25 What if I'm right, and someone all the time—
Don't hold my arm!"

                          "I say it's someone passing."

"You speak as if this were a traveled road.
You forget where we are. What is beyond

From THE POETRY OF ROBERT FROST edited by Edward Connery Lathem. Copyright 1930, 1939, © 1969 by Holt, Rinehart and Winston. Copyright © 1958 by Robert Frost. Copyright © 1967 by Lesley Frost Ballantine. Reprinted by permission of the Estate of Robert Frost, Holt, Rinehart and Winston and Jonathan Cape Ltd., publishers.

That he'd be going to or coming from
At such an hour of night, and on foot too?
What was he standing still for in the bushes?''

''It's not so very late—it's only dark.
There's more in it than you're inclined to say.
Did he look like——?''

       ''He looked like anyone. *woman*
I'll never rest tonight unless I know.
Give me the lantern.''

       ''You don't want the lantern.'' *Joel*

She pushed past him and got it for herself.

''You're not to come,'' she said. ''This is my business. *woman*
If the time's come to face it, I'm the one
To put it the right way. He'd never dare—
Listen! He kicked a stone. Hear that, hear that!
He's coming towards us. Joel, *go* in—please.
Hark!—I don't hear him now. But please go in.''

''In the first place you can't make me believe it's——'' *47 Joel*

''It is—or someone else he's sent to watch.
And now's the time to have it out with him
While we know definitely where he is. *woman*
Let him get off and he'll be everywhere
Around us, looking out of trees and bushes
Till I shan't dare to set a foot outdoors.
And I can't stand it. Joel, let me go!''

''But it's nonsense to think he'd care enough.'' *55 Joel*

''You mean you couldn't understand his caring. *woman*
Oh, but you see he hadn't had enough—
Joel, I won't—I won't—I promise you.
We mustn't say hard things. You mustn't either.''

60 "I'll be the one, if anybody goes!
But you give him the advantage with this light.
What couldn't he do to us standing here!
And if to see was what he wanted, why,
He has seen all there was to see and gone."

65 He appeared to forget to keep his hold,
But advanced with her as she crossed the grass.

"What do you want?" she cried to all the dark.
She stretched up tall to overlook the light
That hung in both hands hot against her skirt.

70 "There's no one; so you're wrong," he said.

                                        "There is.—

What do you want?" she cried, and then herself
Was startled when an answer really came.

"Nothing." It came from well along the road.

75 She reached a hand to Joel for support:
The smell of scorching woolen made her faint.
"What are you doing round this house at night?"

"Nothing." A pause: there seemed no more to say.

And then the voice again: "You seem afraid.
80 I saw by the way you whipped up the horse.
I'll just come forward in the lantern-light
And let you see."

                    "Yes, do.—Joel, go back!"

She stood her ground against the noisy steps
85 That came on, but her body rocked a little.

"You see," the voice said.

                            "Oh." She looked and looked.

"You don't see—I've a child here by the hand.
A robber wouldn't have his family with him."

90 "What's a child doing at this time of night——?"

12 TURNABOUT

1. What are the visual details presented at the beginning of the poem that suggest the isolation and loneliness of the poem's setting?

2. What are the indications that the woman fears that someone she knows, someone out of her past, is hiding in the dark nearby?

3. In line 55, Joel says to the woman: "But it's nonsense to think he'd care enough." Explain what he means, and discuss the woman's reply, lines 56–59.

4. (a) What is the woman's attitude when she discovers that all she has seen or heard was a man out on a walk with his son? (b) Does she relax or remain tense? Discuss.

5. (a) Describe the emotional state of the woman at the end of the poem. (b) What happens to the lantern? Discuss.

Robert Frost 1874 · 1963

Although we seem to hear a shrewd Yankee or New England voice in Frost's poetry, he was actually born in San Francisco. However, he moved to Massachusetts at the age of eleven, and his poems tend to be set in New England, especially on the farm or in the rural area.

Frost married at twenty, studied at Harvard for two years and then supported himself at a number of odd jobs before settling down on a New Hampshire farm. After eleven years of farming and writing poetry, Frost had little success to show for his efforts: his farm was a failure and only the local newspaper would accept his poems for publication. In a discouraged mood he moved to England where he offered his collected work to a publisher. The book came out as *A Boy's Will* in 1913 and was immediately recognized for its fresh, original poetry. Frost followed this with *North of Boston* (1914).

Frost, now famous, returned home in 1915. He was to become one of the most popular poets in America. In 1924 he won the first of several Pulitzer Prizes for his poetry. In 1961 he was invited to read a poem at the inauguration ceremonies of President John F. Kennedy.

man { "Out walking. Every child should have the memory
Of at least one long-after-bedtime walk.
What, son?"

woman {
95   "Then I should think you'd try to find
Somewhere to walk——"

                                      "The highway, as it happens—
We're stopping for the fortnight down at Dean's."

14 days

"But if that's all—Joel—you realize—
You won't think anything. You understand?
100 You understand that we have to be careful.
This is a very, very lonely place.—
Joel!" She spoke as if she couldn't turn.
The swinging lantern lengthened to the ground,
It touched, it struck, it clattered and went out.

Sorrow Rides a Fast Horse

Dorothy Gilman Butters

When my mother died everyone in Green Valley said what a selfless and patient woman she had been, and how wonderfully she had managed to raise two sons alone. "A modest, uncomplaining woman," the minister said at her funeral. "A woman who was born in this town and who died in this town and never went beyond it, but cultivated wisdom in her own small garden."

When he said this my brother Rufus nudged me and smiled. People forget, of course—and anyway, the minister had lived in Green Valley for only twelve years, so he couldn't have known. Certainly Mother would never have told him about what Rufus and I tacitly referred to as That Year; when it was over, Mother never talked of it with us or anyone. I don't think she was ashamed or sorry so much as embarrassed about it because she could not explain her actions even to herself. Only once did she even admit that it had taken place, and I can imagine the effort this cost her. It happened when I was in the ninth grade at Green Valley School and Miss Larkin showed us a film slide of the Taj Mahal. She made a few remarks about it, saying she was sorry she could not show us a picture of the interior, but that no photographs of it had as yet been allowed.

I raised my hand and told her that inside it was glittering and white, with words from the Koran[1] carved on the walls, and flower designs, and colored stones set into the marble.

"And from what book did you get that, John?"

"I didn't get it from a book," I told her. "I've been there. I've seen the Taj Mahal."

After school Miss Larkin took me aside and told me sternly that I must not tell lies like that; I had done it only to gain attention, but people would like me much better if I told the truth. "Now I want you to admit that you've never visited the Taj Mahal."

"But I have," I protested.

She rapped my knuckles and said I would have to stay after school every day until I confessed to the class that I had never seen the

Taj Mahal and had not been telling the truth. I almost lost my paper route from being punished and that was how Mother learned about it. The next day she walked into Miss Larkin's room looking pale and nervous. Standing just inside the door she said stiffly, "Miss Larkin, John was not lying; he has seen the Taj Mahal," and without another word she walked out of the room.

Since that day two wars ago the boys and men of Green Valley have seen quite a few exotic corners of the earth, but when I was a child no one in Green Valley traveled abroad. There was neither the time nor the money for such frivolity. The town was—and still is—farmland with only a few stores, two churches and one school. My father taught in that school until one day he was reading lines from "Kubla Khan" to his class and reached the words "Down to a sunless sea" and crumpled suddenly to the floor. Three hours later he died of a cerebral hemorrhage.

My brother Rufus was seven and I was nine. It's difficult to realize that my mother was only thirty-one. She didn't cry when they told her; she stiffened as if she had been hit, her chin went up and her eyes glittered strangely. The first thing she did when everyone had gone was to go into the kitchen and begin scrubbing the floor. Even after the relatives arrived nobody could make her stop working; our Aunt Agatha said she was like a woman possessed.

After the funeral we were glad to go back to school because it seemed to us we had lost a mother, too; when we spoke to her she looked at us blankly, as if she'd forgotten who we were. She was still that way when the insurance man arrived. He spent an hour in the study with Mother and when he left she looked chilled.

"What's that pink paper you've got?" Rufus asked.

"Sorrow Rides a Fast Horse" by Dorothy Gilman Butters. Copyright © 1962 by The Curtis Publishing Co. Appeared originally in the LADIES HOME JOURNAL. Reprinted by permission of McIntosh and Otis, Inc.

1. *Koran* (kô rän'), the sacred text of the Moslems. It is the standard by which Moslems live.

"It's a check," Mother said, staring down at it contemptuously. "A check for fifteen thousand dollars. When I think of what it could have bought us—the things we could have done together——" For one moment I thought she was going to cry and then her face froze and she walked back into the kitchen. But the check must have put the idea into her mind; here was all this money, so utterly meaningless to her now that she wanted only to destroy it, and if not to destroy at least abuse it. And besides, she had cleaned the house from attic to cellar and there was nothing left to clean.

Two weeks later Rufus and I came home from school to find Mother standing in the hall with three suitcases on the floor. She was dressed in her good black coat and the plain blue dress that she wore to Sunday school. In those days her brown hair was parted in the center and pulled into a tight bun at her neck, but little tendrils always succeeded in escaping to soften her small, delicate-boned face. "You won't be going to school tomorrow," she told us. "We're going away."

"When will we be back?" I asked.

She gave me that impatient blind glance that I was growing accustomed to now. "I don't know when we'll be back," she said in a voice that meant that she didn't care when we came back. "We're going around the world."

"I can't go around the world tomorrow," I told her. "I've got an arithmetic exam."

"I'm sorry," she said politely. "But we are leaving in one hour and we are going around the world."

It was late October when we landed in England, and in London we settled into a hotel room and Mother made arrangements for two weeks of sight-seeing. After we'd watched the changing of the guard at the palace Rufus and I decided England might be fun, but after four days of London Mother decided we must go to Wales. A week later we were in Holland and soon after that we left for Austria. I remember that we spent Christmas in Paris, but we had no sooner visited the Eiffel Tower and the Bastille

than Mother announced that we must pack our bags again. That was the way it was all through the winter and spring—we packed and unpacked our bags through Spain, Portugal and Morocco. We were like bees flitting nervously from flower to flower: one week riding a camel in Morocco, the next week a rented bicycle in Italy. Rome held us briefly, but Mother found Naples too beautiful and so we did not even unpack our bags there but left immediately for Florence. Then we moved to Greece, Rufus and I picking up foreign words like crumbs begged from shopkeepers, concierges, sailors and chambermaids. We behaved very badly as well, I remember, and despaired when Mother did not notice. We were alone, really alone, for the first time in our young and sheltered lives and we resented being shut out of Mother's life. But in the manner of children everywhere, I suppose some kind of adjustment took place in us. It was to me that Rufus looked for comfort, and I to him; and if we hated Mother's indifference we also took advantage of it, eating sweets when we chose and going to bed when we pleased and saying "No" to her in half a dozen languages.

In July we came to Baghdad, a city of houses the color of yellow sand, and of blazing sun and minarets puncturing the sky with their polished gold domes. The streets were narrow and dim, overflowing with dust, sheep and people, the men with tender dark eyes, the women soft and mysterious behind veils. In the *sugs* Rufus and I ate yogurt with our fingers from earthenware pots, we drank bitterly strong coffee and sat cross-legged for hours watching men work gold or silver into filigree or hammer out huge jugs of copper. We did not go back to our hotel except at night. There were other Americans in that hotel because the first oil well had been brought in only a few years earlier, but we scorned these men; they talked only of geological surveys and gushers and pipelines.

No one had questioned Mother until we reached Baghdad, when an English colonel stopped one night beside our table in the dining room. It was Rufus's eighth birthday and we· were

attempting some kind of celebration. The colonel told Mother that Rufus reminded him of his grandson, and after a few minutes he sat down and asked us where we were going. Mother explained that we were on our way to India to see the Taj Mahal and to spend a week in Kashmir. But first, she added, we were going across the mountains to Tehran and then to Meshed to see the place where Harun al-Rashid, the caliph of the *Arabian Nights*,[2] was buried.

The colonel's jaw dropped. "Across the mountains! What on earth can you be thinking of? This isn't England, you know."

"I didn't think it was," Mother told him with asperity.

"You're in Asia now. Those mountains are full of smugglers and thieves—not safe at all. Unthinkable. I can't imagine who planned your itinerary."

"My husband did," said Mother in an even voice. "Some years ago."

The colonel snorted. "Well, you can't just look at a map and go the shortest way in these countries. If you won't listen to me I'll go to your consul first thing in the morning and tell him what you're up to. He'll stop you."

But of course by the next day we were gone. Mother had already visited the consulates and she had had the foresight to acquire a visa for Persia and a man to drive us across the border and over the mountains. In those days the idea of a woman traveling alone in Asia with two children was so unthinkable that it must never have occurred to anyone—except the colonel—to ask her questions. I think the authorities, most of whom spoke little or no English, assumed Mother was traveling with one child and a husband, and Mother did not discourage them. Certainly she did not look like an adventuress and she met no one wise enough to see her ruthlessness. They did not know that Mother was courting self-destruction. As for endangering the lives of two children, no appeal in that direction could have touched her because she was, as Aunt Agatha said, a woman possessed. We scarcely existed for her then.

Our driver was an Afghan named Mohammed Aslam and there was so much affection in his first glance at us that we stopped acting like spoiled and precocious children. As Mother handed him our three suitcases, she inquired—dutifully and with not much interest—if there really were thieves in the mountains ahead.

Aslam gave her a gay smile accompanied by a shrug. "A few, perhaps. The people are poor, poorer than anybody else in that country. But in my car, we go fast."

We looked at his car, a patched and ancient Ford truck. "She goes," he told us proudly, patting its fender. And indeed she did go; and did not break down until we needed her most.

A child does not remember the same things an adult remembers. You may take a child to the Louvre, and he will remember the guard who picked his nose, or the organ grinder on the street outside, or the chocolate treat on the way home. Only the adults remember the *Mona Lisa*.[3] For us this journey into Persia was Aslam, dust and heat and picnics eaten beside the truck. In this queer, convulsed corner of the world even Mother seemed more cheerful, as if its bleakness matched hers. We slept for two nights on rugs beside the car with a canvas stretched from the truck to a pole. No one passed us along the way; we might have been the only four people in the world. At dawn we would eat *mast*, a kind of curds dried into a hard white ball, and Mother and Aslam would drink *chai*[4] while we had milk from a goatskin kept cool in a bucket of water. Then we would be off, climbing slowly toward the mountain range before us. It was barren, desolate country covered not with scrub but with thistles, as tall as a man and bearing blossoms the size of an apple. The truck gave out when we had reached what seemed like the top of the world. It simply stopped. We piled out, trying not to look into the canyon below, and waited while Aslam

---

2. *the Arabian Nights,* a collection of old tales from Arabia, Persia, and India dating from the tenth century.

3. *Mona Lisa* (mō'nə lē'zə), a famous portrait by Leonardo da Vinci that hangs in the Louvre, an art museum, in Paris.

4. *chai* (chāy), tea.

cheerfully peered under and into the engine. At last he shook his head. *"No benzine."*

"You're out of gas?"

"Bali." He led us to the rear and showed us the gas tank, which had a hole in it the size of a twenty-five-cent piece.

Mother appeared unconcerned; she asked Aslam what he proposed to do next. He replied—still very cheerfully—that we must not worry, he would get us to Hamadan, *inshallah.* I did not remind Mother that *inshallah* meant if God wills it. He asked for money, which Mother trustingly gave him, and said he would be back in a few hours with donkeys. Five hours later, when we were nearly prostrate from the heat, he did indeed return, from heaven knows where, leading four emaciated donkeys. He had bought them in a Lur village some miles away and he said he would return them when he came back for his truck. The donkeys, Aslam told me, were for my *mader,* my *barader* and me; upon the fourth he would pile our baggage and food and water while he himself would walk. Although we protested at this he was very insistent, saying that he could walk faster than any of us. I did not realize until later that he was afraid. It did not occur to us that in these mountains a man with enough money to buy donkeys draws attention to himself.

We made poor time, but we traveled until long past sunset. The border was far behind us now. Another day's traveling, Aslam said, and we would reach Kermanshah, where he could purchase *benzine* and—he hoped—the means to repair his tank. In the meantime we would stop here—we had reached a plateau rimmed with jagged rocks—and cook a little rice and spread our rugs. He began to make a small fire, leaning over it, blowing on it and crooning to it. Mother sat slumped on her donkey, too tired to dismount, while Rufus and I stood beside ours wondering how to tether them.

It was several moments before we realized we were not alone.

There were six of them, and they had stepped out of the darkness like wraiths. The poverty of them, and the desolateness of our surroundings, made my heart jump in a sickening fashion. They were bearded, fierce and ragged. They wore loose, pantaloonlike black trousers, but neither sashes nor shirts. Only three of them owned turbans. They looked so terribly poor—and so fierce—that I suddenly realized how wealthy we must look to them with our rugs and our donkeys.

"Who are they?" asked Mother with a faint look of surprise.

Aslam stood up cautiously and spoke to them. The tallest of the six men—heavily bearded and wearing a turban so that only his eyes and the sharpness of his cheekbones showed—replied at some length. When he had finished speaking he laughed and showed Aslam the heavy stick he carried in one hand.

"Who are they?" repeated Mother, still not afraid.

Aslam looked a little sick. "Bandits."

"Then give them food," Mother said impatiently.

Aslam said uneasily, "They do not want food."

"Then give them what money we have."

Still Aslam hesitated.

"Well?" asked Mother curtly. "What is it they want?"

Keeping his eyes on the ground, Aslam said, "They want you and the children as well as the food and money. I have told them you are American, but they do not know what American is."

Mother frowned. "They intend to *capture* us?"

Aslam gave her a fleeting look of surprise. "They have already captured us."

"But what on earth do they want us for?"

Aslam's eyes returned to the ground. He said nothing, which was thoughtful of him, for none of the possibilities would have pleased us. The leader of the bandits stepped forward and made a gesture to Mother to get down from her donkey. She stared at him unbelievingly and then she turned to look at the five other men and at Rufus and me. Her gaze moved from us to the deep night sky and then to the jagged black rocks and I saw a shudder run through her as if she were shaking herself out of a deep trance. The blind look had gone from her eyes. I realized that at last she was clearly seeing us and her surroundings. Such a look of horror crossed her face that I thought she was going to scream.

"Please," Aslam begged in a low voice. "There is no hope just now. Wait. Do nothing to resist. These men are dangerous."

Mother seemed dazed. "Not resist? Aslam, they must not capture us!"

Aslam said sadly. "It must be your *qismat*—your fate—to stop here."

Mother gave a bitter, half-strangled laugh. Her cheeks were flushed and her hair undone; she looked wild and strange. "My *qismat*?" she said harshly. "Tell this man I must travel like the wind—that is my *qismat*. Tell him," she went on fiercely, "that Sorrow rides behind me on a fast horse—if he listens closely he may hear the hoofbeats. Tell him that if he captures me he will capture Sorrow as well—because where I go Sorrow follows and where I stop Sorrow will stop."

Where did she find these words? I don't know. My mother had never spoken in that manner before and I never heard her speak that way again. Aslam obediently translated her words for the bandit chief and I saw him narrow his eyes. I wondered if instead of capturing us they might kill us then and there. The bandits began to speak among themselves and to gesticulate, one of them pointing in the direction from which we had come, and another giving us an angry, accusing glance. After interminable moments the bandit chief turned to Mother and spoke.

Aslam said breathlessly, "He says it has been a hard year, with many people dead in their village. Sheep have sickened and died. He says they do not wish for more Sorrow. If Sorrow follows behind you then you must leave these mountains at once. You must not stop even to sleep."

Mother closed her eyes. She looked suddenly drained.

"He and his men will guide us out of the mountains to speed us on our way."

Mother opened her eyes and said with dignity, "Tell him that we are ready to go."

The bandits were as good as their word. All night we rode behind them and when dawn came we were only an hour from Kermanshah. We dismounted and the bandits took the donkeys from us, as well as our food and money, but left us our baggage. As they turned to go the bandit chief walked up to Mother and gave her a hard, calm, searching glance. Aslam, translating his words, said, "He wants you to know that his wife died last month and a son last year. He is well acquainted with Sorrow. He has taken your food and money, but he gives you the gift of a copper water jug. Which he probably captured from somebody else," Aslam added dryly. "He says to you '*Istali mashi*,' which means 'May you never be tired.' In return you must say to him '*Kwar mashi*,' which means 'May you never be poor.' "

There were tears in Mother's eyes. "*Kwar mashi*," she replied to the bandit chief.

We stood and watched them ride away on our donkeys and then Mother said quietly, "I think it is time we began making arrangements to go home now."

We had left Green Valley in October and we returned in October and when we entered our front yard Mother looked at the sagging front steps and said in a matter-of-fact voice, "You and I will have to mend those tomorrow, John." She took off her black coat and hung it in the hall closet and said to Rufus, "You're beginning to look like your father, Rufus." Then she went upstairs to unpack our suitcases, still only three in number because Mother had not brought home any Persian rugs or Haviland china or any of the souvenirs that tourists collect; there was only the copper jug which she wrapped and put away in a chest. To the neighbors she said, "We did a little traveling, here and there." And in the spring she went to work in the public library and never, never did she talk to us of That Year so that after a while it seemed to Rufus and me like a dream that we happened to dream at the same time.

After the funeral Rufus and I came back to the empty house and rebuilt the fire on the kitchen hearth and made coffee. When it had been poured we sat quietly for a few minutes, neither of us speaking, and then Rufus got up and went to the chest in the living room and brought back a bulky package of flannel and newspaper. He unwrapped the copper jug.

" 'A quiet, uneventful life,' " I quoted dryly.

Rufus nodded. "She would have agreed with the minister, you know."

"It was insane, every moment of it," I said. "We were fortunate to escape with our lives."

Rufus smiled. "There is a proverb that says to nearly lose your life is to find it. Of course it was madness, all of it. And yet——"

"Yes?" I said curiously, for it had been a long time since we had talked of this.

He said softly, "We learned from her how perverse, how unpredictable, how astonishing and how courageous a human being can be."

I lifted my cup. "To our legacy, then," I said, smiling at him. *"Istali mashi."*

"Kwar mashi," he replied, and we drank to That Year. □□

Discussion

1. (a) When the narrator gives his class and his teacher a description of the interior of the Taj Mahal, what is the reaction of the teacher? (b) What does the narrator's mother do? Explain and discuss.

2. When the father died, he was teaching "Kubla Khan" in school. "Kubla Khan," a poem by Samuel Taylor Coleridge (1772–1834) describes the Mongolian king Kubla Khan's city of Xanadu where he built a great palace ("stately pleasure-dome") amid a mysteriously romantic setting: the "sacred river" Alph ran "through caverns measureless to man/ Down to a sunless sea." (a) What might you infer from the description of the father's death about his personality and ambition? (b) How does it relate to the trip the mother plans after his death?

3. (a) What is the mother's immediate reaction to the news of her husband's death? (b) Why is the insurance money "meaningless" to her? (c) Why does she decide to take her two sons out of school to make a trip around the world?

4. In the paragraph listing all the foreign places they visited, the narrator says: "Rome held us briefly, but Mother found Naples too beautiful and so we did not even unpack our bags there but left immediately for Florence." Explain and discuss.

5. At the moment of greatest peril on the trip, the mother saves her family by telling the bandits that she is pursued by sorrow. (a) What is the reaction of the bandits? (b) Why does the author choose this episode as the source for the title? Explain and discuss.

6. The story opens and closes with an account of the funeral of the mother which takes place long after the principal events of the story. This "frame" for the story presents the minister's view of the mother. By the "close" of the story, the reader has quite a contrasting view. Indeed, the main story presents a kind of *turnabout* in the characterization of the mother. Explain and discuss.

Vocabulary · Context

These aids can help you understand words you don't know:

CONTEXT: the setting the word appears in; other words or ideas in the sentence, paragraph, or selection. STRUCTURE: the arrangement and meaning of parts of words (root words and affixes). PRONUNCIATION: Use the dictionary when you need help with pronunciation. DICTIONARY: If the meaning can't be determined by using context or structure clues, consult the dictionary.

Read the following quotations from "Sorrow Rides a Fast Horse." If there is enough information in the sentence to determine the meaning of the italicized word, write what you think the word means on a separate sheet of paper. If there is not enough information, write "no" on the paper. Then check your Glossary to be sure you know the meanings and pronunciations of *all* the italicized words.

1. "In those days her brown hair was parted in the center and pulled into a tight bun at her neck, but little *tendrils* always succeeded in escaping to soften her small, delicate-boned face."

2. "We were like bees *flitting* nervously from flower to flower."

3. "In July we came to Baghdad, a city of houses the color of yellow sand, and of blazing sun and *minarets* puncturing the sky with their polished gold domes."

4. "It was barren, *desolate* country covered not with scrub but with thistles, as tall as a man and bearing blossoms the size of an apple."

5. ". . . he did indeed return, from heaven knows where, leading four *emaciated* donkeys."

6. "The bandits began to speak among themselves and to *gesticulate*, one of them pointing in the direction from which we had come. . . ."

7. "Three hours later he died of a cerebral *hemorrhage*."

8. "There were six of them, and they had stepped out of the darkness like *wraiths*."

9. "I can't imagine who planned your *itinerary*."

10. "Certainly Mother would never have told him about what Rufus and I *tacitly* referred to as That Year."

Dorothy Gilman Butters
1923 ·

Butters began her career by writing for children and young people; then, shortening her name to Dorothy Gilman, she wrote a series of novels about Mrs. Pollifax for an older audience. She has written: "When I switched to writing adult books . . . I conscientiously abbreviated my name so that there would be no mix-up. I find now that I have only confused the postman because young people are a large part of Mrs. Pollifax's 'audience,' so to speak. I think this reinforces my belief that I write the kind of book I would love to find available, and failing to find it, write it myself."

Born in New Brunswick, New Jersey, Butters attended the Pennsylvania Academy of Fine Arts and the University of Pennsylvania. She published her first work *(Enchanted Caravan)* in 1949. *The Unexpected Mrs. Pollifax* (1966) was made into a movie in 1970. Other Mrs. Pollifax books include *A Palm for Mrs. Pollifax* (1973).

Skins

Adele Seronde

Once
    this rug was blanket,
    cover to my life.
It kept me warm—
5 It slept where I slept,
    rode with me.
It told my story
    in a shout,
    a wild, strong war-cry
10   to the world!
The zig-zag reds were voices
    of the storm,
    the eagle,
    waters of the rain,
15   and hoof-beats to the stars.

Now
    my rugs
    are hung like skins
    in white men's
20   houses——

Discussion

1. There are two lines in "Skins" which contain only single words—"Once" and "Now." Discuss the probable reasons for the poet using only one word in each of these lines.

2. (a) In line 5, with what does the speaker endow the rug? **(b)** What do the symbols on the rug suggest and how do they tell the speaker's story?

3. In the closing lines of the poem, the speaker says that the rugs are now hung in white men's houses "like skins." Skins normally are hung on walls as trophies after an animal has been killed. What is the effect of this simile at this point in the poem? Why has the poet used it as her title?

Extension · Writing

Museums, art galleries, public buildings, and homes often have on display, in cabinets or hanging on walls, items that had deep meaning for the original owner, but which have lost that original meaning now and are looked upon as interesting or pretty or beautiful objects of design. Choose some such object, in your possession or elsewhere, and recreate as briefly and vividly as you can the meaning it *once* had for its original owner (perhaps yourself), and the meaning it *now* has for its present owner—or for someone viewing it without awareness of its deeply personal history. It may be a spear in the museum, an African mask in the art gallery, a miniature car in your room, a rag doll gathering dust in the closet, a work of art painted by you in the first grade and now hanging in your mother's kitchen. . . .

Reprinted from ASK A CACTUS ROSE, by Adele Seronde, with the permission of the Wenkhart Publishing Company, 4 Shady Hill Square, Cambridge, Massachusetts, 02138.
For author biography, see page 246.

See **SATIRE** Handbook of Literary Terms

No People Need Apply

Mike Royko

The manager of a high-rise building on Lake Shore Drive recently sent this letter to his tenants:

"Dear Tenant:

"We have been receiving numerous complaints on the misuse of the lobbies by adults as well as children.

"We must ask, therefore, that 'Lobby Sitting' be discontinued.

"Please note under Rules and Regulations:

"Children shall not be permitted to loiter or play on the stairways, halls, porches or court areas or in public places generally used by the public or other tenants.

"The sidewalks, entryways, passages, vestibules, halls and stairways outside of the several apartments shall not be used for any other purpose than ingress and egress to and from the respective rooms or apartments.

"We have been asked by many, why we have sofas and chairs in the lobby if we do not permit their use.

"It is the intention of the owners that seating be available for the FEW MINUTES that a guest may be waiting for a tenant, or that a tenant and guest be waiting for a taxi or driver to pick them up, and to enhance our lobby.

"We are sure you will agree that we are constantly extending efforts to maintain our lobbies and public areas in a manner that will be pleasing to you and reflect the prestige of our building. It is our sincere hope that you will cooperate with us."

The letter angered a lady who lives in the building. She said it was directed at the elderly people, who, during the great blizzard, had no place to go. So they sat in the lobby just to get out of their apartments for a few hours.

The lady sent it to me because she felt I would share her anger.

I can't get angry about the letter because I think I understand the feelings of the building

From I MAY BE WRONG, BUT I DOUBT IT by Mike Royko. Copyright © 1968 Mike Royko. Reprinted by permission of Contemporary Books, Inc.

manager and the people who complained to him about all those old people hanging around the lobby.

Life just happens to be different in a high-rise than, say, in a bungalow or three-flat neighborhood.

And High-Rise Man sees things—himself included—in a different way.

High-Rise Man is like his building—soaring, lean, modern, gracious, cool, handsome, push-button, filter-tipped, a symbol of today and today's young, calorie-free living.

In the morning, he can leap out of bed and stand there in his shorts, looking out of his sweeping glass window at the sun rising over Lake Michigan.

At night, with the lights dimmed, he might stand there sipping something-on-the-rocks, listening to something tasteful on his stereo, gazing down at the twinkling lights on Lake Shore Drive. With a slight smile, he thinks:

"This is It. And I have made It."

Contrast him to Bungalow Man and Three-Flat Man. We think of ourselves as kind of squat, pot-bellied, ordinary, brick, mortar, sidewalks-by-WPA[1]—just like the real estate.

The sight of old people is not offensive to Three-Flat Man and Bungalow Man because even when he is young he thinks he is getting old.

Besides, old people are part of Three-Flat Man's world. They're always there, sitting on the front steps, watering a lawn, watering a dog, taking a walk for the paper, complaining about somebody's punk kids.

But when High-Rise Man and his High-Rise Mate step out of the cab, nod to the doorman's respectful greeting and stride through their lobby, it can be jarring—shocking—to see a bunch of old people sitting around, dozing, knitting, cackling, or even, heaven forbid, coughing.

Not in their lean, young, soaring world.

Children are just as distasteful. When you see a child, you think of runny noses, scabby knees, diapers, boisterous behavior—none of which belongs in the world of muted tones, indirect lighting, thick-rugged hallways and gleaming lobbies.

This is a problem, of course, because old people do live in those buildings. And a few children, too.

And it seems somewhat harsh to bar them from the lobbies entirely.

Possibly the building managers could work out some sort of schedule, as second lieutenants used to do with the day rooms in the service.

They might tell them something like this:

"Dear Tenant:

"It has come to our attention that due to the cold weather some of our elderly tenants would like to leave their apartments and sit in the lobby.

"Therefore we have amended our rules to permit 'Limited Lobby Sitting.'

"No more than six (6) elderly people will be permitted to sit in the lobby at one time.

"They will space themselves and will use those chairs that are arranged to face AWAY from the main entrance.

"Lobby Sitting will not be permitted during morning hours when tenants are leaving for their offices or during evening hours when dinner guests might be arriving.

"It is NOT allowed on Friday and Saturday nights.

"Lobby Sitting privileges will be revoked, of course, for violations of the above or for repeated complaints of cackling, knitting, dozing, coughing or cracking sounds from joints.

"Regarding children: We suggest that tenants who possess them consider giving them away."

□□

---

1. **WPA,** Work Projects Administration. A federal agency in charge of public works established during the Depression to relieve national unemployment.

Mutt of the Year

Mike Royko

Someone ought to sponsor a new kind of dog show. Maybe I'll do it myself. Better yet, the *Daily News* will do it. That ought to surprise some of the editors.

The obvious need for a new form of dog competition occurred to me after I read accounts of the International Dog Show held here over the weekend.

It sounded like a good show, but it was just like most of the others. The dogs were pure-bred aristocrats with names like Merry Rover of Valley Run, Molley Haven Sugar and Gala Cairns Redstar.

To get into the show, the dog owners must submit proof of ancestry. (The dog's ancestry, I mean. The owners don't have to prove anything about their own.)

These shows are fine and some of the dogs may even enjoy themselves, but my dog show would be just as interesting and even more exciting.

It would be open only to mixed-breed mutts, and the more mixed the better.

Instead of Merry Rover of Valley Run, we'd have Spot of Armitage Avenue.

Any dog that doesn't look like three different breeds couldn't get in. There even would be a special award for the dog who is so mixed that he looks like a goat or something.

Dogs would not be judged solely on the basis of their muttiness, although it would be of great importance in the winning of points. A dog whose legs were of uneven length and thus walked in a circle would naturally have a scoring advantage over a dog who walked sideways.

There would be obedience trials, work dog competition, sporting dog tests, and such things. But our competition would be more meaningful than that of the purebred dog shows. They have competition for sheepdogs, and how many people in Chicago keep sheep?

Our standards of obedience and performance

Reprinted from UP AGAINST IT by Mike Royko. Published by the Henry Regnery Company. Copyright © 1967 by Henry Regnery Company. By permission of Contemporary Books, Inc.

would be up-to-date. Some of the possible categories follow:

Sporting Dogs: This would be open to the greatest modern sporting dog of them all—the dog that runs on the field during a football game.

Six judges, dressed like football officials, would chase each entry around the judging area. The dog that survived longest would be the champion. The judge who survived longest would get to kick the dog that survived longest.

Work Dogs: Entries in this field would be the noblest of all the modern work dogs—the tavern dog.

They would be judged for fierceness of gaze, loudness of bark, lightness of sleep, and quickness of bite.

Any tavern dog that did not try to bite a judge would be disqualified. Extra points would be given to tavern dogs that try to bite other tavern dogs. Bonus points would go to dogs that bite their owners.

Non-working Dogs: Eligible for this award would be all house or back-yard dogs.

They will be awarded points for their ability to withstand ear-pulling, tail-twisting and rib-tickling by children without biting them. The dog that takes the most without going mad would receive an award. Children who are bitten would receive first aid, a citation, and a good lesson.

Points also would be awarded to house dogs for their willingness to eat leftovers, including peanut-butter-and-jelly sandwich crusts, cold pizza, tuna-fish salad, cottage cheese, and Sugar Pops. What's good enough for me is good enough for them.

Obedience: All dogs will be expected to respond to the following commands:

Lie down, speak, shut up, get off the couch, get off the bed, get on the porch, get in the yard, get in the house, get in the kitchen, get in the basement, get out of here, and get.

Finally, there will be a special award, a trophy known as the Royko Cup.

It will go to the dog who demonstrates his ability to learn nothing.

He must prove that he barks only at passing airplanes, sleeps through burglaries, howls endlessly when left alone, prefers a new rug to an old fire plug, is affectionate to mice while trying to bite friends and relatives, snores, snarls, and snatches food from the table.

Of course, we might have to let in some of those tiny, fuzzy purebred dogs for that one.

□□

Discussion · *No People ...*

1. Assume that you are a tenant receiving a letter like the one presented at the beginning of Royko's piece. How would you react? Explain and discuss.

2. Royko describes "High-Rise Man" as "like his building—soaring, lean, modern, gracious, cool, handsome, push-button, filter-tipped," while he describes "Bungalow Man and Three-Flat Man" as "kind of squat, pot-bellied, ordinary, brick, mortar, side-walks-by-WPA—just like the real estate." (a) At first glance, which of these types seems more attractive? (b) Which of them does Royko actually support over the other? Explain and discuss.

3. As a satirist, Royko throughout seems to be sympathetic with the side or group he is criticizing and poking fun at. At the end, for example, he offers a letter that he says will prove helpful for the building managers of high-rise buildings. What is Royko's real purpose in this letter in contrast with what he says is his purpose? Discuss.

Discussion · *Mutt of the Year*

1. What does Royko think is wrong with the typical dog show?

2. What changes would Royko make in dog shows?

3. (a) Is Royko being unnecessarily cruel in any of his "rules"? **(b)** What is his purpose in suggesting such rules?

4. (a) What type of dog would win the Royko Cup? **(b)** What attitude of Royko's is revealed by this prize? **(c)** Do you agree with him? Why or why not?

Vocabulary · Dictionary

Using the Glossary, determine if the following statements about the italicized words are true or false. On a separate sheet of paper write "T" or "F" after the number of the statement. Be sure you can spell and pronounce each italicized word.

1. The word *boisterous* would have been totally unfamiliar to a person who spoke Middle English.

2. One who *loiters* through the day probably does not get much accomplished.

3. The *egress* is an exotic bird first brought to this country by P. T. Barnum.

4. *Enhance* comes from the Old French meaning to "raise up."

5. *Ingress* and *entrance* are synonyms.

6. The state of Bengal in India and the word *bungalow* have nothing in common.

7. The words *vestibule* and *vestments* have the same Latin root.

8. *Muted* colors are bright and shiny.

Extension · Writing

In a *turnabout*, assume that you are a dog in charge of a "human show." What would be your rules and regulations? What categories would you devise? How would you award points?

Mike Royko 1932 ·

No visit to Chicago would be complete without buying the *Chicago Sun-Times* and reading Mike Royko's daily column. Each day he writes of Chicago's politicians, people, and folkways with an acid wit.

A native Chicagoan, he worked his way up from neighborhood newspapers to a leading daily. He had been with the *Chicago Daily News* from 1959 until its demise in 1978. In 1972 he received the Pulitzer Prize for his book on the late Mayor Richard J. Daley, *Boss.*

His columns are full of Chicago characters, including a creation named Slats Grobnick, a boy who liked to spend entire days avoiding the cracks in the sidewalks of the city.

This Is Just to Say

William Carlos Williams

I have eaten
the plums
that were in
the icebox

5 and which
you were probably
saving
for breakfast

Forgive me
10 they were delicious
so sweet
and so cold.

Variation on a Theme
By William Carlos Williams

Tino Villanueva

I have eaten
the *tamales*
that were on
the stove heating

5 and which
you were probably
having
for dinner

Perdóname
10 they were *riquísimos*[1]
so juicy
and so steaming hot.

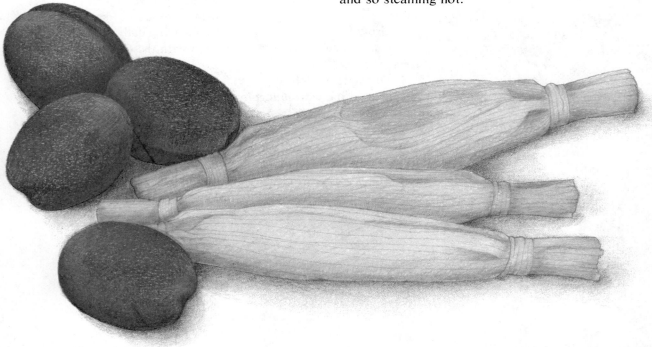

William Carlos Williams, COLLECTED EARLIER POEMS. Copyright 1938 by New Directions Publishing Corporation. Reprinted by permission of New Directions Publishing Corporation.

Copyright © 1974 by Tino Villanueva. Originally appeared in TEJIDOS, University of Texas-Austin (Vol. 1, No. 2, March 1974). Reprinted by permission of the author.

1. *riquísimos* (rē kē'sē môs), delicious. *[Spanish]*

Discussion · *This Is ...*

1. William Carlos Williams believed that poetry was not so much for the special occasion as for the ordinary occasion. Reconstruct out of your imagination what might have been the occasion of the writing of this poem. Note that the poem begins not with the first line but with the title.

2. Is there a reason for dividing the poem into three stanzas, rather, say, than into two or four? Discuss.

3. Williams believed that the visual impression of the poem—its organization into lines on the page—was very important to the poem's effect. Try rearranging the words in the lines and consider the different effects. For example:

> I have
> Eaten the
> Plums that were
> In the icebox

Discussion · *Variation ...*

1. Villanueva's title reveals that he has taken Williams's poem as a model. What are the similarities and the variations? Discuss.

2. In the last stanza Villanueva introduces two Spanish words: *Perdóname*—forgive me; and *riquísimos*—very tasty or delicious. Thus the foreign words are simply translations of Williams's English words. Why, in your opinion, does the poet switch from English to Spanish?

3. Of the following motives that Villanueva might have had in writing his poem, which seems closest to your view of his poem? **(a)** He wanted to prove he was as good a poet as Williams. **(b)** He wanted to try out a poetic exercise. **(c)** He wanted to show that tamales taste as good as plums. **(d)** He wanted to suggest that the experience of Williams's poem had some universal aspects, understandable to people of different cultures. Discuss.

Extension · Writing

William Carlos Williams lifted many simple experiences out of his own life and embodied them in poems. He rarely used rhyme, but he was careful about the placement of words in lines, aware that the location of a word often emphasized or deemphasized it. Try your hand at writing a short poem about some ordinary experience in the Williams style: answering to a wrong number on the telephone; eating an apple on the porch steps; checking out a strange book from the library; finding a red marble lying in the dirt; breaking a glass while getting a drink of water; dropping an egg on the kitchen floor. . . .

William Carlos Williams
1883 · 1963

William Carlos Williams advised the poet to write on "things with which he is familiar, simple things—at the same time to detach them from ordinary experience to the imagination." "This Is Just to Say" is one of the poems in which Williams begins with simple things, a familiar situation, and attempts to transfer the subject to the realm of the imagination.

Williams spent his life as a doctor in Rutherford, New Jersey, writing his poetry whenever he found time in his busy schedule.

Tino Villanueva 1941 ·

With the publication of his collection of poetry *Hay Otra Voz Poems* in 1971, Villanueva was acclaimed to be one of the best of the many contemporary Mexican American poets.

Born in San Marcos, Texas, he currently teaches in the Spanish Department at Boston University and serves as program director for "La Hora Hispana," a Harvard University radio broadcast for the Spanish-speaking community.

The Man Called Dead

Pearl S. Buck

Drake Forrester woke on Monday morning with more than his usual reluctance. On Saturdays and Sundays his agent closed his office and for two days he knew he could not ask the question or receive the answer. The question was always the same, and so was the answer.

"Have you heard of anything, Nick?"

"No, Drake, sorry, not yet, I have all sorts of lines out, as I told you, but no fish."

The next two sentences were likewise always the same.

"Thanks, Nick. If there is the slightest chance——"

"I know, I know, old man. I'd be on your doorstep in five minutes."

There might or might not follow the next hesitating words.

"Had I better tell you where I'll be today?"

"No, no, it's not that close, old man."

He was never anywhere but in his one-room apartment in this third-rate apartment house, unless he went out for a walk or a cheap meal somewhere. He was finished, he was through, the early promise had never been fulfilled, the parts he had played so brilliantly, almost up to the lead in the last play, had not led anywhere. He was not too old yet, barely forty-five, but the big chance had never come. He had made the most of opportunity, but the lead part, the humorous, sophisticated, delightful part that he knew he could do was simply not popular any more. Playwrights weren't interested. They wrote about raw brutal lustful boys. That he was not and that he could not be. He was born out of his time, too late or too early. The civilizing influence of the old world was gone and the new American civilization had not yet arrived, that was how he excused himself. There was no place for him.

It was fortunate indeed that he had never married, that he and Sara had agreed to wait. Then she had married another man, someone he did not know. He did not blame her, five years was too long to wait, and there was nothing in prospect, even then. Years ago that was, twelve years and three months and two days. He had not even seen her picture in the papers since her husband died two years, four months and six days ago, and he did not write to her.

He got up unwillingly and went to the door for the morning paper. The moment of greatest comfort in his dreary day was when he crept back into his still warm bed with the morning paper. This morning his bed was an especial refuge. It was raining, he saw, as he shut the window against the raw spring air. At least he had the shelter of this room, this bed, and he had been wise enough so that he would not starve. One meal a day and the meager rent were assured. There was no particular joy in the barren security, but it meant that he could be indifferent about getting up and going out on a bad day.

He piled the two thin pillows under the wall bedlight, opened the paper, turned to the theater page and read it closely and thoroughly. No news there. The season's plays were probably settled by now and his only chance was with the summer playhouse. He must talk with Nick about that and urge him, Nick was getting careless, the old bonds of friendship and past success were wearing down. Yet he dared not go to another agent, if indeed one would take him on. Nick knew him, at least. He did not have to explain what he could do.

"The Man Called Dead," slightly adapted from pp. 161-175 of THE LOVERS AND OTHER STORIES (The John Day Company). Copyright © 1977 by The Pearl S. Buck Foundation, Inc. Reprinted by permission of Thomas Y. Crowell Company, Inc., The Pearl S. Buck Foundation Inc. and Eyre Methuen Ltd., London.

At this moment the bedlight, always uneasy upon the plaster wall, chose to fall from its hook. He threw down the paper in sudden anger and sprang up to set it back, when he saw his name leap at him from the scattered pages.

DRAKE FORRESTER FOUND DEAD
IN HIS APARTMENT

It was a small headline on the back page. He seized the paper and took it to the window, and read his own obituary. "Drake Forrester, an actor, was found dead in his bed this morning by an elevator man, who brought him his usual morning paper. Mr. Forrester was well known in former years in successful Broadway plays. He received offers from Hollywood which he did not accept, preferring to remain on the legitimate stage. In recent years——"

The paper fell from his hand. He rushed to the telephone to call up Nick. This had to be contradicted immediately, Nick must send out a press release, he would sue the newspaper.

A nasal voice replied, "Nicholas Jansen Agency."

"Oh yes," he said, stammering as he always did when he was upset. "Is Mr. Jansen in?"

"Mr. Jansen won't be in today."

"Oh—do you know where he can be reached?"

"He can't be reached. He is spending the weekend in the country with an important client."

"Oh——"

He hesitated and then not knowing what else to say to the cold voice he muttered thanks and hung up and after another moment he went back to bed, covered himself up and shut his eyes. The paper fell on the floor and he gave himself up to loneliness.

Who cared whether it was true or not? Nobody had cared for a long time. His sister he had not heard from in years. She was married and lived in Texas. His parents had died when he was in his twenties, thank God, at the time it had seemed he would inevitably be famous. The theater was wickedly consuming, one had no life outside it, family and friends had fallen away.

He might as well be dead.

It was a strange feeling this being dead. Though he breathed and was awake in this room where he had lived so long, he was dead. His dramatic mind began to stir. He had read stories, he had even once seen a play on this very situation, and the man who was called dead had begun a new and completely free life, all the old debts cancelled, the failures erased. He might so welcome his freedom, he might do something entirely new, even take a new name and disappear from all he had known. He saw himself roaming about the world, a different person in one city or another, London, Paris, Venice, or even just Chicago or San Francisco.

There was no difficulty. He did not want to do anything except theater. Whatever else he attempted it would all end in a room like this somewhere, an agent trying to find him a job, and would an agent even try to find an unknown man a job? At least Drake Forrester had been somebody once, there was a memory.

It had been a long time since he had wept, but he wept now, only a few tears and not exactly for himself, but for anybody like him anywhere. He was not unique, of course. There was no use fooling himself. He had a little flair, a tiny talent that, combined with youth and extreme good looks—oh, he had been good-looking, still was— enough to carry him a little beyond the average, but it had not been enough and would never be enough for more than that.

So why not die? It would be easy, he had thought of it as anyone alone and unsuccessful thinks of it, not as something he would ever do, but still a possibility. He had thought of it sometimes at night when he took his sleeping pills. He held death in the palm of his hand, he had mused, gazing down on the white pellets, not with any reality in his mind, but with his little flair for drama, thinking that if he should so choose, he could do it.

Now someone else had done it for him, someone with his name. He took up the paper and read again. No reason was given for his death. It was simply announced with the few details about his former success on the stage and his gradual retirement. It was quite dignified, and if he died now, actually, the effect would be spoiled. This shabby room, his continual hounding of Nick, the ragged shirts and torn pajamas, the disgusting private details which he could keep hidden while he lived, but dead he must reveal. He ought really to be grateful that someone had died so nicely in his place. They had the address right, this street, this house.

He grinned, his lips twisted, and suddenly he felt hungry. He would get up, he would make his coffee and toast over the gas ring and he would never call Nick up again. He might leave here, he might go west tomorrow, saunter into Hollywood, later, quite on his own, and get any kind of a job around the sets, even a janitor's job. Nothing mattered, since his name was dead.

While he was drinking his coffee at his bedside table, the telephone rang suddenly. He got up and went to it. An unknown voice, a woman's voice, cried out, "Who is this, please?"

His name flew to his tongue and he checked it. "Whom do you want?" he growled.

"I've just seen the paper. I used to know Drake Forrester, years ago. We were in the same cast of a play. He was a good actor and I've often wondered—and now he's dead!"

He hesitated and then he said firmly, in the same deep voice, "Sorry, Madame, you have the wrong number." He hung up and sat down on his bed. But it was wonderful, nevertheless. Who could she have been? He was a good actor, she had not forgotten. He sat staring at the blank wall, trying to place the voice, and not being able to. Well, one person remembered. He felt cheered by so much and looked out of the window to see if it was still raining. On clear mornings he usually took a walk down the street.

It was still raining and he went back to bed and had scarcely settled himself when he heard a knock on the door. He got up again and opened it and there stood the janitor, looking surly and holding a small box of flowers.

"Oh, thanks," Drake said. "Wait a minute."

He went to his trousers hung over the chair and took out a dime. "Thanks a lot," he said.

The door shut and he opened the box of flowers. They were white roses and snapdragons with asparagus fern. There was an envelope and in it a card, "In memory of a swell time" the card said, and under it were signed seven names. He remembered them, people who had had bit parts in *The Red Circle*, the year it was almost a hit. It had been a mystery play, and he was just the husband of the murdered woman, not the lead. Still the run had been good and he had saved his money, thinking still that he and Sara would be married. That was the year she had married Harrison Page. It did not matter now. If he had been successful he would probably have been married to someone.

He put the flowers into the tin wastepaper basket, half filled it with water and set it in the window. He decided not to go back to bed, but to get up and go out. It was April and the sky was beginning to clear. He took a shower in the bathroom down the hall and came back and dressed carefully, and by the time he reached the street the clouds were white and ragged and scraps of blue sky were showing.

He took his usual walk around six blocks and since nobody knew him by name nobody was surprised to see him. He bought a copy of a small theatrical magazine, wondered if it were too cold yet to sit on a park bench and read, and decided it was and went back to his room. Not to call Nick gave him nothing at all to do, but he had made up his mind. He was not going to call Nick. When he felt like it he would consider further the question of where he would go, and maybe he would not go anywhere.

When he reached his room an envelope was stuck under his door, a telegram. He picked it up, tore it open and saw it was from Nick, a frantic appeal. "For heaven's sake, call me up. Been trying to get you for hours. Took the first train to town."

He sat down, his hat still on his head. Did this mean Nick knew he was dead or did not? Probably he had seen the news and did not believe it. Or maybe he thought someone was with him, he had never revealed to Nick the way he lived, and Nick supposed he had a friend. Nick knew he had some money but he did not know how little. He decided again not to call Nick up. Without taking his hat off he put the telegram beside the flowers and went out again.

Back on the park bench, he read the magazine from cover to cover. Then he sat awhile looking thoughtfully about at other men on the park benches. He recognized several of them, and he supposed they recognized him but they had never spoken to each other and there was no reason why they should do so now. It was about noon and he decided that he would get some lunch in an automat nearby and then go back to his room and sleep. He felt tired with the uncertainty of his emotions. It was an experience to be dead, he thought, and grinned again to himself.

When he went into the old apartment house the janitor came shambling out. "Must be your birthday or something," he said. "Two more boxes of flowers come while you was gone, and three telegrams."

"It's an anniversary," Drake said. He fumbled for another dime and gave it to the janitor and loaded himself with the boxes, put the telegrams in his pocket and went upstairs. This was getting funny, his room full of flowers and telegrams. It was like being back in the theater in his dressing room. Congratulations on being dead!

But he was touched, for all that. He had thought himself completely forgotten, and now he knew he was not. He opened the flowers and put them into the tin wastepaper basket with the others, pale yellow roses and white spirea from the director of his first play, and spring flowers from the star in *The Red Circle*, the man who murdered the wife. The telegrams were from members of the casts of his other plays and from a girl who used to work in Nick's office, who he knew well enough had once dreamed about him, only in those days he was still getting over Sara. The card was handwritten, "In fondest memory, Louise." But he had always called her Miss Silverstein.

The room looked festive and cheerful. He had not made the bed, often he did not make it, but just got into it again the way he had left it, but now he made it carefully and found an old handkerchief and dusted the table, the window sill and the bureau. After some thought he took the yellow roses and spirea and put them in a milk bottle and set them on the bureau.

Then the telephone began to ring and kept on ringing until either he had to go out again or answer it. He took up the receiver cautiously.

"Hello," he said in a voice not at all like his own. But it was not Nick. It was a woman and her voice was gentle.

"Hello, is this where Drake Forrester used to live?"

"It is," he answered. Then he recognized the voice. His heart gave a fierce leap. It was Sara! She had the loveliest voice he had ever heard.

"I have only just read the dreadful news," the gentle voice said. "Will you tell me where the services are to be? I used to know him years ago. I loved him very much, and I still do, though now I can never tell him."

He could not speak. What could he say? Then silly words burst from him. "Why didn't you tell him?"

She was surprised. "Are you his friend?"

"In a way. He told me about you."

"Oh, did he—he didn't forget?"

"Never!"

He was shocked at what was going on. He was weaving a new web, entangling himself beyond rescue.

"Oh, would you come and tell me about him?" she pleaded.

"Where are you?"

She gave him a street number far uptown, a long journey from where he stood. "I don't know just when——" So he began.

"Oh, come now," she begged. "I must know

everything. Then I can explain to you why—you see, I lost him, I mean, after my husband died I didn't know where to turn. Besides, I never saw his name anywhere until this morning, and then I knew really that I meant all along to find him. I suppose I just kept dreaming."

"I'll come," he promised. He hung up the receiver. Though he had committed himself, he might yet break his promise, but he knew where she was and sooner or later, however much he delayed, he knew as he knew himself that he would be on her threshold, ringing the bell, waiting for the moment of her recognition. He had to come back to life.

The telephone was ringing and on the chance that it might be her again he took it up impulsively and was caught. "Hello!" he cried too eagerly.

It was Nick, exasperated. "Of all the nonsense! Where have you been all morning? I knew you weren't dead."

"How did you know it?" he demanded. He felt injured. Did Nick think he hadn't the courage——

"For a while I thought maybe it was true, you old fake," Nick said. "Then I read the news item again and saw it couldn't be you. They had you sixty-five—didn't you notice?"

"No," Drake said.

"You never could remember figures," Nick said impatiently. "They had you born in 1887. I knew you weren't born then. I've done too much publicity for you. I've been busy all morning. The newspaper is going to correct the error tomorrow. Seems some fellow down in Virginia had your name and the newspaper mixed him up with you and used your obituary from the files. Well, it's done you a lot of good anyway. I've got you a part."

"A part?"

"Yeah, a good one, not starring, but a solid part. New play, *South Side of the Moon*, looks good too. Summer tryouts, of course, then probably Broadway. Producer says he used to know you, he called me up to tell me he was sorry he hadn't kept up with you, says he could have used you, if he'd known, so I said to give me a few minutes. You come right up here, Drake, and I'll have the contract ready. We'll sew things up. I'm not going to let any grass grow, not from now on."

Drake wavered. He could not be in two places at once. Either he went to Sara first, or he went to Nick first. The decision was close, he was always an actor, and he had not for a long time been a lover. Could the old role be revived? His dramatic imagination leaped ahead. He saw himself in Sara's hall, or perhaps in her living room, waiting for her, and then she came down the stairs, looking as beautiful as ever. He would stand perfectly still, waiting, and then when she saw him she would cry out.

"Oh Drake, darling—but how is this?"

"Somebody else died, Sara, not me."

He closed his eyes to kiss her and felt her soft lips. Sara was one of those soft women—the sweetest lips he had ever kissed.

"Hey, you asleep?" Nick bellowed in his ear.

"I can't come right away, Nick. I have an important engagement."

"What engagement?" Nick said indignantly. "What's more important than a contract?"

"Just this engagement," Drake said gaily. "But hold the contract, Nick. I'll get there sometime, today, tomorrow, one of these days."

He hung up and stood still, dreaming. He'd get there today, of course. When he and Sara had sat down on the sofa side by side, when he had kissed her again and again, when they had lunched together and told each other everything, he would glance at his watch and cry out.

"By gad, darling, I have an important engagement—I entirely forgot. You make me forget everything."

"A play, Drake?"

"Yes, *South Side of the Moon*, a new thing— it looks good."

"Come back soon." That is what she would say. "I'm so proud of you, Drake." That is what she would say.

"I'll come back," he would promise. "We'll dine together, shall we? We'll make our plans."

"I'll be waiting for you." That was what she would say, in her soft voice. It was softer than it used to be.

He bustled about the room, getting himself ready. He had one new shirt. He always kept one new shirt, just in case he might get an interview with a casting director. He began all over with another shower and a shave and then the new shirt and his better suit. He always kept one better suit. Then he hesitated. What about taking her something? He looked about the room at his few books, his small mementos, and then cried out aloud, snapping his thumb and finger, "Of course, the flowers!" He swept them all together, recovered a box he had thrown in the corner, packed them into it and tied the string carefully. Then he reached into his closet and took out a cane which he had not used for years, a slender bamboo cane tipped with imitation ivory which he had carried as the husband in the play. Pausing at the mirror he looked into it and saw someone he had not seen for a long time, a tall thin fellow whose pale face was alert and smiling, whose dark eyes were bright, a debonair sort of fellow, after all.

He smiled at the face, pleased at the resurrection. It was not bad, considering how dead he had been.

"Greetings," he said pleasantly to the face, and putting on his hat he tilted it slightly to one side and left the room. □□

Could This Have Really Happened?

While reading a story, many readers ask themselves, "Could this have really happened?" In the case of the story, "The Man Called Dead," the question would be "Is it possible that a newspaper would print an obituary of someone still alive?"

It is, and it has happened. To show that Pearl Buck's story is not purely imaginary, here are two instances where living people saw their obituaries in print.

Hemingway (1899–1961) once found himself "called dead." On a flight across Uganda, Africa, in 1953, the writer endured two plane crashes in a row. Newspapers and magazines all over the world printed the death notices. When Hemingway saw them, he was sobered. But before reporters he is said to have remarked, "My luck she is running good."

Mark Twain (1835–1910) used the publication of his demise as an excuse for laughter. While abroad in Europe in 1897, stories were appearing in the press that he had died. Twain responded waggishly to the inquiry of a reporter: "The reports of my death are greatly exaggerated."

Discussion

1. When Drake Forrester reads about his death, he is shocked and tries to phone his agent. But then, as he muses over the matter, he thinks of those who, their deaths announced, have gone out into the world and created new lives for themselves. Why doesn't Forrester seize this opportunity for himself?

2. Forrester next thinks how easy it would be to simply die. There is something clean-cut about the way his death has been announced. Now he could actually die. Why doesn't he take this path?

3. As the telephone calls begin and the flowers start to arrive, Forrester's attitude changes. Explain and discuss.

4. (a) What evidence early in the story shows that Forrester is still in love with Sara? (b) When she calls after reading about his death, what is his reaction and what does it suggest about his feelings?

5. What evidence is there at the end of the story that Forrester has been changed by his "death," especially in his response to his agent's request that he come over right away to sign a contract for a part in a play?

6. What evidence is there in the conclusion of the story that Forrester has not "died" but has been "reborn" by his "death"?

Pearl Buck 1892 · 1973

Daughter of missionaries, Buck lived in China until she attended college in the United States. Returning to China, she taught at several colleges and universities and began the writing that was to bring her fame. In 1931 she won the Pulitzer Prize, and in 1938 she was awarded the coveted Nobel Prize for Literature, the first American woman to be so honored.

See **CHARACTERIZATION** Handbook of Literary Terms

Waiting for Her Train

Audrey M. Lee

She sits in Thirtieth Street Station watching the newsman over the three-screen television. She is waiting for her train to come in. The station vibrates with arrival and departure of trains. Hers does not arrive. But she has time. Other people are waiting, too. Expectant. Anxious. They have schedules to meet. Destinations. They have purchased tickets—round trip or one-way. She has not purchased her ticket yet. A ticket represents a destination. She has not decided upon her destination. But who is to know . . .

She recognizes the old woman wearing two dresses and two sweaters and carrying the shopping bag full of her possessions. She will not be as obvious as the old lady. There will never be a vagrant look about her. She has locked her possessions in one of the station lockers. Her presence in the station is temporary—just until her train comes in. And for all anyone knows, her baggage is being shipped ahead of her. She is waiting for her train no matter *what* anyone might think.

The railroad workers for the day shift are coming into the station. They are looking at her as usual. They think they know but they don't. Those tolerant looks that express knowing—as if she were a distant relative in their house. A poor distant relative who has had a bad stroke of luck. What of it? She has had a taste of the finer things. She has been to the Art Museum, stood among the Picassos and the Powells—and oh too many paintings to be mentioned. The fact remains that she has been. She knows something about fashion, too. About designing. About labels—labels tell so much about quality. And they lend respectability to clothing. She has no proof that she knows, except the dress she is wearing. Her creditors have reclaimed all the others, along with the shoes. They were right, of course. But they couldn't deny she had discriminating taste. But that is behind her. She must look to the future.

At eight o'clock the Horn and Hardart Restaurant will open. She will go there as usual. And afterwards—well, she would see.

Copyright © 1971 by Audrey M. Lee. Reprinted by permission.

"North Philadelphia. Trenton. Princeton. Newark. New York. Now loading on platform number three."

Not her train. She is waiting for something more exotic. A tropic island with palm trees. There are so many people going places. And so many people returning. She likes this time of morning. Her train would come in the morning. It would pull into the station on velvet springs. And it would purr, not screech. Her man would be waiting with her bags. And she would be clothed in quiet elegance, the labels of the day's fashion turned in, reassuring against her skin, the quality turned out for everyone to see. That would teach the know-alls. The railroad workers who passed her bench, throwing their tolerant glances. That would prove that she had been waiting for her train after all. That she was going somewhere.

Horn and Hardart opens. She gets up from the bench, brushes the wrinkles that resist her pressure. When she bought the dress it was wrinkle-resistant. She puts on her soiled gloves and respectable walk, feeling the kinks loosen in her knees, giving them a jerk or two when no one is looking. She picks up a newspaper from a bench. Someone is always leaving a newspaper. Then she checks the return coin slots of the telephones. No forgotten dimes. She will not have coffee this morning.

Inside Horn and Hardart, she is reading the specials posted on the menu. Later on breakfast will cost more. She is giving the menu a respectable glance, demonstrating her discriminating taste with proper deliberation. Then with the same deliberating eye, she looks at the long line of people waiting to take advantage of the early morning special breakfasts. A glass of water will do until the line is shorter. That is her reasoning. She tugs decisively at her glove and fills her glass with cool water from the fountain and sits down to a table near the window to read the newspaper. But first she will make the table ready for breakfast. She lays knife, fork and spoon, the napkin. There.

The newspaper. She will choose a supermarket to visit from those advertised. She wonders how many different supermarkets she has shopped in over the past.

Nine o'clock. She is entering the supermarket. She fills her cart with steaks, chops, parsley, fruit. She will eat an orange while she shops. Cheese—she would taste a piece of cheese, too. Not the same brand she had yesterday at the other market. This cheese is sharper. Raisin bread. She will eat a slice or two.

She opens a jar of herring. Herring for breakfast—oh well, one eats what one finds convenient. Besides, fish is a necessary part of the diet, too. The manager is smiling and handing her glove to her.

"Looks like you're having your breakfast..."

Kidding her, of course. People are always chewing on something when they go to market. "Yes. You have good herring." The compliment pleases him. "Very good herring," she is saying for emphasis. He is smiling and walking away.

Bananas—bananas are filling. She needs something that will fill her. Meanwhile, she must appear in earnest. She must fill her cart with household articles. A mop handle and mop. That would look impressive jutting from the cart. There—now another bite of banana. Paper napkins from the shelf. Table salt. Black pepper. Paprika . . .

She swallows the last of the banana. Then she puts on her gloves, pushes the cartful of groceries to the front of the store, places it in a respectful position just to one side of the checkout counter, out of the path of shoppers waiting in line for the cashier. And in a respectable voice:

"Cashier—I forgot my purse—I wonder if you would be kind enough to let my cart stay here until I return . . ."

"Certainly, madam."

"I appreciate it. Thanks so much." She burps. Bananas take a while to digest. But she has time. She hurries from the market. She does not want the manager to see her leaving. He might suggest sending the groceries to her—sweet of him, of course—but how could she explain—what could she say—that she was waiting for a train? Well, she had escaped now. Explanations are not necessary.

In D-D's Department Store she stands before the cosmetics counter, trying on a sample lipstick. She doesn't like it well enough to buy it. She tries the expensive face powder which the saleslady mixes for her. A spoonful of white powder. A spoonful of pinkish powder, mint-colored powder. Then blending them with a spatula.

"You look absolutely gorgeous—this is wonderful and it's good for your skin. Put this on and wipe it dry—work that in—truly pink would be equal to your natural——"

"I was looking for something quick and easy. I don't have time to do much in the morning . . ."

"Try this," dipping the spoon into the powder. Wiping the spoon and dipping it into another powder. "This has orange in it. You have to use it sparingly—you need some color—it's a sample portion. Try it out at home—try them both—and see how you like them."

"Thank you very much. Maybe I can come back tomorrow—if I decide I like the way it looks on me. These lights—if I were only at home . . ."

"You'll like it."

One mirror is seldom true. One has to consider the majority of mirrors. She smiles at the woman. Then she walks toward the perfumes. Aura of Emotion—Charles of the Ritz—Desert Flower—Desert Flower is too incongruous a name to be considered by a bench sitter. Still she must try something new. Yesterday it was Heaven Scent. Today—well—it would depend—Chantilly—she felt like *Chantilly*—but first . . . She looked at the bottles of perfume and toilet water, picked them up, read their labels. She is a discriminating shopper. All the bottles scrutinized. She picks up the spray bottle of Chantilly. Poof—savors the scent with a sensitive and discriminating nose. That is what she wants. She sprays her ears, wrists, clothing. All very quickly

and tastefully. Subtly. She wants to be sure of catching the scent.

"It smells good. May I show you something, madam? We have the talcum, too. It will make a nice set . . ."

She is very discriminating, so she will not answer right away. She has not made up her mind—not really—Chanel No. 5. Intimate.

"Excuse me a minute, madam. I'll wait on this customer—I know you want to take your time—when you decide . . ."

Poof. Chantilly behind her ears once more. Subtly. Discriminatingly. The saleslady is busy. Several customers are waiting. She pulls her gloves securely over her hands, resumes her respectable posture and walks out of the store. The scent does indeed smell good on. Now she will return to the station and wash her gloves. She will lay them on the bench to dry. If only she had a portable hair dryer, she could wash her hair. But portable hair dryers are made for people of means—not for people of predicament.

Back at the station powder room. She washes her gloves, touches her hair, and checks her makeup. The powder goes well with her complexion. And so does the lipstick. She checks her purse, making certain she still has the samples in her purse, touches her hair again, approves. Still she would like to get her hair washed and styled. She will think of a way. But having the new makeup and the perfume makes her feel somewhat refreshed. She will settle down on a bench to watch the pictures, plan the dinner menu, decide upon the evening's entertainment.

And of course, she will watch the evening flow of men and women in and out of the station. But before that, she will check the coin return slots of the telephones. Nothing yet. She will have to wait for her coffee a little longer. The best time to check the slots is just after the rush hour. She might even be able to afford two cups of coffee. And who is there to deny that her train might have arrived by then. □□

From the Author

I first wrote this story on June 28, 1967. I sent it out to publications thirty-three times and it was rejected thirty-three times, including four rejections from one and the same magazine, before it was published [in a] 1971 anthology.

It is one of my purely fictional short stories. I have seen men and women in train stations searching telephones for forgotten coins. I have seen men and women sitting in Horn and Hardart, who, obviously, have no money to buy food. And I have seen shoppers who have money eat foods from supermarket shelves while they are shopping; and they never pay for the food which they have eaten.

It is one of those stories which came to me before any conscious idea. That is, the first line came to me, while I was either sitting at my desk or in transit. I don't remember. I do know that it was born on the type-writer, without any urging from me, that I wrote it out of creative mischief; and I had fun writing it. That it was born of my imagination, which is the true ingredient of creative writing, as opposed to stories based on actual events but fictionalized. Because most of my writing calls upon my imagination, I do not write every day. I must also be moved to write (some people call it inspiration); so I do not force myself to write when I do not feel like doing it.

Discussion

1. As the story opens, the woman is waiting in the station for a train—or is she? (a) What is she doing at the station? (b) When does the reader discover the truth about the woman?

2. At the Horn and Hardart cafeteria, what does the woman do to suggest that she is a regular customer?

3. What is the woman's real purpose at the supermarket, and what does she do to deflect attention from her purpose?

4. What does the woman do at the department store to get what she wants?

5. (a) As we see her back at the station at the end of the story, what is the attitude of the woman toward what she has done? (b) Does she have any feelings of guilt?

6. (a) What do you think the author's attitude is toward the woman's behavior? (b) What do you think of the woman's behavior?

Vocabulary · Context

Be sure you know the meanings and pronunciations of the following words. Use your Glossary for reference. Choose the correct words from the list to complete the sentences, and write those words on a separate sheet of paper.

discriminating   predicament
incongruous   savor
jutted   scrutinize

1. This store's basement has some great bargains, but one must _____ everything for possible flaws.

2. Dickens's account of a Christmas dinner is so vivid that one can virtually _____ the aromas and flavors.

3. It was natural for the girl to have _____ taste in clothes since her mother had been a noted dress designer.

4. The western hero's strong jaw _____ out in silhouette against the flaming sky.

5. The small group of cacti in the rose bed seemed an _____ touch even for the eccentric owner of the garden.

Long Distance

Carole Gregory

That phone call, the one that you wait for
but never expect to come
was phoned today. And
that voice, the voice you ache for
5 but seldom expect to hear
spoke today. And that
loneliness, the loneliness you hurt from
but always held inside,
flies out like thin stones across water.

Discussion

1. What ideas do you get
from this poem as to who
the caller and the person
called might be?

2. Do you think the image
of the word "stones" in
the last line is a good one?
What would the effect be
if the word were changed
to "leaves" for example?

"Long Distance" by Carole Gregory from
NINE BLACK POETS. Copyright 1968.
Reprinted by permission of Moore Publishing
Company, Durham, NC.

See **PROTAGONIST/ANTAGONIST** Handbook of Literary Terms

Twelve Angry Men

Reginald Rose

Descriptions of Jurors

FOREMAN. *A small, petty man who is impressed with the authority he has and handles himself quite formally. Not overly bright, but dogged.*

JUROR NUMBER TWO. *A meek, hesitant man who finds it difficult to maintain any opinions of his own. Easily swayed and usually adopts the opinion of the last person to whom he has spoken.*

JUROR NUMBER THREE. *A very strong, very forceful, extremely opinionated man within whom can be detected a streak of sadism. A humorless man who is intolerant of opinions other than his own and accustomed to forcing his wishes and views upon others.*

JUROR NUMBER SEVEN. *A loud, flashy, glad-handed salesman type who has more important things to do than to sit on a jury. He is quick to show temper, quick to form opinions on things about which he knows nothing. Is a bully and, of course, a coward.*

JUROR NUMBER EIGHT. *A quiet, thoughtful, gentle man. A man who sees all sides of every question and constantly seeks the truth. A man of strength tempered with compassion. Above all, a man who wants justice to be done and will fight to see that it is.*

JUROR NUMBER NINE. *A mild, gentle old man, long since defeated by life and now merely waiting to die. A man who recognizes himself for what he is and mourns the days when it would have been possible to be courageous without shielding himself behind his many years.*

JUROR NUMBER FOUR. *Seems to be a man of wealth and position. A practiced speaker who presents himself well at all times. Seems to feel a little bit above the rest of the jurors. His only concern is with the facts in this case, and he is appalled at the behavior of the others.*

JUROR NUMBER FIVE. *A naïve, very frightened young man who takes his obligations in this case very seriously, but who finds it difficult to speak up when his elders have the floor.*

JUROR NUMBER SIX. *An honest but dull-witted man who comes upon his decisions slowly and carefully. A man who finds it difficult to create positive opinions, but who must listen to and digest and accept those opinions offered by others which appeal to him most.*

JUROR NUMBER TEN. *An angry, bitter man. A man who antagonizes almost at sight. A bigot who places no values on any human life save his own. A man who has been nowhere and is going nowhere and knows it deep within him.*

JUROR NUMBER ELEVEN. *A refugee from Europe who had come to this country in 1941. A man who speaks with an accent and who is ashamed, humble, almost subservient to the people around him, but who will honestly seek justice because he has suffered through so much injustice.*

JUROR NUMBER TWELVE. *A slick, bright advertising man who thinks of human beings in terms of percentages, graphs, and polls and has no real understanding of people. A superficial snob, but trying to be a good fellow.*

Act One

Fade in[1] on a jury box. Twelve men are seated in it, listening intently to the voice of the JUDGE as he charges them.[2] We do not see the JUDGE. He speaks in slow, measured tones and his voice is grave. The camera drifts over the faces of the JURYMEN as the JUDGE speaks and we see that most of their heads are turned to camera's left. SEVEN looks down at his hands. THREE looks off in another direction, the direction in which the defendant would be sitting. TEN keeps moving his head back and forth nervously. The JUDGE drones on.

JUDGE. Murder in the first degree—premeditated homicide—is the most serious charge tried in our criminal courts. You've heard a long and complex case, gentlemen, and it is now your duty to sit down to try and separate the facts from the fancy. One man is dead. The life of another is at stake. If there is a reasonable doubt in your minds as to the guilt of the accused . . . then you must declare him not guilty. If, however, there is no reasonable doubt, then he must be found guilty. Whichever way you decide, the verdict must be unanimous. I urge you to deliberate honestly and thoughtfully. You are faced with a grave responsibility. Thank you, gentlemen.

(There is a long pause.)

CLERK *(droning).* The jury will retire.

(And now, slowly, almost hesitantly, the members of the jury begin to rise. Awkwardly, they file out of the jury box and off camera to the left. Camera holds on jury box, then fades out.)

(Fade in on a large, bare, unpleasant-looking room. This is the jury room in the county criminal court of a large Eastern city. It is about 4:00 P.M. The room is furnished with a long conference table and a dozen chairs. The walls are bare, drab, and badly in need of a fresh coat of paint. Along one wall is a row of windows which look out on the skyline of the city's financial district. High on another wall is an electric clock. A washroom opens off the jury room. In one corner of the room is a water fountain. On the table are
pads, pencils, ashtrays. One of the windows is open. Papers blow across the table and onto the floor as the door opens. Lettered on the outside of the door are the words "Jury Room." A uniformed GUARD holds the door open. Slowly, almost self-consciously, the twelve JURORS file in. The GUARD counts them as they enter the door, his lips moving, but no sound coming forth. Four or five of the JURORS light cigarettes as they enter the room. FIVE lights his pipe, which he smokes constantly throughout the play. TWO and TWELVE go to the water fountain, NINE goes into the washroom, the door of which is lettered "Men." Several of the JURORS take seats at the table. Others stand awkwardly around the room. Several look out the windows. These are men who are ill at ease, who do not really know each other to talk to, and who wish they were anywhere but here. SEVEN, standing at window, takes out a pack of gum, takes a piece, and offers it around. There are no takers. He mops his brow.)*

SEVEN *(to SIX).* Y'know something? It's hot. *(SIX nods.)* You'd think they'd at least air-condition the place. I almost dropped dead in court.

(SEVEN opens the window a bit wider. The GUARD looks them over and checks his count. Then, satisfied, he makes ready to leave.)

GUARD. Okay, gentlemen. Everybody's here. If there's anything you want, I'm right outside. Just knock.

(He exits, closing the door. Silently they all look at the door. We hear the lock clicking.)

FIVE. I never knew they locked the door.

TEN *(blowing nose).* Sure, they lock the door. What did you think?

FIVE. I don't know. It just never occurred to me.

(Some of the JURORS are taking off their jackets.

Twelve Angry Men from SIX TELEVISION PLAYS by Reginald Rose. Reprinted by permission of International Creative Management. Copyright © 1956 by Reginald Rose.

1. **Fade in.** This is one of several terms that indicate the way in which the television camera functions. When the camera "fades in," it gradually brings the picture into focus. When the camera "fades out," the picture disappears, leaving a blank screen.

2. **he charges them.** He tells them what their duties are as jurors.

Others are sitting down at the table. They still are reluctant to talk to each other. FOREMAN *is at head of table, tearing slips of paper for ballots. Now we get a close shot of* EIGHT.[3] *He looks out the window. We hear* THREE *talking to* TWO.)

THREE. Six days. They should have finished it in two. Talk, talk, talk. Did you ever hear so much talk about nothing?

TWO (*nervously laughing*). Well . . . I guess . . . they're entitled.

THREE. Everybody gets a fair trial. (*He shakes his head.*) That's the system. Well, I suppose you can't say anything against it.

(TWO *looks at him nervously, nods, and goes over to water cooler. Cut to shot of* EIGHT *staring out window. Cut to table.[4]* SEVEN *stands at the table, putting out a cigarette.*)

SEVEN (*to* TEN). How did you like that business about the knife? Did you ever hear a phonier story?

TEN (*wisely*). Well, look, you've gotta expect that. You know what you're dealing with.

SEVEN. Yeah, I suppose. What's the matter, you got a cold?

TEN (*blowing*). A lulu. These hot-weather colds can kill you.

(SEVEN *nods sympathetically.*)

FOREMAN (*briskly*). All right, gentlemen. Let's take seats.

SEVEN. Right. This better be fast. I've got tickets to *The Seven Year Itch*[5] tonight. I must be the only guy in the whole world who hasn't seen it yet. (*He laughs and sits down.*) Okay, your honor, start the show.

(*They all begin to sit down. The* FOREMAN *is seated at the head of the table.* EIGHT *continues to look out the window.*)

FOREMAN (*to* EIGHT). How about sitting down? (EIGHT *doesn't hear him.*) The gentleman at the window.

(EIGHT *turns, startled.*)

FOREMAN. How about sitting down?

EIGHT. Oh, I'm sorry.

(*He heads for a seat.*)

TEN (*to* SIX). It's tough to figure, isn't it? A kid kills his father. Bing! Just like that. Well, it's the element. They let the kids run wild. Maybe it serves 'em right.

FOREMAN. Is everybody here?

TWELVE. The old man's inside.

(*The* FOREMAN *turns to the washroom just as the door opens.* NINE *comes out, embarrassed.*)

FOREMAN. We'd like to get started.

NINE. Forgive me, gentlemen. I didn't mean to keep you waiting.

FOREMAN. It's all right. Find a seat.

(NINE *heads for a seat and sits down. They look at the* FOREMAN *expectantly.*)

FOREMAN. All right. Now, you gentlemen can handle this any way you want to. I mean, I'm not going to make any rules. If we want to discuss it first and then vote, that's one way. Or we can vote right now to see how we stand.

SEVEN. Let's vote now. Who knows, maybe we can all go home.

TEN. Yeah. Let's see who's where.

THREE. Right. Let's vote now.

FOREMAN. Anybody doesn't want to vote?

(*He looks around the table. There is no answer.*)

Okay, all those voting guilty raise your hands.

(*Seven or eight hands go up immediately. Several others go up more slowly. Everyone looks around the table. There are two hands not raised,* NINE'*s and* EIGHT'*s.* NINE'*s hand goes up slowly now as the* FOREMAN *counts.*)

FOREMAN. . . . Nine . . . ten . . . eleven . . . That's eleven for guilty. Okay. Not guilty? (EIGHT'*s hand is raised.*) One. Right. Okay. Eleven to one, guilty. Now we know where we are.

THREE. Somebody's in left field. (*To* EIGHT) You think he's not guilty?

EIGHT (*quietly*). I don't know.

THREE. I never saw a guiltier man in my life. You

---

3. *a close shot of Eight,* a head-and-shoulders view of *Eight.*

4. *Cut to shot of Eight. . . . Cut to table.* The word *cut* indicates an immediate switch from one camera to another camera in order to show what is happening on another part of the television stage.

5. *The Seven Year Itch,* a comedy that opened on Broadway in 1952.

sat right in court and heard the same thing I did. The man's a dangerous killer. You could see it.

EIGHT. He's nineteen years old.

THREE. That's old enough. He knifed his own father. Four inches into the chest. An innocent little nineteen-year-old kid. They proved it a dozen different ways. Do you want me to list them?

EIGHT. No.

TEN *(to* EIGHT*).* Well, do you believe his story?

EIGHT. I don't know whether I believe it or not. Maybe I don't.

SEVEN. So what'd you vote not guilty for?

EIGHT. There were eleven votes for guilty. It's not so easy for me to raise my hand and send a boy off to die without talking about it first.

SEVEN. Who says it's easy for me?

EIGHT. No one.

SEVEN. What, just because I voted fast? I think the guy's guilty. You couldn't change my mind if you talked for a hundred years.

EIGHT. I don't want to change your mind. I just want to talk for a while. Look, this boy's been kicked around all his life. You know, living in a slum, his mother dead since he was nine. That's not a very good head start. He's a tough, angry kid. You know why slum kids get that way? Because we knock 'em on the head once a day, every day. I think maybe we owe him a few words. That's all.

(He looks around the table. Some of them look back coldly. Some cannot look at him. Only NINE *nods slowly.* TWELVE *doodles steadily.* FOUR *begins to comb his hair.)*

TEN. I don't mind telling you this, mister. We don't owe him a thing. He got a fair trial, didn't he? You know what that trial cost? He's lucky he got it. Look, we're all grownups here. You're not going to tell us that we're supposed to believe him, knowing what he is. I've lived among 'em all my life. You can't believe a word they say. You know that.

NINE *(to* TEN *very slowly).* I don't know that. What a terrible thing for a man to believe! Since when is dishonesty a group characteristic?

You have no monopoly on the truth——

THREE *(interrupting).* All right. It's not Sunday. We don't need a sermon.

NINE. What this man says is very dangerous——

*(*EIGHT *puts his hand on* NINE's *arm and stops him. Somehow his touch and his gentle expression calm the old man. He draws a deep breath and relaxes.)*

FOUR. I don't see any need for arguing like this. I think we ought to be able to behave like gentlemen.

SEVEN. Right!

FOUR. If we're going to discuss this case, let's discuss the facts.

FOREMAN. I think that's a good point. We have a job to do. Let's do it.

ELEVEN *(with accent).* If you gentlemen don't mind, I'm going to close the window. *(He gets up and does so.) (Apologetically)* It was blowing on my neck. *(*TEN *blows his nose fiercely.)*

TWELVE. I may have an idea here. I'm just thinking out loud now, but it seems to me that it's up to us to convince this gentleman— *(indicating* EIGHT*)*—that we're right and he's wrong. Maybe if we each took a minute or two, you know, if we sort of try it on for size——

FOREMAN. That sounds fair enough. Supposing we go once around the table.

SEVEN. Okay, let's start it off.

FOREMAN. Right. *(To* TWO*)* I guess you're first.

TWO *(timidly).* Oh. Well . . . *(Long pause)* I just think he's guilty. I thought it was obvious. I mean nobody proved otherwise.

EIGHT *(quietly).* Nobody has to prove otherwise. The burden of proof is on the prosecution. The defendant doesn't have to open his mouth. That's in the Constitution. The Fifth Amendment.[6] You've heard of it.

TWO *(flustered).* Well, sure, I've heard of it. I know what it is. I . . . what I meant . . . well, anyway, I think he was guilty.

---

6. **The Fifth Amendment,** the amendment that guarantees that a person on trial for a criminal offense cannot be forced to testify against oneself.

THREE. Okay, let's get to the facts. Number one, let's take the old man who lived on the second floor right underneath the room where the murder took place. At ten minutes after twelve on the night of the killing he heard loud noises in the upstairs apartment. He said it sounded like a fight. Then he heard the kid say to his father, "I'm gonna kill you." A second later he heard a body falling, and he ran to the door of his apartment, looked out, and saw the kid running down the stairs and out of the house. Then he called the police. They found the father with a knife in his chest.

FOREMAN. And the coroner fixed the time of death at around midnight.

THREE. Right. Now what else do you want?

FOUR. The boy's entire story is flimsy. He claimed he was at the movies. That's a little ridiculous, isn't it? He couldn't even remember what pictures he saw.

THREE. That's right. Did you hear that? (To FOUR) You're absolutely right.

TEN. Look, what about the woman across the street? If her testimony don't prove it, then nothing does.

TWELVE. That's right. She saw the killing, didn't she?

FOREMAN. Let's go in order.

TEN (loud). Just a minute. Here's a woman who's lying in bed and can't sleep. It's hot, you know. (He gets up and begins to walk around, blowing his nose and talking.) Anyway, she looks out the window, and right across the street she sees the kid stick the knife into his father. She's known the kid all his life. His window is right opposite hers, across the el tracks, and she swore she saw him do it.

EIGHT. Through the windows of a passing elevated train.

TEN. Okay. And they proved in court that you can look through the windows of a passing el train at night and see what's happening on the other side. They proved it.

EIGHT. I'd like to ask you something. How come you believed her? She's one of "them" too, isn't she?

(TEN walks over to EIGHT.)

TEN. You're a pretty smart fellow, aren't you?

FOREMAN (rising). Now take it easy.

(THREE gets up and goes to TEN.)

THREE. Come on. Sit down. (He leads TEN back to his seat.) What're you letting him get you all upset for? Relax.

(TEN and THREE sit down.)

FOREMAN. Let's calm down now. (To FIVE) It's your turn.

FIVE. I'll pass it.

FOREMAN. That's your privilege. (To SIX) How about you?

SIX (slowly). I don't know. I started to be convinced, you know, with the testimony from those people across the hall. Didn't they say something about an argument between the father and the boy around seven o'clock that night? I mean, I can be wrong.

ELEVEN. I think it was eight o'clock. Not seven.

EIGHT. That's right. Eight o'clock. They heard the father hit the boy twice and then saw the boy walk angrily out of the house. What does that prove?

SIX. Well, it doesn't exactly prove anything. It's just part of the picture. I didn't say it proved anything.

FOREMAN. Anything else?

SIX. No.

(SIX goes to the water fountain.)

FOREMAN (to SEVEN). All right. How about you?

SEVEN. I don't know, most of it's been said already. We can talk all day about this thing, but I think we're wasting our time. Look at the kid's record. At fifteen he was in reform school. He stole a car. He's been arrested for mugging. He was picked up for knife-fighting. I think they said he stabbed somebody in the arm. This is a very fine boy.

EIGHT. Ever since he was five years old his father beat him up regularly. He used his fists.

SEVEN. So would I! A kid like that.

THREE. You're right. It's the kids. The way they are—you know? They don't listen. (Bitter) I've got a kid. When he was eight years old he ran away from a fight. I saw him. I was so ashamed, I told him right out, "I'm gonna make a man out of you or I'm gonna bust you up into little pieces trying." When he was fifteen he hit me in the face. He's big, you know. I haven't seen him in three years. Rotten kid! You work your heart out. . . . *(Pause)* All right. Let's get on with it. *(Looks away embarrassed.)*

FOUR. We're missing the point here. This boy—let's say he's a product of a filthy neighborhood and a broken home. We can't help that. We're not here to go into reasons why slums are breeding grounds for criminals. They are. I know it. So do you. The children who come out of slum backgrounds are potential menaces to society.

TEN. You said it there. I don't want any part of them, believe me.

(There is a dead silence for a moment, and then FIVE *speaks haltingly.)*

FIVE. I've lived in a slum all my life——

TEN. Oh, now wait a second!

FIVE. I used to play in a back yard that was filled with garbage. Maybe it still smells on me.

FOREMAN. Now let's be reasonable. There's nothing personal——*(*FIVE *stands up.)*

FIVE. There is something personal!

(Then he catches himself and, seeing everyone looking at him, sits down, fists clenched.)

THREE *(persuasively)*. Come on, now. He didn't mean you, feller. Let's not be so sensitive. . . .

(There is a long pause.)

ELEVEN. I can understand this sensitivity.

FOREMAN. Now let's stop the bickering. We're wasting time. *(To* EIGHT*)* It's your turn.

EIGHT. All right. I had a peculiar feeling about this trial. Somehow I felt that the defense counsel never really conducted a thorough cross-examination. I mean, he was appointed by the court to defend the boy. He hardly seemed interested. Too many questions were left unasked.

THREE *(annoyed)*. What about the ones that were asked? For instance, let's talk about that cute little switch-knife.[7] You know, the one that fine upright kid admitted buying.

EIGHT. All right. Let's talk about it. Let's get it in here and look at it. I'd like to see it again, Mr. Foreman.

(The FOREMAN *looks at him questioningly and then gets up and goes to the door. During the following dialogue the* FOREMAN *knocks, the* GUARD *comes in, the* FOREMAN *whispers to him, the* GUARD *nods and leaves, locking the door.)*

THREE. We all know what it looks like. I don't see why we have to look at it again. *(To* FOUR*)* What do you think?

FOUR. The gentleman has a right to see exhibits in evidence.

THREE *(shrugging)*. Okay with me.

FOUR *(to* EIGHT*)*. This knife is a pretty strong piece of evidence, don't you agree?

EIGHT. I do.

FOUR. The boy admits going out of his house at eight o'clock after being slapped by his father.

EIGHT. Or punched.

FOUR. Or punched. He went to a neighborhood store and bought a switch-knife. The storekeeper was arrested the following day when he admitted selling it to the boy. It's a very unusual knife. The storekeeper identified it and said it was the only one of its kind he had in stock. Why did the boy get it? *(Sarcastically)* As a present for a friend of his, he says. Am I right so far?

EIGHT. Right.

THREE. You bet he's right. *(To all)* Now listen to this man. He knows what he's talking about.

FOUR. Next, the boy claims that on the way home the knife must have fallen through a hole in his coat pocket, that he never saw it again. Now there's a story, gentlemen. You know what actually happened. The boy took the knife home and a few hours later stabbed his father with it and even remembered to wipe off the fingerprints.

(The door opens and the GUARD *walks in with an oddly designed knife with a tag on it.* FOUR *gets up and takes it from him. The* GUARD *exits.)*

---

7. **switch-knife,** switchblade, a pocketknife with a blade that springs out.

FOUR. Everyone connected with the case identified this knife. Now are you trying to tell me that someone picked it up off the street and went up to the boy's house and stabbed his father with it just to be amusing?

EIGHT. No, I'm saying that it's possible that the boy lost the knife and that someone else stabbed his father with a similar knife. It's possible.

(FOUR *flips open the knife and jams it into the table.*)

FOUR. Take a look at that knife. It's a very strange knife. I've never seen one like it before in my life. Neither had the storekeeper who sold it to him.

(EIGHT *reaches casually into his pocket and withdraws an object. No one notices this. He stands up quietly.*)

FOUR. Aren't you trying to make us accept a pretty incredible coincidence?

EIGHT. I'm not trying to make anyone accept it. I'm just saying it's possible.

THREE (*shouting*). And I'm saying it's not possible.

(EIGHT *swiftly flicks open the blade of a switchknife and jams it into the table next to the first one. They are exactly alike. There are several gasps and everyone stares at the knife. There is a long silence.*)

THREE (*slowly, amazed*). What are you trying to do?

TEN (*loud*). Yeah, what is this? Who do you think you are?

FIVE. Look at it! It's the same knife!

FOREMAN. Quiet! Let's be quiet.

(*They quiet down.*)

FOUR. Where did you get it?

EIGHT. I got it last night in a little junk shop around the corner from the boy's house. It cost two dollars.

THREE. Now listen to me! You pulled a real smart trick here, but you proved absolutely zero. Maybe there are ten knives like that, so what?

EIGHT. Maybe there are.

THREE. The boy lied and you know it.

EIGHT. He may have lied. (*To* TEN) Do you think he lied?

TEN (*violently*). Now that's a stupid question. Sure he lied!

EIGHT (*to* FOUR). Do you?

FOUR. You don't have to ask me that. You know my answer. He lied.

EIGHT (*to* FIVE). Do you think he lied?

(FIVE *can't answer immediately. He looks around nervously.*)

FIVE. I . . . I don't know.

SEVEN. Now wait a second. What are you, the guy's lawyer? Listen, there are still eleven of us who think he's guilty. You're alone. What do you think you're gonna accomplish? If you want to be stubborn and hang this jury,[8] he'll be tried again and found guilty, sure as he's born.

EIGHT. You're probably right.

SEVEN. So what are you gonna do about it? We can be here all night.

NINE. It's only one night. A man may die.

(SEVEN *glares at* NINE *for a long while, but has no answer.* EIGHT *looks closely at* NINE *and we can begin to sense a rapport[9] between them. There is a long silence. Then suddenly everyone begins to talk at once.*)

THREE. Well, whose fault is that?

SIX. Do you think maybe if we went over it again? What I mean is——

TEN. Did anyone force him to kill his father? (*To* THREE) How do you like him? Like someone forced him!

ELEVEN. Perhaps this is not the point.

FIVE. No one forced anyone. But listen——

TWELVE. Look, gentlemen, we can spitball all night here.

TWO. Well, I was going to say——

SEVEN. Just a minute. Some of us've got better things to do than sit around a jury room.

FOUR. I can't understand a word in here. Why do we all have to talk at once?

---

8. **hang this jury,** keep this jury from reaching a verdict. A jury that fails to reach a verdict is called a "hung" jury.

9. *rapport* (ra pôr'), agreement, harmony.

FOREMAN. He's right. I think we ought to get on with it.

(EIGHT has been listening to this exchange closely.)

THREE *(to EIGHT)*. Well, what do you say? You're the one holding up the show.

EIGHT *(standing)*. I've got a proposition to make.

(We catch a close shot of FIVE looking steadily at him as he talks. FIVE, seemingly puzzled, listens closely.)

EIGHT. I want to call for a vote. I want you eleven men to vote by secret ballot. I'll abstain. If there are still eleven votes for guilty, I won't stand alone. We'll take in a guilty verdict right now.

SEVEN. Okay. Let's do it.

FOREMAN. That sounds fair. Is everyone agreed? *(They all nod their heads. EIGHT walks over to the window, looks out for a moment and then faces them.)*

FOREMAN. Pass these along.

(The FOREMAN passes ballot slips to all of them, and now EIGHT watches them tensely as they begin to write.)

(Fade out)

notes and comments

Words in the Courtroom

If you were a juror deciding the guilt or innocence of the accused, you would need to understand the meanings of many words as they are used in a court of law. With a man's life in the balance, you would be obligated to use these words with absolute precision. You would need to understand, for example, the precise difference between *homicide* and *premeditated homicide*. Do you?

As a juror, you would need to understand the meaning of the word *reasonable* in the phrase "reasonable doubt." Why is the meaning of this word significant?

Before voting guilty, or not guilty, a juror must consider the evidence that was given during the trial. What distinction is there between the meanings of *evidence, testimony,* and *proof*?

How many meanings can be cited for the words *acquittal, defendant, defense, jury, prosecution, verdict*? Which meanings would be used in a court of law?

Discussion

1. As the play begins, the JUDGE is charging the twelve jurors. What are his specific instructions?

2. (a) How might the jury room itself, the time, and the weather affect the jurors? **(b)** Which juror is particularly anxious to reach a quick decision? Why?

3. Before the first vote is taken, what do you learn about **(a)** the nature of the crime, and **(b)** the defendant?

4. (a) What is the result of the first vote? **(b)** Which juror seems the least confident of his vote? **(c)** What reasons does EIGHT give to account for his vote? **(d)** How do the jurors react to EIGHT's statements?

5. In order to convince EIGHT of the defendant's guilt, the jurors decide to discuss the facts of the case. **(a)** How does TWO interpret the facts? How does EIGHT answer TWO's interpretation? **(b)** What is the testimony cited by THREE? How do the FOREMAN and FOUR support THREE's statement? **(c)** What is the testimony cited by

TEN? By SIX? How does EIGHT counter their statements?

6. (a) What comments do SEVEN, THREE, and FOUR make about the defendant? **(b)** Do their comments pertain to the facts of the case? Explain. **(c)** Why does FIVE react as he does?

7. (a) How does EIGHT describe his reaction to the trial? **(b)** How does THREE react to EIGHT's comments?

8. (a) Why is the switch-knife an important exhibit in evidence? **(b)** What was the defendant's testimony about the switch-knife? **(c)** How do FOUR and EIGHT differ in their interpretation of this testimony?

9. (a) What is the dramatic climax, that is, the point of most intense excitement, of Act One? **(b)** How do the jurors react to this incident? **(c)** What does EIGHT prove by his action? **(d)** What does this incident reveal about EIGHT's motives?

10. (a) What proposition does EIGHT make to his fellow jurors? **(b)** How do you think FOUR, THREE, FIVE, and NINE will vote on the second ballot? Cite specific passages from the play to account for your answer.

Act Two

Fade in on same scene, no time lapse. EIGHT *stands tensely watching as the* JURORS *write on their ballots. He stays perfectly still as one by one they fold the ballots and pass them along to the* FOREMAN. *The* FOREMAN *takes them, riffles through the folded ballots, counts eleven and now begins to open them. He reads each one out loud and lays it aside. They watch him quietly, and all we hear is his voice and the sound of* TWO *sucking on a cough drop.*

FOREMAN. Guilty. Guilty. Guilty. Guilty. Guilty. Guilty. Guilty. Guilty. Guilty.

(He pauses at the tenth ballot and then reads it.) Not Guilty. *(THREE slams down hard on the table. The FOREMAN opens the last ballot.)* Guilty.

TEN *(angry).* How do you like that!

SEVEN. Who was it? I think we have a right to know.

ELEVEN. Excuse me. This was a secret ballot. We agreed on this point, no? If the gentleman wants it to remain secret——

THREE *(standing up angrily).* What do you mean? There are no secrets in here! I know who it was. *(He turns to FIVE.)* What's the matter with you? You come in here and you vote guilty and then this slick preacher starts to tear your heart out with stories about a poor little kid who just couldn't help becoming a murderer.

So you change your vote. If that isn't the most sickening——

(FIVE stares at THREE, frightened at this outburst.)

FOREMAN. Now hold it.

THREE. Hold it? We're trying to put a guilty man into the chair where he belongs—and all of a sudden we're paying attention to fairy tales.

FIVE. Now just a minute——

ELEVEN. Please. I would like to say something here. I have always thought that a man was entitled to have unpopular opinions in this country. This is the reason I came here. I wanted to have the right to disagree. In my own country, I am ashamed to say——

TEN. What do we have to listen to now—the whole history of your country?

SEVEN. Yeah, let's stick to the subject. *(To FIVE)* I want to ask you what made you change your vote.

(There is a long pause as SEVEN and FIVE eye each other angrily.)

NINE *(quietly).* There's nothing for him to tell you. He didn't change his vote. I did. *(There is a pause.)* Maybe you'd like to know why.

THREE. No, we wouldn't like to know why.

FOREMAN. The man wants to talk.

NINE. Thank you. *(Pointing at EIGHT)* This gentleman chose to stand alone against us. That's his

right. It takes a great deal of courage to stand alone even if you believe in something very strongly. He left the verdict up to us. He gambled for support and I gave it to him. I want to hear more. The vote is ten to two.

TEN. That's fine. If the speech is over, let's go on.

(FOREMAN *gets up, goes to door, knocks, hands* GUARD *the tagged switch-knife and sits down again.*)

THREE (to FIVE). Look, buddy, I was a little excited. Well, you know how it is. I . . . I didn't mean to get nasty. Nothing personal. (FIVE *looks at him.*)

SEVEN (to EIGHT). Look, supposing you answer me this. If the kid didn't kill him, who did?

EIGHT. As far as I know, we're supposed to decide whether or not the boy on trial is guilty. We're not concerned with anyone else's motives here.

NINE. Guilty beyond a reasonable doubt. This is an important thing to remember.

THREE (to TEN). Everyone's a lawyer. (To NINE) Supposing you explain what your reasonable doubts are.

NINE. This is not easy. So far, it's only a feeling I have. A feeling. Perhaps you don't understand.

TEN. A feeling! What are we gonna do, spend the night talking about your feelings? What about the facts?

THREE. You said a mouthful. (To NINE) Look, the old man heard the kid yell, "I'm gonna kill you." A second later he heard the father's body falling, and he saw the boy running out of the house fifteen seconds after that.

TWELVE. That's right. And let's not forget the woman across the street. She looked into the open window and saw the boy stab his father. She saw it. Now if that's not enough for you . . .

EIGHT. It's not enough for me.

SEVEN. How do you like him? It's like talking into a dead phone.

FOUR. The woman saw the killing through the windows of a moving elevated train. The train had five cars, and she saw it through the windows of the last two. She remembers the most insignificant details.

(*Cut to close shot of* TWELVE *who doodles a picture of an el train on a scrap of paper.*)

THREE. Well, what have you got to say about that?

EIGHT. I don't know. It doesn't sound right to me.

THREE. Well, supposing you think about it. (To TWELVE) Lend me your pencil.

(TWELVE *gives it to him. He draws a tick-tack-toe square on the same sheet of paper on which* TWELVE *has drawn the train. He fills in an X, hands the pencil to* TWELVE.)

THREE. Your turn. We might as well pass the time.

(TWELVE *takes the pencil.* EIGHT *stands up and snatches the paper away.* THREE *leaps up.*)

THREE. Wait a minute!

EIGHT (*hard*). This isn't a game.

THREE (*angry*). Who do you think you are?

SEVEN (*rising*). All right, let's take it easy.

THREE. I've got a good mind to walk around this table and belt him one!

FOREMAN. Now, please. I don't want any fights in here.

THREE. Did ya see him? The nerve! The absolute nerve!

TEN. All right. Forget it. It don't mean anything.

SIX. How about sitting down.

THREE. This isn't a game. Who does he think he is?

(*He lets them sit him down.* EIGHT *remains standing, holding the scrap of paper. He looks at it closely now and seems to be suddenly interested in it. Then he throws it back toward* THREE. *It lands in center of table.* THREE *is angered again at this, but* FOUR *puts his hand on his arm.* EIGHT *speaks now and his voice is more intense.*)

EIGHT (to FOUR). Take a look at that sketch. How long does it take an elevated train going at top speed to pass a given point?

FOUR. What has that got to do with anything?

EIGHT. How long? Guess.

FOUR. I wouldn't have the slightest idea.

EIGHT (to FIVE). What do you think?

FIVE. About ten or twelve seconds, maybe.

EIGHT. I'd say that was a fair guess. Anyone else?

ELEVEN. I would think about ten seconds, perhaps.

TWO. About ten seconds.

FOUR. All right. Say ten seconds. What are you getting at?

EIGHT. This. An el train passes a given point in ten seconds. That given point is the window of the room in which the killing took place. You can almost reach out of the window of that room and touch the el. Right? (Several of them nod.) All right. Now let me ask you this. Did anyone here ever live right next to the el tracks? I have. When your window is open and the train goes by, the noise is almost unbearable. You can't hear yourself think.

TEN. Okay. You can't hear yourself think. Will you get to the point?

EIGHT. The old man heard the boy say, "I'm going to kill you," and one second later he heard a body fall. One second. That's the testimony, right?

TWO. Right.

EIGHT. The woman across the street looked through the windows of the last two cars of the el and saw the body fall. Right? The *last two* cars.

TEN. What are you giving us here?

EIGHT. An el takes ten seconds to pass a given point or two seconds per car. That el had been going by the old man's window for at least six seconds, and maybe more, before the body fell, according to the woman. The old man would have had to hear the boy say, "I'm going to kill you," while the front of the el was roaring past his nose. It's not possible that he could have heard it.

THREE. What d'ya mean! Sure he could have heard it.

EIGHT. Could he?

THREE. He said the boy yelled it out. That's enough for me.

NINE. I don't think he could have heard it.

TWO. Maybe he didn't hear it. I mean with the el noise——

THREE. What are you people talking about? Are you calling the old man a liar?

FIVE. Well, it stands to reason.

THREE. You're crazy. Why would he lie? What's he got to gain?

NINE. Attention, maybe.

THREE. You keep coming up with these bright sayings. Why don't you send one in to a newspaper? They pay two dollars.

(EIGHT *looks hard at* THREE *and then turns to* NINE.)

EIGHT (softly). Why might the old man have lied? You have a right to be heard.

NINE. It's just that I looked at him for a very long time. The seam of his jacket was split under the arm. Did you notice that? He was a very old man with a torn jacket, and he carried two canes. I think I know him better than anyone here. This is a quiet, frightened, insignificant man who has been nothing all his life, who has never had recognition—his name in the newspapers. Nobody knows him after seventy-five years. That's a very sad thing. A man like this needs to be recognized. To be questioned, and listened to, and quoted just once. This is very important.

TWELVE. And you're trying to tell us he lied about a thing like this just so that he could be important?

NINE. No, he wouldn't really lie. But perhaps he'd make himself believe that he heard those words and recognized the boy's face.

THREE (loud). Well, that's the most fantastic story I've ever heard. How can you make up a thing like that? What do you know about it?

NINE (low). I speak from experience. (There is a long pause. Then the FOREMAN clears his throat.)

FOREMAN (to EIGHT). All right. Is there anything else?

(EIGHT *is looking at* NINE. TWO *offers the* FOREMAN *a box of cough drops. The* FOREMAN *pushes it away.*)

TWO (hesitantly). Anybody . . . want a cough . . . drop?

FOREMAN (sharply). Come on. Let's get on with it.

EIGHT. I'll take one. (TWO almost gratefully slides him one along the table.) Thanks. (TWO nods and EIGHT puts the cough drop into his mouth.)

EIGHT. Now. There's something else I'd like to point out here. I think we proved that the old man couldn't have heard the boy say, "I'm going to kill you," but supposing he really did hear it? This phrase: how many times has each of you used it? Probably hundreds. "If you do that once more, Junior, I'm going to murder you." "Come on, Rocky, kill him!" We say it every day. This doesn't mean that we're going to kill someone.

THREE. Wait a minute. The phrase was "I'm going to kill you," and the kid screamed it out at the top of his lungs. Don't try and tell me he didn't mean it. Anybody says a thing like that the way he said it—they mean it.

TEN. And how they mean it!

EIGHT. Well, let me ask you this. Do you really think the boy would shout out a thing like that so the whole neighborhood would hear it? I don't think so. He's much too bright for that.

TEN (exploding). Bright! He's a common, ignorant slob. He don't even speak good English!

ELEVEN (slowly). He doesn't even speak good English.

(TEN stares angrily at ELEVEN, and there is silence for a moment. Then FIVE looks around the table nervously.)

FIVE. I'd like to change my vote to not guilty.

(THREE gets up and walks to the window, furious, but trying to control himself.)

FOREMAN. Are you sure?

FIVE. Yes. I'm sure.

FOREMAN. The vote is nine to three in favor of guilty.

SEVEN. Well, if that isn't the end. (To FIVE) What are you basing it on? Stories this guy—(indicating EIGHT)—made up! He oughta write for Amazing Detective Monthly. He'd make a fortune. Listen, the kid had a lawyer, didn't he? Why didn't his lawyer bring up all these points?

FIVE. Lawyers can't think of everything.

SEVEN. Oh, brother! (To EIGHT) You sit in here and pull stories out of thin air. Now we're supposed to believe that the old man didn't get up out of bed, run to the door, and see the kid beat it downstairs fifteen seconds after the killing. He's only saying he did to be important.

FIVE. Did the old man say he ran to the door?

SEVEN. Ran. Walked. What's the difference? He got there.

FIVE. I don't remember what he said. But I don't see how he could run.

FOUR. He said he went from his bedroom to the front door. That's enough, isn't it?

EIGHT. Where was his bedroom again?

TEN. Down the hall somewhere. I thought you remembered everything. Don't you remember that?

EIGHT. No. Mr. Foreman, I'd like to take a look at the diagram of the apartment.

SEVEN. Why don't we have them run the trial over just so you can get everything straight?

EIGHT. Mr. Foreman——

FOREMAN (rising). I heard you.

(The FOREMAN gets up, goes to door during following dialogue. He knocks on door, GUARD opens it, he whispers to GUARD, GUARD nods and closes door.)

THREE (to EIGHT). All right. What's this for? How come you're the only one in the room who wants to see exhibits all the time?

FIVE. I want to see this one, too.

THREE. And I want to stop wasting time.

FOUR. If we're going to start wading through all that nonsense about where the body was found . . .

EIGHT. We're not. We're going to find out how a man who's had two strokes in the past three years, and who walks with a pair of canes, could get to his front door in fifteen seconds.

THREE. He said twenty seconds.

TWO. He said fifteen.

THREE. How does he know how long fifteen seconds is? You can't judge that kind of a thing.

NINE. He said fifteen. He was positive about it.

THREE (angry). He's an old man. You saw him. Half the time he was confused. How could he be positive about . . . anything?

(THREE looks around sheepishly, unable to cover up his blunder. The door opens and the GUARD walks in, carrying a large pen-and-ink diagram of the apartment. It is a railroad flat. A bedroom faces the el tracks. Behind it is a series of rooms off a long hall. In the front bedroom is a diagram of the spot where the body was found. At the back of the apartment we see the entrance into the apartment hall from the building hall. We see a flight of stairs in the building hall. The diagram is clearly labeled and included in the information on it are the dimensions of the various rooms. The GUARD gives the diagram to the FOREMAN.)

GUARD. This what you wanted?

FOREMAN. That's right. Thank you.

(The GUARD nods and exits. EIGHT goes to FOREMAN and reaches for it.)

EIGHT. May I?

(The FOREMAN nods. EIGHT takes the diagram and sets it up on a chair so that all can see it. EIGHT looks it over. Several of the JURORS get up to see it better. THREE, TEN, and SEVEN, however, barely bother to look at it.)

SEVEN (to TEN). Do me a favor. Wake me up when this is over.

EIGHT (ignoring him). All right. This is the apartment in which the killing took place. The old man's apartment is directly beneath it and exactly the same. (Pointing) Here are the el tracks. The bedroom. Another bedroom. Living room. Bathroom. Kitchen. And this is the hall. Here's the front door to the apartment. And here are the steps. (Pointing to front bedroom and then front door) Now the old man was in bed in this room. He says he got up, went out into the hall, down the hall to the front door, opened it, and looked out just in

time to see the boy racing down the stairs. Am I right?

THREE. That's the story.

EIGHT. Fifteen seconds after he heard the body fall.

ELEVEN. Correct.

EIGHT. His bed was at the window. It's—(looking closer)—twelve feet from his bed to the bedroom door. The length of the hall is forty-three feet, six inches. He had to get up out of bed, get his canes, walk twelve feet, open the bedroom door, walk forty-three feet, and open the front door—all in fifteen seconds. Do you think this possible?

TEN. You know it's possible.

ELEVEN. He can only walk very slowly. They had to help him into the witness chair.

THREE. You make it sound like a long walk. It's not.

(EIGHT gets up, goes to the end of the room, and takes two chairs. He puts them together to indicate a bed.)

NINE. For an old man who uses canes, it's a long walk.

THREE (to EIGHT). What are you doing?

EIGHT. I want to try this thing. Let's see how long it took him. I'm going to pace off twelve feet— the length of the bedroom. (He begins to do so.)

THREE. You're crazy. You can't re-create a thing like that.

ELEVEN. Perhaps if we could see it . . . this is an important point.

THREE (mad). It's a ridiculous waste of time.

SIX. Let him do it.

EIGHT. Hand me a chair. (Someone pushes a chair to him.) All right. This is the bedroom door. Now how far would you say it is from here to the door of this room?

SIX. I'd say it was twenty feet.

TWO. Just about.

EIGHT. Twenty feet is close enough. All right, from here to the door and back is about forty feet. It's shorter than the length of the hall, wouldn't you say that?

NINE. A few feet, maybe.

TEN. Look, this is absolutely insane. What makes you think you can——

EIGHT. Do you mind if I try it? According to you, it'll only take fifteen seconds. We can spare that. *(He walks over to the two chairs now and lies down on them.)* Who's got a watch with a second hand?

TWO. I have.

EIGHT. When you want me to start, stamp your foot. That'll be the body falling. Time me from there. *(He lies down on the chairs.)* Let's say he keeps his canes right at his bedside. Right?

TWO. Right!

EIGHT. Okay. I'm ready.

(They all watch carefully. TWO *stares at his watch, waiting for the second hand to reach sixty. Then, as it does, he stamps his foot loudly.* EIGHT *begins to get up. Slowly he swings his legs over the edges of the chairs, reaches for imaginary canes, and struggles to his feet.* TWO *stares at the watch.* EIGHT *walks as a crippled old man would walk, toward the chair which is serving as the bedroom door. He gets to it and pretends to open it.)*

TEN *(shouting).* Speed it up. He walked twice as fast as that.

*(*EIGHT, *not having stopped for this outburst, begins to walk the simulated forty-foot hallway.)*

ELEVEN. This is, I think, even more quickly than the old man walked in the courtroom.

EIGHT. If you think I should go faster, I will.

(He speeds up his pace slightly. He reaches the door and turns now, heading back, hobbling as an old man would hobble, bent over his imaginary canes. They watch him tensely. He hobbles back to the chair, which also serves as the front door. He stops there and pretends to unlock the door. Then he pretends to push it open.)

EIGHT *(loud).* Stop.

TWO. Right.

EIGHT. What's the time?

TWO. Fifteen . . . twenty . . . thirty . . . thirty-one seconds exactly.

ELEVEN. Thirty-one seconds.

(Some of the JURORS *adlib[1] their surprise to each other.)*

EIGHT. It's my guess that the old man was trying to get to the door, heard someone racing down the stairs, and assumed that it was the boy.

---

1. **adlib,** from the Latin *ad libitum,* to make up words or gestures that are not in the script.

SIX. I think that's possible.

THREE (infuriated). Assumed? Now, listen to me, you people. I've seen all kinds of dishonesty in my day . . . but this little display takes the cake. (To FOUR) Tell him, will you?

(FOUR sits silently. THREE looks at him and then he strides over to EIGHT.)

THREE. You come in here with your heart bleeding all over the floor about slum kids and injustice and you make up these wild stories, and you've got some soft-hearted old ladies listening to you. Well I'm not. I'm getting real sick of it. (To all) What's the matter with you people? This kid is guilty! He's got to burn! We're letting him slip through our fingers here.

EIGHT (calmly). Our fingers. Are you his executioner?

THREE (raging). I'm one of 'em.

EIGHT. Perhaps you'd like to pull the switch.

THREE (shouting). For this kid? You bet I'd like to pull the switch!

EIGHT. I'm sorry for you.

THREE (shouting). Don't start with me.

EIGHT. What it must feel like to want to pull the switch!

THREE. Shut up!

EIGHT. You're a sadist.

THREE (louder). Shut up!

EIGHT (strong). You want to see this boy die because you personally want it—not because of the facts.

THREE (shouting). Shut up!

(He lunges at EIGHT, but is caught by two of the JURORS and held. He struggles as EIGHT watches calmly.)

THREE (screaming). Let me go! I'll kill him. I'll kill him!

EIGHT (softly). You don't really mean you'll kill me, do you?

(THREE stops struggling now and stares at EIGHT. All the JURORS watch in silence as we fade out.)

Discussion

1. How does the result of the second vote create a conflict between juror THREE and jurors FIVE, ELEVEN, and NINE?

2. (a) What evidence does EIGHT offer first to discount the old man's testimony? (b) What is the connection between the el train's noise and the old man's testimony?

3. Reread (54 b, line 16) the comments NINE makes about the old man. Are NINE's comments based on fact or do they reflect his personal feelings? Explain.

4. (a) What is the significance of TEN's comment that the defendant "don't even speak good English"? (b) How does this comment affect ELEVEN? FIVE? (c) Is the comment consistent with TEN's previous behavior? Why or why not?

5. How does EIGHT interpret the result of his timed experiment?

6. (a) In Act Two THREE contradicts his earlier views. In what ways? (b) How do you think each juror would vote at the end of Act Two?

From the Author

Twelve Angry Men is the only play I've written which has any relation at all to actual personal experience. A month or so before I began the play I sat on the jury of a manslaughter case in New York's General Sessions Court. This was my first experience on a jury, and it left quite an impression on me. The receipt of my jury notice activated many grumblings and mutterings, most of which began with lines like "Eight million people in New York and they have to call me!" All the prospective jurors I met in the waiting room the first day I appeared had the same grim, horribly persecuted attitude. But, strangely, the moment I walked into the courtroom to be empaneled and found myself facing a strange man whose fate was suddenly more or less in my hands, my entire attitude changed. I was hugely impressed with the almost frightening stillness of the courtroom, the impassive, masklike face of the judge, the brisk, purposeful scurrying of the various officials in the room, and the absolute finality of the decision I and my fellow jurors would have to make at the end of the trial. I doubt whether I have ever been so impressed in my life with a role I had to play, and I suddenly became so earnest that, in thinking about it later, I probably was unbearable to the eleven other jurors.

It occurred to me during the trial that no one anywhere ever knows what goes on inside a jury room but the jurors, and I thought then that a play taking place entirely within a jury room might be an exciting and possibly moving experience for an audience.

Actually, the outline of *Twelve Angry Men*, which I began shortly after the trial ended, took longer to write than the script itself. The movements in the play were so intricate that I wanted to have them down on paper to the last detail before I began the construction of the dialogue. I worked on the idea and outline for a week and was stunned by the time I was finished to discover that the outline was twenty-seven typewritten pages long. The average outline is perhaps five pages long, and many are as short as one or two pages. This detailed setting down of the moves of the play paid off, however. The script was written in five days and could have been done in four had I not written it approximately fifteen pages too long.

In writing *Twelve Angry Men* I attempted to blend four elements which I had seen at work in the jury room during my jury service. These elements are: (a) the evidence as remembered and interpreted by each individual juror (the disparities here were incredible); (b) the relationship of juror to juror in a life-and-death situation; (c) the emotional pattern of each individual juror; and (d) physical problems such as the weather, the time, the uncomfortable room, etc. All of these elements are of vital importance in any jury room, and all of them presented excellent dramatic possibilities.

From the Author's Commentary on *Twelve Angry Men* from SIX TELEVISION PLAYS by Reginald Rose. Reprinted by permission of International Famous Agency. Copyright © 1956 by Reginald Rose.

Act Three

Fade in on same scene. No time lapse. THREE *glares angrily at* EIGHT. *He is still held by two* JURORS. *After a long pause, he shakes himself loose and turns away. He walks to the windows. The other* JURORS *stand around the room now, shocked by this display of anger. There is silence. Then the door opens and the* GUARD *enters. He looks around the room.*

GUARD. Is there anything wrong, gentlemen? I heard some noise.

FOREMAN. No. There's nothing wrong. *(He points to the large diagram of the apartment.)* You can take that back. We're finished with it.

(The GUARD *nods and takes the diagram. He looks curiously at some of the* JURORS *and exits. The* JURORS *still are silent. Some of them slowly begin to sit down.* THREE *still stands at the window. He turns around now. The* JURORS *look at him.)*

THREE *(loud).* Well, what are you looking at?

(They turn away. He goes back to his seat now. Silently the rest of the JURORS *take their seats.* TWELVE *begins to doodle.* TEN *blows his nose, but no one speaks. Then, finally——)*

FOUR. I don't see why we have to behave like children here.

ELEVEN. Nor do I. We have a responsibility. This is a remarkable thing about democracy. That we are . . . what is the word? . . . Ah, notified! That we are notified by mail to come down to this place and decide on the guilt or innocence of a man we have not known before. We have nothing to gain or lose by our verdict. This is one of the reasons why we are strong. We should not make it a personal thing.

(There is a long, awkward pause.)

TWELVE. Well—we're still nowhere. Who's got an idea?

SIX. I think maybe we should try another vote. Mr. Foreman?

FOREMAN. It's all right with me. Anybody doesn't want to vote?

(He looks around the table.)

SEVEN. All right, let's do it.

THREE. I want an open ballot. Let's call out our votes. I want to know who stands where.

FOREMAN. That sounds fair. Anyone object? *(No one does.)* All right. I'll call off your jury numbers.

(He takes a pencil and paper and makes marks now in one of two columns after each vote.)

FOREMAN. I vote guilty. Number Two?

TWO. Not guilty.

FOREMAN. Number Three?

THREE. Guilty.

FOREMAN. Number Four?

FOUR. Guilty.

FOREMAN. Number Five?

FIVE. Not guilty.

FOREMAN. Number Six?

SIX. Not guilty.

FOREMAN. Number Seven?

SEVEN. Guilty.

FOREMAN. Number Eight?

EIGHT. Not guilty.

FOREMAN. Number Nine?

NINE. Not guilty.

FOREMAN. Number Ten?

TEN. Guilty.

FOREMAN. Number Eleven?

ELEVEN. Not guilty.

FOREMAN. Number Twelve?

TWELVE. Guilty.

FOUR. Six to six.

TEN *(mad).* I'll tell you something. The crime is being committed right in this room.

FOREMAN. The vote is six to six.

THREE. I'm ready to walk into court right now and declare a hung jury. There's no point in this going on any more.

SEVEN. I go for that, too. Let's take it in to the judge and let the kid take his chances with twelve other guys.

FIVE *(to* SEVEN). You mean you still don't think there's room for reasonable doubt?

SEVEN. No, I don't.

ELEVEN. I beg your pardon. Maybe you don't understand the term "reasonable doubt."

SEVEN *(angry).* What do you mean I don't understand it? Who do you think you are to talk to me like that? *(To all)* How do you like this guy? He comes over here running for his life, and before he can even take a big breath he's telling us how to run the show. The arrogance of him!

FIVE (to SEVEN). Wait a second. Nobody around here's asking where you came from.

SEVEN. I was born right here.

FIVE. Or where your father came from. . . . (He looks at SEVEN, who doesn't answer but looks away.) Maybe it wouldn't hurt us to take a few tips from people who come running here! Maybe they learned something we don't know. We're not so perfect!

ELEVEN. Please—I am used to this. It's all right. Thank you.

FIVE. It's not all right!

SEVEN. Okay, okay, I apologize. Is that what you want?

FIVE. That's what I want.

FOREMAN. All right. Let's stop the arguing. Who's got something constructive to say?

TWO (hesitantly). Well, something's been bothering me a little . . . this whole business about the stab wound and how it was made, the downward angle of it, you know?

THREE. Don't tell me we're gonna start that. They went over it and over it in court.

TWO. I know they did—but I don't go along with it. The boy is five feet eight inches tall. His father was six two. That's a difference of six inches. It's a very awkward thing to stab *down* into the chest of someone who's half a foot taller than you are.

(THREE *jumps up, holding the knife.*)

THREE. Look, you're not going to be satisfied till you see it again. I'm going to give you a demonstration. Somebody get up.

(He looks around the table. EIGHT *stands up and walks toward him.* THREE *closes the knife and puts it in his pocket. They stand face to face and look at each other for a moment.*)

THREE. Okay. (To TWO) Now watch this. I don't want to have to do it again. (He crouches down now until he is quite a bit shorter than EIGHT.) Is that six inches?

TWELVE. That's more than six inches.

THREE. Okay, let it be more.

(He reaches into his pocket and takes out the knife. He flicks it open, changes its position in his hand, and holds the knife aloft, ready to stab. He and EIGHT look steadily into each other's eyes. Then he stabs downward, hard.)

TWO (shouting). Look out!

(He stops short just as the blade reaches EIGHT's chest. THREE laughs.)

SIX. That's not funny.

FIVE. What's the matter with you?

THREE. Now just calm down. Nobody's hurt, are they?

EIGHT (low). No. Nobody's hurt.

THREE. All right. There's your angle. Take a look at it. Down and in. That's how I'd stab a taller man in the chest, and that's how it was done. Take a look at it and tell me I'm wrong.

(TWO doesn't answer. THREE looks at him for a moment, then jams the knife into the table, and sits down. They all look at the knife.)

SIX. Down and in. I guess there's no argument.

(EIGHT picks the knife out of the table and closes it. He flicks it open and, changing its position in his hand, stabs downward with it.)

EIGHT (to SIX). Did you ever stab a man?

SIX. Of course not.

EIGHT (to THREE). Did you?

THREE. All right, let's not be silly.

EIGHT. Did you?

THREE (loud). No, I didn't!

EIGHT. Where do you get all your information about how it's done?

THREE. What do you mean? It's just common sense.

EIGHT. Have you ever seen a man stabbed?

THREE (pauses and looks around the room nervously). No.

EIGHT. All right. I want to ask you something. The boy was an experienced knife fighter. He was even sent to reform school for knifing someone, isn't that so?

TWELVE. That's right.

EIGHT. Look at this. (EIGHT closes the knife, flicks it open, and changes the position of the knife so that he can stab overhanded.) Doesn't it seem like an awkward way to handle a knife?

THREE. What are you asking me for?

(EIGHT *closes the blade and flicks it open, holds it ready to slash underhanded.*)

FIVE. Wait a minute! What's the matter with me? Give me that. (*He reaches out for the knife.*)

EIGHT. Have you ever seen a knife fight?

FIVE. Yes, I have.

EIGHT. In the movies?

FIVE. In my back yard. On my stoop. In the vacant lot across the street. Too many of them. Switch-knives came with the neighborhood where I lived. Funny I didn't think of it before. I guess you try to forget those things. (*Flicking the knife open*) Anyone who's ever used a switch-knife would never have stabbed downward. You don't handle a switch-knife that way. You use it underhanded.

EIGHT. Then he couldn't have made the kind of wound which killed his father.

FIVE. No. He couldn't have. Not if he'd ever had any experience with switch-knives.

THREE. I don't believe it.

TEN. Neither do I. You're giving us a lot of mumbo jumbo.

EIGHT (*to* TWELVE). What do you think?

TWELVE (*hesitantly*). Well . . . I don't know.

EIGHT (*to* SEVEN). What about you?

SEVEN. Listen, I'll tell you something. I'm a little sick of this whole thing already. We're getting nowhere fast. Let's break it up and go home. I'm changing my vote to not guilty.

THREE. You're what?

SEVEN. You heard me. I've had enough.

THREE. What do you mean, you've had enough? That's no answer.

ELEVEN (*angry*). I think perhaps you're right. This is not an answer. (*To* SEVEN) What kind of a man are you? You have sat here and voted guilty with everyone else because there are some theater tickets burning a hole in your pocket. Now you have changed your vote for the same reason. I do not think you have the right to play like this with a man's life. This is an ugly and terrible thing to do.

SEVEN. Now wait a minute . . . you can't talk like that to me.

ELEVEN (*strong*). I can talk like that to you! If you want to vote not guilty, then do it because you are convinced the man is not guilty. If you believe he is guilty, then vote that way. Or don't you have the . . . the . . . guts—the guts to do what you think is right?

SEVEN. Now listen . . .

ELEVEN. Is it guilty or not guilty?

SEVEN (*hesitantly*). I told you. Not . . . guilty.

ELEVEN (*hard*). Why?

SEVEN. I don't have to——

ELEVEN. You have to! Say it! Why?

(*They stare at each other for a long while.*)

SEVEN (*low*). I . . . don't think . . . he's guilty.

EIGHT (*fast*). I want another vote.

FOREMAN. Okay, there's another vote called for. I guess the quickest way is a show of hands. Anybody object? (*No one does.*) All right. All those voting not guilty, raise your hands.

(TWO, FIVE, SIX, SEVEN, EIGHT, NINE, *and* ELEVEN *raise their hands immediately. Then, slowly,* TWELVE *raises his hand. The* FOREMAN *looks around the table carefully and then he too raises his hand. He looks around the table, counting silently.*)

FOREMAN. Nine. (*The hands go down.*) All those voting guilty.

(THREE, FOUR, *and* TEN *raise their hands.*)

FOREMAN. Three. (*They lower their hands.*) The vote is nine to three in favor of acquittal.

TEN. I don't understand you people. How can you believe this kid is innocent? Look, you know how those people lie. I don't have to tell you. They don't know what the truth is. And lemme tell you, they—(FIVE *gets up from table, turns his back to it, and goes to window.*)—don't need any real big reason to kill someone either. You know, they get drunk, and *bang*, someone's lying in the gutter. Nobody's blaming them. That's how they are. You know what I mean? Violent! (NINE *gets up and does the same. He is followed by* ELEVEN.)

TEN. Human life don't mean as much to them as it does to us. Hey, where are you going? Look, these people are drinking and fighting all the time, and if somebody gets killed, so somebody gets killed. They don't care. Oh, sure, there are some good things about them, too. Look, I'm the first to say that. (EIGHT *gets up, and then* TWO *and* SIX *follow him to the window.)*

TEN. I've known a few who were pretty decent, but that's the exception. Most of them, it's like they have no feelings. They can do anything. What's going on here?

(The FOREMAN *gets up and goes to the window, followed by* SEVEN *and* TWELVE.)

TEN. I'm speaking my piece, and you—Listen to me! They're no good. There's not a one of 'em who's any good. We better watch out. Take it from me. This kid on trial . . .

*(*THREE *sits at table toying with the knife and* FOUR *gets up and starts for the window. All have their backs to* TEN.)

TEN. Well, don't you know about them? Listen to me! What are you doing? I'm trying to tell you something. . . .

*(*FOUR *stands over him as he trails off. There is a dead silence. Then* FOUR *speaks softly.)*

FOUR. I've had enough. If you open your mouth again, I'm going to split your skull.

*(*FOUR *stands there and looks at him. No one moves or speaks.* TEN *looks at him, then looks down at the table.)*

TEN *(softly).* I'm only trying to tell you . . .

(There is a long pause as FOUR *stares down at* TEN.)

FOUR *(to all).* All right. Sit down everybody.

(They all move back to their seats. When they are all seated, FOUR *then sits down.)*

FOUR *(quietly).* I still believe the boy is guilty of murder. I'll tell you why. To me, the most damning evidence was given by the woman across the street who claimed she actually saw the murder committed.

THREE. That's right. As far as I'm concerned, that's the most important testimony.

EIGHT. All right. Let's go over her testimony. What exactly did she say?

FOUR. I believe I can recount it accurately. She said that she went to bed at about eleven o'clock that night. Her bed was next to the open window, and she could look out of the window while lying down and see directly into the window across the street. She tossed and turned for over an hour, unable to fall asleep. Finally she turned toward the window at about twelve-ten and, as she looked out, she saw the boy stab his father. As far as I can see, this is unshakable testimony.

THREE. That's what I mean. That's the whole case.

*(*FOUR *takes off his eyeglasses and begins to polish them, as they all sit silently watching him.)*

FOUR *(to the* JURY). Frankly, I don't see how you can vote for acquittal. *(To* TWELVE) What do you think about it?

TWELVE. Well . . . maybe . . . there's so much evidence to sift.

THREE. What do you mean, maybe? He's absolutely right. You can throw out all the other evidence.

FOUR. That was my feeling.

*(*TWO, *polishing his glasses, squints at clock, can't see it.* SIX *watches him closely.)*

TWO. What time is it?

ELEVEN. Ten minutes of six.

TWO. It's late. You don't suppose they'd let us go home and finish it in the morning. I've got a kid with mumps.

FIVE. Not a chance.

SIX *(to* TWO). Pardon me. Can't you see the clock without your glasses?

TWO. Not clearly. Why?

SIX. Oh, I don't know. Look, this may be a dumb thought, but what do you do when you wake up at night and want to know what time it is?

TWO. What do you mean? I put on my glasses and look at the clock.

SIX. You don't wear them to bed.

TWO. Of course not. No one wears eyeglasses to bed.

TWELVE. What's all this for?

SIX. Well, I was thinking. You know the woman who testified that she saw the killing wears glasses.

THREE. So does my grandmother. So what?

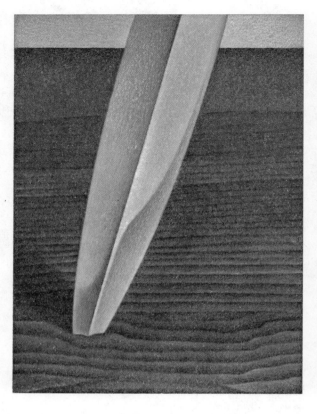 

EIGHT. Your grandmother isn't a murder witness.

SIX. Look, stop me if I'm wrong. This woman wouldn't wear her eyeglasses to bed, would she?

FOREMAN. Wait a minute! Did she wear glasses at all? I don't remember.

ELEVEN *(excited).* Of course she did. The woman wore bifocals. I remember this very clearly. They looked quite strong.

NINE. That's right. Bifocals. She never took them off.

FOUR. She did wear glasses. Funny. I never thought of it.

EIGHT. Listen, she wasn't wearing them in bed. That's for sure. She testified that in the midst of her tossing and turning she rolled over and looked casually out the window. The murder was taking place as she looked out, and the lights went out a split second later. She couldn't have had time to put on her glasses. Now maybe she honestly thought she saw the boy kill his father. I say that she saw only a blur.

THREE. How do you know what she saw? Maybe she's far-sighted. *(He looks around. No one answers.)*

THREE *(loud).* How does he know all these things?

(There is silence.)

EIGHT. Does anyone think there still is not a reasonable doubt?

(He looks around the room, then squarely at TEN. TEN *looks down and shakes his head no.)*

THREE *(loud).* I think he's guilty.

EIGHT *(calmly).* Does anyone else?

FOUR *(quietly).* No. I'm convinced.

EIGHT *(to* THREE*).* You're alone.

THREE. I don't care whether I'm alone or not! I have a right.

EIGHT. You have a right.

(There is a pause. They all look at THREE.*)*

THREE. Well, I told you I think the kid's guilty. What else do you want?

EIGHT. Your arguments. *(They all look at* THREE.*)*

THREE. I gave you my arguments.

EIGHT. We're not convinced. We're waiting to hear them again. We have time.

*(*THREE *runs to* FOUR *and grabs his arm.)*

THREE *(pleading).* Listen. What's the matter with you? You're the guy. You made all the arguments. You can't turn now. A guilty man's gonna be walking the streets. A murderer. He's got to die! Stay with me.

FOUR. I'm sorry. There's a reasonable doubt in my mind.

EIGHT. We're waiting.

*(*THREE *turns violently on him.)*

THREE *(shouting).* Well, you're not going to intimidate me! *(They all look at* THREE.*)* I'm entitled to my opinion! *(No one answers him.)* It's gonna be a hung jury! That's it!

EIGHT. There's nothing we can do about that, except hope that some night, maybe in a few months, you'll get some sleep.

FIVE. You're all alone.

NINE. It takes a great deal of courage to stand alone.

*(*THREE *looks around at all of them for a long time. They sit silently, waiting for him to speak, and all of them despise him for his stubbornness. Then, suddenly, his face contorts as if he is about to cry, and he slams his fist down on the table.)*

THREE *(thundering).* All right!

*(*THREE *turns his back on them. There is silence for a moment and then the* FOREMAN *goes to the door and knocks on it. It opens. The* GUARD *looks in and sees them all standing. The* GUARD *holds the door for them as they begin slowly to file out.* EIGHT *waits at the door as the others file past him. Finally he and* THREE *are the only ones left.* THREE *turns around and sees that they are alone. Slowly he moves toward the door. Then he stops at the table. He pulls the switch-knife out of the table and walks over to* EIGHT *with it. He holds it in the approved knife-fighter fashion and looks long and hard at* EIGHT, *pointing the knife at his belly.* EIGHT *stares back. Then* THREE *turns the knife around.* EIGHT *takes it by the handle.* THREE *exits.* EIGHT *closes the knife, puts it away and, taking a last look around the room, exits, closing the door. The camera moves in close on the littered table in the empty room, and we clearly see a slip of crumpled paper on which are scribbled the words "Not guilty.")*

(Fade out)

☐☐

notes and comments

The Jurors

When Reginald Rose began writing *Twelve Angry Men,* he knew that his play could not exceed fifty minutes. Faced with the time limits of television, many dramatists would present a limited number of characters. Rose, on the other hand, not only presents twelve jurors, but he keeps all twelve on the scene continuously.

It must have been obvious to Rose that he could not fully characterize twelve men in a fifty-minute play. He must have known that his jurors could be little more than *character types.* Early in Act One, for example, EIGHT (The Just Man) emerges as the hero; THREE (The Sadist) emerges as the villain. What single word would you use to describe SEVEN? TEN?

Character types are a device almost as old as English drama itself. In many medieval plays, *vices* (such as Ignorance and Shame) and *virtues* (such as Humility and Mercy) appear as real people. Rose borrows this device and then carries it one step further by assigning numbers instead of names to his characters.

Discussion

1. In the beginning of Act Three the jurors vote for the third time. (a) What is the result of the third vote? (b) Which jurors have changed their votes?

2. FIVE provides information that discounts an important piece of testimony. (a) What information does FIVE provide? (b) Is he qualified to speak as an expert? Why or why not? (c) Is FIVE's ability to provide this information too coincidental to be believable? Explain.

3. (a) In what way is SEVEN's willingness to change his vote consistent with his earlier behavior? (b) Why does ELEVEN question SEVEN so closely?

4. What is the result of the fourth vote?

5. How do the other jurors react to TEN's statements of his true feelings?

6. (a) Why does FOUR feel that he still cannot vote for acquittal? (b) What significant observation does SIX make at this point?

7. As the play draws to its close, THREE stands alone in his conviction that the boy is guilty. (a) Do you think THREE was pressured into agreeing with the majority? Explain your answer. (b) What does THREE reveal about himself in changing his vote?

8. Did the jury prove that the defendant was not guilty? Cite passages which will support your answer.

Vocabulary
Pronunciation and Context

Write the following words on a separate sheet of paper. Divide the words into syllables and put the stress marks after each accented syllable. Then use each word in a sentence that shows you understand the meaning of the word. Underline the vocabulary words in your sentences. Be sure you can pronounce and spell all the vocabulary words.

Example: pros′e cu′tion
The witness for the *prosecution* gave such strong evidence that the lawyer for the defense did not dare try to cross-examine him.

appall	sadism
bigot	superficial
dogged	testimony
premeditate	verdict

Reginald Rose 1920 ·

Rose sold his first television script, which he had written in his spare time, in 1951. He wrote *Twelve Angry Men* in 1954 for television; later he wrote the script for the motion-picture version and then another script for the stage version. Among his numerous awards are three Emmies, one for *Twelve Angry Men* and two for the television series *The Defenders*. He has written feature films as well as television plays.

1: Turnabout

CONTENT REVIEW

I. A turnabout can be pleasant, horrible, surprising, commonplace, puzzling. It can also be caused by someone, something, an accident, chance, or apparently nothing. Discuss the precise nature of the *turnabouts* indicated in the following works, exploring their emotional impact and the causes (sometimes multiple) that lie behind them.

1. In "The Monkey's Paw," Mr. White, urged on by his son, expects his first wish to bring him money to pay for his house. But. . . .

2. In "The Fear," the man and woman expect the figure lurking in the dark to be someone they know out of the woman's past. But. . . .

3. In "Sorrow Rides a Fast Horse," the narrator and his brother expect, after being captured by the bandits, that they will be held prisoners and treated brutally. But. . . .

4. In "Skins," after seeing that the rug means warmth and identity and life to the narrator, we expect its fate to be in some way noble. But then. . . .

5. In "No People Need Apply," Mike Royko says he understands the manager's feelings. But. . . .

6. In "This Is Just to Say," we might imagine someone coming down to breakfast and heading toward the icebox to take out some plums. Instead, this imaginary person finds a note (the poem). . . .

7. In "Variation on a Theme by William Carlos Williams," someone passes through the kitchen and checks the pan on the stove containing the tamales. Beside it is a note (the poem). . . .

8. In "The Man Called Dead," Drake Forrester is outraged when he sees the story about his death in the newspaper. After a while, however. . . .

9. When we first see the woman in "Waiting for Her Train," we think that she is going to catch a train for some destination, as yet undecided. But as we read on. . . .

10. In "Long-Distance," you are waiting for a phone call that you never expect to come. But then. . . .

11. In *Twelve Angry Men*, the first vote of the jury shows eleven in favor of a guilty verdict, and one in favor of a not guilty verdict. The situation looks hopeless for the defendant in the trial. But then. . . .

II. *Twelve Angry Men*

1. As a dramatist sets his major conflicts in motion, he provides whatever background information his audience needs to understand the characters and their actions. Such explanatory information is called the *exposition* of the play, most of which occurs during the first act. **(a)** In *Twelve Angry Men*, what information about the trial does Rose provide while the jurors are still in the courtroom? **(b)** While they are assembling in the jury room? **(c)** After they vote for the first time?

2. Review, if necessary, the article on *Protagonist/Antagonist* in the Handbook of Literary Terms. **(a)** Who is the protagonist in *Twelve Angry Men?* Who (or what) is the antagonist in the play? **(b)** Suggest a substitute title for *Twelve Angry Men* that reflects the identity of the protagonist.

3. The conflict of a play creates several moments of dramatic climax—moments that excite the audience. Which do you consider to be the most exciting moments in *Twelve Angry Men?* Explain.

INTERPRETATION: NEW MATERIAL

Read the story, then answer the questions.

The Interlopers
Saki

In a forest of mixed growth somewhere on the eastern spurs of the Carpathians,[1] a man stood one winter night watching and listening, as though he waited for some beast of the woods to come within the range of his vision, and later, of his rifle. But the game for whose presence he kept so keen an outlook was none that figured in the sportsman's calendar as lawful and proper for the chase; Ulrich von Gradwitz[2] patrolled the dark forest in quest of a human enemy.

The forest lands of Gradwitz were of wide extent and well stocked with game; the narrow strip of precipitous woodland that lay on its outskirts was not remarkable for the game it harbored or the shooting it afforded, but it was the most jealously guarded of all its owner's territorial possessions. A famous lawsuit, in the days of his grandfather, had wrested it from the illegal possession of a neighboring family of petty landowners; the dispossessed party had never acquiesced in the judgment of the courts, and a long series of poaching affrays[3] and similar scandals had embittered the relationships between the families for three generations. The neighbors' feud had grown into a personal one since Ulrich had come to be head of his family; if there was a man in the world whom he detested and wished ill to, it was Georg Znaeym,[4] the inheritor of the quarrel and the tireless game snatcher and raider of the disputed border forest.

The feud might, perhaps, have died down or been compromised if the personal ill will of the two men had not stood in the way; as boys they had thirsted for one another's blood; as men each prayed that misfortune might fall on the other; and this wind-scourged winter night Ulrich had banded together his foresters to watch the dark forest, not in quest of four-footed quarry, but to keep a lookout for the prowling thieves whom he suspected of being afoot from across the land boundary. The roebuck, which usually kept in the sheltered hollows during a storm-wind, were running like driven things tonight; and there was movement and unrest among the creatures that were wont to sleep through the dark hours. Assuredly there was a disturbing element in the forest, and Ulrich could guess the quarter from whence it came.

He strayed away by himself from the watchers whom he had placed in ambush on the crest of the hill, and wandered far down the steep slopes amid the wild tangle of undergrowth, peering through the tree trunks and listening through the whistling and skirling of the wind and the restless beating of the branches for sight or sound of the marauders. If only on this wild night, in this dark, lone spot, he might come across Georg Znaeym, man to man, with none to witness—that was the wish that was uppermost in his thoughts. And as he stepped round the trunk of a huge beech, he came face to face with the man he sought.

The two enemies stood glaring at one another for a long, silent moment. Each had a rifle in his hand; each had hate in his heart and murder uppermost in his mind. The chance had come to give full play to the passions of a lifetime. But a man who has been brought up under the code of a restraining civilization cannot easily nerve himself to shoot down his neighbor in cold blood and without a word spoken, except for an offense against his hearth and honor. And before the moment of hesitation had given way to action, a deed of nature's own violence overwhelmed them both. A fierce shriek of the storm

From THE COMPLETE SHORT STORIES OF SAKI (H. H. Munro). All rights reserved. Reprinted by permission of The Viking Press.

1. *Carpathians* (kär pā'thē ənz), mountain chain extending from northern Rumania to Czechoslovakia.

2. *Ulrich von Gradwitz* (ül'rik fən gräd'vits).

3. *poaching affrays.* The dispossessed family retaliated by trespassing on the land to hunt game.

4. *Georg Znaeym* (gā'ôrg znä'im).

had been answered by a splitting crash over their heads; and ere they could leap aside, a mass of falling beech tree had thundered down on them. Ulrich von Gradwitz found himself stretched on the ground, one arm numb beneath him and the other held almost as helpless in a tight tangle of forked branches, while both legs were pinned beneath the fallen mass. His heavy shooting boots had saved his feet from being crushed to pieces; but if his fractures were not so serious as they might have been, at least it was evident that he could not move from his present position till someone came to release him. The descending twigs had slashed the skin of his face, and he had to wink away some drops of blood from his eyelashes before he could take in a general view of the disaster. At his side, so near that under ordinary circumstances he could almost have touched him, lay Georg Znaeym, alive and struggling, but obviously as helplessly pinioned down as himself. All round them lay a thick-strewn wreckage of splintered branches and broken twigs.

Relief at being alive and exasperation at his captive plight brought a strange medley of pious thank offerings and sharp curses to Ulrich's lips. Georg, who was nearly blinded with the blood which trickled across his eyes, stopped his struggling for a moment to listen and then gave a short, snarling laugh.

"So you're not killed, as you ought to be; but you're caught, anyway," he cried; "caught fast. Ho, what a jest, Ulrich von Gradwitz snared in his stolen forest. There's real justice for you!"

And he laughed again, mockingly and savagely.

"I'm caught in my own forest land," retorted Ulrich. "When my men come to release us, you will wish, perhaps, that you were in a better plight than caught poaching on a neighbor's land. Shame on you!"

Georg was silent for a moment; then he answered quietly:

"Are you sure that your men will find much to release? I have men, too, in the forest tonight, close behind me; and *they* will be here first and do the releasing. When they drag me out from under these branches, it won't need much clumsiness on their part to roll this mass of trunk right over on the top of you. Your men will find you dead under a fallen beech tree. For form's sake I shall send my condolences to your family."

"It is a useful hint," said Ulrich fiercely. "My men had orders to follow in ten minutes' time, seven of which must have gone by already; and when they get me out—I will remember the hint. Only as you will have met your death poaching on my lands, I don't think I can decently send any message of condolence to your family."

"Good," snarled Georg, "good. We'll fight this quarrel out to the death—you and I and our foresters, with no cursed interlopers to come between us. Death to you, Ulrich von Gradwitz!"

"The same to you, Georg Znaeym, forest thief, game snatcher!"

Both men spoke with the bitterness of possible defeat before them, for each knew that it might be long before his men would seek him out or find him; it was a bare matter of chance which party would arrive first on the scene.

Both had now given up the useless struggle to free themselves from the mass of wood that held them down; Ulrich limited his endeavors to an effort to bring his one partially free arm near enough to his outer coat pocket to draw out his wine flask. Even when he had accomplished that operation, it was long before he could manage the unscrewing of the stopper or get any of the liquid down his throat. But what a Heaven-sent draft it seemed! It was an open winter, and little snow had fallen as yet, hence the captives suffered less from the cold than might have been the case at that season of the year; nevertheless, the wine was warming and reviving to the wounded man, and he looked across with something like a throb of pity to where his enemy lay, barely keeping the groans of pain and weariness from crossing his lips.

"Could you reach this flask if I threw it over to you?" asked Ulrich suddenly. "There is good wine in it, and one may as well be as comfortable as one can. Let us drink, even if tonight one of us dies.''

''No, I can scarcely see anything, there is so much blood caked round my eyes,'' said Georg; ''and in any case I don't drink wine with an enemy.''

Ulrich was silent for a few minutes and lay listening to the weary screeching of the wind. An idea was slowly forming and growing in his brain, an idea that gained strength every time that he looked across at the man who was fighting so grimly against pain and exhaustion. In the pain and languor that Ulrich himself was feeling, the old fierce hatred seemed to be dying down.

''Neighbor,'' he said presently, ''do as you please if your men come first. It was a fair compact. But as for me, I've changed my mind. If my men are the first to come, you shall be the first to be helped, as though you were my guest. We have quarreled like devils all our lives over this stupid strip of forest where the trees can't even stand upright in a breath of wind. Lying here tonight, thinking, I've come to think that we've been rather fools; there are better things in life than getting the better of a boundary dispute. Neighbor, if you will help me to bury the old quarrel I—I will ask you to be my friend.''

Georg Znaeym was silent for so long that Ulrich thought, perhaps, he had fainted with the pain of his injuries. Then he spoke slowly and in jerks:

''How the whole region would stare and gabble if we rode into the market square together. No one living can remember seeing a Znaeym and a Von Gradwitz talking to one another in friendship. And what peace there would be among the forester folk if we ended our feud tonight. And if we choose to make peace among our people, there is none other to interfere, no interlopers from outside. . . . You would come and keep the Sylvester night[5] beneath my roof, and I would come and feast on some high day at your castle. . . . I would never fire a shot on your land, save when you invited me as a guest; and you should come and shoot

with me down in the marshes where the wild fowl are. In all the countryside there are none that could hinder if we willed to make peace. I never thought to have wanted to do other than hate you all my life; but I think I have changed my mind about things, too, this last half-hour. And you offered me your wine flask. . . . Ulrich von Gradwitz, I will be your friend.''

For a space both men were silent, turning over in their minds the wonderful changes that this dramatic reconciliation would bring about. In the cold, gloomy forest, with the wind tearing in fitful gusts through the naked branches and whistling around the tree trunks, they lay and waited for the help that would now bring release and succor to both parties. And each prayed a private prayer that his men might be the first to arrive, so that he might be the first to show honorable attention to the enemy that had become a friend.

Presently, as the wind dropped for a moment, Ulrich broke silence.

''Let's shout for help,'' he said; ''in this lull our voices may carry a little way.''

''They won't carry far through the trees and undergrowth,'' said Georg; ''but we can try. Together, then.''

The two raised their voices in a prolonged hunting call.

''Together again,'' said Ulrich a few minutes later, after listening in vain for an answering halloo.

''I heard something that time, I think,'' said Ulrich.

''I heard nothing but the pestilential wind,'' said Georg hoarsely.

There was silence again for some minutes, and then Ulrich gave a joyful cry.

''I can see figures coming through the wood. They are following in the way I came down the hillside.''

Both men raised their voices in as loud a shout as they could muster.

''They hear us! They've stopped. Now they

---

5. Sylvester night, New Year's Eve. Festivities honor St. Sylvester, Bishop of Rome (A.D. 314–335).

see us. They're running down the hill toward us," cried Ulrich.

"How many of them are there?" asked Georg.

"I can't see distinctly," said Ulrich; "nine or ten."

"Then they are yours," said Georg; "I had only seven out with me."

"They are making all the speed they can, brave lads," said Ulrich gladly.

"Are they your men?" asked Georg. "Are they your men?" he repeated impatiently as Ulrich did not answer.

"No," said Ulrich with a laugh, the idiotic chattering laugh of a man unstrung with hideous fear.

"Who are they?" asked Georg quickly, straining his eyes to see what the other would gladly not have seen.

"Wolves!" □□

On a separate sheet of paper write the word or phrase that best answers the questions. Do not write in your book.

1. What seemingly assured the continuing of the feud?

2. Why do the men not shoot immediately when they meet under the beech tree?

3. What is Ulrich's first thought after the tree traps him?

4. What is the turning point in the men's relationship?

5. How would a change of heart on the part of Gradwitz and Znaeym affect the inhabitants of the region?

6. What is the weather the night of the men's meeting? How does it affect the story?

7. There are three conflicts in "The Interlopers." Which situation is an example of man against man? of man against nature? of man against himself?

8. Georg speaks of "interlopers" two times (pages 69 and 70). Whom does he mean? Who are the interlopers ultimately?

9. Which man's thinking is revealed to the reader?

10. What is ironic about the ending of the story? (If necessary, review *Irony* in the Handbook of Literary Terms.)

Unit 1, Test II
COMPOSITION

From the assignments below choose one to write about.

1. Choose three of the selections in the unit and discuss the reasons for the turnabouts in them. Assume you are writing for your classmates.

2. Decide which story in the unit you liked least and tell why that story did not appeal to you and how you would change it to your liking. Assume you are writing for your classmates.

3. Contrast the different cultures and the ways conflict between cultures is treated in any two of the following selections: "Sorrow Rides a Fast Horse," "Skins," and "No People Need Apply." Assume you are writing a magazine article for the general public.

4. Write three short news stories and headlines as they might appear after the events in "The Interlopers," *Twelve Angry Men,* and "Sorrow Rides a Fast Horse." Be sure to follow the style of newspaper stories.

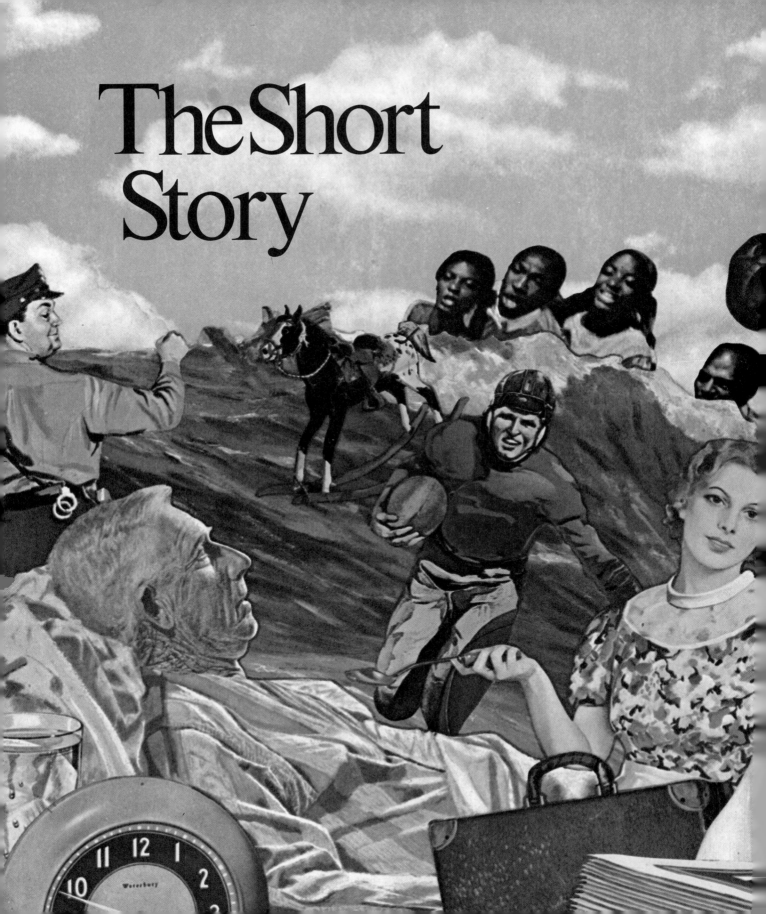

The Short Story

GROWTH

Through the Tunnel

Doris Lessing

Going to the shore on the first morning of the vacation, the young English boy stopped at a turning of the path and looked down at a wild and rocky bay, and then over to the crowded beach he knew so well from other years. His mother walked on in front of him, carrying a bright striped bag in one hand. Her other arm, swinging loose, was very white in the sun. The boy watched that white, naked arm, and turned his eyes, which had a frown behind them, toward the bay and back again to his mother. When she felt he was not with her, she swung around. "Oh, there you are, Jerry!" she said. She looked impatient, then smiled. "Why, darling, would you rather not come with me? Would you rather——" She frowned, conscientiously worrying over what amusements he might secretly be longing for, which she had been too busy or too careless to imagine. He was very familiar with that anxious, apologetic smile.

Contrition sent him running after her. And yet, as he ran, he looked back over his shoulder at the wild bay; and all morning, as he played on the safe beach, he was thinking of it.

Next morning, when it was time for the routine of swimming and sunbathing, his mother said, "Are you tired of the usual beach, Jerry? Would you like to go somewhere else?"

"Oh, no!" he said quickly, smiling at her out of that unfailing impulse of contrition—a sort of chivalry. Yet, walking down the path with her, he blurted out, "I'd like to go and have a look at those rocks down there."

She gave the idea her attention. It was a wild-looking place, and there was no one there; but she said, "Of course, Jerry. When you've had

"Through the Tunnel" from THE HABIT OF LOVING by Doris Lessing (1957). Copyright © 1955 by Doris Lessing. Originally appeared in THE NEW YORKER and reprinted by permission of Thomas Y. Crowell Company, Inc.

enough, come to the big beach. Or just go straight back to the villa, if you like." She walked away, that bare arm, now slightly reddened from yesterday's sun, swinging. And he almost ran after her again, feeling it unbearable that she could go by herself, but he did not.

She was thinking. Of course he's old enough to be safe without me. Have I been keeping him too close? He mustn't feel he ought to be with me. I must be careful.

He was an only child, eleven years old. She was a widow. She was determined to be neither possessive nor lacking in devotion. She went worrying off to her beach.

As for Jerry, once he saw that his mother had gained her beach, he began the steep descent to the bay. From where he was, high up among red-brown rocks, it was a scoop of moving bluish green fringed with white. As he went lower, he saw that it spread among small promontories and inlets of rough, sharp rock, and the crisping, lapping surface showed stains of purple and darker blue. Finally, as he ran sliding and scraping down the last few yards, he saw an edge of white surf and the shallow, luminous movement of water over white sand, and, beyond that, a solid, heavy blue.

He ran straight into the water and began swimming. He was a good swimmer. He went out fast over the gleaming sand, over a middle region where rocks lay like discolored monsters under the surface, and then he was in the real sea—a warm sea where irregular cold currents from the deep water shocked his limbs.

When he was so far out that he could look back not only on the little bay but past the promontory that was between it and the big beach, he floated on the buoyant surface and looked for his mother. There she was, a speck of yellow under an umbrella that looked like a slice of orange peel. He swam back to shore, relieved at being sure she was there, but all at once very lonely.

On the edge of a small cape that marked the side of the bay away from the promontory was a loose scatter of rocks. Above them, some boys were stripping off their clothes. They came running, naked, down to the rocks. The English boy swam toward them, but kept his distance at a stone's throw. They were of that coast; all of them were burned smooth dark brown and speaking a language he did not understand. To be with them, of them, was a craving that filled his whole body. He swam a little closer; they turned and watched him with narrowed, alert dark eyes. Then one smiled and waved. It was enough. In a minute, he had swum in and was on the rocks beside them, smiling with a desperate, nervous supplication. They shouted cheerful greetings at him; and then, as he preserved his nervous, uncomprehending smile, they understood that he was a foreigner strayed from his own beach, and they proceeded to forget him. But he was happy. He was with them.

They began diving again and again from a high point into a well of blue sea between rough, pointed rocks. After they had dived and come up, they swam around, hauled themselves up, and waited their turn to dive again. They were big boys—men, to Jerry. He dived, and they watched him; and when he swam around to take his place, they made way for him. He felt he was accepted and he dived again, carefully, proud of himself.

Soon the biggest of the boys poised himself, shot down into the water, and did not come up. The others stood about, watching. Jerry, after waiting for the sleek brown head to appear, let out a yell of warning; they looked at him idly and turned their eyes back toward the water. After a long time, the boy came up on the other side of a big dark rock, letting the air out of his lungs in a sputtering gasp and a shout of triumph. Immediately the rest of them dived in. One moment, the morning seemed full of chattering boys; the next, the air and the surface of the water were empty. But through the heavy blue, dark shapes could be seen moving and groping.

Jerry dived, shot past the school of underwater swimmers, saw a black wall of rock looming at him, touched it, and bobbed up at once to the surface, where the wall was a low barrier he could see across. There was no one visible; under him, in the water, the dim shapes of the swimmers had disappeared. Then one, and then another of the boys came up on the far side of the barrier of rock, and he understood that they had swum through some gap or hole in it. He plunged down again. He could see nothing through the stinging salt water but the blank rock. When he came up the boys were all on the diving rock, preparing to attempt the feat again. And now, in a panic of failure, he yelled up, in English, "Look at me! Look!" and he began splashing and kicking in the water like a foolish dog.

They looked down gravely, frowning. He knew the frown. At moments of failure, when he clowned to claim his mother's attention, it was with just this grave, embarrassed inspection that she rewarded him. Through his hot shame, feeling the pleading grin on his face like a scar that he could never remove, he looked up at the group of big brown boys on the rock and shouted, "*Bonjour! Merci! Au revoir! Monsieur, monsieur!*" while he hooked his fingers round his ears and waggled them.

Water surged into his mouth; he choked, sank, came up. The rock, lately weighted with boys, seemed to rear up out of the water as their weight was removed. They were flying down past him, now, into the water; the air was full of falling bodies. Then the rock was empty in the hot sunlight. He counted one, two, three. . . .

At fifty, he was terrified. They must all be drowning beneath him, in the watery caves of the rock! At a hundred, he stared around him at the empty hillside, wondering if he should yell for help. He counted faster, faster, to hurry them up, to bring them to the surface quickly, to drown them quickly—anything rather than the terror of counting on and on into the blue emptiness of the morning. And then, at a hundred and sixty, the water beyond the rock was full of boys blowing like brown whales. They swam back to the shore without a look at him.

He climbed back to the diving rock and sat down, feeling the hot roughness of it under his thighs. The boys were gathering up their bits of clothing and running off along the shore to another promontory. They were leaving to get away from him. He cried openly, fists in his eyes. There was no one to see him, and he cried himself out.

It seemed to him that a long time had passed, and he swam out to where he could see his mother. Yes, she was still there, a yellow spot under an orange umbrella. He swam back to the big rock, climbed up, and dived into the blue pool among the fanged and angry boulders. Down he went, until he touched the wall of rock again. But the salt was so painful in his eyes that he could not see.

He came to the surface, swam to shore and went back to the villa to wait for his mother. Soon she walked slowly up the path, swinging her striped bag, the flushed, naked arm dangling beside her. "I want some swimming goggles," he panted, defiant and beseeching.

She gave him a patient inquisitive look as she said casually, "Well, of course, darling."

But now, now, now! He must have them this minute, and no other time. He nagged and pestered until she went with him to a shop. As soon as she had bought the goggles, he grabbed them from her hand as if she were going to claim them for herself, and was off, running down the steep path to the bay.

Jerry swam out to the big barrier rock, adjusted the goggles, and dived. The impact of the water broke the rubber-enclosed vacuum, and the goggles came loose. He understood that he must swim down to the base of the rock from the surface of the water. He fixed the goggles tight and firm, filled his lungs, and floated, face down, on the water. Now, he could see. It was as if he had eyes of a different kind—fish eyes that showed everything clear and delicate and wavering in the bright water.

Under him, six or seven feet down, was a floor of perfectly clean, shining white sand, rippled firm and hard by the tides. Two grayish shapes steered there, like long, rounded pieces of wood or slate. They were fish. He saw them nose toward each other, poise motionless, make a dart forward, swerve off, and come around again. It was like a water dance. A few inches above them the water sparkled as if sequins were dropping through it. Fish again—myriads of minute fish, the length of his fingernail, were drifting through the water, and in a moment he could feel the innumerable tiny touches of them against his limbs. It was like swimming in flaked silver. The great rock the big boys had swum through rose sheer out of the white sand—black, tufted lightly with greenish weed. He could see no gap in it. He swam down to its base.

Again and again he rose, took a big chestful of air, and went down. Again and again he groped over the surface of the rock, feeling it, almost hugging it in the desperate need to find the entrance. And then, once, while he was clinging to the black wall, his knees came up and he shot his feet out forward and they met no obstacle. He had found the hole.

He gained the surface, clambered about the stones that littered the barrier rock until he found a big one, and, with this in his arms, let himself down over the side of the rock. He dropped, with the weight, straight to the sandy floor. Clinging tight to the anchor of stone, he lay on his side and looked in under the dark shelf at the place where his feet had gone. He could see the hole. It was an irregular, dark gap; but he could not see deep into it. He let go of his anchor, clung with his hands to the edges of the hole, and tried to push himself in.

He got his head in, found his shoulders jammed, moved them in sidewise, and was inside as far as his waist. He could see nothing ahead. Something soft and clammy touched his mouth; he saw a dark frond moving against the grayish rock, and panic filled him. He thought of octopuses, of clinging weed. He pushed himself out backward and caught a glimpse, as he retreated, of a harmless tentacle of seaweed drifting in the mouth of the tunnel. But it was enough. He reached the sunlight, swam to shore, and lay on the diving rock. He looked down into the blue well of water. He knew he must find his way through that cave, or hole, or tunnel, and out the other side.

First, he thought, he must learn to control his breathing. He let himself down into the water with another big stone in his arms, so that he could lie effortlessly on the bottom of the sea. He counted. One, two, three. He counted steadily. He could hear the movement of blood in his chest. Fifty-one, fifty-two. . . . His chest was hurting. He let go of the rock and went up into the air. He saw that the sun was low. He rushed to the villa and found his mother at her supper. She said only "Did you enjoy yourself?" and he said "Yes."

All night the boy dreamed of the water-filled cave in the rock, and as soon as breakfast was over he went to the bay.

That night, his nose bled badly. For hours he had been underwater, learning to hold his breath, and now he felt weak and dizzy. His mother said, "I shouldn't overdo things, darling, if I were you."

That day and the next, Jerry exercised his lungs as if everything, the whole of his life, all that he would become, depended upon it. Again his nose bled at night, and his mother insisted on his coming with her the next day. It was a torment to him to waste a day of his careful self-training, but he stayed with her on that other beach, which now seemed a place for small children, a place where his mother might lie safe in the sun. It was not his beach.

He did not ask for permission, on the following day, to go to his beach. He went, before his mother could consider the complicated rights and wrongs of the matter. A day's rest, he discovered, had improved his count by ten. The big boys had made the passage while he counted a hundred and sixty. He had been counting fast, in his fright. Probably now, if he tried, he could get through that long tunnel, but he was not going to try yet. A curious, most unchildlike persistence, a controlled impatience, made him wait. In the meantime, he lay underwater on the white sand, littered now by stones he had brought down from the upper air, and studied the entrance to the tunnel. He knew every jut and corner of it, as far as it was possible to see. It was as if he already felt its sharpness about his shoulders.

He sat by the clock in the villa, when his mother was not near, and checked his time. He was incredulous and then proud to find he could hold his breath without strain for two minutes. The words "two minutes," authorized by the clock, brought close the adventure that was so necessary to him.

In another four days, his mother said casually one morning, they must go home. On the day before they left, he would do it. He would do it if it killed him, he said defiantly to himself. But two days before they were to leave—a day of triumph when he increased his count by fifteen— his nose bled so badly that he turned dizzy and had to lie limply over the big rock like a bit of seaweed, watching the thick red blood flow on the rock and trickle slowly down to the sea. He was frightened. Supposing he turned dizzy in the tunnel? Supposing he died there, trapped? Supposing—his head went around, in the hot sun, and he almost gave up. He thought he would return to the house and lie down, and next summer, perhaps, when he had another year's growth in him—*then* he would go through the hole.

But even after he had made the decision, or thought he had, he found himself sitting up on the rock and looking down into the water; and he knew that now, this moment, when his nose had only just stopped bleeding, when his head was still sore and throbbing—this was the moment when he would try. If he did not do it now, he never would. He was trembling with fear that he would not go; and he was trembling with horror at that long, long tunnel under the rock, under the sea. Even in the open sunlight, the barrier rock seemed very wide and very heavy; tons of rock pressed down on where he would go. If he died there, he would lie until one day—perhaps not before next year—those big boys would swim into it and find it blocked.

He put on his goggles, fitted them tight, tested the vacuum. His hands were shaking. Then he chose the biggest stone he could carry and slipped over the edge of the rock until half of him was in the cool, enclosing water and half in the hot sun. He looked up once at the empty sky, filled his lungs once, twice, and then sank fast to the bottom with the stone. He let it go and began to count. He took the edges of the hole in his hands and drew himself into it, wriggling his shoulders in sidewise as he remembered he must, kicking himself along with his feet.

Soon he was clear inside. He was in a small rock-bound hole filled with yellowish-gray water. The water was pushing him up against the roof. The roof was sharp and pained his back. He pulled himself along with his hands—fast, fast—and used his legs as levers. His head knocked against something; a sharp pain dizzied him. Fifty, fifty-one, fifty-two. . . . He was without light, and the water seemed to press upon him with the weight of rock. Seventy-one, seventy-two. . . . There was no strain on his lungs. He felt like an inflated balloon, his lungs were so light and easy, but his head was pulsing.

He was being continually pressed against the sharp roof, which felt slimy as well as sharp. Again he thought of octopuses, and wondered if the tunnel might be filled with weed that could tangle him. He gave himself a panicky, convulsive kick forward, ducked his head, and swam. His feet and hands moved freely, as if in open water. The hole must have widened out. He thought he must be swimming fast, and he was frightened of banging his head if the tunnel narrowed.

A hundred, a hundred and one. . . . The water paled. Victory filled him. His lungs were beginning to hurt. A few more strokes and he would be out. He was counting wildly; he said a hundred and fifteen, and then, a long time later, a hundred and fifteen again. The water was a clear jewel-green all around him. Then he saw, above his head, a crack running up through the rock. Sunlight was falling through it, showing the clean, dark rock of the tunnel, a single mussel shell, and darkness ahead.

He was at the end of what he could do. He looked up at the crack as if it were filled with air and not water, as if he could put his mouth to it to draw in air. A hundred and fifteen, he heard himself say inside his head—but he had said that long ago. He must go on into the blackness ahead, or he would drown. His head was swelling, his lungs cracking. A hundred and fifteen, a hundred and fifteen pounded through his head, and he feebly clutched at rocks in the dark, pulling himself forward, leaving the brief space of sunlit water behind. He felt he was dying. He was no longer quite conscious. He struggled on in the darkness between lapses into unconsciousness. An immense, swelling pain filled his head, and then the darkness cracked with an explosion of green light. His hands, groping forward, met nothing; and his feet, kicking back, propelled him out into the open sea.

He drifted to the surface, his face turned up to the air. He was gasping like a fish. He felt he would sink now and drown; he could not swim the few feet back to the rock. Then he was clutching it and pulling himself up on to it. He lay face down, gasping. He could see nothing but a red-veined, clotted dark. His eyes must have burst, he thought; they were full of blood. He tore off his goggles and a gout of blood went into the sea. His nose was bleeding, and the blood had filled the goggles.

He scooped up handfuls of water from the cool, salty sea, to splash on his face, and did not know whether it was blood or salt water he tasted. After a time, his heart quieted, his eyes cleared, and he sat up. He could see the local boys diving and playing half a mile away. He did not want them. He wanted nothing but to get back home and lie down.

In a short while, Jerry swam to shore and climbed slowly up the path to the villa. He flung himself on his bed and slept, waking at the sound of feet on the path outside. His mother was coming back. He rushed to the bathroom, thinking she must not see his face with bloodstains, or tearstains, on it. He came out of the bathroom and met her as she walked into the villa, smiling, her eyes lighting up.

"Have a nice morning?" she asked, laying her hand on his warm brown shoulder a moment.

"Oh, yes, thank you," he said.

"You look a bit pale." And then, sharp and anxious, "How did you bang your head?"

"Oh, just banged it," he told her.

She looked at him closely. He was strained; his eyes were glazed-looking. She was worried. And then she said to herself, Oh, don't fuss! Nothing can happen. He can swim like a fish.

They sat down to lunch together.

"Mummy," he said, "I can stay under water for two minutes—three minutes, at least." It came bursting out of him.

"Can you, darling?" she said. "Well, I shouldn't overdo it. I don't think you ought to swim any more today."

She was ready for a battle of wills, but he gave in at once. It was no longer of the least importance to go to the bay. □□

Discussion

1. (a) Describe the relationship between Jerry and his mother at the beginning of the story. (b) To what extent is the relationship a consequence of Jerry's being without a father? Explain.

2. (a) Under what circumstances does Jerry happen to encounter the group of older boys? (b) What seems to be their attitude toward the younger boy? Explain. (c) What signs of immaturity does Jerry display first in front of the boys and then immediately after they leave?

3. (a) Describe the preparations Jerry makes to conquer the underwater tunnel. (b) What risks to his health does the boy take in undergoing these preparations? (c) If Jerry had had numerous friends his own age, do you believe he would have taken the same risks? Explain.

4. (a) Describe Jerry's state of mind and his physical condition at the time he decides that he must immediately try swimming the tunnel. (b) What physical and mental experiences does he have while inside the tunnel?

5. How will Jerry's relationship to his mother and to others change as a consequence of his mastering the tunnel? Explain.

6. Describe situations in the story that indicate that each of the following adjectives might apply to Jerry at one time or another: (a) *immature,* (b) *impatient,* (c) *persistent,* (d) *foolhardy,* (e) *courageous,* (f) *mature.*

Doris Lessing 1919 ·

The daughter of an Army captain, Lessing was born in Kermanshah, Iran. The family moved to Africa shortly afterwards, where she was educated at a convent and girls' school in Salisbury, Northern Rhodesia.

Her first novel, *The Grass Is Singing* (1950), was highly acclaimed. In 1952 she began a series of novels called *Children of Violence.* Her books deal with the problems of blacks and whites in the rapidly changing society of Africa. *African Stories* (1964), an anthology of short stories, contains some of her best portrayals of the problems of South Africa. In the introduction to that collection, she comments: "Writers brought up in Africa have many advantages—being at the centre of a modern battlefield; part of a society in rapid, dramatic change."

See **THEME** Handbook of Literary Terms

Shaving

Leslie Norris

Earlier, when Barry had left the house to go to the game, an overnight frost had still been thick on the roads, but the brisk April sun had soon dispersed it, and now he could feel the spring warmth on his back through the thick tweed of his coat. His left arm was beginning to stiffen up where he'd jarred it in a tackle, but it was nothing serious. He flexed his shoulders against the tightness of his jacket and was surprised again by the unexpected weight of his muscles, the thickening strength of his body. A few years back, he thought, he had been a small, unimportant boy, one of a swarming gang laughing and jostling to school, hardly aware that he possessed an identity. But time had transformed him. He walked solidly now, and often alone. He was tall, strongly made, his hands and feet were adult and heavy, the rooms in which all his life he'd moved had grown too small for him. Sometimes a devouring restlessness drove him from the house to walk long distances in the dark. He hardly understood how it had happened. Amused and quiet, he walked the High Street among the morning shoppers.

He saw Jackie Bevan across the road and remembered how, when they were both six years old, Jackie had swallowed a pin. The flustered teachers had clucked about Jackie as he stood there, bawling, cheeks awash with tears, his nose wet. But now Jackie was tall and suave, his thick, pale hair sleekly tailored, his gray suit enviable. He was talking to a girl as golden as a daffodil.

"Hey, hey!" called Jackie. "How's the athlete, how's Barry boy?"

He waved a graceful hand at Barry.

"Come and talk to Sue," he said.

Barry shifted his bag to his left hand and walked over, forming in his mind the answers he'd make to Jackie's questions.

"Did we win?" Jackie asked. "Was the old Barry Stanford magic in glittering evidence yet once more this morning? Were the invaders sent hunched and silent back to their hovels in the

"Shaving" by Leslie Norris, ATLANTIC, April 1977. Copyright, © 1977, by Leslie Norris. Reprinted by permission of Brandt & Brandt.

hills? What was the score? Give us an epic account, Barry, without modesty or delay. This is Sue, by the way."

"I've seen you about," the girl said.

"You could hardly miss him," said Jackie. "Four men, roped together, spent a week climbing him—they thought he was Everest. He ought to carry a warning beacon, he's a danger to aircraft."

"Silly," said the girl, smiling at Jackie. "He's not much taller than you are."

She had a nice voice too.

"We won," Barry said. "Seventeen points to three, and it was a good game. The ground was hard, though."

He could think of nothing else to say.

"Let's all go for a frivolous cup of coffee," Jackie said. "Let's celebrate your safe return from the rough fields of victory. We could pour libations all over the floor for you."

"I don't think so," Barry said. "Thanks. I'll go straight home."

"Okay," said Jackie, rocking on his heels so that the sun could shine on his smile. "How's your father?"

"No better," Barry said. "He's not going to get better."

"Yes, well," said Jackie, serious and uncomfortable, "tell him my mother and father ask about him."

"I will," Barry promised. "He'll be pleased."

Barry dropped the bag in the front hall and moved into the room which had been the dining room until his father's illness. His father lay in the white bed, his long body gaunt, his still head scarcely denting the pillow. He seemed asleep, thin blue lids covering his eyes, but when Barry turned away he spoke.

"Hullo, son," he said. "Did you win?"

His voice was a dry, light rustling, hardly louder than the breath which carried it. Its sound moved Barry to a compassion that almost unmanned him, but he stepped close to the bed and looked down at the dying man.

"Yes," he said. "We won fairly easily. It was a good game."

His father lay with his eyes closed, inert, his breath irregular and shallow.

"Did you score?" he asked.

"Twice," Barry said. "I had a try in each half."

He thought of the easy certainty with which he'd caught the ball before his second try; casually, almost arrogantly he had taken it on the tips of his fingers, on his full burst for the line, breaking the fullback's tackle. Nobody could have stopped him. But watching his father's weakness he felt humble and ashamed, as if the morning's game, its urgency and effort, was not worth talking about. His father's face, fine-skinned and pallid, carried a dark stubble of beard, almost a week's growth, and his obstinate, strong hair stuck out over his brow.

"Good," said his father, after a long pause. "I'm glad it was a good game."

Barry's mother bustled about the kitchen, a tempest of orderly energy.

"Your father's not well," she said. "He's down today, feels depressed. He's a particular man, your father. He feels dirty with all that beard on him."

She slammed shut the stove door.

"Mr. Cleaver was supposed to come up and shave him," she said, "and that was three days ago. Little things have always worried your father, every detail must be perfect for him."

Barry filled a glass with milk from the refrigerator. He was very thirsty.

"I'll shave him," he said.

His mother stopped, her head on one side.

"Do you think you can?" she asked. "He'd like it if you can."

"I can do it," Barry said.

He washed his hands as carefully as a surgeon. His father's razor was in a blue leather case, hinged at the broad edge and with one hinge broken. Barry unfastened the clasp and took out the razor. It had not been properly cleaned after its last use and lather had stiffened into hard yellow rectangles between the teeth of the guard. There were water-shaped rust stains, brown as chocolate, on the surface of the blade. Barry removed it, throwing it in the wastebin. He washed the razor until it glistened, and dried it on a soft towel, polishing the thin handle, rubbing its metal head to a glittering shine. He took a new blade from its waxed envelope, the paper clinging to the thin metal. The blade was smooth and flexible to the touch, the little angles of its cutting clearly defined. Barry slotted it into the grip of the razor, making it snug and tight in the head.

The shaving soap, hard, white, richly aromatic, was kept in a wooden bowl. Its scent was immediately evocative and Barry could almost see his father in the days of his health, standing before his mirror, thick white lather on his face and neck. As a little boy Barry had loved the generous perfume of the soap, had waited for his father to lift the razor to his face, for one careful stroke to take away the white suds in a clean revelation of the skin. Then his father would renew the lather with a few sweeps of his brush, one with an ivory handle and the bristles worn, which he still used.

His father's shaving mug was a thick cup, plain and serviceable. A gold line ran outside the rim of the cup, another inside, just below the lip. Its handle was large and sturdy, and the face of the mug carried a portrait of the young Queen Elizabeth II, circled by a wreath of leaves, oak perhaps, or laurel. A lion and unicorn balanced precariously on a scroll above her crowned head, and the Union Jack, the Royal Standard, and other flags were furled each side of the portrait. And beneath it all, in small black letters, ran the legend: "Coronation June 2nd 1953." The cup was much older than Barry. A pattern of faint translucent cracks, fine as a web, had worked itself haphazardly, invisibly almost, through the white glaze. Inside, on the bottom, a few dark bristles were lying, loose and dry. Barry shook them out, then held the cup in his hand, feeling its solidness. Then he washed it ferociously, until it was clinically clean.

Methodically he set everything on a tray,

razor, soap, brush, towels. Testing the hot water with a finger, he filled the mug and put that, too, on the tray. His care was absorbed, ritualistic. Satisfied that his preparations were complete, he went downstairs, carrying the tray with one hand.

His father was waiting for him. Barry set the tray on a bedside table and bent over his father, sliding an arm under the man's thin shoulders, lifting him without effort so that he sat against the high pillows.

"You're strong . . ." his father said. He was as breathless as if he'd been running.

"So are you," said Barry.

"I was," his father said. "I used to be strong once."

He sat exhausted against the pillows.

"We'll wait a bit," Barry said.

"You could have used your electric razor," his father said. "I expected that."

"You wouldn't like it," Barry said. "You'll get a closer shave this way."

He placed the large towel about his father's shoulders.

"Now," he said, smiling down.

The water was hot in the thick cup. Barry wet the brush and worked up the lather. Gently he built up a covering of soft foam on the man's chin, on his cheeks and his stark cheekbones.

"You're using a lot of soap," his father said.

"Not too much," Barry said. "You've got a lot of beard."

His father lay there quietly, his wasted arms at his sides.

"It's comforting," he said. "You'd be surprised how comforting it is."

Barry took up the razor, weighing it in his hand, rehearsing the angle at which he'd use it. He felt confident.

"If you have prayers to say, . . ." he said.

"I've said a lot of prayers," his father answered.

Barry leaned over and placed the razor delicately against his father's face, setting the head

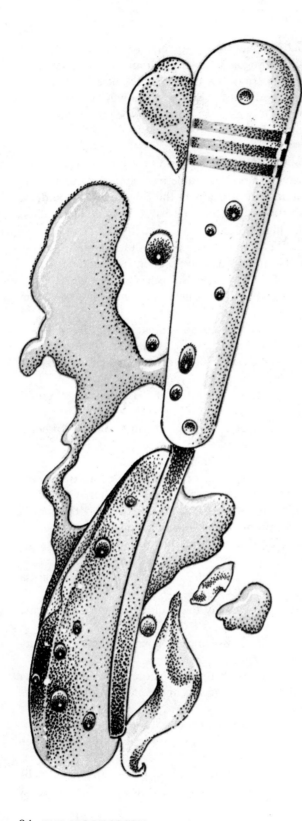

accurately on the clean line near the ear where the long hair ended. He held the razor in the tips of his fingers and drew the blade sweetly through the lather. The new edge moved light as a touch over the hardness of the upper jaw and down to the angle of the chin, sliding away the bristles so easily that Barry could not feel their release. He sighed as he shook the razor in the hot water, washing away the soap.

"How's it going?" his father asked.

"No problem," Barry said. "You needn't worry."

It was as if he had never known what his father really looked like. He was discovering under his hands the clear bones of the face and head; they became sharp and recognizable under his fingers. When he moved his father's face a gentle inch to one side, he touched with his fingers the frail temples, the blue veins of his father's life. With infinite and meticulous care he took away the hair from his father's face.

"Now for your neck," he said. "We might as well do the job properly."

"You've got good hands," his father said. "You can trust those hands, they won't let you down."

Barry cradled his father's head in the crook of his left arm, so that the man could tilt back his head, exposing the throat. He brushed fresh lather under the chin and into the hollows alongside the stretched tendons. His father's throat was fleshless and vulnerable, his head was a hard weight on the boy's arm. Barry was filled with unreasoning protective love. He lifted the razor and began to shave.

"You don't have to worry," he said. "Not at all. Not about anything."

He held his father in the bend of his strong arm and they looked at each other. Their heads were very close.

"How old are you?" his father said.

"Seventeen," Barry said. "Near enough seventeen."

"You're young," his father said, "to have this happen."

"Not too young," Barry said. "I'm bigger than most men."

"I think you are," his father said.

He leaned his head tiredly against the boy's shoulder. He was without strength, his face was cold and smooth. He had let go all his authority, handed it over. He lay back on his pillow, knowing his weakness and his mortality, and looked at his son with wonder, with a curious humble pride.

"I won't worry then," he said. "About anything."

"There's no need," Barry said. "Why should you worry?"

He wiped his father's face clean of all soap with a damp towel. The smell of illness was everywhere, overpowering even the perfumed lather. Barry settled his father down and took away the shaving tools, putting them by with the same ceremonial precision with which he'd prepared them: the cleaned and glittering razor in its broken case; the soap, its bowl wiped and dried, on the shelf between the brush and the coronation mug; all free of taint. He washed his hands and scrubbed his nails. His hands were firm and broad, pink after their scrubbing. The fingers were short and strong, the little fingers slightly crooked, and soft dark hair grew on the backs of his hands and his fingers just above the knuckles. Not long ago they had been small bare hands, not very long ago.

Barry opened wide the bathroom window. Already, although it was not yet two o'clock, the sun was retreating and people were moving briskly, wrapped in their heavy coats against the cold that was to come. But now the window was full in the beam of the dying sunlight, and Barry stood there, illuminated in its golden warmth for a whole minute, knowing it would soon be gone. □□

Discussion

1. In the opening paragraph of the story, we read of the protagonist, Barry: "Sometimes a devouring restlessness drove him from the house to walk long distances in the dark. He hardly understood how it had happened." By the end of the story we have come to know Barry rather well. What do you believe is the restlessness devouring and driving him?

2. In the scene with his old friend Jackie Bevan and Sue, how does Barry show his maturity and sense of responsibility?

3. Describe the relationship between father and son as it emerges in the scene in which Barry skillfully and gently shaves his father.

4. Near the end of the story, we are told that the father "had let go all his authority, handed it over." Explain.

5. Is this story about "shaving" or something else? Explain what you think the author is trying to communicate.

Leslie Norris 1921 ·

Primarily a poet, Leslie Norris has said that he writes "slowly and with great pain, about six poems a year." He was born in Wales and went to school in Coventry, England, and to the University of Southampton. He served in the Royal Air Force from 1940–1942.

His books of poems have included *The Ballad of Billy Rose* (1964), *The Loud Winter* (1967), and *Ransoms* (1970). He has written plays for the BBC. His collection of stories, *Sliding,* appeared in 1976.

Lamb to the Slaughter

Roald Dahl

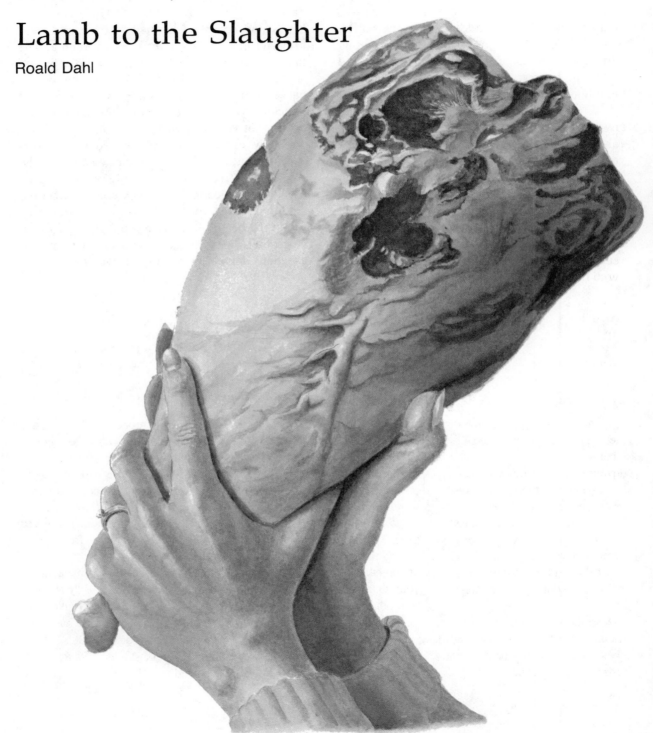

The room was warm and clean, the curtains drawn, the two table lamps alight—hers and the one by the empty chair opposite. On the sideboard behind her, two tall glasses, soda water, whiskey. Fresh ice cubes in the Thermos bucket.

Mary Maloney was waiting for her husband to come home from work.

Now and again she would glance up at the clock, but without anxiety, merely to please herself with the thought that each minute gone by made it nearer the time when he would come. There was a slow smiling air about her, and about everything she did. The drop of the head as she bent over her sewing was curiously tranquil. Her skin—for this was her sixth month with child—had acquired a wonderful translucent quality, the mouth was soft, and the eyes, with their new placid look, seemed larger, darker than before.

When the clock said ten minutes to five, she began to listen, and a few moments later, punctually as always, she heard the tires on the gravel outside, and the car door slamming, the footsteps passing the window, the key turning in the lock. She laid aside her sewing, stood up, and went forward to kiss him as he came in.

"Hullo darling," she said.

"Hullo," he answered.

She took his coat and hung it in the closet. Then she walked over and made the drinks, a strongish one for him, a weak one for herself; and soon she was back again in her chair with the sewing, and he in the other, opposite, holding the tall glass with both his hands, rocking it so the ice cubes tinkled against the side.

For her, this was always a blissful time of day. She knew he didn't want to speak much until the first drink was finished, and she, on her side, was content to sit quietly, enjoying his company after the long hours alone in the house. She loved to luxuriate in the presence of this man, and to feel—almost as a sunbather feels the sun—that warm male glow that came out of him to her when they were alone together. She loved him for the way he sat loosely in a chair, for the

way he came in a door, or moved slowly across the room with long strides. She loved the intent, far look in his eyes when they rested on her, the funny shape of the mouth, and especially the way he remained silent about his tiredness, sitting still with himself until the whiskey had taken some of it away.

"Tired darling?"

"Yes," he said. "I'm tired." And as he spoke, he did an unusual thing. He lifted his glass and drained it in one swallow although there was still half of it, at least half of it left. She wasn't really watching him, but she knew what he had done because she heard the ice cubes falling back against the bottom of the empty glass when he lowered his arm. He paused a moment, leaning forward in the chair, then he got up and went slowly over to fetch himself another.

"I'll get it!" she cried, jumping up.

"Sit down," he said.

When he came back, she noticed that the new drink was dark amber with the quantity of whiskey in it.

"Darling, shall I get your slippers?"

"No."

She watched him as he began to sip the dark yellow drink, and she could see little oily swirls in the liquid because it was so strong.

"I think it's a shame," she said, "that when a policeman gets to be as senior as you, they keep him walking about on his feet all day long."

He didn't answer, so she bent her head again and went on with her sewing; but each time he lifted the drink to his lips, she heard the ice cubes clinking against the side of the glass.

"Darling," she said. "Would you like me to get you some cheese? I haven't made any supper because it's Thursday."

"No," he said.

"If you're too tired to eat out," she went on, "it's still not too late. There's plenty of meat and stuff in the freezer, and you can have it right here and not even move out of the chair."

Copyright 1953 by Roald Dahl. Reprinted from SOMEONE LIKE YOU, by Roald Dahl, by permission of Alfred A. Knopf, Inc. and Murray Pollinger Literary Agent.

Her eyes waited on him for an answer, a smile, a little nod, but he made no sign.

"Anyway," she went on, "I'll get you some cheese and crackers first."

"I don't want it," he said.

She moved uneasily in her chair, the large eyes still watching his face. "But you *must* have supper. I can easily do it here. I'd like to do it. We can have lamb chops. Or pork. Anything you want. Everything's in the freezer."

"Forget it," he said.

"But darling, you *must* eat! I'll fix it anyway, and then you can have it or not, as you like."

She stood up and placed her sewing on the table by the lamp.

"Sit down," he said. "Just for a minute, sit down."

It wasn't till then that she began to get frightened.

"Go on," he said. "Sit down."

She lowered herself back slowly into the chair, watching him all the time with those large, bewildered eyes. He had finished the second drink and was staring down into the glass, frowning.

"Listen," he said. "I've got something to tell you."

"What is it, darling? What's the matter?"

He had now become absolutely motionless, and he kept his head down so that the light from the lamp beside him fell across the upper part of his face, leaving the chin and mouth in shadow. She noticed there was a little muscle moving near the corner of his left eye.

"This is going to be a bit of a shock to you, I'm afraid," he said. "But I've thought about it a good deal and I've decided the only thing to do is tell you right away. I hope you won't blame me too much."

And he told her. It didn't take long, four or five minutes at most, and she sat very still through it all, watching him with a kind of dazed horror as he went further and further away from her with each word.

"So there it is," he added. "And I know it's kind of a bad time to be telling you, but there simply wasn't any other way. Of course I'll give you money and see you're looked after. But there needn't really be any fuss. I hope not anyway. It wouldn't be very good for my job."

Her first instinct was not to believe any of it, to reject it all. It occurred to her that perhaps he hadn't even spoken, that she herself had imagined the whole thing. Maybe, if she went about her business and acted as though she hadn't been listening, then later, when she sort of woke up again, she might find none of it had ever happened.

"I'll get the supper," she managed to whisper, and this time he didn't stop her.

When she walked across the room she couldn't feel her feet touching the floor. She couldn't feel anything at all—except a slight nausea and a desire to vomit. Everything was automatic now—down the steps to the cellar, the light switch, the deep freeze, the hand inside the cabinet taking hold of the first object it met. She lifted it out, and looked at it. It was wrapped in paper, so she took off the paper and looked at it again.

A leg of lamb.

All right then, they would have lamb for supper. She carried it upstairs, holding the thin bone-end of it with both her hands, and as she went through the living-room, she saw him standing over by the window with his back to her, and she stopped.

"For heaven's sake," he said, hearing her, but not turning round. "Don't make supper for me. I'm going out."

At that point, Mary Maloney simply walked up behind him and without any pause she swung the big frozen leg of lamb high in the air and brought it down as hard as she could on the back of his head.

She might just as well have hit him with a steel club.

She stepped back a pace, waiting, and the funny thing was that he remained standing there for at least four or five seconds, gently swaying. Then he crashed to the carpet.

The violence of the crash, the noise, the small

table overturning, helped bring her out of the shock. She came out slowly, feeling cold and surprised, and she stood for a while blinking at the body, still holding the ridiculous piece of meat tight with both hands.

All right, she told herself. So I've killed him.

It was extraordinary, now, how clear her mind became all of a sudden. She began thinking very fast. As the wife of a detective, she knew quite well what the penalty would be. That was fine. It made no difference to her. In fact, it would be a relief. On the other hand, what about the child? What were the laws about murderers with unborn children? Did they kill them both— mother and child? Or did they wait until the tenth month? What did they do?

Mary Maloney didn't know. And she certainly wasn't prepared to take a chance.

She carried the meat into the kitchen, placed it in a pan, turned the oven on high, and shoved it inside. Then she washed her hands and ran upstairs to the bedroom. She sat down before the mirror, tidied her hair, touched up her lips and face. She tried a smile. It came out rather peculiar. She tried again.

"Hullo Sam," she said brightly, aloud.

The voice sounded peculiar too.

"I want some potatoes please, Sam. Yes, and I think a can of peas."

That was better. Both the smile and the voice were coming out better now. She rehearsed it several times more. Then she ran downstairs, took her coat, went out the back door, down the garden, into the street.

It wasn't six o'clock yet and the lights were still on in the grocery shop.

"Hullo Sam," she said brightly, smiling at the man behind the counter.

"Why, good evening, Mrs. Maloney. How're you?"

"I want some potatoes please, Sam. Yes, and I think a can of peas."

The man turned and reached up behind him on the shelf for the peas.

"Patrick's decided he's tired and doesn't want to eat out tonight," she told him. "We usually go out Thursdays, you know, and now he's caught me without any vegetables in the house."

"Then how about meat, Mrs. Maloney?"

"No, I've got meat, thanks. I got a nice leg of lamb from the freezer."

"Oh."

"I don't much like cooking it frozen, Sam, but I'm taking a chance on it this time. You think it'll be all right?"

"Personally," the grocer said, "I don't believe it makes any difference. You want these Idaho potatoes?"

"Oh yes, that'll be fine. Two of those."

"Anything else?" The grocer cocked his head on one side, looking at her pleasantly. "How about afterwards? What you going to give him for afterwards?"

"Well—what would you suggest, Sam?"

The man glanced around his shop. "How about a nice big slice of cheesecake? I know he likes that."

"Perfect," she said. "He loves it."

And when it was all wrapped and she had paid, she put on her brightest smile and said, "Thank you, Sam. Goodnight."

"Goodnight, Mrs. Maloney. And thank *you.*"

And now, she told herself as she hurried back, all she was doing now, she was returning home to her husband and he was waiting for his supper; and she must cook it good, and make it as tasty as possible because the poor man was tired, and if, when she entered the house, she happened to find anything unusual, or tragic, or terrible, then naturally it would be a shock and she'd become frantic with grief and horror. Mind you, she wasn't *expecting* to find anything. She was just going home with the vegetables. Mrs. Patrick Maloney going with the vegetables on Thursday evening to cook supper for her husband.

That's the way, she told herself. Do everything right and natural. Keep things absolutely natural and there'll be no need for any acting at all.

Therefore, when she entered the kitchen by the back door, she was humming a little tune to herself and smiling.

"Patrick!" she called. "How are you, darling?"

She put the parcel down on the table and went through into the living room; and when she saw him lying there on the floor with his legs doubled up and one arm twisted back underneath his body, it really was rather a shock. All the old love and longing for him welled up inside her, and she ran over to him, knelt down beside him, and began to cry her heart out. It was easy. No acting was necessary.

A few minutes later she got up and went to the phone. She knew the number of the police station, and when the man at the other end answered, she cried to him, "Quick! Come quick! Patrick's dead!"

"Who's speaking?"

"Mrs. Maloney. Mrs. Patrick Maloney."

"You mean Patrick Maloney's dead?"

"I think so," she sobbed. "He's lying on the floor and I think he's dead."

"Be right over," the man said.

The car came very quickly, and when she opened the front door, two policemen walked in. She knew them both—she knew nearly all the men at that precinct—and she fell right into Jack Noonan's arms, weeping hysterically. He put her gently into a chair, then went over to join the other one, who was called O'Malley, kneeling by the body.

"Is he dead?" she cried.

"I'm afraid he is. What happened?"

Briefly, she told her story about going out to the grocer and coming back to find him on the floor. While she was talking, crying and talking, Noonan discovered a small patch of congealed blood on the dead man's head. He showed it to O'Malley who got up at once and hurried to the phone.

Soon, other men began to come into the house. First a doctor, then two detectives, one of whom she knew by name. Later, a police photographer arrived and took pictures, and a man who knew about fingerprints. There was a great deal of whispering and muttering beside the corpse, and the detectives kept asking her a lot of questions. But they always treated her kindly. She told her story again, this time right from the beginning, when Patrick had come in, and she was sewing, and he was tired, so tired he hadn't wanted to go out for supper. She told how she'd put the meat in the oven—"it's there now, cooking"—and how she'd slipped out to the grocer for vegetables, and come back to find him lying on the floor.

"Which grocer?" one of the detectives asked.

She told him, and he turned and whispered something to the other detective who immediately went outside into the street.

In fifteen minutes he was back with a page of notes, and there was more whispering, and through her sobbing she heard a few of the whispered phrases—". . . acted quite normal . . . very cheerful . . . wanted to give him a good supper . . . peas . . . cheesecake . . . impossible that she . . ."

After a while, the photographer and the doctor departed and two other men came in and took the corpse away on a stretcher. Then the fingerprint man went away. The two detectives remained, and so did the two policemen. They were exceptionally nice to her, and Jack Noonan asked if she wouldn't rather go somewhere else, to her sister's house perhaps, or to his own wife who would take care of her and put her up for the night.

No, she said. She didn't feel she could move even a yard at the moment. Would they mind awfully if she stayed just where she was until she felt better. She didn't feel too good at the moment, she really didn't.

Then hadn't she better lie down on the bed? Jack Noonan asked.

No, she said. She'd like to stay right where she was, in this chair. A little later perhaps, when she felt better, she would move.

So they left her there while they went about their business, searching the house. Occasionally one of the detectives asked her another question. Sometimes Jack Noonan spoke to her gently as he passed by. Her husband, he told her, had been killed by a blow on the back of the head administered with a heavy blunt instrument, almost certainly a large piece of metal. They were looking for the weapon. The murderer may have taken it with him, but on the other hand he may've thrown it away or hidden it somewhere on the premises.

"It's the old story," he said. "Get the weapon, and you've got the man."

Later, one of the detectives came up and sat beside her. Did she know, he asked, of anything in the house that could've been used as the weapon? Would she mind having a look around to see if anything was missing—a very big spanner, for example, or a heavy metal vase.

They didn't have any heavy metal vases, she said.

"Or a big spanner?"

She didn't think they had a big spanner. But there might be some things like that in the garage.

The search went on. She knew that there were other policemen in the garden all around the house. She could hear their footsteps on the gravel outside, and sometimes she saw the flash of a torch through a chink in the curtains. It began to get late, nearly nine she noticed by the clock on the mantel. The four men searching the rooms seemed to be growing weary, a trifle exasperated.

"Jack," she said, the next time Sergeant Noonan went by. "Would you mind giving me a drink?"

"Sure I'll give you a drink. You mean this whiskey?"

"Yes please. But just a small one. It might make me feel better."

He handed her the glass.

"Why don't you have one yourself," she said. "You must be awfully tired. Please do. You've been very good to me."

"Well," he answered. "It's not strictly allowed, but I might take just a drop to keep me going."

One by one the others came in and were persuaded to take a little nip of whiskey. They stood around rather awkwardly with the drinks in their hands, uncomfortable in her presence, trying to say consoling things to her. Sergeant Noonan wandered into the kitchen, came out quickly and said, "Look, Mrs. Maloney. You know that oven of yours is still on, and the meat still inside."

"Oh *dear* me!" she cried. "So it is!"

"I better turn it off for you, hadn't I?"

"Will you do that, Jack. Thank you so much."

When the sergeant returned the second time, she looked at him with her large, dark, tearful eyes. "Jack Noonan," she said.

"Yes?"

"Would you do me a small favour—you and these others?"

"We can try, Mrs. Maloney."

"Well," she said. "Here you all are, and good friends of dear Patrick's too, and helping to catch the man who killed him. You must be terrible hungry by now because it's long past your suppertime, and I know Patrick would never forgive me, God bless his soul, if I allowed you to remain in his house without offering you decent hospitality. Why don't you eat up that lamb that's in the oven. It'll be cooked just right by now."

"Wouldn't dream of it," Sergeant Noonan said.

"Please," she begged. "Please eat it. Personally I couldn't touch a thing, certainly not what's been in the house when he was here. But it's all right for you. It'd be a favour to me if you'd eat it up. Then you can go on with your work again afterwards."

There was a good deal of hesitating among the four policemen, but they were clearly hungry, and in the end they were persuaded to go into the kitchen and help themselves. The woman stayed where she was, listening to them through the open door, and she could hear them speaking among themselves, their voices thick and sloppy because their mouths were full of meat.

"Have some more, Charlie?"

"No. Better not finish it."

"She *wants* us to finish it. She said so. Be doing her a favour."

"Okay then. Give me some more."

"That's a big club the guy must've used to hit poor Patrick," one of them was saying. "The doc says his skull was smashed all to pieces just like from a sledgehammer."

"That's why it ought to be easy to find."

"Exactly what I say."

"Whoever done it, they're not going to be carrying a thing like that around with them longer than they need."

One of them belched.

"Personally, I think it's right here on the premises."

"Probably right under our very noses. What you think, Jack?"

And in the other room Mary Maloney began to giggle.

□□

Discussion

1. (a) What evidence is there early in the story that Mary Maloney loved her husband? (b) What motivates her to kill her spouse? (c) Was the slaying premeditated or spontaneous? Explain.

2. Cite the evidence that indicates that Mary carefully planned her alibi.

3. Would this story have been strengthened or weakened (a) if Patrick Maloney had been a banker rather than a policeman? (b) if the author had told the reader what Patrick told Mary? (c) if the last line of the story had been eliminated?

4. (a) Before one has read the story, what meaning has the title? (b) After one has finished the story, what additional meaning does the title have? (c) Are both meanings appropriate to the story? Explain.

5. What does the last line of the story seem to imply?

Roald Dahl 1916 ·

Born in Llandaff, South Wales, the first part of Dahl's career was with Shell Oil in British East Africa from 1932 to 1939. After Hitler's invasion of Poland in 1939, Dahl joined the Royal Air Force, where he served six years.

A collection of short stories, *Someone Like You* (1953), plus regular appearances in *The New Yorker,* acquainted United States readers with him. *Kiss, Kiss* (1960) was another impressive story anthology that added to his reputation.

Dahl married the actress Patricia Neal in 1953 and they presently live in England with their four children. Dahl is also author of several books for children, including the original story for the film *Willie Wonka and the Chocolate Factory.*

See **PLOT** Handbook of Literary Terms

Footfalls

Wilbur Daniel Steele

This is not an easy story; not a road for tender or for casual feet. Better the meadows. Let me warn you, it is as hard as that old man's soul and as sunless as his eyes. It has its inception in catastrophe, and its end in an act of almost incredible violence; between them it tells barely how one long blind can become also deaf and dumb.

He lived in one of those old Puritan sea towns where the strain has come down austere and moribund, so that his act would not be quite unbelievable. Except that the town is no longer Puritan and Yankee. It has been betrayed; it has become an outpost of the Portuguese islands.

This man, this blind cobbler himself, was a Portuguese from St. Michael, in the Western Islands,[1] and his name was Boaz Negro.

He was happy. An unquenchable exuberance lived in him. When he arose in the morning he made vast, as it were, uncontrollable, gestures with his stout arms. He came into his shop singing. His voice, strong and deep as the chest from which it emanated, rolled out through the doorway and along the street, and the fishermen, done with their morning work and lounging and

Copyright 1929, 1957 by Wilbur Daniel Steele, reprinted by permission of Harold Matson Co. Inc.

1. St. Michael, in the Western Islands, St. Michael or São Miguel (souɴ mi gel'), largest island of the Azores (ə zôrz'), a group of islands in the Atlantic Ocean west of and belonging to Portugal.

smoking along the wharves, said, "Boaz is to work already." Then they came up to sit in the shop.

In that town a cobbler's shop is a club. One sees the interior always dimly thronged. They sit on the benches watching the artisan at his work for hours, and they talk about everything in the world. A cobbler is known by the company he keeps.

Boaz Negro kept young company. He would have nothing to do with the old. On his own head the gray hairs sat thickly.

He had a grown son. But the benches in his shop were for the lusty and valiant young, men who could spend the night drinking, and then at three o'clock in the morning turn out in the rain and dark to pull at the weirs, sing songs, buffet one another among the slippery fish in the boat's bottom, and make loud jokes about the fundamental things, love and birth and death. Hearkening to their boasts and strong prophecies, his breast heaved and his heart beat faster. He was a large, full-blooded fellow, fashioned for exploits; the flame in his darkness burned higher even to hear of them.

It is scarcely conceivable how Boaz Negro could have come through this much of his life still possessed of that unquenchable and priceless exuberance; how he would sing in the dawn; how, simply listening to the recital of deeds in gale or brawl, he could easily forget himself a blind man, tied to a shop and a last; easily make of himself a lusty young fellow breasting the sunlit and adventurous tide of life.

He had had a wife, whom he had loved. Fate, which had scourged him with the initial scourge of blindness, had seen fit to take his Angelina away. He had had four sons. Three, one after another, had been removed, leaving only Manuel, the youngest. Recovering slowly, with agony, from each of these recurrent blows, his unquenchable exuberance had lived. And there was another thing quite as extraordinary. He had never done anything but work, and that sort of thing may kill the flame where an abrupt catastrophe fails. Work in the dark. Work, work, work! And accompanied by privation, an almost miserly scale of personal economy. Yes, indeed, he had "skinned his fingers," especially in the earlier years. When it tells most.

How he had worked! Not alone in the daytime, but also sometimes, when orders were heavy, far into the night. It was strange for one, passing along that deserted street at midnight, to hear issuing from the black shop of Boaz Negro the rhythmical tap-tap-tap of hammer on wooden peg.

Nor was that sound all: no man in town could get far past that shop in his nocturnal wandering unobserved. No more than a dozen footfalls, and from the darkness Boaz' voice rolled forth, fraternal, stentorian, "Good night, Antone!" "Good night to you, Caleb Snow!"

To Boaz Negro it was still broad day.

Now, because of this, he was what might be called a substantial man. He owned his place, his shop, opening on the sidewalk, and behind it the dwelling house with trellised galleries upstairs and down.

And there was always something for his son, a "piece for the pocket," a dollar, five, even a ten-dollar bill if he had "got to have it." Manuel was "a good boy." Boaz not only said this, he felt that he was assured of it in his understanding, to the infinite peace of his heart.

It was curious that he should be ignorant only of the one nearest to him. Not because he was physically blind. Be certain he knew more of other men and of other men's sons than they or their neighbors did. More, that is to say, of their hearts, their understandings, their idiosyncrasies, and their ultimate weight in the balance pan of eternity.

His simple explanation of Manuel was that Manuel "wasn't too stout." To others he said this, and to himself. Manuel was not indeed too robust. How should he be vigorous when he never did anything to make him so? He never worked. Why should he work, when existence was provided for, and when there was always that "piece for the pocket"? Even a ten-dollar bill on a Saturday night! No, Manuel "wasn't too stout."

In the shop they let it go at that. The missteps and frailties of everyone else in the world were canvassed there with the most shameless publicity. But Boaz Negro was a blind man, and in a sense their host. Those reckless, strong young fellows respected and loved him. It was allowed to stand at that. Manuel was "a good boy." Which did not prevent them, by the way, from joining later in the general condemnation of that father's laxity—"the ruination of the boy!"

"He should have put him to work, that's what."

"He should have said to Manuel, 'Look here, if you want a dollar, go earn it first.'"

As a matter of fact, only one man ever gave Boaz the advice direct. That was Campbell Wood. And Wood never sat in that shop.

In every small town there is one young man who is spoken of as "rising." As often as not he is not a native, but "from away."

In this town Campbell Wood was that man. He had come from another part of the state to take a place in the bank. He lived in the upper story of Boaz Negro's house, the ground floor now doing for Boaz and the meager remnant of his family. The old woman who came in to tidy up for the cobbler looked after Wood's rooms as well.

Dealing with Wood, one had first of all the sense of his incorruptibility. A little ruthless perhaps, as if one could imagine him, in defense of his integrity, cutting off his friend, cutting off his own hand, cutting off the very stream flowing out from the wellsprings of human kindness. An exaggeration, perhaps.

He was by long odds the most eligible young man in town, good-looking in a spare, ruddy, sandy-haired Scottish fashion, important, incorruptible, "rising." But he took good care of his heart. Precisely that; like a sharp-eyed duenna to his own heart. One felt that there was the man, if ever was the man, who held his destiny in his own hand. Failing, of course, some quite gratuitous and unforeseeable catastrophe.

Not that he was not human, or even incapable of laughter or passion. He was, in a way, immensely accessible. He never clapped one on the shoulder; on the other hand, he never failed to speak. Not even to Boaz.

Returning from the bank in the afternoon, he had always a word for the cobbler. Passing out again to supper at his boarding place, he had another, about the weather, the prospects of rain. And if Boaz were at work in the dark when he returned from an evening at the board of trade, there was a "Good night, Mr. Negro!"

On Boaz' part, his attitude toward his lodger was curious and paradoxical. He did not pretend to anything less than reverence for the young man's position; precisely on account of that position he was conscious toward Wood of a vague distrust. This was because he was an uneducated fellow.

To the uneducated the idea of large finance is as uncomfortable as the idea of the Law. It must be said for Boaz that, responsive to Wood's unfailing civility, he fought against this sensation of dim and somehow shameful distrust.

Nevertheless his whole parental soul was in arms that evening, when Wood, returning from the bank and finding the shop empty of loungers, paused a moment to propose the bit of advice already referred to.

"Haven't you ever thought of having Manuel learn the trade?"

A suspicion, a kind of premonition, lighted the fires of defense.

"Shoemaking," said Boaz, "is good enough for a blind man."

"Oh, I don't know. At least it's better than doing nothing at all."

Boaz' hammer was still. He sat silent, monumental. Outwardly. For once his unfailing response "Manuel ain't too stout, you know," had failed him. Perhaps it had become suddenly inadequate.

He hated Wood; he despised Wood; more than ever before, a hundredfold more, quite abruptly, he distrusted Wood.

How could a man say such things as Wood had said? And where Manuel himself might hear!

Where Manuel had heard! Boaz' other emotions—hatred and contempt and distrust—were overshadowed. Sitting in darkness, no sound had come to his ears, no footfall, no infinitesimal creaking of a floor plank. Yet by some sixth uncanny sense of the blind he was aware that Manuel was standing in the dusk of the entry joining the shop to the house.

Boaz made a Herculean effort. The voice came out of his throat, harsh, bitter, and loud enough to have carried ten times the distance to his son's ears.

"Manuel is a good boy!"

"Yes—h'm—yes—I suppose so."

Wood shifted his weight. He seemed uncomfortable.

"Well. I'll be running along, I—ugh! Heavens!"

Something was happening. Boaz heard exclamations, breathings, the rustle of sleeve cloth in large frantic, and futile graspings—all without understanding. Immediately there was an impact on the floor, and with it the unmistakable clink of metal. Boaz even heard that the metal was minted, and that the coins were gold. He un-

derstood. A coin sack, gripped not quite carefully enough for a moment under the other's overcoat, had shifted, slipped, escaped, and fallen.

And Manuel had heard!

It was a dreadful moment for Boaz, dreadful in its native sense, as full of dread. Why? It was a moment of horrid revelation, ruthless clarification. His son, his link with the departed Angelina, that "good boy"—Manuel standing in the shadow of the entry, visible alone to the blind, had heard the clink of falling gold, and—*and Boaz wished that he had not!*

There, amazing, disconcerting, destroying, stood the sudden fact.

Sitting as impassive and monumental as ever, his strong, bleached hands at rest on his work, round drops of sweat came out on Boaz' forehead. He scarcely took the sense of what Wood was saying. Only fragments.

"Government money, understand—for the breakwater workings—huge—too many people know here, everywhere—don't trust the safe—tin safe—'Noah's Ark'—give you my word—heavens, no!"

It boiled down to this—the money, more money than was good for that antiquated "Noah's Ark" at the bank, and whose contemplated sojourn there overnight was public to too many minds—in short, Wood was not only incorruptible, he was canny. To what one of those minds, now, would it occur that he should take away that money bodily, under casual cover of his coat, to his own lodgings behind the cobblershop of Boaz Negro? For this one, this important night!

He was sorry the coin sack had slipped, because he did not like to have the responsibility of secret sharer cast upon anyone, even upon Boaz, even by accident. On the other hand, how tremendously fortunate that it had been Boaz and not another. So far as that went, Wood had no more anxiety now than before. One incorruptible knows another.

"I'd trust you, Mr. Negro" (that was one of the fragments which came and stuck in the cobbler's brain), "as far as I would myself. As long as it's only you. I'm just going up here and throw it under the bed. Oh, yes, certainly."

Boaz ate no supper. For the first time in his life food was dry in his gullet. Even under those other successive crushing blows of fate the full and generous habit of his functionings had carried on unabated; he had always eaten what was set before him. Tonight, over his untouched plate, he watched Manuel with his sightless eyes, keeping track of his every mouthful, word, intonation, breath. What profit he expected to extract from this catlike surveillance it is impossible to say.

When they arose from the supper table, Boaz made another Herculean effort: "Manuel, you're a good boy!"

The formula had a quality of appeal, of despair, and of command.

"Manuel, you should be short of money, maybe. Look, what's this? A tenner?[2] Well, there's a piece for the pocket; go and enjoy yourself."

He would have been frightened had Manuel, upsetting tradition, declined the offering. With the morbid contrariness of the human imagination, the boy's avid grasping gave him no comfort.

He went out into the shop, where it was already dark, drew to him his last, his tools, mallets, cutters, pegs, leather. And having prepared to work, he remained idle. He found himself listening.

It has been observed that the large phenomena of sunlight and darkness were nothing to Boaz Negro. A busy night was broad day. Yet there was a difference; he knew it with the blind man's eyes, the ears.

Day was a vast confusion, or rather a wide fabric, of sounds; great and little sounds all woven together, voices, footfalls, wheels, far-off whistles and foghorns, flies buzzing in the sun. Night was another thing. Still there were voices and footfalls, but rarer, emerging from the large, pure body of silence as definite, surprising, and yet familiar entities.

Tonight there was an easterly wind, coming off the water and carrying the sound of waves. So far as other fugitive sounds were concerned it was the same as silence. The wind made little difference to the ears. It nullified, from one direction at least, the other two visual processes of the blind, the sense of touch and the sense of smell. It blew away from the shop, toward the living-house.

As had been said, Boaz found himself listening, scrutinizing with an extraordinary attention, this immense backgound of sound. He heard footfalls. The story of that night was written, for him, in footfalls.

He heard them moving about the house, the lower floor, prowling here, there, halting for long spaces, advancing, retreating softly on the planks. About this aimless, interminable perambulation there was something to twist the nerves, something led and at the same time driven like a succession of frail and indecisive charges.

Boaz lifted himself from his chair. All his impulse called him to make a stir, join battle,

2. **tenner,** ten-dollar bill. [Slang]

cast in the breach the reinforcement of his presence, authority, good will. He sank back again; his hands fell down. The curious impotence of the spectator held him.

He heard footfalls, too, on the upper floor, a little fainter, borne to the inner rather than the outer ear, along the solid causeway of partitions and floor, the legs of his chair, the bony framework of his body. Very faint indeed. Sinking back easily into the background of the wind. They, too, came and went, this room, that, to the passage, the stairhead, and away. About them, too, there was the same quality of being led and at the same time of being driven.

Time went by. In his darkness it seemed to Boaz that hours must have passed. He heard voices. Together with the footfalls, the abrupt, brief, and (in view of Wood's position) astounding interchange of sentences made up his history of the night. Wood must have opened the door at the head of the stair; by the sound of his voice he would be standing there, peering below perhaps, perhaps listening.

"What's wrong down there?" he called. "Why don't you go to bed?"

After a moment, came Manuel's voice, "Ain't sleepy."

"Neither am I. Look here, do you like to play cards?"

"What kind? Euchre! I like euchre all right. Or pitch."

"Well, what would you say to coming up and having a game of euchre then, Manuel? If you can't sleep?"

"That'd be all right."

The lower footfalls ascended to join the footfalls on the upper floor. There was the sound of a door closing.

Boaz sat still. In the gloom he might have been taken for a piece of furniture, of machinery, an extraordinary lay figure,[3] perhaps, for the trying on of the boots he made. He seemed scarcely to breathe, only the sweat starting from his brow giving him an aspect of life.

---

3. *lay figure*, jointed model of a human body.

He ought to have run, and leaped up that inner stair and pounded with his fists on that door. He seemed unable to move. At rare intervals feet passed on the sidewalk outside, just at his elbow, so to say, and yet somehow, tonight, immeasurably far away. Beyond the orbit of the moon. He heard Rugg, the policeman, noting the silence of the shop, muttering, "Boaz is to bed tonight," as he passed.

The wind increased. It poured against the shop with its deep, continuous sound of a river. Submerged in its body, Boaz caught the note of the town bell striking midnight.

Once more, after a long time, he heard footfalls. He heard them coming around the corner of the shop from the house, footfalls half swallowed by the wind, passing discreetly, without haste, retreating, merging step by step with the huge, incessant background of the wind.

Boaz' muscles tightened all over him. He had the impulse to start up, to fling open the door, shout into the night, "What are you doing? Stop there! Say! What are you doing and where are you going?"

And as before, the curious impotence of the spectator held him motionless. He had not stirred in his chair. And those footfalls, upon

which hinged, as it were, that momentous decade of his life, were gone.

There was nothing to listen for now. Yet he continued to listen. Once or twice, half arousing himself, he drew toward him his unfinished work. And then relapsed into immobility.

As has been said, the wind, making little difference to the ears, made all the difference in the world with the sense of feeling and the sense of smell. From the one important direction of the house. That is how it could come about that Boaz Negro could sit, waiting and listening to nothing in the shop, and remain ignorant of disaster until the alarm had gone away and come back again, pounding, shouting, clanging.

"Fire!" he heard them bawling in the street. *"Fire! Fire!"*

Only slowly did he understand that the fire was in his own house.

There is nothing stiller in the world than the skeleton of a house in the dawn after a fire. It is as if everything living, positive, violent, had been completely drained in the one flaming act of violence, leaving nothing but negation till the end of time. It is worse than a tomb. A monstrous stillness! Even the footfalls of the searchers cannot disturb it, for they are separate and superficial. In its presence they are almost frivolous.

Half an hour after dawn the searchers found the body, if what was left from that consuming ordeal might be called a body. The discovery came as a shock. It seemed incredible that the occupant of that house, no cripple or invalid but an able man in the prime of youth, should not have awakened and made good his escape. It was the upper floor which had caught; the stairs had stood to the last. It was beyond calculation. Even if he had been asleep!

And he had not been asleep. This second and infinitely more appalling discovery began to be known. Slowly. By a hint, a breath of rumor here; there an allusion, half taken back. The man, whose incinerated body still lay curled in its bed of cinders, had been dressed at the moment of disaster; even to the watch, the cuff buttons, the studs, the very scarf pin. Fully clothed to the last detail, precisely as those who had dealings at the bank might have seen Campbell Wood any weekday morning for the past eight months. A man does not sleep with his clothes on. The skull of the man had been broken, as if with a blunt instrument of iron. On the charred lacework of the floor lay the leg of an old andiron with which Boaz Negro and his Angelina had set up housekeeping in that new house.

It needed only Mr. Asa Whitelaw, coming up the street from that gaping "Noah's Ark" at the bank, to round out the scandalous circle of circumstance.

"Where is Manuel?"

Boaz Negro still sat in his shop, impassive, monumental, his thick, hairy arms resting on the arms of his chair. The tools and materials of his work remained scattered about him, as his irresolute gathering of the night before had left them. Into his eyes no change could come. He had lost his house, the visible monument of all those years of "skinning his fingers." It would seem that he had lost his son. And he had lost something incalculably precious—that hitherto unquenchable exuberance of the man.

"Where is Manuel?"

When he spoke his voice was unaccented and stale, like the voice of a man already dead.

"Yes, where is Manuel?"

He had answered them with their own question.

"When did you last see him?"

Neither he nor they seemed to take note of that profound irony.

"At supper."

"Tell us, Boaz; you knew about this money?"

The cobbler nodded his head.

"And did Manuel?"

He might have taken sanctuary in a legal doubt. How did he know what Manuel knew? Precisely! As before, he nodded his head.

"After supper, Boaz, you were in the shop? But you heard something?"

He went on to tell them what he had heard: the footfalls, below and above, the extraordinary conversation which had broken for a moment the silence of the inner hall. The account was bare, the phrases monosyllabic. He reported only what had been registered on the sensitive tympanums of his ears, to the last whisper of footfalls stealing past the dark wall of the shop. Of all the formless tangle of thoughts, suspicions, interpretations, and the special and personal knowledge given to the blind which moved in his brain, he said nothing.

He shut his lips there. He felt himself on the defensive. Just as he distrusted the higher ramifications of finance (his house had gone down uninsured), so before the rites and processes of that inscrutable creature, the Law, he felt himself menaced by the invisible and the unknown, helpless, oppressed; in an abject sense, skeptical.

"Keep clear of the Law!" they had told him in his youth. The monster his imagination had summoned up then still stood beside him in his age.

Having exhausted his monosyllabic and superficial evidence, they could move him no further. He became deaf and dumb. He sat before them, an image cast in some immensely heavy stuff, inanimate. His lack of visible emotion impressed them. Remembering his exuberance, it was only the stranger to see him unmoving and unmoved. Only once did they catch sight of something beyond. As they were preparing to leave, he opened his mouth. What he said was like a swan song[4] to the years of his exuberant happiness. Even now there was no color of expression in his words, which sounded mechanical.

"Now I have lost everything. My house. My last son. Even my honor. You would not think I would like to live. But I go to live. I go to work. That *cachorra*,[5] one day he shall come back again, in the dark night, to have a look. I shall go to show you all. That *cachorra!*"

(And from that time on, it was noted, he never referred to the fugitive by any other name than *cachorra*, which is a kind of dog. "That *cachorra!*" As if he had forfeited the relationship not only of the family, but of the very genus, the very race! "That *cachorra!*")

He pronounced this resolution without passion. When they assured him that the culprit would come back again indeed, much sooner than he expected, "with a rope around his neck," he shook his head slowly.

"No, you shall not catch that *cachorra* now. But one day——"

There was something about its very colorlessness which made it sound oracular. It was at least prophetic. They searched, laid their traps, proceeded with all the placards, descriptions, rewards, clues, trails. But on Manuel Negro they never laid their hands.

Months passed and became years. Boaz Negro did not rebuild his house. He might have done so, out of his earnings, for upon himself he spent scarcely anything, reverting to his old habit of almost miserly economy. Yet perhaps it would have been harder after all. For his earnings were less and less. In that town a cobbler who sits in an empty shop is apt to want for trade. Folk take their boots to mend where they take their bodies to rest and their minds to be edified.

No longer did the walls of Boaz' shop resound to the boastful recollections of young men. Boaz had changed. He had become not only different, but opposite. A metaphor will do best. The spirit of Boaz Negro had been a meadowed hillside giving upon the open sea, the sun, the warm, wild winds from beyond the blue horizon. And covered with flowers, always hungry and thirsty for the sun and the fabulous wind and bright showers of rain. It had become an intrenched camp, lying silent, sullen, verdureless, under a gray sky. He stood solitary against the world. His approaches were closed. He was blind, and he was also deaf and dumb.

Against that what can young fellows do who wish for nothing but to rest themselves and talk about their friends and enemies? They had come

---

4. *a swan song,* a farewell. This expression came into being because a swan is fabled to sing a song when it is dying.
5. *cachorra* (kä chôr′rä). [Portuguese]

and they had tried. They had raised their voices even higher than before. Their boasts had grown louder, more presumptuous, more preposterous, until, before the cold separation of that unmoving and as if contemptuous presence in the cobbler's chair, they burst of their own air, like toy balloons. And they went and left Boaz alone.

There was another thing which served, if not to keep them away, at least not to entice them back. That was the aspect of the place. It was not cheerful. It invited no one. In its way that fire-bitten ruin grew to be almost as great a scandal as the act itself had been. It was plainly an eyesore. A valuable property, on the town's main thoroughfare—and an eyesore! The neighboring owners protested.

Their protestations might as well have gone against a stone wall. That man was deaf and dumb. He had become, in a way, a kind of vegetable, for the quality of a vegetable is that, while it is endowed with life, it remains fixed in one spot. For years Boaz was scarcely seen to move foot out of that shop that was left him, a small, square, blistered promontory on the shores of ruin.

He must indeed have carried out some rudimentary sort of domestic program under the debris at the rear (he certainly did not sleep or eat in the shop). One or two lower rooms were left fairly intact. The outward aspect of the place was formless; it grew to be no more than a mound in time; the charred timbers, one or two still standing, lean and naked against the sky, lost their blackness and faded to a silvery gray. It would have seemed strange, had they not grown accustomed to the thought, to imagine that blind man, like a mole, or some slow slug, turning himself mysteriously in the bowels of that gray mound—that time-silvered "eyesore."

When they saw him, however, he was in the shop. They opened the door to take in their work (when other cobblers turned them off), and they saw him seated in his chair in the half-darkness, his whole person, legs, torso, neck, head, as motionless as the vegetable of which we have

spoken—only his hands and his bare arms endowed with visible life. The gloom had bleached the skin to the color of damp ivory, and against the background of his immobility they moved with a certain amazing monstrousness, interminably. No, they were never still. One wondered what they could be at. Surely he could not have had enough work now to keep those insatiable hands so monstrously in motion. Even far into the night. Tap-tap-tap! Blows continuous and powerful. On what? On nothing? On the bare iron last? And for what purpose? To what conceivable end?

Well, one could imagine those arms, growing paler, also growing thicker and more formidable with that unceasing labor; the muscles feeding themselves, omnivorously on their own waste, the cords toughening, the bone tissues revitalizing themselves without end. One could imagine the whole aspiration of that mute and motionless man pouring itself out into those pallid arms, and the arms taking it up with a kind of blind greed. Storing it up. Against a day!

"That *cachorra!* One day——"

What were the thoughts of this man? What moved within that motionless cranium covered

with long hair? Who can say? Behind everything, of course, stood that bitterness against the world—the blind world—blinder than he would ever be. And against "that *cachorra.*" But this was no longer a thought; it was the man.

Just as all muscular aspiration flowed into his arms, so all the energies of his senses turned to his ears. The man had become, you might say, two arms and two ears. Can you imagine a man listening, intently, through the waking hours of nine years?

Listening to footfalls. Marking with a special emphasis of concentration the beginning, rise, full passage, falling away, and dying of all footfalls. By day, by night, winter and summer and winter again. Unraveling the skein of foot-falls passing up and down the street!

For three years he wondered when they would come. For the next three years he wondered if they would ever come. It was during the last three that a doubt began to trouble him. It gnawed at his huge moral strength. Like a hidden seepage of water, it undermined (in anticipation) his terrible resolution. It was a sign, perhaps of age, a slipping away of the reckless infallibility of youth.

Supposing, after all, that his ears should fail him. Supposing they were capable of being tricked, without his being able to know it. Supposing that that *cachorra* should come and go, and he, Boaz, living in some vast delusion, some unrealized distortion of memory, should let him pass unknown. Supposing precisely this thing had already happened!

Or the other way around. What if he should hear the footfalls coming, even into the very shop itself? What if he should be as sure of them as of his own soul? What, then, if he should strike? And what then, if it were not that *cachorra* after all? How many tens and hundreds of millions of people were there in the world? Was it possible for them all to have footfalls distinct and different?

Then they would take him and hang him. And that *cachorra* might then come and go at his own will, undisturbed.

As he sat there sometimes the sweat rolled down his nose, cold as rain.

Supposing!

Sometimes, quite suddenly, in broad day, in the booming silence of the night, he would start. Not outwardly. But beneath the pale integument of his skin all his muscles tightened and his nerves sang. His breathing stopped. It seemed almost as if his heart stopped.

Was that it? Were those the feet, there emerging faintly from the distance? Yes, there was something about them. Yes! Memory was in travail. Yes, yes, yes! No! How could he be sure? Ice ran down into his empty eyes. The footfalls were already passing. They were gone, swallowed up already by time and space. Had that been that *cachorra?*

Nothing in his life had been so hard to meet as this insidious drain of distrust in his own powers; this sense of a traitor within the walls. His iron-gray hair had turned white. It was always this now, from the beginning of the day to the end of the night: How was he to know? How was he to be inevitably, unshakably sure?

Curiously, after all this purgatory of doubts, he did know them. For a moment at least, when he had heard them, he was sure. It was on an evening of the winter holidays, the Portuguese festival of *Menin' Jesus.*[6] Christ was born again in a hundred mangers on a hundred tiny altars; there was cake and wine; songs went shouting by to the accompaniment of mandolins and tramping feet. The wind blew cold under a clear sky. In all the houses there were lights; even in Boaz Negro's shop a lamp was lit just now, for a man had been in for a pair of boots which Boaz had patched. The man had gone out again. Boaz was thinking of blowing out the light. It meant nothing to him.

He leaned forward, judging the position of the lamp chimney by the heat on his face, and puffed out his cheeks to blow. Then his cheeks collapsed suddenly, and he sat back again.

It was not odd that he had failed to hear the footfalls until they were actually within the door. A crowd of merrymakers was passing just then; their songs and tramping almost shook the shop.

Boaz sat back. Beneath his passive exterior his nerves thrummed; his muscles had grown as hard as wood. Yes! Yes! But no! He had heard nothing; no more than a single step, a single foot pressure on the planks within the door. Dear God! He could not tell!

Going through the pain of an enormous effort, he opened his lips.

"What can I do for you?"

"Well, I—I don't know. To tell the truth——"

The voice was unfamiliar, but it might be assumed. Boaz held himself. His face remained blank, interrogating, slightly helpless.

"I am a little deaf," he said. "Come nearer."

The footfalls came halfway across the intervening floor, and there appeared to hesitate. The voice, too, had a note of uncertainty.

"I was just looking around. I have a pair of— well, you mend shoes?"

Boaz nodded his head. It was not in response to the words, for they meant nothing. What he had heard was the footfalls on the floor.

Now he was sure. As has been said, for a moment at least after he had heard them he was unshakably sure. The congestion of his muscles

had passed. He was at peace.

The voice became audible once more. Before the massive preoccupation of the blind man it became still less certain of itself.

"Well, I haven't got the shoes with me. I was—just looking around."

It was amazing to Boaz, this miraculous sensation of peace.

"Wait!" Then, bending his head as if listening to the winter wind, "It's cold tonight. You've left the door open. But wait!" Leaning down, his hand fell on a rope's end hanging by the chair. The gesture was one continuous, undeviating movement of the hand. No hesitation. No groping. How many hundreds, how many thousands of times, had his hand schooled itself in that gesture!

A single strong pull. With a little *bang* the front door had swung to and latched itself. Not only the front door. The other door, leading to the rear, had closed, too, and latched itself with a little *bang*. And leaning forward from his chair, Boaz blew out the light.

There was not a sound in the shop. Outside, feet continued to go by, ringing on the frozen road; voices were lifted; the wind hustled about the corners of the wooden shell with a continuous, shrill note of whistling. All of this outside, as on another planet. Within the blackness of the shop the complete silence persisted.

Boaz listened. Sitting on the edge of his chair, half crouching, his head, with its long, unkempt, white hair, bent slightly to one side, he concentrated upon this chambered silence the full power of his senses. He hardly breathed. The other person in that room could not be breathing at all, it seemed.

No, there was not a breath, not the stirring of a sole on wood, not the infinitesimal rustle of any fabric. It was as if, in this utter stoppage of sound, even the blood had ceased to flow in the veins and arteries of that man, who was like a rat caught in a trap.

It was appalling even to Boaz; even to the

---

6. *festival of Menin' Jesus* (mən nēn′ zhə süs′), a Christmas festival brought to Massachusetts by early Protuguese settlers.

cat. Listening became more than a labor. He began to have to fight against a growing impulse to shout out loud, to leap, sprawl forward without aim in that unstirred darkness—do something. Sweat rolled down from behind his ears, into his shirt collar. He gripped the chair arms. To keep quiet, he sank his teeth into his lower lip. He would not! He would not!

And of a sudden he heard before him, in the center of the room, an outburst of breath, an outrush from lungs in the extremity of pain, thick, laborious, fearful. A coughing up of dammed air.

Pushing himself from the arms of the chair, Boaz leaped.

His fingers, passing swiftly through the air, closed on something. It was a sheaf of hair, bristly and thick. It was a man's beard.

On the road outside, up and down the street for a hundred yards, merrymaking people turned to look at one another. With an abrupt cessation of laughter, of speech. Inquiringly. Even with an unconscious dilation of the pupils of their eyes.

"What was that?"

There had been a scream. There could be no doubt of that. A single, long-drawn note. Immensely high-pitched. Not as if it were human.

"What was that? Where'd it come from?"

Those nearest said it came from the cobblershop of Boaz Negro.

They went and tried the door. It was closed, even locked, as if for the night. There was no light behind the window shade. But Boaz would not have a light. They beat on the door. No answer.

But from where, then, had that prolonged, as if animal, note come?

They ran about, penetrating into the side lanes, interrogating, prying. Coming back at last, inevitably, to the neighborhood of Boaz Negro's shop.

The body lay on the floor at Boaz' feet, where it had tumbled down slowly after a moment from the spasmodic embrace of his arms, those ivory-colored arms which had beaten so long upon the bare iron surface of a last. Blows continuous and powerful. It seemed incredible. They were so weak now. They could not have lifted the hammer now.

But that beard! That bristly, thick, square beard of a stranger!

His hands remembered it. Standing with his shoulders fallen forward and his weak arms hanging down, Boaz began to shiver. The whole thing was incredible. What was on the floor there, upheld in the vast gulf of darkness, he could not see. Neither could he hear it, smell it. Nor (if he did not move his foot) could he feel it. What he did not hear, smell, or touch did not exist. It was not there. Incredible!

But that beard! All the accumulated doubtings of those years fell down upon him. After all, the thing he had been so fearful of in his weak imaginings had happened. He had killed a stranger. He, Boaz Negro, had murdered an innocent man!

And all on account of that beard. His deep panic made him light-headed. He began to confuse cause and effect. If it were not for that beard, it would have been that *cachorra.*

On this basis he began to reason with a crazy directness. And to act. He went and pried open the door into the entry. From a shelf he took down his razor. A big, heavyheeled strop. His hands began to hurry. And the mug, half full of soap. And water. It would have to be cold water. But after all, he thought (light-headedly), at this time of night——

Outside, they were at the shop again. The crowd's habit is to forget a thing quickly, once it is out of sight and hearing. But there had been something about that solitary cry which continued to bother them, even in memory. Where had it been? Where had it come from? And those who stood nearest the cobblershop were heard again. They were certain now, dead certain. They could swear!

In the end they broke down the door.

If Boaz heard them, he gave no sign. An absorption as complete as it was monstrous wrapped him. Kneeling in the glare of the lantern they had brought, as impervious as his own shadow sprawling behind him, he continued to shave the dead man on the floor.

No one touched him. Their minds and imaginations were arrested by the gigantic proportions of the act. The unfathomable presumption of the act. As throwing murder in their faces to the tune of a jig in a barbershop. It is a fact that none of them so much as thought of touching him. No less than all of them, together with all other men, shorn of their imaginations—that is to say, the expressionless and imperturbable creature of the Law—would be sufficient to touch that ghastly man.

On the other hand, they could not leave him alone. They could not go away. They watched. They saw the damp lather-soaked beard of that victimized stranger falling away, stroke by stroke of the flashing, heavy razor. The dead denuded by the blind!

It was seen that Boaz was about to speak. It was something important he was about to utter; something, one would say, fatal. The words would not come all at once. They swelled his cheeks out. His razor was arrested. Lifting his face, he encircled the watchers with a gaze at once of imploration and of command. As if he could see them. As if he could read his answer in the expressions of their faces.

"Tell me one thing now. Is it that *cachorra?*"

For the first time those men in the room made sounds. They shuffled their feet. It was as if an uncontrollable impulse to ejaculation, laughter, derision, forbidden by the presence of death, had gone down into their boot soles.

"Manuel?" one of them said. "You mean *Manuel?*"

Boaz laid the razor down on the floor beside its work. He got up from his knees slowly, as if his joints hurt. He sat down in his chair, rested his hands on the arms, and once more encircled the company with his sightless gaze.

"Not Manuel. Manuel was a good boy. But tell me now, is it that *cachorra?*"

Here was something out of their calculations; something for them, mentally, to chew on.

Mystification is a good thing sometimes. It gives the brain a fillip, stirs memory, puts the gears of imagination in mesh. One man, an old, tobacco-chewing fellow, began to stare harder at the face on the floor. Something moved in his intellect.

"No, but look here now——"

He had even stopped chewing. But he was forestalled by another.

"Say now, if it don't look like that fellow Wood, himself. The bank fellow—that was burned—remember? Himself."

"That *cachorra* was not burned. Not that Wood. You darned fool!"

Boaz spoke from his chair. They hardly knew his voice, emerging from its long silence; it was so didactic and arid.

"That *cachorra* was not burned. It was my boy that was burned. It was that *cachorra* called my boy upstairs. That *cachorra* killed my boy. That *cachorra* put his clothes on my boy, and he set my house on fire. I knew that all the time. Because when I heard those feet come out of my house and go away, I knew they were the feet of that *cachorra* from the bank. I did not know where he was going to. Something said to me— you better ask him where he is going to. But then

I said, you are foolish. He had the money from the bank. I did not know. And then my house was on fire. No, it was not my boy that went away; it was that *cachorra* all the time. You darned fools! Did you think I was waiting for my own boy?

"Now I show you all," he said at the end. "And now I can get hanged."

No one ever touched Boaz Negro for that murder. For murder it was in the eye and letter of the Law. The Law in a small town is sometimes a curious creature; it is sometimes blind only in one eye.

Their minds and imaginations in that town were arrested by the romantic proportions of the act. Simply, no one took it up. I believe the man, Wood, was understood to have died of heart failure.

When they asked Boaz why he had not told what he knew as to the identity of that fugitive in the night, he seemed to find it hard to say exactly. How could a man of no education define for them his own but half-defined misgivings about the Law, his sense of oppression, con-straint, and awe, of being on the defensive, even, in an abject way, his skepticism? About his wanting, come what might, to "keep clear of the Law"?

He did say this, "You would have laughed at me."

And this, "If I told folks it was Wood went away, then I say he would not dare come back again."

That was the last. Very shortly he began to refuse to talk about the thing at all. The act was completed. Like the creature of fable, it had consumed itself. Out of that old man's con-sciousness it had departed. Amazingly. Like a dream dreamed out.

Slowly at first, in a makeshift, piece-at-a-time, poor man's way, Boaz commenced to rebuild his house. That "eyesore" vanished.

And slowly at first, like the miracle of a green shoot pressing out from the dead earth, that priceless and unquenchable exuberance of the man was seen returning. Unquenchable, after all.

□□

Discussion

1. In the first paragraph of "Footfalls," the author briefly outlines the action of the story. It begins, he says, in "catas-trophe"; it ends in "an act of almost incredible violence"; and it tells how a blind man "can become also deaf and dumb." Now that you have read the whole story, justify Steele's outline by citing the exact events he refers to in each quoted phrase.

2. (a) Describe Boaz' attitude toward Manuel as the story opens. (b) How do the townspeople react to this attitude? (c) Does Boaz ever cease to feel that "Manuel is a good boy"? Explain.

3. When Campbell Wood is introduced into the story, what is Boaz' opinion of him? Why?

4. (a) At the time of the fire, what evidence seemed to point to Manuel's guilt? (b) What secret knowledge did Boaz possess? (c) Why did he withhold it?

5. The emotional impact of "Footfalls" depends upon the reader's accepting Manuel's guilt just as the townspeople do. What factors in the story make the reader accept Manuel's guilt?

6. Now that you have answered the previous question, do you feel the author deceived you or that you deceived yourself? In an-swering, consider the way the author uses the word *incorruptibil-ity* (95b, 1) when he describes Campbell Wood.

Vocabulary
Structure and Dictionary

Use your Glossary to do the following exercises. Be sure you can spell and pronounce each vocabulary word.

A. The words below have prefixes and Latin roots. On your paper make three columns. Write the prefix in one column, the Latin root in the second, and the meaning of the word in the third.

For the word *inanimate* your paper would look like this:

in *anima* lifeless

The words are:

1. infallible **2.** omnivorous **3.** inscrutable **4.** incinerate

B. The words below are *derivatives,* words formed by adding suffixes to other words. On your paper write the original words.

1. ramifications **2.** rudimentary **3.** spasmodic **4.** derision **5.** aspiration

Now write the *derivative* from the list just above, that fits correctly into each sentence below.

6. Of course, this is just a _____ outline, but it does give a general idea of what the play is about.

7. In theory your idea is simple, but in actual practice all of its _____ make it quite complex.

8. The woman's childhood _____, to become a physician, was realized by her daughter.

9. There was _____ applause for the actors, but on the whole the show was not well received.

10. Mike's idea for a better mousetrap met with such _____ that he destroyed the model.

Wilbur Daniel Steele
1886 · 1970

Steele was born in Greensboro, North Carolina. After completing studies in Denver, Boston, Paris, and New York for a career in art, he joined an artists' colony in Massachusetts. There, in 1912, he wrote a short story which was later published in the *Atlantic Monthly.* The story won such favorable notice that Steele abandoned his art career for writing. Although he also wrote successful novels and plays, Steele won greatest fame for his carefully planned and well-wrought short stories. After years of travel in various parts of the world, Steele settled in Lyme, Connecticut.

notes and comments

Characterization

A major task of the short-story writer is to develop the personality of his main character. Boaz Negro comes alive because Steele shows the *traits* of personality that make him act, think, and feel as he does.

Throughout the story, the author *labels* Boaz with the descriptive phrase "unquenchable exuberance." Why is this label an important one in guiding the reader to a sound appreciation of Boaz' character?

Steele also uses *direct comments* to develop a significant trait. He tells us Boaz is diligent: "How he had worked! Not alone in the daytime, but . . . far into the night."

In addition to a label and direct comments, Steele reveals the cobbler through *dialogue* and *action.* For example, what Boaz says—and what others say about him—reveal his devotion to Manuel. Boaz insists that Manuel isn't "too stout" and "is a good boy" while the townspeople criticize Boaz' indulgence: "He should have put him to work." To "hear" these remarks is to understand how Boaz could spend those long years waiting for the *cachorra.* After the fire, Boaz listens for the *cachorra's* footfalls. What does this reveal about Boaz' character?

A writer may use one or several of these methods to develop a single trait. Which method or methods does Steele use to indicate Boaz' distrust of the Law?

A writer seldom develops secondary characters as fully as he does a main character. Compare the extent of the development of Wood and Manuel with that of Boaz Negro.

A Short Return

Durango Mendoza

I

I had gone home again. It was my last day.

In the kitchen Mom was cleaning up, and Edmund, who was on vacation, had gone up town. It was mid-morning and the kids were all in school, and in the quiet of the front room I slept. I began to dream, and in my dream I was again that boy—six years old that year and in another town.

We lived in the dusty country town where nothing ever happened to stir the town's aged population. Youth left quickly there. But that was many years ago, and I was just a little boy.

The streets of our town were plain dirt and dusty gravel and they had no names. We did have a main street which was called "Main Street," but that was the only one named. I sometimes wondered how strangers ever found their way around or where anyone lived. But then I never saw many strangers, except when they stopped at Sanford's station for gas or soda pop. The number nine highway ran straight past our tired little town of unnamed streets.

I used to stand by the big black gas tank next to the Neon Cafe and count the different kinds of cars that whizzed by. They were all full of strangers and didn't often stop. And so I wondered why, because there did not seem to be many other places in the world besides Dustin, Oklahoma. It was certainly the only place *I* had ever been.

I asked my brother once where everybody was going, and why they didn't stop for a while. He said that Dustin was nothing to the world, but I couldn't see how that could be. It was the only place I knew and it couldn't be that no one else knew it. I knew it.

"Not everybody is you," he said. "There are other people who don't live like we do. People who aren't like us. People who live in way off places like—like New York and California. See?"

"A Short Return" by Durango Mendoza. Copyright © 1979 by Durango Mendoza. Reprinted by permission.

I didn't really see, but I said I did anyway and asked him how come he knew so much about it. He'd never been any place that I hadn't.

"I know because I read about them," he said. "Besides, the teacher at school said so too."

And so I had to believe it, because Bobby Joe was ten years old, and I couldn't start school until September.

We lived just one block from the north end of Main Street, but even then we were in the last house. Our family was my older sister and brother, Mom and me. Then there was our stepfather, Edmund, and our little half-sister, Linda Beth. Mom belonged to both parts of the family.

We used to have a real father, but he left before I was born. Bobby Joe and Rita said they could remember him, and Rita said that she hated him because he left. I didn't like him at all, except when I was lonesome and by myself. But I was not unhappy. I was too young to be sad, but I could feel very sorry for myself.

Sometimes when he was up town or at an Indian church, people would ask Edmund about our father. He would get very angry, but he would never say anything. We could tell he was mad, because he would not even say much to Mom. He hardly ever spoke to us three kids after Linda Beth was born. And after the time he hit Mom for telling him that his sister Ida was too nosey, he said nothing at all to us. Mom told us not to ever call him "daddy" again, and he got even madder. "They better!" he had said. But we didn't, and I wished that day that I could have gone to school with Bobby Joe and Rita. It was too cold to go outside.

Our house was gray, square, and had a very high peaked roof. Under the roof was an attic, and it was big and filled with dust and dusty boxes and empty jars. The attic had no floor, only the ceiling below, and I used to sneak up to its peacefulness and sit just as quietly as the dust and feel alone. It had one small dusty window where I could sit and watch the road that ran in front of our house. It was old and gravel and went nowhere.

Sometimes I would think of money, fine houses, cars, daddies, and families. To feel nasty and bad I would smoke cigarette butts. Then I didn't think I was a good boy, but everyone else thought I was.

We were very poor, and I wore striped overalls and homemade shirts of flannel. In the winter I wore a mackinaw coat and high-top brown leather work shoes that had funny round hard toes. But in the summer I ran around in my dusty, and as Mom would say, "rusty" feet. We also ate the same things for dinner as for supper. We had pinto beans and fried potatoes with gravy and flat bread. Breakfast was dried milk and bread which tasted much better with sugar.

I didn't have toys, so whenever Edmund bought Linda Beth some new ones, I usually played with the old ones when he was not at home. When he was at home I often just went away by myself and was quiet. But if he was asleep I sat at the kitchen table and talked with Mom while she cooked or sewed. I liked to do that more than most other things.

Rita was always off somewhere with her girl friends, but Bobby Joe played with me a lot after school. He would always make me cry though, and then Mom would have to get after him and he would go off by himself and not let me sit with him. Then I wished I did not have to cry. I knew I cried too much but I did it anyway.

One day I was playing on the front-room bed with Linda Beth and her toys and accidentally made her cry. I had taken one of her new toys and she was angry. She was still very young.

Edmund had just gotten back from town and was in the kitchen with Mom so I tried to hush her up. I was scared. She got down off the bed and ran into the kitchen and told on me. I was very tight inside. I sat very still and strained to hear. Then I heard him talking to Mom in Creek and I could not understand what he was saying, but his voice was mean.

"But he takes care of her all day when everyone else is gone!" Mom said, and she began to cry and try to take up for me. I heard a sharp noise and I tried to stop listening.

Linda Beth cried even louder. Then she suddenly stopped and ran from the kitchen.

Quickly I slipped out of the front door with my throat clogged with a hurt lump. Overhead the sky was hidden by a light, dry overcast. I passed around the corner of the house and a breeze touched lightly my hot cheeks. I went into the high weeds of the side lot and found a spot to sit down. The harsh smelling weeds rustled softly and my whole body ached as I tried to cry. Soon I grew very tired and went to sleep.

When I woke up the sky had gotten darker and the glow of the sun had moved west. My body was stiff and chilled, my cheeks felt dry and dusty, and my eyes hurt in the light. I moved around, stood up, and pushed the rough stalks out of my way. The ache was beginning to come back into the space behind my eyes, and my mouth was dry.

Then I saw the house. It stood there, ugly and gray, its high shingled roof coming to a peak against the light gray sky. The wind had died for a moment, and in the silence I was suddenly afraid. My skin tingled as I walked toward the house, and I hoped that Edmund would not be there. The two west windows looked at me and I stopped, then turned away, and walked down to the next street corner to sit on the culvert and wait for Bobby Joe to come home from school.

Soon I saw Bobby Joe and Rita coming up the sidewalk and went to meet them.

"Let's go down and watch the cars go by, Bobby," I said, when they had gotten close enough. "Rita can take your books back to the house."

"What the heck for?" he demanded. I told him what had happened. "Okay," he said. "Come on."

We sat for a while identifying the cars as they zoomed past. Chevrolet. Dodge. A brand new Cadillac.

"Looks like some rich movie star," said Bobby Joe.

"Boy, I sure'd like to be a movie star," I said.

"You can't be a movie star."

"Why not?"

He looked at me.

"How come?" I wanted to know.

"Did you ever see an Indian movie star? A real Indian movie star?"

I thought about that. I hadn't seen any movies, but Rita had some movie magazines.

"Nope," I said at last, unable to remember, but still trying.

We sat for a while doing nothing. Bobby Joe was quiet like when Mom got after him for beating on me, but he didn't make me go away. I was glad about that.

"What are you going to do when you grow up, Bobby Joe?" I asked because I knew he liked to talk about things like that.

"Oh, I don't know," he mused, "go into the Air Force, I guess." Bobby Joe had a scrapbook full of airplane pictures, and he was always drawing them. We talked for a time about how much money test pilots made just for flying a new jet a few hours a week.

"What are you going to do with all that money, Bobby Joe? Save it?" Mom always told us to save our money.

"Some of it," he answered. "But I'd spend the rest."

"What would you get with it? Would you buy me a bicycle?"

"Sure," he said, and I grinned. "Then I'd get a new house for Mom, a new car—a sports car— you know, one of those new sports cars——"

"Mom'd like a station wagon," I said. "You'd get Mom a station wagon too, wouldn't you?"

"Sure, the first thing. That's what I meant."

We talked for a while, but then we were silent and I knew he didn't want to talk about when we grew up.

"Would you like to go away, like Rita says she wants to? To Canada?"

"I'm going to get to go to California when I get old enough. Mom wants to send me to a boarding school in Riverside."

"Can I go when you do?" I asked. I always

went where he did, except school, and I could start that in September.

" 'Course. One of these days we'll both go all over the place. California, New York, Canada—everywhere! We'll never come back!"

"Yeah!" I agreed. But then I remembered. "But won't we have to see Mom and them?"

"Heck, we'll take them along," he said, and that pleased me. I began to think about it.

But again we were silent. For a long while we sat under the black gas tank and watched the cars whizz by. The wind had been blowing steadily and the overcast was breaking up. In the west the sun was just above the hills. It was getting to be supper time and we would have to go home soon. Then Bobby Joe spoke.

"So Mom an' Edmund had a fight, huh?"

"Yep." And we both thought about it. I began to remember the day. I began to get very lonesome.

"Bobby Joe?"

"Yeah?"

"I didn't mean to make Linda Beth cry, so why did Edmund have to get so mad?"

"Because he's not our real father and when he knows it he don't like us. Mom says that some people tell him that our real daddy comes down here sometimes."

"But he don't, does he?"

"Naw, what for? He left, didn't he?"

"But if he don't hang around, why does Edmund get so mad?"

"I don't know. Just mean, I guess. I don't know."

"Would you like to see him again?" I asked after while.

"Who?"

"Our real daddy."

"Would you?"

"Not if you don't."

Bobby Joe said nothing.

"Huh?"

"What?"

"I said, would you like to see him again?"

"I don't know," he said, quietly, so I couldn't know either.

"How come?"

"I said, I don't know!"

"Okay."

We sat in the twilight and talked very little. The wind blew soft and cooler in the dusk. Soon we got up and started for home.

We never went to California. But when Rita and Bobby Joe graduated, I went to live with them in Kansas City. Mom, Edmund, and the kids who followed Linda Beth moved to another town fourteen miles north of Dustin, where Edmund worked in a smelter. Times got a little better.

II

When I woke up, Edmund was back and Mom was still ironing by the front door. The apartment was otherwise quiet.

"Did you have a good nap?" Mom asked, smiling at me.

"Sure did," I said, sitting up and stretching. I swung my legs off the bed and felt very refreshed.

"Edmund says a bus left at eight, and the next one won't go until four this afternoon."

"I think I'd better start back sooner than that, Mom. I won't get to K.C. until the wee hours of the morning if I start so late. I ought to hitchhike to Tulsa at least. I know a bus leaves there about one."

"You ought not to hitchhike, Son. It's too dangerous," she said, trying not to sound reproving. She never scolded me anymore, so I tried not to take advantage. I didn't want her to worry, so I told her it was all right.

"I've been all the way to New York and back this summer that way, Mom, and here I am. Anyway, Tulsa's only sixty miles away, and I can make that in two hours easy. I have to get settled; school starts in a couple of days. Besides," I added, "I've already promised to take the bus all the way to K.C. from Tulsa."

She turned to Edmund and spoke.

"When does Dick come through town on his way to Tulsa? Pretty soon?"

"No," he began, "he don't get by 'til after

three. He don't always stop, but he said he would today. Last time I seen him he told me he'd be by. He said, 'I'll be by Monday.' "

"That'd be too late," I said, speaking to Mom. "It's only ten-thirty now, so I could make it to Tulsa by one easy. I sure hate to have to spend all that money for bus fare when I don't have to. I could buy a shirt with what it takes to get to Tulsa. A couple of tee shirts, anyway."

Edmund said something to Mom in Creek, and she spoke to me.

"Edmund said he'll give you bus fare if you wait and take the bus. I think you should."

I thought for a moment and decided against it.

"You don't have to do that," I said, looking at Mom. "The kids need it more than I do. But I'll think on it some more."

Mom knew I had already made up my mind to hitchhike, and Edmund told her again that his brother would be by after three.

"He ought to be careful," he said, speaking of me. "It shore can get rough sometimes." And he lapsed into Creek as he recalled some experience of his past.

I listened for a moment, but then I lay back on the bed and thought about how things had changed since I had lived away the last four years. Mom had seemed to get much older, and ever since all the smaller kids had started to school, she missed her three oldest even more.

I remembered her saying once that she had a dream about us. She said that in her dream Rita had died. "I just couldn't live if anything ever happened to one of my children," she had said. "It would kill me." Linda Beth told me that Mom often spoke to Edmund about us, and I knew that she always prayed for us.

In the last few years I noticed that Edmund often sat in the kitchen alone, almost completely ignored by his three children. His two daughters seldom spoke to him other than to ask for money or permission to go somewhere. Only his youngest, Edmund Jr., his only son, gave him much attention.

I sometimes found myself wanting to tell the girls to show more respect for their father. And then one night I saw the second oldest put a note for school money in his coffee pot. She had signed it: "Yours truly, Rosellen." Later, his oldest, Linda Beth, referred to him as "Edmund" when she was talking to Mom. But I knew I could not make them understand, nor could I myself forget the past. For I knew it was not their fault, and the truth made me helpless.

A truck roared down the hill and shifted gears as it drifted around the sharp curve at the bottom, and still shifting, it roared anew as it strained past the apartment and was gone.

I sat up again.

Edmund had gone somewhere and Mom still ironed by the front door. The apartment was quiet and a breeze blew gently through the open windows of the back room. Outside the sky was clear, and near the open windows I saw the leafy branches of the tree that stood there.

"Well, Mom," I said, "I guess I'll go now." She put aside her iron and picked up another piece of clothing. "Am I all packed?" I asked, knowing that I was, for I remembered her the night before, carefully placing my starched and ironed clothes in my suitcase. I knew also that she had put in a new tube of toothpaste and a new bar of soap. She also had given me Junior's old clipboard and one of Linda Beth's mechanical pencils. "They don't need them," she had said.

I took my clean jacket from where she had hung it, and took my suitcase to the doorway. Mom had turned off her iron and was putting on a light sweater. She looked very alone.

"Let me carry your suitcase," she said.

"That's okay, Mom, I've got it," I said, and we walked down the dim hall and the creaking stairs and stepped out onto the sidewalk.

Edmund was standing just outside the doorway. Past him the highway curved sharply just before reaching the railroad tracks and turned again at the top of the hill before it stretched out past the smelter and on to Tulsa.

I stood silent for a moment and felt awkward.

Then I turned to Mom, and as she always did when one of her children went away again, she shook my hand.

"Be careful," she said.

" 'Bye, Mom," I said, and smiled, looking at the ground.

I took my suitcase and glanced up. Edmund was standing near Mom and almost directly in front of me, his face impassive. As strange as it seemed to me that he stood with Mom to see me off, I felt no intrusion. I thought to shake his hand also, but instead I turned quickly and crossed the highway and did not look back until I had gone around the curve. When I glanced back they still stood together, looking after me. I lifted my arm, but a truck lumbered by and I dropped my arm and continued on out of their sight. □□

Discussion

1. In Part I of the story, the narrator dreams of the time when he was six years old and his family lived in Dustin, Oklahoma. How, at that time, does he feel about his town? How does his view of Dustin differ from that of his older brother?

2. What was Edmund's relationship with his stepchildren as the narrator remembers it?

3. How does the incident with Linda Beth and her toys show the relationships in the family?

4. As the narrator and his older brother watch the cars go by, what do they reveal about their ambitions for the future?

5. In Part II the narrator emerges from the dream and memory of the past and makes his plans to go back to Kansas City and school. How do the incidents portrayed in Part II reveal the relationship of the narrator and his stepfather Edmund? Discuss.

Extension · Writing

In "A Short Return" the narrator and Bobby Joe have ambitions to become a movie star and an Air Force pilot. In a brief essay describe an ambition you had as a child or a current ambition, and explain how it was born, grew, and developed.

Durango Mendoza 1945 ·

Born in Oklahoma of Native American descent (Creek tribe), Mendoza was educated at the University of Missouri and the Art Institute of Chicago. His various works may be found in the *Prairie Schooner* and other university publications.

notes and comments

From the Author

As a young adult, my childhood was remembered as a series of emotional high and low spots. . . . These . . . early years are all colored by the perspective of an introverted child. It seemed that the sightlines of my vision of the world slanted upward from me— things and people and events loomed over me . . . the ground, the grass, and the details of floor-level life were closely sensed.

The time came when I began to realize that my perspective grew less and less slanted as I grew, both physically and emotionally. . . . one day I crossed the plane between childhood and maturity and began to feel that I could comfortably look backward and forward . . . and, if not understand them, at least sense that life had different meaning for different people at different times.

This is the state of mind I was exploring when I wrote "A Short Return." I did not analyze it then, but the process—taking a series of emotional vignettes and giving them a time, a setting, and characters—enabled me to express my feelings about the past and look to the future with my emotional accounts balanced.

Is the story based on real-life situations? Yes, if memory serves and has survived the child.

A Visit to Grandmother

William Melvin Kelley

Chig knew something was wrong the instant his father kissed her. He had always known his father to be the warmest of men, a man so kind that when people ventured timidly into his office, it took only a few words from him to make them relax, and even laugh. Doctor Charles Dunford cared about people.

But when he had bent to kiss the old lady's black face, something new and almost ugly had come into his eyes: fear, uncertainty, sadness, and perhaps even hatred.

Ten days before in New York, Chig's father had decided suddenly he wanted to go to Nashville to attend his college class reunion, twenty years out. Both Chig's brother and sister, Peter and Connie, were packing for camp and besides were too young for such an affair. But Chig was seventeen, had nothing to do that summer, and his father asked if he would like to go along. His father had given him additional reasons: "All my running buddies got their diplomas and were snapped up by them crafty young gals, and had kids within a year—now all those kids, some of them gals, are your age."

The reunion had lasted a week. As they packed for home, his father, in a far too offhand way, had suggested they visit Chig's grandmother. "We're this close. We might as well drop in on her and my brothers."

So, instead of going north, they had gone farther south, had just entered her house. And Chig had a suspicion now that the reunion had been only an excuse to drive south, that his father had been heading to this house all the time.

His father had never talked much about his family, with the exception of his brother, GL, who seemed part con man, part practical joker and part Don Juan; he had spoken of GL with the kind of indulgence he would have shown a cute, but ill-behaved and potentially dangerous, five-year-old.

Chig's father had left home when he was fifteen. When asked why, he would answer: "I wanted to go to school. They didn't have a Negro high school at home, so I went up to Knoxville and lived with a cousin and went to school."

They had been met at the door by Aunt Rose, GL's wife, and ushered into the living room. The old lady had looked up from her seat by the window. Aunt Rose stood between the visitors.

The old lady eyed his father. "Rose, who that? Rose?" She squinted. She looked like a doll, made of black straw, the wrinkles in her face running in one direction like the head of a broom. Her hair was white and coarse and grew out straight from her head. Her eyes were brown—the whites, too, seemed light brown—and were hidden behind thick glasses, which remained somehow on a tiny nose. "That Hiram?" That was another of his father's brothers. "No, it ain't Hiram; too big for Hiram." She turned then to Chig. "Now that man, he look like Eleanor, Charles' wife, but Charles wouldn't never send my grandson to see me. I never even hear from Charles." She stopped again.

"It Charles, Mama. That who it is." Aunt Rose, between them, led them closer. "It Charles come all the way from New York to see you, and brung little Charles with him."

The old lady stared up at them. "Charles? Rose, that really Charles?" She turned away, and reached for a handkerchief in the pocket of her clean, ironed, flowered housecoat, and wiped her eyes. "God have mercy, Charles." She spread her arms up to him, and he bent down and kissed her cheek. That was when Chig saw his face, grimacing. She hugged him; Chig watched the muscles in her arms as they tightened around his father's neck. She half rose out of her chair. "How are you, son?"

Chig could not hear his father's answer.

She let him go, and fell back into her chair, grabbing the arms. Her hands were as dark as the wood, and seemed to become part of it. "Now, who that standing there? Who that man?"

"That's one of your grandsons, Mama." His father's voice cracked. "Charles Dunford, junior. You saw him once, when he was a baby, in Chicago. He's grown now."

"A Visit to Grandmother," copyright © 1964 by William Melvin Kelley from DANCERS ON THE SHORE by William Melvin Kelley. Reprinted by permission of Doubleday & Company, Inc. and A. D. Peters & Co. Ltd.

"I can see that, boy!" She looked at Chig squarely. "Come here, son, and kiss me once." He did. "What they call you? Charles too?"

"No, ma'am, they call me Chig."

She smiled. She had all her teeth, but they were too perfect to be her own. "That's good. Can't have two boys answering to Charles in the same house. Won't nobody at all come. So you that little boy. You don't remember me, do you. I used to take you to church in Chicago, and you'd get up and hop in time to the music. You studying to be a preacher?"

"No, ma'am. I don't think so. I might be a lawyer."

"You'll be an honest one, won't you?"

"I'll try."

"Trying ain't enough! You be honest, you hear? Promise me. You be honest like your daddy."

"All right. I promise."

"Good. Rose, where's GL at? Where's that thief? He gone again?"

"I don't know, Mama." Aunt Rose looked embarrassed. "He say he was going by his liquor store. He'll be back."

"Well, then where's Hiram? You call up those boys, and get them over here—now! You got enough to eat? Let me go see." She started to get up. Chig reached out his hand. She shook him off. "What they tell you about me, Chig? They tell you I'm all laid up? Don't believe it. They don't know nothing about old ladies. When I want help, I'll let you know. Only time I'll need help getting anywheres is when I dies and they lift me into the ground."

She was standing now, her back and shoulders straight. She came only to Chig's chest. She squinted up at him. "You eat much? Your daddy ate like two men."

"Yes, ma'am."

"That's good. That means you ain't nervous. Your mama, she ain't nervous. I remember that. In Chicago, she'd sit down by a window all afternoon and never say nothing, just knit." She smiled. "Let me see what we got to eat."

"I'll do that, Mama." Aunt Rose spoke softly. "You haven't seen Charles in a long time. You sit and talk."

The old lady squinted at her. "You can do the cooking if you promise it ain't because you think I can't."

Aunt Rose chuckled. "I know you can do it, Mama."

"All right. I'll just sit and talk a spell." She sat again and arranged her skirt around her short legs.

Chig did most of the talking, told all about himself before she asked. His father only spoke when he was spoken to, and then, only one word at a time, as if by coming back home, he had become a small boy again, sitting in the parlor while his mother spoke with her guests.

When Uncle Hiram and Mae, his wife, came they sat down to eat. Chig did not have to ask about Uncle GL's absence; Aunt Rose volunteered an explanation: "Can't never tell where the man is at. One Thursday morning he left here and next thing we knew, he was calling from Chicago, saying he went up to see Joe Louis fight. He'll be here though; he ain't as young and footloose as he used to be." Chig's father had mentioned driving down that GL was about five years older than he was, nearly fifty.

Uncle Hiram was somewhat smaller than Chig's father; his short-cropped kinky hair was half grey, half black. One spot, just off his forehead, was totally white. Later, Chig found out it had been that way since he was twenty. Mae (Chig could not bring himself to call her Aunt) was a good deal younger than Hiram, pretty enough so that Chig would have looked at her twice on the street. She was a honey-colored woman, with long eyelashes. She was wearing a white sheath.

At dinner, Chig and his father sat on one side, opposite Uncle Hiram and Mae; his grandmother and Aunt Rose sat at the ends. The food was good; there was a lot and Chig ate a lot. All through the meal, they talked about the family as it had been thirty years before, and particularly about the young GL. Mae and Chig asked questions; the old lady answered; Aunt Rose directed the discussion, steering the old lady onto the best stories; Chig's father laughed from time to time; Uncle Hiram ate.

"Why don't you tell them about the horse, Mama?" Aunt Rose, over Chig's weak protest, was spooning mashed potatoes onto his plate. "There now, Chig."

"I'm trying to think." The old lady was holding her fork halfway to her mouth, looking at them over her glasses. "Oh, you talking about that crazy horse GL brung home that time."

"That's right, Mama." Aunt Rose nodded and slid another slice of white meat on Chig's plate.

Mae started to giggle. "Oh, I've heard this. This is funny, Chig."

The old lady put down her fork and began: Well, GL went out of the house one day with an old, no-good chair I wanted him to take over to the church for a bazaar, and he met up with this man who'd just brung in some horses from out West. Now, I reckon you can expect one swindler to be in every town, but you don't rightly think there'll be two, and heaven forbid they should ever meet—but they did, GL and his chair, this man and his horses. Well, I wished I'd-a been there; there must-a been some mighty high-powered talking going on. That man with his horses, he told GL them horses was half-Arab, half-Indian, and GL told that man the chair was an antique he'd stole from some rich white folks. So they swapped. Well, I was a-looking out the window and seen GL dragging this animal to the house. It looked pretty gentle and its eyes was most closed and its feet was shuffling.

"GL, where'd you get that thing?" I says.

"I swapped him for that old chair, Mama," he says. "And made myself a bargain. This is even better than Papa's horse."

Well, I'm a-looking at this horse and noticing how he be looking more and more wide-awake every minute, sort of warming up like a teakettle until, I swears to you, that horse is blowing steam out its nose.

"Come on, Mama," GL says, "come on and I'll take you for a ride." Now George, my husband, God rest his tired soul, he'd brung home this white folks' buggy which had a busted wheel and fixed it and was to take it back that day and GL says: "Come on, Mama, we'll use this fine buggy and take us a ride."

"GL," I says, "no, we ain't. Them white folks'll burn us alive if we use their buggy. You just take that horse right on back." You see, I was sure that boy'd come by that animal ungainly.

"Mama, I can't take him back," GL says.

"Why not?" I says.

"Because I don't rightly know where that man is at," GL says.

"Oh," I says. "Well, then I reckon we stuck with it." And I turned to go back into the house because it was getting late, near dinner time, and I was cooking for ten.

"Mama," GL says to my back. "Mama, ain't you coming for a ride with me?"

"Go on, boy. You ain't getting me inside kicking range of that animal." I was eying that beast and it was boiling hotter all the time. I reckon maybe that man had drugged it. "That horse is wild, GL," I says.

"No, he ain't. He ain't. That man say he is buggy and saddle broke and as sweet as the inside of a apple."

My oldest girl, Essie, had-a come out on the porch and she says: "Go on, Mama. I'll cook. You ain't been out the house in weeks."

"Sure, come on, Mama," GL says. "There ain't nothing to be fidgety about. This horse is gentle as a rose petal." And just then that animal snorts so hard it sets up a little dust storm around its feet.

"Yes, Mama," Essie says, "you can see he gentle." Well, I looked at Essie and then at that horse because I didn't think we could be looking at the same animal. I should-a figured how Essie's eyes ain't never been so good.

"Come on, Mama," GL says.

"All right," I says. So I stood on the porch and watched GL hitching that horse up to the white folks' buggy. For a while there, the animal was pretty quiet, pawing a little, but not much. And I was feeling a little better about riding with GL behind that crazy-looking horse. I could see how GL was happy I was going with him. He was scurrying around that animal buckling buckles and strapping straps, all the time smiling, and that made me feel good.

Then he was finished, and I must say, that horse looked mighty fine hitched to that buggy and I knew anybody what climbed up there would look pretty good too. GL came around and stood at the bottom of the steps, and took off his hat and bowed and said: "Madam," and reached out his hand to me and I was feeling real elegant like a fine lady. He helped me up to the seat and then got up beside me and we moved out down our alley. And I remember how black folks come out on their porches and shook their heads, saying: "Will you *look* at Eva Dunford, the fine lady! Don't she look good sitting up there!" And I pretended not to hear and sat up straight and proud.

We rode on through the center of town, up Market Street, and all the way out where Hiram is living now, which in them days was all woods, there not being even a farm in sight and that's when that horse must-a first realized he weren't at all broke or tame or maybe thought he was back out West again, and started to gallop.

"GL," I says, "now you ain't joking with your mama, is you? Because if you is, I'll strap you purple if I live through this."

Well, GL was pulling on the reins with all his meager strength, and yelling, "Whoa, you. Say now, whoa!" He turned to me just long enough to say, "I ain't fooling with you, Mama. Honest!"

I reckon that animal weren't too satisfied with the road, because it made a sharp right turn just then, down into a gulley and struck out across a hilly meadow. "Mama," GL yells. "Mama, do something!"

I didn't know what to do, but I figured I had to do something so I stood up, hopped down onto the horse's back and pulled it to a stop. Don't ask me how I did that; I reckon it was that I was a

mother and my baby asked me to do something, is all.

"Well, we walked that animal all the way home; sometimes I had to club it over the nose with my fist to make it come, but we made it, GL and me. You remember how tired we was, Charles?"

"I wasn't here at the time." Chig turned to his father and found his face completely blank, without even a trace of a smile or a laugh.

"Well, of course you was, son. That happened in . . . in . . . it was a hot summer that year and——"

"I left here in June of that year. You wrote me about it."

The old lady stared past Chig at him. They all turned to him; Uncle Hiram looked up from his plate.

"Then you don't remember how we all laughed?"

"No, I don't, Mama. And I probably wouldn't have laughed. I don't think it was funny." They were staring into each other's eyes.

"Why not, Charles?"

"Because in the first place, the horse was gained by fraud. And in the second place, both of you might have been seriously injured or even killed." He broke off their stare and spoke to himself more than to any of them: "And if I'd done it, you would've beaten me good for it."

"Pardon?" The old lady had not heard him; only Chig had heard.

Chig's father sat up straight as if preparing to debate. "I said that if I had done it, if I had done just exactly what GL did, you would have beaten me good for it, Mama." He was looking at her again.

"Why you say that, son?" She was leaning toward him.

"Don't you know? Tell the truth. It can't hurt me now." His voice cracked, but only once. "If GL and I did something wrong, you'd beat me first and then be too tired to beat him. At dinner, he'd always get seconds and I wouldn't. You'd do things with him, like ride in that buggy, but if I wanted you to do something with me, you were always too busy." He paused and considered whether to say what he finally did say: "I cried when I left here. Nobody loved me, Mama. I cried all the way up to Knoxville. That was the last time I ever cried in my life."

"Oh, Charles." She started to get up, to come around the table to him.

He stopped her. "It's too late."

"But you don't understand."

"What don't I understand? I understood then; I understand now."

Tears now traveled down the lines in her face, but when she spoke, her voice was clear. "I thought you knew. I had ten children. I had to give all of them what they needed most." She nodded. "I paid more mind to GL. I had to. GL could-a ended up swinging if I hadn't. But you was smarter. You was more growed up than GL when you was five and he was ten, and I tried to show you that by letting you do what you wanted to do."

"That's not true, Mama. You know it. GL was light-skinned and had good hair and looked almost white and you loved him for that."

"Charles, no. No, son. I didn't love any one of you more than any other."

"That can't be true." His father was standing now, his fists clenched tight. "Admit it, Mama . . . please!" Chig looked at him, shocked; the man was actually crying.

"It may not-a been right what I done, but I ain't no liar." Chig knew she did not really understand what had happened, what he wanted of her. "I'm not lying to you, Charles."

Chig's father had gone pale. He spoke very softly. "You're about thirty years too late, Mama." He bolted from the table. Silverware and dishes rang and jumped. Chig heard him hurrying up to their room.

They sat in silence for a while and then heard a key in the front door. A man with a new, lacquered straw hat came in. He was wearing brown and white two-tone shoes with very pointed toes and a white summer suit. "Say now! Man! I heard my brother was in town. Where he at? Where that rascal?"

He stood in the doorway, smiling broadly, an engaging, open, friendly smile, the innocent smile of a five-year-old. □□

Discussion

1. List at least three functions served by the opening paragraph of "A Visit to Grandmother."

2. Chig sees "fear, uncertainty, sadness, and perhaps even hatred" in his father's eyes. Show how Dr. Dunford reveals these emotions.

3. In paragraphs four and five, it becomes clear that for Dr. Dunford the class reunion was just an excuse to go home. (a) What does Dunford want—or expect to get—from the visit? (b) What does he want Mama to admit to?

(c) Dr. Dunford's last words are, "You're about thirty years too late, Mama." Thirty years too late for what?

4. (a) What do you learn about GL in the last sentence? (b) Did both GL and the doctor get what they needed from Mama? (c) Which man is better off? Why?

William Melvin Kelley 1937 ·

Although many of his stories have southern settings, Kelley was born in New York City. When he created a fictional southern state in his first novel, *A Different Drummer,* he had spent only two weeks in the South. "A Negro knows the South by osmosis," he said. Kelley studied at Harvard and later taught at a university in New York State. His stories in *Dancers on the Shore* won the *Transatlantic Review* Award, and his novels include *A Drop of Patience* and *dem.*

notes and comments

From the Author

Kelley has this to say about "A Visit to Grandmother": "I think it is important for any reader to remember that fiction is *not* reality. Prose fiction is the attempt, preferably by one man ('committee'-written fiction does not work) to put the real world into words. That very act separates fiction from fact. But at the same time a writer does this, he is also trying to create a world which reflects and comments on the real world. So, in a strange way, as a glass bottle is just as *real* as a human being, so fiction is as real in its

way as reality. It is just another kind of reality. The reason I'm saying all this is to stop you at the start from reading 'A Visit to Grandmother' as fact. It is *based* on certain actual events from my life, and from my father's, but these events have been shaped in my writer's imagination, and by my personal view of the world, to make a definite point which the reader should be able to understand without my help. If you want some facts, here they are. When I was about fourteen, my father and I did drive South to

see his relatives, and mine. But by that time, my father's mother was already dead. My idea of her comes from photographs I've seen of her. Long after I took the trip, I was told about my father's boyhood by some people who had known him when he was a boy. I took these various elements, bits and snatches of stories, and made them into a story about a man who had been living most of his adult life with misconceptions about his childhood and how his mother felt about him."

See **SETTING** Handbook of Literary Terms

Of Dry Goods and Black Bow Ties

Yoshiko Uchida[1]

Long after reaching the age of sixty, when my father was persuaded at last to wear a conservative four-in-hand tie, it was not because of his family's urging, but because Mr. Shimada (I shall call him that), had died. Until then, for some forty years, my father had always worn a plain black bow tie, a formality which was required on his first job in America and which he had continued to observe as faithfully as his father before him had worn his samurai sword.

My father came to America in 1906 when he was not yet twenty-one. Sailing from Japan on a small six-thousand-ton ship which was buffeted all the way by rough seas, he landed in Seattle on a bleak January day. He revived himself with the first solid meal he had enjoyed in many days, and then allowed himself one day of rest to restore his sagging spirits. Early on the second morning, wearing a stiff new bowler, he went to see Mr. Shozo Shimada to whom he carried a letter of introduction.

At that time, Shozo Shimada was Seattle's most successful Japanese business man. He owned a chain of dry goods stores which extended not only from Vancouver to Portland, but to cities in Japan as well. He had come to America in 1880, penniless but enterprising, and sought work as a laborer. It wasn't long, however, before he saw the futility of trying to compete with American laborers whose bodies were twice his in muscle and bulk. He knew he would never go far as a laborer, but he did possess another skill that could give him a start toward better things. He knew how to sew. It was a matter of expediency over masculine pride. He set aside his shovel, bought a second-hand sewing machine, and hung a dressmaker's sign in his window. He was in business.

In those days, there were some Japanese women in Seattle who had neither homes nor families nor sewing machines, and were delighted to find a friendly Japanese person to do

"Of Dry Goods and Black Bow Ties" by Yoshiko Uchida. Copyright © 1979 by Yoshiko Uchida. Reprinted by permission.

1. **Yoshiko Uchida** (yōsh′kō ū chē dä).

some sewing for them. They flocked to Mr. Shimada with bolts of cloth, elated to discover a dressmaker who could speak their native tongue and, although a male, sew western-styled dresses for them.

Mr. Shimada acquainted himself with the fine points of turning a seam, fitting sleeves, and coping with the slippery folds of silk, and soon the women told their friends and gave him enough business to keep him thriving and able to establish a healthy bank account. He became a trusted friend and confidante to many of them and soon they began to bring him what money they earned for safekeeping.

"Keep our money for us, Shimada-san,"[2] they urged, refusing to go to American banks whose tellers spoke in a language they could not understand.

At first the money accumulated slowly and Mr. Shimada used a pair of old socks as a repository, stuffing them into a far corner of his drawer beneath his union suits. But after a time, Mr. Shimada's private bank began to overflow and he soon found it necessary to replenish his supply of socks.

He went to a small dry goods store downtown, and as he glanced about at the buttons, threads, needles and laces, it occurred to him that he owed it to the women to invest their savings in a business venture with more future than the dark recesses of his bureau drawer. That night he called a group of them together.

"Think, ladies," he began. "What are the two basic needs of the Japanese living in Seattle? Clothes to wear and food to eat," he answered himself. "Is that not right? Every man must buy a shirt to put on his back and pickles and rice for his stomach."

The women marveled at Mr. Shimada's cleverness as he spread before them his fine plans for a Japanese dry goods store that would not only carry everything available in an American dry goods store, but Japanese foodstuff as well. That was the beginning of the first Shimada Dry Goods Store on State Street.

By the time my father appeared, Mr. Shi-mada had long since abandoned his sewing machine and was well on his way to becoming a business tycoon. Although he had opened cautiously with such stock items as ginghams, flannel, handkerchiefs, socks, shirts, overalls, umbrellas and ladies' silk and cotton stockings, he now carried tins of salt rice crackers, bottles of soy sauce, vinegar, ginger root, fish-paste cakes, bean paste, Japanese pickles, dried mushrooms, salt fish, red beans, and just about every item of canned food that could be shipped from Japan. In addition, his was the first Japanese store to install a U.S. Post Office Station, and he thereby attained the right to fly an American flag in front of the large sign that bore the name of his shop.

When my father first saw the big American flag fluttering in front of Mr. Shimada's shop, he was overcome with admiration and awe. He expected that Mr. Shozo Shimada would be the finest of Americanized Japanese gentlemen, and when he met him, he was not disappointed.

Although Mr. Shimada was not very tall, he gave the illusion of height because of his erect carriage. He wore a spotless black alpaca suit, an immaculate white shirt and a white collar so stiff it might have overcome a lesser man. He also wore a black bow tie, black shoes that buttoned up the side and a gold watch whose thick chain looped grandly on his vest. He was probably in his fifties then, a ruddy-faced man whose hair, already turning white, was parted carefully in the center. He was an imposing figure to confront a young man fresh from Japan with scarcely a future to look forward to. My father bowed, summoned as much dignity as he could muster, and presented the letter of introduction he carried to him.

Mr. Shimada was quick to sense his need. "Do you know anything about bookkeeping?" he inquired.

"I intend to go to night school to learn this very skill," my father answered.

---

2. **Shimada-san** (shē mä dä sän). *San*, a polite form of address usually added to given and surnames of both men and women. [*Japanese*]

Mr. Shimada could assess a man's qualities in a very few minutes. He looked my father straight in the eye and said, "Consider yourself hired." Then he added, "I have a few basic rules. My employees must at all times wear a clean white shirt and a black bow tie. They must answer the telephone promptly with the words, 'Good morning or good afternoon, Shimada's Dry Goods,' and they must always treat each customer with respect. It never hurts to be polite," he said thoughtfully. "One never knows when one might be indebted to even the lowliest of beggars."

My father was impressed with these modest words from a man of such success. He accepted them with a sense of mission and from that day was committed to white shirts and black bow ties, and treated every customer, no matter how humble, with respect and courtesy. When, in later years, he had his own home, he never failed to answer the phone before it could ring twice if at all possible.

My father worked with Mr. Shimada for ten years, becoming first the buyer for his Seattle store and later, manager of the Portland branch. During this time Mr. Shimada continued on a course of exhilarated expansion. He established two Japanese banks in Seattle, bought a fifteen-room house outside the dreary confines of the Japanese community and dressed his wife and daughter in velvets and ostrich feathers. When his daughter became eighteen, he sent her to study in Paris, and the party he gave on the eve of her departure, hiring musicians, as well as caterers to serve roast turkey, venison, baked ham and champagne, seemed to verify rumors that he had become one of the first Japanese millionaires of America.

In spite of his phenomenal success, however, Mr. Shimada never forgot his early friends nor lost any of his generosity, and this, ironically enough, was his undoing. Many of the women for whom he had once sewn dresses were now well established, and they came to him requesting loans with which they and their husbands might open grocery stores and laundries and shoe repair shops. Mr. Shimada helped them all

and never demanded any collateral. He operated his banks on faith and trust and gave no thought to such common prudence as maintaining a reserve.

When my father was called to a new position with a large Japanese firm in San Francisco, Mr. Shimada came down to Portland to extend personally his good wishes. He took Father to a Chinese dinner and told him over the peanut duck and chow mein that he would like always to be considered a friend.

"If I can ever be of assistance to you," he said, "don't ever hesitate to call." And with a firm shake of the hand, he wished my father well.

That was in 1916. My father wrote regularly to Mr. Shimada telling him of his new job, of his bride, and later, of his two children. Mr. Shimada did not write often, but each Christmas he sent a box of Oregon apples and pears, and at New Year's a slab of heavy white rice paste from his Seattle shop.

In 1929 the letters and gifts stopped coming and Father learned from friends in Seattle that both of Mr. Shimada's banks had failed.[3] He immediately dispatched a letter to Mr. Shimada, but it was returned unopened. The next news he had was that Mr. Shimada had had to sell all of his shops. My father was now manager of the San Francisco branch of his firm. He wrote once more asking Mr. Shimada if there was anything he could do to help. The letter did not come back, but there was no reply, and my father did not write again. After all, how do you offer help to the head of a fallen empire? It seemed almost irreverent.

It was many years later that Mr. Shimada appeared one night at our home in Berkeley. In the dim light of the front porch my mother was startled to see an elderly gentleman wearing striped pants, a morning coat and a shabby black hat. In his hand he carried a small black satchel. When she invited him inside, she saw that the

3. **In 1929 . . . banks had failed.** There were many bank failures in the U.S. at this time. From the end of 1929 through the 1930s there was a period of low business activity, called the Great Depression.

morning coat was faded, and his shoes badly in need of a shine.

"I am Shimada," he announced with a courtly bow, and it was my mother who felt inadequate to the occasion. She hurriedly pulled off her apron and went to call my father. When he heard who was in the living room, he put on his coat and tie before going out to greet his old friend.

Mr. Shimada spoke to them about Father's friends in Seattle and about his daughter who was now married and living in Denver. He spoke of a typhoon that had recently swept over Japan, and he drank the tea my mother served and ate a piece of her chocolate cake. Only then did he open his black satchel.

"I thought your girls might enjoy these books," he said, as he drew out a brochure describing *The Book of Knowledge.*

"Fourteen volumes that will tell them of the wonders of this world." He spread his arms in a magnificent gesture that recalled his eloquence of the past. "I wish I could give them to your children as a personal gift," he added softly.

Without asking the price of the set, my father wrote a check for one hundred dollars and gave it to Mr. Shimada.

Mr. Shimada glanced at the check and said, "You have given me fifty dollars too much." He seemed troubled for only a moment, however, and quickly added, "Ah, the balance is for a deposit, is it? Very well, yours will be the first deposit in my next bank."

"Is your home still in Seattle then?" Father asked cautiously.

"I am living there, yes," Mr. Shimada answered.

And then, suddenly overcome with memories of the past, he spoke in a voice so low he could scarcely be heard.

"I paid back every cent," he murmured. "It took ten years, but I paid it back. All of it. I owe nothing."

"You are a true gentleman, Shimada-san," Father said. "You always will be." Then he pointed to the black tie he wore, saying, "You see, I am still one of the Shimada men."

That was the last time my father saw Shozo Shimada. Some time later he heard that he had returned to Japan as penniless as the day he set out for America.

It wasn't until the Christmas after we heard of Mr. Shimada's death that I ventured to give my father a silk four-in-hand tie. It was charcoal gray and flecked with threads of silver. My father looked at it for a long time before he tried it on, and then fingering it gently, he said, "Well, perhaps it is time now that I put away my black bow ties."

□□

Discussion

1. What enabled Mr. Shimada to rise to such an eminent position in America?

2. When the narrator's father, a freshly arrived immigrant from Japan, reported to work for Mr. Shimada, the latter set forth his "basic rules." Relate these rules to the title of the story.

3. What caused the fall of Mr. Shimada's fortunes?

4. (a) What happened when the narrator's father tried to help Mr. Shimada in his misfortune? (b) How did the narrator's father finally help Mr. Shimada?

5. In the final scene portraying Mr. Shimada selling *The Book of Knowledge* door to door, in what ways did he appear changed and in what ways did he appear to be the same?

Read the following sentences. If the meaning of the italicized words can be determined from their contexts, write what you think the meaning is on a separate sheet of paper. If the meaning cannot be determined fully enough for your purposes, look up the word in your Glossary and then use it in a sentence of your own. Be sure you can spell and pronounce all the italicized words.

1. We sailed from Japan on a small ship that was so *buffeted* all the way by rough seas that we were seasick.

2. Early in the morning, he arrived wearing a stiff new *bowler.*

3. He has become a trusted friend and *confidante* to all of the students.

4. Although Linda is not very tall, she gives the illusion of height because of her erect *carriage.*

5. My uncle bowed, *mustered* as much dignity as he could, and introduced his wife to the queen.

6. Mr. Shimada helped everyone and never demanded any *collateral.*

7. The small wooden chest in later years became a *repository* for the treasured love letters.

8. The grand party he gave last week seemed to *verify* rumors that he had become a millionaire.

9. We were *exhilarated* by our early morning walk.

10. The *prudence* of the buyer was revealed when the cold spell hit, and hers was the only store in town to have a complete stock of sweaters.

Yoshiko Uchida 1921 •

During World War II, in 1942, Uchida was evacuated with others of Japanese descent from California to Utah, where she taught second grade at the relocation camp. Born in Alameda, California, she had graduated from the University of California just before this disruption of her life.

Shortly after her wartime experiences, she began writing Japanese folk tales. She went to Japan on a Ford Foundation Research Fellowship in 1952 and stayed for two years. She speaks both Japanese and French.

notes and comments

From the Author

For Yoshiko Uchida, living is a joy, and writing an affirmation of life's positive values.

Uchida has written twenty books for adolescents and younger children, including *Journey to Topaz* and *Samurai of Gold Hill.* They reflect her proud identity as a Japanese American, an identity she hopes to reaffirm among the third- and fourth-generation Japanese Americans growing up today.

Uchida is well suited to this task, having been raised by *Issei* (first generation) parents with strong ties to both the old Japanese and the new American ways. They maintained many Japanese traditions which Uchida remembers with fondness. Moreover, both of her grandfathers were samurai who lived at the tail end of the feudal system in Japan. Thus, both Christian and samurai values were transmitted to Uchida as a child.

According to Uchida, the samurai were much more than the violent warriors our modern stereotype makes them out to be. "They were members of the military class, but, as retainers to the great nobles, were considered to be an elite, intellectual group as well. They were trained in literature, the arts, and Chinese philosophy. Their code included the values of discipline, loyalty, respect for elders, and being strong, yet having a heart that could understand beauty."

Her book-oriented mother found time to read Japanese stories to her daughters, as well as to write her own poems. This undoubtedly influenced Uchida, who remembers her first book, which she wrote on brown wrapping paper at the age of ten.

Average Waves in Unprotected Waters

Anne Tyler

As soon as it got light, Bet woke him and dressed him, and then she walked him over to the table and tried to make him eat a little cereal. He wouldn't, though. He could tell something was up. She pressed the edge of the spoon against his lips till she heard it click on his teeth, but he just looked off at a corner of the ceiling—a knobby child with great glassy eyes and her own fair hair. Like any other nine-year-old, he wore a striped shirt and jeans, but the shirt was too neat and the jeans too blue, unpatched and unfaded, and would stay that way till he outgrew them. And his face was elderly—pinched, strained, tired—though it should have looked as unused as his jeans. He hardly ever changed his expression.

She left him in his chair and went to make the beds. Then she raised the yellowed shade, rinsed a few spoons in the bathroom sink, picked up some bits of magazines he'd torn the night before. This was a rented room in an ancient, crumbling house, and nothing you could do to it would lighten its cluttered look. There was always that feeling of too many lives layered over other lives, like the layers of brownish wallpaper her child had peeled away in the corner by his bed.

She slipped her feet into flat-heeled loafers and absently patted the front of her dress, a worn beige knit she usually saved for Sundays. Maybe she should take it in a little; it hung from her shoulders like a sack. She felt too slight and frail, too wispy for all she had to do today. But she reached for her coat anyhow, and put it on and tied a blue kerchief under her chin. Then she went over to the table and slowly spun, modeling the coat. "See, Arnold?" she said. "We're going out."

Arnold went on looking at the ceiling, but his gaze turned wild and she knew he'd heard.

She fetched his jacket from the closet—brown corduroy, with a hood. It had set her back half a week's salary. But Arnold didn't like it; he always wanted his old one, a little red duffel coat he'd long ago outgrown. When she came toward him, he started moaning and rocking and shaking his head. She had to struggle to stuff his arms in the sleeves. Small though he was, he was strong, wiry; he was getting to be too much for her. He shook free of her hands and ran over to his bed. The jacket was on, though. It wasn't buttoned, the collar was askew, but never mind; that just made him look more real. She always felt bad at how he stood inside his clothes, separate from them, passive, unaware of all the buttons and

Copyright © 1977 by Anne Tyler. Reprinted by permission of Russell & Volkening, Inc. as agents for the author. Originally in THE NEW YORKER.

snaps she'd fastened as carefully as she would a doll's.

She gave a last look around the room, checked to make sure the hot plate was off, and then picked up her purse and Arnold's suitcase. "Come along, Arnold," she said.

He came, dragging out every step. He looked at the suitcase suspiciously, but only because it was new. It didn't have any meaning for him. "See?" she said. "It's yours. It's Arnold's. It's going on the train with us."

But her voice was all wrong. He would pick it up, for sure. She paused in the middle of locking the door and glanced over at him fearfully. Anything could set him off nowadays. He hadn't noticed, though. He was too busy staring around the hallway, goggling at a freckled, walnut-framed mirror as if he'd never seen it before. She touched his shoulder. "Come, Arnold," she said.

They went down the stairs slowly, both of them clinging to the sticky mahogany railing. The suitcase banged against her shins. In the entrance hall, old Mrs. Puckett stood waiting outside her door—a huge, soft lady in a black crêpe dress and orthopedic shoes. She was holding a plastic bag of peanut-butter cookies, Arnold's favorites. There were tears in her eyes. "Here, Arnold," she said, quavering. Maybe she felt to blame that he was going. But she'd done

the best she could: babysat him all these years and only given up when he'd grown too strong and wild to manage. Bet wished Arnold would give the old lady some sign—hug her, make his little crowing noise, just take the cookies, even. But he was too excited. He raced on out the front door, and it was Bet who had to take them. "Well, thank you, Mrs. Puckett," she said. "I know he'll enjoy them later."

"Oh, no . . ." said Mrs. Puckett, and she flapped her large hands and gave up, sobbing.

They were lucky and caught a bus first thing. Arnold sat by the window. He must have thought he was going to work with her; when they passed the red-and-gold Kresge's sign, he jabbered and tried to stand up. "No, honey," she said, and took hold of his arm. He settled down then and let his hand stay curled in hers awhile. He had very small, cool fingers, and nails as smooth as thumbtack heads.

At the train station, she bought the tickets and then a pack of Wrigley's spearmint gum. Arnold stood gaping at the vaulted ceiling, with his head flopped back and his arms hanging limp at his sides. People stared at him. She would have liked to push their faces in. "Over here, honey," she said, and she nudged him toward the gate, straightening his collar as they walked.

He hadn't been on a train before and acted a little nervous, bouncing up and down in his seat and flipping the lid of his ashtray and craning forward to see the man ahead of them. When the train started moving, he crowed and pulled at her sleeve. "That's right, Arnold. Train. We're taking a trip," Bet said. She unwrapped a stick of chewing gum and gave it to him. He loved gum. If she didn't watch him closely, he sometimes swallowed it—which worried her a little because she'd heard it clogged your kidneys; but at least it would keep him busy. She looked down at the top of his head. Through the blond prickles of his hair, cut short for practical reasons, she could see his skull bones moving as he chewed. He was so thin-skinned, almost transparent; sometimes she imagined she could see the blood traveling in his veins.

When the train reached a steady speed, he grew calmer, and after a while he nodded over against her and let his hands sag on his knees. She watched his eyelashes slowly drooping—two colorless, fringed crescents, heavier and heavier, every now and then flying up as he tried to fight off sleep. He had never slept well, not ever, not even as a baby. Even before they'd noticed anything wrong, they'd wondered at his jittery, jerky catnaps, his tiny hands clutching tight and springing open, his strange single wail sailing out while he went right on sleeping. Avery said it gave him the chills. And after the doctor talked to them Avery wouldn't have anything to do with Arnold anymore—just walked in wide circles around the crib, looking stunned and sick. A few weeks later, he left. She wasn't surprised. She even knew how he felt, more or less. Halfway, he blamed her; halfway, he blamed himself. You can't believe a thing like this will just fall on you out of nowhere.

She'd had moments herself of picturing some kind of evil gene in her husband. All his fault. But other times she was sure the gene was hers. It seemed so natural; she never could do anything as well as most people. And then other times she blamed their marriage. They'd married too young, against her parents' wishes. All she'd wanted was to get away from home. Now she couldn't remember why. What was wrong with home? She thought of her parents' humped green trailer, perched on cinder blocks near a forest of masts in Salt Spray, Maryland. At this distance (parents dead, trailer rusted to bits, even Salt Spray changed past recognition), it seemed to her that her old life had been beautifully free and spacious. She closed her eyes and saw wide gray skies. Everything had been ruled by the sea. Her father (who'd run a fishing boat for tourists) couldn't arrange his day till he'd heard the marine forecast—the wind, the tides, the small-craft warnings, the height of average waves in unprotected waters. He loved to fish, offshore and on, and he swam every chance he could get. He'd tried to teach her to bodysurf, but it hadn't worked out. There was something about the breakers: she just gritted her teeth and stood staunch and let them slam into her. As if standing staunch were a virtue, really. She couldn't explain it. Her father thought she was scared, but it wasn't that at all.

She'd married Avery against their wishes and been sorry ever since—sorry to move so far from home, sorrier when her parents died within a year of each other, sorriest of all when the marriage turned grim and cranky. But she never would have thought of leaving him. It was Avery who left; she would have stayed forever. In fact, she did stay on in their apartment for months after he'd gone, though the rent was far too high. It wasn't that she expected him back. She just took some comfort from enduring.

Arnold's head snapped up. He looked around him and made a gurgling sound. His chewing gum fell onto the front of his jacket. "Here, honey," she told him. She put the gum in her ashtray. "Look out the window. See the cows?"

He wouldn't look. He began bouncing in his seat, rubbing his hands together rapidly.

"Arnold? Want a cookie?"

If only she'd brought a picture book. She'd meant to and then forgot. She wondered if the train people sold magazines. If she let him get too bored, he'd go into one of his tantrums, and then she wouldn't be able to handle him. The doctor had given her pills just in case, but she was always afraid that while he was screaming he would choke on them. She looked around the car. "Arnold," she said, "see the . . . see the hat with feathers on? Isn't it pretty? See the red suitcase? See the, um . . ."

The car door opened with a rush of clattering wheels and the conductor burst in, singing "Girl of my dreams, I love you." He lurched down the aisle, plucking pink tickets from the back of each seat. Just across from Bet and Arnold, he stopped. He was looking down at a tiny lady in a purple coat, with a fox fur piece biting its own tail around her neck. "You!" he said.

The lady stared straight ahead.

"You, I saw you. You're the one in the washroom."

A little muscle twitched in her cheek.

"You got on this train in Beulah, didn't you. Snuck in the washroom. Darted back like you thought you could put something over on me. I saw that bit of purple! Where's your ticket gone to?"

She started fumbling in a blue cloth purse. The fumbling went on and on. The conductor shifted his weight.

"Why!" she said finally. "I must've left it back in my other seat."

"What other seat?"

"Oh, the one back . . ." She waved a spidery hand.

The conductor sighed. "Lady," he said, "you owe me money."

"I do no such thing!" she said. "Viper! Monger! Hitler!" Her voice screeched up all at once; she sounded like a parrot. Bet winced and felt herself flushing, as if *she* were the one. But then at her shoulder she heard a sudden, rusty clang, and she turned and saw that Arnold was laughing. He had his mouth wide open and his tongue curled, the way he did when he watched "Sesame Street." Even after the scene had worn itself out, and the lady had paid and the conductor had moved on, Arnold went on chortling and

la-la-ing, and Bet looked gratefully at the little lady, who was settling her fur piece fussily and muttering under her breath.

From the Parkinsville Railroad Station, which they seemed to be tearing down or else remodelling—she couldn't tell which—they took a taxicab to Parkins State Hospital. "Oh, I been out there many and many a time," said the driver. "Went out there just the other——"

But she couldn't stop herself; she had to tell him before she forgot. "Listen," she said, "I want you to wait for me right in the driveway. I don't want you to go on away."

"Well, fine," he said.

"Can you do that? I want you to be sitting right by the porch or the steps or whatever, right where I come out of, ready to take me back to the station. Don't just go off and——"

"I *got* you, I got you," he said.

She sank back. She hoped he understood.

Arnold wanted a peanut-butter cookie. He was reaching and whimpering. She didn't know what to do. She wanted to give him anything he asked for, anything; but he'd get it all over his face and arrive not looking his best. She couldn't stand it if they thought he was just ordinary and unattractive. She wanted them to see how small and neat he was, how somebody cherished him. But it would be awful if he went into one of his rages. She broke off a little piece of cookie from the bag. "Here," she told him. "Don't mess, now."

He flung himself back in the corner and ate it, keeping one hand flattened across his mouth while he chewed.

The hospital looked like someone's great, pillared mansion, with square brick buildings all around it. "Here we are," the driver said.

"Thank you," she said. "Now you wait here, please. Just wait till I get——"

"*Lady,*" he said. "I'll wait."

She opened the door and nudged Arnold out ahead of her. Lugging the suitcase, she started toward the steps. "Come on, Arnold," she said.

He hung back.

"Arnold?"

Maybe he wouldn't allow it, and they would go on home and never think of this again.

But he came, finally, climbing the steps in his little hobbled way. His face was clean, but there were a few cookie crumbs on his jacket. She set down the suitcase to brush them off. Then she buttoned all his buttons and smoothed his shirt collar over his jacket collar before she pushed open the door.

In the admitting office, a lady behind a wooden counter showed her what papers to sign. Secretaries were clacketing typewriters all around. Bet thought Arnold might like that, but instead he got lost in the lights—chilly, hanging ice-cube-tray lights with a little flicker to them. He gazed upward, looking astonished. Finally a flat-fronted nurse came in and touched his elbow. "Come along, Arnold. Come, Mommy. We'll show you where Arnold is staying," she said.

They walked back across the entrance hall, then up wide marble steps with hollows worn in them. Arnold clung to the bannister. There was a smell Bet hated, pine-oil disinfectant, but Arnold didn't seem to notice. You never knew; sometimes smells could just put him in a state.

The nurse unlocked a double door that had chicken-wired windows. They walked through a corridor, passing several fat, ugly women in shapeless gray dresses and ankle socks. "Ha!" one of the women said, and fell giggling into the arms of a friend. The nurse said, *"Here* we are." She led them into an enormous hallway lined with little white cots. Nobody else was in it; there wasn't a sign that children lived here except for a tiny cardboard clown picture hanging on one vacant wall. "This one is your bed, Arnold," said the nurse. Bet laid the suitcase on it. It was made up so neatly, the sheets might have been painted on. A steely-gray blanket was folded across the foot. She looked over at Arnold, but he was pivoting back and forth to hear how his new sneakers squeaked on the linoleum.

"Usually," said the nurse, "we like to give new residents six months before the family visits. That way they settle in quicker, don't you see." She turned away and adjusted the clown picture, though as far as Bet could tell it was fine the way it was. Over her shoulder, the nurse said, "You can tell him goodbye now, if you like."

"Oh," Bet said. "All right." She set her hands on Arnold's shoulders. Then she laid her face against his hair, which felt warm and fuzzy. "Honey," she said. But he went on pivoting. She straightened and told the nurse, "I brought his special blanket."

"Oh, fine," said the nurse, turning toward her again. "We'll see that he gets it."

"He always likes to sleep with it; he has ever since he was little."

"All right."

"Don't wash it. He hates if you wash it."

"Yes. Say goodbye to Mommy now, Arnold."

"A lot of times he'll surprise you. I mean there's a whole lot to him. He's not just——"

"We'll take very good care of him, Mrs. Blevins, don't worry."

"Well," she said. "'Bye, Arnold."

She left the ward with the nurse and went down the corridor. As the nurse was unlocking the doors for her, she heard a single, terrible scream, but the nurse only patted her shoulder and pushed her gently on through.

In the taxi, Bet said, "Now, I've just got fifteen minutes to get to the station. I wonder if you could hurry?"

"Sure thing," the driver said.

She folded her hands and looked straight ahead. Tears seemed to be coming down her face in sheets.

Once she'd reached the station, she went to the ticket window. "Am I in time for the twelve-thirty-two?" she asked.

"Easily," said the man. "It's twenty minutes late."

"What?"

"Got held up in Norton somehow."

"But you can't!" she said. The man looked startled. She must be a sight, all swollen-eyed and wet-cheeked. "Look," she said, in a lower voice. "I figured this on purpose. I chose the one train from Beulah that would let me catch another one back without waiting. I do not want to sit and wait in this station."

"Twenty *minutes,* lady. That's all it is."

"What am I going to do?" she asked him.

He turned back to his ledgers.

She went over to a bench and sat down. Ladders and scaffolding towered above her, and only ten or twelve passengers were dotted through the rest of the station. The place looked bombed out—nothing but a shell. "Twenty minutes!" she said aloud. "What am I going to do?"

Through the double glass doors at the far end of the station, a procession of gray-suited men arrived with briefcases. More men came behind them, dressed in work clothes, carrying folding chairs, black trunklike boxes with silver hinges, microphones, a wooden lectern, and an armload of bunting. They set the lectern down in the center of the floor, not six feet from Bet. They draped the bunting across it—an arc of red, white, and blue. Wires were connected, floodlights were lit. A microphone screeched. One of the workmen said, "Try her, Mayor." He held the microphone out to a fat man in a suit, who cleared his throat and said, "Ladies and gentlemen, on the occasion of the expansion of this fine old railway station——"

"Sure do get an echo here," the workman said. "Keep on going."

The Mayor cleared his throat again. "If I may," he said, "I'd like to take about twenty minutes of your time, friends."

He straightened his tie. Bet blew her nose, and then she wiped her eyes and smiled. They had come just for her sake, you might think. They were putting on a sort of private play. From now on, all the world was going to be like that—just something on a stage, for her to sit back and watch. □□

Discussion

1. As Bet is leaving the apartment building with Arnold, Mrs. Puckett stands at her door and offers the boy a bag of his favorite cookies. (a) How does Arnold respond to her? (b) What has been Mrs. Puckett's relationship with Arnold, and why is she now sobbing?

2. On the train Arnold becomes restless and Bet is afraid he will throw one of his tantrums. What engages his attention causing him to burst out in a peal of laughter? Discuss.

3. At the Parkins State Hospital, Bet gives Arnold's favorite blanket to the nurse and explains that he likes to sleep with it and he does not want it washed. Do you think Arnold will be given his blanket? Support your opinion.

4. When Bet gets back to the station alone and discovers that her train will be twenty minutes late, why does she panic?

5. (a) What happens to fill up the twenty minutes? (b) How does Bet plan to deal with life from then on? Discuss.

6. The title of the story is analogous to Bet's life. What comparisons are being made?

Anne Tyler 1941 ·

About her story "Average Waves . . . ," Tyler says that special children like Arnold used to go to her school, and she has thought about these children and their mothers for years. "The picture of this child came to me so vividly," she says; "I felt I knew exactly how small and cool his fingers would feel in mine as we climbed the stairs to say good-bye."

Tyler's novels include *If Morning Ever Comes* (1964), *The Tin Can Tree* (1965), *A Slipping-Down Life* (1970), and *Searching for Caleb* (1976).

See **MOOD** Handbook of Literary Terms

The Life You Save May Be Your Own

Flannery O'Connor

The old woman and her daughter were sitting on their porch when Mr. Shiftlet came up their road for the first time. The old woman slid to the edge of her chair and leaned forward, shading her eyes from the piercing sunset with her hand. The daughter could not see far in front of her and continued to play with her fingers. Although the old woman lived in this desolate spot with only her daughter and she had never seen Mr. Shiftlet before, she could tell, even from a distance, that he was a tramp and no one to be afraid of. His left coat sleeve was folded up to show there was only half an arm in it and his gaunt figure listed slightly to the side as if the breeze were pushing him. He had on a black town suit and a brown felt hat that was turned up in the front and down in the back and he carried a tin tool box by a handle. He came on, at an amble, up her road, his face turned toward the sun which appeared to be balancing itself on the peak of a small mountain.

The old woman didn't change her position until he was almost into her yard; then she rose with one hand fisted on her hip. The daughter, a large girl in a short blue organdy dress, saw him all at once and jumped up and began to stamp and point and make excited speechless sounds.

Mr. Shiftlet stopped just inside the yard and set his box on the ground and tipped his hat at her as if she were not in the least afflicted; then he turned toward the old woman and swung the hat all the way off. He had long black slick hair that hung flat from a part in the middle to beyond the tips of his ears on either side. His face descended in forehead for more than half its length and ended suddenly with his features just balanced over a jutting steel-trap jaw. He seemed to be a young man but he had a look of

Copyright, 1953, by Flannery O'Connor. Reprinted from her volume A GOOD MAN IS HARD TO FIND AND OTHER STORIES by permission of Harcourt Brace Jovanovich, Inc. and Harold Matson Co., Inc.

composed dissatisfaction as if he understood life thoroughly.

"Good evening," the old woman said. She was about the size of a cedar fence post and she had a man's gray hat pulled down low over her head.

The tramp stood looking at her and didn't answer. He turned his back and faced the sunset. He swung both his whole and his short arm up slowly so that they indicated an expanse of sky and his figure formed a crooked cross. The old woman watched him with her arms folded across her chest as if she were the owner of the sun, and the daughter watched, her head thrust forward and her fat helpless hands hanging at the wrists. She had long pink-gold hair and eyes as blue as a peacock's neck.

He held the pose for almost fifty seconds and then he picked up his box and came on to the porch and dropped down on the bottom step. "Lady," he said in a firm nasal voice, "I'd give a fortune to live where I could see me a sun do that every evening."

"Does it every evening," the old woman said and sat back down. The daughter sat down too and watched him with a cautious sly look as if he were a bird that had come up very close. He leaned to one side, rooting in his pants pocket, and in a second he brought out a package of chewing gum and offered her a piece. She took it and unpeeled it and began to chew without taking her eyes off him. He offered the old woman a piece but she only raised her upper lip to indicate she had no teeth.

Mr. Shiftlet's pale sharp glance had already passed over everything in the yard—the pump near the corner of the house and the big fig tree that three or four chickens were preparing to roost in—and had moved to a shed where he saw the square rusted back of an automobile. "You ladies drive?" he asked.

"That car ain't run in fifteen years," the old woman said. "The day my husband died, it quit running."

"Nothing is like it used to be, lady," he said. "The world is almost rotten."

"That's right," the old woman said. "You from around here?"

"Name Tom T. Shiftlet," he murmured, looking at the tires.

"I'm pleased to meet you," the old woman said. "Name Lucynell Crater and daughter Lucynell Crater. What you doing around here, Mr. Shiftlet?"

He judged the car to be about a 1928 or '29 Ford. "Lady," he said, and turned and gave her his full attention, "lemme tell you something. There's one of these doctors in Atlanta that's taken a knife and cut the human heart—the human heart," he repeated, leaning forward, "out of a man's chest and held it in his hand," and he held his hand out, palm up, as if it were slightly weighted with the human heart, "and studied it like it was a day-old chicken, and lady," he said, allowing a long significant pause in which his head slid forward and his clay-colored eyes brightened, "he don't know no more about it than you or me."

"That's right," the old woman said.

"Why, if he was to take that knife and cut into every corner of it, he still wouldn't know no more than you or me. What you want to bet?"

"Nothing," the old woman said wisely. "Where you come from, Mr. Shiftlet?"

He didn't answer. He reached into his pocket and brought out a sack of tobacco and a package of cigarette papers and rolled himself a cigarette, expertly with one hand, and attached it in a hanging position to his upper lip. Then he took a box of wooden matches from his pocket and struck one on his shoe. He held the burning match as if he were studying the mystery of flame while it traveled dangerously toward his skin. The daughter began to make loud noises and to point to his hand and shake her finger at him, but when the flame was just before touching him, he leaned down with his hand cupped over it as if he were going to set fire to his nose and lit the cigarette.

He flipped away the dead match and blew a stream of gray into the evening. A sly look came over his face. "Lady," he said, "nowadays, people'll do anything anyways. I can tell you my name is Tom T. Shiftlet and I come from Tarwater, Tennessee, but you never have seen me before: how you know I ain't lying? How you know my name ain't Aaron Sparks, lady, and I come from Singleberry, Georgia, or how you know it's not George Speeds and I come from Lucy, Alabama, or how you know I ain't Thompson Bright from Toolafalls, Mississippi?''

''I don't know nothing about you,'' the old woman muttered, irked.

''Lady,'' he said, ''people don't care how they lie. Maybe the best I can tell you is, I'm a man; but listen lady,'' he said and paused and made his tone more ominous still, ''what is a man?''

The old woman began to gum a seed. ''What you carry in that tin box, Mr. Shiftlet?'' she asked.

''Tools,'' he said, put back. ''I'm a carpenter.''

''Well, if you come out here to work, I'll be able to feed you and give you a place to sleep but I can't pay. I'll tell you that before you begin,'' she said.

There was no answer at once and no particular expression on his face. He leaned back against the two-by-four that helped support the porch roof. ''Lady,'' he said slowly, ''there's some men that some things mean more to them than money.'' The old woman rocked without comment and the daughter watched the trigger that moved up and down in his neck. He told the old woman then that all most people were interested in was money, but he asked what a man was made for. He asked her if a man was made for money, or what. He asked her what she thought she was made for but she didn't answer, she only sat rocking and wondered if a one-armed man could put a new roof on her garden house. He asked a lot of questions that she didn't answer. He told her that he was twenty-eight years old and had lived a varied life. He had been a gospel singer, a foreman on the railroad, an assistant in an undertaking parlor, and he had come over the radio for three months with Uncle Roy and his Red Creek Wranglers. He said he had fought and bled in the Arm Service of his country and visited every foreign land and that everywhere he had seen people that didn't care if they did a thing one way or another. He said he hadn't been raised thataway.

A fat yellow moon appeared in the branches of the fig tree as if it were going to roost there with the chickens. He said that a man had to escape to the country to see the world whole and that he wished he lived in a desolate place like this where he could see the sun go down every evening like God made it to do.

''Are you married or are you single?'' the old woman asked.

There was a long silence. ''Lady,'' he asked finally, ''where would you find you an innocent woman today? I wouldn't have any of this trash I could just pick up.''

The daughter was leaning very far down, hanging her head almost between her knees, watching him through a triangular door she had made in her overturned hair; and she suddenly fell in a heap on the floor and began to whimper. Mr. Shiftlet straightened her out and helped her get back in the chair.

''Is she your baby girl?'' he asked.

''My only,'' the old woman said, ''and she's the sweetest girl in the world. I wouldn't give her up for nothing on earth. She's smart too. She can sweep the floor, cook, wash, feed the chickens, and hoe. I wouldn't give her up for a casket of jewels.''

''No,'' he said kindly, ''don't ever let any man take her away from you.''

''Any man come after her,'' the old woman said, '' 'll have to stay around the place.''

Mr. Shiftlet's eye in the darkness was focused on a part of the automobile bumper that glittered in the distance. ''Lady,'' he said, jerking his short arm up as if he could point with it to her house and yard and pump, ''there ain't a broken thing on this plantation that I couldn't fix for you, one-arm jackleg or not. I'm a man,'' he said with a sullen dignity, ''even if I ain't a whole one. I got,'' he said, tapping his knuckles on the floor to emphasize the immensity of what he was going to say, "a moral intelligence!" and his face pierced out of the darkness into a shaft of doorlight and he stared at her as if he were astonished himself at this impossible truth.

The old woman was not impressed with the phrase. "I told you you could hang around and work for food," she said, "if you don't mind sleeping in that car yonder."

"Why listen, Lady," he said with a grin of delight, "the monks of old slept in their coffins!"

"They wasn't as advanced as we are," the old woman said.

The next morning he began on the roof of the garden house while Lucynell, the daughter, sat on a rock and watched him work. He had not been around a week before the change he had made in the place was apparent. He had patched the front and back steps, built a new hog pen, restored a fence, and taught Lucynell, who was completely deaf and had never said a word in her life, to say the word "bird." The big rosy-faced girl followed him everywhere, saying "Burrttddt ddbirrrttdt," and clapping her hands. The old woman watched from a distance, secretly pleased. She was ravenous for a son-in-law.

Mr. Shiftlet slept on the hard narrow back seat of the car with his feet out the side window. He had his razor and a can of water on a crate that served him as a bedside table and he put up a piece of mirror against the back glass and kept his coat neatly on a hanger that he hung over one of the windows.

In the evenings he sat on the steps and talked while the old woman and Lucynell rocked violently in their chairs on either side of him. The old woman's three mountains were black against the dark blue sky and were visited off and on by various planets and by the moon after it had left the chickens. Mr. Shiftlet pointed out that the reason he had improved this plantation was because he had taken a personal interest in it. He said he was even going to make the automobile run.

He had raised the hood and studied the mechanism and he said he could tell that the car had been built in the days when cars were really built. You take now, he said, one man puts in one bolt and another man puts in another bolt and another man puts in another bolt so that it's a man for a bolt. That's why you have to pay so much for a car: you're paying all those men. Now if you didn't have to pay but one man, you could get you a cheaper car and one that had had a personal interest taken in it, and it would be a better car. The old woman agreed with him that this was so.

Mr. Shiftlet said that the trouble with the world was that nobody cared, or stopped and took any trouble. He said he never would have been able to teach Lucynell to say a word if he hadn't cared and stopped long enough.

"Teach her to say something else," the old woman said.

"What you want her to say next?" Mr. Shiftlet asked.

The old woman's smile was broad and toothless and suggestive. "Teach her to say 'sugarpie,' " she said.

Mr. Shiftlet already knew what was on her mind.

The next day he began to tinker with the automobile and that evening he told her that if she would buy a fan belt, he would be able to make the car run.

The old woman said she would give him the money. "You see that girl yonder?" she asked, pointing to Lucynell who was sitting on the floor a foot away, watching him, her eyes blue even in the dark. "If it was ever a man wanted to take her away, I would say, 'No man on earth is going to take that sweet girl of mine away from me!' but if he was to say, 'Lady, I don't want to take her away, I want her right here,' I would say, 'Mister, I don't blame you none. I wouldn't pass up a chance to live in a permanent place and get the sweetest girl in the world myself. You ain't no fool.' I would say?"

"How old is she?" Mr. Shiftlet asked casually.

"Fifteen, sixteen," the old woman said. The girl was nearly thirty but because of her innocence it was impossible to guess.

"It would be a good idea to paint it too," Mr. Shiftlet remarked. "You don't want it to rust out."

"We'll see about that later," the old woman said.

The next day he walked into town and returned with the parts he needed and a can of gasoline. Late in the afternoon, terrible noises issued from the shed and the old woman rushed out of the house, thinking Lucynell was somewhere having a fit. Lucynell was sitting on a chicken crate, stamping her feet and screaming, "Burrddtttt! bddurrddtttt!" but her fuss was drowned out by the car. With a volley of blasts it emerged from the shed, moving in a fierce and stately way. Mr. Shiftlet was in the driver's seat, sitting very erect. He had an expression of serious modesty on his face as if he had just raised the dead.

That night, rocking on the porch, the old woman began her business at once. "You want you an innocent woman, don't you?" she asked sympathetically. "You don't want none of this trash."

"No'm, I don't," Mr. Shiftlet said.

"One that can't talk," she continued, "can't sass you back or use foul language. That's the kind for you to have. Right there," and she pointed to Lucynell sitting cross-legged in her chair, holding both feet in her hands.

"That's right," he admitted. "She wouldn't give me any trouble."

"Saturday," the old woman said, "you and her and me can drive into town and get married."

Mr. Shiftlet eased his position on the steps.

"I can't get married right now," he said. "Everything you want to do takes money and I ain't got any."

"What you need with money?" she asked.

"It takes money," he said. "Some people'll do anything anyhow these days, but the way I think, I wouldn't marry no woman that I couldn't take on a trip like she was somebody. I mean take her to a hotel and treat her. I wouldn't marry the Duchesser Windsor,"[1] he said firmly, "unless I could take her to a hotel and give her something good to eat.

"I was raised thataway and there ain't a thing I can do about it. My old mother taught me how to do."

"Lucynell don't even know what a hotel is," the old woman muttered. "Listen here, Mr. Shiftlet," she said, sliding forward in her chair, "you'd be getting a permanent house and a deep well and the most innocent girl in the world. You don't need no money. Lemme tell you something: there ain't any place in the world for a poor disabled friendless drifting man."

The ugly words settled in Mr. Shiftlet's head like a group of buzzards in the top of a tree. He didn't answer at once. He rolled himself a cigarette and lit it and then he said in an even voice, "Lady, a man is divided into two parts, body and spirit."

The old woman clamped her gums together.

"A body and a spirit," he repeated. "The body, lady, is like a house: it don't go anywhere; but the spirit, lady, is like a automobile: always on the move, always . . ."

"Listen, Mr. Shiftlet," she said, "my well never goes dry and my house is always warm in the winter and there's no mortgage on a thing about this place. You can go to the court house and see for yourself. And yonder under that shed is a fine automobile." She laid the bait carefully. "You can have it painted by Saturday. I'll pay for the paint."

In the darkness, Mr. Shiftlet's smile stretched like a weary snake waking up by a fire. After a second he recalled himself and said, "I'm only saying a man's spirit means more to him than anything else. I would have to take my wife off for the weekend without no regards at all for cost. I got to follow where my spirit says to go."

---

1. **Duchesser Windsor,** the Duchess of Windsor (Wallis Warfield Simpson), the widow of the Duke of Windsor, who was King Edward VIII of England before renouncing the throne to marry Simpson, a commoner.

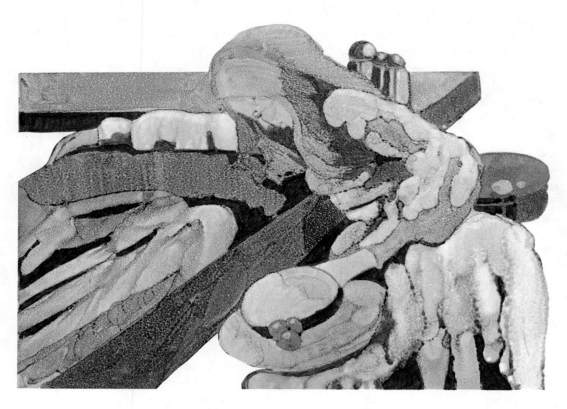

"I'll give you fifteen dollars for a weekend trip," the old woman said in a crabbed voice. "That's the best I can do."

"That wouldn't hardly pay for more than the gas and the hotel," he said. "It wouldn't feed her."

"Seventeen-fifty," the old woman said. "That's all I got so it isn't any use you trying to milk me. You can take a lunch."

Mr. Shiftlet was deeply hurt by the word "milk." He didn't doubt that she had more money sewed up in her mattress but he had already told her he was not interested in her money. "I'll make that do," he said and rose and walked off without treating with her further.

On Saturday the three of them drove into town in the car that the paint had barely dried on and Mr. Shiftlet and Lucynell were married in the Ordinary's office while the old woman witnessed. As they came out of the courthouse, Mr. Shiftlet began twisting his neck in his collar. He looked morose and bitter as if he had been insulted while someone held him. "That didn't satisfy me none," he said. "That was just something a woman in an office did, nothing but paper work and blood tests. What do they know about my blood? If they was to take my heart and cut it out," he said, "they wouldn't know a thing about me. It didn't satisfy me at all."

"It satisfied the law," the old woman said sharply.

"The law," Mr. Shiftlet said and spit. "It's the law that don't satisfy me."

He had painted the car dark green with a yellow band around it just under the windows. The three of them climbed in the front seat and the old woman said, "Don't Lucynell look pretty? Looks like a baby doll." Lucynell was dressed up in a white dress that her mother had uprooted from a trunk and there was a Panama hat on her head with a bunch of red wooden cherries on the brim. Every now and then her placid expression was changed by a sly isolated little thought like a shoot of green in the desert. "You got a prize!" the old woman said.

Mr. Shiftlet didn't even look at her.

They drove back to the house to let the old woman off and pick up the lunch. When they were ready to leave, she stood staring in the window of the car, with her fingers clenched around the glass. Tears began to seep sideways out of her eyes and run along the dirty creases in her face. "I ain't ever been parted with her for two days before," she said.

Mr. Shiftlet started the motor.

"And I wouldn't let no man have her but you because I seen you would do right. Good-by, Sugarbaby," she said, clutching at the sleeve of the white dress. Lucynell looked straight at her and didn't seem to see her there at all. Mr. Shiftlet eased the car forward so that she had to move her hands.

The early afternoon was clear and open and surrounded by pale blue sky. Although the car would go only thirty miles an hour, Mr. Shiftlet imagined a terrific climb and dip and swerve that went entirely to his head so that he forgot his morning bitterness. He had always wanted an automobile but he had never been able to afford one before. He drove very fast because he wanted to make Mobile by nightfall.

Occasionally he stopped his thought long enough to look at Lucynell in the seat beside him. She had eaten the lunch as soon as they were out of the yard and now she was pulling the cherries off the hat one by one and throwing them out the window. He became depressed in spite of the car. He had driven about a hundred miles when he decided that she must be hungry again and at the next small town they came to, he stopped in front of an aluminum-painted eating place called The Hot Spot and took her in and ordered her a plate of ham and grits. The ride had made her sleepy and as soon as she got up on the stool, she rested her head on the counter and shut her eyes. There was no one in The Hot Spot but Mr. Shiftlet and the boy behind the counter, a pale youth with a greasy rag hung over his shoulder. Before he could dish up the food, she was snoring gently.

"Give it to her when she wakes up," Mr. Shiftlet said. "I'll pay for it now."

The boy bent over her and stared at the long pink-gold hair and the half-shut sleeping eyes. Then he looked up and stared at Mr. Shiftlet. "She looks like an angel of Gawd," he murmured.

"Hitchhiker," Mr. Shiftlet explained. "I can't wait. I got to make Tuscaloosa."

The boy bent over again and very carefully touched his finger to a strand of the golden hair and Mr. Shiftlet left.

He was more depressed than ever as he drove on by himself. The late afternoon had grown hot and sultry and the country had flattened out. Deep in the sky a storm was preparing very slowly and without thunder as if it meant to drain every drop of air from the earth before it broke. There were times when Mr. Shiftlet preferred not to be alone. He felt too that a man with a car had a responsibility to others and he kept his eye out for a hitchhiker. Occasionally he saw a sign that warned: "Drive carefully. The life you save may be your own."

The narrow road dropped off on either side into dry fields and here and there a shack or a filling station stood in a clearing. The sun began to set directly in front of the automobile. It was a reddening ball that through his windshield was slightly flat on the bottom and top. He saw a boy in overalls and a gray hat standing on the edge of the road and he slowed the car down and stopped in front of him. The boy didn't have his hand raised to thumb the ride, he was only standing there, but he had a small cardboard suitcase and his hat was set on his head in a way to indicate that he had left somewhere for good. "Son," Mr. Shiftlet said, "I see you want a ride."

The boy didn't say he did or he didn't but he opened the door of the car and got in, and Mr. Shiftlet started driving again. The child held the suitcase on his lap and folded his arms on top of it. He turned his head and looked out the window away from Mr. Shiftlet. Mr. Shiftlet felt oppressed. "Son," he said after a minute, "I got the best old mother in the world so I reckon you only got the second best."

The boy gave him a quick dark glance and then turned his face back out the window.

"It's nothing so sweet," Mr. Shiftlet continued, "as a boy's mother. She taught him his first prayers at her knee, she give him love when no other would, she told him what was right and what wasn't, and she seen that he done the right thing. Son," he said, "I never rued a day in my life like the one I rued when I left that old mother of mine."

The boy shifted in his seat but he didn't look at Mr. Shiftlet. He unfolded his arms and put one hand on the door handle.

"My mother was a angel of Gawd," Mr. Shiftlet said in a very strained voice. "He took her from heaven and giver to me and I left her." His eyes were instantly clouded over with a mist of tears. The car was barely moving.

The boy turned angrily in the seat. "You go to the devil!" he cried. "My old woman is a flea bag and yours is a stinking pole cat!" and with that he flung the door open and jumped out with his suitcase into the ditch.

Mr. Shiftlet was so shocked that for about a hundred feet he drove along slowly with the door still open. A cloud, the exact color of the boy's hat and shaped like a turnip, had descended over the sun, and another, worse looking, crouched behind the car. Mr. Shiftlet felt that the rottenness of the world was about to engulf him. He raised his arm and let it fall again to his breast. "Oh Lord!" he prayed. "Break forth and wash the slime from this earth!"

The turnip continued slowly to descend. After a few minutes there was a guffawing peal of thunder from behind and fantastic raindrops, like tin-can tops, crashed over the rear of Mr. Shiftlet's car. Very quickly he stepped on the gas and with his stump sticking out the window he raced the galloping shower into Mobile. □□

Discussion

1. What is the attitude of Mrs. Crater toward her daughter?

2. What kind of a person has Mr. Shiftlet shown himself to be up to the time of his marriage with Lucynell?

3. What evidence is there that Mr. Shiftlet's conscience is bothering him after he abandons Lucynell in the eating place?

4. It is after Mr. Shiftlet has abandoned Lucynell that he sees the sign, "Drive carefully. The life you save may be your own." Discuss this episode and how the story's title might apply to Mr. Shiftlet.

Extension · Writing

Review *Mood* in the Handbook of Literary Terms. Select examples from "The Life You Save May Be Your Own" that you feel were especially effective in contributing to the mood of the selection.

Flannery O'Connor
1925 · 1964

A Southern writer noted for her Gothic stories and grotesque characters, Flannery O'Connor always considered herself a Christian writer whose faith was implicit in the stories she wrote. She was born in Georgia and after college there studied at the University of Iowa Writer's Workshop. Her first novel, *Wise Blood* (1952), has become a modern classic. It was followed by a collection of stories, *A Good Man Is Hard to Find* (1955), and a second novel, *The Violent Bear It Away* (1960).

OBSESSIONS

The Secret Life of Walter Mitty

James Thurber

We're going through!'' The Commander's voice was like thin ice breaking. He wore his full-dress uniform, with the heavily braided white cap pulled down rakishly over one cold gray eye. ''We can't make it, sir. It's spoiling for a hurricane, if you ask me.'' ''I'm not asking you, Lieutenant Berg,'' said the Commander. ''Throw on the power light! Rev her up to 8500! We're going through!'' The pounding of the cylinders increased: ta-pocketa-pocketa-pocketa-*pocketa-pocketa*. The Commander stared at the ice forming on the pilot window. He walked over and twisted a row of complicated dials. ''Switch on No. 8 auxiliary!'' he shouted. ''Switch on No. 8 auxiliary!'' repeated Lieutenant Berg. ''Full strength in No. 3 turret!'' shouted the Commander. ''Full strength in No. 3 turret!'' The crew, bending to their various tasks in the huge, hurtling eight-engined Navy hydroplane, looked at each other and grinned. ''The Old Man'll get us through,'' they said to one another. ''The Old Man ain't afraid of Hell!''

''Not so fast! You're driving too fast!'' said Mrs. Mitty. ''What are you driving so fast for?''

''Hmm?'' said Walter Mitty. He looked at his wife, in the seat beside him, with shocked astonishment. She seemed grossly unfamiliar, like a strange woman who had yelled at him in a crowd: ''You were up to fifty-five,'' she said. ''You know I don't like to go more than forty. You were up to fifty-five.'' Walter Mitty drove on toward Waterbury in silence, the roaring of the SN202 through the worst storm in twenty years of Navy flying fading in the remote, intimate airways of his mind. ''You're tensed up again,'' said Mrs. Mitty. ''It's one of your days. I wish you'd let Dr. Renshaw look you over.''

Walter Mitty stopped the car in front of the building where his wife went to have her hair done. ''Remember to get those overshoes while

Copyright 1943 James Thurber. Copyright © 1970 Helen Thurber. From MY WORLD AND WELCOME TO IT, published by Harcourt Brace Jovanovich, Inc. Originally printed in THE NEW YORKER. Also appearing in VINTAGE THURBER, Vol. I by James Thurber, copyright © 1963 Hamish Hamilton Ltd. Reprinted by permission.

I'm having my hair done," she said. "I don't need overshoes," said Mitty. She put her mirror back into her bag. "We've been all through that," she said, getting out of the car. "You're not a young man any longer." He raced the engine a little. "Why don't you wear your gloves? Have you lost your gloves?" Walter Mitty reached in a pocket and brought out the gloves. He put them on, but after she had turned and gone into the building and he had driven on to a red light, he took them off again. "Pick it up, brother!" snapped a cop as the light changed, and Mitty hastily pulled on his gloves and lurched ahead. He drove around the streets aimlessly for a time, and then he drove past the hospital on his way to the parking lot.

. . . "It's the millionaire banker, Wellington McMillan," said the pretty nurse. "Yes?" said Walter Mitty, removing his gloves slowly. "Who has the case?" "Dr. Renshaw and Dr. Benbow, but there are two specialists here, Dr. Remington from New York and Mr. Pritchard-Mitford from London. He flew over." A door opened down a long, cool corridor and Dr. Renshaw came out. He looked distraught and haggard. "Hello, Mitty," he said, "We're having the devil's own time with McMillan, the millionaire banker and close personal friend of Roosevelt. Obstreosis of the ductal tract. Tertiary.[1] Wish you'd take a look at him." "Glad to," said Mitty.

In the operating room there were whispered introductions: "Dr. Remington, Dr. Mitty. Mr. Pritchard-Mitford, Dr. Mitty." "I've read your book on streptothricosis," said Pritchard-Mitford, shaking hands. "A brilliant performance, sir." "Thank you," said Walter Mitty. "Didn't know you were in the States, Mitty," grumbled Remington. "Coals to Newcastle, bringing Mitford and me up here for a tertiary." "You are very kind," said Mitty. A huge, complicated machine, connected to the operating table, with many tubes and wires, began at this moment to go pocketa-pocketa-pocketa. "The new anesthetizer is giving way!" shouted an intern. "There is no one in the East who knows how to fix it!" "Quiet, man!" said Mitty, in a low, cool voice. He sprang to the machine, which was now going pocketa-pocketa-queep-pocketa-queep. He began fingering delicately a row of glistening dials. "Give me a fountain pen!" he snapped. Someone handed him a fountain pen. He pulled a faulty piston out of the machine and inserted the pen in its place. "That will hold for ten minutes," he said. "Get on with the operation." A nurse hurried over and whispered to Renshaw, and Mitty saw the man turn pale. "Coreopsis has set in," said Renshaw nervously. "If you would take over, Mitty?" Mitty looked at him and at the craven figure of Benbow, who drank, and at the grave, uncertain faces of the two great specialists. "If you wish," he said. They slipped a white gown on him; he adjusted a mask and drew on thin gloves; nurses handed him shining . . .

"Back it up, Mac! Look out for that Buick!" Walter Mitty jammed on the brakes. "Wrong lane, Mac," said the parking-lot attendant, looking at Mitty closely. "Gee. Yeh," muttered Mitty. He began cautiously to back out of the lane marked "Exit Only." "Leave her sit there," said the attendant. "I'll put her away." Mitty got out of the car. "Hey, better leave the key." "Oh," said Mitty, handing the man the ignition key. The attendant vaulted into the car, backed it up with insolent skill, and put it where it belonged.

They're so damn cocky, thought Walter Mitty, walking along Main Street; they think they know everything. Once he had tried to take his chains off, outside New Milford, and he had got them wound around the axles. A man had had to come out in a wrecking car and unwind them, a young, grinning garageman. Since then Mrs. Mitty always made him drive to a garage to have the chains taken off. The next time, he thought, I'll wear my right arm in a sling; they won't grin at me then. I'll have my right arm in a sling and they'll see I couldn't possibly take the chains off myself. He kicked at the slush on the

---

1. **Obstreosis of the ductal tract. Tertiary.** The diagnosis that the imaginary Dr. Renshaw is giving to Walter Mitty is complete nonsense.

sidewalk. "Overshoes," he said to himself, and he began looking for a shoe store.

When he came out into the street again, with the overshoes in a box under his arm, Walter Mitty began to wonder what the other thing was his wife had told him to get. She had told him twice, before they set out from their house for Waterbury. In a way he hated these weekly trips to town—he was always getting something wrong. Kleenex, he thought, Squibb's, razor blades? No. Toothpaste, toothbrush, bicarbonate, carborundum, initiative and referendum? He gave it up. But she would remember it. "Where's the what's-its-name?" she would ask. "Don't tell me you forgot the what's-its-name." A newsboy went by shouting something about the Waterbury trial.

. . . "Perhaps this will refresh your memory." The District Attorney suddenly thrust a heavy automatic at the quiet figure on the witness stand. "Have you ever seen this before?" Walter Mitty took the gun and examined it expertly. "This is my Webley-Vickers 50.80," he said calmly. An excited buzz ran around the courtroom. The judge rapped for order. "You are a crack shot with any sort of firearms, I believe?" said the District Attorney, insinuatingly. "Objection!" shouted Mitty's attorney. "We have shown that the defendant could not have fired the shot. We have shown that he wore his right arm in a sling on the night of the fourteenth of July." Walter Mitty raised his hand briefly and the bickering attorneys were stilled. "With any known make of gun," he said evenly, "I could have killed Gregory Fitzhurst at three hundred feet *with my left hand.*" Pandemonium broke loose in the courtroom. A woman's scream rose above the bedlam and suddenly a lovely, dark-haired girl was in Walter Mitty's arms. The District Attorney struck at her savagely. Without rising from his chair, Mitty let the man have it on the point of the chin. "You miserable cur!"

"Puppy biscuit," said Walter Mitty. He stopped walking and the buildings of Waterbury rose up out of the misty courtroom and sur-

rounded him again. A woman who was passing laughed. "He said 'Puppy biscuit,' " she said to her companion. "That man said 'Puppy biscuit' to himself." Walter Mitty hurried on. He went into an A. & P., not the first one he came to but a smaller one farther up the street. "I want some biscuit for small, young dogs," he said to the clerk. "Any special brand, sir?" The greatest pistol shot in the world thought a moment. "It says 'Puppies Bark for It' on the box," said Walter Mitty.

His wife would be through at the hairdresser's in fifteen minutes, Mitty saw in looking at his watch, unless they had trouble drying it; sometimes they had trouble drying it. She didn't like to get to the hotel first; she would want him to be there waiting for her as usual. He found a big leather chair in the lobby, facing a window, and he put the overshoes and the puppy biscuit on the floor beside it. He picked up an old copy of *Liberty* and sank down into the chair. "Can Germany Conquer the World Through the Air?" Walter Mitty looked at the pictures of bombing planes and of ruined streets.

. . . "The cannonading has got the wind up in young Raleigh, sir," said the sergeant. Captain Mitty looked up at him through tousled hair. "Get him to bed," he said wearily. "With the others. I'll fly alone." "But you can't, sir," said the sergeant anxiously. "It takes two men to handle that bomber and the Archies are pounding hell out of the air. Von Richtman's circus is between here and Saulier." "Somebody's got to get that ammunition dump," said Mitty. "I'm going over. Spot of brandy?" He poured a drink for the sergeant and one for himself. War thundered and whined around the dugout and battered at the door. There was a rending of wood and splinters flew through the room. "A bit of a near thing," said Captain Mitty carelessly. "The box barrage is closing in," said the sergeant. "We only live once, Sergeant," said Mitty, with his faint fleeting smile. "Or do we?" He poured another brandy and tossed it off. "I never see a man could hold his brandy like you, sir," said the sergeant. "Begging your pardon, sir." Captain Mitty stood up and strapped on his huge Webley-Vickers automatic. "It's forty kilometers through hell, sir," said the sergeant. Mitty finished one last brandy. "After all," he said softly, "what isn't?" The pounding of the cannon increased; there was the rat-tat-tatting of machine guns, and from somewhere came the menacing pocketa-pocketa-pocketa of the new flame throwers. Walter Mitty walked to the door of the dugout humming "Auprès de Ma Blonde."[2] He turned and waved to the sergeant. "Cheerio!" he said. . . .

Something struck his shoulder. "I've been looking all over this hotel for you," said Mrs. Mitty. "Why do you have to hide in this old chair? How did you expect me to find you?" "Things close in," said Walter Mitty vaguely. "What?" Mrs. Mitty said. "Did you get the what's-its-name? The puppy biscuit? What's in that box?" "Overshoes," said Mitty. "Couldn't you have put them on in the store?" "I was thinking," said Walter Mitty. "Does it ever occur to you that I am sometimes thinking?" She looked at him. "I'm going to take your temperature when I get you home," she said.

They went out through the revolving doors that made a faintly derisive whistling sound when you pushed them. It was two blocks to the parking lot. At the drugstore on the corner she said, "Wait here for me. I forgot something. I won't be a minute." She was more than a minute. Walter Mitty lighted a cigarette. It began to rain, rain with sleet in it. He stood up against the wall of the drugstore, smoking. . . . He put his shoulders back and his heels together. "To hell with the handkerchief," said Walter Mitty scornfully. He took one last drag on his cigarette and snapped it away. Then, with that faint, fleeting smile playing about his lips, he faced the firing squad; erect and motionless, proud and disdainful, Walter Mitty the Undefeated, inscrutable to the last. □□

---

2. **Auprès de Ma Blonde** (ō prä′də ma blon′də), title of a French song, "Near My Blonde."

Discussion

1. Describe the two Walter Mittys, that of the real world and that of fantasy.

2. When Mitty's wife asks him why he never wears his gloves, Mitty first puts them on, then takes them off, and then puts them on again. How does this behavior characterize him?

3. Give examples of the way Thurber connects the events of Walter Mitty's real life with the events of his imaginary life.

4. What purpose do Walter Mitty's dreams serve for him?

James Thurber 1894 · 1961

Probably the foremost American humorist of the twentieth century, Thurber was born and grew up in Columbus, Ohio, worked for a time as a newspaperman in Paris and New York, and became associated with *The New Yorker* magazine shortly after its founding in 1925. He remained a contributor until his death.

His pieces were collected and published in a series of books, including *The Seal in the Bedroom and Other Predicaments* (1932), and *My World—and Welcome to It* (1942).

He was a talented cartoonist as well, and often illustrated his own stories. He was especially good at bestowing personality upon dogs with a few simple strokes of the pen, as in *Men, Women, and Dogs* (1943).

Walter Mitty is one of the most beloved and best-known Thurber characters, and the story was made into a full-length film in 1949.

Philip Wedge

E. B. White

To the friends of Philip Wedge, his gradual withdrawal from human society was the cause of some wonderment. Most of them were bothered less by his having renounced the world than by their not knowing why. One explanation was that he had taken up with a woman. A few people said money had something to do with it.

Both explanations were absurd. I knew Wedge well, and got wind of some of the little matters that eventually drove him into a kind of retirement. For one thing, he had a curious feeling in regard to his nose, being often troubled with the suspicion that there was a black smudge on the side of it. This suspicion was usually groundless, but used to attack him suddenly, unsettling him and causing him embarrassment and physical discomfort. I have seen him, dining with a large company, twist quickly in his chair and point questioningly at his nose. Assured by the person next to him that the nose was spotless, he would remain uneasy and would close first one eye, then the other, in an attempt to peer downward and sideways at the suspected member. After almost throwing his eyeballs out of their sockets, he would dip his napkin fiercely in a tumbler and dab hard at his nose, reddening it and surprising the whole company.

That was only one thing that troubled him. He was also subject to the suspicion that he had feathers on his back. One of a group of persons in a drawing-room, he would without warning throw his right hand desperately over his left shoulder, and flick at his back, in real terror. This feeling was not without some basis in fact, for at one time the pillow in his bed had developed a leak and for a period of about a week he had found feathers here and there on his person. The pillow had been discarded, of course, but he seemed unable to forget the feathers, and never could believe he was quite without them.

Wedge had difficulty keeping appointments—a failing which further explains his reclusion. He was at heart a romantic fellow and had built up a strange myth about the telephone: he could not bear to think of its ringing when he was not there to answer it, lest the message be one which might change the whole course of his life. His modest apartment was on the fourth floor, and he once told me that he never left it—to keep a date or for any other reason—but that he felt, after shutting the door, that the phone was ringing. Sometimes the suspicion did not take hold of him until he was down three flights of stairs, when he would turn and spring like a goat back up the stairs, fumble madly with his key, and burst into the room to find all quiet. Often this furious ascent would so derange his clothes that he would have to make a complete change, and once or twice, he confided, it had so exhausted him that he had to lie down.

I can't help thinking that Wedge's pet turtle had something to do with his taking the veil. He kept the little beast in an old photograph-developer pan, and fed it bits of beef which he brought from restaurants as often as he remembered to. Unfortunately, he had never devised a satisfactory method of carrying the morsels home, but almost invariably wrapped them in his handkerchief when he thought no one was looking, and replaced the handkerchief in his hip-pocket. This would have been a decent enough expedient had Wedge always gone directly home from the restaurant, but frequently he was diverted, and I happen to know of several occasions when he pulled out his handkerchief—in the lobby of a theatre, in a club, in a cab—and out dropped beef on the floor. Rather than admit

"Philip Wedge" (pp. 209-214) from QUO VADIMUS? by E. B. White. Copyright 1929, 1957 by E. B. White. Originally appeared in THE NEW YORKER and reprinted by permission of Harper & Row, Publishers, Inc.

to owning a turtle, Wedge preferred to let the matter stand without any explanation; but it unnerved him, and people never understood.

He was a nervous person, anyway. I recall (now that I'm thinking about these things) a day, probably three years ago, when he and I were walking together down Sixth Avenue. As we passed a letter-box, Wedge dropped a letter in— a slight incident which I thought nothing of until, a block later, Wedge suddenly turned and darted back along the sidewalk, twisting and turning and looking from the rear very like a madman. When he reached the letter-box, he seized the slot and jiggled it viciously a dozen times, glancing in finally to see that it was empty. When he joined me again he seemed tired and spent. He told me, in a jerky, shy manner, that he frequently was bothered by the fear that his letter had not been properly posted, and found it necessary to rush back and make sure that it had dropped all the way down into the box.

I shall not call up all Wedge's peculiarities; yet I can hardly omit mention of his phobia about oranges and grapefruit. He delighted in the taste of citrus fruits, and preferred to eat them with a spoon rather than drink the juice; yet I know for a fact that he could not get halfway through an orange without imagining that he had swallowed a pit. The moment this thought took hold of him, he laid down his spoon and puckered his throat into a bad knot, trying to reclaim the imaginary object from his esophagus. This set him against oranges and disturbed his digestion. When other persons were present at table, their astonishment increased his agony.

For all the absurdity of these fears, I suspect Wedge would still not have isolated himself from society had it not been for another peculiarity of his—which I shall explain as delicately as I can. (He told me the main facts himself, so I am not guessing.) At various times in his life, Wedge had courted ladies, with rather a positive grace for so excitable a man. And of course, in going about, he had had occasion to kiss many of them— which he managed with more amiability than passion. By dint of confining his affectionate

regard to one lady at a time, and to none very long, he managed to come through his affairs with no very great remorse or embarrassment. Shortly before his renunciation of society, he was kissing a fine woman in a perfectly creditable manner when (possibly as a result of a phrase he had read somewhere and remembered) the suspicion overcame him that his consort had opened her eyes, in the midst of the kiss, and was calmly regarding him. There was no way definitely to confirm or disprove the suspicion, for Wedge felt that he was ethically unwarranted in opening his own eyes, as well as biologically incapable of it. Therefore, the suspicion remained to trouble him and make all further companionship with the opposite sex unthinkable.

He now lives quietly with his turtle. By divorcing his friends he has probably added to his tranquillity; and I suspect he hasn't changed much but still goes about dabbing his nose, whacking feathers from his back, rushing upstairs to a silent and scornful telephone, jiggling letter-boxes, choking over his orange, and pulling from his hip-pocket a handkerchief from which falls a little morsel of beef. I rather liked him.

□□

Discussion

1. Philip Wedge's withdrawal from society resulted from the fears that he developed over a period of time. On what are these fears based?

2. How do the fears affect Wedge's behavior?

3. After summing up the peculiar behavior of Wedge at the end of the story, the narrator concludes: "I rather liked him." (a) Why do you think he does? (b) How would *you* react to Wedge?

Extension · Writing

Think over all the interesting people you have known, read, or heard about, and select one whose behavior you found fascinating. Reconstruct from your memory the actions and incidents in which the character of this person seemed most fully revealed. Then try your hand at a brief character sketch. Change the name, the place, the date, and even the action or event if it will make the portrait you are painting more vivid.

E. B. White 1899 ·

Like James Thurber, E. B. White is a humorist who writes with serious purpose.

Born in Mt. Vernon, New York, White early in his career started contributing to *The New Yorker,* becoming responsible for the opening section, "Talk of the Town." His books include *One Man's Meat* (1942), and *The Second Tree from the Corner* (1954). White has also written children's books, the most notable of which is *Charlotte's Web* (1952), a book as popular with adults as with children.

Tom Edison's Shaggy Dog

Kurt Vonnegut, Jr.

Two old men sat on a park bench one morning in the sunshine of Tampa, Florida—one trying doggedly to read a book he was plainly enjoying while the other, Harold K. Bullard, told him the story of his life in the full, round, head tones of a public address system. At their feet lay Bullard's Labrador retriever, who further tormented the aged listener by probing his ankles with a large, wet nose.

Bullard, who had been, before he retired, successful in many fields, enjoyed reviewing his important past. But he faced the problem that complicates the lives of cannibals—namely: that a single victim cannot be used over and over. Anyone who had passed the time of day with him and his dog refused to share a bench with them again.

So Bullard and his dog set out through the park each day in quest of new faces. They had had good luck this morning, for they had found this stranger right away, clearly a new arrival in Florida, still buttoned up tight in heavy serge, stiff collar and necktie, and with nothing better to do than read.

"Yes," said Bullard, rounding out the first hour of his lecture, "made and lost five fortunes in my time."

"So you said," said the stranger, whose name Bullard had neglected to ask. "Easy, boy. No, no, no, boy," he said to the dog, who was growing more aggressive toward his ankles.

"Oh? Already told you that, did I?" said Bullard.

"Twice."

"Two in real estate, one in scrap iron, and one in oil and one in trucking."

"So you said."

"I did? Yes, guess I did. Two in real estate, one in scrap iron, one in oil, and one in trucking. Wouldn't take back a day of it."

"No, I suppose not," said the stranger. "Pardon me, but do you suppose you could move your dog somewhere else? He keeps——"

"Him?" said Bullard, heartily. "Friendliest dog in the world. Don't need to be afraid of him."

"I'm not afraid of him. It's just that he drives me crazy, sniffing at my ankles."

"Plastic," said Bullard, chuckling.

"What?"

"Plastic. Must be something plastic on your garters. By golly, I'll bet it's those little buttons. Sure as we're sitting here, those buttons must be plastic. That dog is nuts about plastic. Don't know why that is, but he'll sniff it out and find it if there's a speck around. Must be a deficiency in his diet, though, by gosh, he eats better than I do. Once he chewed up a whole plastic humidor. Can you beat it? *That's* the business I'd go into now, by glory, if the pill rollers hadn't told me to let up, to give the old ticker a rest."

"You could tie the dog to that tree over there," said the stranger.

"Tom Edison's Shaggy Dog." Copyright 1953 by Kurt Vonnegut, Jr. Originally published in COLLIER'S. Reprinted from the book WELCOME TO THE MONKEY HOUSE by Kurt Vonnegut, Jr. by permission of Delacorte Press/Seymour Lawrence and Jonathan Cape Ltd.

"I get so darn sore at all the youngsters these days!" said Bullard. "All of 'em mooning around about no frontiers any more. There never have been so many frontiers as there are today. You know what Horace Greeley[1] would say today?"

"His nose is wet," said the stranger, and he pulled his ankles away, but the dog humped forward in patient pursuit. "Stop it, boy!"

"His wet nose shows he's healthy," said Bullard. " 'Go plastic, young man!' That's what Greeley'd say. 'Go atom, young man!' "

The dog had definitely located the plastic buttons on the stranger's garters and was cocking his head one way and another, thinking out ways of bringing his teeth to bear on those delicacies.

"Scat!" said the stranger.

" 'Go electronic, young man!' " said Bullard. "Don't talk to me about no opportunity any more. Opportunity's knocking down every door in the country, trying to get in. When I was young, a man had to go out and find opportunity and drag it home by the ears. Nowadays——"

"Sorry," said the stranger, evenly. He slammed his book shut, stood and jerked his ankle away from the dog. "I've got to be on my way. So good day, sir."

He stalked across the park, found another bench, sat down with a sigh and began to read. His respiration had just returned to normal, when he felt the wet sponge of the dog's nose on his ankles again.

"Oh—it's you!" said Bullard, sitting down beside him. "He was tracking you. He was on the scent of something, and I just let him have his head. What'd I tell you about plastic?" He looked about contentedly. "Don't blame you for moving on. It was stuffy back there. No shade to speak of and not a sign of a breeze."

"Would the dog go away if I bought him a humidor?" said the stranger.

"Pretty good joke, pretty good joke," said Bullard, amiably. Suddenly he clapped the stranger on his knee. "Sa-ay, you aren't in plastics, are you? Here I've been blowing off about plastics, and for all I know that's your line."

"My line?" said the stranger crisply, laying down his book. "Sorry—I've never had a line. I've been a drifter since the age of nine, since Edison set up his laboratory next to my home, and showed me the intelligence analyzer."

"Edison?" said Bullard. "Thomas Edison, the inventor?"

"If you want to call him that, go ahead," said the stranger.

"If I *want* to call him that?"—Bullard guffawed—"I guess I just will! Father of the light bulb and I don't know what all."

"If you want to think he invented the light bulb, go ahead. No harm in it." The stranger resumed his reading.

"Say, what is this?" said Bullard, suspiciously. "You pulling my leg? What's this about an intelligence analyzer? I never heard of that."

"Of course you haven't," said the stranger. "Mr. Edison and I promised to keep it a secret. I've never told anyone. Mr. Edison broke his promise and told Henry Ford, but Ford made him promise not to tell anybody else—for the good of humanity."

Bullard was entranced. "Uh, this intelligence analyzer," he said, "it analyzed intelligence, did it?"

"It was an electric butter churn," said the stranger.

"Seriously now," Bullard coaxed.

"Maybe it *would* be better to talk it over with someone," said the stranger. "It's a terrible thing to keep bottled up inside me, year in and year out. But how can I be sure that it won't go any further?"

"My word as a gentleman," Bullard assured him.

"I don't suppose I could find a stronger guarantee than that, could I?" said the stranger, judiciously.

"There is no stronger guarantee," said Bullard, proudly. "Cross my heart and hope to die!"

"Very well." The stranger leaned back and

---

1. *Horace Greeley* (1811–1872), U.S. journalist, editor, and political leader who advised people to seek opportunities in the West with his often quoted "Go West, young man, go West."

closed his eyes, seeming to travel backward through time. He was silent for a full minute, during which Bullard watched with respect.

"It was back in the fall of eighteen seventy-nine," said the stranger at last, softly. "Back in the village of Menlo Park, New Jersey. I was a boy of nine. A young man we all thought was a wizard had set up a laboratory next door to my home, and there were flashes and crashes inside, and all sorts of scary goings on. The neighborhood children were warned to keep away, not to make any noise that would bother the wizard.

"I didn't get to know Edison right off, but his dog Sparky and I got to be steady pals. A dog a whole lot like yours, Sparky was, and we used to wrestle all over the neighborhood. Yes, sir, your dog is the image of Sparky."

"Is that so?" said Bullard, flattered.

"Gospel," replied the stranger. "Well, one day Sparky and I were wrestling around, and we wrestled right up to the door of Edison's laboratory. The next thing I knew, Sparky had pushed me in through the door, and bam! I was sitting on the laboratory floor, looking up at Mr. Edison himself."

"Bet he was sore," said Bullard, delighted.

"You can bet I was scared," said the stranger. "I thought I was face to face with Satan himself. Edison had wires hooked to his ears and running down to a little black box in his lap! I started to scoot, but he caught me by my collar and made me sit down.

" 'Boy,' said Edison, 'it's always darkest before the dawn. I want you to remember that.'

" 'Yes, sir,' I said.

" 'For over a year, my boy,' Edison said to me, 'I've been trying to find a filament that will last in an incandescent lamp. Hair, string, splinters—nothing works. So while I was trying to

think of something else to try, I started tinkering with another idea of mine, just letting off steam. I put this together,' he said, showing me the little black box. 'I thought maybe intelligence was just a certain kind of electricity, so I made this intelligence analyzer here. It works! You're the first one to know about it, my boy. But I don't know why you shouldn't be. It will be your generation that will grow up in the glorious new era when people will be as easily graded as oranges.' "

"I don't believe it!" said Bullard.

"May I be struck by lightning this very instant!" said the stranger. "And it did work, too. Edison had tried out the analyzer on the men in his shop, without telling them what he was up to. The smarter a man was, by gosh, the farther the needle on the indicator in the little black box swung to the right. I let him try it on me, and the needle just lay where it was and trembled. But dumb as I was, then is when I made my one and only contribution to the world. As I say, I haven't lifted a finger since."

"Whadja do?" said Bullard, eagerly.

"I said, 'Mr. Edison, sir, let's try it on the dog.' And I wish you could have seen the show that dog put on when I said it! Old Sparky barked and howled and scratched to get out. When he saw we meant business, that he wasn't going to get out, he made a beeline right for the intelligence analyzer and knocked it out of Edison's hands. But we cornered him, and Edison held him down while I touched the wires to his ears. And would you believe it, that needle sailed clear across the dial, way past a little red pencil mark on the dial face!"

"The dog busted it," said Bullard.

" 'Mr. Edison, sir,' I said, 'what's that red mark mean?'

" 'My boy,' said Edison, 'it means that the instrument is broken, because that red mark is me.' "

"I'll say it was broken," said Bullard.

The stranger said gravely, "But it wasn't broken. No, sir. Edison checked the whole thing, and it was in apple-pie order. When Edison told me that, it was then that Sparky, crazy to get out, gave himself away."

"How?" said Bullard, suspiciously.

"We really had him locked in, see? There were three locks on the door—a hook and eye, a bolt, and a regular knob and latch. That dog stood up, unhooked the hook, pushed the bolt back and had the knob in his teeth when Edison stopped him."

"No!" said Bullard.

"Yes!" said the stranger, his eyes shining. "And then is when Edison showed me what a great scientist he was. He was willing to face the truth, no matter how unpleasant it might be.

" 'So!' said Edison to Sparky. 'Man's best friend, huh? Dumb animal, huh?'

"That Sparky was a caution. He pretended not to hear. He scratched himself and bit fleas and went around growling at ratholes—anything to get out of looking Edison in the eye.

" 'Pretty soft, isn't it, Sparky?' said Edison. 'Let somebody else worry about getting food, building shelters and keeping warm, while you sleep in front of a fire or go chasing after the girls or raise hell with the boys. No mortgages, no politics, no war, no work, no worry. Just wag the old tail or lick a hand, and you're all taken care of.'

" 'Mr. Edison,' I said, 'do you mean to tell me that dogs are smarter than people?'

" 'Smarter?' said Edison. 'I'll tell the world! And what have I been doing for the past year? Slaving to work out a light bulb so dogs can play at night!'

" 'Look, Mr. Edison,' said Sparky, 'why not——' "

"Hold on!" roared Bullard.

"Silence!" shouted the stranger, triumphantly. " 'Look, Mr. Edison,' said Sparky, 'why not keep quiet about this? It's been working out to everybody's satisfaction for hundreds of thousands of years. Let sleeping dogs lie. You forget all about it, destroy the intelligence analyzer, and I'll tell you what to use for a lamp filament.' "

"Hogwash!" said Bullard, his face purple.

The stranger stood. "You have my solemn word as a gentleman. That dog rewarded *me* for my silence with a stock-market tip that made me independently wealthy for the rest of my days. And the last words that Sparky ever spoke were to Thomas Edison. 'Try a piece of carbonized cotton thread,' he said. Later, he was torn to bits by a pack of dogs that had gathered outside the door, listening."

The stranger removed his garters and handed them to Bullard's dog. "A small token of esteem, sir, for an ancestor of yours who talked himself to death. Good day." He tucked his book under his arm and walked away. □□

Discussion

1. Why does the stranger grow restless in the company of Harold K. Bullard and his dog?

2. When the stranger tries to leave Bullard, by moving to another bench, Bullard and his dog follow. How does Bullard explain his following the stranger?

3. When asked his line, the stranger answers: "I've never had a line. I've been a drifter since the age of nine, since Edison set up his laboratory next to my home, and showed me the intelligence analyzer." (a) How does Bullard react to this speech? (b) Are there any clues in the speech that suggest it is not to be taken at face value by the reader? (c) The speech may be seen as a turning of the tables in the story. Explain.

4. After the needle of the "intelligence analyzer" had "sailed across the dial" for Edison's dog, how did Sparky "prove" his intelligence?

5. (a) When does Bullard begin to see that his leg is being pulled and that for a change he has become the victim of an exaggerated tale? (b) What is the stranger's reaction to Bullard's skepticism?

Extension · Speaking

Assume that you have run into a Harold K. Bullard type on a park bench and that you must start talking in order to prevent him from boring you to death. Invent a "shaggy dog" story (some openers are suggested below) that will keep your acquaintance off-balance long enough for you to make your escape. Present your story in front of the class.

My pet fly was learning to fly in loops . . .

There is this strange frog that lives in the backyard that sings . . .

Some university lab has finally gotten a porpoise and a chimp talking to each other . . .

At the supermarket, the frozen peas were telling the string beans . . .

My stuffed bear wanted to go to the stuffed animal circus . . .

Kurt Vonnegut 1922 ·

Vonnegut fought in World War II and was taken prisoner by the Germans and held in Dresden, a city that was destroyed in a fire-bombing by the Allied Air Force. Vonnegut and his fellow prisoners were being held underground in meat storage vaults and survived the fire-bombing. But the event scarred his imagination and shaped his fiction, and became the central event of his novel *Slaughterhouse Five* (1969).

Vonnegut borrowed many of his writing techniques from science fiction and some from advertising, a field he tried before turning to fiction. His early novel, *Cat's Cradle* (1963), became an underground favorite with American youth. Other books like *Mother Night* (1966) and *Welcome to the Monkey House* (1968) established his reputation as an important contemporary fiction writer. His work is noted for its grim humor, as well as its breezy style.

Gwilan's Harp

Ursula K. Le Guin

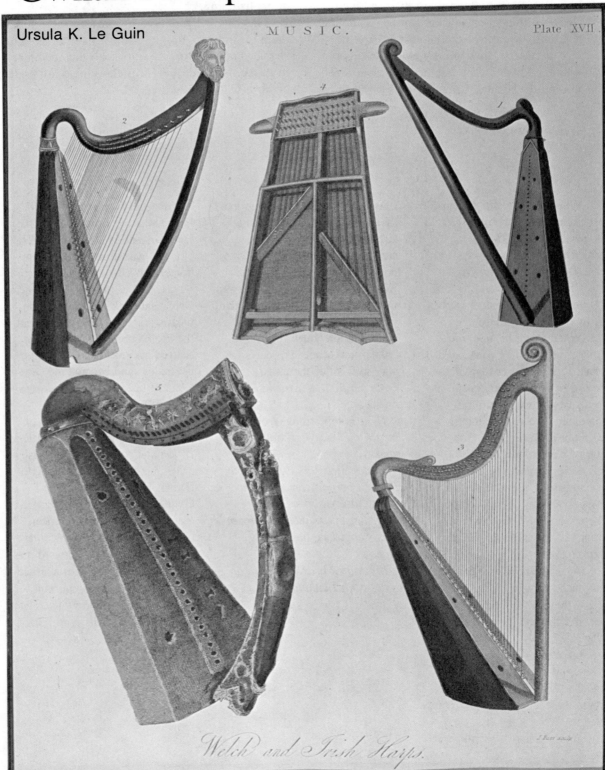

Encyclopaedia Londinensis, 1818, Courtesy of the Art Institute of Chicago, Gift of Mrs. Charles H. Swift.

Welch and Irish Harps.

The harp had come to Gwilan from her mother, and so had her mastery of it, people said. "Ah," they said when Gwilan played, "you can tell, that's Diera's touch," just as their parents had said when Diera played, "Ah, that's the true Penlin touch!" Gwilan's mother had had the harp from Penlin, a musician's dying gift to the worthiest of pupils. From a musician's hands Penlin too had received it; never had it been sold or bartered for, nor any value put upon it that can be said in numbers. A princely and most incredible instrument it was for a poor harper to own. The shape of it was perfection, and every part was strong and fine: the wood as hard and smooth as bronze, the fittings of ivory and silver. The grand curves of the frame bore silver mountings chased with long intertwining lines that became waves and the waves became leaves, and the eyes of gods and stags looked out from among the leaves that became waves and the waves became lines again. It was the work of great craftsmen, you could see that at a glance, and the longer you looked the clearer you saw it. But all this beauty was practical, obedient, shaped to the service of sound. The sound of Gwilan's harp was water running and rain and sunlight on the water, waves breaking and the foam on the brown sands, forests, the leaves and branches of the forest and the shining eyes of gods and stags among the leaves when the wind blows in the valleys. It was all that and none of that. When Gwilan played, the harp made music; and what is music but a little wrinkling of the air?

Play she did, wherever they wanted her. Her singing voice was true but had no sweetness, so when it was songs and ballads she accompanied the singers. Weak voices were borne up by her playing, fine voices gained a glory from it; the loudest, proudest singers might keep still a verse to hear her play alone. She played with flute and reed-flute and tambour, and the music made for the harp to play alone, and the music that sprang up of itself when her fingers touched the strings. At weddings and festivals it was, "Gwilan will be here to play," and at music-day competitions, "When will Gwilan play?"

She was young; her hands were iron and her touch was silk; she could play all night and the next day too. She travelled from valley to valley, from town to town, stopping here and staying there and moving on again with other musicians on their wanderings. They walked, or a wagon was sent for them, or they got a lift on a farmer's cart. However they went, Gwilan carried her harp in its silk and leather case at her back or in her hands. When she rode she rode with the harp and when she walked she walked with the harp and when she slept, no, she didn't sleep with the harp, but it was there where she could reach out and touch it. She was not jealous of it, and would change instruments with another harper gladly; it was a great pleasure to her when at last they gave her back her own, saying with sober envy, "I never played so fine an instrument." She kept it clean, the mountings polished and strung it with the harp strings made by old Uliad, which cost as much apiece as a whole set of common harp strings. In the heat of summer she carried it in the shade of her body; in the bitter winter it shared her cloak. In a firelit hall she did not sit with it very near the fire, nor yet too far away, for changes of heat and cold would change the voice of it, and perhaps harm the frame. She did not look after herself with half the care. Indeed she saw no need to. She knew there were other harpers, and would be other harpers; most not as good, some better. But the harp was the best. There had not been and there would not be a better. Delight and service were due and fitting to it. She was not its owner but its player. It was her music, her joy, her life, the noble instrument.

She was young; she travelled from town to town; she played *A Fine Long Life* at weddings and *The Green Leaves* at festivals. There were funerals, with the burial feast, the singing of elegies, and Gwilan to play the Lament of Orioth, the music that crashes and cries out like the sea and the sea birds, bringing relief and a

"Gwilan's Harp" by Ursula K. Le Guin, REDBOOK, May 1977. Copyright © 1977 by Ursula K. Le Guin. Reprinted by permission of the author and the author's agent, Virginia Kidd.

burst of tears to the grief-dried heart. There were music-days, with a rivalry of harpers and a shrilling of fiddlers and a mighty outshouting of tenors. She went from town to town in sun and rain, the harp on her back or in her hands. So she was going one day to the yearly music-day at Comin, and the landowner of Torm Vale was giving her a lift; a man who so loved music that he had traded a good cow for a bad horse, since the cow would not take him where he could hear music played. It was he and Gwilan in a rickety cart, and the lean-necked roan stepping out down the steep, sunlit road from Torm.

A bear in the forest by the road, or a bear's ghost, or the shadow of a hawk: the horse shied half across the road. Torm had been discussing music deeply with Gwilan, waving his hands to conduct a choir of voices, and the reins went flipping out of those startled hands. The horse jumped like a cat, and ran. At the sharp curve of the road the cart swung round and smashed against the rocky cutting. A wheel leapt free and rolled, rocking like a top, for a few yards. The roan went plunging and sliding down the road with half the wrecked cart dragging behind, and was gone, and the road lay silent in the sunlight between the forest trees.

Torm had been thrown from the cart, and lay stunned for a minute or two.

Gwilan had clutched the harp to her when the horse shied, but had lost hold of it in the smash. The cart had tipped over and dragged on it. It was in its case of leather and embroidered silk, but when, one-handed, she got the case out from under the wheel and opened it, she did not take out a harp, but a piece of wood, and another piece, and a tangle of strings, and a sliver of ivory, and a twisted shell of silver chased with lines and leaves and eyes, held by a silver nail to a fragment of the frame.

It was six months without playing after that, since her arm had broken at the wrist. The wrist healed well enough, but there was no mending the harp; and by then the landowner of Torm had asked her if she would marry him, and she had said yes. Sometimes she wondered why she had said yes, having never thought much of marriage before, but if she looked steadily into her own mind she saw the reason why. She saw Torm on the road in the sunlight kneeling by the broken harp, his face all blood and dust, and he was weeping. When she looked at that she saw that the time for rambling and roving was over and gone. One day is the day for moving on, and overnight, the next day, there is no more good in moving on, because you have come where you were going to.

Gwilan brought to the marriage a gold piece, which had been the prize last year at Four Valleys music-day; she had sewn it to her bodice as a brooch, because where on earth could you spend a gold piece. She also had two silver pieces, five coppers, and a good winter cloak. Torm contributed house and household, fields and forests, four tenant farmers even poorer than himself, twenty hens, five cows and forty sheep.

They married in the old way, by themselves, over the spring where the stream began, and came back and told the household. Torm had never suggested a wedding, with singing and harp-playing, never a word of all that. He was a man you could trust, Torm was.

What began in pain, in tears, was never free from the fear of pain. The two of them were gentle to each other. Not that they lived together thirty years without some quarreling. Two rocks sitting side by side would get sick of each other in thirty years, and who knows what they say now and then when nobody is listening. But if people trust each other they can grumble, and a good bit of grumbling takes the fuel from wrath. Their quarrels went up and burned out like bits of paper, leaving nothing but a feather of ash, a laugh in bed in the dark. Torm's land never gave more than enough, and there was no money saved. But it was a good house, and the sunlight was sweet on those high stony fields. There were two sons, who grew up into cheerful sensible men. One had a taste for roving, and the other was a farmer born; but neither had any gift of music.

Gwilan never spoke of wanting another harp.

But about the time her wrist was healed, old Uliad had a travelling musician bring her one on loan; when he had an offer to buy it at its worth, he sent for it back again. At that time Torm would have it that there was money from selling three good heifers to the landowner of Comin High Farm, and that the money should buy a harp, which it did. A year or two later an old friend, a flute-player still on his travels and rambles, brought her a harp from the south as a present. The three-heifers harp was a common instrument, plain and heavy; the Southern harp was delicately carved and gilt, but cranky to tune and thin of voice. Gwilan could draw sweetness from the one and strength from the other. When she picked up a harp, or spoke to a child, it obeyed her.

She played at all festivities and funerals in the neighborhood, and with the musician's fees she bought good strings; not Uliad's strings, though, for Uliad was in his grave before her second child was born. If there was a music-day nearby, she went to it with Torm. She would not play in the competitions, not for fear of losing but because she was not a harper now, and if they did not know it, she did. So they had her judge the competitions, which she did well and mercilessly. Often in the early years musicians would stop by on their travels, and stay two or three nights at Torm; with them she would play the Hunts of Orioth, the Dances of Cail, the difficult and learned music of the North, and learn from them the new songs. Even on winter evenings there was music in the house of Torm: she playing the harp—usually the three-heifers one, sometimes the fretful Southerner—and Torm's good tenor voice, and the boys singing, first in sweet treble, later on in husky, unreliable baritone; one of the farm's men was a lively fiddler; and the shepherd Keth, when he was there, played on the pipes, though he never could tune them to anyone else's note. "It's our own music-day tonight," Gwilan would say. "Put another log on the fire, Torm, and sing *The Green Leaves* with me, and the boys will take the descant."

Her wrist that had been broken grew a little stiff as the years went on; then the arthritis came into her hands. The work she did in house and farm was not easy work. But then who, looking at a hand, would say it was made to do easy work? You can see from the look of it that it is meant to do difficult things, that it is the noble, willing servant of the heart and mind. But the best servants get clumsy as the years go on. Gwilan could still play the harp, but not as well as she had played, and she did not much like half-measures. So the two harps hung on the wall, though she kept them tuned. About that time the younger son went wandering off to see what things looked like in the north, and the elder married and brought his bride to Torm. Old Keth was found dead up on the mountain in the spring rain, his dog crouched silent by him and the sheep nearby. And the drouth came, and the good year, and the poor year, and there was food to eat and to be cooked and clothes to wear and to be washed, poor year or good year. In the depth of a winter Torm took ill. He went from a cough to a high fever to quietness, and died while Gwilan sat beside him.

Thirty years, how can you say how long that is, and yet no longer than the saying of it: thirty years. How can you say how heavy the weight of thirty years is, and yet you can hold all of them together in your hand lighter than a bit of ash, briefer than a laugh in the dark. The thirty years began in pain; they passed in peace, contentment. But they did not end there. They ended where they began.

Gwilan got up from her chair and went into the hearth room. The rest of the household were asleep. In the light of her candle she saw the two harps hung against the wall, the three-heifers harp and the gilded Southern harp, the dull music and the false music. She thought, "I'll take them down at last and smash them on the hearthstone, crush them till they're only bits of wood and tangles of wire, like my harp." But she did not. She could not play them at all any more; her hands were far too stiff. It is silly to smash an instrument you cannot even play.

"There is no instrument left that I can play," Gwilan thought, and the thought hung in her mind for a while like a long chord, till she knew the notes that made it. "I thought my harp was myself. But it was not. It was destroyed, I was not. I thought Torm's wife was myself, but she was not. He is dead, I am not. I have nothing left at all now but myself. The wind blows from the valley, and there's a voice on the wind, a bit of a tune. Then the wind falls, or changes. The work has to be done, and we did the work. It's their turn now for that, the children. There's nothing left for me to do but sing. I never could sing. But you play the instrument you have."

So she stood by the cold hearth and sang the melody of Orioth's Lament. The people of the household wakened in their beds and heard her singing, all but Torm; but he knew that tune already. The untuned strings of the harps hung on the wall wakened and answered softly, voice to voice, like eyes that shine among the leaves when the wind is blowing. □□

Discussion

1. On what various occasions does Gwilan play the harp?

2. (a) Why does Gwilan decide to marry Torm? (b) What does the author mean when she states that such a decision indicates "you have come where you were going to" (154 b, line 10)?

3. (a) How would you describe Gwilan and Torm's marriage? (b) What is meant by the statement, "a good bit of grumbling takes the fuel from wrath" (154 b, 3)? (c) Reread 155b, 1. In what sense could it be said of their thirty years of marriage, "They ended where they began"?

4. This might be viewed as a story of a woman's life in terms of the harps she plays and the music she makes. Explain how each of the following represents a stage in Gwilan's life: (a) the first harp—a strong, beautiful, family heirloom which is eventually destroyed; (b) the "three-heifers harp"—a plain, common instrument purchased by Torm with his farm savings; (c) Gwilan's sons' singing—"first in sweet treble, later on in husky, unreliable baritone"; (d) Gwilan's observation, "There is no instrument left that I can play"; (e) her decision, "There's nothing left for me to do but sing."

5. At the end of the story, Gwilan states: "But you play the instrument you have." (a) How does this observation apply to Gwilan? (b) In what sense could this statement be said to apply to life in general?

Extension · Writing

Le Guin describes music in terms of "water running," "waves breaking," leaves blowing in the wind, and "a little wrinkling of the air." (a) Explain whether you think her choice of images effectively portrays the idea of music. (b) Imagine that you were asked to describe music to a deaf person. What images would you use to convey your own ideas of music. (Remember that in your written description you must appeal to senses other than that of sound.)

Ursula K. Le Guin 1929 ·

Originally, Le Guin's interests were in the French language, and she majored in this subject while at Radcliffe College. However, her literary talents soon came to dominate her career.

At first, she wrote only science fiction and was very popular. But fantasy came more and more to be her major interest, and today she is recognized as one of the top imaginative writers in America.

Le Guin reads "Gwilan's Harp" on a recording released in 1977 by Caedmon Records (# TC 1556).

The Ballad of the Harp-Weaver

Edna St. Vincent Millay

During the Middle Ages the stories of a community were in the oral tradition; a domestic tragedy, a heroic deed, or perhaps a tale of magic, of the supernatural—all became the material for a local poet from which to fashion a ballad. These ballads were meant to be sung.

In England, during the eighteenth and early nineteenth centuries some of the romantic poets adopted the ballad form. (Such imitations are of known authorship and are called literary ballads.) In America, the form was first used during the Revolution to tell the story of the war and the feelings of the people about it. There followed ballads of the pioneer, the cowboy, the homesteader, and many other people.

Among twentieth-century American poets who used the form to tell a story is Edna St. Vincent Millay. As you read her "Ballad of the Harp-Weaver," keep in mind Le Guin's "Gwilan's Harp." How are the two selections alike? What are the time and place settings? How are the scenes in each made vivid? What kinds of imagery do the writers use? What is *mystic* about each of the selections? Do you think one form is more effective than the other in telling stories such as these? Could "Gwilan's Harp" be retold in ballad form? Would the "Ballad of the Harp-Weaver" make a good short story?

"Son," said my mother,
  When I was knee-high,
"You've need of clothes to
    cover you,
And not a rag have I.

5 "There's nothing in the house
  To make a boy breeches,
Nor shears to cut a cloth with
  Nor thread to take stitches.

"There's nothing in the house
10   But a loaf-end of rye,
And a harp with a woman's
    head
    Nobody will buy,"
  And she began to cry.

That was in the early fall.
15   When came the late fall,
"Son," she said, "the sight of
    you
  Makes your mother's blood
    crawl—

"Little skinny shoulder blades
  Sticking through your
    clothes!
20 And where you'll get a jacket
    from
  God above knows.

"It's lucky for me, lad,
  Your daddy's in the ground
And can't see the way I let
25   His son go around!"
  And she made a queer
    sound.

That was in the late fall.
  When the winter came,
I'd not a pair of breeches
30   Nor a shirt to my name.

I couldn't go to school,
  Or out of doors to play.
And all the other little boys
  Passed our way.

35 "Son," said my mother,
  "Come, climb into my lap,
And I'll chafe your little bones
  While you take a nap."

And, oh, but we were silly
40   For half an hour or more,
Me with my long legs
  Dragging on the floor,

A-rock-rock-rocking
  To a mother-goose rhyme!
45 Oh, but we were happy
  For half an hour's time!

But there was I, a great boy,
  And what would folks say
To hear my mother singing me
50   To sleep all day,
  In such a daft way?

From COLLECTED POEMS, Harper & Row. Copyright 1922, 1950 by Edna St. Vincent Millay. Reprinted by permission of Norma Millay Ellis.

Men say the winter
   Was bad that year;
Fuel was scarce,
55   And food was dear.

A wind with a wolf's head
   Howled about our door,
And we burned up the chairs
   And sat upon the floor.

60 All that was left us
   Was a chair we couldn't
      break,
And the harp with a woman's
      head
   Nobody would take,
   For song or pity's sake.

65 The night before Christmas
   I cried with the cold,
I cried myself to sleep
   Like a two-year-old.

And in the deep night
70   I felt my mother rise,
And stare down upon me
   With love in her eyes.

I saw my mother sitting
   On the one good chair,
75 A light falling on her
   From I couldn't tell where,

Looking nineteen,
   And not a day older,
And the harp with a woman's
      head
80   Leaned against her
      shoulder.

Her thin fingers, moving
   In the thin, tall strings,
Were weav-weav-weaving
   Wonderful things.

85 Many bright threads,
   From where I couldn't see,
Were running through the
      harp-strings
   Rapidly,

And gold threads whistling
90   Through my mother's hand.
I saw the web grow,
   And the pattern expand.

She wove a child's jacket,
   And when it was done
95 She laid it on the floor
   And wove another one.

She wove a red cloak
   So regal to see,
"She's made it for a king's
      son,"
100   I said, "and not for me."
   But I knew it was for me.

She wove a pair of breeches
   Quicker than that!
She wove a pair of boots
105   And a little cocked hat.

She wove a pair of mittens,
   She wove a little blouse,
She wove all night
   In the still, cold house.

110 She sang as she worked,
   And the harp-strings spoke;
Her voice never faltered,
   And the thread never broke.
   And when I awoke—

115 There sat my mother
   With the harp against her
      shoulder,
Looking nineteen
   And not a day older,

A smile about her lips,
120   And a light about her head,
And her hands in the harp-
      strings
   Frozen dead.

And piled up beside her
   And toppling to the skies,
125 Were the clothes of a king's
      son,
   Just my size.

Extension · Writing

Suppose that you answered "yes" to the questions "Could 'Gwilan's Harp' be retold in ballad form?" "Would the 'Ballad of the Harp-Weaver' make a good short story?" Select one of the two to retell. Write a paragraph or two establishing setting for "The Ballad of the Harp-Weaver" or write two or three ballad stanzas beginning the story of "Gwilan's Harp."

Emergency Society

Uta Frith

It was emergency time again. Everybody got together their red-and-white-striped gear, their heart-shaped first aid boxes, their miniature emergency weapons kits. Some people also reached down such extras as umbrellas, gas masks, diving suits, asbestos overalls, spiked shoes, stilts, and the like—but these were optional.

Everybody loved emergency time, especially the children. It was a time for dressing up, for action, and there was always the chance that something absolutely new, something really surprising would happen.

Spinelli, recently retired from public office, chose to stay at home, close beside his radio and his huge, glowing television set. On-the-spot newsflashes were being transmitted continuously. The excitement was terrific, as it always was when emergency time had been announced.

What would it be this time? Bets were placed, computers and public opinion polls were consulted. Astrologers pronounced remarkable divinations, newspapers gave authoritative reports from special correspondents. Intuitions were widely exchanged. Everybody, but everybody, had a pet hypothesis. Some people firmly believed that the worst—that is, whatever they feared the most—would undoubtedly come to pass. Some maintained the belief that it would happen to the others, not to them. A large group was convinced that punishment was imminent for all wrongdoers and that general repentance should prevail.

As Spinelli remembered from his own youth, such intense and active entertainment was no more than dreamed of by the theatrical and cinema industries of the distant past. The anticipation alone counted for more than any circus spectacular presented by a Roman emperor. The people themselves were in the arena, arbitrary spectators and actors, victims or victors determined by the mysterious plans of the Council.

With millions of other viewers, Spinelli watched flashbacks and highlights of emergencies of the last decade. He knew, all the viewers knew, that each time they survived unscathed they formed the true emergency society. Twice, Spinelli himself had been decorated as a hero: in the Great Flood he had organized a rescue fleet to pluck scores of people from the foaming torrents, and during the Locust Plague he had flown insecticide into the afflicted areas at considerable risk to his own safety.

Emergency, of course, was not without its lighter side. Spinelli laughed and laughed again at the well-loved scenes from the Raccoon Invasion, when hundreds of raccoons had been parachuted into suburban gardens, and the Custard Pie Orgy, when pies had been flung by the million in one huge comedy.

There were dramatic sequences, too, from the day when Russian roulette was played by every hundredth person in the telephone directory, and there were pictures of the foot-and-mouth disease, the collapsing blocks of flats, the special earthquakes, and so on. The television interviewer approached a man swathed in bearskins: "So you think there'll be a new Ice Age

"Emergency Society" by Uta Frith. © 1975 by Uta Frith and reprinted from *Antigrav* by permission of the author and Philip Strick.

this time?'' ''It was bound to happen sooner or later,'' the man replied, shrugging the fur around his ears. ''I can already feel the cold, can't you?'' In the background, a wild figure could be glimpsed shouting that the plagues of Egypt[1] were about to return.

Spinelli liked the news best on these occasions—better, if the truth be told, than the spectacle itself. He was looking forward to all the papers the next day; the heroes would be announced, the victims mourned. Even if there was grief and loss in some places, the following week would be celebrated by all the happy people who had truly emerged. It was miraculous how human ingenuity, organization and adaptability saved the community from disaster every time. No disaster was ever bad enough to make any difference to economic expansion or population increase.

''Hard times,'' a businessman observed on the cascading screen not far from Spinelli's nose,

''have always been a blessing to us. People get together and help each other. All the petty squabbles of weeks past are forgotten when we put on our emergency kit. United we are strong.'' He was leading his entire staff towards one of the football stadiums, where whole communities would often gather to watch, entranced, the events unfolding on the giant televideo panoramas.

How true, Spinelli thought. He himself was a founder member of the party that had introduced emergency. ''Already fifty years ago,'' said the television interviewer, ''psychologists proved that the destructive impulses in man, allowed for centuries to burst out in unmotivated violence and irrational acts of warfare, could be channeled into useful paths. Creative energy, in-

---

1. **Plagues of Egypt.** In the Biblical account, God inflicted ten plagues on Egypt when the pharaoh refused to let Moses and the Israelites leave Egypt.

telligence, presence of mind, courage, honor, selfless sacrifice, discipline—once these qualities were almost forgotten. But now, thanks to emergency, they have returned to enrich our civilization.''

Spinelli recalled his student days when, longing for purpose and excitement, he and his friends would stage demonstrations and riots in order to capture the flavor of real and personal involvement. How often they had been stunned at the indifference they had encountered! Yes, it had all changed now; the party had helped to bring sense and meaning to everyday life.

It was in this moment of contentment that Spinelli was destined to take the role of victim for the first and last time in his existence. As in millions of other homes, his television set exploded. □□

Discussion

1. An emergency is usually thought of as a spontaneous situation, often a disaster, that arouses anxiety. Judging by the reaction to the announcement "emergency time again," what has the word come to mean to the people in "Emergency Society"?

2. Throughout the story there are references to past emergencies (a) What is the nature of these emergencies? (b) What do they reveal about the nature of emergencies in this society?

3. As Spinelli listens to television, he hears an explanation of the virtues of the periodic emergencies. (a) According to this explanation, how do the emergencies help the community? (b) How do the emergencies help deal with man's "destructive impulses"? (c) Are these so-called virtues really horrors? Discuss.

4. What is ironic about Spinelli being a victim of "emergency time"?

Extension · Writing

The surprise ending of "Emergency Society" turns upon a fictional destructive use of television.

Of the uses being made of television by today's society, select the one that you feel is the most constructive. Write a short essay explaining its use and why you feel it is effective.

Uta Frith 1941 ·

Born in southwest Germany, Frith studied art history and psychology, first at the University of Saarbruecken, then at the University of London, where she received a doctorate in abnormal psychology in 1969. Since then she has been a research psychologist investigating the development of perception and thinking in children.

Her writing mainly consists of scientific papers. However, since attending evening classes in science fiction in 1974, she has also become interested in other forms of writing. She enjoys traveling, cooking, and playing piano duets. She lives in South London with her husband and three-year-old son.

HUNGER

Travels

Alice Walker

Mama," a half-naked little boy called as they walked up to the porch, "it's some people out here, and one of 'em is that woman in the cap."

The wooden steps were broken and the porch sagged. In the front room a thin young man worked silently in a corner. In front of him was a giant pile of newspapers that looked as though they'd been salvaged from the hands of children who ate dinner over the funnies. Meridian and Truman watched the man carefully smooth out the paper, gather ten sheets, then twenty, and roll them into a log around which he placed a red rubber band. When he finished the "log" he stacked it, like a piece of wood, on top of the long pile of such "logs" that ran across one side of the poorly furnished, rather damp and smelly room.

Through the inner door he had a view of his wife—when he turned around to put the paper on the pile—lying on the bed. He nodded to them that they should enter his wife's room.

"How're you?" asked Meridian, as she and Truman looked about for chairs.

"Don't sit there," the woman said to Truman, who sat in a straight chair the young son brought. "You blocks my view of my husband."

"I'm sorry," said Truman, quickly moving.

"I'm feelin' a little better today," said the woman, "a little better." Her small black face was childlike, all bony points and big brown eyes that never left her husband's back.

"My husband Johnny went out and got me some venison and made me up a little stew. I think that's helping me to git my strength up some." She laughed, for no reason that her visitors could fathom. It was a soft, intimate chuckle, weak but as if she wanted them to understand she could endure whatever was wrong.

"Where did he get deer this time of year?" asked Truman.

From MERIDIAN copyright © 1976 by Alice Walker. Reprinted by permission of Harcourt Brace Jovanovich, Inc. and Andre Deutsch Limited.

"Don't tell anybody," the sick woman chuckled again, slyly, "but he went hunting out at one of those places where the sign says 'Deer Crossin'.' If we had a refrigerator we wouldn't need any more meat for the rest of the year. Johnny——" she began, showing all her teeth as one hand clutched the bedspread with the same intensity as her rather ghastly smile.

"Did you say somethin', Agnes?" asked Johnny, getting up from his chore with the newspapers and coming to stand at the foot of the bed. "You hongry again?"

"I gets full just lookin' at you, sugah," said the sick woman coquettishly. "That's about the only reason I hate to die," she said, looking at her visitors for a split second, "I won't be able to see my ol' good-lookin' man."

"Shoot," said Johnny, going back to the other room.

"He used to be a worker at the copper plant, used to make wire. They fired him 'cause he wouldn't let the glass in front of his table stay covered up. You know in the plant they don't want the working folks to look at nothing but what's right on the table in front of them. But my Johnny said he wasn't no mule to be wearing blinders. He wanted to see a little bit of grass, a little bit of sky. It was bad enough being buried in the basement over there, but they wanted to even keep out the sun." She looked at her husband's back as if she could send her fingers through her eyes.

"What does he do with the newspapers?" asked Truman.

"Did you see how many he has?" asked the woman. "You should see the room behind this one. Rolled newspapers up to the ceiling. Half the kitchen is rolled newspapers." She chuckled hoarsely. "So much industry in him. Why, in the wintertime he and little Johnny will take them logs around to folks with fireplaces and sell 'em for a nickel apiece and to colored for only three pennies."

"Hummm——" said Meridian. "Maybe we could help him roll a few while we're here. We just came by to ask if you all want to register to vote, but I think we could roll a few newspapers while you think about it."

"Vote?" asked the woman, attempting to raise her voice to send the question to her husband. Then she lay back. "Go on in there and git a few pages," she said.

As soon as she touched the newspapers Meridian realized Johnny must have combed the city's garbage cans, trash heaps, and department store alleys for them. Many were damp and even slimy, as if fish or worse had been wrapped in them. She began slowly pressing the papers flat, then rolling them into logs.

The sick woman was saying, "I have this dream that if the Father blesses me I'll die the week before the second Sunday in May because I want to be buried on Mother's Day. I don't know why I want that, but I do. The pain I have is like my kidneys was wrapped in that straining gauze they use in dairies to strain milk, and something is squeezing and squeezing them. But when I die, the squeezing will stop. Round Mother's Day, if the merciful Father say so."

"Mama's goin' to heaven," said Johnny Jr., who came to roll the papers Meridian had smoothed.

"She's already sweet like an angel," said Meridian impulsively, rubbing his hair and picking away the lint, "like you."

"What good is the vote, if we don't own nothing?" asked the husband as Truman and Meridian were leaving. The wife, her eyes steadily caressing her husband's back, had fallen asleep, Johnny Jr. cuddled next to her on the faded chenille bedspread. In winter the house must be freezing, thought Truman, looking at the cracks in the walls; and now, in spring, it was full of flies.

"Do you want free medicine for your wife? A hospital that'll take black people through the front door? A good school for Johnny Jr. and a job no one can take away?"

"You know I do," said the husband sullenly.

"Well, voting probably won't get it for you, not in your lifetime," Truman said, not knowing whether Meridian intended to lie and claim it would.

"What *will* it get me but a lot of trouble," grumbled the husband.

"I don't know," said Meridian. "It may be useless. Or maybe it can be the beginning of the use of your voice. You have to get used to using your voice, you know. You start on simple things and move on. . . ."

"No," said the husband, "I don't have time for foolishness. My wife is dying. My boy don't have shoes. Go somewhere else and find somebody that ain't got to work all the time for pennies, like I do."

"Okay," said Meridian. Surprised, Truman followed as she calmly walked away.

"What's this here?" asked the husband ten minutes later as they came through his front door with two bags of food.

"To go with the venison." Meridian grinned.

"I ain't changed my mind," said the husband, with a suspicious peek into the bags.

And they did not see him again until the Monday after Mother's Day, when he brought them six rabbits already skinned and ten newspaper logs; and under the words WILL YOU BE BRAVE ENOUGH TO VOTE in Meridian's yellow pad, he wrote his name in large black letters. □□

Discussion

1. Why has the husband, Johnny, lost his job? What does the episode reveal about his character?

2. What does the sick woman dream about? What does this dream reveal about her personality?

3. Why does Johnny, after saying he won't vote, change his mind and sign up to vote? What is the significance of Johnny's appearing the Monday after Mother's Day?

Alice Walker 1944 •

Walker was born in Eatonton, Georgia, and attended Sarah Lawrence College, graduating in 1966. By the age of twenty-nine, she had written five books. From 1968 to 1970 she was a teacher of writing and black literature at Jackson State College and Tougaloo College, Mississippi. Since 1972, she has taught at Wellesley College and the University of Massachusetts.

Her fiction titles include *The Third Life of Grange Copland* (1970), *Revolutionary Petunias* (1973), and *In Love and Trouble: Stories of Black Women* (1973). Her biography of Langston Hughes appeared in 1973.

See **SYMBOL** Handbook of Literary Terms

The Rocking-Horse Winner

D. H. Lawrence

There was a woman who was beautiful, who started with all the advantages, yet she had no luck. She married for love, and the love turned to dust. She had bonny children, yet she felt they had been thrust upon her, and she could not love them. They looked at her coldly, as if they were finding fault with her. And hurriedly she felt she must cover up some fault in herself. Yet what it was that she must cover up she never knew. Nevertheless, when her children were present, she always felt the centre of her heart go hard. This troubled her, and in her manner she was all the more gentle and anxious for her children, as if she loved them very much. Only she herself knew that at the centre of her heart was a hard little place that could not feel love, no, not for anybody. Everybody else said of her: "She is such a good mother. She adores her children." Only she herself, and her children themselves, knew it was not so. They read it in each other's eyes.

There was a boy and two little girls. They lived in a pleasant house, with a garden, and they had discreet servants, and felt themselves superior to anyone in the neighbourhood.

Although they lived in style, they felt always an anxiety in the house. There was never enough money. The mother had a small income, and the

From THE COMPLETE SHORT STORIES OF D. H. LAWRENCE, Vol. III. Copyright 1933 by the Estate of D. H. Lawrence, © 1961 by Angelo Ravagli and C. M. Weekley, Executors of the Estate of Frieda Lawrence Ravagli. Reprinted by permission of The Viking Press and Laurence Pollinger Ltd.

father had a small income, but not nearly enough for the social position which they had to keep up. The father went into town to some office. But though he had good prospects, these prospects never materialized. There was always the grinding sense of the shortage of money, though the style was always kept up.

At last the mother said: "I will see if *I* can't make something." But she did not know where to begin. She racked her brains and tried this thing and the other, but could not find anything successful. The failure made deep lines come into her face. Her children were growing up, they would have to go to school. There must be more money, there must be more money. The father, who was always very handsome and expensive in his tastes, seemed as if he never *would* be able to do anything worth doing. And the mother, who had a great belief in herself, did not succeed any better, and her tastes were just as expensive.

And so the house came to be haunted by the unspoken phrase: There *must* be more money! There *must* be more money! The children could hear it all the time, though nobody said it aloud. They heard it at Christmas, when the expensive and splendid toys filled the nursery. Behind the shining modern rocking horse, behind the smart doll's-house, a voice would start whispering: "There *must* be more money! There *must* be more money!" And the children would stop playing, to listen for a moment. They would look into each other's eyes, to see if they had all heard. And each one saw in the eyes of the other two that they too had heard. "There *must* be more money! There *must* be more money!"

It came whispering from the springs of the still-swaying rocking horse, and even the horse, bending his wooden, champing head, heard it. The big doll, sitting so pink and smirking in her new pram, could hear it quite plainly, and seemed to be smirking all the more self-consciously because of it. The foolish puppy, too, that took the place of the teddy-bear, he was looking so extraordinarily foolish for no other reason but that he heard the secret whisper all over the house: "There *must* be more money!"

Yet nobody ever said it aloud. The whisper was everywhere, and therefore no one spoke it. Just as no one ever says: "We are breathing!" in spite of the fact that breath is coming and going all the time.

"Mother," said the boy Paul one day, "why don't we keep a car of our own? Why do we always use uncle's, or else a taxi?"

"Because we're the poor members of the family," said the mother.

"But why *are* we, mother?"

"Well—I suppose," she said slowly and bitterly, "it's because your father has no luck."

The boy was silent for some time.

"Is luck money, mother?" he asked, rather timidly.

"No, Paul. Not quite. It's what causes you to have money."

"Oh!" said Paul vaguely. "I thought when Uncle Oscar said *filthy lucker,* it meant money."

"*Filthy lucre* does mean money," said the mother. "But it's lucre, not luck."

"Oh!" said the boy. "Then what is luck, mother?"

"It's what causes you to have money. If you're lucky you have money. That's why it's better to be born lucky than rich. If you're rich, you may lose your money. But if you're lucky, you will always get more money."

"Oh! Will you? And is father not lucky?"

"Very unlucky, I should say," she said bitterly.

The boy watched her with unsure eyes.

"Why?" he asked.

"I don't know. Nobody ever knows why one person is lucky and another unlucky."

"Don't they? Nobody at all? Does nobody know?"

"Perhaps God. But He never tells."

"He ought to, then. And aren't you lucky either, mother?"

"I can't be, if I married an unlucky husband."

"But by yourself, aren't you?"

"I used to think I was, before I married. Now I think I am very unlucky indeed."

"Why?"

"Well—never mind! Perhaps I'm not really," she said.

The child looked at her, to see if she meant it. But he saw, by the lines of her mouth, that she was only trying to hide something from him.

"Well, anyhow," he said stoutly, "I'm a lucky person."

"Why?" said his mother, with a sudden laugh.

He stared at her. He didn't even know why he had said it. "God told me," he asserted, brazening it out.

"I hope He did, dear!" she said, again with a laugh, but rather bitter.

"He did, mother!"

"Excellent!" said the mother, using one of her husband's exclamations.

The boy saw she did not believe him; or, rather, that she paid no attention to his assertion. This angered him somewhat, and made him want to compel her attention.

He went off by himself, vaguely, in a childish way, seeking for the clue to "luck." Absorbed, taking no need of other people, he went about with a sort of stealth, seeking inwardly for luck. He wanted luck, he wanted it, he wanted it. When the two girls were playing dolls in the nursery, he would sit on his big rocking horse, charging madly into space, with a frenzy that made the little girls peer at him uneasily. Wildly the horse careered, the waving dark hair of the boy tossed, his eyes had a strange glare in them. The little girls dared not speak to him.

When he had ridden to the end of his mad little journey, he climbed down and stood in front of his rocking horse, staring fixedly into its lowered face. Its red mouth was slightly open, its big eye was wide and glassy-bright.

"Now!" he would silently command the snorting steed. "Now, take me to where there is luck! Now take me."

And he would slash the horse on the neck with the little whip he had asked Uncle Oscar for. He *knew* the horse could take him to where there was luck, if only he forced it. So he would mount again, and start on his furious ride, hoping at last to get there. He knew he could get there.

"You'll break your horse, Paul!" said the nurse.

"He's always riding like that! I wish he'd leave off!" said his elder sister Joan.

But he only glared down on them in silence. Nurse gave him up. She could make nothing of him. Anyhow he was growing beyond her.

One day his mother and his Uncle Oscar came in when he was on one of his furious rides. He did not speak to them.

"Hallo, you young jockey! Riding a winner?" said his uncle.

"Aren't you growing too big for a rocking horse? You're not a very little boy any longer, you know," said his mother.

But Paul only gave a blue glare from his big, rather close-set eyes. He would speak to nobody when he was in full tilt. His mother watched him with an anxious expression on her face.

At last he suddenly stopped forcing his horse into the mechanical gallop, and slid down. "Well, I got there!" he announced fiercely, his blue eyes still flaring, and his sturdy long legs straddling apart.

"Where did you get to?" asked his mother.

"Where I wanted to go," he flared back at her.

"That's right, son!" said Uncle Oscar. "Don't you stop till you get there. What's the horse's name?"

"He doesn't have a name," said the boy.

"Gets on without all right?" asked the uncle.

"Well, he has different names. He was called Sansovino last week."

"Sansovino, eh? Won the Ascot.[1] How did you know his name?"

"He always talks about horse races with Bassett," said Joan.

---

1. **Ascot,** a horse race. Other races mentioned are the Lincoln, Leger, and Derby.

The uncle was delighted to find that his small nephew was posted with all the racing news. Bassett, the young gardener, who had been wounded in the left foot in the war and had got his present job through Oscar Cresswell, whose batman[2] he had been, was a perfect blade of the "turf." He lived in the racing events, and the small boy lived with him.

Oscar Cresswell got it all from Bassett.

"Master Paul comes and asks me, so I can't do more than tell him, sir," said Bassett, his face terribly serious, as if he were speaking of religious matters.

"And does he ever put anything on a horse he fancies?"

"Well—I don't want to give him away—he's a young sport, a fine sport, sir. Would you mind asking him himself? He sort of takes a pleasure in it, and perhaps he'd feel I was giving him away, sir, if you don't mind."

Bassett was serious as a church.

The uncle went back to his nephew, and took him off for a ride in the car.

"Say, Paul, old man, do you ever put anything on a horse?" the uncle asked.

The boy watched the handsome man closely.

"Why, do you think I oughtn't to?" he parried.

"Not a bit of it! I thought perhaps you might give me a tip for the Lincoln."

The car sped on into the country, going down to Uncle Oscar's place in Hampshire.

"Honour bright?" said the nephew.

"Honour bright, son!" said the uncle.

"Well, then. Daffodil."

"Daffodil! I doubt it, sonny. What about Mirza?"

"I only know the winner," said the boy. "That's Daffodil."

"Daffodil, eh?"

There was a pause. Daffodil was an obscure horse comparatively.

"Uncle!"

"Yes, son?"

"You won't let it go any further, will you? I promised Bassett."

"Bassett be . . . , old man! What's he got to do with it?"

"We're partners. We've been partners from the first. Uncle, he lent me my first five shillings, which I lost. I promised him, honour bright, it was only between me and him; only you gave me that ten-shilling note I started winning with, so I thought you were lucky. You won't let it go any further, will you?"

The boy gazed at his uncle from those big, hot, blue eyes, set rather close together. The uncle stirred and laughed uneasily.

"Right you are, son! I'll keep your tip private. Daffodil, eh! How much are you putting on him?"

"All except twenty pounds,"[3] said the boy. "I keep that in reserve."

The uncle thought it a good joke.

"You keep twenty pounds in reserve, do you, you young romancer? What are you betting, then?"

"I'm betting three hundred," said the boy gravely. "But it's between you and me, Uncle Oscar! Honour bright?"

The uncle burst into a roar of laughter.

"It's between you and me all right, you young Nat Gould,"[4] he said, laughing. "But where's your three hundred?"

"Bassett keeps it for me. We're partners."

"You are, are you! And what is Bassett putting on Daffodil?"

"He won't go quite as high as I do, I expect. Perhaps he'll go a hundred and fifty."

"What, pennies?" laughed the uncle.

"Pounds," said the child, with a surprised look at his uncle. "Bassett keeps a bigger reserve than I do."

Between wonder and amusement Uncle Oscar was silent. He pursued the matter no further, but he determined to take his nephew

---

2. *batman.* Bassett had been Cresswell's servant while the latter served in the army.

3. *twenty pounds.* At the time of this story, the English pound was worth nearly five dollars in United States currency.

4. *Nat Gould,* journalist, author, and highly respected racing authority.

with him to the Lincoln races.

"Now son," he said, "I'm putting twenty on Mirza, and I'll put five for you on any horse you fancy. What's your pick?"

"Daffodil, uncle."

"No, not the fiver on Daffodil!"

"I should if it was my own fiver," said the child.

"Good! Good! Right you are! A fiver for me and a fiver for you on Daffodil."

The child had never been to a race meeting before, and his eyes were blue fire. He pursed his mouth tight, and watched. A Frenchman just in front had put his money on Lancelot. Wild with excitement, he flayed his arms up and down, yelling *"Lancelot! Lancelot!"* in his French accent.

Daffodil came in first, Lancelot second, Mirza third. The child, flushed and with eyes blazing, was curiously serene. His uncle brought him four five-pound notes, four to one.

"What am I to do with these?" he cried, waving them before the boy's eyes.

"I suppose we'll talk to Bassett," said the boy. "I expect I have fifteen hundred now; and twenty in reserve; and this twenty."

His uncle studied him for some moments.

"Look here, son!" he said. "You're not serious about Bassett and that fifteen hundred, are you?"

"Yes, I am. But it's between you and me, uncle. Honour bright!"

"Honour bright all right, son! But I must talk to Bassett."

"If you'd like to be a partner, uncle, with Bassett and me, we could all be partners. Only, you'd have to promise, honour bright, uncle, not to let it go beyond us three. Bassett and I are lucky, and you must be lucky, because it was your ten shillings I started winning with. . . ."

Uncle Oscar took both Bassett and Paul into Richmond Park[5] for an afternoon, and there they talked.

"It's like this, you see, sir," Bassett said. "Master Paul would get me talking about racing events, spinning yarns, you know, sir. And he was always keen on knowing if I'd made or if I'd lost. It's about a year since, now, that I put five shillings on Blush of Dawn for him—and we lost. Then the luck turned, with that ten shillings he

5. *Richmond Park,* a deer park just outside of London.

had from you, that we put on Singhalese. And since that time it's been pretty steady, all things considering. What do you say, Master Paul?"

"We're all right when we're sure," said Paul. "It's when we're not quite sure that we go down."

"Oh, but we're careful then," said Bassett.

"But when are you *sure?*" smiled Uncle Oscar.

"It's Master Paul, sir," said Bassett, in a secret, religious voice. "It's as if he had it from heaven. Like Daffodil, now, for the Lincoln. That was as sure as eggs."

"Did you put anything on Daffodil?" asked Oscar Cresswell.

"Yes, sir. I made my bit."

"And my nephew?"

Bassett was obstinately silent, looking at Paul.

"I made twelve hundred, didn't I, Bassett? I told uncle I was putting three hundred on Daffodil."

"That's right," said Bassett, nodding.

"But where's the money?" asked the uncle.

"I keep it safe locked up, sir. Master Paul he can have it any minute he likes to ask for it."

"What, fifteen hundred pounds?"

"And twenty! And *forty,* that is, with the twenty he made on the course."

"It's amazing!" said the uncle.

"If Master Paul offers you to be partners, sir, I would if I were you; if you'll excuse me," said Bassett.

Oscar Cresswell thought about it.

"I'll see the money," he said.

They drove home again, and sure enough, Bassett came round to the garden-house with fifteen hundred pounds in notes. The twenty pounds reserve was left with Joe Glee, in the Turf Commission deposit.[6]

"You see, it's all right, uncle, when I'm *sure!* Then we go strong, for all we're worth. Don't we, Bassett?"

"We do that, Master Paul."

"And when are you sure?" said the uncle, laughing.

"Oh, well, sometimes I'm *absolutely* sure, like about Daffodil," said the boy; "and sometimes I have an idea; and sometimes I haven't even an idea, have I, Bassett? Then we're careful, because we mostly go down."

"You do, do you! And when you're sure, like about Daffodil, what makes you sure, sonny?"

"Oh, well, I don't know," said the boy uneasily. "I'm sure, you know, uncle; that's all."

"It's as if he had it from heaven, sir," Bassett reiterated.

"I should say so!" said the uncle.

But he became a partner. And when the Leger was coming on, Paul was "sure" about Lively Spark, which was a quite inconsiderable horse. The boy insisted on putting a thousand on the horse, Bassett went for five hundred, and Oscar Cresswell two hundred. Lively Spark came in first, and the betting had been ten to one against him. Paul had made ten thousand.

"You see," he said, "I was absolutely sure of him."

Even Oscar Cresswell had cleared two thousand.

"Look here, son," he said, "this sort of thing makes me nervous."

"It needn't, uncle! Perhaps I shan't be sure again for a long time."

"But what are you going to do with your money?" asked the uncle.

"Of course," said the boy, "I started it for mother. She said she had no luck, because father is unlucky, so I thought if *I* was lucky, it might stop whispering."

"What might stop whispering?"

"Our house. I *hate* our house for whispering."

"What does it whisper?"

"Why—why"—the boy fidgeted—"why, I don't know. But it's always short of money, you know, uncle."

"I know it, son, I know it."

---

6. *Turf Commission deposit,* a type of bank in which English bettors deposit betting funds.

"You know people send mother writs,[7] don't you, uncle?"

"I'm afraid I do," said the uncle.

"And then the house whispers, like people laughing at you behind your back. It's awful, that is! I thought if I was lucky . . ."

"You might stop it," added the uncle.

The boy watched him with big blue eyes, that had an uncanny cold fire in them, and he said never a word.

"Well, then!" said the uncle. "What are we doing?"

"I shouldn't like mother to know I was lucky," said the boy.

"Why not, son?"

"She'd stop me."

"I don't think she would."

"Oh!"—and the boy writhed in an odd way— "I *don't* want her to know, uncle."

"All right, son! We'll manage it without her knowing."

They managed it very easily. Paul, at the other's suggestion, handed over five thousand pounds to his uncle, who deposited it with the family lawyer, who was then to inform Paul's mother that a relative had put five thousand pounds into his hands, which sum was to be paid out a thousand pounds at a time, on the mother's birthday, for the next five years.

"So she'll have a birthday present of a thousand pounds for five successive years," said Uncle Oscar. "I hope it won't make it all the harder for her later."

Paul's mother had her birthday in November. The house had been "whispering" worse than ever lately, and, even in spite of his luck, Paul could not bear up against it. He was very anxious to see the effect of the birthday letter, telling his mother about the thousand pounds.

When there were no visitors, Paul now took his meals with his parents, as he was beyond the nursery control. His mother went into town nearly every day. She had discovered that she had an odd knack of sketching furs and dress materials, so she worked secretly in the studio of a friend who was the chief "artist" for the leading drapers. She drew the figures of ladies in furs and ladies in silk and sequins for the newspaper advertisements. This young woman artist earned several thousand pounds a year, but Paul's mother only made several hundreds, and she was again dissatisfied. She so wanted to be first in something, and she did not succeed, even in making sketches for drapery advertisements.

She was down to breakfast on the morning of her birthday. Paul watched her face as she read her letters. He knew the lawyer's letter. As his mother read it, her face hardened and became more expressionless. Then a cold, determined look came on her mouth. She hid the letter under the pile of others, and said not a word about it.

"Didn't you have anything nice in the post for your birthday, mother?" said Paul.

"Quite moderately nice," she said, her voice cold and absent.

She went away to town without saying more.

But in the afternoon Uncle Oscar appeared. He said Paul's mother had had a long interview with her lawyer, asking if the whole five thousand could not be advanced at once, as she was in debt.

"What do you think, uncle?" said the boy.

"I leave it to you, son."

"Oh, let her have it, then! We can get some more with the other," said the boy.

"A bird in the hand is worth two in the bush, laddie!" said Uncle Oscar.

"But I'm sure to *know* for the Grand National; or the Lincolnshire; or else the Derby. I'm sure to know for *one* of them," said Paul.

So Uncle Oscar signed the agreement, and Paul's mother touched the whole five thousand. Then something very curious happened. The voices in the house suddenly went mad, like a chorus of frogs on a spring evening. There were certain new furnishings, and Paul had a tutor. He was *really* going to Eton, his father's school, in the following autumn. There were flowers in the

---

7. writs, legal documents. Here the term is used to mean that legal action is about to be taken to collect unpaid bills.

winter, and a blossoming of the luxury Paul's mother had been used to. And yet the voices in the house, behind the sprays of mimosa and almond blossom, and from under the piles of iridescent cushions, simply trilled and screamed in a sort of ecstasy. "There *must* be more money! Oh-h-h; there *must* be more money! Oh, now, now-w! Now-w-w—there *must* be more money!—more than ever! More than ever!"

It frightened Paul terribly. He studied away at his Latin and Greek with his tutors. But his intense hours were spent with Bassett. The Grand National had gone by: he had not "known," and had lost a hundred pounds. Summer was at hand. He was in agony for the Lincoln. But even for the Lincoln he didn't "know," and he lost fifty pounds. He became wild-eyed and strange, as if something were going to explode in him.

"Let it alone, son! Don't you bother about it!" urged Uncle Oscar. But it was as if the boy couldn't really hear what his uncle was saying.

"I've got to know for the Derby! I've got to know for the Derby!" the child reiterated, his big blue eyes blazing with a sort of madness.

His mother noticed how overwrought he was.

"You'd better go to the seaside. Wouldn't you like to go now to the seaside, instead of waiting? I think you'd better," she said, looking down at him anxiously, her heart curiously heavy because of him.

But the child lifted his uncanny blue eyes.

"I couldn't possibly go before the Derby, mother!" he said. "I couldn't possibly!"

"Why not?" she said, her voice becoming heavy when she was opposed. "Why not? You can still go from the seaside to see the Derby with your Uncle Oscar, if that's what you wish. No need for you to wait here. Besides, I think you care too much about these races. It's a bad sign. My family has been a gambling family, and you won't know till you grow up how much damage it has done. But it has done damage. I shall have to send Bassett away, and ask Uncle Oscar not to talk racing to you, unless you promise to be reasonable about it; go away to the seaside and forget it. You're all nerves!"

"I'll do what you like, mother, so long as you don't send me away till after the Derby," the boy said.

"Send you away from where? Just from this house?"

"Yes," he said, gazing at her.

"Why, you curious child, what makes you care about this house so much, suddenly? I never knew you loved it."

He gazed at her without speaking. He had a secret within a secret, something he had not divulged, even to Bassett or to his Uncle Oscar.

But his mother, after standing undecided and a little bit sullen for some moments, said:

"Very well, then! Don't go to the seaside till after the Derby, if you don't wish it. But promise me you won't let your nerves go to pieces. Promise you won't think so much about horse racing and *events* as you call them!"

"Oh, no," said the boy casually. "I won't think much about them, mother. You needn't worry. I wouldn't worry, mother, if I were you."

"If you were me and I were you," said his mother, "I wonder what we *should* do!"

"But you know you needn't worry, mother, don't you?" the boy repeated.

"I should be awfully glad to know it," she said wearily.

"Oh, well, you *can,* you know. I mean, you *ought* to know you needn't worry," he insisted.

"Ought I? Then I'll see about it," she said.

Paul's secret of secrets was his wooden horse, that which had no name. Since he was emancipated from a nurse and a nursery-governess, he had had his rocking horse removed to his own bedroom at the top of the house.

"Surely, you're too big for a rocking horse!" his mother had remonstrated.

"Well, you see, mother, till I can have a *real* horse, I like to have *some* sort of animal about," had been his quaint answer.

"Do you feel he keeps you company?" she laughed.

"Oh, yes! He's very good, he always keeps me company, when I'm there," said Paul.

So the horse, rather shabby, stood in an arrested prance in the boy's bedroom.

The Derby was drawing near, and the boy grew more and more tense. He hardly heard what was spoken to him, he was very frail, and his eyes were really uncanny. His mother had sudden strange seizures of uneasiness about him. Sometimes, for half-an-hour, she would feel a sudden anxiety about him that was almost anguish. She wanted to rush to him at once, and know he was safe.

Two nights before the Derby, she was at a big party in town, when one of her rushes of anxiety about her boy, her first-born, gripped her heart till she could hardly speak. She fought with the feeling, might and main, for she believed in common sense. But it was too strong. She had to leave the dance and go downstairs to telephone to the country. The children's nursery-governess was terribly surprised and startled at being rung up in the night.

"Are the children all right, Miss Wilmot?"

"Oh, yes, they are quite all right."

"Master Paul? Is he all right?"

"He went to bed as right as a trivet. Shall I run up and look at him?"

"No," said Paul's mother reluctantly. "No! Don't trouble. It's all right. Don't sit up. We shall be home fairly soon." She did not want her son's privacy intruded upon.

"Very good," said the governess.

It was about one o'clock when Paul's mother and father drove up to their house. All was still. Paul's mother went to her room and slipped off her white fur cloak. She had told her maid not to wait up for her. She heard her husband downstairs, mixing a whiskey-and-soda.

And then, because of the strange anxiety at her heart, she stole upstairs to her son's room. Noiselessly she went along the upper corridor. Was there a faint noise? What was it?

She stood, with arrested muscles, outside his door, listening. There was a strange, heavy, and yet not loud noise. Her heart stood still. It was a soundless noise, yet rushing and powerful. Something huge, in violent, hushed motion. What was it? What in God's name was it? She ought to know. She felt that she knew the noise. She knew what it was.

Yet she could not place it. She couldn't say what it was. And on and on it went, like a madness.

Softly, frozen with anxiety and fear, she turned the door handle.

The room was dark. Yet in the space near the window, she heard and saw something plunging to and fro. She gazed in fear and amazement.

Then suddenly she switched on the light, and saw her son, in his green pajamas, madly surging on the rocking horse. The blaze of light suddenly lit him up, as he urged the wooden horse, and lit her up, as she stood, blonde, in her dress of pale green and crystal, in the doorway.

"Paul!" she cried. "Whatever are you doing?"

"It's Malabar!" he screamed, in a powerful, strange voice. "It's Malabar!"

His eyes blazed at her for one strange and senseless second, as he ceased urging his wooden horse. Then he fell with a crash to the ground, and she, all her tormented motherhood flooding upon her, rushed to gather him up.

But he was unconscious, and unconscious he remained, with some brain-fever. He talked and tossed, and his mother sat stonily by his side.

"Malabar! It's Malabar! Bassett, Bassett, I *know*! It's Malabar!"

So the child cried, trying to get up and urge the rocking horse that gave him his inspiration.

"What does he mean by Malabar?" asked the heart-frozen mother.

"I don't know," said the father stonily.

"What does he mean by Malabar?" she asked her brother Oscar.

"It's one of the horses running for the Derby," was the answer.

And, in spite of himself, Oscar Cresswell spoke to Bassett, and himself put a thousand on Malabar: at fourteen to one.

The third day of the illness was critical: they were waiting for a change. The boy, with his rather long, curly hair, was tossing ceaselessly on the pillow. He neither slept nor regained consciousness, and his eyes were like blue stones. His mother sat, feeling her heart had gone, turned actually into a stone.

In the evening, Oscar Cresswell did not come, but Bassett sent a message, saying could he come up for one moment, just one moment? Paul's mother was very angry at the intrusion, but on second thought she agreed. The boy was the same. Perhaps Bassett might bring him to consciousness.

The gardener, a shortish fellow with a little brown moustache, and sharp little brown eyes, tiptoed into the room, touched his imaginary cap to Paul's mother, and stole to the bedside, staring with glittering, smallish eyes, at the tossing, dying child.

"Master Paul!" he whispered. "Master Paul! Malabar came in first all right, a clean win. I did as you told me. You've made over seventy thousand pounds, you have; you've got over eighty thousand. Malabar came in all right, Master Paul."

"Malabar! Malabar! Did I say Malabar, mother? Did I say Malabar? Do you think I'm lucky, mother? I knew Malabar, didn't I? Over eighty thousand pounds! I call that lucky, don't you, mother? Over eighty thousand pounds! I knew, didn't I know I knew? Malabar came in all right. If I ride my horse till I'm sure, then I tell you, Bassett, you can go as high as you like. Did you go for all you were worth, Bassett?"

"I went a thousand on it, Master Paul."

"I never told you, mother, that if I can ride my horse, and *get* there, then I'm absolutely sure—oh, absolutely! Mother, did I ever tell you? I *am* lucky!"

"No, you never did," said the mother.

But the boy died in the night.

And even as he lay dead, his mother heard her brother's voice saying to her: "My God, Hester, you're eighty-odd thousand to the good, and a poor devil of a son to the bad. But, poor devil, poor devil, he's best gone out of a life where he rides his rocking horse to find a winner." □□

Discussion

1. (a) What causes the "hard little place" at the center of the mother's heart? **(b)** How does her attitude affect her children? **(c)** Although the children's father is mentioned in the story, he never actually appears. Why might Lawrence have excluded him from the story?

2. (a) What causes the whispering Paul and his sisters hear? **(b)** Why does it frighten them? **(c)** Why do the adults fail to hear the whispering?

3. (a) Why does Paul become so determined to have luck? **(b)** How does he go about getting it?

4. (a) What causes the whispering to grow louder after Paul gives his mother five thousand pounds? **(b)** How does Paul react to the increased whispering?

5. Shortly before Paul dies, his mother hears him on his rocking horse. What similarities exist between the effect of the noise made by the rocking horse on her and the effect of the house's whispering on Paul?

6. Reread the passages that deal with Paul's eyes, paying special attention to the adjectives used to describe them. How do the feelings reflected in his eyes show the changes he undergoes?

7. (a) What elements of fantasy does the story contain? **(b)** Do these fantastic elements strengthen or weaken the story? Justify your answer. **(c)** These elements of fantasy are also symbolic of what?

8. Defend or criticize this statement: "Money is the root of all evil" is an adequate statement of the theme of "The Rocking-Horse Winner."

Vocabulary
Context and Dictionary

Each of the following words appears in "The Rocking-Horse Winner." Look up the words in your Glossary. When you have determined the meanings, rewrite each sentence to include the appropriate word in the place of the italicized word or phrase. Be sure you can spell and pronounce each word. You will not need all the words for the sentences.

parry   overwrought
discreet   remonstrate
smirk   uncanny

1. In the confusion of her embarrassment, Lola felt the judges were *grinning unpleasantly* at her.

2. She is a sensible person, and we can depend upon her to be *cautious* in this rather delicate matter of the company's merger.

3. The celebrity managed to *turn aside* the interviewer's prying questions without appearing cross.

4. Chloe maintains that there is nothing *supernatural* in her ability to sense when the telephone is about to ring.

5. Uncle Ralph used to try to *reason with* my naughty cousins, but Aunt Kate's method was to send them to their rooms to think by themselves.

David Herbert Lawrence
1885 · 1930

Lawrence was born in the small provincial town of Eastwood, England. His father, a coal miner, was uneducated, unrefined, and unambitious. His mother, a woman of some education and fierce ambitions, felt vastly superior to her husband. Mrs. Lawrence looked to David and an older brother to compensate for her bad marriage, and, when the brother died, she poured her affections and ambitions entirely upon David. This unhappy relationship was aggravated by poverty and the father's drinking; Lawrence's childhood was a wretched one.

After completing his education, Lawrence went to work in a local warehouse—a job that did not please his mother. After a few months, he left the warehouse to work as a teacher, a profession he followed for a number of years. During these years he wrote, and with the publication of his first work and his mother's death he left teaching to spend his time writing.

Lawrence was only forty-five when he died of the tuberculosis that had long been threatening him.

CONTENT REVIEW

1. (a) In what ways do the boys in "Through the Tunnel" and "Shaving" grow? **(b)** Is each aware of his growth? Explain. **(c)** Which parent is more aware of a change: Jerry's mother or Barry's father? How do you know?

2. Both "Lamb to the Slaughter" and "Footfalls" have surprise endings. **(a)** In which story is the ending ironic? What makes it so? **(b)** Why might the ending of the other story be called poignant and moving?

3. (a) In "A Short Return," "A Visit to Grandmother," and "Of Dry Goods and Black Bow Ties," children come to a new awareness about their parents and the lives they've lived. What insights do the children gain? What effect do they have on the parent-son/daughter relationship? **(b)** Both the grandmother in "A Visit . . ." and Shozo Shimada in "Of Dry Goods . . ." are alike in that they are strong disciplinarians and basically good people. What difference in their personalities has a lasting effect on the fathers in each story? Discuss.

4. (a) Both "Average Waves in Unprotected Waters" and "The Life You Save May Be Your Own" show how hard it can be to find a way to help a child who has severe problems or handicaps. How do Bet and Mrs. Crater show their love? **(b)** Both mothers suffer anguish in letting go of their children: as Arnold is left at the hospital, and as Lucynell goes off married to Mr. Shiftlet. What concerns do they have about their children? What seems to be in store for Arnold and Lucynell?

5. (a) What character traits of Walter Mitty, Philip Wedge, and Harold K. Bullard have been exaggerated to create humor? **(b)** What, in the personality and/or situation of each man, might one sympathize with?

6. (a) What are the rituals in "Gwilan's Harp"? in "Emergency Society"? **(b)** The fictional worlds of "Gwilan's Harp" and "Emergency Society" are radically different in a number of ways. What are they? For example, consider time and place. **(c)** Why do you think such different stories were paired?

7. (a) Both "Travels" and "The Rocking-Horse Winner" are about families who need more money. Compare and contrast the needs and the effect of these desires on the families. **(b)** Both Johnny Jr. in "Travels" and Paul in "The Rocking-Horse Winner" are drawn into the problems of the adults around them. How does their involvement in the problem affect them? Discuss.

The Miraculous Phonograph Record of 1921

William Saroyan

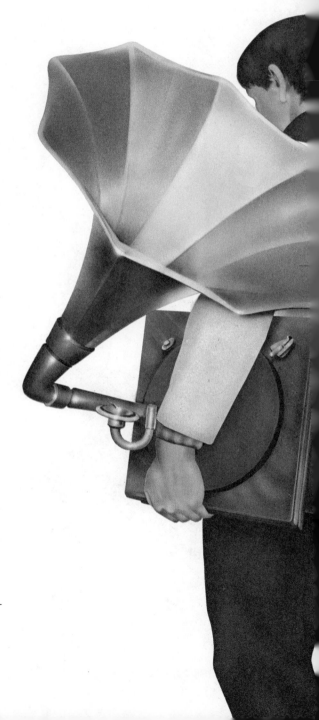

Read the following story, then answer the questions about it.

Sometime soon after I was thirteen years old in 1921 I rode home from the heart of Fresno with a wind-up Victor phonograph under my arm, hitched above my hipbone, and one Victor record. On a bicycle, that is.

The bicycle went to pieces from the use I gave it as a Postal Telegraph messenger.

The phonograph developed motor trouble soon after my first book was published; and while I was traveling in Europe for the first time, in 1935, it was given to the Salvation Army.

But I still have the record, and I have a special fondness for it.

The reason I have a special fondness for it is that whenever I listen to it, I remember what happened when I reached home with the phonograph and the record.

The phonograph had cost ten dollars, the record seventy-five cents, both brand-new. I had earned the money as a messenger in my first week of work, plus four and a quarter, which I had in my pocket.

My mother had just got home from Guggenheim's, where, judging from the expression on her face, she had been packing figs in eight-ounce packs, which I knew was the weight and size that was least desired by the packers, because a full day of hard work doing eight-ounce packs, at so much per pack, meant only about a dollar and a half, or at the most two dollars, whereas, if they were packing four-ounce packs, they could earn three and sometimes even four dollars, which in those days was good money, and welcome, especially as the work at Guggenheim's, or at any of the other dried-fruit packing houses such as Rosenberg's or Inderrieden's, was seasonal, and the season was never long.

When I walked into the house, all excited about the phonograph hitched to my hip, my mother gave me a look that suggested an eight-ounce day. She said nothing, however, and I

"The Miraculous Phonograph Record of 1921" by William Saroyan. From the SATURDAY EVENING POST, October, 1963. Copyright 1963 by The Curtis Publishing Company. Reprinted by permission of the author.

said nothing, as I placed the phonograph on the round table in the parlor, checked it for any accidents to exposed parts that might have happened in transit, found none, lifted the record from the turntable where the girl in the store had fixed it with two big rubber bands, examined both sides of it, and noticed that my mother was watching. While I was still cranking the machine, she spoke at last, softly and politely, which I knew meant she didn't like the looks of things.

She spoke in Armenian.

"Willie, what is that you have there?"

"This is called a phonograph."

"Where did you get this phonograph?"

"I got it from Sherman, Clay, on Broadway."

"The people at Sherman, Clay—did they *give* you this phonograph?"

"No, I paid for it."

"How much did you pay, Willie?"

"Ten dollars."

"Ten dollars is a lot of money in this family. Did you *find* the ten dollars in the street perhaps?"

"No, I got the ten dollars from my first week's pay as a messenger. And I paid seventy-five cents for the record."

"And how much money have you brought home for the whole family—for rent and food and clothing—out of your first week's pay?"

"Four dollars and twenty-five cents. My pay is fifteen dollars a week."

Now, the record is on the machine, and I am about to put the needle to the revolving disc when I suddenly notice that I had better forget it and get out of there, which I do, and just in time, too. The screen door of the back porch slams once for me, and then once for my mother.

As I race around the house, I become aware of two things: (1) that it's a beautiful evening, and (2) that Levon Kemalyan's father, who is a very dignified man, is standing in front of his house across the street with his mouth a little open, watching. Well, he's an elder at the First Armenian Presbyterian Church; he isn't from Bitlis,[1] as we are; he's not a Saroyan, and this sort of thing comes as a surprise to him. Surely Takoohi Saroyan and her son are not racing around their house for exercise, or in an athletic contest of some kind, so why are they running?

In a spirit of neighborliness I salute Mr. Kemalyan as I race to the front porch and back into the parlor, where I quickly put needle to disc, and hurry to the dining room, from whence I can

---

1. **Bitlis** (bit lis'), a province and city in E. Turkey heavily settled by Armenians. Armenia, an ancient country, is now a region in Turkey, Iran, and the Soviet Union.

both witness the effect of the music on my mother, and, if necessary, escape to the back porch, and out into the yard again.

The music of the record begins to come from the machine just as my mother gets back into the parlor.

For a moment it looks as if she is going to ignore the music and continue the chase, and then suddenly it happens, the thing that makes the record something to remember and cherish forever.

My mother comes to a halt, perhaps only to catch her breath, perhaps to listen to the music; there's still no way of telling for sure.

As the music moves along, I can't help noticing that my mother is either too tired to run any more or is actually listening. And then I notice that she is *very definitely* listening. I watch her turn from the chase to the machine. I watch her take one of the six cane chairs that have remained in the family from the time of my father, from 1911, and move it to the round table. I watch her sit down. I notice now that her expression no longer suggests that she is tired and angry. I remember the man in the Bible who was mad and was comforted by somebody playing a harp.[2] I stand in the doorway to the parlor, and when the record ends I go to the machine, lift the needle from the disc and stop the motor.

Without looking at me, my mother says, this time in English, "All right, we keep this." And then in softly spoken Armenian, "Play it again, I beg of you."

I quickly give the crank a few spins and put needle to disc again.

This time when the needle comes to the end of the record my mother says, "Show me how it's done." I show her, and she starts the record a third time for herself.

Well, of course the music *is* beautiful, but only a moment ago she had been awfully mad at me for what she had felt had been the throwing-away of most of my week's wages for some kind of ridiculous piece of junk. And then she had heard the music; she had got the message, and the message had informed her that not only had the money *not* been thrown away, it had been wisely invested.

She played the record six times while I sat at the table in the dining room looking through a small catalogue of records given to me free of charge by the girl at Sherman, Clay, and then she said, "You have brought home only the one record?"

"Well, there's another song on the other side."

---

2. I remember . . . harp. Saul, first king of Israel, was comforted by the songs and harp of the shepherd boy David.

I went back to the machine, turned the record over, and put it in place.

"What is this other one?"

"Well, it's called 'Song of India.' I've never heard it. At the store I listened only to the first one, which is called 'Cho-Cho-San.' "[3]

"What is the meaning of *that*—'Cho-Cho-San'?"

"It's just the name of the song, I guess. Would you like to hear the other one, 'Song of India'?"

"I beg of you."

Now, as the other members of the family came home, they heard music coming from the parlor, and when they went in they saw the brand-new phonograph, and my mother sitting on the cane chair, directly in front of it, listening.

Why wouldn't that record be something I would want to keep as long as possible, and something I deeply cherish? Almost instantly it had won over my mother to art, and for all I know marked the point at which she began to suspect that her son rightfully valued some things higher than he valued money, and possibly even higher than he valued food, drink, shelter, and clothing.

A week later she remarked to everybody during supper that the time had come to put some of the family money into a second record, and she wanted to know what was available. I got out the catalogue and went over the names, but they meant nothing to her, so she told me to just go to the store and pick out something *hrashali,* the Armenian word for miraculous, which I was happy to do.

Now, as I listen to the record again, forty-two years later, and try to guess what happened, I think it was the banjo beat that got my mother, that spoke directly to her as if to one long known, deeply understood, and totally loved; the banjo chords just back of the clarinet that remembered everything gone, accepted everything present, and waited for anything more still to come, echoing in and out of the story of the Japanese girl betrayed by the American sailor, the oboe saying words and the saxophone choking on swallowed emotion: "Fox Trot (On Melodies by G. Puccini, arranged by Hugo Frey) Paul Whiteman and His Orchestra. 18777-A."

After that, whenever other members of the family attacked me for some seeming eccentricity, my mother always patiently defended me until she lost her temper, whereupon she shouted, "He is not a businessman, thank God."

□□

---

3. *"Song of India"* . . . *"Cho-Cho-San."* The record mentioned here is a popular arrangement of tunes from longer works of music.

Short Answer

Write the word or phrase that best answers the questions.

1. The author tells us the incident takes place in 1921. What are some details in the story that indicate that this happened some years ago?

2. What is the economic situation of the family at the time the story takes place? List as many reasons for your answer as you can.

3. What kind of person is Takoohi Saroyan? List some examples from the story that support your answer.

4. What is the tone of the narration as the author describes running around the house with his mother chasing him?

5. Where does the turning point come in the story?

6. What does the author think the music symbolized to his mother?

7. Why does the author think the record was "miraculous"?

8. What did the author's mother mean by her last statement in the story?

Unit 2, Test II
COMPOSITION

From the assignments below choose one to write about.

1. Choose any three of the characters from the stories and explain why you would like to have them for your friends.

2. The narrator of "A Short Return" tells the story from his own point of view. Using your imagination and any clues from the story, explain why you think Edmund, the stepfather, acted as he did when the narrator was a child.

3. Many of the stories in the unit are concerned with the relationship between parent and child. Choose any three of the following stories and compare and contrast the parent-child relationships in them: "Footfalls," "A Visit to Grandmother," "Shaving," "Average Waves in Unprotected Waters," "The Rocking-Horse Winner," "Through the Tunnel," and "The Miraculous Phonograph Record of 1921." You may wish to include such topics as loyalty, the child's becoming an adult, misunderstanding between parent and child, and over-or under-indulgence.

4. Write an editorial condemning or approving the "emergencies" in "Emergency Society," the latest of which took the life of the founder, Spinelli.

5. Mr. Shimada in "Of Dry Goods and Black Bow Ties" and Mr. Shiftlet in "The Life You Save . . ." are both hard-working men who achieve their goals. Compare and contrast their characters. Try to include answers to the following questions: What are their aims? How do they go about achieving their aims? How do they deal with subsequent disappointment?

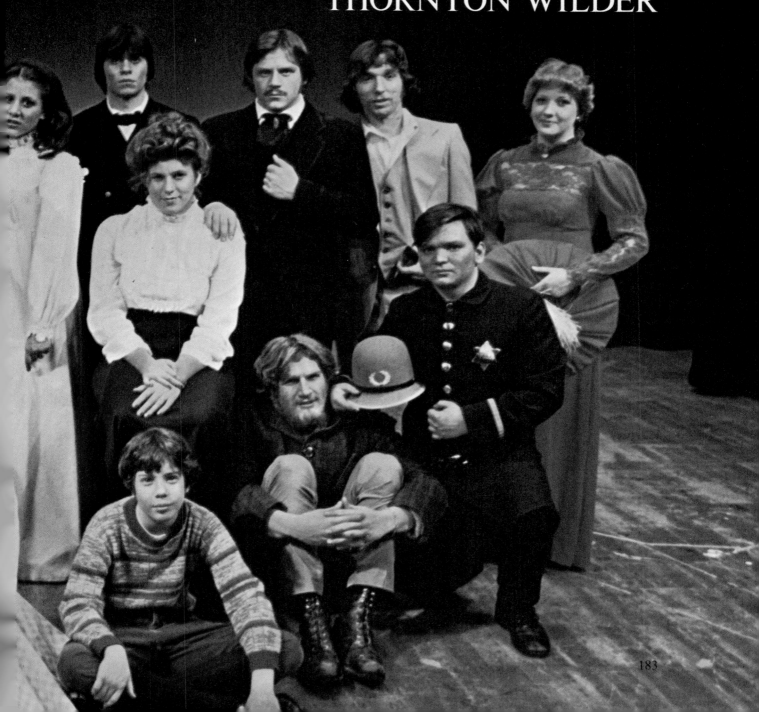

Act I

Characters (in the order of their appearance)

STAGE MANAGER

DR. GIBBS

JOE CROWELL

HOWIE NEWSOME

MRS. GIBBS

MRS. WEBB

GEORGE GIBBS

REBECCA GIBBS

WALLY WEBB

EMILY WEBB

PROFESSOR WILLARD

MR. WEBB

WOMAN IN THE BALCONY

MAN IN THE AUDITORIUM

LADY IN THE BOX

SIMON STIMSON

MRS. SOAMES

CONSTABLE WARREN

SI CROWELL

THREE BASEBALL PLAYERS

SAM CRAIG

JOE STODDARD

The entire play takes place in Grover's Corners, New Hampshire.

No curtain.
No scenery.
The audience, arriving, sees an empty stage in half-light.
Presently the STAGE MANAGER, *hat on and pipe in mouth, enters and begins placing a table and three chairs downstage left, and a table and three chairs downstage right. He also places a low bench at the corner of what will be the Webb house, left.*
"Left" and "right" are from the point of view of the actor facing the audience. "Up" is toward the back wall.
As the house lights go down he has finished setting the stage and leaning against the right proscenium pillar watches the late arrivals in the audience.
When the auditorium is in complete darkness he speaks:

STAGE MANAGER. This play is called "Our Town." It was written by Thornton Wilder; produced and directed by A. . . . (or: produced by A. . . .; directed by B. . . .). In it you will see Miss C. . . .; Miss D. . . .; Miss E. . . .; and Mr. F. . . .; Mr. G. . . .; Mr. H. . . .; and many others. The name of the town is Grover's Corners, New Hampshire—just across the Massachusetts line: latitude 42 degrees 40 minutes; longitude 70 degrees 37 minutes. The First Act shows a day in our town. The day is May 7, 1901. The time is just before dawn. (*A rooster crows.*) The sky is beginning to show some streaks of light over in the East there, behind our mount'in. The morning star always gets wonderful bright the minute before it has to go,—doesn't it? (*He stares at it for a moment, then goes upstage.*)

(Play) OUR TOWN by Thornton Wilder. Copyright © 1938, 1957 by Thornton Wilder. Reprinted by permission of Harper & Row, Publishers, Inc. and Penguin Books Ltd.

Caution! OUR TOWN is the sole property of the author and is fully protected by copyright. It may not be acted by professionals or amateurs without formal permission and the payment of a royalty. All rights, including professional, amateur, stock, radio and television, broadcasting, motion picture, recitation, lecturing, public reading, and the rights of translation into foreign languages are reserved. All professional inquiries should be addressed to the author's agent: Harold Freedman, Brandt & Brandt Dramatic Department, Inc., 101 Park Avenue, New York 10017, N.Y. All requests for amateur rights should be addressed to Samuel French, 25 West 45th Street, New York 10019, N.Y.

Well, I'd better show you how our town lies. Up here—*(That is: parallel with the back wall.)* is Main Street. Way back there is the railway station; tracks go that way. Polish Town's across the tracks, and some Canuck[1] families. *(Toward the left.)* Over there is the Congregational Church; across the street's the Presbyterian. Methodist and Unitarian are over there. Baptist is down in the holla' by the river. Catholic Church is over beyond the tracks. Here's the Town Hall and Post Office combined; jail's in the basement. Bryan once made a speech from these very steps here. Along here's a row of stores. Hitching posts and horse blocks in front of them. First automobile's going to come along in about five years—belonged to Banker Cartwright, our richest citizen . . . lives in the big white house up on the hill. Here's the grocery store and here's Mr. Morgan's drugstore. Most everybody in town manages to look into those two stores once a day. Public School's over yonder. High School's still farther over. Quarter of nine mornings, noontimes, and three o'clock afternoons, the hull town can hear the yelling and screaming from those schoolyards. *(He approaches the table and chairs downstage right.)* This is our doctor's house,—Doc Gibbs'. This is the back door. *(Two arched trellises, covered with vines and flowers, are pushed out, one by each proscenium pillar.)* There's some scenery for those who think they have to have scenery. This is Mrs. Gibbs' garden. Corn . . . peas . . . beans . . . hollyhocks . . . heliotrope . . . and a lot of burdock. *(Crosses the stage.)* In those days our newspaper come out twice a week—the Grover's Corners *Sentinel*—and this is Editor Webb's house. And this is Mrs. Webb's garden. Just like Mrs. Gibbs', only it's got a lot of sunflowers, too. *(He looks upward, center stage.)* Right here . . .'s a big butternut tree. *(He returns to his place by the right proscenium pillar and looks at the audience for a minute.)*

Nice town, y'know what I mean? Nobody very remarkable ever come out of it, s'far as we know. The earliest tombstones in the cemetery up there on the mountain say 1670-1680—they're Grovers and Cartwrights and Gibbses and Herseys—same names as are around here now. Well, as I said: it's about dawn. The only lights on in town are in a cottage over by the tracks where a Polish mother's just had twins. And in the Joe Crowell house, where Joe Junior's getting up so as to deliver the paper. And in the depot, where Shorty Hawkins is gettin' ready to flag the 5:45 for Boston. *(A train whistle is heard. The* STAGE MANAGER *takes out his watch and nods.)* Naturally, out in the country—all around—there've been lights on for some time, what with milkin's and so on. But town people sleep late.

So—another day's begun. There's Doc Gibbs comin' down Main Street now, comin' back from that baby case. And here's his wife comin' downstairs to get breakfast.

MRS. GIBBS, *a plump, pleasant woman in the middle thirties, comes "downstairs" right. She pulls up an imaginary window shade in her kitchen and starts to make a fire in her stove.* Doc Gibbs died in 1930. The new hospital's named after him. Mrs. Gibbs died first—long time ago, in fact. She went out to visit her daughter, Rebecca, who married an insurance man in Canton, Ohio, and died there—pneumonia—but her body was brought back here. She's up in the cemetery there now—in with a whole mess of Gibbses and Herseys—she was Julia Hersey 'fore she married Doc Gibbs in the Congregational Church over there. In our town we like to know the facts about everybody. There's Mrs. Webb, coming downstairs to get her breakfast, too.—That's Doc Gibbs. Got that call at half past one this morning. And there comes Joe Crowell, Jr., delivering Mr. Webb's *Sentinel*.

DR. GIBBS *has been coming along Main Street from the left. At the point where he would turn to approach his house, he stops, sets down*

---

1. **Canuck**, a derogatory term for a Canadian.

his—imaginary—black bag, takes off his hat, and rubs his face with fatigue, using an enormous handkerchief.

MRS. WEBB, *a thin, serious, crisp woman, has entered her kitchen, left, tying on an apron. She goes through the motions of putting wood into a stove, lighting it, and preparing breakfast. Suddenly,* JOE CROWELL, JR., *eleven, starts down Main Street from the right, hurling imaginary newspapers into doorways.*

JOE CROWELL, JR. Morning, Doc Gibbs.

DR. GIBBS. Morning, Joe.

JOE CROWELL, JR. Somebody been sick, Doc?

DR. GIBBS. No. Just some twins born over in Polish Town.

JOE CROWELL, JR. Do you want your paper now?

DR. GIBBS. Yes, I'll take it.—Anything serious goin' on in the world since Wednesday?

JOE CROWELL, JR. Yessir. My schoolteacher, Miss Foster,'s getting married to a fella over in Concord.

DR. GIBBS. I declare.—How do you boys feel about that?

JOE CROWELL, JR. Well, of course, it's none of my business—but I think if a person starts out to be a teacher, she ought to stay one.

DR. GIBBS. How's your knee, Joe?

JOE CROWELL, JR. Fine, Doc, I never think about it at all. Only like you said, it always tells me when it's going to rain.

DR. GIBBS. What's it telling you today? Goin' to rain?

JOE CROWELL, JR. No, sir.

DR. GIBBS. Sure?

JOE CROWELL, JR. Yessir.

DR. GIBBS. Knee ever make a mistake?

JOE CROWELL, JR. No, sir. (JOE *goes off.* DR. GIBBS *stands reading his paper.*)

STAGE MANAGER. Want to tell you something about that boy Joe Crowell there. Joe was awful bright—graduated from high school here, head of his class. So he got a scholarship to Massachusetts Tech. Graduated head of his class there, too. It was all wrote up in the Boston paper at the time. Goin' to be a great engineer, Joe was. But the war broke out and he died in France.—All that education for nothing.

HOWIE NEWSOME (*off left*). Giddap, Bessie! What's the matter with you today?

STAGE MANAGER. Here comes Howie Newsome, deliverin' the milk.

HOWIE NEWSOME, *about thirty, in overalls, comes along Main Street from the left, walking beside an invisible horse and wagon and carrying an imaginary rack with milk bottles. The sound of clinking milk bottles is heard. He leaves some bottles at Mrs. Webb's trellis, then, crossing the stage to Mrs. Gibbs', he stops center to talk to Dr. Gibbs.*

HOWIE NEWSOME. Morning, Doc.

DR. GIBBS. Morning, Howie.

HOWIE NEWSOME. Somebody sick?

DR. GIBBS. Pair of twins over to Mrs. Goruslawski's.

HOWIE NEWSOME. Twins, eh? This town's gettin' bigger every year.

DR. GIBBS. Goin' to rain, Howie?

HOWIE NEWSOME. No, no. Fine day—that'll burn through. Come on, Bessie.

DR. GIBBS. Hello Bessie. (*He strokes the horse, which has remained up center.*) How old is she, Howie?

HOWIE NEWSOME. Going on seventeen. Bessie's all mixed up about the route ever since the Lockharts stopped takin' their quart of milk every day. She wants to leave 'em a quart just the same—keeps scolding me the hull trip. (*He* *reaches Mrs. Gibbs' back door. She is waiting for him.)*

MRS. GIBBS. Good morning, Howie.

HOWIE NEWSOME. Morning, Mrs. Gibbs. Doc's just comin' down the street.

MRS. GIBBS. Is he? Seems like you're late today.

HOWIE NEWSOME. Yes. Somep'n went wrong with the separator. Don't know what 'twas. *(He passes Dr. Gibbs up center.)* Doc!

DR. GIBBS. Howie!

MRS. GIBBS *(calling upstairs).* Children! Children! Time to get up.

HOWIE NEWSOME. Come on, Bessie! *(He goes off right.)*

MRS. GIBBS. George! Rebecca!

DR. GIBBS *arrives at his back door and passes through the trellis into his house.*

MRS. GIBBS. Everything all right, Frank?

DR. GIBBS. Yes. I declare—easy as kittens.

MRS. GIBBS. Bacon'll be ready in a minute. Set down and drink your coffee. You can catch a couple hours' sleep this morning, can't you?

DR. GIBBS. Hm! . . . Mrs. Wentworth's coming at eleven. Guess I know what it's about, too. Her stummick ain't what it ought to be.

MRS. GIBBS. All told, you won't get more'n three hours' sleep. Frank Gibbs, I don't know what's goin' to become of you. I do wish I could get you to go away someplace and take a rest. I think it would do you good.

MRS. WEBB. Emileeee! Time to get up! Wally! Seven o'clock!

MRS. GIBBS. I declare, you got to speak to George. Seems like something's come over him lately. He's no help to me at all. I can't even get him to cut me some wood.

DR. GIBBS *(washing and drying his hands at the sink.* MRS. GIBBS *is busy at the stove).* Is he sassy to you?

MRS. GIBBS. No. He just whines! All he thinks about is that baseball—George! Rebecca! You'll be late for school.

DR. GIBBS. M-m-m . . .

MRS. GIBBS. George!

DR. GIBBS. George, look sharp!

GEORGE'S VOICE. Yes, Pa!

DR. GIBBS *(as he goes off the stage).* Don't you hear your mother calling you? I guess I'll go upstairs and get forty winks.

MRS. WEBB. Walleee! Emileee! You'll be late for school! Walleee! You wash yourself good or I'll come up and do it myself.

REBECCA GIBBS' VOICE. Ma! What dress shall I wear?

MRS. GIBBS. Don't make a noise. Your father's been out all night and needs his sleep. I washed and ironed the blue gingham for you special.

REBECCA. Ma, I hate that dress.

MRS. GIBBS. Oh, hush-up-with-you.

REBECCA. Every day I go to school dressed like a sick turkey.

MRS. GIBBS. Now, Rebecca, you always look *very* nice.

REBECCA. Mama, George's throwing soap at me.

MRS. GIBBS. I'll come and slap the both of you,— that's what I'll do.

A factory whistle sounds. The CHILDREN *dash in and take their places at the tables. Right,* GEORGE, *about sixteen, and* REBECCA, *eleven. Left,* EMILY *and* WALLY, *same ages. They carry strapped schoolbooks.*

STAGE MANAGER. We've got a factory in our town too—hear it? Makes blankets. Cartwrights own it and it brung 'em a fortune.

MRS. WEBB. Children! Now I won't have it. Breakfast is just as good as any other meal and I won't have you gobbling like wolves. It'll stunt your growth,—that's a fact. Put away your book, Wally.

WALLY. Aw, Ma! By ten o'clock I got to know all about Canada.

MRS. WEBB. You know the rule's well as I do—no books at table. As for me, I'd rather have my children healthy than bright.

EMILY. I'm both, Mama: you know I am. I'm the brightest girl in school for my age. I have a wonderful memory.

MRS. WEBB. Eat your breakfast.

WALLY. I'm bright, too, when I'm looking at my stamp collection.

MRS. GIBBS. I'll speak to your father about it when

he's rested. Seems to me twenty-five cents a week's enough for a boy your age. I declare I don't know how you spend it all.

GEORGE. Aw, Ma,—I gotta lotta things to buy.

MRS. GIBBS. Strawberry phosphates—that's what you spend it on.

GEORGE. I don't see how Rebecca comes to have so much money. She has more'n a dollar.

REBECCA (spoon in mouth, dreamily). I've been saving it up gradual.

MRS. GIBBS. Well, dear, I think it's a good thing to spend some every now and then.

REBECCA. Mama, do you know what I love most in the world—do you?—Money.

MRS. GIBBS. Eat your breakfast.

THE CHILDREN. Mama, there's first bell.—I gotta hurry.—I don't want any more.—I gotta hurry.

The CHILDREN *rise, seize their books and dash out through the trellises. They meet, down center, and chattering, walk to Main Street, then turn left. The* STAGE MANAGER *goes off, unobtrusively, right.*

MRS. WEBB. Walk fast, but you don't have to run. Wally, pull up your pants at the knee. Stand up straight, Emily.

MRS. GIBBS. Tell Miss Foster I send her my best congratulations—can you remember that?

REBECCA. Yes, Ma.

MRS. GIBBS. You look real nice, Rebecca. Pick up your feet.

ALL. Good-by.

MRS. GIBBS *fills her apron with food for the chickens and comes down to the footlights.*

MRS. GIBBS. Here, chick, chick, chick. No, go away, you. Go away. Here, chick, chick, chick. What's the matter with *you?* Fight, fight, fight,—that's all you do. Hm . . . *you* don't belong to me. Where'd you come from? *(She shakes her apron.)* Oh, don't be so scared. Nobody's going to hurt you. (MRS. WEBB *is sitting on the bench by her trellis, stringing beans.)* Good morning, Myrtle. How's your cold?

MRS. WEBB. Well, I still get that tickling feeling in my throat. I told Charles I didn't know as I'd go to choir practice tonight. Wouldn't be any use.

MRS. GIBBS. Have you tried singing over your voice?

MRS. WEBB. Yes, but somehow I can't do that and stay on the key. While I'm resting myself I thought I'd string some of these beans.

MRS. GIBBS (rolling up her sleeves as she crosses the stage for a chat). Let me help you. Beans have been good this year.

MRS. WEBB. I've decided to put up forty quarts if it kills me. The children say they hate 'em, but I notice they're able to get 'em down all winter. *(Pause. Brief sound of chickens cackling.)*

MRS. GIBBS. Now, Myrtle. I've got to tell you something, because if I don't tell somebody I'll burst.

MRS. WEBB. Why, Julia Gibbs!

MRS. GIBBS. Here, give me some more of those beans. Myrtle, did one of those secondhand-furniture men from Boston come to see you last Friday?

MRS. WEBB. No-o.

MRS. GIBBS. Well, he called on me. First I thought he was a patient wantin' to see Dr. Gibbs. 'N he wormed his way into my parlor, and, Myrtle Webb, he offered me three hundred and fifty dollars for Grandmother Wentworth's highboy, as I'm sitting here!

MRS. WEBB. Why, Julia Gibbs!

MRS. GIBBS. He did! That old thing! Why, it was so big I didn't know where to put it and I almost give it to Cousin Hester Wilcox.

MRS. WEBB. Well, you're going to take it, aren't you?

MRS. GIBBS. I don't know.

MRS. WEBB. You don't know—three hundred and fifty dollars! What's come over you?

MRS. GIBBS. Well, if I could get the Doctor to take the money and go away someplace on a real trip, I'd sell it like that.—Y'know, Myrtle, it's been the dream of my life to see Paris, France.—Oh, I don't know. It sounds crazy, I suppose, but for years I've been promising myself that if we ever had the chance——

MRS. WEBB. How does the Doctor feel about it?

MRS. GIBBS. Well, I did beat about the bush a little and said that if I got a legacy—that's the way I put it—I'd make him take me somewhere.

MRS. WEBB. M-m-m . . . What did he say?

MRS. GIBBS. You know how he is. I haven't heard a serious word out of him since I've known him. No, he said, it might make him discontented with Grover's Corners to go traipsin' about Europe; better let well enough alone, he says. Every two years he makes a trip to the battlefields of the Civil War and that's enough treat for anybody, he says.

MRS. WEBB. Well, Mr. Webb just *admires* the way Dr. Gibbs knows everything about the Civil War. Mr. Webb's a good mind to give up Napoleon and move over to the Civil War, only Dr. Gibbs being one of the greatest experts in the country just makes him despair.

MRS. GIBBS. It's a fact! Dr. Gibbs is never so happy as when he's at Antietam or Gettysburg. The times I've walked over those hills, Myrtle, stopping at every bush and pacing it all out, like we were going to buy it.

MRS. WEBB. Well, if that secondhand man's really serious about buyin' it, Julia, you sell it. And then you'll get to see Paris, all right. Just keep droppin' hints from time to time—that's how I got to see the Atlantic Ocean, y'know.

MRS. GIBBS. Oh, I'm sorry I mentioned it. Only it seems to me that once in your life before you die you ought to see a country where they don't talk in English and don't even want to. *The* STAGE MANAGER *enters briskly from the right. He tips his hat to the ladies, who nod their heads.*

STAGE MANAGER. Thank you, ladies. Thank you very much. *(MRS. GIBBS and MRS. WEBB gather up their things, return into their homes and disappear.)* Now we're going to skip a few hours. But first we want a little more information about the town, kind of a scientific account, you might say. So I've asked Professor Willard of our State University to sketch in a few details of our past history here. Is Professor Willard here? *(PROFESSOR WILLARD, a rural*

savant, pince-nez on a wide satin ribbon, enters from the right with some notes in his hand.) May I introduce Professor Willard of our State University. A few brief notes, thank you, Professor,—unfortunately our time is limited.

PROFESSOR WILLARD. Grover's Corners . . . let me see . . . Grover's Corners lies on the old Pleistocene granite of the Appalachian range. I may say it's some of the oldest land in the world. We're very proud of that. A shelf of Devonian basalt crosses it with vestiges of Mesozoic shale, and some sandstone outcroppings; but that's all more recent: two hundred, three hundred million years old. Some highly interesting fossils have been found . . . I may say: unique fossils . . . two miles out of town, in Silas Peckham's cow pasture. They can be seen at the museum in our University at any time—that is, at any reasonable time. Shall I read some of Professor Gruber's notes on the meteorological situation—mean precipitation, et cetera?

STAGE MANAGER. Afraid we won't have time for that, Professor. We might have a few words on the history of man here.

PROFESSOR WILLARD. Yes . . . anthropological data: Early Amerindian stock. Cotahatchee tribes . . . no evidence before the tenth century of this era . . . hm . . . now entirely disappeared . . . possible traces in three families. Migration toward the end of the seventeenth century of English brachiocephalic blue-eyed stock . . .

for the most part. Since then some Slav and Mediterranean——

STAGE MANAGER. And the population, Professor Willard?

PROFESSOR WILLARD. Within the town limits: 2,640.

STAGE MANAGER. Just a moment, Professor. *(He whispers into the professor's ear.)*

PROFESSOR WILLARD. Oh, yes, indeed?—The population, *at the moment,* is 2,642. The Postal District brings in 507 more, making a total of 3,149.—Mortality and birth rates: constant.—By MacPherson's gauge: 6.032.

STAGE MANAGER. Thank you very much, Professor. We're all very much obliged to you, I'm sure.

PROFESSOR WILLARD. Not at all, sir; not at all.

STAGE MANAGER. This way, Professor, and thank you again. *(Exit* PROFESSOR WILLARD.*)* Now the political and social report: Editor Webb.—Oh, Mr. Webb?

MRS. WEBB *appears at her back door.*

MRS. WEBB. He'll be here in a minute. . . . He just cut his hand while he was eatin' an apple.

STAGE MANAGER. Thank you, Mrs. Webb.

MRS. WEBB. Charles! Everybody's waitin'. *(Exit* MRS. WEBB.*)*

STAGE MANAGER. Mr. Webb is Publisher and Editor of the Grover's Corners *Sentinel.* That's our local paper, y'know.

MR. WEBB *enters from his house, pulling on his coat. His finger is bound in a handkerchief.*

MR. WEBB. Well . . . I don't have to tell you that we're run here by a Board of Selectmen.—All males vote at the age of twenty-one. Women vote indirect. We're lower middle class: sprinkling of professional men . . . ten per cent illiterate laborers. Politically, we're eighty-six per cent Republicans; six per cent Democrats; four per cent Socialists; rest, indifferent. Religiously, we're eighty-five per cent Protestants; twelve per cent Catholics; rest, indifferent.

STAGE MANAGER. Have you any comments, Mr. Webb?

MR. WEBB. Very ordinary town, if you ask me. Little better behaved than most. Probably a lot duller. But our young people here seem to like it well enough. Ninety per cent of 'em graduating from high school settle down right here to live—even when they've been away to college.

STAGE MANAGER. Now, is there anyone in the audience who would like to ask Editor Webb anything about the town?

WOMAN IN THE BALCONY. Is there much drinking in Grover's Corners?

MR. WEBB. Well, ma'am, I wouldn't know what you'd call *much.* Satiddy nights the farmhands meet down in Ellery Greenough's stable and holler some. We've got one or two town drunks, but they're always having remorses every time an evangelist comes to town. No, ma'am, I'd say likker ain't a regular thing in the home here, except in the medicine chest. Right good for snake bite, y'know—always was.

BELLIGERENT MAN AT BACK OF AUDITORIUM. Is there no one in town aware of——

STAGE MANAGER. Come forward, will you, where we can all hear you—What were you saying?

BELLIGERENT MAN. Is there no one in town aware of social injustice and industrial inequality?

MR. WEBB. Oh, yes, everybody is—somethin' terrible. Seems like they spend most of their time talking about who's rich and who's poor.

BELLIGERENT MAN. Then why don't they do something about it? *(He withdraws without waiting for an answer.)*

MR. WEBB. Well, I dunno. . . . I guess we're all hunting like everybody else for a way the diligent and sensible can rise to the top and the lazy and quarrelsome can sink to the bottom. But it ain't easy to find. Meanwhile, we do all we can to help those that can't help themselves and those that can we leave alone.—Are there any other questions?

LADY IN A BOX. Oh, Mr. Webb? Mr. Webb, is there any culture or love of beauty in Grover's Corners?

MR. WEBB. Well, ma'am, there ain't much—not in the sense you mean. Come to think of it, there's some girls that play the piano at High School Commencement; but they ain't happy about it. No, ma'am, there isn't much culture; but maybe this is the place to tell you that we've got a lot of pleasures of a kind here: we like the sun comin' up over the mountain in the morning, and we all notice a good deal about the birds. We pay a lot of attention to them. And we watch the change of the seasons; yes, everybody knows about them. But those other things—you're right, ma'am,—there ain't much.—*Robinson Crusoe* and the Bible; and Handel's ''Largo,'' we all know that; and Whistler's ''Mother''—those are just about as far as we go.

LADY IN A BOX. So I thought. Thank you, Mr. Webb.

STAGE MANAGER. Thank you, Mr. Webb. (MR. WEBB *retires.*) Now, we'll go back to the town. It's early afternoon. All 2,642 have had their dinners and all the dishes have been washed. (MR. WEBB, *having removed his coat, returns and starts pushing a lawn mower to and fro beside his house.*) There's an early-afternoon calm in our town: a buzzin' and a hummin' from the school buildings; only a few buggies on Main Street—the horses dozing at the hitching posts; you all remember what it's like. Doc Gibbs is in his office, tapping people and making them say ''ah.'' Mr. Webb's cuttin' his lawn over there; one man in ten thinks it's a privilege to push his own lawn mower. No, sir. It's later than I thought. There are the children coming home from school already. *Shrill girls' voices are heard, off left.* EMILY *comes along Main Street, carrying some books. There are some signs that she is imagining herself to be a lady of startling elegance.*

EMILY. I *can't*, Lois. I've got to go home and help my mother. I *promised.*

MR. WEBB. Emily, walk simply. Who do you think you are today?

EMILY. Papa, you're terrible. One minute you tell me to stand up straight and the next minute you call me names. I just don't listen to you. (*She gives him an abrupt kiss.*)

MR. WEBB. Golly, I never got a kiss from such a great lady before. (*He goes out of sight.* EMILY *leans over and picks some flowers by the gate of her house.*)

GEORGE GIBBS *comes careening down Main Street. He is throwing a ball up to dizzying heights, and waiting to catch it again. This sometimes requires his taking six steps backward. He bumps into an* OLD LADY *invisible to us.*

GEORGE. Excuse me, Mrs. Forrest.

STAGE MANAGER (*as Mrs. Forrest*). Go out and play in the fields, young man. You got no business playing baseball on Main Street.

GEORGE. Awfully sorry, Mrs. Forrest.—Hello, Emily.

EMILY. H'lo.

GEORGE. You made a fine speech in class.

EMILY. Well . . . I was really ready to make a speech about the Monroe Doctrine, but at the last minute Miss Corcoran made me talk about the Louisiana Purchase instead. I worked an awful long time on both of them.

GEORGE. Gee, it's funny, Emily. From my window up there I can just see your head nights when you're doing your homework over in your room.

EMILY. Why, can you?

GEORGE. You certainly do stick to it, Emily. I don't see how you can sit still that long. I guess you like school.

EMILY. Well, I always feel it's something you have to go through.

GEORGE. Yeah.

EMILY. I don't mind it really. It passes the time.

GEORGE. Yeah.—Emily, what do you think? We might work out a kinda telegraph from your window to mine; and once in a while you could give me a kinda hint or two about one of those algebra problems. I don't mean the answers, Emily, of course not . . . just some little hint . . .

EMILY. Oh, I think *hints* are allowed.—So—ah—if you get stuck, George, you whistle to me; and I'll give you some hints.

GEORGE. Emily, you're just naturally bright, I guess.

EMILY. I figure that it's just the way a person's born.

GEORGE. Yeah. But, you see, I want to be a farmer, and my Uncle Luke says whenever I'm ready I can come over and work on his farm and if I'm any good I can just gradually have it.

EMILY. You mean the house and everything?
Enter MRS. WEBB *with a large bowl and sits on the bench by her trellis.*

GEORGE. Yeah. Well, thanks . . . I better be getting out to the baseball field. Thanks for the talk, Emily.—Good afternoon, Mrs. Webb.

MRS. WEBB. Good afternoon, George.

GEORGE. So long, Emily.

EMILY. So long, George.

MRS. WEBB. Emily, come and help me string these beans for the winter. George Gibbs let himself have a real conversation, didn't he? Why, he's growing up. How old would George be?

EMILY. I don't know.

MRS. WEBB. Let's see. He must be almost sixteen.

EMILY. Mama, I made a speech in class today and I was very good.

MRS. WEBB. You must recite it to your father at supper. What was it about?

EMILY. The Louisiana Purchase. It was like silk off a spool. I'm going to make speeches all my life.—Mama, are these big enough?

MRS. WEBB. Try and get them a little bigger if you can.

EMILY. Mama, will you answer me a question, serious?

MRS. WEBB. Seriously, dear—not serious.

EMILY. Seriously,—will you?

MRS. WEBB. Of course, I will.

EMILY. Mama, am I good looking?

MRS. WEBB. Yes, of course you are. All my children have got good features; I'd be ashamed if they hadn't.

EMILY. Oh, Mama, that's not what I mean. What I mean is: am I *pretty?*

MRS. WEBB. I've already told you, yes. Now that's enough of that. You have a nice young pretty face. I never heard of such foolishness.

EMILY. Oh, Mama, you never tell us the truth about anything.

MRS. WEBB. I *am* telling you the truth.

EMILY. Mama, were *you* pretty?

MRS. WEBB. Yes, I was, if I do say it. I was the prettiest girl in town next to Mamie Cartwright.

EMILY. But, Mama, you've got to say *some*thing about me. Am I pretty enough . . . to get anybody . . . to get people interested in me?

MRS. WEBB. Emily, you make me tired. Now stop it. You're pretty enough for all normal purposes.—Come along now and bring that bowl with you.

EMILY. Oh, Mama, you're no help at all.

STAGE MANAGER. Thank you. Thank you! That'll do. We'll have to interrupt again here. Thank you, Mrs. Webb; thank you, Emily. (MRS. WEBB *and* EMILY *withdraw.)* There are some more things we want to explore about this town. *(He comes to the center of the stage. During the following speech the lights gradually dim to darkness, leaving only a spot on him.)* I think this is a good time to tell you that the Cartwright interests have just begun building a new bank in Grover's Corners—had to go to Vermont for the marble, sorry to say. And they've asked a friend of mine what they should put in the cornerstone for people to dig up . . . a thousand years from now. . . . Of course, they've put in a copy of the *New York Times* and a copy of Mr. Webb's *Sentinel*. . . . We're kind of interested in this because some scientific fellas have found a way of painting all that reading matter with a glue—a silicate glue—that'll make it keep a thousand—two thousand years. We're putting in a Bible . . . and the Constitution of the United States—and a copy of William Shakespeare's plays. What do you say, folks? What do you think? Y'know—Babylon once had two million people in it, and all we know about 'em is the names of the kings and some copies of wheat contracts . . . and contracts for the sale of slaves. Yet every night all those families sat down to supper, and the father came home from his work, and the smoke went up the chimney,—same as here. And even in Greece and Rome, all we know about the *real* life of the people is what we can piece together out of the joking poems and the comedies they wrote for the theatre back then. So I'm going to have a copy of this play put in the cornerstone and the people a thousand years from now'll know a few simple facts about us—more than the Treaty of Versailles and the Lindbergh flight. See what I mean? So—people a thousand years from now—this is the way we were in the provinces north of New York at the beginning of the twentieth century.—This is the way we were: in our growing up and in our marrying and in our living and in our dying. *(A choir partially concealed in the orchestra pit has begun singing "Blessed Be the Tie That Binds."* SIMON STIMSON *stands directing them. Two ladders have been pushed onto the stage; they serve as indication of the second story in the Gibbs and Webb houses.* GEORGE *and* EMILY *mount them, and apply themselves to their schoolwork.* DR. GIBBS *has entered and is seated in his kitchen reading.)* Well!—good deal of time's gone by. It's evening. You can hear choir practice going on in the Congregational Church. The children are at home doing their schoolwork. The day's running down like a tired clock.

SIMON STIMSON. Now look here, everybody. Music come into the world to give pleasure.—Softer! Softer! Get it out of your heads that music's only good when it's loud. You leave loudness to the Methodists. You couldn't beat 'em, even if you wanted to. Now again. Tenors!

GEORGE. Hssst! Emily!

EMILY. Hello.

GEORGE. Hello.

EMILY. I can't work at all. The moonlight's so *terrible.*

GEORGE. Emily, did you get the third problem?

EMILY. Which?

GEORGE. The *third?*

EMILY. Why, yes, George—that's the easiest of them all.

GEORGE. I don't see it. Emily, can you give me a hint?

EMILY. I'll tell you one thing: the answer's in yards.

GEORGE. ! ! ! In yards? How do you mean?

EMILY. In *square* yards.

GEORGE. Oh . . . in square yards.

EMILY. Yes, George, don't you see?

GEORGE. Yeah.

EMILY. In square yards of *wallpaper.*

GEORGE. Wallpaper,—oh, I see. Thanks a lot, Emily.

EMILY. You're welcome. My, isn't the moonlight *terrible?* And choir practice going on.—I think if you hold your breath you can hear the train all the way to Contoocook. Hear it?

GEORGE. M-m-m—What do you know!

EMILY. Well, I guess I better go back and try to work.

GEORGE. Good night, Emily. And thanks.

EMILY. Good night, George.

SIMON STIMSON. Before I forget it: how many of you will be able to come in Tuesday afternoon and sing at Fred Hersey's wedding?—show your hands. That'll be fine; that'll be right nice. We'll do the same music we did for Jane Trowbridge's last month.—Now we'll do: "Art Thou Weary; Art Thou Languid?" It's a question, ladies and gentlemen, make it talk. Ready.

DR. GIBBS. Oh, George, can you come down a minute?

GEORGE. Yes, Pa. *(He descends the ladder.)*

DR. GIBBS. Make yourself comfortable, George; I'll only keep you a minute. George, how old are you?

GEORGE. I? I'm sixteen, almost seventeen.

DR. GIBBS. What do you want to do after school's over?

GEORGE. Why, you know, Pa. I want to be a farmer on Uncle Luke's farm.

DR. GIBBS. You'll be willing, will you, to get up early and milk and feed the stock . . . and you'll be able to hoe and hay all day?

GEORGE. Sure, I will. What are you . . . what do you mean, Pa?

DR. GIBBS. Well, George, while I was in my office today I heard a funny sound . . . and what do you think it was? It was your mother chopping wood. There you see your mother—getting up early; cooking meals all day long; washing and ironing;—and still she has to go out in the back yard and chop wood. I suppose she just got

tired of asking you. She just gave up and decided it was easier to do it herself. And you eat her meals, and put on the clothes she keeps nice for you, and you run off and play baseball,—like she's some hired girl we keep around the house but that we don't like very much. Well, I knew all I had to do was call your attention to it. Here's a handkerchief, son. George, I've decided to raise your spending money twenty-five cents a week. Not, of course, for chopping wood for your mother, because that's a present you give her, but because you're getting older—and I imagine there are lots of things you must find to do with it.

GEORGE. Thanks, Pa.

DR. GIBBS. Let's see—tomorrow's your payday. You can count on it—Hmm. Probably Rebecca'll feel she ought to have some more too. Wonder what could have happened to your mother. Choir practice never was as late as this before.

GEORGE. It's only half past eight, Pa.

DR. GIBBS. I don't know why she's in that old choir. She hasn't any more voice than an old crow. . . . Traipsin' around the streets at this hour of the night . . . Just about time you retired, don't you think?

GEORGE. Yes, Pa. (GEORGE *mounts to his place on the ladder.)*

Laughter and good nights can be heard on stage left and presently MRS. GIBBS. MRS. SOAMES, *and* MRS. WEBB *come down Main Street. When they arrive at the corner of the stage they stop.*

MRS. SOAMES. Good night, Martha. Good night, Mr. Foster.

MRS. WEBB. I'll tell Mr. Webb; I *know* he'll want to put it in the paper.

MRS. GIBBS. My, it's late!

MRS. SOAMES. Good night, Irma.

MRS. GIBBS. Real nice choir practice, wa'n't it? Myrtle Webb! Look at that moon, will you! Tsk-tsk-tsk. Potato weather, for sure. *(They are silent a moment, gazing up at the moon.)*

MRS. SOAMES. Naturally I didn't want to say a word

about it in front of those others, but now we're alone—really, it's the worst scandal that ever was in this town!

MRS. GIBBS. What?

MRS. SOAMES. Simon Stimson!

MRS. GIBBS. Now, Louella!

MRS. SOAMES. But, Julia! To have the organist of a church *drink* and *drunk* year after year. You know he was drunk tonight.

MRS. GIBBS. Now, Louella! We all know about Mr. Stimson, and we all know about the troubles he's been through, and Dr. Ferguson knows too, and if Dr. Ferguson keeps him on there in his job the only thing the rest of us can do is just not to notice it.

MRS. SOAMES. *Not to notice it!* But it's getting worse.

MRS. WEBB. No, it isn't, Louella. It's getting better. I've been in that choir twice as long as you have. It doesn't happen anywhere near so often. . . . My, I hate to go to bed on a night like this.—I better hurry. Those children'll be sitting up till all hours. Good night, Louella. *(They all exchange good nights. She hurries downstage, enters her house and disappears.)*

MRS. GIBBS. Can you get home safe, Louella?

MRS. SOAMES. It's as bright as day. I can see Mr. Soames scowling at the window now. You'd think we'd been to a dance the way the menfolk carry on.

More good nights. MRS. GIBBS *arrives at her home and passes through the trellis into the kitchen.*

MRS. GIBBS. Well, we had a real good time.

DR. GIBBS. You're late enough.

MRS. GIBBS. Why, Frank, it ain't any later 'n usual.

DR. GIBBS. And you stopping at the corner to gossip with a lot of hens.

MRS. GIBBS. Now, Frank, don't be grouchy. Come out and smell the heliotrope in the moonlight. *(They stroll out arm in arm along the footlights.)* Isn't that wonderful? What did you do all the time I was away?

DR. GIBBS. Oh, I read—as usual. What were the girls gossiping about tonight?

MRS. GIBBS. Well, believe me, Frank—there is something to gossip about.

DR. GIBBS. Hmm! Simon Stimson far gone, was he?

MRS. GIBBS. Worst I've ever seen him. How'll that end, Frank? Dr. Ferguson can't forgive him forever.

DR. GIBBS. I guess I know more about Simon Stimson's affairs than anybody in this town. Some people ain't made for small-town life. I don't know how that'll end; but there's nothing we can do but just leave it alone. Come, get in.

MRS. GIBBS. No, not yet . . . Frank, I'm worried about you.

DR. GIBBS. What are you worried about?

MRS. GIBBS. I think it's my duty to make plans for you to get a real rest and change. And if I get that legacy, well, I'm going to insist on it.

DR. GIBBS. Now, Julia, there's no sense in going over that again.

MRS. GIBBS. Frank, you're just *unreasonable!*

DR. GIBBS *(starting into the house).* Come on, Julia, it's getting late. First thing you know you'll catch cold. I gave George a piece of my mind tonight. I reckon you'll have your wood chopped for a while anyway. No, no, start getting upstairs.

MRS. GIBBS. Oh, dear. There's always so many things to pick up, seems like. You know, Frank, Mrs. Fairchild always locks her front door every night. All those people up that part of town do.

DR. GIBBS *(blowing out the lamp).* They're all getting citified, that's the trouble with them. They haven't got nothing fit to burgle and everybody knows it. *(They disappear.)*

REBECCA *climbs up the ladder beside* GEORGE.

GEORGE. Get out, Rebecca. There's only room for one at this window. You're always spoiling everything.

REBECCA. Well, let me look just a minute.

GEORGE. Use your own window.

REBECCA. I did, but there's no moon there. . . . George, do you know what I think, do you? I think maybe the moon's getting nearer

and nearer and there'll be a big 'splosion.

GEORGE. Rebecca, you don't know anything. If the moon were getting nearer, the guys that sit up all night with telescopes would see it first and they'd tell about it, and it'd be in all the newspapers.

REBECCA. George, is the moon shining on South America, Canada, and half the whole world?

GEORGE. Well—prob'ly is.

The STAGE MANAGER *strolls on. Pause. The sound of crickets is heard.*

STAGE MANAGER. Nine thirty. Most of the lights are out. No, there's Constable Warren trying a few doors on Main Street. And here comes Editor Webb, after putting his newspaper to bed.

MR. WARREN, *an elderly policeman, comes along Main Street from the right,* MR. WEBB *from the left.*

MR. WEBB. Good evening, Bill.

CONSTABLE WARREN. Evenin', Mr. Webb.

MR. WEBB. Quite a moon!

CONSTABLE WARREN. Yepp.

MR. WEBB. All quiet tonight?

CONSTABLE WARREN. Simon Stimson is rollin' around a little. Just saw his wife movin' out to hunt for him so I looked the other way—there he is now.

SIMON STIMSON *comes down Main Street from the left, only a trace of unsteadiness in his walk.*

MR. WEBB. Good evening, Simon . . . Town seems to have settled down for the night pretty well.

. . . (SIMON STIMSON *comes up to him and pauses a moment and stares at him, swaying slightly.*) Good evening . . . Yes, most of the town's settled down for the night, Simon. . . . I guess we better do the same. Can I walk along a ways with you? (SIMON STIMSON *continues on his way without a word and disappears at the right.*) Good night.

CONSTABLE WARREN. I don't know how that's goin' to end, Mr. Webb.

MR. WEBB. Well, he's seen a peck of trouble, one thing after another. . . . Oh, Bill . . . if you see my boy smoking cigarettes, just give him a word, will you? He thinks a lot of you, Bill.

CONSTABLE WARREN. I don't think he smokes no cigarettes, Mr. Webb. Leastways, not more'n two or three a year.

MR. WEBB. Hm . . . I hope not.—Well, good night, Bill.

CONSTABLE WARREN. Good night, Mr. Webb. *(Exit.)*

MR. WEBB. Who's that up there? Is that you, Myrtle?

EMILY. No, it's me, Papa.

MR. WEBB. Why aren't you in bed?

EMILY. I don't know. I just can't sleep yet, Papa. The moonlight's so *won*-derful. And the smell of Mrs. Gibbs' heliotrope. Can you smell it?

MR. WEBB. Hm . . . Yes. Haven't any troubles on your mind, have you, Emily?

EMILY. *Troubles,* Papa? *No.*

MR. WEBB. Well, enjoy yourself, but don't let your mother catch you. Good night, Emily.

EMILY. Good night, Papa.

MR. WEBB *crosses into the house, whistling "Blessed Be the Tie That Binds" and disappears.*

REBECCA. I never told you about that letter Jane Crofut got from her minister when she was sick. He wrote Jane a letter and on the envelope the address was like this: It said: Jane Crofut; The Crofut Farm; Grover's Corners; Sutton County; New Hampshire; United States of America.

GEORGE. What's funny about that?

REBECCA. But listen, it's not finished: the United States of America; Continent of North America; Western Hemisphere; the Earth; the Solar System; the Universe; the Mind of God— that's what it said on the envelope.

GEORGE. What do you know!

REBECCA. And the postman brought it just the same.

GEORGE. What do you know!

STAGE MANAGER. That's the end of the First Act, friends. You can go and smoke now, those that smoke.

Discussion

Act I

1. The Stage Manager in *Our Town* has a leading part, but he does not play a major character in the plot of the play. Citing examples from the play, describe his various functions as (a) a source of information about the town and its people, (b) a mover or manipulator of the action, and (c) a player of minor parts.

2. Rather early in the first act it becomes clear that the playwright wishes to focus on two Grover's Corners families; he selects two households, the Gibbses and the Webbs. (a) Point out the differences between the two families, particularly their professions and family members. (b) Discuss the similarities between the two families. (c) Discuss the possible reasons for Wilder presenting the family scenes simultaneously or in tandem, the focus shifting from one side of the stage to another as the families engage in similar activities.

3. By the end of the first act, it seems clear that Emily Webb and George Gibbs are major characters in the play. What can you find in the two following scenes that suggest their relationship will be of concern in Acts II and III: (a) the scene in which George suggests they "work out a kinda telegraph" to communicate between their windows; (b) the scene in which Emily helps George with an arithmetic problem.

4. Professor Willard appears briefly in one scene, to "sketch in a few details of our past history here." (a) What is the nature of his information? (b) What relevance does it have to the play?

5. In one scene, members of the audience ask questions about Grover's Corners. (a) What do the answers to the questions reveal about the town? (b) How do the answers compare with your image of Grover's Corners?

6. At one point the Stage Manager tells the audience what items Grover's Corners plans to put in the new bank's cornerstone, to be opened in a thousand years. (a) What are the items? (b) What would they reveal about the town and country in that distant time? (c) Why does the Stage Manager decide to include a copy of *Our Town*?

7. Early in the play, to emphasize the involvement of the people of Grover's Corners in simple and ordinary routines, Wilder introduces two minor characters. (a) Who are they and what work do they do? (b) How do their scenes convey to the audience a sense of their individuality?

8. Two additional minor characters appear near the end of the act—Mrs. Soames, a member of the church choir, and Simon Stimson, the organist. (a) What traits characterize each of them? (b) What appears to be their function in the play?

9. In the final scene of Act I, Rebecca Gibbs tells her brother George about the peculiar address the minister used in his letter to Jane Crofut, starting with "The Crofut Farm" and ending with the "Mind of God." (a) What is George's reaction to his sister's story? (b) How does the story suggest that *Our Town* is about more than just Grover's Corners?

Act II

The tables and chairs of the two kitchens are still on the stage.
The ladders and the small bench have been withdrawn. The STAGE MANAGER *has been at his accustomed place watching the audience return to its seats.*

STAGE MANAGER. Three years have gone by. Yes, the sun's come up over a thousand times. Summers and winters have cracked the mountains a little bit more and the rains have brought down some of the dirt. Some babies that weren't even born before have begun talking regular sentences already; and a number of people who thought they were right young and spry have noticed that they can't bound up a flight of stairs like they used to, without their heart fluttering a little. All that can happen in a thousand days. Nature's been pushing and contriving in other ways, too: a number of young people fell in love and got married. Yes, the mountain got bit away a few fractions of an inch; millions of gallons of water went by the mill; and here and there a new home was set up under a roof. Almost everybody in the world gets married,—you know what I mean? In our town there aren't hardly any exceptions. Most everybody in the world climbs into their graves married.

The First Act was called the Daily Life. This act is called Love and Marriage. There's another act coming after this: I reckon you can guess what that's about.

So: It's three years later. It's 1904. It's July 7th, just after High School Commencement. That's the time most of our young people jump up and get married. Soon as they've passed their last examinations in solid geometry and Cicero's Orations, looks like they suddenly feel themselves fit to be married. It's early morning. Only this time it's been raining. It's been pouring and thundering. Mrs. Gibbs' garden, and Mrs. Webb's here: drenched. All those bean poles and pea vines: drenched. All yesterday over there on Main Street, the rain looked like curtains being blown along. Hm . . . it may begin again any minute. There! You can hear the 5:45 for Boston.

MRS. GIBBS *and* MRS. WEBB *enter their kitchens and start the day as in the First Act.*

And there's Mrs. Gibbs and Mrs. Webb come down to make breakfast, just as though it were an ordinary day. I don't have to point out to the women in my audience that those ladies they see before them, both of those ladies cooked three meals a day—one of 'em for twenty years, the other for forty—and no summer vacation. They brought up two children apiece, washed, cleaned the house,—and *never a nervous breakdown.*

It's like what one of those Middle West poets said: You've got to love life to have life, and you've got to have life to love life. . . . It's what they call a vicious circle.

HOWIE NEWSOME *(off stage left).* Giddap, Bessie!

STAGE MANAGER. Here comes Howie Newsome delivering the milk. And there's Si Crowell delivering the papers like his brother before him.

SI CROWELL *has entered hurling imaginary newspapers into doorways;* HOWIE NEWSOME *has come along Main Street with Bessie.*

SI CROWELL. Morning, Howie.

HOWIE NEWSOME. Morning, Si.—Anything in the papers I ought to know?

SI CROWELL. Nothing much, except we're losing about the best baseball pitcher Grover's Corners ever had—George Gibbs.

HOWIE NEWSOME. Reckon he is.

SI CROWELL. He could hit and run bases, too.

HOWIE NEWSOME. Yep. Mighty fine ball player.—Whoa! Bessie! I guess I can stop and talk if I've a mind to!

SI CROWELL. I don't see how he could give up a thing like that just to get married. Would you, Howie?

HOWIE NEWSOME. Can't tell, Si. Never had no talent that way. (CONSTABLE WARREN *enters. They exchange good mornings.)* You're up early, Bill.

CONSTABLE WARREN. Seein' if there's anything I can do to prevent a flood. River's been risin' all night.

HOWIE NEWSOME. Si Crowell's all worked up here about George Gibbs' retiring from baseball.

CONSTABLE WARREN. Yes, sir; that's the way it goes. Back in '84 we had a player, Si—even George Gibbs couldn't touch him. Name of Hank Todd. Went down to Maine and become a parson. Wonderful ball player.—Howie, how does the weather look to you?

HOWIE NEWSOME. Oh, 'tain't bad. Think maybe it'll clear up for good. (CONSTABLE WARREN *and* SI CROWELL *continue on their way.* HOWIE NEWSOME *brings the milk first to Mrs. Gibbs' house. She meets him by the trellis.*)

MRS. GIBBS. Good morning, Howie. Do you think it's going to rain?

HOWIE NEWSOME. Morning, Mrs. Gibbs. It rained so heavy, I think maybe it'll clear up.

MRS. GIBBS. Certainly hope it will.

HOWIE NEWSOME. How much did you want today?

MRS. GIBBS. I'm going to have a houseful of relations, Howie. Looks to me like I'll need three-a-milk and two-a-cream.

HOWIE NEWSOME. My wife says to tell you we both hope they'll be very happy, Mrs. Gibbs. Know they *will.*

MRS. GIBBS. Thanks a lot, Howie. Tell your wife I hope she gits there to the wedding.

HOWIE NEWSOME. Yes, she'll be there; she'll be there if she kin. (HOWIE NEWSOME *crosses to Mrs. Webb's house.*) Morning, Mrs. Webb.

MRS. WEBB. Oh, good morning, Mr. Newsome. I told you four quarts of milk, but I hope you can spare me another.

HOWIE NEWSOME. Yes'm . . . and the two of cream.

MRS. WEBB. Will it start raining again, Mr. Newsome?

HOWIE NEWSOME. Well. Just sayin' to Mrs. Gibbs as how it may lighten up. Mrs. Newsome told me to tell you as how we hope they'll both be very happy, Mrs. Webb. Know they *will.*

MRS. WEBB. Thank you, and thank Mrs. Newsome and we're counting on seeing you at the wedding.

HOWIE NEWSOME. Yes, Mrs. Webb. We hope to git there. Couldn't miss that. Come on, Bessie. (*Exit* HOWIE NEWSOME.)

DR. GIBBS *descends in shirt sleeves, and sits down at his breakfast table.*

DR. GIBBS. Well, Ma, the day has come. You're losin' one of your chicks.

MRS. GIBBS. Frank Gibbs, don't you say another word. I feel like crying every minute. Sit down and drink your coffee.

DR. GIBBS. The groom's up shaving himself—only there ain't an awful lot to shave. Whistling and singing, like he's glad to leave us.—Every now and then he says "I do" to the mirror, but it don't sound convincing to me.

MRS. GIBBS. I declare, Frank, I don't know how he'll get along. I've arranged his clothes and seen to it he's put warm things on,—Frank! they're too *young.* Emily won't think of such things. He'll catch his death of cold within a week.

DR. GIBBS. I was remembering my wedding morning, Julia.

MRS. GIBBS. Now don't start that, Frank Gibbs.

DR. GIBBS. I was the scaredest young fella in the State of New Hampshire. I thought I'd make a mistake for sure. And when I saw you comin' down that aisle I thought you were the prettiest girl I'd ever seen, but the only trouble was that I'd never seen you before. There I was in the Congregational Church marryin' a total stranger.

MRS. GIBBS. And how do you think I felt!—Frank, weddings are perfectly awful things. Farces,—that's what they are! (*She puts a plate before him.*) Here, I've made something for you.

DR. GIBBS. Why, Julia Hersey—French toast!

MRS. GIBBS. 'Tain't hard to make and I had to do *some*thing. (*Pause.* DR. GIBBS *pours on the syrup.*)

DR. GIBBS. How'd you sleep last night, Julia?

MRS. GIBBS. Well, I heard a lot of the hours struck off.

DR. GIBBS. Ye-e-s! I get a shock every time I think

of George setting out to be a family man—that great gangling thing!—I tell you Julia, there's nothing so terrifying in the world as a *son*. The relation of father and son is the darndest, awkwardest——

MRS. GIBBS. Well, mother and daughter's no picnic, let me tell you.

DR. GIBBS. They'll have a lot of troubles, I suppose, but that's none of our business. Everybody has a right to their own troubles.

MRS. GIBBS *(at the table, drinking her coffee, meditatively).* Yes . . . people are meant to go through life two by two. 'Tain't natural to be lonesome. *(Pause.* DR. GIBBS *starts laughing.)*

DR. GIBBS. Julia, do you know one of the things I was scared of when I married you?

MRS. GIBBS. Oh, go along with you!

DR. GIBBS. I was afraid we wouldn't have material for conversation more'n'd last us a few weeks. *(Both laugh.)* I was afraid we'd run out and eat our meals in silence, that's a fact.—Well, you and I been conversing for twenty years now without any noticeable barren spells.

MRS. GIBBS. Well,—good weather, bad weather—'tain't very choice, but I always find something to say. *(She goes to the foot of the stairs.)* Did you hear Rebecca stirring around upstairs?

DR. GIBBS. No. Only day of the year Rebecca hasn't been managing everybody's business up there. She's hiding in her room.—I got the impression she's crying.

MRS. GIBBS. Lord's sakes!—This has got to stop.—

Rebecca! Rebecca! Come and get your breakfast.

GEORGE *comes rattling down the stairs, very brisk.*

GEORGE. Good morning, everybody. Only five more hours to live. *(Makes the gesture of cutting his throat, and a loud "k-k-k," and starts through the trellis.)*

MRS. GIBBS. George Gibbs, where are you going?

GEORGE. Just stepping across the grass to see my girl.

MRS. GIBBS. Now, George! You put on your overshoes. It's raining torrents. You don't go out of this house without you're prepared for it.

GEORGE. Aw, Ma. It's just a *step!*

MRS. GIBBS. George! You'll catch your death of cold and cough all through the service.

DR. GIBBS. George, do as your mother tells you! *(*DR. GIBBS *goes upstairs.)*

GEORGE *returns reluctantly to the kitchen and pantomimes putting on overshoes.*

MRS. GIBBS. From tomorrow on you can kill yourself in all weathers, but while you're in my house you'll live wisely, thank you.—Maybe Mrs. Webb isn't used to callers at seven in the morning.—Here, take a cup of coffee first.

GEORGE. Be back in a minute. *(He crosses the stage, leaping over the puddles.)* Good morning, Mother Webb.

MRS. WEBB. Goodness! You frightened me!—Now, George, you can come in a minute out of the wet, but you know I can't ask you in.

GEORGE. Why not——?

MRS. WEBB. George, you know's well as I do: the groom can't see his bride on his wedding day, not until he sees her in church.

GEORGE. Aw!—that's just a superstition.—Good morning, Mr. Webb.

Enter MR. WEBB.

MR. WEBB. Good morning, George.

GEORGE. Mr. Webb, you don't believe in that superstition, do you?

MR. WEBB. There's a lot of common sense in some superstitions, George. *(He sits at the table, facing right.)*

MRS. WEBB. Millions have folla'd it, George, and you don't want to be the first to fly in the face of custom.

GEORGE. How is Emily?

MRS. WEBB. She hasn't waked up yet. I haven't heard a sound out of her.

GEORGE. Emily's *asleep!!!*

MRS. WEBB. No wonder! We were up 'til all hours, sewing and packing. Now I'll tell you what I'll do; you set down here a minute with Mr. Webb and drink this cup of coffee; and I'll go upstairs and see she doesn't come down and surprise you. There's some bacon, too; but don't be long about it. (*Exit* MRS. WEBB.)

Embarrassed silence. MR. WEBB *dunks doughnuts in his coffee. More silence.*

MR. WEBB (*suddenly and loudly*). Well, George, how are you?

GEORGE (*startled, choking over his coffee*). Oh, fine, I'm fine. (*Pause.*) Mr. Webb, what sense could there be in a superstition like that?

MR. WEBB. Well, you see,—on her wedding morning a girl's head's apt to be full of . . . clothes and one thing and another. Don't you think that's probably it?

GEORGE. Ye-e-s. I never thought of that.

MR. WEBB. A girl's apt to be a mite nervous on her wedding day. (*Pause.*)

GEORGE. I wish a fellow could get married without all that marching up and down.

MR. WEBB. Every man that's ever lived has felt that way about it, George; but it hasn't been any use. It's the womenfolk who've built up weddings, my boy. For a while now the women have it all their own. A man looks pretty small at a wedding, George. All those good women standing shoulder to shoulder making sure that the knot's tied in a mighty public way.

GEORGE. But . . . you *believe* in it, don't you, Mr. Webb?

MR. WEBB (*with alacrity*). Oh, yes; *oh, yes.* Don't you misunderstand me, my boy. Marriage is a wonderful thing,—wonderful thing. And don't you forget that, George.

GEORGE. No, sir.—Mr. Webb, how old were you when you got married?

MR. WEBB. Well, you see: I'd been to college and I'd taken a little time to get settled. But Mrs. Webb—she wasn't much older than what Emily is. Oh, age hasn't much to do with it, George,—not compared with . . . uh . . . other things.

GEORGE. What were you going to say, Mr. Webb?

MR. WEBB. Oh, I don't know.—Was I going to say something? (*Pause.*) George, I was thinking the other night of some advice my father gave me when I got married. Charles, he said, Charles, start out early showing who's boss, he said. Best thing to do is to give an order, even if it don't make sense; just so she'll learn to obey. And he said: if anything about your wife irritates you—her conversation, or anything—just get up and leave the house. That'll make it clear to her, he said. And, oh, yes! he said never, *never* let your wife know how much money you have, never.

GEORGE. Well, Mr. Webb . . . I don't think I could . . .

MR. WEBB. So I took the opposite of my father's advice and I've been happy ever since. And let that be a lesson to you, George, never to ask advice on personal matters.—George, are you going to raise chickens on your farm?

GEORGE. What?

MR. WEBB. Are you going to raise chickens on your farm?

GEORGE. Uncle Luke's never been much interested, but I thought——

MR. WEBB. A book came into my office the other day, George, on the Philo System of raising chickens. I want you to read it. I'm thinking of beginning in a small way in the back yard, and I'm going to put an incubator in the cellar——

Enter MRS. WEBB.

MRS. WEBB. Charles, are you talking about that old incubator again? I thought you two'd be talking about things worth while.

MR. WEBB *(bitingly)*. Well, Myrtle, if you want to give the boy some good advice, I'll go upstairs and leave you alone with him.

MRS. WEBB *(pulling* GEORGE *up)*. George, Emily's got to come downstairs and eat her breakfast. She sends you her love but she doesn't want to lay eyes on you. Good-by.

GEORGE. Good-by.

GEORGE *crosses the stage to his own home, bewildered and crestfallen. He slowly dodges a puddle and disappears into his house.*

MR. WEBB. Myrtle, I guess you don't know about that older superstition.

MRS. WEBB. What do you mean, Charles?

MR. WEBB. Since the cave men: no bridegroom should see his father-in-law on the day of the wedding, or near it. Now remember that.

Both leave the stage.

STAGE MANAGER. Thank you very much, Mr. and Mrs. Webb.—Now I have to interrupt again here. You see, we want to know how all this began—this wedding, this plan to spend a lifetime together. I'm awfully interested in how big things like that begin. You know how it is: you're twenty-one or twenty-two and you make some decisions; then whisssh! you're seventy: you've been a lawyer for fifty years, and that white-haired lady at your side has eaten over fifty thousand meals with you. How do such things begin? George and Emily are going to show you now the conversation they had when they first knew that . . . that . . . as the saying goes . . . they were meant for one another. But before they do it I want you to try and remember what it was like to have been very young. And particularly the days when you were first in love; when you were like a person sleepwalking, and you didn't quite see the street you were in, and didn't quite hear everything that was said to you. You're just a little bit crazy. Will you remember that, please? Now they'll be coming out of high school at three o'clock. George has just been elected President of the Junior Class, and as it's June, that means he'll be President of the Senior Class all next year. And Emily's just been elected Secretary and Treasurer. I don't have to tell you how important that is. *(He places a board across the backs of two chairs, which he takes from those at the Gibbs family's table. He brings two high stools from the wings and places them behind the board. Persons sitting on the stools will be facing the audience. This is the counter of Mr. Morgan's drugstore. The sounds of young people's voices are heard off left.)* Yepp,—there they are coming down Main Street now.

EMILY, *carrying an armful of—imaginary— schoolbooks, comes along Main Street from the left.*

EMILY. I can't, Louise. I've got to go home. Good-by. Oh, Ernestine! Ernestine! Can you come over tonight and do Latin? Isn't that Cicero the worst thing—! Tell your mother you *have* to. G'by. G'by, Helen. G'by, Fred.

GEORGE, *also carrying books, catches up with her.*

GEORGE. Can I carry your books home for you, Emily?

EMILY *(coolly)*. Why . . . uh . . . Thank you. It isn't far. *(She gives them to him.)*

GEORGE. Excuse me a minute, Emily.—Say, Bob, if I'm a little late, start practice anyway. And give Herb some long high ones.

EMILY. Good-by, Lizzy.

GEORGE. Good-by, Lizzy.—I'm awfully glad you were elected, too, Emily.

EMILY. Thank you.

They have been standing on Main Street, almost against the back wall. They take the first steps toward the audience when GEORGE *stops and says:*

GEORGE. Emily, why are you mad at me?

EMILY. I'm not mad at you.

GEORGE. You've been treating me so funny lately.

EMILY. Well, since you ask me, I might as well say it right out, George,— *(She catches sight of a teacher passing.)* Good-by, Miss Corcoran.

GEORGE. Good-by, Miss Corcoran.—Wha—what is it?

EMILY *(not scoldingly; finding it difficult to say).* I don't like the whole change that's come over you in the last year. I'm sorry if that hurts your feelings, but I've got to—tell the truth and shame the devil.

GEORGE. A *change?*—Wha—what do you mean?

EMILY. Well, up to a year ago I used to like you a lot. And I used to watch you as you did everything . . . because we'd been friends so long . . . and then you began spending all your time at *baseball* . . . and you never stopped to speak to anybody any more. Not even to your own family you didn't . . . and, George, it's a fact, you've got awful conceited and stuck-up, and all the girls say so. They may not say so to your face, but that's what they say about you behind your back, and it hurts me to hear them say it, but I've got to agree with them a little. I'm sorry if it hurts your feelings . . . but I can't be sorry I said it.

GEORGE. I . . . I'm glad you said it, Emily. I never thought that such a thing was happening to me. I guess it's hard for a fella not to have faults creep into his character.

They take a step or two in silence, then stand still in misery.

EMILY. I always expect a man to be perfect and I think he should be.

GEORGE. Oh . . . I don't think it's possible to be perfect, Emily.

EMILY. Well, my *father* is, and as far as I can see *your* father is. There's no reason on earth why you shouldn't be, too.

GEORGE. Well, I feel it's the other way round. That men aren't naturally good; but girls are.

EMILY. Well, you might as well know right now that I'm not perfect. It's not as easy for a girl to be perfect as a man, because we girls are more—more—nervous.—Now I'm sorry I said all that about you. I don't know what made me say it.

GEORGE. Emily,——

EMILY. Now I can see it's not the truth at all. And I suddenly feel that it isn't important, anyway.

GEORGE. Emily . . . would you like an ice-cream soda, or something, before you go home?

EMILY. Well, thank you. . . . I would.

They advance toward the audience and make an abrupt right turn, opening the door of Morgan's drugstore. Under strong emotion, EMILY *keeps her face down.* GEORGE *speaks to some passers-by.*

GEORGE. Hello, Stew,—how are you?—Good afternoon, Mrs. Slocum.

The STAGE MANAGER, *wearing spectacles and assuming the role of Mr. Morgan, enters abruptly from the right and stands between the audience and the counter of his soda fountain.*

STAGE MANAGER. Hello, George. Hello, Emily.— What'll you have?—Why, Emily Webb,— what you been crying about?

GEORGE. *(He gropes for an explanation.)* She . . . she just got an awful scare, Mr. Morgan. She almost got run over by that hardware-store wagon. Everybody says that Tom Huckins drives like a crazy man.

STAGE MANAGER *(drawing a drink of water).* Well, now! You take a drink of water, Emily. You look all shook up. I tell you, you've got to look both ways before you cross Main Street these days. Gets worse every year.—What'll you have?

EMILY. I'll have a strawberry phosphate, thank you, Mr. Morgan.

GEORGE. No, no, Emily. Have an ice-cream soda with me. Two strawberry ice-cream sodas, Mr. Morgan.

STAGE MANAGER (working the faucets). Two strawberry ice-cream sodas, yes sir. Yes, sir. There are a hundred and twenty-five horses in Grover's Corners this minute I'm talking to you. State Inspector was in here yesterday. And now they're bringing in these auto-mo-biles, the best thing to do is to just stay home. Why, I can remember when a dog could go to sleep all day in the middle of Main Street and nothing come along to disturb him. (He sets the imaginary glasses before them.) There they are. Enjoy 'em. (He sees a customer, right.) Yes, Mrs. Ellis. What can I do for you? (He goes out right.)

EMILY. They're so expensive.

GEORGE. No, no,—don't you think of that. We're celebrating our election. And then do you know what else I'm celebrating?

EMILY. N-no.

GEORGE. I'm celebrating because I've got a friend who tells me all the things that ought to be told me.

EMILY. George, please don't think of that. I don't know why I said it. It's not true. You're——

GEORGE. No, Emily, you stick to it. I'm glad you spoke to me like you did. But you'll see: I'm going to change so quick—you bet I'm going to change. And, Emily, I want to ask you a favor.

EMILY. What?

GEORGE. Emily, if I go away to State Agriculture College next year, will you write me a letter once in a while?

EMILY. I certainly will. I certainly will, George . . . (Pause. They start sipping the sodas through the straws.) It certainly seems like being away three years you'd get out of touch with things.

Maybe letters from Grover's Corners wouldn't be so interesting after a while. Grover's Corners isn't a very important place when you think of all—New Hampshire; but I think it's a very nice town.

GEORGE. The day wouldn't come when I wouldn't want to know everything that's happening here. I know that's true, Emily.

EMILY. Well, I'll try to make my letters interesting. (Pause.)

GEORGE. Y'know. Emily, whenever I meet a farmer I ask him if he thinks it's important to go to Agriculture School to be a good farmer.

EMILY. Why, George——

GEORGE. Yeah, and some of them say that it's even a waste of time. You can get all those things, anyway, out of the pamphlets the government sends out. And Uncle Luke's getting old,—he's about ready for me to start in taking over his farm tomorrow, if I could.

EMILY. My!

GEORGE. And, like you say, being gone all that time . . . in other places and meeting other people . . . Gosh, if anything like that can happen I don't want to go away. I guess new people aren't any better than old ones. I'll bet they almost never are. Emily . . . I feel that you're as good a friend as I've got. I don't need to go and meet the people in other towns.

EMILY. But, George, maybe it's very important for you to go and learn all that about—cattle judging and soils and those things. . . . Of course, I don't know.

GEORGE (after a pause, very seriously). Emily, I'm going to make up my mind right now. I won't go. I'll tell Pa about it tonight.

EMILY. Why, George, I don't see why you have to decide right now. It's a whole year away.

GEORGE. Emily, I'm glad you spoke to me about that . . . that fault in my character. What you said was right; but there was one thing wrong in it, and that was when you said that for a year I wasn't noticing people, and . . . you, for instance. Why, you say you were watching me when I did everything . . . I was doing the same about you all the time. Why, sure,—I always thought about you as one of the chief people I thought about. I always made sure where you were sitting on the bleachers, and who you were with, and for three days now I've been trying to walk home with you; but something's always got in the way. Yesterday I was standing over against the wall waiting for you, and you walked home with *Miss Corcoran.*

EMILY. George! . . . Life's awful funny! How could I have known that? Why, I thought——

GEORGE. Listen, Emily, I'm going to tell you why I'm not going to Agriculture School. I think that once you've found a person that you're very fond of . . . I mean a person who's fond of you, too, and likes you enough to be interested in your character . . . Well, I think that's just as important as college is, and even more so. That's what I think.

EMILY. I think it's awfully important, too.

GEORGE. Emily.

EMILY. Y-yes, George.

GEORGE. Emily, if I *do* improve and make a big change . . . would you be . . . I mean: *could* you be . . .

EMILY. I . . . I am now; I always have been.

GEORGE (*pause*). So I guess this is an important talk we've been having.

EMILY. Yes . . . yes.

GEORGE (*takes a deep breath and straightens his back*). Wait just a minute and I'll walk you home. (*With mounting alarm he digs into his pockets for the money. The* STAGE MANAGER *enters, right.* GEORGE, *deeply embarrassed, but direct, says to him*) Mr. Morgan, I'll have to go home and get the money to pay you for this. It'll only take me a minute.

STAGE MANAGER (*pretending to be affronted*). What's that? George Gibbs, do you mean to tell me——!

GEORGE. Yes, but I had reasons, Mr. Morgan.— Look, here's my gold watch to keep until I come back with the money.

STAGE MANAGER. That's all right. Keep your watch. I'll trust you.

GEORGE. I'll be back in five minutes.

STAGE MANAGER. I'll trust you ten years, George,— not a day over.—Got all over your shock, Emily?

EMILY. Yes, thank you, Mr. Morgan. It was nothing.

GEORGE (*taking up the books from the counter*). I'm ready.

They walk in grave silence across the stage and pass through the trellis at the Webbs' back door and disappear. The STAGE MANAGER *watches them go out, then turns to the audience, removing his spectacles.*

STAGE MANAGER. Well,——(*He claps his hands as a signal.*) Now we're ready to get on with the wedding. (*He stands waiting while the set is prepared for the next scene.* STAGEHANDS *remove the chairs, tables and trellises from the Gibbs and Webb houses. They arrange the pews for the church in the center of the stage. The congregation will sit facing the back wall. The aisle of the church starts at the center of the back wall and comes toward the audience. A small platform is placed against the back wall on which the* STAGE MANAGER *will stand later, playing the minister. The image of a stained-glass window is cast from a lantern slide upon the back wall. When all is ready the* STAGE MANAGER *strolls to the center of the stage, down front, and musingly, addresses the audience.*) There are a lot of things to be said about a wedding; there are a lot of thoughts that go on during a wedding. We can't get them

all into one wedding, naturally, and especially not into a wedding at Grover's Corners, where they're awfully plain and short. In this wedding I play the minister. That gives me the right to say a few more things about it. For a while now, the play gets pretty serious. Y'see, some churches say that marriage is a sacrament. I don't quite know that that means, but I can guess. Like Mrs. Gibbs said a few minutes ago: People were made to live two-by-two. This is a good wedding, but people are so put together that even at a good wedding there's a lot of confusion way down deep in people's minds and we thought that that ought to be in our play, too.

The real hero of this scene isn't on the stage at all, and you know who that is. It's like what one of those European fellas said: every child born into the world is nature's attempt to make a perfect human being. Well, we've seen nature pushing and contriving for some time now. We all know that nature's interested in quantity; but I think she's interested in quality, too,—that's why I'm in the ministry. And don't forget all the other witnesses at this wedding,—the ancestors. Millions of them. Most of them set out to live two-by-two, also. Millions of them.

Well, that's all my sermon. 'Twan't very long, anyway.

The organ starts playing Handel's "Largo." The congregation streams into the church and sits in silence. Church bells are heard. MRS.

GIBBS *sits in the front row, the first seat on the aisle, the right section; next to her are* REBECCA *and* DR. GIBBS. *Across the aisle* MRS. WEBB, WALLY *and* MR. WEBB. *A small choir takes its place, facing the audience under the stained-glass window.* MRS. WEBB, *on the way to her place, turns back and speaks to the audience.*

MRS. WEBB. I don't know why on earth I should be crying. I suppose there's nothing to cry about. It came over me at breakfast this morning; there was Emily eating her breakfast as she's done for seventeen years and now she's going off to eat it in someone else's house. I suppose that's it. And Emily! She suddenly said: I can't eat another mouthful, and she put her head down on the table and *she* cried. *(She starts toward her seat in the church, but turns back and adds)* Oh, I've got to say it: you know, there's something downright cruel about sending our girls out into marriage this way. I hope some of her girl friends have told her a thing or two. It's cruel, I know, but I couldn't bring myself to say anything. I went into it blind as a bat myself. *(In half-amused exasperation.)* The whole world's wrong, that's what's the matter. There they come. *(She hurries to her place in the pew.)*

GEORGE *starts to come down the right aisle of the theatre, through the audience. Suddenly* THREE MEMBERS *of his baseball team appear by the right proscenium pillar and start whistling and catcalling to him. They are dressed for the ball field.*

THE BASEBALL PLAYERS. Eh, George, George! Hsst—yaow! Look at him, fellas—he looks scared to death. Yaow! George, don't look so innocent, you old geezer. We know what you're thinking. Don't disgrace the team, big boy. Whoo-oo-oo.

STAGE MANAGER. All right! All right! That'll do. That's enough of that. (*Smiling, he pushes them off the stage. They lean back to shout a few more catcalls.*) There used to be an awful lot to that kind of thing at weddings in the old days,—Rome, and later. We're more civilized now,—so they say.

The choir starts singing "Love Divine, All Love Excelling——" GEORGE has reached the stage. He stares at the congregation a moment, then takes a few steps of withdrawal, toward the right proscenium pillar. His mother, from the front row, seems to have felt his confusion. She leaves her seat and comes down the aisle quickly to him.

MRS. GIBBS. George! George! What's the matter?

GEORGE. Ma, I don't want to grow old. Why's everybody pushing me so?

MRS. GIBBS. Why, George . . . you wanted it.

GEORGE. No, Ma, listen to me——

MRS. GIBBS. No, no, George,—you're a man now.

GEORGE. Listen, Ma,—for the last time I ask you . . . All I want to do is to be a fella——

MRS. GIBBS. George! If anyone should hear you! Now stop. Why, I'm ashamed of you!

GEORGE. (*He comes to himself and looks over the scene.*) What? Where's Emily?

MRS. GIBBS (*relieved*). George! You gave me such a turn.

GEORGE. Cheer up, Ma. I'm getting married.

MRS. GIBBS. Let me catch my breath a minute.

GEORGE (*comforting her*). Now, Ma, you save Thursday nights. Emily and I are coming over to dinner every Thursday night . . . you'll see. Ma, what are you crying for? Come on; we've got to get ready for this.

MRS. GIBBS, *mastering her emotion, fixes his tie and whispers to him. In the meantime,* EMILY, *in white and wearing her wedding veil, has*

come through the audience and mounted onto the stage. She too draws back, frightened, when she sees the congregation in the church. The choir begins: "Blessed Be the Tie That Binds."

EMILY. I never felt so alone in my whole life. And George over there, looking so . . . ! I *hate* him. I wish I were dead. Papa! Papa!

MR. WEBB (*leaves his seat in the pews and comes toward her anxiously*). Emily! Emily! Now don't get upset. . . .

EMILY. But, Papa,—I don't want to get married. . . .

MR. WEBB. Sh—sh—Emily. Everything's all right.

EMILY. Why can't I stay for a while just as I am? Let's go away,——

MR. WEBB. No, no, Emily. Now stop and think a minute.

EMILY. Don't you remember that you used to say,—all the time you used to say—all the time: that I was *your* girl! There must be lots of places we can go to. I'll work for you. I could keep house.

MR. WEBB. Sh . . . You mustn't think of such things. You're just nervous, Emily. (*He turns and calls*): George! George! Will you come here a minute? (*He leads her toward George.*) Why you're marrying the best young fellow in the world. George is a fine fellow.

EMILY. But Papa,——

MRS. GIBBS *returns unobtrusively to her seat.* MR. WEBB *has one arm around his daughter.*

He places his hand on GEORGE's *shoulder.*

MR. WEBB. I'm giving away my daughter, George. Do you think you can take care of her?

GEORGE. Mr. Webb, I want to . . . I want to try. Emily, I'm going to do my best. I love you, Emily. I need you.

EMILY. Well, if you love me, help me. All I want is someone to love me.

GEORGE. I will, Emily. Emily, I'll try.

EMILY. And I mean for *ever.* Do you hear? For ever and ever.

They fall into each other's arms. The march from Lohengrin *is heard. The* STAGE MANAGER, *as* CLERGYMAN, *stands on the box, up center.*

MR. WEBB. Come, they're waiting for us. Now you know it'll be all right. Come, quick.

GEORGE *slips away and takes his place beside the* STAGE MANAGER-CLERGYMAN. EMILY *proceeds up the aisle on her father's arm.*

STAGE MANAGER. Do you, George, take this woman, Emily, to be your wedded wife, to have . . .

MRS. SOAMES *has been sitting in the last row of the congregation. She now turns to her neighbors and speaks in a shrill voice. Her chatter drowns out the rest of the clergyman's words.*

MRS. SOAMES. Perfectly lovely wedding! Loveliest wedding I ever saw. Oh, I do love a good wedding, don't you? Doesn't she make a lovely bride?

GEORGE. I do.

STAGE MANAGER. Do you, Emily, take this man, George, to be your wedded husband,——

Again his further words are covered by those of MRS. SOAMES.

MRS. SOAMES. Don't know *when* I've seen such a lovely wedding. But I always cry. Don't know why it is, but I always cry. I just like to see young people happy, don't you? Oh, I think it's lovely.

The ring. The kiss. The stage is suddenly arrested into silent tableau. The STAGE MANAGER, *his eyes on the distance, as though to himself:*

STAGE MANAGER. I've married over two hundred couples in my day. Do I believe in it? I don't know. M. . . . marries N. . . . millions of them. The cottage, the go-cart, the Sunday-afternoon drives in the Ford, the first rheumatism, the grandchildren, the second rheumatism, the deathbed, the reading of the will,——*(He now looks at the audience for the first time, with a warm smile that removes any sense of cynicism from the next line.)* Once in a thousand times it's interesting.

—Well, let's have Mendelssohn's ''Wedding March''!

The organ picks up the March. The BRIDE *and* GROOM *come down the aisle, radiant, but trying to be very dignified.*

MRS. SOAMES. Aren't they a lovely couple? Oh, I've never been to such a nice wedding. I'm sure they'll be happy. I always say: *happiness,* that's the great thing! The important thing is to be happy.

The BRIDE *and* GROOM *reach the steps leading into the audience. A bright light is thrown upon them. They descend into the auditorium and run up the aisle joyously.*

STAGE MANAGER. That's all the Second Act, folks. Ten minutes' intermission.

Discussion

Act II

1. In his opening speech, the Stage Manager tells us that Act I was called "Daily Life," and Act II "Love and Marriage." And then he says, "There's another act coming after this: I reckon you can guess what that's about." (a) How and why are these titles appropriate? (b) What do you think Act III will be about? Why?

2. As in Act I, the paperboy and the milkman appear early and briefly in Act II. How are their actions similar and how are they different from those of Act I?

3. George is not allowed to see his bride the morning of the wedding, and he is left alone with her father, Mr. Webb. Discuss the nature of the advice that Mr. Webb gives his future son-in-law.

4. In the scene that shows how their love began, Emily tells George how, in the last year, he has changed. (a) What does Emily tell George, and why is she so frank? (b) What is George's reaction? Explain.

5. In the scene in the drugstore, George makes up his mind quite suddenly not to go to college and reaches an understanding with Emily. (a) What causes George to change his mind about college? (b) Do you think George makes the right decision? Discuss.

6. When the Stage Manager turns into the minister to preside at George and Emily's wedding, he says in his sermon: "The real hero of this scene isn't on the stage at all, and you know who that is. It's like what one of those European fellas said: every child born into the world is nature's attempt to make a perfect human being. Well, we've seen nature pushing and contriving for some time now." Who is the "real hero"? Explain.

7. Just before the wedding, neither George nor Emily seem to want to go through with it. (a) Why are they suddenly reluctant? (b) How do they overcome these feelings?

8. Mrs. Soames's chatter and comments tend to drown out the wedding ceremony for the audience. What appears to be Mrs. Soames's dramatic function in this closing scene?

9. Near the end of the act, the scene is "suddenly arrested into silent tableau," and the Stage Manager talks to the audience about marriage, concluding: "Once in a thousand times it's interesting." (a) What does he seem to be saying about life? (b) about marriage? (c) What might his words foreshadow?

Act III

During the intermission the audience has seen the STAGEHANDS *arranging the stage. On the right-hand side, a little right of the center, ten or twelve ordinary chairs have been placed in three openly spaced rows facing the audience.*

These are graves in the cemetery.

Toward the end of the intermission the ACTORS *enter and take their places. The front row contains: toward the center of the stage, an empty chair; then* MRS. GIBBS; SIMON STIMSON.

The second row contains, among others, MRS. SOAMES. *The third row has* WALLY WEBB.

The dead do not turn their heads or their eyes to right or left, but they sit in a quiet without stiffness. When they speak their tone is matter-of-fact, without sentimentality and, above all, without lugubriousness.

The STAGE MANAGER *takes his accustomed place and waits for the house lights to go down.*

STAGE MANAGER. This time nine years have gone by, friends—summer, 1913. Gradual changes in Grover's Corners. Horses are getting rarer. Farmers coming into town in Fords. Everybody locks their house doors now at night. Ain't been any burglars in town yet, but everybody's heard about 'em. You'd be surprised, though—on the whole, things don't change much around here.

This is certainly an important part of Grover's Corners. It's on a hilltop—a windy hilltop—lots of sky, lots of clouds,—often lots of sun and moon and stars. You come up here, on a fine afternoon and you can see range on range of hills—awful blue they are—up there by Lake Sunapee and Lake Winnipesaukee . . . and way up, if you've got a glass, you can see the White Mountains and Mt. Washington—where North Conway and Conway is. And, of course, our favorite mountain, Mt. Monadnock,'s right here—and all these towns that lie around it: Jaffrey, 'n East Jaffrey, 'n Peterborough, 'n Dublin; and *(then pointing down in the audience)* there, quite a ways

down, is Grover's Corners. Yes, beautiful spot up here. Mountain laurel and li-lacks. I often wonder why people like to be buried in Wood-lawn and Brooklyn when they might pass the same time up here in New Hampshire. Over there—*(pointing to stage left)* are the old stones,—1670, 1680. Strong-minded people that come a long way to be independent. Summer people walk around there laughing at the funny words on the tombstones . . . it don't do any harm. And genealogists come up from Boston—get paid by city people for looking up their ancestors. They want to make sure they're Daughters of the American Revolution and of the *Mayflower*. . . . Well, I guess that don't do any harm, either. Wherever you come near the human race, there's layers and layers of nonsense. . . .

Over there are some Civil War veterans. Iron flags on their graves . . . New Hampshire boys . . . had a notion that the Union ought to be kept together, though they'd never seen more than fifty miles of it themselves. All they knew was the name, friends—the United States of America. The United States of America. And they went and died about it.

This here is the new part of the cemetery. Here's your friend Mrs. Gibbs. 'N let me see—here's Mr. Stimson, organist at the Congregational Church. And Mrs. Soames who enjoyed the wedding so—you remember? Oh, and a lot of others. And Editor Webb's boy, Wallace, whose appendix burst while he was on a Boy Scout trip to Crawford Notch. Yes, an awful lot of sorrow has sort of quieted down up here. People just wild with grief have brought their relatives up to this hill. We all know how it is . . . and then time . . . and sunny days . . . and rainy days . . . 'n snow . . . We're all glad they're in a beautiful place and we're coming up here ourselves when our fit's over.

Now there are some things we all know, but we don't take'm out and look at'm very often. We all know that *something* is eternal. And it ain't houses and it ain't names, and it ain't earth, and it ain't even the stars . . . everybody knows in their bones that *something* is eternal, and that something has to do with human beings. All the greatest people ever lived have been telling us that for five thousand years and yet you'd be surprised how people are always losing hold of it. There's something way down deep that's eternal about every human being. *(Pause.)*

You know as well as I do that the dead don't stay interested in us living people for very long. Gradually, gradually, they lose hold of the earth . . . and the ambitions they had . . . and the pleasures they had . . . and the things they suffered . . . and the people they loved. They get weaned away from earth—that's the way I put it,—weaned away. And they stay here while the earth part of 'em burns away, burns out; and all that time they slowly get indifferent to what's goin' on in Grover's Corners. They're waitin' for something that they feel is comin'. Something important, and great. Aren't they waitin' for the eternal part in them to come out clear? Some of the things they're going to say maybe'll hurt your feelings—but that's the way it is: mother 'n daughter . . . husband 'n wife . . . enemy 'n enemy . . . money 'n miser . . . all those terribly important things kind of grow pale around here. And what's left when memory's gone, and your identity, Mrs. Smith? *(He looks at the audience a minute, then turns to the stage.)* Well! There are some *living* people. There's Joe Stoddard,

our undertaker, supervising a new-made grave. And here comes a Grover's Corners boy, that left town to go out West.

JOE STODDARD *has hovered about in the background.* SAM CRAIG *enters left, wiping his forehead from the exertion. He carries an umbrella and strolls front.*

SAM CRAIG. Good afternoon, Joe Stoddard.

JOE STODDARD. Good afternoon, good afternoon. Let me see now: do I know you?

SAM CRAIG. I'm Sam Craig.

JOE STODDARD. Gracious sakes' alive! Of all people! I should'a knowed you'd be back for the funeral. You've been away a long time, Sam.

SAM CRAIG. Yes, I've been away over twelve years. I'm in business out in Buffalo now, Joe. But I was in the East when I got news of my cousin's death, so I thought I'd combine things a little and come and see the old home. You look well.

JOE STODDARD. Yes, yes, can't complain. Very sad, our journey today, Samuel.

SAM CRAIG. Yes.

JOE STODDARD. Yes, yes. I always say I hate to supervise when a young person is taken. They'll be here in a few minutes now. I had to come here early today—my son's supervisin' at the home.

SAM CRAIG *(reading stones)*. Old Farmer McCarty, I used to do chores for him—after school. He had the lumbago.

JOE STODDARD. Yes, we brought Farmer McCarty here a number of years ago now.

SAM CRAIG *(staring at Mrs. Gibbs' knees)*. Why, this is my Aunt Julia . . . I'd forgotten that she'd . . . of course, of course.

JOE STODDARD. Yes, Doc Gibbs lost his wife two-three years ago . . . about this time. And today's another pretty bad blow for him, too.

MRS. GIBBS *(to Simon Stimson, in an even voice)*. That's my sister Carey's boy, Sam . . . Sam Craig.

SIMON STIMSON. I'm always uncomfortable when *they're* around.

MRS. GIBBS. Simon.

SAM CRAIG. Do they choose their own verses much, Joe?

JOE STODDARD. No . . . not usual. Mostly the bereaved pick a verse.

SAM CRAIG. Doesn't sound like Aunt Julia. There aren't many of those Hersey sisters left now. Let me see: where are . . . I wanted to look at my father's and mother's . . .

JOE STODDARD. Over there with the Craigs . . . Avenue F.

SAM CRAIG (reading Simon Stimson's epitaph). He was organist at church, wasn't he?—Hm, drank a lot, we used to say.

JOE STODDARD. Nobody was supposed to know about it. He'd seen a peck of trouble. (Behind his hand.) Took his own life, y' know?

SAM CRAIG. Oh, did he?

JOE STODDARD. Hung himself in the attic. They tried to hush it up, but of course it got around. He chose his own epy-taph. You can see it there. It ain't a verse exactly.

SAM CRAIG. Why, it's just some notes of music—what is it?

JOE STODDARD. Oh, I wouldn't know. It was wrote up in the Boston papers at the time.

SAM CRAIG. Joe, what did she die of?

JOE STODDARD. Who?

SAM CRAIG. My cousin.

JOE STODDARD. Oh, didn't you know? Had some trouble bringing a baby into the world. 'Twas her second, though. There's a little boy 'bout four years old.

SAM CRAIG (opening his umbrella). The grave's going to be over there?

JOE STODDARD. Yes, there ain't much more room over here among the Gibbses, so they're opening up a whole new Gibbs section over by Avenue B. You'll excuse me now. I see they're comin'.

From left to center, at the back of the stage, comes a procession. FOUR MEN *carry a casket, invisible to us. All the rest are under umbrellas. One can vaguely see:* DR. GIBBS, GEORGE, *the* WEBBS, *etc. They gather about a grave in the back center of the stage, a little to the left of center.*

MRS. SOAMES. Who is it, Julia?

MRS. GIBBS (without raising her eyes). My daughter-in-law, Emily Webb.

MRS. SOAMES (a little surprised, but no emotion). Well, I declare! The road up here must have been awful muddy. What did she die of, Julia?

MRS. GIBBS. In childbirth.

MRS. SOAMES. Childbirth. (Almost with a laugh.) I'd forgotten all about that. My, wasn't life awful—(With a sigh.) and wonderful.

SIMON STIMSON (with a sideways glance). Wonderful, was it?

MRS. GIBBS. Simon! Now, remember!

MRS. SOAMES. I remember Emily's wedding. Wasn't it a lovely wedding! And I remember her reading the class poem at Graduation Exercises. Emily was one of the brightest girls ever graduated from High School. I've heard Principal Wilkins say so time after time. I called on them at their new farm, just before I died. Perfectly beautiful farm.

A WOMAN FROM AMONG THE DEAD. It's on the same road we lived on.

A MAN AMONG THE DEAD. Yepp, right smart farm.

They subside. The group by the grave starts singing "Blessed Be the Tie That Binds."

A WOMAN AMONG THE DEAD. I always liked that hymn. I was hopin' they'd sing a hymn.

Pause. Suddenly EMILY *appears from among the umbrellas. She is wearing a white dress.*

Her hair is down her back and tied by a white ribbon like a little girl. She comes slowly, gazing wonderingly at the dead, a little dazed. She stops halfway and smiles faintly. After looking at the mourners for a moment, she walks slowly to the vacant chair beside Mrs. Gibbs and sits down.

EMILY *(to them all, quietly, smiling).* Hello.

MRS. SOAMES. Hello, Emily.

A MAN AMONG THE DEAD. Hello, M's Gibbs.

EMILY *(warmly).* Hello, Mother Gibbs.

MRS. GIBBS. Emily.

EMILY. Hello. *(With surprise.)* It's raining. *(Her eyes drift back to the funeral company.)*

MRS. GIBBS. Yes . . . They'll be gone soon, dear. Just rest yourself.

EMILY. It seems thousands and thousands of years since I . . . Papa remembered that that was my favorite hymn. Oh, I wish I'd been here a long time. I don't like being new here.—How do you do, Mr. Stimson?

SIMON STIMSON. How do you do, Emily.

EMILY *continues to look about her with a wondering smile; as though to shut out from her mind the thought of the funeral company she starts speaking to Mrs. Gibbs with a touch of nervousness.*

EMILY. Mother Gibbs, George and I have made that farm into just the best place you ever saw. We thought of you all the time. We wanted to show you the new barn and a great long cement drinking fountain for the stock. We bought that out of the money you left us.

MRS. GIBBS. I did?

EMILY. Don't you remember, Mother Gibbs—the legacy you left us? Why, it was over three hundred and fifty dollars.

MRS. GIBBS. Yes, yes, Emily.

EMILY. Well, there's a patent device on the drinking fountain so that it never overflows, Mother Gibbs, and it never sinks below a certain mark they have there. It's fine. *(Her voice trails off and her eyes return to the funeral group.)* It won't be the same to George without me, but it's a lovely farm. *(Suddenly she looks directly at Mrs. Gibbs.)* Live people don't understand, do they?

MRS. GIBBS. No, dear—not very much.

EMILY. They're sort of shut up in little boxes, aren't they? I feel as though I knew them last a thousand years ago . . . My boy is spending the day at Mrs. Carter's. *(She sees* MR. CARTER *among the dead.)* Oh, Mr. Carter, my little boy is spending the day at your house.

MR. CARTER. Is he?

EMILY. Yes, he loves it there—Mother Gibbs, we have a Ford, too. Never gives any trouble. I don't drive, though. Mother Gibbs, when does this feeling go away?—Of being . . . one of *them?* How long does it . . . ?

MRS. GIBBS. Sh! dear. Just wait and be patient.

EMILY *(with a sigh).* I know.—Look, they're finished. They're going.

MRS. GIBBS. Sh——

The umbrellas leave the stage. DR. GIBBS *has come over to his wife's grave and stands before it a moment.* EMILY *looks up at his face.* MRS. GIBBS *does not raise her eyes.*

EMILY. Look! Father Gibbs is bringing some of my flowers to you. He looks just like George, doesn't he? Oh, Mother Gibbs, I never realized before how troubled and how . . . how in the dark live persons are. Look at him. I loved him so. From morning till night, that's all they are—troubled. DR. GIBBS *goes off.*

THE DEAD. Little cooler than it was.—Yes, that rain's cooled it off a little. Those northeast

winds always do the same thing, don't they? If it isn't a rain, it's a three-day blow.——

A patient calm falls on the stage. The STAGE MANAGER *appears at his proscenium pillar, smoking.* EMILY *sits up abruptly with an idea.*

EMILY. But, Mother Gibbs, one can go back; one can go back there again . . . into living. I feel it. I know it. Why just then for a moment I was thinking about . . . about the farm . . . and for a minute I *was* there, and my baby was on my lap as plain as day.

MRS. GIBBS. Yes, of course you can.

EMILY. I can go back there and live all those days over again . . . why not?

MRS. GIBBS. All I can say is, Emily, don't.

EMILY. *(She appeals urgently to the stage manager.)* But it's true, isn't it? I can go and live . . . back there . . . again.

STAGE MANAGER. Yes, some have tried—but they soon come back here.

MRS. GIBBS. Don't do it, Emily.

MRS. SOAMES. Emily, don't. It's not what you think it'd be.

EMILY. But I won't live over a sad day. I'll choose a happy one—I'll choose the day I first knew that I loved George. Why should that be painful?

THEY *are silent. Her question turns to the stage manager.*

STAGE MANAGER. You not only live it; but you watch yourself living it.

EMILY. Yes?

STAGE MANAGER. And as you watch it, you see the thing that they—down there—never know. You see the future. You know what's going to happen afterwards.

EMILY. But is that—painful? Why?

MRS. GIBBS. That's not the only reason why you shouldn't do it, Emily. When you've been here longer you'll see that our life here is to forget all that, and think only of what's ahead, and be ready for what's ahead. When you've been here longer you'll understand.

EMILY *(softly).* But, Mother Gibbs, how can I *ever* forget that life? It's all I know. It's all I had.

MRS. SOAMES. Oh, Emily. It isn't wise. Really, it isn't.

EMILY. But it's a thing I must know for myself. I'll choose a happy day, anyway.

MRS. GIBBS. *No!*—At least, choose an unimportant day. Choose the least important day in your life. It will be important enough.

EMILY *(to herself).* Then it can't be since I was married; or since the baby was born. *(To the stage manager, eagerly.)* I can choose a birthday at least, can't I?—I choose my twelfth birthday.

STAGE MANAGER. All right. February 11th, 1899. A Tuesday.—Do you want any special time of day?

EMILY. Oh, I want the whole day.

STAGE MANAGER. We'll begin at dawn. You remember it had been snowing for several days; but it had stopped the night before, and they had begun clearing the roads. The sun's coming up.

EMILY *(with a cry; rising).* There's Main Street . . . why, that's Mr. Morgan's drugstore before he changed it! . . . And there's the livery stable.

The stage at no time in this act has been very dark; but now the left half of the stage gradually becomes very bright—the brightness of a crisp winter morning. EMILY *walks toward Main Street.*

STAGE MANAGER. Yes, it's 1899. This is fourteen years ago.

EMILY. Oh, that's the town I knew as a little girl. And, *look,* there's the old white fence that used to be around our house. Oh, I'd forgotten that! Oh, I love it so! Are they inside?

STAGE MANAGER. Yes, your mother'll be coming downstairs in a minute to make breakfast.

EMILY *(softly).* Will she?

STAGE MANAGER. And you remember: your father had been away for several days; he came back on the early-morning train.

EMILY. No . . . ?

STAGE MANAGER. He'd been back to his college to make a speech—in western New York, at Clinton.

EMILY. Look! There's Howie Newsome. There's our policeman. But he's *dead;* he *died.*

The voices of HOWIE NEWSOME, CONSTABLE WARREN *and* JOE CROWELL, JR., *are heard at the left of the stage.* EMILY *listens in delight.*

HOWIE NEWSOME. Whoa, Bessie!—Bessie! 'Morning, Bill.

CONSTABLE WARREN. Morning, Howie.

HOWIE NEWSOME. You're up early.

CONSTABLE WARREN. Been rescuin' a party; darn near froze to death, down by Polish Town thar. Got drunk and lay out in the snowdrifts. Thought he was in bed when I shook'm.

EMILY. Why, there's Joe Crowell. . . .

JOE CROWELL. Good morning, Mr. Warren. 'Morning, Howie.

MRS. WEBB *has appeared in her kitchen, but* EMILY *does not see her until she calls.*

MRS. WEBB. Chil-*dren!* Wally! Emily! . . . Time to get up.

EMILY. Mama, I'm here! Oh! how young Mama looks! I didn't know Mama was ever that young.

MRS. WEBB. You can come and dress by the kitchen fire, if you like; but hurry. *(HOWIE NEWSOME has entered along Main Street and brings the milk to Mrs. Webb's door.)* Good morning, Mr. Newsome. Whhhh—it's cold.

HOWIE NEWSOME. Ten below by my barn, Mrs. Webb.

MRS. WEBB. Think of it! Keep yourself wrapped up. *(She takes her bottles in, shuddering.)*

EMILY *(with an effort).* Mama, I can't find my blue hair ribbon anywhere.

MRS. WEBB. Just open your eyes, dear, that's all. I laid it out for you special—on the dresser, there. If it were a snake it would bite you.

EMILY. Yes, yes . . .

She puts her hand on her heart. MR. WEBB *comes along Main Street, where he meets* CONSTABLE WARREN. *Their movements and voices are increasingly lively in the sharp air.*

MR. WEBB. Good morning, Bill.

CONSTABLE WARREN. Good morning, Mr. Webb. You're up early.

MR. WEBB. Yes, just been back to my old college in New York State. Been any trouble here?

CONSTABLE WARREN. Well, I was called up this mornin' to rescue a Polish fella—darn near froze to death he was.

MR. WEBB. We must get it in the paper.

CONSTABLE WARREN. 'Twan't much.

EMILY *(whispers).* Papa.

MR. WEBB *shakes the snow off his feet and enters his house.* CONSTABLE WARREN *goes off, right.*

MR. WEBB. Good morning, Mother.

MRS. WEBB. How did it go, Charles?

MR. WEBB. Oh, fine, I guess. I told'm a few things.—Everything all right here?

MRS. WEBB. Yes—can't think of anything that's happened, special. Been right cold. Howie Newsome says it's ten below over to his barn.

MR. WEBB. Yes, well, it's colder than that at Hamilton College. Students' ears are falling off. It ain't Christian.—Paper have any mistakes in it?

MRS. WEBB. None that I noticed. Coffee's ready when you want it. *(He starts upstairs.)* Charles! Don't forget; it's Emily's birthday. Did you remember to get her something?

MR. WEBB *(patting his pocket).* Yes, I've got something here. *(Calling up the stairs.)* Where's my girl? Where's my birthday girl? *(He goes off left.)*

MRS. WEBB. Don't interrupt her now, Charles. You can see her at breakfast. She's slow enough as it is. Hurry up, children! It's seven o'clock. Now, I don't want to call you again.

EMILY *(softly, more in wonder than in grief).* I can't bear it. They're so young and beautiful. Why did they ever have to get old? Mama, I'm here. I'm grown up. I love you all, everything.—I can't look at everything hard enough. *(She looks questioningly at the* STAGE MANAGER, *saying or suggesting: "Can I go in?" He nods briefly. She crosses to the inner door to the kitchen, left of her mother, and as though entering the room, says, suggesting the voice of a girl of twelve)* Good morning, Mama.

MRS. WEBB *(crossing to embrace and kiss her; in her characteristic matter-of-fact manner).* Well, now, dear, a very happy birthday to my girl and many happy returns. There are some surprises waiting for you on the kitchen table.

EMILY. Oh, Mama, you *shouldn't* have. *(She throws an anguished glance at the stage manager.)* I can't—I can't.

MRS. WEBB *(facing the audience, over her stove).* But birthday or no birthday, I want you to eat your breakfast good and slow. I want you to grow up and be a good strong girl. That in the blue paper is from your Aunt Carrie; and I reckon you can guess who brought the postcard album. I found it on the doorstep when I brought in the milk—George Gibbs . . . must have come over in the cold pretty early . . . right nice of him.

EMILY *(to herself).* Oh, George! I'd forgotten that. . . .

MRS. WEBB. Chew that bacon good and slow. It'll help keep you warm on a cold day.

EMILY *(with mounting urgency).* Oh, Mama, just look at me one minute as though you really saw me. Mama, fourteen years have gone by. I'm dead. You're a grandmother, Mama. I married George Gibbs, Mama. Wally's dead, too. Mama, his appendix burst on a camping trip to North Conway. We felt just terrible about it—don't you remember? But, just for a moment now we're all together. Mama, just for a moment we're happy. *Let's look at one another.*

MRS. WEBB. That in the yellow paper is something I found in the attic among your grandmother's things. You're old enough to wear it now, and I thought you'd like it.

EMILY. And this is from you. Why, Mama, it's just lovely and it's just what I wanted. It's beautiful!

She flings her arms around her mother's neck. Her MOTHER *goes on with her cooking, but is pleased.*

MRS. WEBB. Well, I hoped you'd like it. Hunted all over. Your Aunt Norah couldn't find one in Concord, so I had to send all the way to Boston. *(Laughing.)* Wally has something for you, too. He made it at manual-training class and he's very proud of it. Be sure you make a big fuss about it.—Your father has a surprise for you, too; don't know what it is myself. Sh—here he comes.

MR. WEBB *(off stage).* Where's my girl? Where's my birthday girl?

EMILY *(in a loud voice to the stage manager).* I can't. I can't go on. It goes so fast. We don't have time to look at one another. *(She breaks down sobbing. The lights dim on the left half of the stage.* MRS. WEBB *disappears.)* I didn't realize. So all that was going on and we never noticed. Take me back—up the hill—to my grave. But first: Wait! One more look. Good-by, Good-by, world. Good-by, Grover's Corners . . . Mama and Papa. Good-by to clocks ticking . . . and Mama's sunflowers. And food and coffee. And new-ironed dresses and hot baths . . . and sleeping and waking up. Oh, earth, you're too wonderful for anybody to realize you. *(She looks toward the stage manager and asks abruptly, through her tears).* Do any human beings ever realize life while they live it?—every, every minute?

STAGE MANAGER. No. *(Pause.)* The saints and poets, maybe—they do some.

EMILY. I'm ready to go back.

(She returns to her chair beside Mrs. Gibbs. Pause.)

MRS. GIBBS. Were you happy?

EMILY. No . . . I should have listened to you. That's all human beings are! Just blind people.

MRS. GIBBS. Look, it's clearing up. The stars are coming out.

EMILY. Oh, Mr. Stimson, I should have listened to them.

SIMON STIMSON *(with mounting violence; bitingly).* Yes, now you know. Now you know! That's what it was to be alive. To move about in a cloud of ignorance; to go up and down trampling on the feelings of those . . . of those about you. To spend and waste time as though you had a million years. To be always at the mercy of one self-centered passion, or another. Now you know—that's the happy existence you wanted to go back to. Ignorance and blindness.

MRS. GIBBS *(spiritedly).* Simon Stimson, that ain't the whole truth and you know it. Emily, look at that star. I forget its name.

A MAN AMONG THE DEAD. My boy Joel was a sailor,—knew 'em all. He'd set on the porch evenings and tell 'em all by name. Yes, sir, wonderful!

ANOTHER MAN AMONG THE DEAD. A star's mighty good company.

A WOMAN AMONG THE DEAD. Yes. Yes, 'tis.

SIMON STIMSON. Here's one of *them* coming.

THE DEAD. That's funny. 'Tain't no time for one of them to be here.—Goodness sakes.

EMILY. Mother Gibbs, it's George.

MRS. GIBBS. Sh, dear. Just rest yourself.

EMILY. It's George.

GEORGE *enters from the left, and slowly comes toward them.*

A MAN FROM AMONG THE DEAD. And my boy, Joel, who knew the stars—he used to say it took millions of years for that speck o' light to git to the earth. Don't seem like a body could believe it, but that's what he used to say—millions of years.

GEORGE *sinks to his knees then falls full length at Emily's feet.*

A WOMAN AMONG THE DEAD. Goodness! That ain't no way to behave!

MRS. SOAMES. He ought to be home.

EMILY. Mother Gibbs?

MRS. GIBBS. Yes, Emily?

EMILY. They don't understand, do they?

MRS. GIBBS. No, dear. They don't understand.

The STAGE MANAGER *appears at the right, one hand on a dark curtain which he slowly draws across the scene. In the distance a clock is heard striking the hour very faintly.*

STAGE MANAGER. Most everybody's asleep in Grover's Corners. There are a few lights on: Shorty Hawkins, down at the depot, has just watched the Albany train go by. And at the livery stable somebody's setting up late and talking.—Yes, it's clearing up. There are the stars—doing their old, old crisscross journeys in the sky. Scholars haven't settled the matter yet, but they seem to think there are no living beings up there. Just chalk . . . or fire. Only this one is straining away, straining away all the time to make something of itself. The strain's so bad that every sixteen hours everybody lies down and gets a rest. *(He winds his watch.)* Hm. . . . Eleven o'clock in Grover's Corners.—You get a good rest, too. Good night.

The End

Thornton Wilder on *OUR TOWN*

Our Town is not offered as a picture of life in a New Hampshire village; or as a speculation about the conditions of life after death (that element I merely took from Dante's *Purgatory*[1]). It is an attempt to find a value above all price for the smallest events in our daily life. I have made the claim as preposterous as possible, for I have set the village against the largest dimensions of time and place. The recurrent words in this play (few have noticed it) are "hundreds," "thousands," and "millions." Emily's joys and griefs, her algebra lessons and her birthday presents—what are they when we consider all the billions of girls who have lived, who are living, and who will live? Each individual's assertion to an absolute reality can only be inner, very inner. And here the method of staging finds its justification—in the first two acts there are at least a few chairs and tables; but when she revisits the earth and the kitchen to which she descended on her twelfth birthday, the very chairs and table are gone. Our claim, our hope, our despair are in the mind—not in things, not in "scenery." Molière[2] said that for the theatre all he needed was a platform and a passion or two. The climax of this play needs only five square feet of boarding and the passion to know what life means to us.

From Preface to THREE PLAYS by Thornton Wilder. Copyright © 1938, 1957 by Thornton Wilder. Reprinted by permission of Harper & Row, Publishers, Inc. and Penguin Books Ltd.

1. *Dante's Purgatory,* the second part of *The Divine Comedy,* a narrative epic by Dante Alighieri (1265–1321). It is considered the greatest poem of the Middle Ages.

2. *Molière,* French actor and playwright (1622–1673).

Discussion

Act III

1. In his introductory remarks, the Stage Manager describes the familiar experience of how the living, after a first wild grief, tend gradually to forget the dead. Then he describes how one might imagine the dead being gradually "weaned away from earth." (a) What in the play prepares you for these "impossible" scenes of the dead? (b) Explore the parallels the Stage Manager draws between the response of the dead to the living and the response of the living to the dead.

2. The first living characters we see in Act III are new to us—Sam Craig and Joe Stoddard. We learn several things from their conversation. What are they? Which advances the dramatic action of the play?

3. When the dead Mrs. Soames hears that Emily died in childbirth, she sighs: "My, wasn't life awful—and wonderful." What does she mean?

4. When the dead Emily appears in the cemetery, she says: "Live people don't understand, do they?" and she adds, "They're sort of shut up in little boxes, aren't they?" What does she mean?

5. Why does Emily choose to relive her twelfth birthday?

6. When Emily relives her twelfth birthday, the first people she sees are Howie Newsome (the milkman), Constable Warren, and Joe Crowell (the paperboy). (a) How does seeing these people affect her? (b) How is George involved in her return?

7. On her day of return, Emily exclaims to her mother: "O, Mama, just look at me one minute as though you really

saw me. Mama, fourteen years have gone by. I'm dead. You're a grandmother, Mama. I married George Gibbs, Mama. Wally's dead.'' **(a)** What is Mrs. Webb's reaction to this speech? **(b)** In what way is this speech the turning point of Emily's day of return?

8. When Emily returns to the dead, Simon Stimson blurts out: ''Now you know—that's the happy existence you wanted to go back to. Ignorance and blindness.'' Mrs. Gibbs chimes in: ''Simon Stimson, that ain't the whole truth and you know it.'' **(a)** Who is right? Explain. **(b)** Did the appearance of George, falling at Emily's feet at the close of the play, affect your answer? If so, how?

Vocabulary
Context, Structure, and Dictionary

A. Use your Glossary to determine the accented syllable of each italicized word below. Then choose the word that rhymes with the accented syllable of each word. Write the appropriate letter and word on your paper.

1. *lugubrious:* **(a)** tug; **(b)** try; **(c)** too; **(d)** tree.

2. *bereave:* **(a)** leave; **(b)** bear; **(c)** rave; **(d)** have.

3. *traipse:* **(a)** wraps; **(b)** fee; **(c)** types; **(d)** grapes.

4. *anguish:* **(a)** fan; **(b)** fish; **(c)** gang; **(d)** pain.

5. *alacrity:* **(a)** track; **(b)** write; **(c)** pal; **(d)** knit.

6. *exertion:* **(a)** hex; **(b)** egg; **(c)** fun; **(d)** her.

7. *diligent:* **(a)** lent; **(b)** twig; **(c)** try; **(d)** pill.

8. *ambitious:* **(a)** lamb; **(b)** us; **(c)** dish; **(d)** lit.

9. *sentimentality:* **(a)** pal; **(b)** time; **(c)** dent; **(d)** fit.

10. *epitaph:* **(a)** laugh; **(b)** fee; **(c)** wit; **(d)** pep.

B. You will need the italicized words from the list above to complete the following sentences. In each case, however, the form of the word must be changed by the addition (or subtraction) of a prefix, suffix, plural, or by the change of tense. Do not use the words as they appear above without altering their form to fit the meaning of the sentences. You will not use all the words.

1. Although Susan is hard-working and has a lot of _____, she always has time for her family and friends.

2. Everyone _____ the utmost effort at the last drive, but the fund is still too low.

3. If we were all as _____ as he is, there would be no greeting-card industry.

4. The _____ of a coyote's howl never fails to send prickles up my spine.

5. In view of his recent sad _____, Peter asked to resign from the prom decoration committee.

6. Her hobby is searching out unusual _____ in old burial grounds.

7. Although they worked _____, they were unable to complete the requirements necessary for entering the contest.

8. While _____ around in southwestern Colorado, we discovered many unusual and fascinating rock formations.

Thornton Wilder has written: "The response we make when we 'believe' a work of the imagination is that of saying: 'This is the way things are. I have always known it without being fully aware that I knew it.' "

Did *Our Town* reveal to you an emotion, a way of thinking, a way of being that you already knew, but did not quite know that you knew? What have you "learned" from *Our Town* about the nature of life (its daily pains and pleasures), the ways of love (its puzzles and ambiguities), the feelings of death (its terrors and sorrows and comforts) that you "already knew"? Select one of the above subjects and write a brief essay of two or three paragraphs describing this new (but really old) knowledge.

Thornton Wilder 1897 · 1975

When *Our Town* was first tried out in Boston in 1938, its reception was so cool that the run was shortened and the play moved to New York. There it received rave reviews, winning the Pulitzer Prize in drama for the year. Ever since 1938, a year has seldom passed without a production somewhere in the world of *Our Town*.

In 1938, Wilder was forty-one years old and had already had a long literary career, but primarily as a novelist. His first novel in 1926, *Cabal*, stirred scarcely a ripple. But in the very next year he published *The Bridge of San Luis Rey*, a story weaving the complex relationships of a group of people who lose their lives when the bridge they are crossing collapses. This novel brought Wilder his first Pulitzer Prize and worldwide recognition.

Born in Madison, Wisconsin, in 1897, Wilder attended schools in China and the U.S., and later studied in Rome. He took degrees at Yale and Princeton. During his early career he taught at various institutions, including the University of Chicago in the 1930s.

In 1942, Wilder won his third Pulitzer Prize for his play *Skin of Our Teeth*, an account of the whole history of mankind through the dramatization of a representative family, the mother and father vaguely evocative of Adam and Eve, their son suggesting Cain, and their maid the eternal siren, Lilith. Wilder's play, *The Matchmaker* (1954), was a reworking of a Broadway flop of 1938, *The Merchant of Yonkers*. It is remembered primarily as the basis for the highly popular musical comedy, *Hello, Dolly!*

In his later years Wilder turned from drama back to the novel. His books, like *The Eighth Day* (1967), attracted both critical readers and popular audiences. At the end of his career he could look back with the satisfaction of a writer who had not followed fashions in literature but had originated them. He was a remarkably independent—and totally committed—artist in words.

3: OUR TOWN

CONTENT REVIEW

1. Consider the meaning of the title of the play. **(a)** What is suggested by the word "Our" in *Our Town?* **(b)** Compare this title with these possible alternatives: "Grover's Corners"; "A Lively Little Burg"; "Long Ago"; "Dullsville, USA." Are they adequate? If not, why not? Suggest your own alternate title.

2. For its time (1938), *Our Town* struck theatergoers as unusual in conception and production. The play did not, like so many of the plays before it, confine itself to a realistic set within a four-wall room (or "box") with one wall removed to enable the audience to see in. Instead, the action flowed between scenes on a bare stage on which the curtain never closed, and the audience used its imagination to fill in whatever was missing in the action. Discuss the ways in which Wilder has used minimum props to suggest rather than re-create places or events—or try your hand at producing one of these scenes for the rest of the class: **(a)** the scene at the windows (on ladders) in Act I, in which Emily and George discuss their homework; **(b)** the drugstore scene in Act II (two stools and a board across chairs), with Emily and George discovering their love for each other; **(c)** the burial scene in Act III (chairs, umbrellas), with Emily moving from the world of the living to the world of the dead.

3. One hymn, "Blessed Be the Tie That Binds," is heard over and over again in the play. **(a)** What are the scenes in which it is heard? **(b)** What is the effect of the repetition of the hymn in these scenes?

4. Often a speech in a play will seem to have a significance beyond its immediate dramatic meaning. How do the following speeches relate to the whole of *Our Town:*

(a) Mr. Webb in Act I, answering the question about culture in Grover's Corners: "No, ma'am, there isn't much culture; but maybe this is the place to tell you that we've got a lot of pleasures of a kind here: we like the sun comin' up over the mountain in the morning, and we all notice a good deal about the birds. We pay a lot of attention to them. And we watch the change of the seasons; yes, everybody knows about them."

(b) The Stage Manager at the opening of Act III: "Now there are some things we all know, but we don't take'm out and look at'm very often. We all know that *something* is eternal. And it ain't houses and it ain't names, and it ain't earth, and it ain't even the stars . . . everybody knows in their bones that *something* is eternal, and that something has to do with human beings. All the greatest people ever lived have been telling us that for five thousand years and yet you'd be surprised how people are always losing hold of it. There's something way down deep that's eternal about every human being."

(c) Emily's farewell speech near the end of the play: "Good-by, good-by, world. Good-by, Grover's Corners . . . Mama and Papa. Good-by to clocks ticking . . . and Mama's sunflowers. And food and coffee. And new-ironed dresses and hot baths . . . and sleeping and waking up. Oh, earth, you're too wonderful for anybody to realize you."

5. Wilder has said that his play is not a "picture of life in a New Hampshire village" nor an exploration of the "conditions of life after death," but rather "an attempt to find a value above all price for the smallest events in our daily life." Review the entire action of the play. Does Wilder's statement conform to your sense of the play and its overall effect? Discuss.

Read the introduction and scene from the play, and then answer the questions.

from The Member of the Wedding

Carson McCullers
Act I

The Member of the Wedding takes place in a small Southern town in 1945. The main character is Frankie Addams, a twelve-year-old girl having a difficult time making the transition from childhood to adolescence. It is late summer, Frankie's best friend has moved away, and Frankie is at loose ends. Her father, a widower, is occupied with his business. The other girls near her age now talk of boys and social clubs, things which as yet have neither her understanding nor her approval, though she very much wants to belong to "something." As a result, Frankie is thrown back on the company of her seven-year-old cousin John Henry and the family's black housekeeper Berenice.

Shortly before the scene presented here, Frankie's brother Jarvis comes home with his fiancee, Janice. They plan to be married in a few days. Frankie's active, romantic imagination is caught, and she falls in love with the idea of the wedding— worrying that she is growing too tall, wishing she hadn't had her hair cut short, wondering if she could change her name to "Jasmine" so that it begins with a "J" like "Jarvis" and "Janice."

Throughout the play there is an undercurrent of the essential loneliness of individuals, whether represented by Frankie, by Berenice who is a widow, or by Honey, Berenice's young foster-brother who leads a wild life two skips ahead of the law.

The scene here opens after Berenice has left Frankie and John Henry out in the backyard awaiting Mr. Addams's arrival home for the evening.

FRANKIE (*looking at the house*). I wonder when that Papa of mine is coming home. He always comes home by dark. I don't want to go into that empty, ugly house all by myself.
JOHN HENRY. Me neither.

Carson McCullers, THE MEMBER OF THE WEDDING. Copyright 1946, as a novel, by Carson McCullers. Copyright 1949, as an unpublished play, by Carson McCullers. Copyright, 1951, by Carson McCullers. Reprinted by permission of New Directions Publishing Corporation and International Creative Management.

FRANKIE (*standing with outstretched arms, and looking around her*). I think something is wrong. It is too quiet. I have a peculiar warning in my bones. I bet you a hundred dollars it's going to storm.

JOHN HENRY. I don't want to spend the night with you.

FRANKIE. A terrible, terrible dog-day storm. Or maybe even a cyclone.

JOHN HENRY. Huh.

FRANKIE. I bet Jarvis and Janice are now at Winter Hill.[1] I see them just plain as I see you. Plainer. Something is wrong. It is too quiet.

(*A clear horn begins to play a blues tune in the distance.*)

JOHN HENRY. Frankie?

FRANKIE. Hush! It sounds like Honey.

(*The horn music becomes jazzy and spangling, then the first blues tune is repeated. Suddenly, while still unfinished, the music stops.* FRANKIE *waits tensely.*)

FRANKIE. He has stopped to bang the spit out of his horn. In a second he will finish. (*After a wait.*) Please, Honey, go on finish!

JOHN HENRY (*softly*). He done quit now.

FRANKIE (*moving restlessly*). I told Berenice that I was leavin' town for good and she did not believe me. Sometimes I honestly think she is the biggest fool that ever drew breath. You try to impress something on a big fool like that, and it's just like talking to a block of cement. I kept on telling and telling and telling her. I told her I had to leave this town for good because it is inevitable. Inevitable.

(MR. ADDAMS *enters the kitchen from the house, calling: "Frankie, Frankie."*)

MR. ADDAMS (*calling from the kitchen door*). Frankie, Frankie.

FRANKIE. Yes, Papa.

MR. ADDAMS (*opening the back door*). You had supper?

FRANKIE. I'm not hungry.

MR. ADDAMS. Was a little later than I intended, fixing a timepiece for a railroad man. (*He goes back through the kitchen and into the hall, calling: "Don't leave the yard!"*)

JOHN HENRY. You want me to get the weekend bag?

FRANKIE. Don't bother me, John Henry. I'm thinking.

JOHN HENRY. What you thinking about?

FRANKIE. About the wedding. About my brother and the bride. Everything's been so sudden today. I never believed before about the fact that the earth turns at the rate of about a thousand miles a day. I didn't understand why it was that if you jumped up in the air you wouldn't land in Selma or Fairview or somewhere else

---

1. **Winter Hill,** the site of Jarvis's army post and town where Janice lives.

instead of the same back yard. But now it seems to me I feel the world going around very fast. *(FRANKIE begins turning around in circles with arms outstretched. JOHN HENRY copies her. They both turn.)* I feel it turning and it makes me dizzy.

JOHN HENRY. I'll stay and spend the night with you.

FRANKIE *(suddenly stopping her turning).* No. I just now thought of something.

JOHN HENRY. You just a little while ago was begging me.

FRANKIE. I know where I'm going.

(There are sounds of CHILDREN playing in the distance.)

JOHN HENRY. Let's go play with the children, Frankie.

FRANKIE. I tell you I know where I'm going. It's like I've known it all my life. Tomorrow I will tell everybody.

JOHN HENRY. Where?

FRANKIE *(dreamily).* After the wedding I'm going with them to Winter Hill. I'm going off with them after the wedding.

JOHN HENRY. You serious?

FRANKIE. Shush, just now I realized something. The trouble with me is that for a long time I have been just an "I" person. All other people can say "we." When Berenice says "we" she means her lodge and church and colored people.[2] Soldiers can say "we" and mean the army. All people belong to a "we" except me.

JOHN HENRY. What are we going to do?

FRANKIE. Not to belong to a "we" makes you too lonesome. Until this afternoon I didn't have a "we," but now after seeing Janice and Jarvis I suddenly realize something.

JOHN HENRY. What?

FRANKIE. I know that the bride and my brother are the "we" of me. So I'm going with them, and joining with the wedding. This coming Sunday when my brother and the bride leave this town, I'm going with the two of them to Winter Hill. And after that to whatever place that they will ever go. *(There is a pause.)* I love the two of them so much and we belong to be together. I love the two of them so much because they are the *we* of me.

THE CURTAIN FALLS.

---

2. *colored people.* This was a term formerly used to designate black people.

1. On what does Frankie base her inference about the weather?

2. The unfinished blues tune and Frankie's feelings about the weather contribute which one of the following to the mood of this scene? (a) a feeling of restlessness; (b) a lazy summer feeling; (c) a feeling of happy anticipation; (d) a sense of horror.

3. We are told in the introduction that Frankie is twelve years old. Which of the following in this scene does *not* reinforce this fact? (a) her turning in circles; (b) her telling Berenice that she is leaving town for good; (c) her plans to go with Janice and Jarvis; (d) her wanting Honey to finish the song.

4. We can infer that Frankie's father is probably a (a) doctor; (b) watchmaker and jeweler; (c) train engineer; (d) jazz musician.

5. John Henry offers to get the weekend bag because (a) he plans to leave home, too; (b) he thinks Frankie is going to leave immediately; (c) Frankie is going to his house to spend the night; (d) only he knows where it is.

6. When Frankie states that "all people belong to a 'we' " she means that (a) most people are lonely; (b) everyone is a member of some club; (c) everyone has someone or a group with which to identify; (d) everyone has a family.

7. What does John Henry assume when he says, "What are we going to do?"

8. What will probably happen to Frankie's plans for going with Janice and Jarvis to Winter Hill?

Unit 3, Test II
COMPOSITION

From the assignments below choose one to write about.

1. Write a three to four paragraph epilogue or afterword to be spoken by the Stage Manager of *Our Town*. Include an account of what you think might have happened to the deeply grieved George, his son, and his farm.

2. Compare and contrast the place where you live with Grover's Corners. In spite of some superficial differences, what are some of the more important similarities?

3. Emily is enabled to relive one day in her life on earth. If the same privilege were granted to you, what day would you choose? Write a letter to a friend explaining the choice of that particular day.

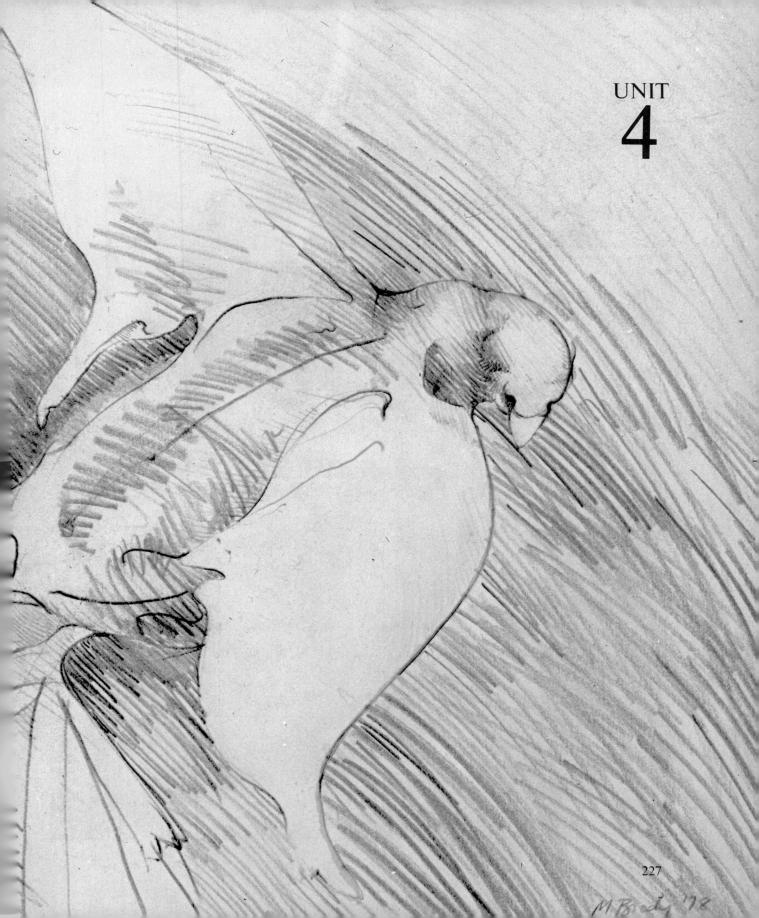

227

Scenes

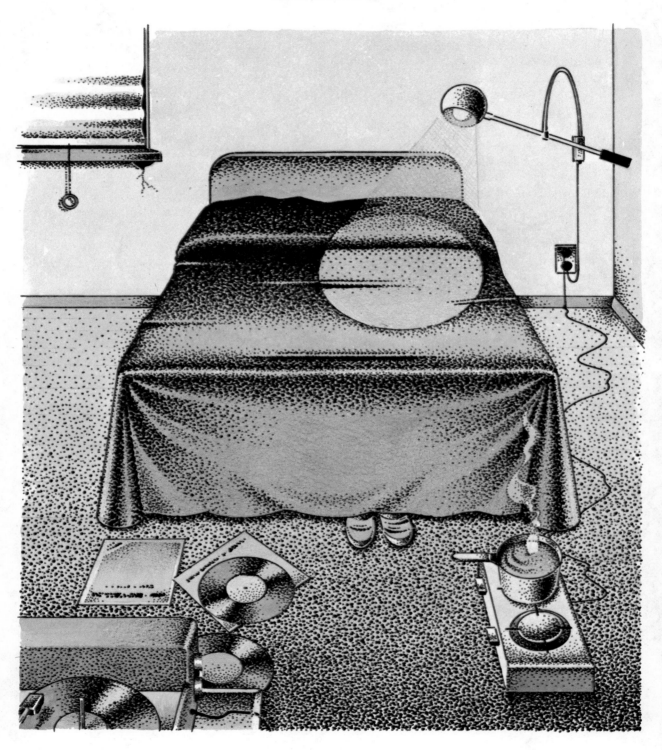

Plucking Out a Rhythm

Lawson Fusao Inada

Discussion

1. What is the scene the poet asks the reader to imagine?

2. What do you think the poet means by line 13?

3. Reread lines 34 and 35. Do you think the poet is being literal, figurative, or both? Explain.

4. Read the poem aloud. How does the movement or pace of the poem change?

Lawson Fusao Inada 1938 ·

Born in Fresno, California, Inada spent the World War II years in a War Relocation Camp for American Japanese. Afterward, his family resettled in the black and Latin section of Fresno where he developed his enthusiasm for music. He attended the University of California at Berkeley as well as other colleges, and he now teaches.

Start with a simple room—
a dullish color—
and draw the one shade down.
Hot plate. Bed.
5 Little phonograph in a corner.

Put in a single figure—
medium weight and height—
but oversize, as a child might.

The features must be Japanese.

10 Then stack a black pompadour on,
and let the eyes
slide behind a night of glass.

The figure is in disguise:

slim green suit
15 for posturing on a bandstand,
the turned-up shoes of Harlem . . .

Then start the music playing—
thick jazz, strong jazz—

and notice that the figure
20 comes to life:

sweating, growling
over an imaginary bass—
plucking out a rhythm—
as the music rises and the room is full,
25 exuding with that rhythm . . .

Then have the shade flap up
and daylight catch him
frozen in that pose

as it starts to snow—
30 thick snow, strong snow—

blowing in the window
while the music quiets,
the room is slowly covered,

and the figure is completely
35 out of sight.

Reprinted by permission of William Morrow & Co., Inc. from BEFORE THE WAR by Lawson Fusao Inada. Copyright © 1971 by Lawson Fusao Inada.

See **METAPHOR** Handbook of Literary Terms

Water Picture

May Swenson

In the pond in the park
all things are doubled:
Long buildings hang and
wriggle gently. Chimneys
5 are bent legs bouncing
on clouds below. A flag
wags like a fishhook
down there in the sky.

The arched stone bridge
10 is an eye, with underlid
in the water. In its lens
dip crinkled heads with hats

that don't fall off. Dogs go by,
barking on their backs.
15 A baby, taken to feed the
ducks, dangles upside-down,
a pink balloon for a buoy.

Treetops deploy a haze of
cherry bloom for roots,
20 where birds coast belly-up
in the glass bowl of a hill;
from its bottom a bunch
of peanut-munching children
is suspended by their
25 sneakers, waveringly.

A swan, with twin necks
forming the figure three,
steers between two dimpled
towers doubled. Fondly
30 hissing, she kisses herself,
and all the scene is troubled:
water-windows splinter,
tree-limbs tangle, the bridge
folds like a fan.

Discussion

1. By the use of language, the poet is able to make the reader visualize and share his or her tastes and experiences. **(a)** To create these pictures for the reader, the poet often compares basically different things. Find at least four comparisons in "Water Picture." **(b)** Which are metaphors? **(c)** Which are similes? (Review *Figurative Language* in the Handbook.)

2. (a) Which comparisons did the artist choose from the poem to illustrate? **(b)** If one of the children (in the picture) on the bridge dropped a pebble into the water, the effect would be the same as which lines of the poem?

Extension · Writing

Put several objects around the edge of a mirror, or dangle them between two mirrors set at angles to each other. Write at least one simile or one metaphor to describe what you see.

"Water Picture" by May Swenson is reprinted by permission of the author from POEMS TO SOLVE, copyright © 1966 by May Swenson, and first published in THE NEW YORKER.

May Swenson 1919 ·

Swenson was born and raised in Logan, Utah, and became a reporter after graduating from college. Her first book was *Another Animal: Poems* (1954). Since then she has received countless awards and scholarships.

See **CACOPHONY/EUPHONY** Handbook of Literary Terms

Thursday's Collection

James W. Thompson

It rolls
upon the hush of morning
ignoring delicate embroidered forms
born of bright beams, descending:
5 spreading a gauze glazing net,
veiling the bald street.

Its giant grey hulk whines
gears grind their metallic chorus
bemoaning a slow advance
10 before rows of three-story houses
(at whose windows, sun beckons!)

Two sullen figures, trailing,
gather rusted containers;
two silent keepers
15 of a whining machine,
whose rotating mouth
tumbles village dross.

From FIRST FIRE, Revised Edition. Copyright
© 1977 James W. Thompson. Published by
Fire Publications, 1977. Reprinted by permission.

Discussion

1. (a) Describe in your own words the way that the speaker seems to regard the morning, **(b)** the truck, and **(c)** the men. What details in each stanza convey these feelings?

2. (a) Read stanzas one and two aloud. In which stanza do the words *sound* harsh and the lines harder to say smoothly? **(b)** Which word, *euphony* or *cacophony*, describes the way stanza one sounds? stanza two?

3. What other machines could be the subject of a poem? To what might one specific machine be compared to show whether you feel positively or negatively about it?

James W. Thompson 1935 ·

After studying at several universities, Thompson decided to learn dance. For a number of years he was a professional dancer and choreographer.

His first book of poetry, *First Fire*, was published in London in 1970. He has also written short stories and a novel.

near El Dorado

Anita Skeen

they nod on & on
warmed into rhythm by the
Kansas sun
necks dipping,
5 rising, dipping
contented to suck long
suck deep
drawing the black stream
from the veins
10 of the Flint Hills[1]

the cattle pretend to be
undisturbed
by their presence
munch yellow grass
15 among the swaying, sleeping shadows
even the sunflowers
stand calmly around them

and i imagine them
watching,
20 rocking,
waiting for darkness
when with slow-motion groans
they uproot themselves
from the land
25 tromp the still flowers
beneath steel hooves &
in magnificent herds
run silently,
boldly
30 on the thin line of
the horizon

"near El Dorado" originally appeared in *Heritage of Kansas,* Vol. 8, No. 4, Winter 1975. Reprinted by permission of the author.

1. **Flint Hills,** a rolling, almost treeless rangeland in central Kansas, the largest area of arable land in the continental United States that has never been broken by a plow.

Discussion

1. (a) What details in the first stanza suggest that the nodding creatures are not animals? **(b)** What do they drink? **(c)** What kind of machines are they?

2. (a) How are the cattle and the sunflowers in stanza two like people? **(b)** How do these details prepare for what happens in stanza three?

3. El Dorado, Kansas, is named after the legendary South American treasure city. How does the title fit the poem?

4. Compare the speaker's attitude toward machines in this poem with the speaker's attitude toward the garbage truck in "Thursday's Collection."

Anita Skeen 1946 ·

Born in Charleston, West Virginia, Skeen has been artist-in-residence at YWCA camps, and has participated in the Poet-in-the-Schools program and in the Squaw Valley, California, Community of Writers.

Currently, she teaches English and creative writing at Wichita State University in Kansas.

See **ONOMATOPOEIA** Handbook of Literary Terms

Cheers

Eve Merriam

The frogs and the serpents each had a football team,
and I heard their cheer leaders in my dream:

"Bilgewater, bilgewater," called the frog,
"Bilgewater, bilgewater,
5 Sis, boom, bog!
Roll 'em off the log,
Slog 'em in the sog,
Swamp 'em, swamp 'em
Muck mire quash!"

10 "Sisyphus, Sisyphus," hissed the snake,
"Sibilant, syllabub,
Syllable-loo-ba-lay.
Scylla and Charybdis,
Sumac, asphodel,
15 How do you spell Success?
With an S-S-S!"

Copyright © 1964 by Eve Merriam. From IT DOESN'T ALWAYS
HAVE TO RHYME. Used by permission of Atheneum Publishers.

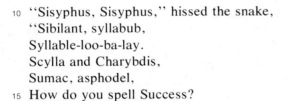

Discussion

1. Read the poem aloud. How are the sounds in the two stanzas different?

2. If, in the last two stanzas, the frog and the snake had not been mentioned by name, how would you know which one was cheering?

Extension · Writing

Try your hand at writing a short poem using words whose sounds suggest their sense.

For starters, you might imitate Merriam's "Cheers" but with a different cast of animal characters, or you might write a stanza on street sounds in a big city. Or, select a subject of your own.

Extension · Speaking

Choose those poems that the class thinks are the most onomatopoetic and read them aloud.

Eve Merriam 1916 ·

Merriam has written advertising copy, radio scripts, newspaper and magazine columns, and she has lectured to various audiences. But she is probably best known for her poetry. Among her recent books is *Growing Up Female in America*.

A devoted outdoorswoman, she keeps fit through walking, biking, and skating. "In my dreams," she says, "I am a proficient ice skater—in real life, I am wobbly but willing."

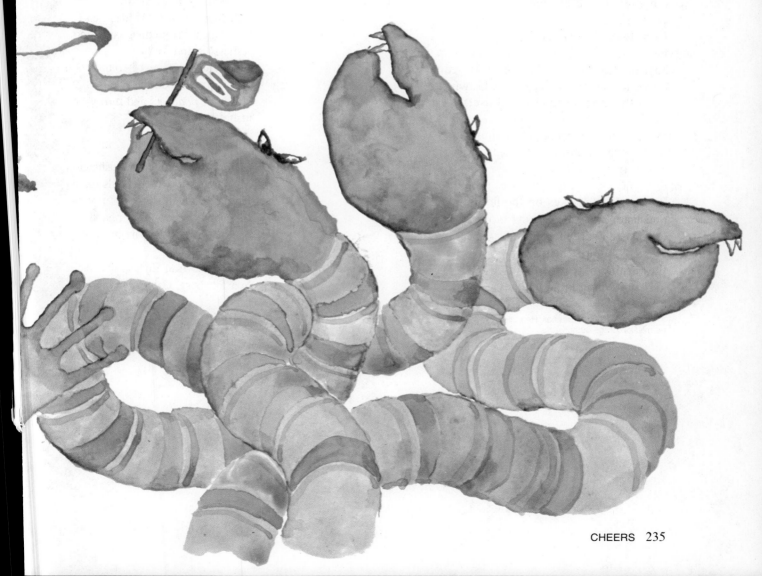

See **CONNOTATION/DENOTATION** Handbook of Literary Terms

The Elk

Hugh McNamar

In winter poachers had used the cabin.
Their empty beer and spaghetti
cans were in one corner,
and fence posts had been burned
5 in the old pot-bellied stove. Some
were left smoldering when,
hearing the truck turn up the road,
the three of them left by the
sun porch door. There,
10 not even gutted or bled,
we found him hanging
from the rafter beam,
hard and turning on the creaking rope.
Just that morning he had probably come
15 down to where the snow was blown
from the grass around the house.

We stayed one weekend in summer
to fish the stream.
Away from the city sounds
20 at night, we could only turn
in our sleeping bags on the floor
and listen: outside insects moved
against the screen; and in such
stillness, almost heard, was
25 the turning of a rope
and something large and restless.

"The Elk" by Hugh McNamar. Reprinted by permission of the author.

Discussion

1. **(a)** What is the difference between a poacher and a hunter? **(b)** What details in the poem justify calling those who killed the elk poachers? **(c)** What seems to outrage the cabin owners most? Why?

2. What difference would it make if the word *toss* replaced the word *turn* in line 20?

3. In addition to the dead elk, what might "something large and restless" stand for?

4. Which aspects of *connotation* and *denotation* do the poet's choice of *poachers* and *turn* illustrate?

Hugh McNamar 1931 ·

Born in the state of Washington, McNamar attended schools there. He has worked as a laborer, cannery employee, and farmhand; and he spent two years in the Army.

He is now an English teacher in a Pittsburg, California, high school.

Abandoned Farmhouse

Ted Kooser

Discussion

1. (a) What story does the poem
tell? (b) What conclusions does
the speaker draw? (c) Do you
think they are reasonable? Why
or why not?

2. What other explanation might
account for the abandoned farm-
house?

Ted Kooser 1939 ·

Kooser's first book, *Official
Entry Blank,* appeared in 1969.
He is a new poet whose work
has been printed in many recent
anthologies.

Born in Ames, Iowa, he has
not moved far from his birthplace:
he now works and lives in Lincoln, Nebraska, where he is an
underwriter for an insurance firm.

He was a big man, says the size of his shoes
on a pile of broken dishes by the house;
a tall man too, says the length of the bed
in an upstairs room; and a good, God-fearing man,
5 says the Bible with a broken back
on the floor below the window, dusty with sun;
but not a man for farming, say the fields
cluttered with boulders and the leaky barn.

A woman lived with him, says the bedroom wall
10 papered with lilacs and the kitchen shelves
covered with oilcloth, and they had a child
says the sandbox made from a tractor tire.
Money was scarce, say the jars of plum preserves
and canned tomatoes sealed in the cellar-hole,
15 and the winters cold, say the rags in the window frames.
It was lonely here, says the narrow gravel road.

Something went wrong, says the empty house
in the weed-choked yard. Stones in the fields
say he was not a farmer; the still-sealed jars
20 in the cellar say she left in a nervous haste.
And the child? Its toys are strewn in the yard
like branches after a storm—a rubber cow,
a rusty tractor with a broken plow,
a doll in overalls. Something went wrong, they say.

"Abandoned Farmhouse" from A LOCAL HABITATION AND A NAME, Solo
Press. Copyright 1974 by Ted Kooser. Reprinted by permission.

Vacation

William Stafford

One scene as I bow to pour her coffee:—

    Three Indians in the scouring drouth
    huddle at a grave scooped in the gravel,
    lean to the wind as our train goes by.
5   Someone is gone.
    There is dust on everything in Nevada.

I pour the cream.

"Vacation" from THE RESCUED YEAR by William Stafford.
Copyright © 1960 by William E. Stafford. Reprinted by permission
of Harper & Row, Publishers, Inc.

Discussion

1. **(a)** Where is the speaker in this poem? **(b)** Does the title give you a clue? Explain.

2. Why are lines 2–6 indented?

3. What is the effect of the speaker mentioning dust being on everything in Nevada and then immediately following with the last line?

4. In light of the title and the scene, what feeling are you left with?

William Stafford 1914 ·

Stafford's first book of poetry was published in 1960, and three years later he won the National Book Award for his volume *Traveling Through the Dark*. In 1970 he served as Consultant in Poetry at the Library of Congress.

One of his concerns as a poet is that his work be unpretentious. His modesty is expressed in his statement, ". . . Of all my writing, only a very small portion goes forth into the world, and of that portion a large part never receives approval."

Looking for Arrowheads

Jim Barnes

Check the horizon for a rise
that should not be there.

Circle until the sun is in your eyes:
long shadows can tell you the lay of stone or bone.

5 Keep your eyes hard against the ground:
never turn for the cracked twig
and know the sky takes care of its own.

Carry a stick grown long enough for prodding:
your vision must be higher than a bent back,
10 or you will lose the perspective
it takes your life to gain.

Know that shapes are various—
fluted, triangular, rectangular,
sunfished, toothed, blunt,
15 some without notch or haft,
some hardly touched by human hand.

If you are lucky,
hold the arrowhead in your good right hand,
raise it to the sun,
20 and give thanks
for the certainty you have come to know
of what may and may not endure.

First appeared in CHICAGO REVIEW, Volume 27, No. 1, 1975, copyright © 1975 by Chicago Review. Reprinted by permission.

Discussion

1. (a) How does the poet convey the impression that the speaker knows what he's talking about? **(b)** Review *Point of View* in the Handbook. In what other poem in SCENES does the poet use the same point of view and a speaker who sounds as authoritative as the arrowhead hunter?

2. Explain what "the perspective/it takes your life to gain" means.

3. (a) What is the speaker's attitude toward the hunt? **(b)** Why does he tell us to raise the arrowheads we find to the sun? Explain in your own words what he says we should give thanks for.

Jim Barnes

Barnes was born in Summerfield, Oklahoma. He spent the 1950s as a lumberjack in western Oregon. Since then he has completed a doctorate in Comparative Literature and has been teaching at Northeast Missouri State University.

Part Choctaw, he is vitally concerned with a sense of earth, with a sense of place. He also edits *The Chariton Review.*

Prayer to the Pacific

Leslie Silko

1

I traveled to the ocean
      distant
            from my southwest land of sandrock
         to the moving blue water
5   Big as the myth of origin.

2

  Pale
pale water in the yellow-white light of
        sun   floating west
           to China
10   where ocean herself was born.
Clouds that blow across the sand are wet.

3

Squat in the wet sand and speak to Ocean:
    I return to you   turquoise   the red coral you sent us,
        sister spirit of Earth.
15 Four round stones in my pocket   I carry back the ocean
      to suck and to taste.

Discussion

1. (a) What words or phrases show that the speaker regards the ocean as if it were a living being? (b) Describe the relationship between the speaker and the ocean and the speaker's attitude toward it.

2. One function of myths is to provide an explanation for what is unknown and mysterious. Find three examples in this poem of such explanations.

Leslie Silko 1948 ·

A descendant of two Native-American, New Mexico tribes, Silko writes fiction, as well as poetry. In *Ceremony*, published in 1977, she draws upon her experience with life on a Navajo reservation for her setting. As in "Prayer to the Pacific," she displays great insight and sympathy for her Native-American characters.

"I write," she says, "because I love the stories, the feelings, the words."

4

Thirty thousand years ago
      Indians came riding across the ocean
      carried by giant sea-turtles.
20 Waves were high that day
      great sea turtles waded slowly out
        from the grey sundown sea.
Grandfather Turtle rolled in the sand four times
      and disappeared
25   swimming into the sun.

5

And so from that time
      immemorial,
        as the old people say,
rainclouds drift from the west
30   gift from the ocean.

6

Green leaves in the wind
Wet earth on my feet
      swallowing raindrops
        clear from China.

"Prayer to the Pacific" by Leslie Silko, CHICAGO REVIEW, Vol. 24, No. 4. Copyright © 1972 by Leslie Silko. Reprinted by permission of the author.

Reflections

Villa R by Paul Klee, By Courtesy of the Kunstmuseum; photograph by Hans Hinz

The Road Not Taken

Robert Frost

Discussion

1. What experience is the poet describing.

2. What might the two roads symbolize?

3. Explain lines 13-15.

4. Reread Frost's biography on page 13. Do you think the speaker in this poem is the poet, Robert Frost? Explain.

Two roads diverged in a yellow wood,
And sorry I could not travel both
And be one traveler, long I stood
And looked down one as far as I could
5 To where it bent in the undergrowth;

Then took the other, as just as fair,
And having perhaps the better claim,
Because it was grassy and wanted wear;
Though as for that, the passing there
10 Had worn them really about the same,

And both that morning equally lay
In leaves no step had trodden black.
Oh! I kept the first for another day!
Yet knowing how way leads on to way,
15 I doubted if I should ever come back.

I shall be telling this with a sigh
Somewhere ages and ages hence:
Two roads diverged in a wood, and I—
I took the one less traveled by,
20 And that has made all the difference.

From THE POETRY OF ROBERT FROST edited by Edward Connery Lathem. Copyright 1916, © 1969 by Holt, Rinehart and Winston. Copyright 1944 by Robert Frost. Reprinted by permission of Holt, Rinehart and Winston, Publishers, the Estate of Robert Frost, and Jonathan Cape Ltd.

For author biography, see page 13.

Woman with Flower

Naomi Long Madgett

I wouldn't coax the plant if I were you.
Such watchful nurturing may do it harm.
Let the soil rest from so much digging
And wait until it's dry before you water it.
5 The leaf's inclined to find its own direction;
Give it a chance to seek the sunlight for itself.

Much growth is stunted by too careful prodding,
Too eager tenderness.
The things we love we have to learn to leave alone.

From STAR BY STAR by Naomi Long Madgett, Detroit, Harlo, 1965, 1970. Reprinted by permission of the author.

Discussion

1. (a) Whether or not the last three lines apply to the growth of a plant, they make sense by themselves. What other things we love might not grow well if we poke them too much or love them too much? **(b)** Do you agree that too much tenderness can be as harmful as too much prodding? Give examples.

2. (a) How could you actually test what the speaker says about a plant? **(b)** Could you make the same kind of test about people? Explain.

3. Which of the following literary techniques has the poet used to express an abstract idea: *satire, symbolism, setting?*

Naomi Long Madgett 1923 •

A full time teacher in Detroit, Madgett has said, "I would rather be a good poet than anything else I can imagine. It pleases me tremendously that my social-worker daughter is becoming a very good poet."

Madgett has been active in Detroit literary groups and has served on the Michigan State Council for the Arts.

See **TONE** Handbook of Literary Terms

Dear Mamá

Oscar Peñaranda

Discussion

1. What do the title and the opening line tell you about the form of the speaker's message and the tone in which it should be read?

2. (a) Describe the speaker's attitude toward Mamá and the other relatives. **(b)** What details in the poem support your inference?

3. (a) How is a casual personal letter different from a formal business letter? **(b)** What specific lines make this poem sound like a personal letter?

Oscar Peñaranda

Born on the island of Leyte, the Philippines, Oscar Peñaranda was educated in Manila until his twelfth year, when his family came to America.

His home has been San Francisco since he was seventeen. He has held a variety of summer jobs: in California fields picking fruits, in Las Vegas as a busboy, and in Alaska's fishing canneries. He currently teaches at San Francisco State University.

. . . .

P.S.
    Tell them I miss
        them all
    and remember well their
5   closeness
    separately surrounding my
    childhood days.

    I would like to extend
    my regards and
10   (let them know:) would
    mention each
    by name
      but won't
    not because of the impossibility
15   of task I know
    every one says that of
    lineage enumerations
    (but it isn't the case here)

    It's just that I
20   don't want a humble
    heart to break should I
    happen

    to miss one

"Dear Mamá" by Oscar Peñaranda. Copyright © 1975 Oscar Peñaranda. Reprinted by permission.

Grandmother

Adele Seronde

Grandmother
of heroes,
Holding all
the past fragments
5   In your heart
As you hold
     the ends
       of home-spun wool,
You must keep weaving,
10 Weaving the tribal rugs
Of dreams

Take all the broken threads—
The blacks and grays—
Weave them with the earth—
15 The browns of wise men,
Whites of age.
And bring in new red strands:
The young.
Tell all the stories over once
     again.
20 Weave in new hope.

Reprinted from ASK A CACTUS ROSE,
by Adele Seronde, with the permission of
the Wenkhart Publishing Company, 4
Shady Hill Square, Cambridge, Massachusetts, 02138.

Discussion

1. (a) For people of all ages and cultures, colors are often symbolic. What do the colors in this poem seem to symbolize? (b) What experiences might they represent?

2. Reread lines 9–11 and 19–20. Why do you think the speaker is so insistent?

3. Do you think the grandmother is the speaker's own? Explain.

Extension · Writing

If you were to draw a color wheel to show how you feel today, and another to show how you feel most of the time, which colors would you use to symbolize which feelings? Which color(s), if any, would dominate? Why? Write a paragraph or two to answer these questions.

Adele Seronde

Seronde has written poetry for children as well as for adults. In *Ask a Daffodil* (1967), a completely phonetic poetry book, she tries "to make real poems . . . for children who are beginning to study sounds." She expresses a hope that applies to all of her own poetry and to poetry in general: "Most of all, I hope you will like them."

The Rabbit

Edna St. Vincent Millay

Hearing the hawk squeal in the high sky
I and the rabbit trembled.
Only the dark small rabbits newly kittled in their neatly
    dissembled
Hollowed nest in the thicket thatched with straw
5 Did not respect his cry.
At least, not that I saw.

But I have said to the rabbit with rage and a hundred times,
    "Hop!
Streak it for the bushes! Why do you sit so still?
You are bigger than a house, I tell you, you are bigger than a
    hill, you are a beacon for air-planes!
10 O indiscreet!
And the hawk and all my friends are out to kill!
Get under cover!" But the rabbit never stirred; she never
    will.

And I shall see again and again the large eye blaze
With death, and gently glaze;
15 The leap into the air I shall see again and again, and the kicking
    feet;
And the sudden quiet everlasting, and the blade of grass green
    in the strange mouth of the interrupted grazer.

From COLLECTED POEMS, Harper & Row. Copyright 1939, 1967 by Edna St. Vincent
Millay and Norma Millay Ellis.

Discussion

1. Why does the speaker's rage seem to be focused on the rabbit instead of on the hawk?

2. What might be the reason for the rabbit not getting under cover?

3. What comment on death do you think the speaker is making in the third stanza?

4. (a) Which words at the ends of lines in each stanza rhyme? **(b)** Did you notice these rhymes when you first read the poem? **(c)** Should rhymes be obvious? Why or why not?

Edna St. Vincent Millay
1892 · 1950

Encouraged to write by her widowed mother, Millay worked hard at her verse while still a teenager. At nineteen, her poem "Renascence" attracted the attention of a patron, who sent her to Vassar College.

After finishing college, she went to New York, where she took up the bohemian life, producing a considerable body of poetry in a short time. In 1923 she won the Pulitzer Prize for *The Harp-Weaver and Other Poems.*

See **PARADOX** Handbook of Literary Terms

Silence

Edgar Lee Masters

I have known the silence of the stars and of the sea,
And the silence of the city when it pauses,
And the silence of a man and a maid,
And the silence for which music alone finds the word,
5 And the silence of the woods before the winds of spring
    begin,
And the silence of the sick
When their eyes roam about the room.
And I ask: For the depths
Of what use is language?
10 A beast of the field moans a few times
When death takes its young:
And we are voiceless in the presence of realities—
We cannot speak.

A curious boy asks an old soldier
15 Sitting in front of the grocery store,
"How did you lose your leg?"
And the old soldier is struck with silence,
Or his mind flies away
Because he cannot concentrate it on Gettysburg.
20 It comes back jocosely
And he says, "A bear bit it off."
And the boy wonders, while the old soldier
Dumbly, feebly, lives over
The flashes of guns, the thunder of cannon,
25 The shrieks of the slain,
And himself lying on the ground,
And the hospital surgeons, the knives,
And the long days in bed.
But if he could describe it all
30 He would be an artist.
But if he were an artist there would be deeper wounds
Which he could not describe.

There is silence of a great hatred,
And the silence of a great love,

1. As the speaker talks about the many kinds of silences, he uses both concrete and abstract ideas. Give examples of each.

2. What do you think the poet is referring to in line 12? Give possible examples.

3. Which of the silences in this poem have you experienced? Explain.

4. (a) How would you state the theme of this poem? **(b)** What about it is paradoxical?

Vocabulary
Context and Dictionary

From the list below choose the words that correctly complete the sentences. Be sure you can spell and pronounce each vocabulary word. You will not use one word.

diverge   intelligible
dross   jocose
enumerate   lineage

1. It seems that many people now are interested in tracing their _____.

2. Maria can _____ a grand duke and a horse thief among her ancestors.

3. The diagram of a family tree with many branches is not always easily _____.

"Silence," reprinted by permission of Mrs. Ellen C. Masters, from SONGS AND SATIRES by Edgar Lee Masters. Copyright 1916, 1944 by Edgar Lee Masters. Published by the Macmillan Company, New York.

4. In our case, the family lines constantly meet and then _____.

5. The hunt itself is fun; John turned up a _____ old cousin with a fund of funny family stories.

Extension · Speaking

Does Masters's poem tend to support or refute the saying that "Silence is golden"? Decide whether you agree or disagree that the statement fits the poem, and be ready to give at least five examples from the poem to prove your point in a contest with persons who take the opposite stand.

Edgar Lee Masters
1868 · 1950

Born in Kansas and reared in Illinois, Masters studied law and built a successful practice in Chicago.

Masters wrote poetry for his own pleasure; his best-known work is *Spoon River Anthology,* a collection of poetic monologues in which the speakers speak their epitaphs from the grave.

35 And the silence of a deep peace of mind,
And the silence of an embittered friendship.
There is the silence of a spiritual crisis,
Through which your soul, exquisitely tortured,
Comes with visions not to be uttered
40 Into a realm of higher life,
And the silence of the gods who understand each other without
    speech.
There is a silence of defeat.
There is the silence of those unjustly punished;
And the silence of the dying whose hand
45 Suddenly grips yours.
There is the silence between father and son,
When the father cannot explain his life,
Even though he be misunderstood for it.
There is the silence that comes between husband and wife,
50 There is the silence of those who have failed;
And the vast silence that covers
Broken nations and vanquished leaders.

There is the silence of Lincoln,
Thinking of the poverty of his youth.
55 And the silence of Napoleon
After Waterloo.
And the silence of Jeanne d'Arc
Saying amid the flames, "Blessed Jesus"—
Revealing in two words all sorrow, all hope.
60 And there is the silence of age,
Too full of wisdom for the tongue to utter it
In words intelligible to those who have not lived
The great range of life.

And there is the silence of the dead.
65 If we who are in life cannot speak
Of profound experiences,
Why do you marvel that the dead
Do not tell you of death?
Their silence shall be interpreted
70 As we approach them.

Hope

Lisel Mueller

It hovers in dark corners
before the lights are turned on,
  it shakes sleep from its eyes
  and drops from mushroom gills,
5   it explodes in the starry heads
      of dandelions turned sages,
         it sticks to the wings of green angels
         that sail from the tops of maples.

It sprouts in each occluded eye
10 of the many-eyed potato,
  it lives in each earthworm segment,
  surviving cruelty,
      it is the motion that runs
      from the eyes to the tail of a dog,
15   it is the mouth that inflates the lungs
      of the child that has just been born.

It is the singular gift
we cannot destroy in ourselves,
the argument that refutes death,
20 the genius that invents the future,
all we know of God.

It is the serum which makes us swear
not to betray one another;
it is in this poem, trying to speak.

Reprinted by permission of Louisiana State University Press from
THE PRIVATE LIFE by Lisel Mueller, copyright © 1976.

Discussion

1. What is the *It* in the first line of the poem?

2. Choose two examples from the first two stanzas, explaining in your own words how *it* influences the existence of living things.

3. In the last two stanzas, the speaker says *it* gives what to human beings?

4. What does the speaker mean by the last line?

Extension · Speaking

Reread the first two lines of "Hope." What might one hope is hovering or perhaps not hovering "in dark corners/before the lights are turned on." Present your ideas to the class.

Lisel Mueller 1924 ·

Born in Hamburg, Germany, Mueller fled from the country with her family in 1939 and settled in Indiana.

After graduating from college, she married and raised a family. Writing poetry came to her much later and grew to be a major interest.

Her latest book, *The Private Life*, won the Lamont Poetry Prize in 1976.

Elegy

for Harriet Tubman and Frederick Douglass[1]

Maya Angelou

I lay down in my grave
and watch my children
grow
Proud blooms
5 above the weeds of death.

Their petals wave
and still nobody
knows the soft black
dirt that is my winding
10 sheet. The worms, my friends,
yet tunnel holes in
bones and through those
apertures I see the rain.
The sunfelt warmth
15 now jabs
within my space and
brings me roots of my
children born.

Their seeds must fall
20 and press beneath
this earth,
and find me where I
wait. My only need to
fertilize their birth.

25 I lay down in my grave
and watch my children
grow.

From OH PRAY MY WINGS ARE GONNA FIT ME WELL, by
Maya Angelou. Copyright © 1975 by Maya Angelou. Reprinted
by permission of Random House, Inc.

1. _Tubman . . . Douglass._ Harriet Tubman (1820-1913),
and Frederick Douglass (1817-1895), black American leaders.
Tubman escaped from slavery in 1849 and successfully led
more than three hundred slaves to freedom. Douglass was
an ex-slave, abolitionist, orator, and writer.

Discussion

1. (a) Read the title of the poem
and the footnote. Who might the
speakers in this poem be? **(b)**
Who are the children? What
makes you think so?

2. What is the tone of the poem:
one of pride, hope, and fulfillment,
or one of defeat and hopelessness?
Explain.

3. In what ways are "Hope"
and "Elegy" similar?

Maya Angelou 1928 ·

Born in St. Louis, Missouri,
Maya Angelou studied music for
seven years before she began to
study dance with Martha Graham
and her company.

In the 1950s Angelou was part
of a national company of _Porgy
and Bess_ that toured Europe and
Africa. Then in the 1960s she
went to Africa and taught at the
University of Ghana.

Her autobiographical book _I
Know Why the Caged Bird Sings_
(1970) was a best seller. Since
then she has published its sequel,
Gather Together in My Name,
and a collection of poetry, _Just
Give Me A Cool Drink of Water
'fore I Diiie._

Reply to the Question:
"How Can You Become a Poet?"

Eve Merriam

take the leaf of a tree
trace its exact shape
the outside edges
and inner lines

5 memorize the way it is fastened to the twig
(and how the twig arches from the branch)
how it springs forth in April
how it is panoplied in July

by late August
10 crumple it in your hand
so that you smell its end-of-summer sadness

chew its woody stem

listen to its autumn rattle

watch as it atomizes in the November air

15 then in winter
when there is no leaf left

invent one

Copyright © 1976 by Eve Merriam. From RAINBOW WRITING.
Used by permission of Atheneum Publishers and Eve Merriam,
c/o International Creative Management.

For author biography, see page 235.

Discussion

1. (a) Explain in your own words the speaker's reply to the question "How Can You Become a Poet?" (b) What is the speaker implying by these suggestions?

2. (a) Of all the things the speaker suggests one should do, which do you think would be the most difficult? (b) Do you think that by following the suggestions one could become a poet? Why or why not?

If There Be Sorrow

Mari Evans

If there be sorrow
let it be
for things undone . . .
undreamed
5   unrealized
      unattained
to these add one:
Love withheld . . .
. . . restrained

"If There Be Sorrow" by Mari Evans
from I AM A BLACK WOMAN, published
by William Morrow and Company, Inc.,
1970. Reprinted by permission of the
author.

Discussion

1. (a) If, in the third line, "un-done" were to read "not done," would this affect the sound and/or sense of the poem? **(b)** What is the effect of the repetition of "un"?

2. How are things that are "un-dreamed," "unrealized," or "unat-tained" different from love being restrained?

3. State the theme of the poem.

Extension · Writing

Using your powers of observa-tion, your memory, and your imagination as Merriam suggests in "Reply to the Question . . . ," write a poem similar in style to Evans's "If There Be Sorrow," but different in theme.

Mari Evans

Diverse in her talents, Evans is fashion designer, musician, teacher, as well as poet. She is currently assistant professor and Writer in Residence at Indiana University, Bloomington.

The book from which this poem was taken won for Evans the Indiana University Writers' Con-ference Award for the most dis-tinguished work of poetry pub-lished by an Indiana author in 1970.

Issues

The Man Who Finds His Son Has Become a Thief

Raymond Souster

Coming into the store at first angry
at the accusation, believing
the word of his boy who has told him,
I didn't steal anything, honest. . . .

5 Then becoming calmer, seeing that anger
won't help in the business, listening patiently
as the other's evidence unfolds, so painfully slow.

Then seeing gradually that evidence
almost as if slowly tightening around the neck
10 of his son, at first circumstantial, then gathering damage,
until there's present guilt's sure odor seeping
into the mind, laying its poison.
                  Suddenly feeling
sick and alone and afraid, as if
15 an unseen hand had slapped him in the face
for no reason whatsoever; wanting to get out
into the street, the night, the darkness, anywhere to hide
the pain that must show to these strangers, the fear.

It must be like this.
20 It could not be otherwise.

From THE COLOUR OF THE TIMES/ TEN ELEPHANTS ON YONGE STREET by Raymond Souster. Reprinted by permission of McGraw-Hill Ryerson Limited.

Discussion

1. What is the issue in this poem?

2. (a) What are the various reactions of the father to the accusation against his son? (b) Why might the father be afraid? (line 14)

3. Reread the last two lines. Who do you think the speaker is in this poem? Why?

Raymond Souster 1921 ·

Born and raised in Toronto, Souster, one of Canada's most familiar poets, has seldom strayed from his native city. He has worked in a bank, flown with the Royal Canadian Air Force, and edited a literary journal.

He is a collector of records and addicted to the game of field hockey.

See **FREE VERSE** Handbook of Literary Terms

Late Rising

Jacques Prévert
translated by Selden Rodman

Terrible
is the soft sound of a hardboiled egg
cracking on a zinc counter
and terrible is that sound
5   when it moves in the memory
of a man who is hungry
Terrible also is the head of a man
the head of a man hungry
when he looks at six o'clock in the morning
10 in a smart shop window and sees
a head the color of dust
But it is not his head he sees
in the window of 'Chez Potin'
he doesn't give a damn
15 for the head of a man
he doesn't think at all
he dreams
imagining another head
calf's-head for instance
20 with vinegar sauce
head of anything edible
and slowly he moves his jaws
slowly slowly
grinds his teeth for the world
25 stands him on his head
without giving him any comeback
so he counts on his fingers one two three
one two three
that makes three days he has been empty
30 and it's stupid to go on saying It can't
go on It can't go on because
it does
Three days
three nights
35 without eating

"Late Rising" by Jacques Prévert, translated by Selden Rodman, from PAROLES DE JACQUES PRÉVERT. © 1949 Editions Gallimard. Reprinted by permission.

Discussion

1. Besides the fact that the sound of an egg being broken is no doubt terrible to a starving man, what in addition is effective about the sound and the sense of the lines ". . . the soft sound of a hardboiled egg/cracking on a zinc counter"?

2. (a) Explain what is meant in line 42. **(b)** How do you interpret lines 55–61?

3. The image of a head recurs throughout the poem. Reread the lines that use this image and explain why you think the poet has chosen to emphasize this part of the body.

4. After reading and discussing the poem, explain what the title means to you.

Jacques Prévert 1900 • 1977

One of France's best-known
screenwriters, Prévert published
his first book of poems, *Paroles*
("Words"), in 1946. It was popular, and he followed it with other
volumes.

Like "Late Rising," his poems
are written with a painter's eye
for detail and color and are often
on the side of the underdog.

and behind those windows
pâté de foie gras[1] wine preserves
dead fish protected by their boxes
boxes in turn protected by windows
40 these in turn watched by the police
police protected in turn by fear
How many guards for six sardines . . .
Then he comes to the lunch counter
coffee-with-cream buttered toast
45 and he begins to flounder
and in the middle of his head
blizzard of words
muddle of words
sardines fed
50 hardboiled eggs coffee-with-cream
coffee black rum food
coffee-with-cream
coffee-with-cream
coffee crime black blood
55 A respectable man in his own neighborhood
had his throat cut in broad daylight
the dastardly assassin stole from him
two bits that is to say
exactly the price of a black coffee
60 two slices of buttered toast
and a nickel left to tip the waiter

Terrible
is the sound of a hardboiled egg
cracking on a zinc counter
65 and terrible is that sound when it moves
in the memory
of a man who is hungry.

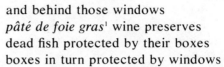

---

1. *pâté de foie gras* (pä tā′ də fwä′grä′), a paste or spread
made of goose livers, considered a delicacy. *[French]*

Harlem

Langston Hughes

What happens to a dream deferred?

Does it dry up
like a raisin in the sun?
Or fester like a sore—
5   And then run?
Does it stink like rotten meat?
Or crust and sugar over—
like a syrupy sweet?

Maybe it just sags
10   like a heavy load.

Or does it explode?

Copyright 1951 by Langston Hughes.
Reprinted from SELECTED POEMS, by
Langston Hughes, by permission of Alfred A.
Knopf, Inc.

Discussion

1. What is the meaning of "deferred"?

2. What kind of dream is the speaker talking about?

3. How does the spacing between stanzas signal the way that you should read the poem?

4. How would you describe the tone of the poem?

Langston Hughes
1902 • 1967

Hughes is perhaps best known as a poet and creator of the short-story character Jesse B. Semple, who met adversity with dignity, wisdom, and humor.

Born in Joplin, Missouri, Hughes attended high school in Cleveland, Ohio, where he began writing poetry. Soon after publishing a play and some poems in 1921, he became part of the Harlem Renaissance, a movement dedicated to publishing black authors.

Toward the end of his career, he devoted his energies to helping young writers and to recording the history and culture of black Americans.

Dolor

Theodore Roethke

Discussion

1. If you do not know the meaning of "dolor," look it up in your Glossary. What do you think this poem will be about?

2. (a) In what places might you find the objects named in lines 1–7? **(b)** What words in the poem show that the speaker feels sad about the work of people who use these things?

3. (a) We are used to thinking about problems such as war, racism, sexism, and poverty as issues. What problem does this poem ask us to consider as an issue? **(b)** Why do you agree or disagree that this issue is worth taking seriously?

Theodore Roethke
1908 · 1963

Roethke grew up in Saginaw, Michigan, and received his education at the University of Michigan and Harvard.

He received numerous honors in his lifetime, including the National Book Award and the Pulitzer Prize for poetry in 1954 for his collection, *The Waking.* At the time of his death, he was professor of English and Poet in Residence at the University of Washington in Seattle.

I have known the inexorable sadness of pencils,
Neat in their boxes, dolor of pad and paper-weight,
All the misery of manilla folders and mucilage,
Desolation in immaculate public places,
5 Lonely reception room, lavatory, switchboard,
The unalterable pathos of basin and pitcher,
Ritual of multigraph, paper-clip, comma,
Endless duplication of lives and objects.
And I have seen dust from the walls of institutions,
10 Finer than flour, alive, more dangerous than silica,
Sift, almost invisible, through long afternoons of tedium,
Dropping a fine film on nails and delicate eyebrows,
Glazing the pale hair, the duplicate grey standard faces.

"Dolor," copyright 1943 Modern Poetry Association, Inc. from THE COLLECTED POEMS OF THEODORE ROETHKE. Reprinted by permission of Doubleday & Company, Inc. and Faber and Faber Ltd.

Hard Questions

Margaret Tsuda

Why wildness?
    Why not mark out the land
    into neat rectangles
    squares and cloverleafs?

5   Put on them cubes
    of varying sizes
    according to use—
    dwellings
        singles/multiples
10   complexes
        commercial/industrial.

    Bale them together
    with bands of roads.

Doesn't that make the land useful?
15   What if a child shall cry
    "I have never known spring!
    I have never seen autumn!"

What is that?
    What if a man shall say
20   "I have never heard
    silence fraught with living
    in swamp or forest!"
    What if the eye shall never see
    marsh birds and muskrats?

25 *What are these?*
    Does not the heart need
    wildness?
    Does not the thought need
    something to rest upon
30   not self-made by man,
    a bosom not his own?

Discussion

1. What opposing views are presented in this poem?
2. Why are these "hard questions"?
3. Does the speaker seem to support one position over the other? Explain.

Margaret Tsuda

Born and raised in New York City, Tsuda studied fine art at Hunter College and later had a career in textile design.

She began publishing poetry in 1969. Her poems, which have been translated into Hindi and many other languages, are collected in *Cry Love Aloud* (1972), and *Urban River* (1976). She illustrates her own books with ink drawings, using a handcut bamboo pen.

Margaret Tsuda and Discovery Books for "Hard Questions" from CRY LOVE ALOUD by Margaret Tsuda, ©1972. Originally appeared in THE LIVING WILDERNESS. Published by The Wilderness Society, Autumn 1970.

The Hand That Signed the Paper

Dylan Thomas

Discussion

1. (a) To whom did the hand that signed the paper belong? (b) What kind of paper was signed?

2. Explain the line "These five kings did a king to death."

3. What do you think is the significance of "sloping shoulder" (line 5) and "The finger joints are cramped with chalk;" (line 6)?

4. Explain what the speaker means in the last two lines of the second stanza.

5. What do you think is the tone of voice behind the lines "Great is the hand that holds dominion over/Man by a scribbled name"?

6. State the author's theme in your own words.

Dylan Thomas
1914 · 1953

Born in Swansea, Wales, Thomas published his first volume of verse, *Eighteen Poems,* in 1934. *Collected Poems* (1953) contains the verse he considered to be his best. His voice play, *Under Milk Wood,* originally written for radio, was produced on Broadway in 1957.

Late in his career, Thomas toured England and America, giving enormously successful poetry readings. He died in New York City while on one of these tours.

The hand that signed the paper felled a city;
Five sovereign fingers taxed the breath,
Doubled the globe of dead and halved a country;
These five kings did a king to death.

5 The mighty hand leads to a sloping shoulder,
The finger joints are cramped with chalk;
A goose's quill has put an end to murder
That put an end to talk.

The hand that signed the treaty bred a fever,
10 And famine grew, and locusts came;
Great is the hand that holds dominion over
Man by a scribbled name.

The five kings count the dead but do not soften
The crusted wound nor stroke the brow;
15 A hand rules pity as a hand rules heaven;
Hands have no tears to flow.

THE POEMS OF DYLAN THOMAS. (British title: COLLECTED POEMS OF DYLAN THOMAS.) Copyright 1939 by New Directions Publishing Corporation. Reprinted by permission of New Directions Publishing Corporation, J. M. Dent & Sons Ltd., and the Trustees for the Copyrights of the late Dylan Thomas.

Homage

Kenneth Fearing

They said to him, "It is a very good thing that you have done,
    yes, both good and great, proving this other passage to
    the Indies. Marvelous," they said. "Very. But where,
    Señor, is the gold?"
5 They said: "We like it, we admire it very much, don't
    misunderstand us, in fact we think it's almost great. But
    isn't there, well, a little too much of this Prince of
    Denmark? After all, there is no one quite like you in
    your lighter vein."
10 "Astonishing," they said. "Who would have thought you had
    it in you, Orville?" They said, "Wilbur, this machine of
    yours is amazing, if it works, and perhaps some day we
    can use it to distribute eggs, or to advertise."

And they were good people, too. Decent people.
15 They did not beat their wives. They went to church. And they
    kept the law.

From NEW AND SELECTED POEMS by Kenneth Fearing. Copyright © 1956 by Kenneth
Fearing. Reprinted by permission of Indiana University Press.

Discussion

1. To whom are "they" speaking in each stanza?

2. (a) Who are "they"? (b) Where can "they" be found?

3. How would you describe the tone in the last stanza?

4. What is the significance of the title?

5. What is the speaker of the poem saying about how contemporaries pay tribute to great achievements of their peers?

Kenneth Fearing
1902 · 1961

Born in Oak Park, Illinois, Fearing was raised in the Midwest and attended the University of Wisconsin. After a brief spell as a journalist in Chicago, Fearing moved to New York City, where he remained the rest of his life.

Angel Arms, his first book of poetry, appeared in 1929. He also wrote a number of novels, including *The Big Clock* (1946), which was made into a movie of the same name in 1948.

His poems often portray the contradictions of the world around us.

The Speaker and the Poet

In reading the poems thus far, you have seen how poets can use elements within a poem to reinforce the sense of the poem. Meter, rhyme, metaphor, or alliteration in themselves are not important; they are important only in the way they contribute to the meaning of the poem. In this essay we will consider one aspect of the poet's craft that might be thought of as being outside the poem and yet governing many of the elements within the poem: the speaking voice that the poet chooses to narrate his message or emotion.

We often make the mistake of thinking that the poem is autobiographical and that the poet is speaking directly to us. This mistake can frequently distort the meaning of the poem and cause us to respond insufficiently or inaccurately to the work.

Maya Angelou dedicates her poem "Elegy" to Harriet Tubman and Frederick Douglass, two black leaders, long dead. The speaker in her poem speaks from the grave. The speaker(s) may or may not be Tubman and Douglass but he or she, or the collective voice of the dead, is certainly black, someone who died before the recent civil rights advance. The voice is proud and fulfilled as it speaks of watching "my children grow." In Naomi Long Madgett's "Woman with Flower" and Jim Barnes's "Looking for Arrowheads," the speakers direct, teach, and admonish the readers. They speak with authority. Jacques Prévert's poem, "Late Rising," relies upon two voices: the first describes from a distance the squalid condition of the starving man; the second, a radio or TV broadcaster, reports the crime; and, finally, the first speaker reappears.

A poet will use different speakers in order to create humor, sadness, or irony, which is a type of figurative language in which the actual intent is expressed in a way that carries the opposite meaning.

The speaker in Margaret Tsuda's poem asks "Hard Questions" that are difficult to answer because of the conflict between society's concern for the environment and the need for industrial growth. The speaker asks questions that make us stop and think.

Frequently, the voice of the speaker is very subtle and disguised so that only with careful study can the reader identify the person the poet has chosen to speak. This speaker will have much to do with whether the poet will write in rhymed iambic pentameter, unrhymed iambic pentameter, or an unrhymed free verse. Also, the speaker will have much to do with the diction of the poem and with the type of figurative language used.

When you read poetry it is wise to read it several times. If possible, read it aloud and ask someone else to read it to you until you can hear the voice of the speaker of the poem. Then you will begin to see how the elements of poetry combine to make sense out of the sound of the language.

Longings

See LYRIC Handbook of Literary Terms

Those Winter Sundays

Robert Hayden

Sundays too my father got up early
and put his clothes on in the blueblack cold,
then with cracked hands that ached
from labor in the weekday weather made
5   banked fires blaze. No one ever thanked him.

I'd wake and hear the cold splintering, breaking.
When the rooms were warm, he'd call,
and slowly I would rise and dress,
fearing the chronic angers of that house,

10 Speaking indifferently to him,
who had driven out the cold
and polished my good shoes as well.
What did I know, what did I know
of love's austere and lonely offices?

Reprinted from ANGLE OF ASCENT, New and Selected Poems by Robert Hayden. By permission of Liveright Publishing Corporation. Copyright © 1975, 1972, 1970, 1966, by Robert Hayden.

Discussion

1. What does the word "too" in the first line tell you?

2. Why do you think "No one ever thanked him"? (line 5)

3. What type of figurative language is used in line 6?

4. What are "chronic angers" of a house?

5. (a) What does the word "offices" mean? (b) Who performed "love's austere and lonely offices"? (c) What were they? (d) Would the word "duties" be as effective? Why or why not?

6. What is the speaker saying about "longing"?

Robert Hayden 1913 •

Hayden's poetry frequently reflected his black heritage, but extended far beyond it. His poems reveal the love and compassion he had for people and the rage he felt against what is mean and petty in human nature. In 1976 he became the first black poet to be appointed Consultant in Poetry to the Library of Congress.

Among Hayden's published works are: *A Ballad of Remembrance* (1962), *Selected Poems* (1966), and *Words in the Mourning Time* (1970).

Driving in Oklahoma

Carter Revard

On humming rubber along this white concrete
    lighthearted between the gravities
of source and destination like a man
    halfway to the moon
5   in this bubble of tuneless whistling
at seventy miles an hour from the windvents,
    over prairie swells rising
    and falling, over the quick offramp
that drops to its underpass and the truck
10   thundering beneath as I cross
with the country music twanging out my windows,
    I'm grooving down this highway feeling
technology is freedom's other name when
                     —a meadowlark
15   comes sailing across my windshield
    with breast shining yellow
    and five notes pierce
    the windroar like a flash
    of nectar on mind
20 gone as the country music swells up and
    drops me wheeling down
    my notch of cement-bottomed sky
    between home and away
               and wanting
25 to move again through country that a bird
    has defined wholly with song
    and maybe next time see how
he flies so easy, when he sings.

From VOICES OF THE RAINBOW edited by Kenneth Rosen. Copyright © 1975 by Kenneth Rosen. Reprinted by permission of The Viking Press.

Discussion

1. What is occurring in the poem?

2. (a) Until the meadowlark flies across the windshield, what has been the speaker's attitude toward technology? **(b)** What does technology seem to give the speaker?

3. (a) How do the sight and sound of the meadowlark affect the speaker? **(b)** Does it seem to change the speaker's attitude in any way? How?

See **RHYTHM** Handbook of Literary Terms

The Stone

Wilfrid Wilson Gibson

"And will you cut a stone for him,
To set above his head?
And will you cut a stone for him—
A stone for him?" she said.

5 Three days before, a splintered rock
Had struck her lover dead—
Had struck him in the quarry dead,
Where, careless of the warning call,
He loitered, while the shot was fired—
10 A lively stripling, brave and tall,
And sure of all his heart desired . . .
A flash, a shock,
A rumbling fall . . .
And, broken 'neath the broken rock,
15 A lifeless heap, with face of clay,
And still as any stone he lay,
With eyes that saw the end of all.

I went to break the news to her:
And I could hear my own heart beat
20 With dread of what my lips might say;
But some poor fool had sped before;
And, flinging wide her father's door,
Had blurted out the news to her,
Had struck her lover dead for her,
25 Had struck the girl's heart dead in her,
Had struck life, lifeless, at a word,
And dropped it at her feet:
Then hurried on his witless way,
Scarce knowing she had heard.
30 And when I came, she stood alone—
A woman, turned to stone:
And, though no word at all she said,
I knew that all was known.

Because her heart was dead,
35 She did not sigh nor moan.

"The Stone" from COLLECTED POEMS by W. W. Gibson.
Reprinted by permission of Macmillan London and Basingstoke.

His mother wept:
She could not weep.
Her lover slept:
She could not sleep.
40 Three days, three nights,
She did not stir:
Three days, three nights,
Were one to her,

Who never closed her eyes
45 From sunset to sunrise,
From dawn to evenfall—
Her tearless, staring eyes,
That, seeing naught, saw all.

The fourth night when I came from work,
50 I found her at my door.
"And will you cut a stone for him?"
She said: and spoke no more:
But followed me, as I went in,
And sank upon a chair;
55 And fixed her grey eyes on my face,
With still, unseeing stare.
And, as she waited patiently,
I could not bear to feel
Those still, grey eyes that followed me,
60 Those eyes that plucked the heart from me,
Those eyes that sucked the breath from me
And curdled the warm blood in me,
Those eyes that cut me to the bone,
And pierced my marrow like cold steel.

65 And so I rose, and sought a stone;
And cut it, smooth and square:

And, as I worked, she sat and watched,
Beside me, in her chair.
Night after night, by candlelight,
70 I cut her lover's name:
Night after night, so still and white,
And like a ghost she came;
And sat beside me, in her chair,
And watched with eyes aflame.
75 She eyed each stroke,
And hardly stirred:
She never spoke
A single word:
And not a sound or murmur broke
80 The quiet, save the mallet-stroke.

With still eyes ever on my hands,
With eyes that seemed to burn my hands,
My wincing, overwearied hands,
She watched, with bloodless lips apart,
85 And silent, indrawn breath:
And every stroke my chisel cut,
Death cut still deeper in her heart:
The two of us were chiselling,
Together, I and death.

90 And when at length the job was done,
And I had laid the mallet by,
As if, at last, her peace were won,
She breathed his name; and, with a sigh,
Passed slowly through the open door;
95 And never crossed my threshold more.

Next night I laboured late, alone,
To cut her name upon the stone.

Discussion

1. (a) Who is the speaker in this poem? (b) How does the speaker relate to the woman?

2. Do you think this poem could be set to music effectively? Why or why not?

3. What words would you use to identify the tone of the poem?

Wilfrid Wilson Gibson
1878 · 1962

Gibson was a prolific poet who began as a romantic verse-writer and turned, in midstream, to become a poet of the people.

His origins, Hexham, in the north of England, gave him the background to write about nature and country people. Yet he first wrote about knights, queens, and historical characters.

In 1910, his book *Daily Bread* turned to everyday life, and thereafter he concerned himself with that subject.

One Perfect Rose

Dorothy Parker

A single flow'r he sent me, since we met.
  All tenderly his messenger he chose;
Deep-hearted, pure, with scented dew still wet—
  One perfect rose.

5 I knew the language of the floweret;
  "My fragile leaves," it said, "his heart enclose."
Love long has taken for his amulet
  One perfect rose.

Why is it no one ever sent me yet
10   One perfect limousine, do you suppose?
Ah no, it's always just my luck to get
  One perfect rose.

From THE PORTABLE DOROTHY PARKER. Copyright 1926, 1954 by Dorothy Parker. Reprinted by permission of The Viking Press and Gerald Duckworth and Company Ltd.

Discussion

1. Identify "his messenger" that "he chose" so carefully.

2. (a) Where in the poem does the mood change? **(b)** How does it change?

3. (a) How would you describe the language in the first two stanzas? **(b)** in the third stanza? **(c)** How does the contrast between style and thought add to its humor?

Dorothy Parker
1893 · 1967

Parker delighted the reading public with her witty, often cynical, verse for many years. Some of her book titles suggest the wry humor that she favored: *Enough Rope, Death and Taxes, Laments for the Living, Not So Deep As A Well,* and *Here Lies.* "One Perfect Rose" is typical of her stabbing wit.

October Journey

Margaret Walker

Traveller take heed for journeys undertaken in the dark of the
      year.
Go in the bright blaze of Autumn's equinox.
Carry protection against ravages of a sun-robber, a vandal,
      and a thief.
Cross no bright expanse of water in the full of the moon.
5 Choose no dangerous summer nights;
no heady tempting hours of spring;
October journeys are safest, brightest, and best.

I want to tell you what hills are like in October
when colors gush down mountainsides
10 and little streams are freighted with a caravan of leaves,
I want to tell you how they blush and turn in fiery shame and
      joy,
how their love burns with flames consuming and terrible
until we wake one morning and woods are like a smoldering
      plain—
a glowing caldron full of jewelled fire;
15 the emerald earth a dragon's eye
the poplars drenched with yellow light
and dogwoods blazing bloody red.
Travelling southward earth changes from gray rock to green
      velvet.
Earth changes to red clay
20 with green grass growing brightly
with saffron skies of evening setting dully
with muddy rivers moving sluggishly.

In the early spring when the peach tree blooms
wearing a veil like a lavender haze
25 and the pear and plum in their bridal hair
gently snow their petals on earth's grassy bosom below
then the soughing breeze is soothing
and the world seems bathed in tenderness,
but in October
30 blossoms have long since fallen.
A few red apples hang on leafless boughs;

From OCTOBER JOURNEY by Margaret Walker. Copyright © 1973 by Margaret Walker
Alexander; Broadside Press, Highland Park, Michigan. Reprinted by permission.

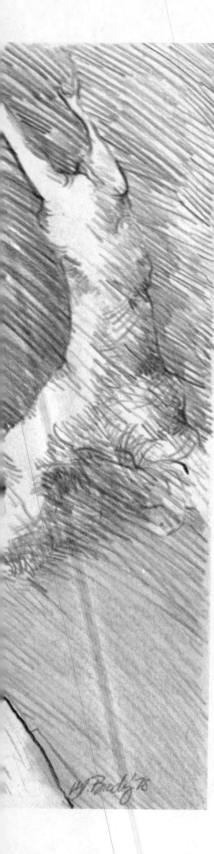

wind whips bushes briskly.
And where a blue stream sings cautiously
a barren land feeds hungrily.
35 An evil moon bleeds drops of death.
The earth burns brown.
Grass shrivels and dries to a yellowish mass.
Earth wears a dun-colored dress
like an old woman wooing the sun to be her lover,
40 be her sweetheart and her husband bound in one.
Farmers heap hay in stacks and bind corn in shocks
against the biting breath of frost.

The train wheels hum, "I am going home, I am going home,
I am moving toward the South."
45 Soon cypress swamps and muskrat marshes
and black fields touched with cotton will appear.
I dream again of my childhood land
of a neighbor's yard with a redbud tree
the smell of pine for turpentine
50 an Easter dress, a Christmas eve
and winding roads from the top of a hill.
A music sings within my flesh
I feel the pulse within my throat
my heart fills up with hungry fear
55 while hills and flatlands stark and staring
before my dark eyes sad and haunting
appear and disappear.

Then when I touch this land again
the promise of a sun-lit hour dies.
60 The greenness of an apple seems
to dry and rot before my eyes.
The sullen winter rains
are tears of grief I cannot shed.
The windless days are static lives.
65 The clock runs down
timeless and still.
The days and nights turn hours to years
and water in a gutter marks the circle of another world
hating, resentful, and afraid,
70 stagnant, and green, and full of slimy things.

Discussion

1. From what part of the country do you think the traveller begins her journey? What lines make you think so?

2. (a) Which images convey the speaker's delight in going home? (b) What kind of experience does she hope to have when she arrives home?

3. (a) How does the tone change in lines 58–70? (b) What words communicate this tone?

4. In your own words, tell the story of the speaker's journey.

Vocabulary · Structure, Pronunciation, and Dictionary

Use your Glossary to answer the questions about the italicized words. Be sure you know the definitions, as well as the spellings.

1. Does the *ch* sound in *chronic* sound like *k* or like *ch* in *chair?*

2. Where is the accent in *inexorable?*

3. *Sough* may be pronounced two ways. Does the first pronunciation rhyme with *bough* or with *rough?*

4. Where is the accent in *amulet?*

5. What is the literal Latin meaning of *equinox?* Does the *e* sound like the *e* in *let* or in *equal?*

6. In *circumstantial* which *c* has an *s* sound? Which a *k* sound?

7. Is the accent in *austere* on the first or second syllable? What is the origin of the word?

8. How many syllables are there in *sovereign?* From what Latin word is it derived?

Margaret Walker 1915 ·

The daughter of a Methodist minister, Walker was born and raised in Birmingham, Alabama. She moved north to attend Northwestern University, near Chicago. Her first book of poetry, *For My People* (1954), grew out of her experiences in the North and the South.

The Old One and the Wind

Clarice Short

Discussion

1. What kinds of things please the old woman? Why do you think they do?

2. What lines imply that the townspeople feel differently about the wind?

3. Reread lines 19–23. (a) What does the wind seem to mean to the old woman? (b) Why might the young not feel the same?

Clarice Short 1910 ·

"The Old One and the Wind" is taken from a volume of poems with the same title by Clarice Short. Throughout this collection, which was published in 1973, she draws upon her own past to make observations about life.

She loves the wind.
There on the edge of the known world, at ninety,
In her tall house, any wildness in the elements
Is as welcome as an old friend.
5 When the surgically patched elms and sycamores
Crack off their heavy limbs in the freak snow storm
Of October, she rejoices; the massy hail
That drives craters into her groomed lawn
Stirs her sluggish heart to a riot of beating.

10 A cluster of cottonwood trees in the swale
Of the prairie, oasis now in a desert of wheat fields,
Is all that is left of the home place. No one
Is left to remember the days there with her:
The playhouse sheltered behind the cowshed,
15 The whirlwinds that made a column of corn shucks,
Winters when snow brushed out all the fences,
Springs when the white of the snow turned to daisies,
Wind-bent as were the urchins who picked them.

To her in her tall house in the tame town, the wind
20 That escapes the windbreaks of man's constructing
Blows from a distance beyond the young's conceiving,
Is rife with excitements of the world's beginning
And its end.

Copyright © 1971 by The Western Humanities Review, reprinted by permission from THE OLD ONE AND THE WIND. POEMS. University of Utah Press, 1973.

Profiles

A Trucker

Thom Gunn

Sometimes it is like a beast
barely controlled by a man.
But the cabin is lofty
as a skull, and all the rest
5 extends from his foot as an
enormous throbbing body:

if he left anything to
chance—see his great frame capsize,
and his rubber limbs explode
10 whirling! and see there follow
a bright fountain of red eyes
tinkling sightless to the road.

Reprinted with the permission of Farrar,
Straus & Giroux, Inc. and Faber and Faber
Ltd. from MY SAD CAPTAINS by Thom
Gunn, Copyright © 1961, 1971, 1973 by
Thom Gunn.

Discussion

1. To what does the "it" in the first line refer?

2. Why do you think the author called this poem "A Trucker" rather than "A Truck"?

3. Describe the speaker's attitude toward the subject of the poem.

4. With what do you associate the phrase "a bright fountain of red eyes tinkling sightless"?

Thom Gunn 1929 ·

One of the "Angry Young Men" of the 1950s in England, Gunn titled his first book *Fighting Terms,* which characterizes much of the mood of his early poetry.

Born Thomson William Gunn at Gravesend, England, Thom Gunn has traveled widely and published a number of poetry books since the fifties. He has taught at the University of California, Berkeley, and presently free-lances while living in San Francisco.

Tightrope Walker

Vernon Scannell

High on the thrilling strand he dances
Laved in white light. The smudged chalk faces
Blur below. His movements scorn
And fluently insult the law
5 That lumps us, munching, on our seats,
Avoiding the question that slyly tweaks:
How much do we want to see him fall?
It's no use saying we don't at all.
We all know that we hate his breed.
10 Prancing the nimble thread he's freed
From what we are and gravity.
And yet we know quite well that he
Started just as we began,
That he is, just like us, a man.
15 (We don't fall off our seats until
We've drunk too much or are feeling ill)
But he has trained the common skill,
Trained and practised; now tonight
It flogs our credence as high and white
20 In the spotlight's talcum he pirouettes,
Lonely, scorning safety nets,
The highly extraordinary man.
But soon, quite softly, boredom starts
Its muffled drilling at our hearts;
25 A frisson of coughs and shuffles moves
Over the crowd like a wind through leaves.
Our eyes slide down the air and walk
Idly round the tent as talk
Hums on denial's monotone.
30 It's just as well the act ends soon
Or we would leave, though not stampede,
Leave furtively in twos and threes,
Absence flooding the canvas house
Where he, alone, all unaware
35 Would go dancing on the almost air
Till fatigue or error dragged him down,
An ordinary man on ordinary ground.

Discussion

1. What law does the tightrope walker "insult"?

2. Does the audience really want to see the tightrope walker fall? Discuss.

3. How does the audience react as the act continues? Why?

4. (a) What statement does this poem make about the attitude of ordinary persons toward extraordinary ones? **(b)** Do you agree or disagree with the statement? Support your opinion.

Vernon Scannell 1922 ·

Scannell at one time was a professional boxer in his native England. But later he went into teaching.

Besides poetry Scannell has also written novels and criticisms, and he has broadcast for the BBC in London.

"Tightrope Walker" by Vernon Scannell, OUTPOSTS, Summer 1964. Copyright © 1965 by Vernon Scannell. Reprinted by permission.

See **ALLITERATION** Handbook of Literary Terms

Part of the Darkness

Isabella Gardner

"Part of the Darkness" by Isabella Gardner from WEST OF CHILDHOOD: POEMS 1950–1965. Copyright © 1965 by Isabella Gardner Tate. Reprinted by permission of Houghton Mifflin Company.

Discussion

1. What was the purpose of the trip to "Wisconsin's Great North woods"?

2. Why do the children boo the bear? Explain.

3. What do you think is the theme of this poem?

4. What do you think the title symbolizes?

5. There are many examples of alliteration in this poem. Select at least two lines in which you think alliteration is especially effective.

Isabella Gardner 1915 ·

The daughter of a Boston investment broker, Gardner attended private schools, but decided not to go on to college. Instead she went to acting school in London.

Though she had been writing before and during her stage career, it was not until the 1950s that her reputation as a poet was established.

I had thought of the bear in his lair as fiercely free, feasting on
    honey and wildwood fruits;
I had imagined a forest lunge, regretting the circus shuffle and
    the zoo's proscribed pursuits.
Last summer I took books and children to Wisconsin's Great
    North woods. We drove
one night through miles of pines and rainy darkness to a
    garbage grove
5 that burgeoned broken crates and bulging paper bags and
    emptied cans of beer,
to watch for native bears, who local guides had told us,
    scavenged there.
After parking behind three other cars (leaving our headlights
    on but dim)
We stumbled over soggy moss to join the families blinking on
    the rim
of mounded refuse bounded east north and west by the
    forest.
10 The parents hushed and warned their pushing children each of
    whom struggled to stand nearest
the arena, and presently part of the darkness humped away
    from the foliage and lumbered bear-shaped
toward the heaping spoilage. It trundled into the litter while we
    gaped,
and for an instant it gaped too, bear-faced, but not a tooth was
    bared. It grovelled
carefully while tin cans clattered and tense tourists tittered.
    Painstakingly it nosed and ravelled
15 rinds and husks and parings, the used and the refused;
    bearskinned and doggedly explored
the second-hand remains while headlights glared and
    flashlights stared and shamed bored
children booed, wishing aloud that it would trudge away so
    they might read its tracks.
They hoped to find an as yet unclassified spoor, certain that no
    authentic bear would turn his back
upon the delicacies of his own domain to flounder where mere
    housewives' leavings rot.
20 I also was reluctant to concede that there is no wild honey in
    the forest and no forest in the bear.
Bereaved, we started home, leaving that animal there.

What She Did in the Morning, I Wouldn't Know, She Was Seated There in the Midst of Her Resilient Symptoms, Always

Merrill Moore

They were like sofa cushions.
She was constantly rearranging them
To form new patterns and support her frame.

Her attention was mainly directed toward herself
5 And some of it, a small part, I would say,
Was aimed at trying to bend others that way,
But few responded, few fulfilled her wish;
She was simply not their kind of dish,
So, she remained, unmarried and complaining.

10 She had a bird, a series of small pets—
A dog, a cat—but none of them ever thrived.
They were, in fact, unusually short-lived.
It almost seemed as if her infections spread.
I was always hearing one of them was dead.

"What She Did in the Morning" by Merrill Moore from SATURDAY REVIEW, June 2, 1956. Copyright © 1956 Saturday Review, Inc. Reprinted by permission of Mrs. Ann Leslie Moore.

Discussion

1. To what does "they" in the first line refer?

2. (a) Have you ever known a person like this? (b) Were her symptoms real or imaginary or could you tell?

3. Does the woman in this poem have any idea of what others think of her? What lines explain her relationship with other people?

4. Do you think her pets were really "short-lived" as a result of her infections? Explain.

Merrill Moore 1903 · 1957

Moore achieved distinction both as a doctor of medicine and as a poet. He began writing verse during his student days at Vanderbilt University and joined with some friends of similar literary interests to found the *Fugitive*, a magazine of poetry and criticism. In his several volumes of poetry, such as *The Noise that Time Makes* (1929) and *It is a Good Deal Later than You Think* (1934), Moore used only one poetic form—the sonnet, or fourteen-line poem. One thousand of his sonnets were published in *M* in 1938.

heritage

Anita Skeen

Discussion

　　1. What kind of work does the speaker's father do? Which details in the poem tell you?

　　2. What is the father's attitude toward his work? How do you know?

　　3. What do lines 24–30 reveal about the way the daughter feels about her father's work?

driving south on route 60 at dawn he would say to me,
my chin hooked over the back of the front seat
a few inches from his ear,
thinking how the lines in the back
5　of his neck were like the deep gullies
that cut through the back hills,
a tense laugh in his voice
"there's where your old man puts in his time"

narrow pipes spit fire at the morning
10　as ovens cough up white-hot coke
rows of stacks, choking
belch out circles of thick breath
holding my nose, swallowing
even closing my eyes
15　does not help:
i still drown
in ammonia and smell
that same smell woven into the fiber
of his heavy wool shirts
20　it fills our house
when he enters each night
and moves with his hands as they
pass food at the supper table

in dreams i climb
25　thin ladders on those big tanks
my bones against their bones
my flesh freezing, weeping
in the winter cold
to toss my orange hat far up
30　far out above the webs of dark steel

"heritage" originally appeared in *The Greenfield Review*, Vol. 5, Nos. 1 & 2, Spring 1976. Reprinted by permission of the author.

For author biography, see page 233.

See **CONSONANCE** Handbook of Literary Terms

Yellow Woman

Genevieve Lim-Jue

I am the daughter of
   seafarers, gold miners, quartz
     miners, railroad miners,
       farmworkers, garment workers,
5   factory workers, restaurant
       workers, laundrymen,
        houseboys, scholars,
          poets, dreamers . . .

   I have seen my father's destiny
10   crushed,
    by the weight of his immigrant dreams
     silently staring
      a heap of yellow misery
      inextricably tangled
15   amongst the sweating, huddled flesh of Utopia.

   I have heard my mother's prayers
    shaped in tombs of darkness
     seen the invisible tears
      trickling down blank cheeks.
20   Heard old women chanting elegies
     from the past,
      beseeching idle gods.
    Neighbors' children mocked their
        bound feet, gnarled hands.

25 Mother was a pioneer
   groping in White Darkness.
    They called her China-Woman
    as she walked quietly alone.
    And in the winter of her isolation I was born—

30   Blood of Asia,
    Flesh of the New World,
     One-hundred-and-twenty-five-
       year-old
    daughter of two worlds
35   struggling
      to embrace
       one.

Discussion

1. In what sense is the speaker the daughter of all people named in stanza one?

2. Look up the meaning of "Utopia" (stanza two) in your Glossary. **(a)** How is Utopia related to the father's "immigrant dreams"? **(b)** Why is the reference to Utopia ironic?

3. What does stanza three tell you about the mother?

4. How is the mother a pioneer?

5. What are the daughter's feelings?

Genevieve Lim-Jue 1946 ·

Lim-Jue grew up in San Francisco's Chinatown, the youngest of seven children. In college she studied theater arts, then dropped out to sing in a rock band.

After working at numerous occupations, she returned to Chinatown, where she began to write. Aside from writing, she is also an avid practitioner of Kung-fu.

"Yellow Woman" by Genevieve Lim-Jue, BRIDGE, February 1975. Copyright © 1975 by Genevieve Lim. Reprinted by permission of the author.

The Other Pioneers

. Roberto Félix Salazar

Discussion

1. (a) Who are the "other pioneers"? **(b)** Which lines tell you? **(c)** List several towns in the Southwest that have "soft-woven, Spanish names."

2. (a) What was the experience of the "other pioneers"? **(b)** Why might the Indians have been cruel?

3. In what way are the experiences of the "other pioneers" and the pioneers in "Yellow Woman" alike? not alike?

Now I must write
Of those of mine who rode these plains
Long years before the Saxon and the Irish came.
Of those who plowed the land and built the towns
5 And gave the towns soft-woven Spanish names.
Of those who moved across the Rio Grande
Toward the hiss of Texas snake and Indian yell.
Of men who from the the earth made thick-walled homes
And from the earth raised churches to their God.
10 And of the wives who bore them sons
And smiled with knowing joy.

They saw the Texas sun rise golden-red with promised
    wealth
And saw the Texas sun sink golden yet, with wealth
    unspent.
"Here," they said. "Here to live and here to love."
15 "Here is the land for our sons and the sons of our sons."
And they sang the songs of ancient Spain
And they made new songs to fit new needs.
They cleared the brush and planted the corn
And saw green stalks turn black from lack of rain.
20 They roamed the plains behind the herds
And stood the Indian's cruel attacks.
There was dust and there was sweat.
And there were tears and the women prayed.

And the years moved on.
25 Those who were first placed in graves
Beside the broad mesquite and the tall nopal.
Gentle mothers left their graces and their arts
And stalwart fathers pride and manly strength.
Salinas, de la Garza, Sánchez, Garcia,
30 Uribe, González, Martinez, de León:
Such were the names of the fathers.
Salinas, de la Garza, Sánchez, Garcia,
Uribe, González, Martinez, de León:
Such are the names of the sons.

"The Other Pioneers," by Roberto Félix Salazar. Appeared in LULAC (League of United Latin American Citizens) *News*, July 1939.

The Way It Is

Gloria Oden

I have always known
that had I been blonde
blue-eyed
with skin fabled white as the unicorn's
5 with cheeks tinted and pearled
as May morning on the lips of a rose
such commercial virtues
could never have led me to assume myself
anywhere near as beautiful as
10 my mother
whose willow fall of black hair
—now pirate silver—
I brushed as a child
(earning five cents)
15 when shaken free from the bun
as wrapped round and pinned
it billowed in a fine mist
from her proud shoulders
to her waist.

20 Brown as I am, she is browner.
Walnut
like the satin leaves of the oak
that fallen overwinter in woods
where night comes quickly
25 and whose wind-peaked piles

deepen the shadows of
such seizure.

Moreover, she is tall.
At her side standing
30 I feel I am still
that scarecrow child of
yesteryear:
owl-eyed
toothed, boned, and angled
35 opposite to her
soft southern presence—
an inaudible allegiance
but sweetening her attendance
upon strangers and friends.

40 Dark hair, dark skin
these are the dominant measures of
my sense of beauty
which explains possibly
why being a black girl
45 in a country of white strangers
I am so pleased with myself.

"The Way It Is" by Gloria Oden. From POETRY IS ALIVE AND WELL AND LIVING IN AMERICA by G. C. Oden and May Swenson. Copyright © 1969 by Media Plus, Inc. Reprinted by permission.

Discussion

1. What advertising phrases might the speaker be thinking of when she refers to blonde, blue-eyed . . . as "commercial virtues"?

2. What is the basis for the speaker's sense of her own beauty?

3. (a) Why do you think the author called this poem "The Way It Is"? (b) What else might it have been titled?

Gloria Oden 1923 ·

Born in Yonkers, New York, Oden graduated from Howard University and its law school. She has been an editor and teacher, as well as writer, and has held a John Hay Whitney Fellowship for creative writing.

See **NARRATIVE POETRY** Handbook of Literary Terms

Eulogy
for a Man from Jalostitlan[1]

Rita Gutierrez-Christensen

1. *Jalostitlan* (hä′lō stē tlän′), a small town in the state of Jalisco, Mexico.

I

My father is dead at 92.
His death, his one selfish act
In his long life
Was his own doing.

5 He planned his death,
The one thing he had control over
By not taking the little pills
That allowed his blood to flow through
His worn and aged arteries.

10 "Please, no eulogy," I told my sisters.
"I can't bear to hear a priest saying
Empty nothings over our father's grave."
His eulogy was carved in our hearts.
How could a priest express how one old man
15 (He was 47 when I was born and I was his oldest.)
Raised four little girls into womanhood
With kindness, wisdom and love?

Two years before, Larry and I
Had taken him to the land of his birth.
20 At first he hesitated—his age, his health,
But then, impulsively and daringly, he said,
"What the helly!"

He sat up front in the truck,
His gray hat turning left and right,
25 Taking in everything.
(No one dared ask him to take his turn
Sitting in the back.)

When we would stop for gas, food or rest,
He'd wander off to speak
30 To someone on the road.

"Eulogy for a Man from Jalostitlan" by Rita Gutierrez-Christensen, GRITO DEL SOL, October-December 1976. Copyright © 1976 by Tonatiuh International, Inc., Berkeley, CA 94704. Reprinted by permission.

Later, he would return
With that someone's story of his life.

When we visited with Tia Maria[2]
His eyes filled with tears and apologies
35 As new friends made gifts of things
He admired on their walls or dining tables.

But the gifts kept coming
As the old man spoke with love
For the land he had not seen
40 In half a century.

He returned home full of tales,
Robust health
And a yearning to return.

The following summer he was disappointed
45 Because we chose instead to go to Oregon.
"But now I know the way," he said,
Threateningly.
My three sisters feared and shook their heads.
We loved him selfishly.
50 (Our mother had died when we were very young.)
We would never let him go alone.

The following June
My father's young neighbor had to make a trip to Mexico.
Her youngest sister was getting married.
55 My father saw his chance.

2. *Tia Maria* (tē yä mä rē yä),
Aunt Maria.

The surgeon had removed a tumor
From his right eye.
"These glasses aren't quite right," he complained.
But we knew that he knew.
60 We were told that he would lose his sight
Within six months, perhaps a year.

The shortness of his breath
We had long been accustomed to.
But what we didn't know
65 Was that the arteries
Were getting harder and less resilient.
We only heard
His laborious breathing
But *he* felt the pain, the dizziness,
70 The loss of balance.
The little pills would help,

The doctors said
(And they did)
But they would not stop
75 The hardening of the arteries
Which like dry irrigation ditches
Were crumbling inside the old man
Who wanted to return once more to Mexico.

Amidst Judy's hot tears,
80 Much family pleading and begging,
My father left for a wedding in Mexico.

(Loretta carefully counted and packed the little pills.)

He returned three weeks later
In a Mexican coffin,
85 Dressed in an elegant Mexican suit
(He always liked nice clothes.)
A trace of a smile on his face
And the bottle of pills unopened.

Later, when the young neighbor returned,
90 We listened greedily of his last days.

How he was up and dressed at four o'clock
The morning of the wedding
To answer the mariachis' gritos[3]
As they came to sing the wedding serenata.

3. *Mariachis' gritos* (mä ryä′chēs grē′tōs). *Mariachis* are small musical groups which play traditional Mexican folksongs. *Gritos* are the soulful shouts characteristic of their singing.

95 "My father thought he was drunk," the neighbor said,
"But I told him, 'No, that's the way he is.' "

She laughed as she told us
How he would introduce her as his wife,
Then watched their uncomfortable expressions
100 As he continued,
"Yes, these two little ones are ours."

We listened how he shopped for gifts—
Shawls, earrings, leather bags—
Gifts for his four daughters and grandchildren.

105 "What do you want, hijita?"[4] he asked me
Via a phone booth in Santa Rosa
(I had planned on going with him
To make sure he'd take the pills, his rest
But my husband had a family business trip
110 And I had to choose.)

"Earrings," I said,
"Big ones and lots of them."
It was the last time I heard
My father's voice.
115 My earrings—lots and big—
Came carefully packed
In an old Christmas card box.

II

The phone calls came late at night.
Loretta said,
120 "My father has just been taken to the hospital."

The second call came an hour later.
"Our father is dead."
We could not talk
The tears were strangling our voices.

125 My daughter woke up and asked
"What's the matter, Mami?"
"Grandpa's dead," I said.
"Grandpa?"
We all thought he'd live forever.
130 "Oh, Mami."
I caught her in my arms

4. *hijita* (ē hē′tä), my little daughter; a term of endearment.

And we both cried for someone we thought
We'd have forever.

The phone calls came.
135 He died, my uncle said,
Saying one last flirtatious jest to the maid.
He died, my aunt said,
Saying to please tell us
That his last thoughts were of us.

140 And all I could think of was . . .

He'll never plant my trees.
My father will never see
The beautiful land we purchased in Santa Rosa.

As each of my sisters bought their family homes
145 My father ceremoniously planted
An olive tree, fruit trees, a walnut tree and cactus.
"With these and beans and tortillas,
You'll never go hungry," he'd say.

My father will never plant my trees . . .

150 Larry and I planted the olive tree.
"When it's grown," I said, "I'll hang
The bell from Taos."
When it rings, I thought,

It'll sing sweet memories
155 Of an old man and his four little girls.

I remembered how we hated to wash dishes.
We had no sink.
Water had to be brought in from the pump,
Heated on a wood stove,
160 Then poured into two pans,
One to wash and one to rinse.

We fussed and whined when it was our turn.
Our tears would stop
When we felt the coin in the bottom of the pan.
165 The value of the coin depended on the number of dishes
And the number of work days my father had put in
As a farm laborer.

The best part was coming home from school on a cold day
And seeing smoke coming from the chimney.
170 Papá was home!
We'd run to a warm house and oatmeal cookies.
(No matter how hard he coaxed,
We seldom ate the oatmeal he cooked for breakfast.
So he made cookies with it instead.)

175 When my father felt rich in time and money
He'd make a capirotada.[5]
I still try to make it from memory,
But even though I follow his very steps:
Corn tortillas on the bottom of the pan,
180 Alternate layers of French bread, longhorn cheese,
Panocha, raisins, canela[6] and canned Pet milk,
It doesn't taste the same.
I used to think that what was missing
Must be the wood stove.

185 On Christmas Eve
My father would bring in the pumpkins
He'd been saving since Halloween,
He'd boil the slices of pumpkin,
Mash the soft orange
190 And serve it with sugar, cinnamon and milk.
This was followed by his capirotada.

On lean days when my father could not work,
We'd all go quail egg hunting along the railroad tracks.

5. capirotada (kä′pē dō tä′dä), a
bread pudding made with bread,
bananas, raisins, milk, and sugar;
traditionally eaten during the Easter
season in Mexican-American communities.

6. panocha . . . canela (pä nō′chä,
kä ne′lä). *Panocha* is raw sugar;
brown sugar. *Canela* is cinnamon
(stick).

On the way we'd pick flowers called Indian Paint Brush.
195 My father would sit and make us crowns
Which we placed on our heads as we hunted for the nests
We sometimes found in the concrete tunnels under the
     tracks
Or in the fig orchards.
We'd separate the tall spring weeds.

200 A squeal of delight meant that one of us had found
What we were looking for.
When we thought we had enough for all of us
We'd go home.
My father would crack the tiny eggs into a bowl
205 (It took eight of the speckled brown, pale blue eggs
To equal one hen's egg.)
Mix cheese, onion, cilantro,[7] oregano and Fresno chiles
Fresh from our garden.
He would salt and pepper the mixture and then poured it
210 Into a frying pan sizzling with hot lard,
Seconds later, our migrant's brunch was ready.

To have sons is an advantage for the migrant farm worker.
While the other men bragged about how much money
Their sons brought in,
215 My father boasted about his quiet life with his four
     daughters
No cars, no booze, no bloody fights.
The men shut their mouths.

7. *cilantro* (sē län′trō), coriander, an herb used for seasoning.

Our girlfriends complained of whippings,
Spying by older brothers.
220 Our father never touched us.
He talked instead and if that failed,
He could always rely on his tsz, tsz,
A sound he made with his tongue
And the roof of his mouth.
225 And so we were brought to reason.

Easter at our barrio[8] church
Celebrated our winter survival as well.
Everyone decked out in their new finery.
One year we had enough money for shoes but not for
      clothes.
230 I looked through my mother's troncón[9]
Where before I had found material or something
I could cut up, but I didn't find anything this time that
I could make dresses with.
Terry and I could do without, but we decided
235 That our two little sisters were still too vulnerable
And had to be protected from the silent barrio snobbery.
(We were too obvious a reminder of hard winters ago and to
      come.)
We looked around and agreed that our bedroom curtains
Would come down.

240 Then we saw our father mending his shoes.
He had not said a word, as usual.
We didn't say a word either
But we put our new spring shoes back into their boxes,
Returned them to the store and handed him the money.
245 "It looks like you need a pair of work shoes, Papá."
We polished our old shoes and celebrated the rising of the
      Christ.

III
Judy was the youngest and the most reluctant to give him
      up.
During the velorio,[10] she insisted that the coffin be opened.
"If I can just touch him, I know I'll be all right."

250 This was impossible, we were told.
Our father had died in a foreign land
And his coffin must remain sealed.
This was also further complicated by the American Embassy
Who, for reasons known only to themselves,

8. *barrio* (bär'yō), neighborhood;
a Mexican-American neighborhood.

9. *troncón* (trōn cōn'), trunk.

10. *velorio* (ve lōr'yō), a wake; the
vigil over a corpse the night before
the funeral.

255 Would not release our father's body.
　　My father would have enjoyed the drama that followed
　　In order to get his body home to us.

　　To this day we still don't understand
　　The American Embassy's rationale but we didn't waste any
　　　　time.
260 "Let's call his congressman,"
　　I, the power-conscious radical said,
　　"This is a small town. We'll threaten him
　　With the Mexican vote."
　　We called the congressman's hometown office.
265 Within minutes Washington was on the phone.
　　Three phone calls later, our father was on his way home.

　　In this rural valley country people sometimes
　　Have to break rules made up by city folk.
　　The mortician in charge, a nice young man,
270 Gave in to Judy's request.

　　The coffin would be opened just before it left the mortuary
　　For the church services.
　　He cautioned Judy about the smell, that the lingering odor
　　Might create an even greater emotional trauma.
275 Judy responded that she understood.
　　Her need to touch my father was great . . .

　　The next morning my father's coffin was opened.
　　There was no smell.
　　We touched our father's hands, kissed his face
280 And said farewell.

　　I, the unbeliever, said to my Catholic sisters
　　"There is a Russian proverb that says
　　That if the body doesn't smell it means that the person is a
　　　　saint."
　　"Ooooh," my sisters said.
285 But didn't we always know that?

　　But now they knew for sure.
　　Their lord had sent them a sign
　　And they were happy.

11. *campo santo* (käm'pō sän'tō),
holy ground; a cemetery.

　　On the way to the campo santo[11] we suddenly remembered
290 The traditional feed.
　　"What are we going to serve all of these people?"

One of us said as we looked at the line of cars and trucks
     behind us.
Neither one of us had given much thought
To the meal following the burial services.
295 We had been too engrossed in helping each other
Maintain the self-control
We'd promised our father
Who disapproved of the hysteria
He had seen at other funerals.

300 And because of this Papacito,
I learned one more of la vida's[12] unexpected surprises.

The funeral was held on a work day.
But the cars and trucks behind us were numerous.
Who were all these people?
305 All of his friends were dead.
My father was the last to go.
We arrived at my father's house.
I was not looking forward to the traditional gathering.
How could anyone eat or socialize at a time like this?
310 And then I knew . . .

My Okie[13] "mother" and "sisters" were already in the
     kitchen.
They had set the tables under my father's walnut trees.
Food was being reheated on the stove,
Pots and pans of menudo, pollo en mole, sopas[14] and salads,
315 Pies, cakes, coffee, punch and beer
Were strewn all over the kitchen and on the tables outside.

12. *la vida's* (lä vē′dä), life's.

13. *Okie*, a term used by Mexican Americans to refer to Anglo-Americans; used affectionately here.

14. *menudo, pollo en mole, sopas* (me nü′dō, pō′yō en mō′lāy, sō′päs). *Menudo* is a traditional Mexican soup made of tripe and hominy; *pollo en mole* is a dish made of chicken with a rich chile sauce, flavored with chocolate. *Sopas* are rice or noodles prepared with special sauces and spices.

My father's friends' children brought the food.
I had not seen many of them since high school.
We ate and talked about how long it had been.
320 We shared stories about our fathers.
And then I knew that this talk and feed was for all our
fathers.
Their concern was our consolation.
They had already suffered their loss.

When my father's meager belongings were shared between
us,
325 I was given my mother's picture I had enlarged and framed for
him.
I asked for and got his old tan working hat
He used while puttering about his yard
And fussing about things that kept breaking down.
My reason was selfish.

15. *cosas de la vida* (kō′säs de lä
vē′ dä), things of life.

330 If las cosas de la vida[15] became too much, in moments of
weakness,
I could bury my face into that old hat and smell my father's
sweat still there.
I have this fantasy that I will muster up the courage and
strength
To go on with the business of living.

When it was all over and we were alone in Judy's kitchen
335 She said, "I'm scared. If only we were as strong and tough as
he."
And I replied, surprising even myself, "We are. He made us
so."

Discussion

1. (a) What is a eulogy? (b) How does this poem meet the definition of eulogy?

2. (a) In what ways were the father and his family of four daughters poor? rich? (b) What specific examples show how love flowed from the father to his daughters, and from the daughters to their father, throughout his lifetime?

3. In what ways does this poem support or contradict your ideas about very old people? about death and people's reactions to death?

4. Why is "Eulogy . . ." a good example of narrative poetry?

Vocabulary · Structure, Pronunciation, and Dictionary

Use your Glossary to answer the following questions about the italicized words. Be sure you know the meanings of the words.

1. What is the Latin root of *audible?* How is the meaning of *audible* changed by the addition of the prefix *in-?*

2. Is the *s* of *resilient* pronounced with an *s* or a *z* sound? What two Latin words form the basis for the word?

3. Is *spoor* pronounced *spùr, spôr,* or *spér?*

4. How many syllables are there in *burgeon?* Is the word derived from the Old English or Old French?

5. Where is the accent in *proscribe?* What does the Latin root *scribere* mean? What other English words have the same root?

6. Is the *g* of *eulogy* pronounced like the *g* in *get* or in *edge?* What two Greek words are the basis for the word?

7. Where is the accent in *credence?* What is the Latin root word? What other English words have the same root?

8. Where is the accent in *inextricable?*

Rita Gutierrez-Christensen

Presently teaching grades 1, 2, and 3 at a Fullerton, California, elementary school, Gutierrez-Christensen has always lived in California.

Born in East Los Angeles, her family moved to Fresno when she was seven, and she graduated from California State University there.

After nineteen years of teaching, she intends to continue in education and in her career as a writer.

4: Poetry

CONTENT REVIEW

1. Which poems in SCENES depict experiences that are easy for you to "see"? Were any hard to "see"? What might have made one poem "easy" and another "hard"?

2. Which poem in REFLECTIONS comes closest to expressing an idea or thought that you have had? What lines in that poem appeal to you most?

3. ISSUES result from conflict. In literature conflict is portrayed generally in one of three ways: person against person, person against nature, and person against self. Reread the poems in this section and identify the type of conflict behind each issue.

4. Compare the issues revealed in "Late Rising," "Harlem," "Hard Questions," and "The Hand That Signed the Paper." **(a)** What do these poems have in common? **(b)** Which poem do you think most convincingly states its issue? **(c)** Which poem do you think discusses an issue most relevant to today's world?

5. **(a)** Explain the kind of LONG-ING in each of the poems in this section. **(b)** Which of the poems in LONGINGS best lend themselves to be used as song lyrics? Explain. **(c)** How many of the poems are about love? Do these particular poems have anything in common besides the subject of love? Explain.

6. **(a)** Which poems in PROFILES give you a new or different way of looking at a person's work, heritage, character, or behavior? If you could choose one of the poets in this section to write a poem about you, your friends, or your family, which poet would you choose? Why? **(b)** Poets use several techniques to reveal the characters they are portraying: (1) the character's own speech, (2) actions, (3) thoughts, (4) description, (5) the poet's attitude toward the character, and (6) other characters' attitudes toward the subject. Select one poem from this section and identify the way or ways in which the poet reveals the subject of the poem.

7. Which poem in each section did you like best? Of those five, did you like one more than the others? Why?

8. Many persons who have never met a poet nonetheless have formed impressions about what people who write poetry are like. What is your impression? What influenced you to form it? Which biographical sketches in this unit come closest to confirming your impressions? Which surprised you most?

Kite

Laura Jensen

Read the poem, then answer the questions.

Dime store. The goldfish swam in the murky
back. I was a child there, where the helmeted
diver bubbled, where, in an enamelled
white basin below, the turtles struggled.
5 They were a moist delight.
And, as I realize,
shaped as a child draws any animal:
round body, legs and head extending.

Kites are separate from toys, for they are
10 Seasonal. Toys are in the inner aisles
that follow age so faithfully a child
might guess what the next step might be.
Of skeins of baby yarn, of bibs and rattles
sings the hardwood floor—of mother. Then
15 of pencils, parties, powder, bobby pins, barrettes.
Suddenly, at the counter, a life has passed—
a history, an age, a generation.

But the kites, like the pleated paper bells,
are Seasonal. Making conversation,
20 the young father tells, "We're not looking
for some expensive kite, now," as his son
and little daughters skip around grandly.

For months it was
Wouldn't your mother like a handkerchief
25 or perhaps a teapot for Christmas?
in the window display,
but now it is kites and flowers.

Not kites in trees or kites like heroines
in wires but the kite that was a speck,
30 the opposite of fishing: to want nothing
caught in anything but the pretty sky,
to reel the color back down again
beside you, a celebrity who tells
what it is like in the altitude.

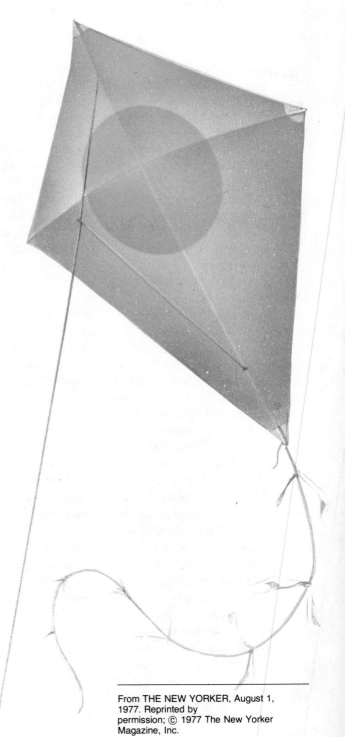

From THE NEW YORKER, August 1,
1977. Reprinted by
permission; © 1977 The New Yorker
Magazine, Inc.

A. Short Answer

On your paper write the word or phrase that best answers the question.

1. List three examples of visual imagery in the first stanza. What is the primary function of this stanza?

2. Reread the second stanza. Why are the kites separate from the toys? What season is the speaker referring to? How is the passage of life symbolized?

3. What might the phrase "like heroines/in wires" (lines 28–29) refer to?

4. How does the speaker indicate the similarity between fishing and kite flying? What does the speaker say is the most important difference?

5. What connotations does the word "celebrity" have that make it an effective word to describe the kite?

6. Of the five divisions in the poetry unit—SCENES, REFLECTIONS, ISSUES, LONGINGS, and PROFILES—in which three might "Kite" effectively be included?

B. Multiple Choice

On the same paper as **A,** write the letter of the word or phrase that best completes the sentence.

7. The poem is written in **(a)** blank verse; **(b)** slant rhyme; **(c)** free verse; **(d)** rhymed couplets.

8. The narrator of "Kite" is probably **(a)** a child; **(b)** an adult; **(c)** a foreign visitor; **(d)** a celebrity.

9. In line 15, "pencils, parties, powder" is an example of **(a)** onomatopoeia; **(b)** metaphor; **(c)** euphony; **(d)** alliteration.

10. Lines 16–17 contain an example of **(a)** figurative language; **(b)** literal language; **(c)** iambic pentameter; **(d)** irony.

11. Line 18 contains an example of **(a)** simile; **(b)** personification; **(c)** comparison; **(d)** hyperbole.

12. "Celebrity" in line 33 is an example of **(a)** hyperbole; **(b)** personification; **(c)** irony; **(d)** stereotype.

Unit 4, Test II
COMPOSITION

From the assignments below choose one to write about.

1. Assume you are asked to write a poem about someone you know well. Keep in mind the various techniques employed by the poets included in the PRO-FILES section of the unit. What would be the title? Would you use euphonious sounds, cacophonous sounds, or both? What colors or objects are particularly representative of the person you wish to portray? What activities does that person pursue? Does he or she have any favorite expressions or sayings? What kind of rhythms would you use? Using these questions as a guide, explain in a composition why your particular choices would help convey an image of your subject to others.

2. You are revising a poetry book. A decision must be made about the poem "October Journey": whether to retain it in the LONGINGS section or to put it in the new SCENES section. Write an explanation of whichever you decide to do with specific references to the poem.

3. Suppose all the poems in the ISSUES section were submitted to a poetry contest for which you are the judge. In a composition, explain your reasons for awarding first, second, third, and honorable-mention prizes. Include in your composition reference to such things as originality of thought, effective use of language, appropriate imagery, and use of sound devices.

GREEK DRAMA
Medea
EURIPIDES

TRANSLATED BY
FREDERIC PROKOSCH

Introduction to Greek Drama

Imagine yourself in the year 431 B.C., in the city of Athens. It is March; the air is pure and cool, a bright spring morning. The great annual festival honoring Dionysus, the ancient Greek god of wine, fertility, and joyous life began three days ago. The image of the god Dionysus sits on its altar in the orchestra waiting "to witness" the next three days of dramatic contests.

A playwright named Euripides[1] is presenting his newest cycle of plays today, among which is *Medea.*[2] He competes with other playwrights, such as Sophocles, for the prestigious ivy wreath that is awarded to the best playwright deemed so by a citizen panel of five judges.

THEATER

The great open-air amphitheater of Athens holds thousands of people in the audience. Because of the religious and civic nature of the festival of Dionysus, everyone is invited and encouraged to attend. On this bright morning businesses and law courts are closed. The admission charge is refunded for those who cannot afford it, and others are compensated for wages lost.

Sitting in the approximately fifty-five rows of seats built into the slope of a hillside are most of the citizens of Athens: a number of school-age boys, most of the voting population, some of the better-educated slaves, and even women (usually barred from most public events).

The spectators look down from their seats in the natural amphitheater to a round space at the bottom called the *orchestra,* behind which is a raised platform and house where the play will be performed.

THE ACTORS

Because the open-air theater is so vast, it is hard to communicate mood and feeling to the distant spectators. In order to improve the spectators' view, the actors must make themselves appear larger than life. To accomplish this, the actors, all men, wear thick-soled boots and great robes with huge sleeves. To communicate expression, they wear stylized masks, some with a calm expression on one side and an angry one on the other, some with a female face and others with a male face.

Although the amphitheater has excellent acoustics, the actors are carefully trained in declamation, for they must be heard by an immense and sometimes noisy audience. To help project their voices, the mouths of the actors' masks are funnel-shaped and act as small megaphones.

THE DIRECTOR

As we await the performance of the play, Euripides, who also directs, trains the chorus, and acts in the dramas, is somewhere behind the stage, engaged in last-minute preparations. He is probably in the *skene,* a small building behind the orchestra used for costume changes and entrances and exits by the characters. It is in front of this small building that the scenes take place in many Greek tragedies, as they do in *Medea.* In fact, in *Medea,* the *skene* serves as Medea's house.

PRIMITIVE ANCESTOR OF GREEK DRAMA

The Dionysian festivals were not always centered around these dramatic contests. In fact, Greek drama as Euripides knew it in 431 B.C. had existed for about seventy years, and had developed

---

1. *Euripides* (yü rip′ ə dēz′) c480?-406? B.C. Greek dramatist.
2. *Medea* (mə dē′ ə).

from choral songs performed by a fifty-member chorus.

This primitive ancestor of Greek drama eventually evolved into the dramatic form Euripides knew. We know of an actor-producer of these choral songs who contributed to the change of choral songs into drama—Thespis. About 534 B.C., Thespis separated himself from the chorus, creating a character. This separation of chorus and character made dialogue possible between the character and the chorus. Thus Greek drama was born.

TRAGEDY

The tragedies were based on the numerous stories and characters of Greek mythology the Greek audiences knew so well. Because of the religious and civic nature of the festival of Dionysus, they were required to be morally instructive as well as entertaining.

The tragedies were not just sad stories of unhappy persons; rather, they were complex studies of the nature of human beings in conflict with themselves, with society, and with the gods.

Tragedies often depicted highborn persons who, because of some tragic flaw or shortcoming in their personalities, made a mistake which brought misery, loss of moral dignity, great sorrow, and suffering. *Medea* is such a play.

When you read the play, imagine it being performed in the great theater of Dionysus for the first time in 431 B.C. The seats are full, the crowd anxious for the start of the play. The flutist who accompanies the songs of the chorus is testing his instrument. . . .

Characters

NURSE
TUTOR
MEDEA
CHORUS *of* CORINTHIAN WOMEN
CHORUS LEADER
CREON
JASON
AEGEUS
The TWO SONS *of* MEDEA *and* JASON
MESSENGER, SERVANTS, ATTENDANTS

As the play opens, the nurse of Medea's children enters and laments the chain of events that has led to the present situation. These background events may be briefly summarized: Pelias, the wicked king of Iolcos, has usurped the throne from his brother and in an attempt to prevent his nephew Jason from

assuming his rightful place as king of Iolcos, commands Jason to go to Colchis, the kingdom of King Aeëtes, to obtain the Golden Fleece, which is greatly valued and closely guarded. Jason constructed his ship, the *Argo*, and sailed to Colchis. King Aeëtes's daughter Medea, a sorceress, falls in love with Jason and helps him get the Golden Fleece by murdering her brother and duping her father. They flee to Iolcos, where Jason claims the throne from Pelias. Pelias resists and Medea, through deception, causes Pelias's own daughters to murder him. Because of this terrible deed, Medea and Jason flee to Corinth, where they live for some years. As the play opens, Jason has abandoned Medea to marry King Creon's daughter. Medea is outraged and seeks revenge.

Medea, translated and copyrighted by Frederic Prokosch (1947) in EURIPIDES, A Great Books Foundation Edition. Published by Henry Regnery Company.

Act One

Scene: Corinth, before the house of Medea.

(The NURSE *enters from the house.)*

NURSE. Jason has betrayed his children and my mistress; he has taken a royal bride to his bed, the daughter of Creon,[3] who is the ruler of this land. And poor Medea, scorned and deserted, can do nothing but appeal to the vows they made to one another, and remind him of the eternal pledge they made with their right hands clasped. And she calls upon the gods to witness how Jason is repaying her for her love. She lies half famished; her body is bowed utterly with grief, wasting away the whole day long. So it has been since she learned that he has betrayed her. Never stirring an eye, never lifting her gaze from the ground; and when her friends speak to her in warning she no more listens than a rock listens, or the surging sea wave. Only now and then she turns her snowy neck and quietly laments, and utters her father's name, and the name of her land and home, which she deserted when she followed the man who now brings her such dishonor.

Pitiful woman! She has learned at last through all her sufferings how lucky are those who have never lost their native land. She has come to feel a hatred for her children, and no longer wants to see them. Indeed, I fear she may be moving toward some dreadful plan, for her heart is violent. She will never submit to this cruel treatment. I know her well: her anger is great, and I know that any man who makes an enemy of her will have it hard. . . . Look, here come the children; they have been playing. Little they know of their mother's misery, little the hearts of the young can guess of sorrow!

(The TUTOR *brings in* MEDEA*'s children.)*

TUTOR. Why are you standing here, in front of the gates? You've been maid for so many years to my mistress; why have you left her alone, then, only to stand outside the gates and lament?

NURSE. Listen, old man, who watches over Jason's sons! It's a sad, sad thing for faithful servants like us to see our master's fortunes meet with disaster; it stirs us to the heart. I am so lost in grief, now, that a longing came over me to step outside the gates, and tell the whole wide world and the heavens of my mistress's sorrows!

TUTOR. Poor lady! Hasn't she ceased her weeping yet?

NURSE. Ceased? Far from it! This is only the beginning; there is far more to come.

TUTOR. Poor, foolish lady. though I shouldn't call her that; but how little she knows of this latest trouble!

NURSE. What do you mean, old man? Come! Don't be afraid to tell me!

3. *Creon* (krē'on), hereditary name of kings of Corinth.

TUTOR. Nothing at all; I should never have mentioned it.

NURSE. No, no, by your wise old beard I beg you, don't hide anything from your fellow servant! Tell me, and, if you wish, I'll keep it secret.

TUTOR. Well, as I was passing the usual place where the old men sit playing draughts,[4] I happened to overhear one of them saying that Creon, king of the land, intends to send these children, and their mother from Corinth, far away into exile. But whether it was the truth he was speaking, I do not know; I hope and pray it wasn't the truth.

NURSE. And will Jason allow this thing to happen to his sons, even though he is on bad terms with their mother?

TUTOR. Old ties give way to new ones; and his love for this family of ours is dying away.

NURSE. Oh, it looks dark indeed for us; new sorrows are being added to old ones, even before the old ones have faded!

TUTOR. Be still, be still; don't whisper a word of it. This isn't the proper time to tell our mistress.

NURSE. O little children, do you hear how your father feels toward you? May evil befall him! But no, he is still my master. Yet how cruelly he has betrayed his dear ones!

TUTOR. And which of us has not done the same? Haven't you learned long ago, my dear, how each man loves himself far more than his neighbor? Some, perhaps, from honest motives; some for private gain. So you see how Jason deserts his children for the pleasure of his new bride.

NURSE. Go back into the house, children; all will be well. Try to keep them out of the way, old man; keep them far from their mother as long as she feels this desperate anger. I have already seen the fire in her eyes as she watched them, almost as though she were wishing them harm. I am sure her anger won't end till she has found a victim. Let's hope the victim will be an enemy, and not a friend!

MEDEA *(from within the house).*

Lost, oh lost! I am lost
In my sufferings. I wish, oh I wish
That I could die. . . .

NURSE.

My dear children, what did I tell you?
Your mother's mind is filled with the wildest
Fancies; her heart is wild with anger!
Run quickly back into the house.
Keep out of her sight. Do not
Go near her. Beware of the wildness
And bitterness of her heart!
Go, quickly, quickly!

4. *draughts* (drafts), the game of checkers.

Oh what will she do, in the pride
And torment of her soul? What
Evil thing will she do?
(The TUTOR *takes the children into the house.)*

MEDEA *(within the house).*

Oh, I have suffered
And suffered enough for all these tears!
I call destruction upon you, all, all of you,
Sons of a doomed mother, and the father too!
May ruin fall on the entire house!

NURSE.

I am full of pity,
Full of deep pity for you! Yet why
Do the children share their father's crime?
Why should you hate them? O my poor children,
I fear some outrage will befall you!
Yes, strange and terrible is the temper of princes.
There is none they need to obey;
There is none that can check them:
There is nothing to control
The madness of their mood.
How much better off are the rest of us
Who've been taught to live equally
With our neighbors! All I wish
Is to grow old quietly, not in pride,
But only in humble security.
It's the moderate thing that always sounds
Best to our ears; and indeed it is
The moderate thing that is best in practice.
For power grows beyond control;
Power brings comfort to no man.
And I say, the greater the power, the greater
The ruin when it finally falls.
(Enter the CHORUS *of* CORINTHIAN WOMEN.*)*

CHORUS OF CORINTHIAN WOMEN.

I heard the voice,
I heard the loud lament
Of the pitiful lady from Colchis:[5]
Oh tell me, mother, is she still
Unquiet? As I stood
By the house with the double gates
I heard the sound of weeping from within.
I grieve for the sorrow of this family
Which I have come to love.

NURSE.

There is no family left; it has gone,

5. *Colchis* (kol′kis), Medea's home-land, a region on the northern shores of the present Black Sea.

It has gone forever. The master now
Has a royal bride in the bed beside him,
And our mistress is withering away
In her chamber, and finds no solace
Or warmth in words
That friends can utter.

MEDEA (*within the house*).

Oh how I wish that a stroke of lightning
Would fall from heaven and shatter my head!
Why should I live any longer?
Death would bring release; in death
I could leave behind me the horror of living.

CHORUS OF CORINTHIAN WOMEN.

Did you hear, almighty Zeus?[6]
O earth, O heaven, did you hear
The cry of woe this woman has uttered?
Oh why, poor lady, should you long
For that unutterable haven of rest?
Death only can bring it; and death comes only too soon!
No, no, there is no need to pray for death.

MEDEA (*within the house*).

Great Themis, O lady Artemis,[7] look down
On all I am suffering; and suffering in spite
Of all the vows my husband made me.
I pray that I may some day see
Him and his bride brought down to ruin
And their palace ruined for all the wrong
They dared to do me without cause.
O my own father, my own country,
Shameful it was of me to leave you,
And to have killed my brother before I left you!

NURSE. Do you hear what she says?

CHORUS OF CORINTHIAN WOMEN.

Go, go, and bring her from the house
That we may see her; speak kindly to her!
Hurry, before she does some violent thing.
I feel her passion rising to a new pitch.

NURSE.

Yes; I shall go; but I deeply doubt
Whether I can persuade my mistress.

(*The* NURSE *goes into the house*.)

CHORUS OF CORINTHIAN WOMEN.

I heard a cry that was heavy and sick with sorrow.
Loud in her bitterness she cries
On the man who betrayed her marriage bed!
Full of her wrongs she cries

6. Zeus (züs), ruler of the Greek gods. He was also the father of many of them.

7. Themis (thē′mis) . . . **Artemis** (är′ tə mis), Greek goddesses. Themis was associated with justice; Artemis with hunting and wild creatures.

To the gods, to Themis, to the bride of Zeus,
To the Keeper of Vows,[8] who brought her away
To the shores of Greece which face the shores of Asia,
Through the straits at night to the gateway opening
On the unlimited salty sea.[9]
(Toward the end of this song, MEDEA *enters from the house.)*

MEDEA. Ladies of Corinth, I have come forth from my house, lest you should feel bitterness toward me; for I know that men often acquire a bad name for their pride—not only the pride they show in public, but also the pride of retirement; those who live in solitude, as I do, are frequently thought to be proud. For there is no justice in the view one man takes of another, often hating him before he has suffered wrong, hating him even before he has seen his true character. Therefore a foreigner above all should fit into the ways of a city. Not even a native citizen, I think, should risk offending his neighbors by rudeness or pride.

But this new thing has fallen upon me so unexpectedly, my strength is broken. O my friends, my life is shattered; my heart no longer longs for the blessings of life, but only for death! There was one man through whom I came to see the world's whole beauty: and that was my husband; and he has turned out utterly evil.

O women, of all creatures that live and reflect, certainly it is we who are the most luckless. First of all, we pay a great price to purchase a husband; and thus submit our bodies to a perpetual tyrant. And everything depends on whether our choice is good or bad—for divorce is not an honorable thing, and we may not refuse to be married. And then a wife is plunged into a way of life and behavior entirely new to her, and must learn what she never learned at home—she must learn by a kind of subtle intuition how to manage the man. And if we have the luck to handle all these things with tact and success, and if the husband is willing to live at our side without resentment, then life can become happy indeed. But if not, I'd rather be dead. A man who is disgusted with what he finds at home, goes forth to put an end to his boredom, and turns to a friend or companion of his own age; while we at home continue to think of him, and of him only.

Still, my friends, I realize that all this applies not to you but to me; you after all have a city of your own, and a family home, and a certain pleasure in life, and the company of your friends. But I am utterly lonely, an exile, cast off by my own husband—nothing but a captive brought here from a foreign land—without a mother or brother, without a single kinsman who can give me refuge in this sea of disaster. Therefore, my ladies, I ask only one thing of you: promise me silence. If I can find some way, some cunning scheme of revenge against my husband for all that he has done to

8. *Keeper of Vows,* refers to Themis, who was considered the patron of oaths and promises.

9. *Through the straits . . . salty sea,* from Colchis, through the straits of the Dardanelles to the Mediterranean.

me, and against the man who gave away his daughter, and against the daughter who is now my husband's wife: then please be silent. For though a woman is timid in everything else, and weak, and terrified at the sight of a sword: still, when things go wrong in this thing of love, no heart is so fearless as a woman's; no heart is so filled with the thought of blood.

CHORUS LEADER. Yes, I promise this. You will be right, Medea, in avenging yourself on your husband. It does not surprise me to see you lost in despair . . . But look! I see Creon, our king, approaching: he will have some news to tell us.

(Enter CREON, *with his following.)*

CREON. Listen to me, Medea! You, with your angry looks and all that bitterness against your husband: I order you to leave my kingdom! I order you to go with both your children into exile, and immediately. This is my decree. And I will not return to my house until I have hurled you beyond the borders of my kingdom.

MEDEA. Oh, now I am lost indeed! This is the end of all things for me! Now my enemies are bearing down on me in all their force; and I have no refuge left in this hour of ruin. And yet, let me ask you this one thing, Creon: why is it, Creon, you are sending me away?

CREON. I am afraid of you. I need no longer pretend otherwise. I am afraid you will do my daughter some mortal harm. And I have many reasons for being afraid of this. You are a cunning woman, Medea, expert in all kinds of magic, so I hear. And you are enraged by the loss of your husband's love. I have also heard them say that you are planning some kind of mischief against Jason and the bride, and the bride's father, myself, as well. It is against these things I take precautions. I tell you, Medea, I'd rather incur your hatred now than be soft-hearted and later learn to regret it.

MEDEA. This is not the first time, Creon! Many times before has this strange reputation done me harm. A sensible man should never nowadays bring up his children to be too clever or exceptional. For one thing, these talents never bring them profit; for another, they end by bringing envy and hatred from others. If you present new ideas to a group of fools, they'll think you ignorant as well as idle. And if your fame should come to exceed the established reputations, they'll hate you for it. This has been my own experience.

Some think me clever, and resent it; some think me not so very clever after all, and disapprove. And you, Creon, are somehow afraid that I may do something to harm you. But you need not worry. It isn't for someone like me to quarrel with kings. After all, why should I? You haven't harmed me. You've allowed your daughter to marry as you saw fit. I hate my husband, certainly;

but as for you, I feel you have acted reasonably enough. I don't grudge you for your good fortune. I wish you luck with your daughter's marriage, Creon, but beg you only, let me live on in this land. I have been wronged, but I shall remain quiet, and submit to those above me.

CREON. Your words are gentle enough, Medea. Yet in my heart I can't help dreading that you are planning some evil; and I trust you now even less than before. It is easier to deal with a quick-tempered man or woman than with one who is subtle and soft-spoken. No. You must go at once. Make no more speeches. It is settled. You are my enemy, and there is nothing you can do to prolong your stay in my country.

MEDEA. I implore you! By your knees, by your newly wed daughter!

CREON. You are wasting your words. You will never persuade me.

MEDEA. Then you'll drive me out without listening to my prayers?

CREON. I shall; for I love my own family more than you.

MEDEA. O my country! How my heart goes back to you now!

CREON. I, too, love my country above all things, except my children.

MEDEA. How cruelly passionate love can deal with men!

CREON. And yet, it all depends on the luck men have.

MEDEA. O Zeus, never forget the man who caused this!

CREON. Go now; go. Spare me this useless trouble.

MEDEA. No trouble, no pain, nothing has been spared me!

CREON. Soon one of my men shall lead you away by force.

MEDEA. Not that, Creon, not that! I beg you, Creon.

CREON. It seems you insist on creating a disturbance.

MEDEA. I will go, I will go. That is not what I intended.

CREON. Why all this commotion, then? What is it you want?

MEDEA. Let me stay here just a single day longer, Creon. Let me stay and think over where I shall go in exile, and how I shall find a living for my children, for whom their father has completely failed to provide. Take pity on them, Creon! You too have children of your own; you too must have a soft place in your heart for them. What happens to me now no longer matters; I only grieve for the suffering that will come to my children.

CREON. I am not a cruel man, Medea. I have often made blunders, out of sheer compassion. Even now I feel I am making a mistake. All the same, have it your way. But let me warn you! If tomorrow at sunrise still finds you and your children within the frontiers of my land, you shall die for it. That is my verdict; it is final. So stay this one day longer, if you must. One day is not enough to bring disaster.

(*Exit* CREON *with his following.*)

CHORUS LEADER.

Pitiful woman! Oh we pity
The sorrows you suffer!
Where will you turn now? Who can help you?
What home remains, what land
Is left to save you from destruction?
O Medea, you have been hurled by heaven
Into an ocean of despair.

MEDEA. Everything has gone wrong. None can deny it. But not quite everything is lost; don't give up hope, my friends! There still are troubles in store for the young bride, and for the bridegroom too. Do you think I would have fawned on that old man without some plan and purpose? Certainly not. I would never have touched him with my hands. But now, although he could have crushed all my plans by instant exile, he has made a fatal error; he has given me one day's reprieve. One day in which I can bring death to the three creatures that I loathe: the father, the bride, my husband.

There are many manners of death which I might use; I don't quite know yet which to try. Shall I set fire to the bridal mansion? Or shall I sharpen a sword and steal into the chamber to the wedding bed and plunge it into their hearts? One thing stands in my way. If I am caught making my way into the bridal room on such an errand, I shall surely be put to death, and my foes will end by triumphing over me. Better to take the shortest way, the way I am best trained in: better to bring them down with poison. That I will do, then. And after that? Suppose them dead. What city will take me in then? What friend will offer me shelter in his land, and safety, and a home? None.

Then best to wait a little longer; perhaps some sure defense will appear, and I can set about this murder in stealth and stillness. And if no help should come from fate, and even if death is certain, still I can take at last the sword in my own hand and go forth boldly to the crime, and kill. Yes, by that dark queen whom I revere above all others, and whom I now invoke to help me, by Hecate[10] who dwells in my most secret chamber: I swear no man shall injure me and not regret it. I will turn their marriage into sorrow and anguish! Go now, go forward to this dangerous deed! The time has come for courage. Remember the suffering they caused you! Never shall you be mocked because of this wedding of Jason's, you who are sprung from a noble father and whose grandfather was the Sun-God[11] himself! You have the skill; what is more, you are a woman: and it's always a woman who is incapable of a noble deed, yet expert in every kind of mischief!

CHORUS OF CORINTHIAN WOMEN.

The sacred rivers are flowing back to their sources!
The order of the world is being reversed!
Now it is men who have grown deceitful,

10. *Hecate* (hek'ə tē), a goddess associated with sorcery and witchcraft.

11. *Sun-God,* Helios (hē' lē os), god of light. He is represented as a strong youth with a crown of rays, driving a four-horse chariot. Each morning he rises from the ocean on the east and drives across the heavens in his glowing chariot, descending at evening into the western sea.

Men who have broken their sacred vows.
The name of woman shall rise to favor
Again; and women once again
Shall rise and regain their honor: never
Again shall ill be said of women!

(As the CHORUS *approaches the end of the song,* JASON *enters.)*

JASON. This is not the first time I have noticed how difficult it is to deal with a violent temper. Ah, Medea, if you had patiently accepted the will of our ruler, you might have stayed on quietly in this land and this house. But now your pointless complaints are driving you into exile. Not that I minded them myself; I didn't mind it at all when you called Jason an evil man. But, considering your references to the King himself, you may count yourself lucky that your punishment is exile. Personally, I have always done my best to calm the King's anger, and would have liked to see you stay on here. But you refused to give up this sort of folly, and kept on slandering him; with the result that you are facing banishment.

Nevertheless, in spite of your behavior, I feel inclined to do you a favor; I have come to make some sort of provision for you and the children, my dear, so that you won't be penniless when you are in exile; for I know that exile will not be easy. And even though you hate me, Medea, my thoughts of you will continue to be friendly as always.

MEDEA. You filthy coward! That is the only name I can find for you, you and your utter lack of manliness! And now you, who are the worst of my enemies, now you too have chosen to come to me! No, it isn't courage which brings you, nor recklessness in facing the friends you have injured; it is worse than that, it is the worst of all human vices: shamelessness. Still, you did well to come to me, for now I can ease my heart by reviling you: and perhaps you too will suffer as you listen.

Let me begin, then, at the very beginning. I saved your life; every Greek who sailed with you on the *Argo* knows I saved you, when you were sent to tame the fire-breathing bulls and to yoke them, and to sow the deadly fields.[12] Yes, and I killed the many-folded serpent who lay guarding the Golden Fleece, forever wakeful, coil upon coil. And I raised a beacon of light to bring you to safety. Freely I deserted my own father and my own home; and followed you to Iolcos, to the hills of Pelion: and all this time my love was stronger than my reason. And I brought death to Pelias by his own daughters' hands;[13] I utterly destroyed the household.

All of these things I did for you, traitor! And you forsook me, and took another wife, even though I had borne your children. Had you been childless, one might have pardoned your wish for a

12. tame . . . the deadly fields, tasks Jason performed in order to get the Golden Fleece.

13. daughter's hands. Medea tricked Pelias's daughters into killing their father.

second wedding. But now all my faith in your vows has vanished. I do not know whether you imagine that the gods by whom you swore have disappeared, or that new rules are now in vogue in such matters; for you must be aware that you have broken your vows to me. Oh this poor right hand, which you so often pressed! These knees, which you so often used to embrace! And all in vain, for it was an evil man that touched me! How wildly all my hopes have fallen through! . . .

And now I am to be cast forth into exile, in utter misery, alone with my children and without a single friend! Oh, this will be a shameful shadow upon you, as you lie in your wedding bed! That your own children, and their mother, who saved your life, should go wandering around the world like beggars! . . . O Zeus, why have you given us a way to tell true gold from the counterfeit, but no way, no emblem branded on a man's body whereby we can tell the true man from the false?

CHORUS LEADER. Dreadful is the anger, and past all healing, when lovers in fury turn against each other!

JASON. The time has come, it seems, when I must speak, and speak well, and like a good helmsman reef up my sail and weather the tempest of your tongue . . . And since you dwell so heavily on all the favors you did me, Medea, I am certain that I owe the safety of my voyage to Aphrodite[14] alone among gods and men. Not that I doubt your skill; but all the same, I prefer not to dwell on this notion that love, with all its irresistible power, compelled you to save my life. I don't think we need go into details. I admit that you meant well, and did your best. But when it comes to this matter of my safety, let me point out that you got rather more than you gave.

First of all, instead of living in a barbaric land, you've come to Greece and enjoyed contact with a country where justice and law prevail, and not brute force; and what is more, the Greeks thought you rather clever. You even acquired a certain fame here. Whereas, if you had stayed on in that outer fringe of the world, your name would now be quite unknown. Frankly, I'd rather have real fame and distinction than mighty stores of gold in my halls or the talent to sing more sweetly than Orpheus.[15] That is my answer to your version of all my labors; remember, it was you who brought up this matter.

As for your bitter attack on my marriage with the princess, I think I can prove first of all that it was a shrewd move; secondly, a thoroughly sober one; and finally, that I did it in your interest and that of your children . . . Wait! Please remain calm . . . Since I had come from Iolcos involved in every kind of trouble, and an exile, what could be luckier for me than marriage with the King's own daughter? Believe me, I have learned how a man's friends

14. *Aphrodite* (af′rə di′tē), the goddess of love and beauty. Aphrodite furnished the love charm to ensure that Medea's passion for Jason would endure so that she would help him secure the Golden Fleece.

15. *Orpheus* (ôr′fē əs), god of music and poetry who played so beautifully that the trees and stones danced to his music and wild beasts were tamed by it.

desert him the moment he is penniless . . . And then I wanted to bring up my sons in a manner worthy of my position; I even hoped that by having more sons, who would live as brothers to yours, we might draw the entire family into harmony, and all be happy. You yourself need no more children, but I would do well to help the sons I have through the sons I hope to have. Do you disagree with all this? You would agree if it weren't for this matter of love which rankles in you. But you women have developed such curious notions; if something happens which upsets your way of love, then all that you once found lovely and desirable you now find hateful. Believe me, it would have been better far if men could have thought up some other way of producing children, and done away with women; then no evil would ever have come to men.

CHORUS LEADER. O Jason, you have given this speech of yours a convincing enough air; and yet I somehow feel, though perhaps I shouldn't say so, that you have acted wickedly in betraying your wife.

MEDEA. I suppose I am different in many ways from most people, for I feel that the worst punishment should fall on the man who speaks brilliantly for an evil cause, the man who knows he can make an evil thing sound plausible and who dares to do so. And still, such a man isn't really so very wise after all. Listen, Jason. You need not bring forth these clever phrases and specious arguments; for a single word from me will destroy you. Consider: had you not been a coward, Jason, you would have spoken frankly to me first, and not concealed your wedding plans from the one who loved you.

JASON. And you, no doubt, would have done all you could to help me, if I had spoken of this matter: you, who even now cannot control the rage in your heart.

MEDEA. It wasn't this that restrained you. No. It was that you thought it might not be altogether proper, as you grew older, to have a foreign wife.

JASON. You may be quite sure of one thing, Medea. It was not because of any woman that I made this royal marriage. It was as I said before: because I wanted security for you, and also to be the father of royal children bound by blood to our two children: a thing which would have brought welfare to all of us.

MEDEA. I don't want the kind of welfare that is brought by suffering. I don't want the kind of safety which ends in sorrow.

JASON. Reflect on that opinion, Medea, it will make you wiser. Don't search for sorrow in prosperity. Don't keep looking for pain in a piece of good luck.

MEDEA. Go on, mock me. You at least have a home to turn to. But I am going into exile, and alone.

JASON. It was you who made this choice; there is no one else to blame.

MEDEA. How so? By marrying and deserting you?

JASON. You called down an evil curse on the royal house.

MEDEA. I have brought a curse to your own house too, I think.

JASON. Well, I don't propose to go into this any further. But if you'd like to take along some of my money into exile, for your own need and that of the children, please say so. I am prepared to be generous on this point, and even to give you letters to friends of mine abroad who will treat you well. It would be madness for you to refuse this offer. It will be to your own gain, Medea, if you give up your anger.

MEDEA. I will never accept favors from friends of yours; and I'll accept nothing from you, so please don't offer it. Gifts from a coward bring luck to no one.

JASON. Very well then. I call upon the gods to witness that I have tried in every way to help you and the children. It is you who refuse my offers. It is you who are stubbornly rejecting your friends. And for this, Medea, you will surely suffer.

MEDEA. Please go! I can see you are longing to be with your new sweetheart. Go, and God help you; you may end by regretting this kind of wedding!

(JASON *goes out.*)

CHORUS OF CORINTHIAN WOMEN.

When love has passed its limits
It brings no longer good:
It brings no peace or comfort to any soul.
Yet while she still moves mildly there is no fire
So sweet as that which is lit by the goddess of love.
Oh never, upon me, Cypris,[16]
Send forth from your golden bow
The unerring arrow poisoned with desire!

(MEDEA *has been sitting in despair on the stairway during this song.* AEGEUS *enters.*)

AEGEUS. Joy to you, Medea! This is the best kind of greeting between old friends!

MEDEA. And joy to you, Aegeus, son of Pandion, King of Athens! How does it happen that you have set foot in this country?

AEGEUS. I have come from the ancient oracles of Phoebus.[17]

MEDEA. And why did you visit that great center of prophecy?

AEGEUS. I went to ask how I might bring fertility to my seed.

MEDEA. Tell me, has your life been childless hitherto?

AEGEUS. Some divine visitation, I think, has made me childless.

MEDEA. Have you a wife, or not?

AEGEUS. I have, Medea.

MEDEA. And what did Phoebus tell you about begetting children?

16. *Cypris* (si′prəs), another name for Aphrodite, goddess of love.

17. *ancient oracles of Phoebus* (fē′-bəs). Aegeus (ē′ jē əs) has been to the temple of Phoebus Apollo at Delphi to hear the prophesies of the god through his priests and priestesses.

AEGEUS. Words far too subtle for any man to understand.

MEDEA. Good luck to you then. And success to your wishes!

AEGEUS. But why do you look so pale and woebegone?

MEDEA. O Aegeus, my husband has turned out to be the vilest of men!

AEGEUS. What do you mean? Tell me what has made you so unhappy.

MEDEA. Jason is wronging me, and utterly without provocation.

AEGEUS. What has he done? Tell me more clearly, Medea.

MEDEA. He has taken another wife to take my place.

AEGEUS. Does he really dare to do such a cruel thing!

MEDEA. He does indeed! He loved me once, but no longer.

AEGEUS. Has he fallen in love?

MEDEA. He's in love with the idea of marrying royalty.

AEGEUS. And who is the father of this princess? Please go on.

MEDEA. Her father is Creon, King of Corinth.

AEGEUS. Indeed, Medea, I understand your grief.

MEDEA. I am lost. And there is more: I am being banished!

AEGEUS. Banished? By whom? This is something new you tell me.

MEDEA. Creon is driving me from Corinth into banishment.

AEGEUS. Does Jason consent? This is a contemptible thing.

MEDEA. Not in so many words, but he has not really opposed it. O Aegeus, I beg you, I implore you, by your beard and by your knees, I beseech you, have pity on me! Have pity on a friend who is in trouble! Don't let me wander about in exile! Let me come to your land of Athens, let me find refuge in your halls! And there, with heaven's consent, you may find your love grow fertile and be blessed with children, and your life at last end happily. You don't know, Aegeus, how good your luck has been, for I shall end your sterility; I shall bring power to your seed; for I know of drugs that can do this.

AEGEUS. There are many reasons, my dear lady, why I should like to do this for you: first, for the sake of the children you promise me (for in that matter, frankly, I'm at my wits' end). But let me state my position. If you arrive in Athens, I shall stand by you as I am bound to do. But I must warn you first, my friend: I won't agree to take you with me. If you arrive at my halls of your own accord, you shall live there in safety; I shan't surrender you to anyone. But you yourself must manage your escape from this land, for I have no wish to incur ill will among my friends here.

MEDEA. Very well. So be it. Make me a formal pledge on this, and I shall be satisfied.

AEGEUS. Do you distrust me? What is it that troubles you?

MEDEA. I trust you, yes. But the house of Pelias, and Creon as well, both detest me. If you are bound to me by an oath, then, when they come to drag me away from your country, I know you will remain true to your vow and stand by me. Whereas, if it's only a promise, you might not be in a position to resist their demands; for I am weak, and they have both money and a royal house to help them.

AEGEUS. You show considerable foresight in these matters, I must say. Still, if you insist, I shan't refuse you. From my own point of view, too, it might be just as well to have an excuse like this oath to present to your enemies . . . Now name your gods.

MEDEA. Swear by the plain of Earth, and by my father's father Helios, the Sun God, and in one sweeping phrase by the whole host of the gods. . . .

AEGEUS. Swear to do what, or not to do what? Tell me.

MEDEA. Swear that you will never cast me from your land, nor ever, as long as you live, allow an enemy of mine to carry me away.

AEGEUS. I swear by the Earth, and by the holy light of Helios, the Sun God, and by the entire host of the gods, that I will abide by the terms you have just made.

MEDEA. Very well. And if you should fail, what curse are you willing to incur?

AEGEUS. Whatever happens to such as disregard the gods.

MEDEA. Go in peace, Aegeus. All is well, now; I shall arrive in your city as soon as I possibly can—after I have done what I must do, and accomplished what I desire.

(AEGEUS *goes out.*)

CHORUS LEADER.

May Hermes,[18] the God of Travelers,
Go with you on your way, Aegeus,
And bring you safely home!
And may you find the thing you have been seeking
For so long; you seem to be a generous man.

MEDEA. O Zeus, and Justice who is the child of Zeus, and light of the Sun God! Now, my friends, has come the hour of my triumph! Now I have started on the road; now I know that I shall bring revenge on the ones I hate. For at the very moment that my doom looked darkest of all, this man Aegeus appeared, like a harbor for all my hopes; and to him I can fasten the cable of my ship when I come to the town and fortress of Pallas Athene.[19]

And now let me tell you all of my plans. Listen; they will not be idle words, or pleasant. I shall send a servant to Jason and ask for an interview. And when he comes, I shall be soft and conciliatory; I shall tell him that I've thought better of it; that I agree; that even the treacherous marriage with the princess, which he is celebrating, strikes me as sensible, and all for the best. However, I shall beg him to let the children stay on here: not that I'd dream of leaving my babies to be insulted in a land that loathes me, but purely as a stratagem; and I shall kill the king's own daughter. For

18. *Hermes* (hėr′mēz), the messenger of the gods, as well as god of travelers and merchants.

19. *Pallas Athene* (pal′əs ə thē′-nē), patron goddess of Athens. Here, Medea means Athens.

I shall send them with gifts in their little hands, to be offered to the bride to preserve them from banishment: a finely woven dress and a golden diadem.[20] And if she takes these things and wears them on her body, she, and whoever touches her, will die in anguish; for I shall rub these things with deadly poison.

That will be that; but it is the next thing I must do which sets me weeping. For I will kill my own children! My own dear children, whom none shall take from me. And when I have brought ruin on the house of Jason, I shall flee from the land and flee from the murder of my children, for it will be a terrible deed to do! It isn't easy, my friends, to bear the insults of one's enemies. And so it shall be. For what have I left in life? I have no land, no home, no harbor to protect me.

What a fool I was to leave my father's house, to put my faith in the words of a Greek! And for this he will pay the penalty, so help me God. Never again will he see his sons alive; never will he have a son by this new bride. For she is doomed to die, and die hideously from the power of my poison. Let no man think I am a feeble, frail-hearted woman who sits with folded hands: no, let them know me for the opposite of that—one who knows how to hurt her enemies and help her friends. It is lives like this that are longest remembered!

CHORUS LEADER. Since you have told us all your plans, let me say this to you: do not do this thing!

MEDEA. There is nothing else I can do. It is forgivable that you should say this: but remember, you have not suffered as I have.

CHORUS LEADER. Woman, can you really bring yourself to destroy your own flesh and blood?

MEDEA. I can; for in that way I can hurt my husband most cruelly.

CHORUS LEADER. And yourself as well! You will be the most miserable of women.

MEDEA. Then I will; no matter. No word of warning now can stop me!

(The NURSE *enters;* MEDEA *turns to her.)*

MEDEA. Go and tell Jason to come to me. And remember, I send you on a mission of great secrecy. Say nothing of the plans I have prepared; don't say a word, if you are loyal to your mistress and loyal to the race of woman!

20. *diadem* (dī'ə dem), a crown or headband usually worn by royalty.

Discussion

1. Medea's nurse serves as her chief servant, governess of the children, and confidante; therefore, she knows Medea well. **(a)** How does she describe Medea's reaction to Jason's abandonment? **(b)** What does she say about Medea's personality and temperament? Which of her statements foreshadow impending events?

2. (a) When Medea addresses the chorus, how does she gain their sympathy? In your answer consider that the chorus consists of Corinthian women. **(b)** What does Medea ask of them?

3. (a) When Creon goes to Medea to order her and her children out of Corinth, why does he particularly fear Medea? **(b)** Does Medea truly mean to be reconciled with Creon or does she have ulterior motives in mind? **(c)** Why does Creon finally agree

to allow Medea to remain in Corinth for twenty-four hours? **(d)** How does his submission to her plea make him a more human character?

4. After Creon leaves, Medea discusses her plans. What do they reveal about her character?

5. (a) When Jason offers Medea some provision for her and her children, does he really have their welfare in mind? Explain. **(b)** What is Medea's response to his offer? **(c)** How does Jason accept Medea's reply?

6. (a) In her encounter with Aegeus, why is Medea especially sensitive regarding the oath she asks him to take? **(b)** In the bargain Aegeus agrees to, why is he so insistent that Medea escape from Corinth by her own means before he will offer her sanctuary in Athens?

Vocabulary
Pronunciation and Dictionary

Use your Glossary to answer the following questions about the italicized words.

1. Would a *tyrant* or an *oracle* be more apt to inflict harsh laws on his or her subjects?

2. Are *treacherous* persons more likely to *slander* or to *solace* their friends?

3. Is a *shrewd* person likely to believe a *specious* story?

4. Where is the primary accent in *conciliatory?* Is the second *c* pronounced like *s* or *k?*

5. Is one more likely to *revere* or to *loathe* an enemy?

6. Is the *g* of *stratagem* pronounced like the *g* in *gum* or in *fudge?*

7. Is it possible for a *plausible* argument to be false?

8. Is the accent in *lament* on the first or second syllable?

notes and comments

The Greek Chorus

As you recall from the introduction to this unit, the ritualistic dancing and singing of the chorus was the center of the early Dionysian festivals until about 534 B.C., while Greek tragedy was in its infancy. As the role of the actors in tragedy increased, the role of the chorus diminished in importance, and its size decreased from fifty members to fifteen; however, the chorus continued to play a vital part in Greek tragedy.

The chorus had two main functions. First, the chorus sang and danced during the interludes between the dialogues. Second, the chorus carried out many dramatic functions in the tragedies. One of its most important roles was that of the "ideal spectator." In this role, the chorus embodied the moral ideas of society and often admonished the characters against breaking these moral laws. In some tragedies, the chorus played a main role. In addition, the chorus

performed very technical functions which aided the movement of the story. For instance, the chorus often announced the entrances and exits of characters, or foreshadowed events in the action. Another technical role it played was to recount or interpret history or past events for the purpose of clarification of the plot.

Act Two

CHORUS OF CORINTHIAN WOMEN.

Oh where can your hand or your heart,
Medea, find the hardness
To do this frightful thing
Against your sons? O how
Can you look on them and yet
Not weep, Medea? How
Can you still resolve to slay them?
Ah, when they fall at your feet
For mercy, you will not be able
To dip your hand in their blood!

(JASON enters.)

JASON. I have come at your bidding, Medea. For although you are full of hatred for me, this small favor I will grant you; I will listen to you, my lady, and hear what new favor you are asking.

MEDEA. Jason, I beg forgiveness for what I have said! Surely you can afford to forgive my bad temper: after all, there has been much love between us! I have reasoned with myself and reproached myself. "Poor fool," I said, "Why am I so distraught? Why am I so bitter against all good advice, why am I so angry at the rulers of this country, and my husband as well, who does the best he can for me in marrying a royal princess, and in having royal children, who will be brothers to my own? Why not stop complaining? What is wrong with me, when the gods are being so generous? Don't I have my children to consider? Don't I realize that we are exiles after all, and in need of friends? . . ."

And when I had thought all this over, Jason, I saw how foolish I'd been, and how silly my anger. So now I agree with you. I think you are well advised in taking this new wife; and I was mad. I should have helped you in your plans; I should have helped arrange the wedding. I should have stood by the wedding bed and been happy to wait on your bride. But we women are—well, I shan't say entirely worthless; but we are what we are. And you men shouldn't stoop to our level: you shouldn't reply to our folly with folly. I give in. I admit I was wrong. I have thought better of it all. . . .

(She turns toward the house.)

Come, come, my children, come out from the house, come and greet your father, and then say good-bye to him. Give up your anger, as your mother does; be friends with him again, be reconciled!

(The TUTOR enters with the children.)

We have made peace now; our bitterness is gone. Take his right hand . . . O God: I can't help thinking of the things that lie dark and hidden in the future! . . . My children, hold out your arms—the way one holds them in farewell after a long, long life . . . I am close to tears, my children! I am full of fear! I have ended my quarrel with your father at last, and look! My eyes are full of tears.

CHORUS LEADER. And our eyes too are filling with tears. O, do not let disasters worse than the present descend on you!

JASON. I approve of your conduct, Medea; not that I blame you for anything in the past. It is natural for a woman to be furious with her husband when he begins to have other affairs. But now your heart has grown more sensible, and your mind is changed for the better; you are behaving like a woman of sense. And of you, my sons, your father will take good care, and make full provision, with the help of God. And I trust that in due time you with your brothers will be among the leading men in Corinth. All you need to do is grow up, my sons; and as for your future, you may leave it safely in the hands of your father, and of those among the gods who love him. I want to see you when you've grown to be men, tall and strong, towering over my enemies! . . . Medea, why are your eyes wet with tears? Why are your cheeks so pale? Why are you turning away? Don't these happy words of mine make you happy?

MEDEA. It is nothing. I was only thinking about these children.

JASON. Take heart, then. I shall look after them well.

MEDEA. I will, Jason. It is not that I don't trust you. Women are weak; and tears come easily to them.

JASON. But why should you feel disturbed about the children?

MEDEA. I gave birth to them, Jason. And when you prayed that they might live long, my heart filled with sorrow to think that all these things must happen . . . Well now: I have told you some of the things I called you here to tell you; now let me tell you the rest. Since the ruler of this land has resolved to banish me, and since I am considered an enemy, I know it will be best for me not to stand in your way, or in the way of the King, by living here. I am going forth from this land into exile. But these children—O let them feel that you are protecting them, and beg of Creon not to banish them!

JASON. I doubt whether I can persuade him; still, I will try.

MEDEA. Or at least ask your wife to beg her father to do this, and give the children reprieve from exile.

JASON. I will try; and with her I think I shall succeed.

MEDEA. She's a woman, after all, and like all other women. And I will help you in this matter; I will send the children to her with gifts far more exquisite, I am sure, than any now to be found among men—a finely woven dress and a diadem of chased gold. There; let one of the servants go and bring me these lovely ornaments.

(One of the SERVANTS *goes into the house.)*

And she'll be happy not in one way, but a thousand! With so splendid a man as you to share her bed, and with this marvelous gown as well, which once the Sun God Helios himself, my father's father, gave his descendants.

(The SERVANT *returns with the poisoned dress and diadem.)*

There, my children, take these wedding presents in your hands and take them as an offering to the royal princess, the lucky bride; give them to her; they are not gifts to be scorned.

JASON. But why do you give them away so rashly, Medea? Do you think the royal palace is lacking in dresses, or in gold? Keep them. Don't give them away. If my wife really loves me, I am sure she values me more highly than gold.

MEDEA. No; don't say that, Jason. For I have heard it said that gifts can persuade even the gods; and men are governed more by gold than by words! Luck has fallen on your bride, and the gods have blessed her fortune. She is young; she's a princess. Yet I'd give not only gold but my life to save my children from exile. Enter that rich palace together, children, and pray to your father's new bride; pray to my mistress, and beg her to save you from banishment. Present this garment to her, and above all let her take the gift from you with her own hands. Go, don't linger. And may you succeed, and bring back to your mother the good news for which she longs!

(Exit JASON, *the* TUTOR, *and the* CHILDREN *bearing the poisoned gifts.)*

CHORUS OF CORINTHIAN WOMEN.
No hope now remains for the children's lives!
No, none. Even now they are moving toward death;
The luckless bride will accept the gown that will kill her,
And take the golden crown, and hold it
In her hand, and over her golden head will
Lift the garment of death!
The grace and glitter of gold will enchant her:
She will put on the golden robe and wear
The golden crown: and deck herself as the bride
Of Death. And thus, pitiful girl,
Will fall in the trap; will fall and perish.
She will never escape.
You likewise, O miserable groom,
Who planned a royal wedding ceremony,
Do not see the doom you are bringing
Upon your sons; and the terrible death
Now lying in wait for your bride. Pity
Upon you! O, how you are fallen!
And I weep for you too, Medea,

O mother who are killing your sons,
Killing in revenge for the loss
Of your love: you whom your lover Jason
Now has deserted and betrayed
To love and marry another mistress!
(Enter TUTOR *with the children.)*

TUTOR. My lady, your children are reprieved from exile. The royal bride was delighted to receive your gifts with her own hands. And there is peace between her and your children . . . Medea! Why are you so distraught at this lucky moment? Why are you turning your head away? Are you not happy to hear this news, my lady?

MEDEA. Oh, I am lost!

TUTOR. That cry does not suit the news I have brought you, surely!

MEDEA. I am lost! I am lost!

TUTOR. Have I told you of some disaster, without knowing it? Was I wrong in thinking that my news was good?

MEDEA. You have said what you have said: I do not wish to blame you.

TUTOR. Then why are you so disturbed? Why are you weeping?

MEDEA. Oh, my old friend, I can't help weeping. It was I, it was I and the gods, who planned these things so badly.

TUTOR. Take heart, Medea. Your sons will bring you back to your home some day.

MEDEA. And I'll bring others back to their homes, long before that happens!

TUTOR. And often before this, mothers have been parted from their sons. Bear your troubles, Medea, as all mortals must bear them.

MEDEA. I will, I will. Go back into the house, and plan your daily work for the children.

(The TUTOR *goes into the house, and* MEDEA *turns to her children.)*

MEDEA. O my children, my children, you will still have a city, you will still have a home where you can dwell forever, far away from me, far forever from your mother! But I am doomed to go in exile to another land, before I can see you grow up and be happy, before I can take pride in you, before I can wait on your brides and make your marriage beds, or hold the torch at your wedding ceremony! What a victim I am of my own self-will! It was all in vain, my children, that I reared you! It was all in vain that I grew weary and worn, and suffered the anguish and pangs of childbirth! O pity me! Once I had great hopes for you; I had hopes that you'd look after me in my old age, and that you'd lovingly deck my body with your own hands when I died, as all men hope and desire. But now my lovely dreams are over. I shall love you both. I shall spend my life in grief and solitude. And never again will you see your mother with your own dear eyes; now you will pass into another kind of life.

Ah, my dear children, why do you look at me like this? Why are you smiling your sweet little smiles at me? Oh children, what can I do? My heart gives way when I see the joy shining in my children's eyes. O women, I cannot do it! . . . Farewell to all my plans! I will take my babies away with me from this land. Why should I hurt their father by hurting them? Why should I hurt myself doubly? No. I cannot do it. I shall say good-bye to my plans . . . And yet—O, what is wrong with me? Am I willing to see my enemies go unpunished? Am I willing to be insulted and laughed at? I shall follow this thing to the end. How weak I am! How weak to let my heart be touched by these soft sentiments! Go back into the house, my children . . . And if anyone prefers not to witness my sacrifice, let him do as he wishes! My poor heart—do not do this thing! My poor heart, have pity on them, let them go, the little children! They'll bring cheer to you, if you let them live with you in exile! . . .

No, by all the avenging Furies,[1] this shall not be! Never shall I surrender my children to the insolence and mockery of my enemies! It is settled. I have made my decision. And since they must die, it is their mother who must kill them. Now there is no escape for the young bride! Already the crown is on her head; already the dress is hanging from her body; the royal bride, the princess is dying! This I know. And now—since I am about to follow a dreadful path, and am sending them on a path still more terrible—I will simply say this: I want to speak to my children.
(She calls and the children come back; she takes them in her arms.)

Come, come, give me your hands, my babies, let your mother kiss you both. O dear little hands, dear little lips: how I have loved them! How fresh and young your eyes look! How straight you stand! I wish you joy with all my heart; but not here; not in this land. All that you had here your father has stolen from you. . . . How good it is to hold you, to feel your soft young cheeks, the warm young sweetness of your breath. . . . Go now; leave me. I cannot look at you any longer . . . I am overcome. . . .
(The children go into the house again.)

Now at last I understand the full evil of what I have planned. At last I see how my passion is stronger than my reason: passion, which brings the worst of woes to mortal man.
(She goes toward the house.)

CHORUS LEADER.
Many a time before
I have gone through subtler reasoning,
Many times I have faced graver questioning

1. **Furies,** three fearsome winged goddesses who pursued and punished wrongdoers.

Than any woman should ever have to face:
But we women have a goddess to help us, too,
And lead us into wisdom.
Not all of us; perhaps not many;
But some women there are who are capable of wisdom.
And I say this: that those who have never
Known the fullness of life and never had children,
Are happier far than those who are parents.
For the childless, who never discover whether
Their children grow up to be a cause for joy or for pain,
Are spared many troubles:
While those who know in their houses
The sweet presence of children—
We have seen how their lives are wasted by worry.
First they fret about how they shall raise them
Properly; and then how to leave them enough
Money to live on; and then they continue
To worry about whether all this labor
Has gone into children that will turn out well
Or turn out ill: and the question remains unanswered.
And let me tell of one more trouble,
The last of all, and common to all mortals:
For suppose you have found enough
For them to live on, and suppose
You have seen them grow up and turn out well;
Still, if fate so decrees it, Death
Will come and tear away your children!
What use is it, then, that the gods
For the sake of children
Should pile on us mortals,
After all other griefs,
This grief for lost children? This grief
Greater by far than any?
(MEDEA *comes out of the house.*)

MEDEA. I have been waiting in suspense, ladies; I have waited long to
learn how things will happen . . . Look! I see one of Jason's
servants coming toward us; he is panting, and the bearer of news,
I think, of bad news . . .

(*A* MESSENGER[2] *rushes in.*)

MESSENGER. Fly, Medea, fly. You have done a terrible thing, a thing
breaking all human laws: fly, and take with you a ship for the
seas, or a chariot for the plains!

MEDEA. Why? What reason have you for asking me to fly?

MESSENGER. She lies dead! The royal princess, and her father Creon
too! They have died: they have been slain by your poisons!

MEDEA. You bring me blessed news! Now and from now on I count

2. **Messenger.** To avoid violence on the stage, Greek dramatists used a "Messenger" to narrate particularly horrible events.

you among my friends, my benefactors!

MESSENGER. What! Are you insane? Are you mad, Medea? You have done an outrage to the royal house: does it make you happy to hear it? Can you hear of this dreadful thing without horror?

MEDEA. I too have words to say in reply to yours. Do not be impatient, my friend. Tell me: how did they die? You will make me doubly happy if you say they died in anguish!

MESSENGER. When those two children, your own babies, Medea, came with their father and entered the palace of the bride, it gave joy to all of us, the servants who have suffered with you; for instantly all through the house we whispered that you had made up your quarrel with your husband. One of us kissed your children's hands, and another their golden hair, and I myself was so overjoyed that I followed them in person to the women's chambers. And there stood our mistress, whom we now serve instead of you; and she kept her eyes fixed longingly on Jason.

When she caught sight of your children, she covered up her eyes, and her face grew pale, and she turned away, filled with petulance at their coming. But your husband tried to soothe the bride's ill humor, and said: "Do not look so unkindly at your friends! Do not feel angry: turn your head to me once more, and think of your husband's friends as your own friends! Accept these gifts, and do this for my sake: beg of your father not to let these children be exiled." And then, when she saw the dress, she grew mild and yielded, and gave in to her husband. And before the father and the children had gone far from her rooms, she took the gorgeous robe and put it on; and she put the golden crown on her curly head, and arranged her hair in the shining mirror, smiling as she saw herself reflected. And then she rose from her chair and walked across the room, stepping softly and delicately on her small white feet, filled with delight at the gift, and glancing again and again at the delicate turn of her ankles.

After that it was a thing of horror we saw. For suddenly her face changed its color, and she staggered back, and began to tremble as she ran, and reached a chair just as she was about to fall to the ground. An old woman servant, thinking no doubt that this was some kind of seizure, a fit sent by Pan,[3] or some other god, cried out a prayer: and then, as she prayed, she saw the flakes of foam flow from her mouth, and her eyeballs rolling, and the blood fade from her face. And then it was a different prayer she uttered, a terrible scream, and one of the women ran to the house of the King, and another to the newly wedded groom to tell him what had happened to the bride; and the whole house echoed as they ran to and fro.

Let me tell you, time enough for a man to walk two hundred yards passed before the poor lady awoke from her trance, with a

3. **Pan,** a goatlike god whose music was said to cause spasms of joy in its hearers.

dreadful scream, and opened her eyes again. A twofold torment was creeping over her. The golden diadem on her head was sending forth a violent stream of flame, and the finely woven dress which your children gave her was beginning to eat into the poor girl's snowy soft flesh. And she leapt from her chair, all on fire, and started to run, shaking her head to and fro, trying to shake off the diadem; but the gold still clung firmly, and as she shook her hair the fire blazed forth with double fury. And then she sank to the ground, helpless, overcome; and past all recognition except to the eye of a father—for her eyes had lost their normal expression, and the familiar look had fled from her face, and from the top of her head a mingled stream of blood and fire was pouring. And it was like the drops falling from the bark of a pine tree when the flesh dropped away from her bones, torn loose by the secret fangs of the poison. And terror kept all of us from touching the corpse, for we were warned by what had happened.

But then her poor father, who knew nothing of her death, came suddenly into the house and stumbled over her body, and cried out as he folded his arms about her, and kissed her, and said: 'O my child, my poor child, which of the gods has so cruelly killed you? Who has robbed me of you, who am old and close to the grave? O my child, let me die with you!' And he grew silent and tried to rise to his feet again, but found himself fastened to the finely spun dress, like vine clinging to a laurel bough, and there was a fearful struggle. And still he tried to lift his knees, and she writhed and clung to him; and as he tugged, he tore the withered flesh from his bones. And at last he could no longer master the pain, and surrendered, and gave up the ghost. So there they are lying together: and it is a sight to send us weeping. . . .

As for you, Medea, I will say nothing of your own problems: you yourself must discover an escape from punishment. I think, and I have always thought, the life of men is a shadow; and I say without fear that those who are wisest among all men, and probe most deeply into the cause of things—they are the ones who suffer most deeply! For, believe me, no man among mortals is happy; if wealth comes to a man, he may be luckier than the rest, but happy—never.

(*Exit* MESSENGER.)

CHORUS LEADER. It seems that heaven has sent, today, a heavy load of evils upon Jason; and he deserves them. Alas, poor girl, poor daughter of Creon! I pity you and your anguish; and now you are gone, all because of your wedding with Jason: gone away to the halls of Hades![4]

MEDEA. Women, the deed shall be done! Swiftly I will go and kill my children, and then leave the land: and not delay nor let them be

4. *halls of Hades* (hā'dēz), the Underworld where Hades, god of the dead, ruled.

killed by a crueler hand. For die they must in any case: and if they must be slain, it is I, their mother who gave them life, who must slay them! O my heart, my heart, arm yourself in steel! Do not shrink back from this hideous thing which has to be done! Come, my hand, and seize the sword, take it and step forward to the place where my life's true sorrow begins! Do not be a coward . . . do not think of the children, and how dear they are to you who are their mother! For one brief day, Medea, forget your children; and then forever after you may mourn; for though you will kill them, they were dear to you, very dear . . . I am a miserable woman!
(With a cry MEDEA *rushes into the house.)*

CHORUS OF CORINTHIAN WOMEN.

O Earth, and the all-brightening
Beam of the Sun, look, look
Upon this lost one, shine upon
This pitiful woman before she raises
Her hand in murder against her sons!
For lo! these are the offspring
Of thine own golden seed, and I fear
That divine blood may now be shed by men!
O Light flung forth by Zeus,
O heavenly Light,
Hold back her hand,
Restrain her, and drive out
This dark demoniac fury from the house!
(A cry is heard from the children within the house.)

CHORUS LEADER.

Listen! Do you hear? Do you hear the children crying?
Hate-hardened heart! O woman born for evil!

1ST SON *(crying within the house).* What can I do? How can I run from mother's hands?

2ND SON *(crying within the house).* I don't know. We are lost, we are lost, brother!

CHORUS LEADER.

Shall I enter the house? Oh surely
I must help! I must save these children from murder!

1ST SON. Help, in the name of heaven! We need your help!

2ND SON. Now, now it's coming closer! The sword is falling!

CHORUS LEADER.

Oh, you must be made of stone or steel,
To kill the fruit of your womb
With your own hands, unhappy woman!
(Enter JASON *with his attendants.)*

JASON. Ladies, you have been sitting near this house! Tell me! Is Medea, is the woman who did this frightful thing, still in the house? Or has she fled already? O believe me, she'll have to hide

deep under the earth, or fly on wings through the sky, if she hopes to escape the vengeance of the royal house! Does she dream, after killing the rulers of the land, that she herself can escape from these halls unpunished? But I am thinking of her far less than of her children; for she herself will duly suffer at the hands of those she wronged. Ladies, I have come to save the lives of my boys, lest the royal house should harm them in revenge for this vile thing done by their mother.

CHORUS LEADER. O Jason, you do not yet know the full depth of your misery, or you would not have spoken those words!

JASON. What do you mean? Is she planning to kill me also?

CHORUS LEADER. Your boys are dead; dead at their mother's hand.

JASON. What have you said, woman? You are destroying me!

CHORUS LEADER. You may be sure of this: your children are dead.

JASON. Oh where did she kill them? Was it here, or in the house?

CHORUS LEADER. Open the doors, and you will see their murdered bodies!

JASON. Open the doors! Unlock the bolts! Undo the fastenings! And let me see this twofold horror! Let me see my murdered boys! Let me look on her whom I shall kill in vengeance!

(His attendants rush to the door. MEDEA *appears above the house in a chariot drawn by dragons. The dead children are at her side.)*

MEDEA. Why do you batter at the doors? Why do you shake these bolts, in quest of the dead and their murderess? You may cease your trouble, Jason; and if there is anything you want to say, then say it! Never again shall you lay your hand on me; so swift is the chariot which my father's father gave me, the Sun God Helios, to save me from my foes!

JASON. Horrible woman! Now you are utterly loathed by the gods, and by me, and by all mankind! You had the heart to stab your children; you, their own mother, and to leave me childless you have done these fearful things, and still you dare to gaze as ever at the sun and the earth! I wish you were dead! Now at last I see clearly what I did not see on the day I brought you, loaded with doom, from your barbarous home to live in Hellas[5]—a traitress to your father and your native land. On me too the gods have hurled the curse which has haunted you. For you killed your own brother[6] at his fireside, and then came aboard our beautiful ship the *Argo.* And that was how it started. And then you married me, and out of your passion bore me children; and now, out of your passion, you have killed them. There is no woman in all of Greece who would dare to do this. And yet I passed them over, and chose you instead; and chose to marry my own doom! I married not a woman, but a monster, wilder of heart than Scylla in the Tyrrhenian Sea![7] But even if I hurled a thousand insults at you,

5. *Hellas* (hel'əs), Greece.

6. *your own brother.* Medea murdered her brother and took his body along as she and Jason escaped by sea. Then she cast parts of the corpse into the sea to delay her father's pursuit.

7. *Scylla* (sil'ə), *in the Tyrrhenian* (tə rē'nē ən) *Sea.* Scylla, like Medea, fell in love with a foreigner—King Minos—which led her to betray her father and city. The gods later transformed her into a monster, stationing her in the Straits of Messina (Sicily) where she fed on mariners passing through.

Medea, I know I could not wound you: your heart is so hard, so utterly hard. Go, you wicked sorceress; I see the stains of your children's blood upon you! Go, all that is left to me now is to mourn. I shall never lie beside my newly wedded love; I shall never have my sons, whom I bred and brought up, alive beside me to say a last farewell! I have lost them forever, and my life is ended.

MEDEA. O Jason, to these words of yours I could make a long reply; but Zeus, the father, himself well knows all that I did for you, and what you did to me. Destiny has refused to let you scorn my love, and lead a life of pleasure, and mock at me; nor were the royal princess and the matchmaker Creon destined to drive me into exile, and then go untormented! Call me a monster if you wish; call me the Scylla in the Tyrrhenian Sea. For now I have torn your heart; and this indeed was destined, Jason!

JASON. You too must feel the pain; you will share my grief, Medea.

MEDEA. Yes, but the pain is milder, since you cannot mock me!

JASON. O my sons, it was an unspeakable mother who bore you!

MEDEA. O my sons, it was really your father who destroyed you!

JASON. But I tell you, it was not my hand that slew them!

MEDEA. No, but your insolence, and your new wedding slew them!

JASON. And you thought this wedding cause enough to kill them?

MEDEA. And you think the anguish of love is trifling for a woman?

JASON. Yes, if her heart is sound: but yours makes all things evil.

MEDEA. Your sons are dead, Jason! Does it hurt you when I say this?

JASON. They will live on, Medea, by bringing suffering on you.

MEDEA. The gods are well aware who caused all this suffering.

JASON. Yes, the gods are well aware. They know your brutal heart.

MEDEA. You too are brutal. And I am sick of your bitter words!

JASON. And I am sick of yours. Oh Medea, it will be easy to leave you.

MEDEA. Easy! Yes! And for me too! What, then, do you want?

JASON. Give me those bodies to bury, and to mourn.

MEDEA. Never! I will bury them myself. I will bring them myself to Hera's temple,[8] which hangs over the Cape, where none of their enemies can insult them, and where none can defile their graves! And in this land of Corinth I shall ordain a holy feast and sacrifice, forever after, to atone for this guilt of killing. And I shall go myself to Athens, to live in the house of Aegeus, the son of Pandion. And I predict that you, as you deserve, will die without honor, and your head crushed by a beam of the shattered *Argo;*[9] and then you will know the bitter end of all my love for you!

JASON. May the avenging fury of our sons destroy you! May Justice

8. *Hera's* (hir'ə) *temple.* Hera, the wife of Zeus, was considered so powerful that none dared profane her temples.

9. *shattered Argo,* a prophecy that later came true, according to legend.

destroy you, and repay blood with blood!

MEDEA. What god, what heavenly power would listen to you? To a breaker of oaths? To a betrayer of love?

JASON. Oh, you are vile! You sorceress! Murderess!

MEDEA. Go to your house. Go, and bury your bride.

JASON. Yes, I shall go, and mourn for my murdered sons.

MEDEA. Wait, do not weep yet, Jason! Wait till age has sharpened your grief!

JASON. Oh my sons, whom I loved! My sons!

MEDEA. It was I, not you, who truly loved them.

JASON. You say you loved them; yet you killed them.

MEDEA. Yes. I killed them to make you suffer.

JASON. Medea, I only long to kiss them one last time.

MEDEA. Now, now, you long to kiss them! Now you long to say farewell: but before, you cast them from you!

JASON. Medea, I beg you, let me touch the little bodies of my boys!

MEDEA. No. Never. You speak in vain.

JASON. O Zeus, high in your heaven, have you heard these words? Have you heard this unutterable cruelty? Have you heard this woman, this monster, this murderess? And now I shall do the only thing I still can do! Yes! I shall cry, I shall cry aloud to heaven, and call on the gods to witness how you killed my sons, and refused to let me kiss them farewell, or touch them, or give them burial! Oh, I'd rather never have seen them live, than have seen them slaughtered so!

(The chariot carries MEDEA *away.)*

CHORUS LEADER.

Many, many are the things
That Zeus determines, high on the Olympian throne;
Many the things beyond men's understanding
That the gods achieve, and bring to pass.
Many the things we think will happen,
Yet never happen.
And many things we thought could never be,
Yet the gods contrive.
Such things have happened on this day,
And in this place![10]

10. *in this place.* With these lines, the chorus marches offstage. This final chorus is called the Exodos (ek'sə dəs).

Discussion

1. Medea dramatically changes her attitude toward Jason when she begs his forgiveness. Why do you think Jason believes her? Cite passages to support your opinion.

2. How does Euripides introduce suspense in the scene in which Medea sends the children off to the royal palace with their father?

3. (a) When the tutor reports the success of the children at the royal palace, why does Medea exhibit such anguish? **(b)** What does her statement to the tutor foreshadow in the following exchange?

TUTOR: Take heart, Medea. Your sons will bring you back to your home some day.

MEDEA: And I'll bring others back to their homes, long before that happens!

4. After the news from the tutor, Medea's resolve to continue with her murderous plan is momentarily weakened. What powerful aspect in Medea's character restrains her from abandoning her plans? Cite passages to support your answer.

Vocabulary
Context and Pronunciation

Answer the following questions about the italicized words. Then choose the correct italicized word to complete each sentence in **B.** Use your Glossary for reference.

A.

1. On page 321, line 45 which homonym of *chase* is the intended word? What is the origin of the word?

2. From what two Latin words is *benefactor* derived?

3. Does the first syllable of *petulance* rhyme with *get* or with *fetch*? Where is the accent?

4. How many syllables are there in *vengeance*?

5. Where is the accent in *distraught*? Is the *gh* silent?

B.

6. The little boy's unknown _____ not only sent him to school, but she also established a trust fund for him.

7. Miranda swore _____ against the family that had dishonestly acquired her father's farm.

8. The jeweler carefully _____ the gold bracelet with an intricate design.

9. Separated from her little girl by the hysterical mob, the _____ woman didn't know what to do.

10. Fritz is usually an easy-going fellow, but he surely exhibits a streak of _____ whenever he doesn't get his own way.

Extension · Writing

Assume that Medea did not escape to Athens, that she was apprehended and jailed and is now on trial for murder. Consider the play to be the testimonial accounts of what occurred according to each character. Assume you are involved in the trial of the *City of Corinth* v. *Medea:*

1. If you were the attorney for the defense, what arguments would you use to defend Medea?

2. If you were the attorney for the prosecution, what arguments would you use to prove her guilty?

Choose one of the stances and write a formal argument, limited to no more than three-hundred words, addressed to the judge and jury of Corinthian men. (At that time, women did not serve on juries.) Do not forget to include an introduction and a conclusion to your statement.

Euripides c480? • 406? B.C.

Euripides, along with Aeschylus and Sophocles, is known as one of the great triad of Greek tragic writers. Euripides was born on the Greek island of Salamis, and lived at a time when Greece was at the pinnacle of its political power and creativity in the arts and philosophy. He was a friend of Socrates, who was reportedly an enthusiastic admirer of his works.

Born into a middle-class, land-holding family, Euripides was a distinguished member of Athenian society. Not only was he a successful and prolific playwright, but he was also an accomplished athlete. Because his parents had received a prophecy that he would win crowns of victory, he was given careful gymnastic training, and did indeed win several athletic victories. He served in the army as a young man and held a priesthood position in the rites of the Delphian Apollo.

In his adult life Euripides avoided society and political life. He lived with his wife and three sons on an estate on the island of Salamis. It was there in a cave, overlooking the sea, he is supposed to have written some of his many plays. Of the total, nineteen are extant in relatively complete form.

About 408 B.C., Euripides was accused of being a traitor because he opposed the war party and questioned the traditional religious beliefs. He went into voluntary exile, and he died shortly after, at the age of seventy-four.

Of the triad, Euripides was the least respectful of the Olympian gods, the most insistent in his social criticism, and the most modern in his appeal. In his long active career, he was awarded the prize for the best drama in the Dionysian competition only four times; but among succeeding generations, he was the most popular tragic poet of Greece, whose plays were most frequently revived and whose plays were most translated and adapted by the Romans.

43 EVRIPIDE

Alinari/EPA, Inc.

5: MEDEA

CONTENT REVIEW

1. There are three main conflicts in the play: **(a)** between husband and wife, **(b)** between man and woman, and **(c)** between alien and native-born citizen. Give examples of each, referring to the text for specific lines.

2. Reread the section on Tragedy in the Introduction. What would you say is the tragic flaw in Medea's personality? Is she ever in conflict with herself? Explain.

3. Review the article about the chorus; then cite three passages in *Medea* which represent three different functions of the chorus.

4. Euripides heightens the tension at several points in *Medea* through the use of dramatic irony. Dramatic irony occurs when the reader or spectator knows more about the true state of affairs than the characters do. Find an example in the play that demonstrates a difference between what a character says and what the reader or spectator knows to be true.

5. Briefly identify each of the following:

Creon	Hades
Thespis	Zeus
Golden Fleece	*Argo*
Tragic Hero/Heroine	Aphrodite
Dionysus	Orpheus

Unit 5, Test I
INTERPRETATION: NEW MATERIAL

from *Alcestis*

Euripides
translated by Richmond Lattimore

The following excerpt comes from *Alcestis* (al ses′ təs), the earliest play of Euripides in existence. It is about self-sacrifice and its rewards, as well as the love between husband and wife. Admetus, king of Thessaly,[1] has been told by the gods that he must die. However, if he finds a suitable substitute, he will be spared. Among his friends, courtiers, and family he finds only his wife Alcestis willing to take his place. In the following section, she gives some of her reasons for doing so as she lies dying.

At the end of the play, Admetus is rewarded for an act of kindness by the return of his wife from Hades. After you have read the selection, answer the questions.

1. *Admetus* (ad mē′təs) *king of Thessaly,* a land of hills and plains in northern Greece. He had gone to Troy with the other Greeks, and was said to have sailed on the ship *Argo,* on its journeys.

He had befriended the god Apollo once, and it was Apollo who had persuaded the other gods to let Admetus escape death, if the king found a suitable substitute.

"Alcestis," by Euripides, translated by Richmond Lattimore in THE COMPLETE GREEK TRAGEDIES, Vol. III, Edited by David Grene and Richmond Lattimore. © 1955 by The University of Chicago. Reprinted by permission.

ALCESTIS.

Somebody has me, somebody takes me away, do you see,
don't you see, to the courts
of dead men. He frowns from under dark
brows. He has wings. It is Death.

5   Let me go, what are you doing, let go.

                                  Such is the road
most wretched I have to walk.

ADMETUS.

Sorrow for all who love you, most of all for me
and for the children. All of us share in this grief.

ALCESTIS.

Let me go now, let me down,
10   flat. I have no strength to stand.
Death is close to me.
The darkness creeps over my eyes. O children,
my children, you have no mother now,
not any longer. Daylight is yours,
15   my children. Look on it and be happy.

ADMETUS.

Ah, a bitter word for me to hear,
heavier than any death of my own.
Before the gods, do not be so harsh
as to leave me, leave your children forlorn.
20   No, up, and fight it.
There would be nothing left of me if you died.
All rests in you, our life, our not
having life. Your love is our worship.

ALCESTIS.

Admetus, you can see how it is with me. Therefore,
25   I wish to have some words with you before I die.
I put you first, and at the price of my own life
made certain you would live and see the daylight. So
I die, who did not have to die, because of you.
I could have taken any man in Thessaly
30   I wished and lived in queenly state here in this house.
But since I did not wish to live bereft of you
and with our children fatherless, I did not spare
my youth, although I had so much to live for. Yet
your father, and the mother who bore you, gave you up,
35   though they had reached an age when it was good to die
and good to save their son and end it honorably.
You were their only one, and they had no more hope
of having other children if you died. That way
I would be living and you would live the rest of our time,
40   and you would not be alone and mourning for your wife

and tending motherless children. No, but it must be
that some god has so wrought that things shall be this way.
So be it. But swear now to do, in recompense,
what I shall ask you—not enough, oh, never enough,
45 since nothing is enough to make up for a life,
but fair, and you yourself will say so, since you love
these children as much as I do; or at least you should.
Keep them as masters in my house, and do not marry
again and give our children to a stepmother
50 who will not be so kind as I, who will be jealous
and raise her hand to your children and mine. Oh no,
do not do that, do not. That is my charge to you.
For the new-come stepmother hates the children born
to a first wife, no viper could be deadlier.
55 The little boy has his father for a tower of strength.
(He can talk with him and be spoken to in turn.)
But you, my darling, what will your girlhood be like,
how will your father's new wife like you? She must not
make shameful stories up about you, and contrive
60 to spoil your chance of marriage in the blush of youth,
because your mother will not be there to help you
when you are married, not be there to give you strength
when your babies are born, when only a mother's help will do.
For I must die. It will not be tomorrow, not
65 the next day, or this month, the horrible thing will come,
but now, at once, I shall be counted among the dead.
Goodbye, be happy, both of you. And you, my husband,
can boast the bride you took made you the bravest wife,
and you, children, can say, too, that your mother was brave.

CHORUS.
70 Fear nothing; for I dare to speak for him. He will
do all you ask. If he does not, the fault is his.

ADMETUS.
It shall be so, it shall be, do not fear, since you
were mine in life, you still shall be my bride in death
and you alone, no other girl in Thessaly
75 shall ever be called wife of Admetus in your place.
There is none such, none so marked out in pride of birth
nor beauty's brilliance, nor in anything else. I have
these children, they are enough; I only pray the gods
grant me the bliss to keep them as we could not keep you.
80 I shall go into mourning for you, not for just
a year, but all my life while it still lasts, my dear,
and hate the woman who gave me birth always, detest
my father. These were called my own people. They were not.
You gave what was your own and dear to buy my life

85 and saved me. Am I not to lead a mourning life
when I have lost a wife like you? I shall make an end
of revelry and entertainment in my house,
the flowers and the music that were found here once.

Write the word or phrase that best answers the questions.

1. List two reasons Alcestis gives for dying in Admetus's place.

2. What does Alcestis say about the refusal of Admetus's parents to die in his place?

3. What does Alcestis request of Admetus in return for her sacrifice?

4. Why does Alcestis worry particularly about her little girl?

5. The chorus speaks only once in this passage. What is its role in this instance?

6. What does Admetus promise Alcestis?

7. Reread lines 16–21. What is ironic about what Admetus is saying?

8. List three differences between Medea and Alcestis. List at least one similarity.

9. List two differences between Jason and Admetus. List one similarity.

10. What figure of speech is used in the first four lines? How does this figure of speech help to set the tone of the passage?

Unit 5, Test II
COMPOSITION

From the following assignments choose one to write about.

1. You are Aegeus. Now that the story of Medea's crime is out, you feel it is necessary to explain your decision to shelter her in your kingdom. Write a press release.

2. The classical Greek theater required a play to have one plot occurring on one day in one place. Discuss *Medea* in terms of this requirement. How are actions that take place long before the play opens incorporated into the play? How does the plot effectively use the rule that the play take place in one day?

3. You are Medea in her old age. Write a commentary on the Corinthian episode, choosing *one* of the following to emphasize: **(a)** whether it was worth the anguish; **(b)** how your life might have been different with your sons; **(c)** how you got along in Aegeus's kingdom; **(d)** your dialogues with the chorus of Corinthian women; **(e)** whether you still feel justified in your actions.

Prose
Forms

VICTORIES

The Letter "A"

Christy Brown

Marvin Kupfer—Newsweek

I was born in the Rotunda Hospital,[1] on June 5th, 1932. There were nine children before me and twelve after me, so I myself belong to the middle group. Out of this total of twenty-two, seventeen lived, but four died in infancy, leaving thirteen still to hold the family fort.

Mine was a difficult birth, I am told. Both mother and son almost died. A whole army of relations queued up outside the hospital until the small hours of the morning, waiting for news and praying furiously that it would be good.

After my birth mother was sent to recuperate for some weeks and I was kept in the hospital while she was away. I remained there for some time, without name, for I wasn't baptized until my mother was well enough to bring me to church.

It was mother who first saw that there was something wrong with me. I was about four months old at the time. She noticed that my head had a habit of falling backward whenever she tried to feed me. She attempted to correct this by placing her hand on the back of my neck to keep it steady. But when she took it away, back it would drop again. That was the first warning sign. Then she became aware of other defects as I got older. She saw that my hands were clenched nearly all of the time and were inclined to twine behind my back, my mouth couldn't grasp the teat of the bottle because even at that early age my jaws would either lock together tightly, so that it was impossible for her to open them, or they would suddenly become limp and fall loose, dragging my whole mouth to one side. At six months I could not sit up without having a mountain of pillows around me. At twelve months it was the same.

Very worried by this, mother told my father her fears, and they decided to seek medical advice without any further delay. I was a little over a year old when they began to take me to

From THE STORY OF CHRISTY BROWN (British title: MY LEFT FOOT) by Christy Brown. Copyright © 1954, 1955 by Christy Brown. Reprinted by permission of Simon & Schuster, a Division of Gulf & Western Corporation, and Martin Secker & Warburg Limited.

1. *Rotunda Hospital,* a hospital in Dublin, Ireland.

hospitals and clinics, convinced that there was something definitely wrong with me, something which they could not understand or name, but which was very real and disturbing.

Almost every doctor who saw and examined me, labeled me a very interesting but also a hopeless case. Many told mother very gently that I was mentally defective and would remain so. That was a hard blow to a young mother who had already reared five healthy children. The doctors were so very sure of themselves that mother's faith in me seemed almost an impertinence. They assured her that nothing could be done for me.

She refused to accept this truth, the inevitable truth—as it then seemed—that I was beyond cure, beyond saving, even beyond hope. She could not and would not believe that I was an imbecile, as the doctors told her. She had nothing in the world to go by, not a scrap of evidence to support her conviction that, though my body was crippled, my mind was not. In spite of all the doctors and specialists told her, she would not agree. I don't believe she knew why— she just knew, without feeling the smallest shade of doubt.

Finding that the doctors could not help in any way beyond telling her not to place her trust in me, or, in other words, to forget I was a human creature, rather to regard me as just something to be fed and washed and then put away again, mother decided there and then to take matters into her own hands. I was *her* child, and therefore part of the family. No matter how dull and incapable I might grow up to be, she was determined to treat me on the same plane as the others, and not as the "queer one" in the back room who was never spoken of when there were visitors present.

That was a momentous decision as far as my future life was concerned. It meant that I would always have my mother on my side to help me fight all the battles that were to come, and to inspire me with new strength when I was almost beaten. But it wasn't easy for her because now the relatives and friends had decided otherwise. They contended that I should be taken kindly,

sympathetically, but not seriously. That would be a mistake. "For your own sake," they told her, "don't look to this boy as you would to the others; it would only break your heart in the end." Luckily for me, mother and father held out against the lot of them. But mother wasn't content just to say that I was not an idiot: she set out to prove it, not because of any rigid sense of duty, but out of love. That is why she was so successful.

At this time she had the five other children to look after besides the "difficult one," though as yet it was not by any means a full house. They were my brothers, Jim, Tony, and Paddy, and my two sisters, Lily and Mona, all of them very young, just a year or so between each of them, so that they were almost exactly like steps of stairs.

Four years rolled by and I was now five, and still as helpless as a newly born baby. While my father was out at bricklaying, earning our bread and butter for us, mother was slowly, patiently pulling down the wall, brick by brick, that seemed to thrust itself between me and the other children, slowly, patiently penetrating beyond the thick curtain that hung over my mind, separating it from theirs. It was hard, heart-breaking work, for often all she got from me in return was a vague smile and perhaps a faint gurgle. I could not speak or even mumble, nor could I sit up without support on my own, let alone take steps. But I wasn't inert or motionless. I seemed, indeed, to be convulsed with movement, wild, stiff, snakelike movement that never left me, except in sleep. My fingers twisted and twitched continually, my arms twined backwards and would often shoot out suddenly this way and that, and my head lolled and sagged sideways. I was a queer, crooked little fellow.

Mother tells me how one day she had been sitting with me for hours in an upstairs room, showing me pictures out of a great big storybook that I had got from Santa Claus last Christmas and telling me the names of the different animals and flowers that were in them, trying without success to get me to repeat them. This had gone on for hours while she talked and laughed with me. Then at the end of it she leaned over me and said gently into my ear:

"Did you like it, Chris? Did you like the bears and the monkeys and all the lovely flowers? Nod your head for yes, like a good boy."

But I could make no sign that I had understood her. Her face was bent over mine hopefully. Suddenly, involuntarily, my queer hand reached up and grasped one of the dark curls that fell in a thick cluster about her neck. Gently she loosened the clenched fingers, though some dark strands were still clutched between them.

Then she turned away from my curious stare and left the room, crying. The door closed behind her. It all seemed hopeless. It looked as though there was some justification for my relatives' contention that I was an idiot and beyond help.

They now spoke of an institution.

"Never!" said my mother almost fiercely, when this was suggested to her. "I know my boy is not an idiot, it is his body that is shattered, not his mind. I'm sure of that."

Sure? Yet inwardly, she prayed God would give her some proof of her faith. She knew it was one thing to believe but quite another thing to prove.

I was now five, and still I showed no real sign of intelligence. I showed no apparent interest in things except with my toes—more especially those of my left foot. Although my natural habits were clean, I could not aid myself, but in this respect my father took care of me. I used to lie on my back all the time in the kitchen or, on bright warm days, out in the garden, a little bundle of crooked muscles and twisted nerves, surrounded by a family that loved me and hoped for me and that made me part of their own warmth and humanity. I was lonely, imprisoned in a world of my own, unable to communicate with others, cut off, separated from them as though a glass wall stood between my existence and theirs, thrusting me beyond the sphere of

their lives and activities. I longed to run about and play with the rest, but I was unable to break loose from my bondage.

Then, suddenly, it happened! in a moment everything was changed, my future life molded into a definite shape, my mother's faith in me rewarded and her secret fear changed into open triumph.

It happened so quickly, so simply after all the years of waiting and uncertainty, that I can see and feel the whole scene as if it had happened last week. It was the afternoon of a cold, gray December day. The streets outside glistened with snow, the white sparkling flakes stuck and melted on the windowpanes and hung on the boughs of the trees like molten silver. The wind howled dismally, whipping up little whirling columns of snow that rose and fell at every fresh gust. And over all, the dull, murky sky stretched like a dark canopy, a vast infinity of grayness.

Inside, all the family were gathered round the big kitchen fire that lit up the little room with a warm glow and made giant shadows dance on the walls and ceiling.

In a corner Mona and Paddy were sitting, huddled together, a few torn school primers before them. They were writing down little sums on to an old chipped slate, using a bright piece of yellow chalk. I was close to them, propped up by a few pillows against the wall, watching.

It was the chalk that attracted me so much. It was a long, slender stick of vivid yellow. I had never seen anything like it before, and it showed up so well against the black surface of the slate that I was fascinated by it as much as if it had been a stick of gold.

Suddenly, I wanted desperately to do what my sister was doing. Then—without thinking or knowing exactly what I was doing, I reached out and took the stick of chalk out of my sister's hand—with my left foot.

I do not know why I used my left foot to do this. It is a puzzle to many people as well as to myself, for, although I had displayed a curious interest in my toes at an early age, I had never attempted before this to use either of my feet in any way. They could have been as useless to me as were my hands. That day, however, my left foot, apparently by its own volition, reached out and very impolitely took the chalk out of my sister's hand.

I held it tightly between my toes, and, acting on an impulse, made a wild sort of scribble with it on the slate. Next moment I stopped, a bit dazed, surprised, looking down at the stick of yellow chalk stuck between my toes, not knowing what to do with it next, hardly knowing how it got there. Then I looked up and became aware that everyone had stopped talking and was staring at me silently. Nobody stirred. Mona, her black curls framing her chubby little face, stared at me with great big eyes and open mouth. Across the open hearth, his face lit by flames, sat my father, leaning forward, hands outspread on his knees, his shoulders tense. I felt the sweat break out on my forehead.

My mother came in from the pantry with a steaming pot in her hand. She stopped midway between the table and the fire, feeling the tension flowing through the room. She followed their stare and saw me in the corner. Her eyes looked from my face down to my foot, with the chalk gripped between my toes. She put down the pot.

Then she crossed over to me and knelt down beside me, as she had done so many times before.

"I'll show you what to do with it, Chris," she said, very slowly and in a queer, choked way, her face flushed as if with some inner excitement.

Taking another piece of chalk from Mona, she hesitated, then very deliberately drew, on the floor in front of me, *the single letter "A."*

"Copy that," she said, looking steadily at me. "Copy it, Christy."

I couldn't.

I looked about me, looked around at the faces that were turned towards me, tense, excited faces that were at that moment frozen, immobile, eager, waiting for a miracle in their midst.

The stillness was profound. The room was full of flame and shadow that danced before my eyes and lulled my taut nerves into a sort of waking sleep. I could hear the sound of the water tap dripping in the pantry, the loud ticking of the clock on the mantelshelf, and the soft hiss and crackle of the logs on the open hearth.

I tried again. I put out my foot and made a wild jerking stab with the chalk which produced a very crooked line and nothing more. Mother held the slate steady for me.

"Try again, Chris," she whispered in my ear. "Again."

I did. I stiffened my body and put my left foot out again, for the third time. I drew one side of the letter. I drew half the other side. Then the stick of chalk broke and I was left with a stump. I wanted to fling it away and give up. Then I felt my mother's hand on my shoulder. I tried once more. Out went my foot. I shook, I sweated and strained every muscle. My hands were so tightly clenched that my fingernails bit into the flesh. I set my teeth so hard that I nearly pierced my lower lip. Everything in the room swam till the faces around me were mere patches of white. But—I drew it—*the letter "A."* There it was on the floor before me. Shaky, with awkward, wobbly sides and a very uneven center line. But it *was* the letter "A." I looked up. I saw my mother's face for a moment, tears on her cheeks. Then my father stooped and hoisted me on to his shoulder.

I had done it! It had started—the thing that was to give my mind its chance of expressing itself. True, I couldn't speak with my lips. But now I would speak through something more lasting than spoken words—written words.

That one letter, scrawled on the floor with a broken bit of yellow chalk gripped between my toes, was my road to a new world, my key to mental freedom. It was to provide a source of relaxation to the tense, taut thing that was I, which panted for expression behind a twisted mouth.

□□

Discussion

1. What convinced the doctors, Christy's relatives, and friends that his case was hopeless?

2. Why did Christy's mother refuse to accept the doctors' diagnosis that Christy was an imbecile?

3. (a) At what point in his account does Christy Brown stop relying on his mother's memory and start relying on his own? (b) Explain why the first part of his story would have been more convincing or less convincing if he had based it on his own memory.

4. What does Christy mean when he says that the letter "A" was the key to his mental freedom?

Vocabulary · Dictionary

For the italicized words below choose first the synonym and then the antonym from the list. Write each group of three words on your paper. Use your Glossary for reference. Be sure you can pronounce and spell each italicized word.

1. *inert*
2. *recuperate*
3. *imbecile*
4. *impertinence*
5. *murky*
6. *molten*
7. *taut*
8. *clench*
9. *momentous*

still	active
sicken	slack
solid	stupid
tight	close (tightly)
dark	trivial
melted	smart
sassiness	release
clear	important
politeness	recover

Extension · Reading

Another moving account of how parents' faith, courage, and imagination enabled their child to achieve independence is *For the Love of Anne,* by Claude De Leusse, Manor Books, 1973.

Christy Brown 1932 ·

Christy Brown, as he writes in "The Letter 'A,' " was born in Dublin, Ireland, the tenth child of the twenty-two his mother would bear. Soon after his birth he was discovered to have cerebral palsy. But the steadfast faith of his mother encouraged him to struggle with this grave handicap and to overcome it.

With the help of physical therapy, he enabled himself to write and type with his feet. Through this arduous method, he wrote an autobiography, *My Left Foot* (1954). Then, in 1970, he finished a novel, *Down All the Days,* which brought him world fame. He has become a serious student of human nature. "I've had no choice but to be an observer," he has said, "always on the outside looking in."

Voice of the Writer

"Cardinals Wipe Out Oilers 5-2."

"Cardinals Defeat Oilers 5-2."

"Enemy Soldiers in Full Scale Retreat."

"Enemy Drops Back to Safer Positions."

"My teacher hates me."

"I failed a test."

Examine the above statements. Which of them would you be more likely to accept as an accurate statement of an event? If you are interested in facts and truths, you will have chosen the more *objective* example.

If an author is impersonal, unbiased, and unemotional, his writing is described as *ob-jective.* Which would you expect to be more objective: an autobiographer, one who writes about himself, or a biographer, one who writes about someone else?

Christy Brown, in "The Letter 'A,' " is writing about one of the most important events in his life: that moment when he was suddenly able to communicate with the world outside his own crippled body. Is it at all possible for a person to write about himself un-emotionally? When a writer allows his feelings and personal biases to affect his choice of words, he is *subjective.*

A good biographer always relies upon facts to write his story. His sources are letters, official documents, eyewitness accounts, and often personal experience with his subject or people and places related to his subject.

As you read this unit, ask yourself, does the author indicate his sources of information? Has he relied completely on facts? Does he at any time bring in his own feelings about his subject?

The line between subjectivity and objectivity is not always clear. As a reader, it is your responsibility to judge each work you read. To do so, you must be alert to the degree of subjectivity of an author.

See **STEREOTYPE** Handbook of Literary Terms

from How Long the Heart Remembers

Mary H. Hollingsworth

On the Fourth of July a circus would be in Fitzgerald and would hold a parade down Main Street in the morning. After its afternoon performance, the town was going to block off Main Street and have a big Fourth of July celebration.

In addition, a pilot had landed an airplane right beside the road on the way to town, and anybody could see it that wanted to.

By the time Papa finished describing the wonders, we were wild with excitement. Who would go? Papa for one, he said, not wanting to miss the day for the world. Lillian, Glory, Gregory and I would be bound to go, but Justin couldn't walk the three miles; so the less said in front of him about the trip the better.

The Fourth of July was a real zippity-do-dah day, bright with sunshine, birds singing, flowers blooming. As we set out for town, Papa's steps were as eager and sprightly as our own. We didn't mind walking the dusty road for three miles.

Papa and Gregory wore their overalls, but we girls felt it was almost a Sunday occasion. Since it was impossible for Lillian to walk very far in her high-heeled, too tight shoes, she went barefoot. Since she did, Glory and I did. But we wore our Sunday voile dresses and Lillian her orange-and-gray checked organdy. We felt dressed up despite our bare feet.

From HOW LONG THE HEART REMEMBERS by Mary H. Hollingsworth, pp. 147-153. Copyright © 1976 by Mary H. Hollingsworth. Reprinted by permission of Houghton Mifflin Company and Julian Bach Literary Agency, Inc.

Though we had never seen an airplane, we knew what it was the minute we saw the strange object in a meadow beside the road. We walked all around it, and climbed on its wings, which were made out of the same kind of cloth as tennis shoes. There were a top and a bottom wing held together with a lot of wires and sticks.

The pilot's seat had no top, and how could the pilot stand the rain?

"He has to," Papa said, "because he has to fight German planes while flying. He has a gun right this side of that stick where he can fire the gun and fly all the same time."

"They guide the plane by that little stick?" Glory asked.

"Yes."

"What if they was in the air and the stick broke?"

"I guess the plane would fall to the ground."

We children decided we wouldn't be pilots, and went on to town for the big wonder; for Papa said elephants, lions, tigers, clowns and a band would be in the parade, and we didn't want to miss that.

There were so many people lining the main street it seemed like Judgment Day. By pushing a little Papa made room for us so we could have a good look at the parade.

First, we heard the band playing the rousing tune of "Dixie," and everyone began singing:

> I wish I was in the land ob cotton,
> Old times dar am not forgotten,
> Look away! Look away!
> Look away! Dixie land!

Then they came in sight, red and blue uniforms, brass flashing, the big drum giving a big, loud boom after each line of the song. The cheering people almost drowned out the music, and we hollered along with the rest.

Then came the elephants, their big ears flopping, dressed in their bright red and green saddles; after them, came the cages on wagons pulled by milk-white or coal-black horses with red tassels bouncing. In the cages we saw lions, tigers, leopards and monkeys.

Following on white horses were beautiful ladies dressed in glittering clothes which hurt the eyes to see. All up and down the line of march funny men tumbled, turning somersaults and cartwheels. They had real white faces, big mouths and noses, and were in ragged clothes. Papa said they were clowns to make people laugh. Some did, but we didn't. We felt sorry for them.

As the parade wound to the ball park where the performance would be held, the crowd followed. But Papa told us sorrowfully, "We can't go in the tent to see the performance. It cost money and I ain't got any. But we can go sit on the benches and listen."

So we did, and could hear the music coming from a tent almost as big as the ball park, and once we were sure we heard a lion roar. But our hearts were heavy.

No more than Papa's. His face wore his saddest look as he said, "Next year, if crops are anyways good, we'll have money to go inside."

Our spirits lifted somewhat. Tired of just listening, we went back to the main street. It was a good thing we did. Someone was giving away balloons, candy and cold drinks; men were busy roping off the street, greasing some pigs and setting up a red, white and blue greased pole with a flag floating at the top. Anyone climbing to the top would win a prize and anyone catching a greased pig could have it, a man said.

Papa said, "I shore would love to have me one of them pigs. We don't have one to kill this fall. But I'm so slow and old I'd never catch one." He looked at Gregory and shook his head; hopefully, he eyed Lillian who could move like a scalded dog when she had a mind to. She was strong enough to hold a good-sized shoat, which those greased pigs were.

She caught his eyes. "Now, Papa, I got my Sunday dress on. Besides, I'm a girl, a grown girl, a young lady!"

In plain disgust he looked at us girls. "I can't

see why in tarnation one of you couldn't have been a boy. Or if Walter had only lived——"

"Who's Walter?" Greg asked.

"Your brother, born 'tween Lillian and Glory. He'd a been just the right age to catch me one of them shoats." He sighed deeply.

A roaring overhead made us look up to the sky where that airplane was soaring like a buzzard. Out of it someone was throwing hundreds of blown-up balloons of all colors. People went wild, trying to catch them.

A man climbed onto a wagon. "Ladees and gentlemen!" he hollered. "I'm gonna turn loose six shoats at that white line you see. Anybody catching one can have it. 'Course you think they's a trick in it, and you think right! Them hogs have been coated with axle grease, and you have to catch 'em with bare hands. Come on, men and boys, try to catch you one of these fine hogs!"

Men and boys jostled their way through the crowd to the line. Suddenly, Lillian joined the jostling and made her way to the line. We saw the man come down from the wagon and talk to her. We saw her talking back. The man shook his head, but she kept talking.

At this unheard-of behavior, a gasp went up from the people, but being in a holiday mood, they shouted, "Let 'er run! Bet she can beat 'em all! Let 'er run!"

The man climbed back on the wagon.

When Lillian toed the line with the male contestants, a loud round of applause rose deafeningly. People began to call out, "Run, girl, run!" "Show 'em, gal!" and various other words of encouragement.

As for us, we stood petrified. Papa's face turned fiery red when she started through the crowd, but now all color drained from it. He stood as a stone, his eyes fixed on Lillian. He didn't know whether to be ashamed or proud, but he knew the reason.

As the squealing shoats were turned loose they were given a sharp slap on their rears to incite speed, and they had a good start before the man said, "Go!" to the contestants.

The pigs showed surprising speed; people lining each side of the street made the hogs go forward, though the width of the street gave them leeway for much zigzagging. Since they were glistening with axle grease, it was easy to keep them spotted if eyes moved fast.

Not so with the chasers. The males wore blue shirts and overalls, and were either tripping over each other or sprawling on the ground in snatching at the pigs.

Only Lillian stood out. Her orange checked dress billowed out behind her; her hair, loosed from its pins, streamed out like a banner. Like the others, time after time she went sprawling with hands clawing empty air; but she was doing as well as the males.

Then a pig was caught, then another, proving the pigs could be.

With hearts in our mouths we watched Lillian. When we saw her sprawl forward again and make no effort to get up, our hearts fell clean to our toes. She was all hunched up, and Papa began running to her. Petrified, we stood, and saw a man go to her and bend down. Fear loosed our feet and we ran after Papa, arriving as soon as he.

The man was helping her to her feet and holding onto something with his other arm. Our hearts almost stopped, but shot as high as the sky when we saw the man put a shoat in Lillian's arms.

The people began shouting and cheering until we couldn't hear a word. She handed the pig to Papa, and we made our way to the sidewalk, people making way as if Lillian was real important.

On the sidewalk she faced Papa, crying a little and wiping her nose and face with her hands, which smeared axle grease on her face. "I may not be a boy," she panted, "but I can do anything a boy can. I caught that hog for you!"

He laid a hand on her shoulder. "You're far better than any son *any* man could have! And you're a far better daughter than I deserve!"

He looked at his second daughter with her black-streaked face, her Sunday dress ruined by gaping holes and axle grease, her honey-colored hair blowing about her face, the blood trickling down a leg from a skinned knee, and love for her flooded him.

Handing the prize to Gloria, he took his bandanna and gently wiped her face, then tied the handkerchief around her skinned knee. Someone handed him a rope with which he securely tied the prize before placing it on the sidewalk.

Somewhat awed by Lillian's feat, people made room for us to watch the boys shinny up the greased pole. Only one reached the top, and his prize was a free ride in the airplane. Personally, we didn't envy him.

The glory of the day was fast fading and faded faster when some men had a water fight with fire hose hooked onto fire wagons. Tiring of spraying one another, they suddenly turned the water on the people. All of us were drenched, and Papa said we'd better go home and get on some dry clothes and pen the pig.

People passing in buggies and wagons gazed, some even slowed, at the man in overalls and straw hat, leading a hog by a rope; a small boy with golden ringlets; a tall girl in a torn and dirty dress with a bandanna tied around one knee; and two young girls in dirty white dresses. All looked as if they had fallen into a creek. Had our somewhat ludicrous appearance been known to us, it wouldn't have mattered, for we had seen and heard wondrous things. ☐☐

Discussion

1. What details show that Mary Hollingsworth is describing events that took place during World War I?

2. (a) Describe the father's attitude toward his daughter. **(b)** Cite details from the text that support your description of his attitude.

3. After Lillian catches a pig, her father exclaims, "You're far better than any son *any* man could have!" **(a)** How do you imagine that Lillian reacted to this extraordinary praise? **(b)** Are there some things that girls should not try to do? If so, what are they, and why shouldn't they try to do these things?

Extension · Speaking

Interview a few twenty- to thirty-year-old men and women and a few who are sixty or more years old to learn how their answers to question 3b compares with your own and those of your classmates.

Mary Hollingsworth

Born in Dahlonega, Georgia. Mary Hollingsworth is a daughter of Clifton and Beulah Phillips Head. She received her education in Georgia, North Carolina, and New Mexico.

A former reporter for newspapers in Chapel Hill and Durham, North Carolina, she is now retired and keeps busy with her hobbies of gardening, birdwatching, and creative writing.

It's funny how sometimes you can forget the most important things.
I forgot that I wasn't the kind of guy who could ever go halfway at anything.

Open Letter to a Young Negro

Jesse Owens

U.P.I.

All black men are insane. . . . Almost any living thing would quickly go mad under the unrelenting exposure to the climate created and reserved for black men in a white racist society. . . . I am secretly pleased about the riots. Nothing would please the tortured man inside me more than seeing bigger and better riots every day."

Those words were spoken by Bob Teague to his young son in *Letters to a Black Boy.* He wrote these letters to "alert" his son to "reality" so that the boy wouldn't "be caught off guard—unprepared and undone."

Are his words true?

Does a black man have to be just about insane to exist in America?

Do all Negroes feel a deep twinge of pleasure every time we see a white man hurt and a part of white society destroyed?

Is reality something so stinking terrible that it'll grab your heart out of your chest with one hand and your manhood with the other if you don't meet it armed like a Nazi storm trooper?

Bob Teague is no "militant." He's a constructive, accomplished journalist with a wife and child. If he feels hate and fear, can *you* ever avoid feeling it?

Whether it's Uncle Tom or ranting rioter doing the talking today, you're told that you'll

Reprinted by permission of William Morrow & Company, Inc. from BLACKTHINK: *My Life as Black Man and White Man* by Jesse Owens and Paul G. Neimark. Copyright © 1970 by Jesse Owens and Paul G. Neimark.

have to be afraid and angry. The only difference is that one tells you to hold it in and the other tells you to let it out. Life is going to be torture because you're a Negro, they all say. They only differ on whether you should grin and bear it or take it out on everyone else. But National Urban League official, Black Panther leader or any of the in-betweens all seem to agree on one thing today: "We must organize around our strongest bond—our blackness."

Is that really our strongest bond? Isn't there something deeper, richer, better in this world than the color of one's skin?

Let me tell you the answer to that. Let me prove it to you so strong and deep that you'll taste it for the days to come. Let me throw my arm around your shoulder and walk you to where so much good is and where the only blackness worth fearing is the black they're trying to color your soul.

Even though you weren't born for ten, maybe twenty years after, you've probably heard the story—the story of the 1936 Olympics and how I managed to come out with four gold medals. A lot of words have been written about those medals and about the one for the broad jump in particular. Because it was during that event that Hitler walked out on me and where, in anger, I supposedly fouled on my first two jumps against his prize athlete, Luz Long. The whole Olympics for me and, symbolically, for my country, seemed to rest on that third jump.

Yes, a lot of words have been written about that day and the days that followed. And they've almost been true, just as it's almost true that sometimes every black man weakens a little and does hate the white man, just as it's almost true that reality is tough at times and does make you want to weaken.

Yet, just like *those* "truths," what was written about me was only a half-truth without some other more important words. I want to say them to you now.

I *was* up against it, but long before I came to the broad jump. Negroes had gone to the Olympics before, and Negroes had won before. But so much more was expected of me. Because this was the time of the most intense conflict between dictatorship and freedom the world had ever known. Adolf Hitler was arming his country against the entire world, and almost everyone sensed it. It was ironic that these last Olympic Games before World War II was to split the earth were scheduled for Berlin, where he would be the host. From the beginning, Hitler had perverted the games into a test between two forms of government, just as he perverted almost everything else he touched.

Almost everything else.

The broad jump preliminaries came before the finals of the other three events I was in—the hundred-meter and two-hundred-meter dashes and the relay. How I did in the broad jump would determine how I did in the entire Olympics. For here was where I held a world record that no one had ever approached before except one man: Luz Long, Hitler's best athlete.

Long, a tall, sandy-haired, perfectly built fellow (the ideal specimen of Hitler's "Aryan supremacy"[1] idea), had been known to jump over twenty-six feet in preparing for the Games. No one knew for sure what he could really do because Hitler kept him under wraps. But stories had filtered out that he had gone as far as I had, farther than anyone else in the world. I was used to hearing rumors like that and tried not to think too much about it. Yet the first time I laid eyes on Long, I sensed that the stories hadn't been exaggerated. After he took his first jump, I knew they hadn't. This man was something. I'd have to set an Olympic record and by no small margin to beat him.

It would be tough. August in Berlin was muggier than May in Ann Arbor or Columbus. Yet the air was cool, and it was hard getting warmed up. The ground on the runway to the broad jump pit wasn't the same consistency as that at home. Long was used to it. I wasn't.

His first jump broke the Olympic record. In the trials!

---

1. *"Aryan"* (är'yən) *supremacy,"* a theory that a so-called race of "Aryans," caucasian primitives, were superior to other races.

Did it worry me a little? More than a little. He was on his home ground and didn't seem susceptible to the pressure. In fact, he'd already done one thing I always tried to do in every jumping event and race I ran: discourage the competition by getting off to a better start.

Well, there was only one way to get back the psychological advantage. Right off the bat I'd have to make a better jump than he did. I didn't want to do it that way—it wasn't wise to use up your energy in preliminaries. Long could afford to showboat in the trials. This was his only event, the one he'd been groomed for under Hitler for years. I had to run three races besides, more than any other athlete on either team.

But I felt I had to make a showing right then. I measured off my steps from the takeoff board and got ready. Suddenly an American newspaperman came up to me. "Is it true, Jesse?" he said.

"Is what true?" I answered.

"That Hitler walked out on you? That he wouldn't watch you jump?"

I looked over at where the German ruler had been sitting. No one was in his box. A minute ago he had been there. I could add two and two. Besides, he'd already snubbed me once by refusing the Olympic Committee's request to have me sit in that box.

This was too much. I was mad, hate-mad, and it made me feel wild. I was going to show him. He'd hear about this jump, even if he wouldn't see it!

I felt the energy surging into my legs and tingling in the muscles of my stomach as it never had before. I began my run, first almost in slow motion, then picking up speed, and finally faster and faster until I was moving almost as fast as I did during the hundred-yard dash. Suddenly the takeoff board was in front of me. I hit it, went up, up high—so high I knew I was outdoing Long and every man who ever jumped.

But they didn't measure it. I heard the referee shout "Foul!" in my ears before I even came down. I had run too fast, been concentrating too

much on a record and not enough on form. I'd gone half a foot over the takeoff board.

All the newspaper stories and books I've ever seen about that Olympic broad jump had me fouling on the next of my three tries, because the writers felt that made the story more dramatic. The truth is I didn't foul at all on my second jump.

I played it safe. Too safe. I was making absolutely sure I didn't foul. All right, I said to myself. Long had won his point. But who would remember the preliminaries tomorrow? It was the finals that counted. I had to make sure I got into those finals. I wasn't going to let him psych me out of it. I wasn't going to let Hitler anger me into throwing away what I'd worked ten years for.

So I ran slower, didn't try to get up as high during my jump.

Well, I said to myself, if I can do twenty-six feet trying my best, I sure ought to be able to do a foot less without much effort. That would be enough to qualify for the finals, and there I'd have three fresh jumps again. That's where I'd take apart Luz Long.

It's funny how sometimes you can forget the most important things. I forgot that I wasn't the kind of guy who could ever go halfway at anything. More than that, no sprinter or jumper can really take just a little bit off the top. It's like taking a little bit off when you're working a mathematical equation or flying an airplane through a storm. You need the total concentration and total effort from beginning to end. One mistake and you're dead. More than that, my whole style was geared to giving everything I had, to using all my speed and energy every second of what I was doing. Once or twice I'd tried a distance race just for kicks. I was miserable at it. If I couldn't go all out all the time, I was no good.

So my second jump was no good.

I didn't foul. But I didn't go far enough to qualify, either. It wasn't just Long and Owens in the event anymore. There were dozens of other participants from other countries, and a bunch of them—too many—were now ahead of me.

I had one jump left.

It wasn't enough.

I looked around nervously, panic creeping into every cell of my body. On my right was Hitler's box. Empty. His way of saying I was a member of an inferior race who would give an inferior performance. In back of that box was a stadium containing more than a hundred thousand people, almost all Germans, all wanting to see me fail. On my right was the broad jump official. Was he fair? Yeah. But a Nazi. If it came to a close call, a hairline win-or-lose decision, deep down didn't he, too, want to see me lose? Worst of all, a few feet away was Luz Long, laughing with a German friend of his, unconcerned, confident, *Aryan*.

They were against me. Every one of them. I was back in Oakville[2] again. I was a nigger.

Did I find some hidden resource deep within me, rise to the occasion and qualify for the finals—as every account of those Olympics says?

No.

I found a hidden resource, but it wasn't inside of me. It was in the most unlikely and revealing place possible.

Time was growing short. One by one the other jumpers had been called and taken their turns. What must have been twenty minutes or half an hour suddenly seemed like only seconds. I was going to be called next. I wasn't ready. I wanted to shout it—*I wasn't ready!*

Then the panic was total. I had to walk in a little circle to keep my legs from shaking, hold my jaw closed tight to stop my teeth from chattering. I didn't know what to do. I was lost, with no Charles Riley to turn to. If I gave it everything I had, I'd foul again. If I played it safe, I wouldn't go far enough to qualify. *And this is what it all comes down to*, I thought to myself. *Ten years and 4,500 miles to make a nigger of myself and not even reach the finals!*

And then I couldn't even think anymore. I started to feel faint, began to gasp for breath. Instinctively, I turned away from everyone so they couldn't see me. But I couldn't help hearing them. The thousands of different noises of the stadium congealed into one droning hum—*ch-ch-ch-ch-ch-ch-ch-ch*, louder and louder in my ears. It was as though they were all chanting it. Hatefully, gleefully. *Ch-ch-ch-ch. Ch-ch-ch-ch. CH-CH-CH-CH.*

Suddenly I felt a firm hand on my arm. I turned and looked into the sky-blue eyes of my worst enemy.

"Hello, Jesse Owens," he said. "I am Luz Long."

I nodded. I couldn't speak.

"Look," he said. "There is no time to waste with manners. What has taken your goat?"

I had to smile a little in spite of myself—hearing his mixed-up American idiom.

"Aww, nothing," I said. "You know how it is."

He was silent for a few seconds. "Yes," he said finally, "I know how it is. But I also know you are a better jumper than this. Now, *what has taken your goat?*"

I laughed out loud this time. But I couldn't tell him, him above all. I glanced over at the broad jump pit. I was about to be called.

Luz didn't waste words, even if he wasn't sure of which ones to use.

"Is it what Reichskanzler[3] Hitler did?" he asked.

I was thunderstruck that he'd say it. "I—" I started to answer. But I didn't know what to say.

"I see," he said, "Look, we talk about that later. Now you must jump. And you must qualify."

"But how?" I shot back.

"I have thought," he said. "You are like I am. You must do it one hundred percent. Cor-

---

2. **Oakville,** Oakville, Alabama, where Jesse Owens was raised.
3. **Reichskanzler** (rīнs' kän slr), Hitler's title as leader of Nazi Germany. It means "Imperial Chancellor."

rect?" I nodded. "Yet you must be sure not to foul." I nodded again, this time in frustration. And as I did, I heard the loudspeaker call my name.

Luz talked quickly. "Then you do both things, Jesse. You remeasure your steps. You take off six inches behind the foul board. You jump as hard as you can. But you need not fear to foul."

All at once the panic emptied out of me like a cloudburst.

Of course!

I jogged over to the runway. I remeasured my steps again. Then I put a towel parallel to the place half a foot before the takeoff board from where I wanted to jump.

I walked back to the starting spot. I began my run, hit the place beside the towel, shot up into the air like a bird and qualified by more than a foot.

The next day I went into the finals of the broad jump and waged the most intense competition of my life with Luz Long. He broke his own personal record and the Olympic record, too, and then I—thanks to him—literally flew to top that. Hours before I had won the hundred meters in 10.3, and then afterward the two hundred meters in 20.7 and helped our team to another gold medal and record in the relay.

During the evenings that framed those days, I would sit with Luz in his space or mine in the Olympic village, and we would form an even more intense friendship. We were sometimes as different inside as we looked on the outside. But the things that were the *same* were much more important to us.

Luz had a wife and a young child, too. His was a son. We talked about everything from athletics to art, but mostly we talked about the future. He didn't say it in so many words, but he seemed to know that war was coming and he would have to be in it. I didn't know then whether the United States would be involved, but I did realize that this earth was getting to be a precarious place for a young man trying to make his way. And, like me, even if war didn't come,

Luz wasn't quite sure how he would make the transformation from athletics to life once the Olympics were over.

We talked, of course, about Hitler and what he was doing. Luz was torn between two feelings. He didn't believe in Aryan supremacy any more than he believed the moon was made of German cheese, and he was disturbed at the direction in which Hitler was going. Yet he loved his country and felt a loyalty to fight for it if it came to that, if only for the sake of his wife and son. I couldn't understand how he could go along with Hitler under any circumstances, though, and I told him so.

He wasn't angry when I said it. He just held out his hands and nodded. He didn't explain because he didn't understand completely himself, just as I couldn't explain to him how the United States tolerated the race situation. So we sat talking about these things, some nights later than two Olympic performers should have. We didn't come up with any final answers then, only with a unique friendship. For we were simply two uncertain young men in an uncertain world. One day we would learn the truth, but in the meantime, we would make some mistakes. Luz's mistake would cost him too much.

Yet we didn't make the mistake of not seeing past each other's skin color to what was within. If we couldn't apply that principle to things on a world scale, we still could live it fully in our own way in the few days we had together, the only days together we would ever have.

We made them count. We crammed as much understanding and fun as we could into every hour. We didn't even stop when we got out on the track. Luz was at my side cheering me on for every event, except the broad jump, of course. There he tried to beat me for all he was worth, but nature had put just a little more spring into my body and I went a handful of inches farther.

After he failed in his last attempt to beat me, he leaped out of the pit and raced to my side. To congratulate me. Then he walked toward the stands pulling me with him while Hitler was glaring, held up my hand and shouted to the gigantic crowd, "Jesse Owens! Jesse Owens!"

The stadium picked it up. "Jesse Owens!" they responded—though it sounded more like *"Jaz-eee-ooh-wenz."* Each time I went for a gold medal and a record in the next three days, the crowd would greet me with *"Jaz-eee-ooh-wenz! Jaz-eee-ooh-wenz!"*

I'd had people cheering me before, but never like this. Many of those men would end up killing my countrymen, and mine theirs, but the truth was that they didn't want to, and would only do it because they "had" to. Thanks to Luz, I learned that the false leaders and sick movements of this earth must be stopped in the beginning, for they turn humanity against itself.

Luz and I vowed to write each other after the Games, and we did. For three years we corresponded regularly, though the letters weren't always as happy as our talks at the Olympics had been. Times were hard for me and harder for Luz. He had had to go into the German army, away from his wife and son. His letters began to bear strange postmarks. Each letter expressed more and more doubt about what he was doing. But he felt he had no other choice. He was afraid for his family if he left the army. And how could they leave Germany? It was Luz's world, just as the South had been the only world for so many Negroes.

The last letter I got from him was in 1939. "Things become more difficult," he said, "and I am afraid, Jesse. Not just the thought of dying. It is that I may die for the wrong thing. But whatever might become of me, I hope only that my wife and son will stay alive. I am asking you who are my only friend outside of Germany, to someday visit them if you are able, to tell them about why I had to do this, and how the good times between us were. Luz."

I answered right away, but my letter came back. So did the next, and the one after. I inquired about Luz through a dozen channels. Nothing. A war was on. Finally, when it was over, I was able to get in touch with Luz's wife and find out what had happened to him. He was buried somewhere in the African desert.

Luz Long had been my competition in the Olympics. He was a white man—a Nazi white man who fought to destroy my country.

I loved Luz Long, as much as my own brothers. I still love Luz Long.

I went back to Berlin a few years ago and met his son, another fine young man. And I told Karl about his father. I told him that, though fate may have thrown us against one another, Luz rose above it, rose so high that I was left with not only four gold medals I would never have had, but with the priceless knowledge that the only bond worth anything between human beings is their humanness.

Today there are times when that bond doesn't seem to exist. I know. I felt the same way before my third jump at the 1936 Olympics, as well as a thousand other times. There've been many moments when I did feel like hating the white man, all white men, felt like giving in to fearful reality once and for all.

But I've learned those moments aren't the real me. And what's true of me is true of most men I've met. My favorite speech in a movie is the scene in *High Noon* when Gary Cooper, alone and hunted by the four sadistic killers, momentarily weakens and saddles a horse to get out of town. Like everyone else, his deputy wants him to do it and helps him. But Cooper finally won't get up on the horse.

"Go on!" his deputy shouts. "Do it!"

"I can't do it," Cooper says.

"You were going to a minute ago!"

"I was tired," Cooper tells him. "A man thinks a lotta things when he's tired. But I *can't do it.*"

We all get tired. But know yourself, know your humanness, and you'll know why you can never finally throw in with the bigotry of black-think. You must not be a Negro. You must be a human being first and last, if not always.

Reach back, Harry Edwards. Reach back inside yourself and grapple for that extra ounce of guts, that last cell of manhood even you didn't know you had, that something that let you stand the pain and beat the ghetto and go on to break the records. Use it now to be totally honest with yourself.

For when the chips are really down, you can either put your skin first or you can go with what's inside it.

Sure, there'll be times when others try to keep you from being human. But remember that prejudice isn't new. It goes way back, just as slavery goes way back, to before there ever was an America. Men have always had to meet insanity without losing their own minds.

That doesn't mean you should stand still for bigotry. Fight it. Fight it for all you're worth. But fight your own prejudice, too. Don't expect protection in your white brother until there's not an ounce of blackthink left in you. And remember that the hardest thing in all of us isn't to fight, but to stop and think. *Black, think* . . . is the opposite of . . . *blackthink.*

I'm not going to play any establishment games with you. My way isn't its own reward. Self-knowledge, getting rid of the bitterness, a better life, are the rewards.

So be a new kind of "militant," an *immoderate moderate,* one hundred percent involved but as a man, not a six-foot hunk of brown wrapping paper, be an extremist when it comes to your ideals, a moderate when it comes to the raising of your fist.

Live every day deep and strong. Don't pass up *your* Olympics and *your* Luz Long. Don't let the blackthinkers sell you out for a masquerade rumble where the real you can never take off the mask.

You see, black *isn't* beautiful.
White isn't beautiful.
Skin-deep is *never* beautiful.

□ □

notes and comments

"He who knows a Why of living surmounts almost every How."
Nietzsche

Yes, but are you willing to die for it?" "That's all very well for you to say, but . . ." "If I were you . . ." "Can you imagine what he did?" "Beautiful!" "The most disgusting thing I ever saw." "It'll never fly, Orville." "Now there is a man's man." "You male chauvinist, you!" "Now, now—no need for violence."

How often have you heard remarks such as the ones above? Have you been able to hear them without reacting in some way? Either you agree with the speaker or you disagree or you say to yourself, "Who cares?" But whichever way you respond, you are responding according to your values.

How does a person develop values? Every moment you live, you are *experiencing* life, and from these experiences, you are *learning.* So, when you have an experience similar to a previous one, you automatically make a *judgment* and *behave* accordingly. The way you behave is a reflection of your *values.*

So it is with an author. Whether he is writing an essay or biography or autobiography, he chooses his words and incidents carefully and then puts them together in a way that will communicate his values.

Making Judgments

When you read Jesse Owens's "Open Letter to a Young Negro," you cannot come away with the idea that he is in favor of violence.

A good author will not necessarily convince you that his values are the correct ones, but he should at least lead you to question yours.

Authors have learned from their experiences and made judgments based upon their values. Now you, as a reader, must judge their values based upon your own experiences and values. If an author has caused you to react in some way and perhaps given you some insight into yourself, then his effort has been successful.

Discussion

1. (a) What caused Jesse Owens almost to foul out in qualifying for the broad jump? **(b)** In what way did Luz Long come to his aid?

2. (a) What could Owens not understand about Long? **(b)** What could Long not understand about Owens?

3. State in your own words what Owens learned from his experience with Long.

4. (a) Does Owens say that blacks should not fight for the rights of blacks? **(b)** Explain his use of the term "immoderate moderate."

5. (a) What do you think is the purpose of an open letter? **(b)** What might the writer achieve through an open letter that he could not achieve in a formal article or essay?

Extension · Writing

1. Choose some aspect of life today which you feel is unjust. Write an open letter to someone you believe will understand your feelings about this issue. Include your own personal experiences relating to the situation and/or the experience.

2. If the last sentence in Jesse Owens's letter "Skin-deep is *never* beautiful" suggests or recalls any experience of your own that reinforces this statement, recount the experience in a letter or essay.

Jesse Owens 1913 ·

A native Alabaman, Jesse Owens first began breaking track records while attending Fairview Junior High in Cleveland, Ohio. Afterwards, he continued breaking them, reaching his peak while at Ohio State University. In one day (May 25, 1935), he broke three world records.

His greatest achievements were at the 1936 Olympic Games in Berlin, which he described in his "Open Letter." There he won four gold medals and embarrassed Adolf Hitler and his "master race" theories.

After graduating from Ohio State in 1937, he retired from sports to work as a businessman, then, as a member of the Illinois Athletic Commission. He devoted his life to promoting sports and assisting promising young athletes.

The Legend of Amelia Earhart

Pete Hamill

Bettmann Archive

Amelia Earhart was born in Atchison, Kansas, on July 24, 1898. Her father Edwin was a railroad lawyer, a small, precise man with a streak of brooding melancholy that he often drowned in hard drinking. Her mother, Amy Otis Earhart, the daughter of the most prominent judge in town, was by all accounts a remarkable woman; influenced by the first wave of American feminism, but still a prisoner of the rigid social codes of her day.

The marriage was tense from the beginning, as Judge Otis attempted to impose his will on the lives of his daughter and her husband. Earhart was away a lot, in his work as a claims agent, and sometimes he took his wife along with him. The result was that Amelia and her younger sister Muriel spent much of their childhood living with their grandparents. Amelia had a rich fantasy life, and lived adventurous summers exploring caves, playing baseball with equipment given to her by her father, reading Scott, Dickens, George Eliot; but she must have learned early on that she was essentially alone.

"I was a horrid little girl," she said later. "Perhaps the fact that I was exceedingly fond of reading made me endurable. With a large library to browse in, I spent many hours not bothering anyone after I once learned to read."

The family moved to Des Moines in 1907, apparently to escape the domination of the grandparents, and on her tenth birthday, Amelia saw her first airplane. That day, her father took her to the Iowa State Fair; it was only five years after the Wright Brothers had first flown at Kitty Hawk (incidentally, with money provided by a Wright sister) and airplanes were a great curiosity. Amelia, however, was not impressed.

"It was a thing of rusty wire and wood," she wrote in 1937. "I was much more interested in an absurd hat made of an inverted peach-basket which I had just purchased for fifteen cents. . . . Today I loathe hats for more than a few minutes on the head and am sure I should pass by the niftiest creation if an airplane were anywhere around."

She went through six schools before finally graduating from Hyde Park High School in Chicago in 1916. In the yearbook she was described as "the girl in brown, who walks alone." Her mother then insisted on sending her to the Ogontz finishing school in Philadelphia, and she was at Ogontz in 1917 when the Americans entered the First World War. At Christmas she traveled to Toronto to visit her sister Muriel, who was then attending St. Margaret's School.

"Canada had been in the war four weary years—years the United States will never appreciate," Amelia wrote later. "Four men on crutches, walking together on King Street in Toronto that winter, was a sight which changed the course of existence for me."

Amelia quit the Ogontz school, and went to work as a nurse's aide for the Canadian Red Cross, caring for shell-shocked veterans. Much of her work was routine and boring, but the impact of sustained intimate contact with these wounded men was clearly profound; in later life, Amelia was a pacifist.

Toronto was also the place where she saw her second airplane, and its impact was considerably different from the one she saw when she was ten.

"A young woman friend and I had gone to the fair grounds to see an exhibition of stunt-flying by one of the aces returned from the war," she remembered later. Amelia and her friend, dressed in their nurses' uniforms, moved to a clearing to get a better view. The pilot went through a repertory of stunts.

"After fifteen or twenty minutes of stunting, the pilot began to dive at the crowd," she wrote. "Looking back as a pilot I think I understand why. He was bored."

Then he saw Amelia and her friend in the open clearing, and started to swoop down on them, too. The friend broke and ran. Amelia stood still, watching the plane come at her.

"I remember the mingled fear and pleasure which surged over me as I watched that small

From "Leather and Pearls: The Cult of Amelia Earhart" by Pete Hamill, *MS.*, September 1976. © 1976 Ms. Magazine Corp. Reprinted by permission.

plane at the top of its earthward swoop. Common sense told me that if something went wrong with the mechanism, or if the pilot lost control, he, the airplane, and I would be rolled up in a ball together. . . . I believe that little red airplane said something to me as it swished by."

The sensuality of that moment of embrace stayed with her all of her life. In the fall of 1919, she moved to New York, and enrolled in a premed course at Columbia University, where she "started in to do the peculiar things they do who would be physicians. I fed orange juice to mice and dissected cockroaches." She took a heavy load of subjects, but she didn't forget flying.

In the summer of 1920, she went on vacation to California, where her parents had moved to start a new life after the death of her grandparents. On that trip, her father took her to an air meet. The planes were old wartime Jennies and Canucks, the pilots all members of that first swaggering generation of barnstormers. The commercial airline industry had not yet been established; the skies were still empty. Amelia was enthralled.

"One thing I knew that day," she wrote. "I wanted to fly." She decided not to return to the university.

At first, she was too shy to ask about flying lessons, afraid that the all-male world of aviation would snicker at the arrival of a woman in the ranks; she had her father ask on her behalf. He arranged for her to take a trial hop, as a passenger. "I am sure he thought one ride would be enough for me," she wrote later, "and he might as well act to cure me promptly."

The pilot was Frank Hawks, a slim, handsome man in the classic *macho* style, who was to become a famous aviator. Hawks insisted that another pilot accompany them on the flight in the event that Amelia turned out to be a "nervous lady." They flew out over the still smog-free green earth of Southern California, with the hills of Hollywood to one side and the vast blue Pacific on the other. Amelia was not a nervous lady. When the plane landed, she was determined to raise the five hundred dollars she would need for a twelve-hour course of instruction.

"Two things deterred me at that moment," she remembered. "One was the tuition fee to be wrung from my father, and the other the determination to look up a woman flier. . . . I felt I should be less self-conscious taking lessons with her, than with the men, who overwhelmed me with their capabilities."

The flier was Neta Snook, the first woman to graduate from the Curtiss School of Aviation, and a good instructor. Amelia took the first of twenty-eight jobs she was to hold in the next years—as a file clerk at the telephone company—in order to pay for her lessons, and Snook extended credit. Amelia, who had once taken a course in auto mechanics just to see what an automobile engine was made of, found herself as interested in the aircraft engines and design as she was in flying itself. When the phone-company money did not cover her expenses, she took another job, driving a truck for a sand and gravel company.

It was an exhilarating time, and Amelia soon was deeply involved in the life of airports. She learned to play rummy with the mechanics. She chopped her hair short, so that her leather helmet fitted snugly.

"I remember so well my first leather coat," she said later. "It was 1922. Somehow I'd contrived to save twenty dollars. With it I bought—at a very special sale—an elegant leather coat. *Patent* leather! Shiny and lovely. But suddenly I saw that it looked *too* new. How were people to think that I was a flier if I was wearing a flying coat that was brand-new? Wrinkles! That was it. There just had to be wrinkles. So—I slept in it for three nights to give my coat a properly veteran appearance."

Meanwhile, Neta Snook had gone broke and was forced to sell her plane. Amelia finally soloed under the guidance of a veteran named John Montijo. But even with her license in her pocket, she still did not know what to do with her life: the commercial aviation business was very young and there was no room in it for women.

Amelia studied photography and worked in a professional darkroom. She had a few secretarial jobs. She plowed all this money into the world of flying. In 1922, in a small open cockpit Kinner Canary, she flew to fourteen thousand feet, establishing her first world's record: highest altitude attained by a woman pilot.

Characteristically, she then tried to break her own record, and almost ended in disaster. "From the sight of cities and the glistening sea two miles below," she wrote about that dangerous attempt, "I plunged into a rolling bank of clouds. There was snow inside. It stung my face and plastered my goggles. At eleven thousand feet the snow changed to sleet, and at about twelve thousand, dense fog enveloped me. Unbelievably—until you've tried it—human sensations fail when one is thus 'blind.' Deprived of a horizon, a flier may lose the feel of his position in space. Was I flying one wing high? Was I turning? I couldn't be sure. I tried to keep the plane in flying trim, with one wish growing stronger every moment—to see the friendly earth again. Spinning was the quickest way down my inexperience could suggest. And so I spun. Seconds seemed very long, until I saw clear weather several thousand feet above the world I knew."

On the ground, the man at the field was angry. "Show a little sense," he said. "Suppose the clouds had closed in until they touched the ground. We'd have had to dig you out in pieces."

"Yes," Amelia said, "I suppose you would."

Flying at last, but with no clear objective in sight, Amelia started feeling like "another sunkist victim of inertia." She had bought a small airplane, but in the spring of 1925, partly because of pressure from her parents and friends, she decided to sell it, buy a car, and drive back to the East Coast; perhaps to become a teacher. Her mother, whose marriage had not improved with a change of locale, went with her on the long drive across the country.

In 1927, after some study at Harvard and Columbia, she went to work as a sixty-dollars-a-month social worker at Denison House in Boston, one of the largest settlement houses in the country. Amelia plunged into the work, dealing with the educational and emotional problems of the immigrant kids who came there every day. But the period wasn't all work; she also bought herself a yellow Kissel convertible, and she would often load it up with the settlement-house kids for rides into the country, or take it out herself when she felt the need for solitude.

She kept up her interest in aviation, but the crowded East Coast was still far behind the open places of the West. She joined the Boston chapter of the National Aeronautic Association, became one of the five board members of an early commercial aircraft concern, and had discussions with another great woman flier of the era, Ruth Nichols, about the need to establish a national association of women pilots. (These talks later led to the founding of the Ninety-Nines, an organization that still exists.) But the days of the flying circuses were fading, buried by a blizzard of new federal and state safety regulations, and the big-money people were moving into the business to ensure ownership of its future. By 1928, her aviation dream had so far receded that Amelia was reduced to being a judge of a model airplane contest sponsored by the Boston Playground Association.

Then one morning, Amelia Earhart received a phone call. "I remember when called to the phone I replied I couldn't answer unless the message was more important than entertaining many little Chinese and Syrian children. The word came assuring me that it was."

The voice on the other end belonged to a press agent named Hilton H. Railey, and he wanted to know whether Amelia was interested in becoming the first woman to fly the Atlantic. At first she thought it was either a joke or a more sinister proposition; on at least two occasions bootleggers had asked her to fly a certain cargo from a certain place to a certain other place. She asked Railey for references. He was legitimate; one of his clients was Commander Richard E.

Byrd. She went to see Railey at his Boston office and started getting the full story.

He told her that a trimotored Fokker, the same airplane that Byrd flew to the South Pole, had recently been purchased by Mrs. Amy Guest. At first Mrs. Guest said that she wanted to fly the Atlantic herself, but her family objected. In those days, even after Lindbergh's historic crossing, the flight was perilous; plane after plane had disappeared in the ocean. Radio equipment was primitive; so was weather information. Deicers had not been developed, so that some planes found themselves paralyzed with up to five hundred pounds of ice.

But Mrs. Guest was determined that a woman should fly the Atlantic. If she could not do it, then it should be someone else. She asked a friend, George Palmer Putnam, to find a suitable woman, and Putnam (whose family owned the publishing concern of G. P. Putnam's) had asked Railey to help. He poked around at Boston airports, and was told about the young woman from Denison House named Amelia Earhart. He was very impressed when he saw her: not by her obvious intelligence, or her more than five hundred hours of flying time, but by her physical resemblance to Charles Lindbergh. Visions of "Lady Lindy" bounced in his head. He reported this to Putnam, and an anxious Amelia was summoned to New York.

"I was interviewed by David T. Laymen, Jr., and John S. Phipps," she wrote, "and found myself in a curious situation. If they did not like me at all, or found me wanting in too many respects, I would be deprived of the trip. If they liked me too well, they might be loath to drown me. It was, therefore, necessary for me to maintain an attitude of impenetrable mediocrity. Apparently I did, because I was chosen."

The weeks that followed were nerve-racking. Amelia, who was to be paid absolutely nothing for the flight, was going only as a passenger. The pilot, a hard-drinking veteran named Wilmer "Bull" Stultz, was being paid twenty thousand dollars; his mechanic, Lou "Slim" Gordon, was to receive five thousand dollars. But the Atlantic had already been flown; the true novelty of this flight was that its passenger was a woman. The sponsors did not want the rest of the world to know their plans, because someone carrying a woman might beat them across the Atlantic; the result was that Amelia was kept away from the airport, where Stultz and Gordon were working on the plane. Among other things, she wrote some "popping off" letters to her parents, in the event that the *Friendship*, as the plane was called, followed so many others into the Atlantic. The letters were sealed and not discovered until 1937.

"Dearest Dad:

"Hooray for the last grand adventure! I wish I had won, but it was worth while anyway. You know that. I have no faith we'll meet anywhere again, but I wish we might.

"Anyway, good-bye and good luck to you.

"Affectionately, your doter. Mill."

To her mother she wrote: "Even though I have lost, the adventure was worth while. Our family tends to be too secure. My life has really been very happy, and I don't mind contemplating its end in the midst of it."

There was a third letter—to her sister Muriel—which was opened and shown to the press on the morning that Amelia and the *Friendship* took off from Boston Harbor.

"Dear Scrappy," it began. "I have tried to play for a large stake and if I succeed all will be well. If I don't, I shall be happy to pop off in the midst of such an adventure. My only regret would be leaving you and mother stranded for a while. . . .

"Sam [Chapman] will tell you the whole story. Please explain all to mother. I couldn't stand the added strain of telling mother and you personally.

"If reporters talk to you, say you knew, if you like . . .   Yours respectfully, Sister."

Throughout the days before departing Boston, the biggest problem was weather.

"When it was right in Boston, the mid-

Atlantic was foreboding," Amelia wrote. "I have a memory of long gray days which had a way of dampening our spirits against our best efforts to be cheerful."

Finally, they departed Boston on June 3, 1928, only to find themselves bogged down for another two weeks in Trespassey, Newfoundland. Stultz could not eat fish, and existed on candy bars and booze; they wandered around the tiny town, examined and reexamined the engines and pontoons, and waited for the weather to break. On the morning of the 17th, they finally took off. Amelia began to keep a detailed log of the flight, which later became a book, *20 Hours, 40 Minutes*. Some excerpts:

"Marvelous shapes in white stand out, some trailing shimmering veils. The clouds look like icebergs in the distance. . . . I think I am happy— sad admission of scant intellectual equipment."

"I am getting housemaid's knee kneeling here gulping beauty."

"How marvelous is a machine and the mind that made it. I am thoroughly occidental in this worship."

"Port motor coughing a bit. Sounds like water. We are going to go into, under, or over a storm. I don't like to, with one motor acting the way it is."

"Himmel! The sea! We are three thousand. Patchy clouds. We have been jazzing from one thousand to five thousand where we now are, to get out of clouds."

"Can't use radio at all. Coming down now in a rather clear spot. Twenty-five hundred feet. Everything sliding forward."

"8:50. Two Boats!!!!"

"Try to get bearing. Radio won't. One hour's gas. Mess. All craft cutting our course. Why?"

The answer to the "Why?" was land. They had made it across the Atlantic, and came down over the harbor of Burry Port, Wales. Amelia Earhart was famous.

The fame was sudden and all-encompassing. She was on all the front pages of the world, posing in a borrowed dress, smiling and giving credit for everything to Stultz and Gordon. As Railey had hoped, the papers started to call her "Lady Lindy." She was feted in London. Her arrival in New York brought the kind of ticker-tape parades reserved for heroes. She was interviewed, photographed, mauled for autographs and souvenirs.

And waiting for her was George Palmer Putnam. He was a promoter, a gifted writer, a bit of a con man, who had been a newspaperman, Mayor of Bend, Oregon, and soldier before joining the family publishing firm. That was the era of adventure, and Putnam concentrated on the great books of exploration. His greatest coup was in signing Lindbergh to write *We* for $100,000, after the famous solo flight. Now he wanted Lady Lindy. Brash, complex, irritating, driven, Putnam was by all accounts a remarkable character. They were married in February, 1931.

Most of her public life is a matter of record, and in the years after her marriage, she lived most of her life in public. She broke record after record; she campaigned for Franklin Roosevelt and once took Eleanor up for a midnight ride; she spoke out on women's issues, looking for "the day when women . . . will be individuals free to live their lives as men are free."

But Amelia always had something more personal to prove. "I wanted to make another flight alone," she wrote. "I wanted to justify myself to myself. I wanted to prove that I deserved at least a small fraction of the nice things said about me. . . . I already had the credit—heaped up and running over. I wanted to deposit a little security to make that credit good. Illogical? Perhaps. Most of the things we want are illogical."

The flight alone was to make up for the *Friendship*. She wanted to cross the Atlantic, flying the plane herself, with no one around to help. Again working in secret, to avoid the added pressure of heavy publicity, she took a Lockheed from Teterboro airport in New Jersey to Harbor Grace, Newfoundland. And on Friday, May 20, 1932, she took off. The journey was rough. Her altimeter failed, so that in fog she could not truly determine how close she was to the ocean. At one point, the plane iced up and went into a spin. "How long we spun I do not know. . . . As we righted and held level again, through the blackness below I could see the whitecaps too close for comfort."

Then a fire broke out in the manifold ring of her engine. "There was nothing to do about it," she said. "There was no use turning back, for I knew I couldn't land at Harbor Grace in the dark even if I could find my way. And I didn't want to roll up in a ball with all that gasoline. . . . So it seemed sensible to keep going."

The fire kept burning in the exhaust manifold, and she discovered she had a leaky fuel gauge. As the hours dragged on, she knew she would soon have to go down. And then she saw land. She circled over green hills, and landed in a pasture. Cows scattered in all directions, and a man came rushing out of a farmhouse.

"I've come from America," Amelia said.

"Do ye be tellin' me that now?" said Dan McCallion, and she knew she was in Ireland. She was exuberant. For the first time, after everything else she had done, Amelia Earhart felt that her fame was for real.

As she moved deeper into her own and the century's thirties, Amelia started to feel that time was beginning to run out. The old flying-by-the-seat-of-the-pants days were clearly over; the commercial giants were beginning to eat up or eliminate their smaller competitors. Amelia continued to set records, from Hawaii to Oakland, from Mexico City to Newark and more. She campaigned for Roosevelt in the 1936 election. She took a job as counselor in careers for women at Purdue University, and, with the financial help of Purdue, began to plan one last flight, in a Lockheed Electra fitted out as a flying laboratory. She wanted to fly around the world at the equator, a distance of 27,000 miles. Others had flown around the world, but only via the shorter northern route.

"I have a feeling," she told a reporter in 1937, "that there is just about one more good flight left in my system, and I hope this trip is it."

The last flight remains mysterious to this day, shrouded in unsolved speculation. Was she on a secret reconnaissance trip for the government; an early intelligence pilot under orders from Roosevelt? Was she captured and imprisoned or killed by the Japanese? No one knows for sure. The first phase of this last adventure ended in March, 1937, when Amelia's overloaded Lockheed Electra crashed on the runway at Pearl Harbor. The plane was badly damaged, but Amelia was not injured. The plane was then taken apart by Lockheed engineers and shipped back to Burbank for repairs. It has never been determined exactly who paid for these repairs.

Between March and June, when the second phase started, a number of events took place. The route was altered, a fact noted by those who speculate about a reconnaissance mission. Instead of traveling around the world by going west, the route was changed to follow an Oakland-Miami-South America-Africa-Asia-Australia course, with the final 2,600-mile hop from Lae, New Guinea, to Howland Island in the mid-Pacific, the most dangerous part of the flight.

In addition, Fred Noonan became the sole navigator. Earlier, Amelia was helped by Paul Mantz on technical matters, and Captain Harry Manning was to be the navigator for part of the flight, with Noonan as his assistant. But Manning canceled after the Honolulu crash, and Mantz was busy on movie work.

Noonan was a legendary character in aviation. He had served as a maritime navigator, transport pilot, navigational instructor, manager of the Port-au-Prince airport in Haiti, and then inspector of all Pan Am airports. He had survived World War I torpedoing, and helped Pan Am map its routes across the Pacific. Nobody knew the Pacific better than Fred Noonan.

Noonan had lost his job with Pan Am because of his heavy drinking, but he had told friends that the flight with Amelia was to be a "second chance." And Amelia insisted she had faith in him.

The official story of the "Last Flight" is told in Amelia's book of that title (compiled by

Putnam after her disappearance from letters, reports, and cables sent along the way). They took off from Miami on June 1 heading south to the equator and east around the world. After a month of grueling flight, they set out on the last lap of the journey. They never reached Howland Island.

There are many theories about the disappearance; writers have gone over the trail in considerable detail. Even Amelia's mother doubted the official version of events. In 1949, she said: "Amelia told me many things, but there were some things she couldn't tell me. I am convinced she was on some sort of a government mission, probably on verbal orders."

If Amelia was on a spy mission, it is most likely that she changed planes in Port Darwin, Australia, picking up another Lockheed Electra specially fitted with cameras. The political rationale for this theory includes Roosevelt's position then: he was unable to end the Depression and wanted heavy defense spending, but faced a Congress reluctant to spend money on guns when there were millions of unemployed Americans walking the streets. If Roosevelt could prove through photographs that Japan was building major naval bases on Saipan and Truk, he would get his defense bill. And in the event that Amelia and Noonan did not make it back, their disappearance would justify a massive sea-and-air search and the Americans could get their photographs anyway.

This in fact is precisely what happened. After the disappearance, a massive sea-and-air search was conducted, covering 400,000 square miles of the Pacific; some sixty-five airplanes were used; American ships moved freely through areas that were previously off limits. In January, Roosevelt got the largest peacetime naval spending bill of his first two administrations.

Meanwhile, there was genuine grief over Amelia's disappearance. Newspapers were full of the story. Tributes poured in. Statues were erected to her. Schools were named for her. After eighteen months, she was declared legally dead. Putnam married twice more, wrote some books, and died in 1950. The commercial airlines froze out women pilots, an event that might not have happened had Amelia still been around to lead a public fight. The old small planes went into the scrap heaps or the museums. Jets arrived. The DC-3 became the 707 which became the 747. Men landed on the moon. America had no women astronauts, and many years elapsed before there was even one woman pilot of a major airline.

And yet, Amelia Earhart seems more alive and more relevant now than she has been since the days of her glory. Perhaps that is why rumors still drift to the surface: she is living in Japan, having survived a wartime concentration camp; she is living in New Jersey, still guarding the secret of her wartime mission by allowing the public to believe her dead. Like male heroes who were thought to live on after death, from Alexander through Zapata,[1] she fulfilled some need in us for the heroic spirit, and so we cannot quite bear to believe that she is gone. □ □

---

1. **Alexander through Zapata,** Alexander the Great (356–323 B.C.) king of Macedonia, one of the greatest leaders of ancient times. Emiliano Zapata (e′mē lyä′nô sä pä′tä) (1879–1919) was a Mexican revolutionist who fought for land reform.

Editor's note: A newspaper article on April 12, 1978, stated that former Air Force pilot Vincent Loomis of Orlando, Florida, had left on a seven-member expedition to find again, a wrecked plane he spotted twenty-five years ago northwest of Howland Island. He believes the plane is Amelia Earhart's.

Discussion

1. What experiences influenced Amelia Earhart's wanting to fly?

2. Explain the meaning of the following statement: "Flying at last, but with no clear objective in sight, Earhart started feeling like 'another sunkist victim of inertia.'"

3. Consider the jobs that Earhart held before her first flight across the Atlantic and her university studies. What do they tell you about her interests and her values?

4. (a) How did you react when you read that Hilton Railey, a press agent, "wanted to know whether Earhart was interested in becoming the first woman to fly the Atlantic"? (b) How did you react when you discovered that she was going only as a passenger?

5. (a) When they reported that she had been the first woman passenger to fly across the Atlantic, why did papers all over the world refer to Earhart as "Lady Lindy"? (b) Explain why you think that "Lady Lindy" was or was not an appropriate title then. (c) Explain why you think "Lady Lindy" is or is not an appropriate title for Amelia Earhart now.

Vocabulary · Pronunciation

Use your Glossary to answer the questions about the pronunciation of each italicized word below. Be sure you know the definition of each, as well as the spelling.

1. Where is the accent in *deter?*

2. Does the first syllable of *exuberant* rhyme with *pecks* or *leg?*

3. How many syllables are in *repertory?* Is the first syllable break following the first *e* or the *p?*

4. Are the syllables of *pontoon* divided between the *n* and *t* or the *t* and *o?*

5. Does the first *c* of *occident* have a *k* or an *s* sound?

6. How many syllables are there in *grueling?*

7. Is the *t* of *inertia* pronounced as *t* or as *sh?*

8. Does the accented syllable of *impenetrable* rhyme with *wren, may,* or *skimp?*

Pete Hamill 1935 ·

Although his formal education was limited, Hamill had always liked to read and write, and by the time he started work at sixteen in the Brooklyn Navy Yard he had been writing and illustrating stories for several years.

Following a stint in the Navy, he enrolled in a night school, where a teacher, Tom McMahon, taught him how to read critically, and how to write. "More than anything else, McMahon taught me that words meant something. They were not typographical ornaments; they were not to be slapped around the page with abandon. They were to be used with care, even love . . ."

When he was twenty-five, Hamill finally got a chance to work as a professional writer, and he has been one ever since. He wrote the article about Amelia Earhart because his ten-year-old daughter was fascinated by her, and because his talks with people who had known Earhart convinced him that she was a genuine hero.

Read the poem "Flight." Then answer the questions below, either in small groups or in a whole class discussion.

1. What ideas or details about Earhart do the poem and the prose selection have in common?

2. What ideas or details about Earhart are in the poem in addition to those in the prose selection?

3. (a) If you could choose only one of these two selections to share with someone who knew nothing about Earhart, which one would you choose? Why? **(b)** If you could select only one of the two to share with someone who already knew a great deal about her, which would you choose? Why?

Flight

for Amelia Earhart

Pamela Alexander

A series of white squares, each
an hour's flying time, each with instructions
in pencil: the organized adventure. "Carelessness
offends the spirit of Ulysses." She suspends herself,
5 as he did, in the elements, finds
reason turns to motion, caution to design.
"One ocean led naturally to
another." The earth led naturally to the sky
after a look at a thing of wood and wire
10 at the state fair in Des Moines, after the sting
of snow blown from the skis of training planes
near Philadelphia.
                 The rumble of the red and gold
Electra wakes the air, shakes stars
15 down their strings until
they hang outside the cockpit, close enough
to touch. The squares, short days,
take turns showing her senses
what to do. The fragrance of blooming
20 orange orchards carries to considerable
altitudes. "No one has seen a tree
who has not seen it from the air, with
its shadow." Lake Chad is huge, shallow,
brightened by the wings of cranes and maribou
25 storks. The Red Sea is blue; the White and Blue Niles,
green; the Amazon delta a party of currents,
brown and yellow, distinct. Beyond

the clutter of sensations, the shriek and clatter
of tools at landing fields, she prepares
30 herself, like the engine, for
one thing. Flight
above the wine-dark shining flood
is order, makes the squares
come and go, makes the plane
35 a tiny gear that turns the world. "Of all those things

"Flight" by Pamela Alexander. From THE ARDIS ANTHOLOGY OF NEW AMERICAN POETRY, Ardis/Ann Arbor. Copyright © 1977 by Ardis. Reprinted by permission of the author.

external to the task at hand, we clutch
what we can.''
                         She leaves the plane briefly to join
a crowd of Javanese walking up a beautiful mountain.
40 They laugh and talk, they carry baskets
and various loads on poles. ''Sometime
I hope to stay somewhere as long as I like.'' For

the last long passage she abandons personal items,
souvenirs; also the parachute, useless over the Pacific.
45 The plane staggers with the weight of fuel.
The squares arrive,
live in her,
subside. The plane
is lighter, then
50 light. The last square has
an island in it, but does not
show her where.

Bettmann Archive

The eyes and ears of the Gestapo were everywhere,
and every day more and more Jews asked her to help them escape.

The Secret Room

Corrie ten Boom
with John and Elizabeth Sherrill

It was Sunday, May 10, 1942, exactly two years after the fall of Holland. The sunny spring skies, the flowers in the lamppost boxes, did not at all reflect the city's mood. German soldiers wandered aimlessly through the streets, some looking as if they had not yet recovered from a hard Saturday night.

Each month the occupation seemed to grow harsher, restrictions more numerous. The latest heartache for Dutchmen was an edict making it a crime to sing the "Wilhelmus," our national anthem.

Father, Betsie, and I were on our way to the Dutch Reformed church in Velsen, a small town not far from Haarlem, where Peter[1] had won the post of organist in competition against forty older and more experienced musicians. The organ at Velsen was one of the finest in the country; though the train seemed slower each time, we went frequently.

Peter was already playing, invisible in the tall organ loft, when we squeezed into the crowded pew. That was one thing the occupation had done for Holland: churches were packed.

After hymns and prayers came the sermon, a good one today, I thought. The closing prayers were said. And then, electrically, the whole church sat at attention. Without preamble, every stop pulled out to full volume, Peter was playing the "Wilhelmus"!

Father, at eighty-two, was the first one on his feet. Now everyone was standing. From somewhere in back of us a voice sang out the words. Another joined in, and another. Then we were all singing together, the full voice of Holland singing her forbidden anthem. We sang at the top of our lungs, sang our oneness, our hope, our love for Queen and country. On this anniversary of defeat it seemed almost for a moment that we were victors.

Afterward we waited for Peter at the small side door of the church. It was a long time before he was free to come away with us, so many people wanted to embrace him, to shake his hand and thump his back. Clearly he was enormously pleased with himself.

But now that the moment had passed I was, as usual, angry with him. The Gestapo[2] was

---

From THE HIDING PLACE by Corrie ten Boom with John and Elizabeth Sherrill. Chosen Books. Copyright © 1971 by Corrie ten Boom and John and Elizabeth Sherrill. Reprinted by permission.

1. Betsie . . . Peter, the author's sister and nephew.

2. Gestapo (gə stä′pō), from the German GEheime STAatsPOlizei ("secret state police"). In existence during the Nazi regime, the Gestapo was known and feared for its brutality.

certain to hear about it, perhaps already had: their eyes and ears were everywhere. For what had Peter risked so much? Not for people's lives but for a gesture. For a moment's meaningless defiance.

At Bos en Hoven Straat, however, Peter was a hero as one by one his family made us describe again what had happened. The only members of the household who felt as I did were the two Jewish women staying at Nollie's. One of these was an elderly Austrian lady whom Willem had sent into hiding here.

The other woman was a young, blonde, blue-eyed Dutch Jew with flawless false identity papers supplied by the Dutch national underground itself. The papers were so good and Annaliese looked so unlike the Nazi stereotype of a Jew, that she went freely in and out of the house, shopping and helping out at the school, giving herself out to be a friend of the family whose husband had died in the bombing of Rotterdam.

I spent an anxious afternoon, tensing at the sound of every motor, for only the police, Germans, and NSBers[3] had automobiles nowadays. But the time came to go home to the Beje[4] and still nothing had happened.

I worried two more days, then decided either Peter had not been reported or that the Gestapo had more important things to occupy them. It was Wednesday morning just as Father and I were unlocking our workbenches that Peter's little sister Cocky burst into the shop.

"Opa! Tante Corrie![5] They came for Peter! They took him away!"

"Who? Where?"

But she didn't know and it was three days before the family learned that he had been taken to the federal prison in Amsterdam.

It was 7:55 in the evening, just a few minutes before the new curfew hour of 8:00. Peter had been in prison for two weeks. Father and Betsie and I were seated around the dining room table, Father replacing watches in their pockets and Betsie doing needlework, our big, black, slightly Persian cat curled contentedly in her lap. A knock on the alley door made me glance in the window mirror. There in the bright spring twilight stood a woman. She carried a small suitcase and—odd for the time of year—wore a fur coat, gloves, and a heavy veil.

I ran down and opened the door. "Can I come in?" she asked. Her voice was high-pitched in fear.

"Of course." I stepped back. The woman looked over her shoulder before moving into the little hallway.

"My name is Kleermaker. I'm a Jew."

"How do you do?" I reached out to take her bag, but she held onto it. "Won't you come upstairs?"

Father and Betsie stood up as we entered the dining room. "Mrs. Kleermaker, my father and my sister."

"I was about to make some tea!" cried Betsie. "You're just in time to join us!"

Father drew out a chair from the table and Mrs. Kleermaker sat down, still gripping the suitcase. The "tea" consisted of old leaves which had been crushed and reused so often they did little more than color the water. But Mrs. Kleermaker accepted it gratefully, plunging into the story of how her husband had been arrested some months before, her son gone into hiding. Yesterday the S.D.—the political police who worked under the Gestapo—had ordered her to close the family clothing store. She was afraid now to go back to the apartment above it. She had heard that we had befriended a man on this street. . . .

"In this household," Father said, "God's people are always welcome."

"We have four empty beds upstairs," said Betsie. "Your problem will be choosing which one to sleep in!"

---

3. **NSBers,** Nationaal Socialistischa Beweging (National Socialist Movement). The members of this Dutch political party collaborated with the Nazis.

4. **Beje** (bāy yāy). The author and her father are watchmakers. The Beje refers to their home and shop.

5. **Opa, Tante Corrie** (ō'pä, tän'te). Grandfather, Aunty Corrie.

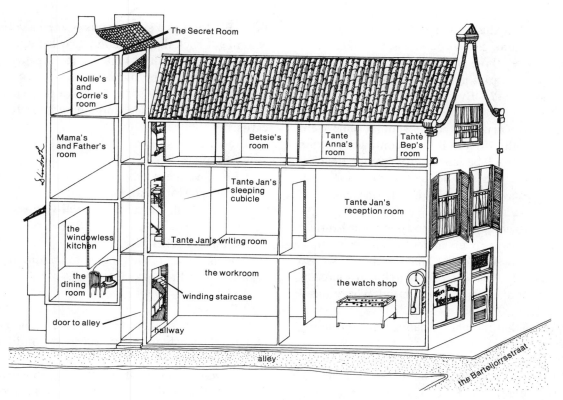

The Secret Room

Nollie's and Corrie's room

Mama's and Father's room

Betsie's room

Tante Anna's room

Tante Bep's room

Tante Jan's sleeping cubicle

Tante Jan's reception room

the windowless kitchen

Tante Jan's writing room

the dining room

the workroom

the watch shop

winding staircase

door to alley

hallway

alley

the Barteljorisstraat

Just two nights later the same scene was repeated. The time was again just before 8:00 on another bright May evening. Again there was a furtive knock at the side door. This time an elderly couple was standing outside.

"Come in!"

It was the same story: the same tight-clutched possessions, the same fearful glance and tentative tread. The story of neighbors arrested, the fear that tomorrow their turn would come.

That night after prayer-time the six of us faced our dilemma. "This location is too dangerous," I told our three guests. "We're half a block from the main police headquarters. And yet I don't know where else to suggest."

Clearly it was time to visit Willem again. So the next day I repeated the difficult trip to Hilversum. "Willem," I said, "we have three Jews staying right at the Beje. Can you get places for them in the country?"

Willem pressed his fingers to his eyes and I noticed suddenly how much white was in his beard. "It's getting harder," he said. "Harder

every month. They're feeling the food shortage now even on the farms. I still have addresses, yes, a few. But they won't take anyone without a ration card."

"Without a ration card! But, Jews aren't issued ration cards!"

"I know." Willem turned to stare out the window. For the first time I wondered how he and Tine were feeding the elderly men and women in their care.

"I know," he repeated. "And ration cards can't be counterfeited. They're changed too often and they're too easy to spot. Identity cards are different. I know several printers who do them. Of course you need a photographer."

A photographer? Printers? What was Willem talking about? "Willem, if people need ration cards and there aren't any counterfeit ones, what do they do?"

Willem turned slowly from the window. He seemed to have forgotten me and my particular problem. "Ration cards?" He gestured vaguely. "You steal them."

I stared at this Dutch Reformed clergyman. "Then, Willem, could you steal . . . I mean . . . could you get three stolen cards?"

"No, Corrie! I'm watched! Don't you understand that? Every move I make is watched!"

He put an arm around my shoulder and went on more kindly. "Even if I can continue working for a while, it will be far better for you to develop your own sources. The less connection with me—the less connection with anyone else—the better."

Joggling home on the crowded train I turned Willem's words over and over in my mind. "Your own sources." That sounded so—so professional. How was I going to find a source of stolen ration cards? Who in the world did I know. . . .

And at that moment a name appeared in my mind.

Fred Koornstra.

Fred was the man who used to read the electric meter at the Beje. The Koornstras had a retarded daughter, now a grown woman, who attended the "church" I had been conducting for the feeble-minded for some twenty years. And now Fred had a new job working for the Food Office. Wasn't it in the department where ration books were issued?

That evening after supper I bumped over the brick streets to the Koornstra house. The tires on my faithful old bicycle had finally given out and I joined the hundreds clattering about town on metal wheel rims. Each bump reminded me jarringly of my fifty years.

Fred, a bald man with a military bearing, came to the door and stared at me blankly when I said I wanted to talk to him about the Sunday service. He invited me in, closed the door, and said, "Now Corrie, what is it you really came to see me about?"

("Lord," I prayed silently, "if it is not safe to confide in Fred, stop this conversation now before it is too late.") "I must first tell you that we've had some unexpected company at the Beje. First it was a single woman, then a couple, when I got back this afternoon, another couple." I paused for just an instant. "They are Jews."

Fred's expression did not change.

"We can provide safe places for these people but they must provide something too. Ration cards."

Fred's eyes smiled. "So. Now I know why you came here."

"Fred, is there any way you can give out extra cards? More than you report?"

"None at all, Corrie. Those cards have to be accounted for a dozen ways. They're checked and double-checked."

The hope that had begun to mount in me tumbled. But Fred was frowning.

"Unless——" he began.

"Unless?"

"Unless there should be a hold-up. The Food Office in Utrecht was robbed last month—but the men were caught."

He was silent a while. "If it happened at noon," he said slowly, "when just the record clerk and I are there . . . and if they found us tied and gagged . . ." He snapped his fingers. "And I know just the man who might do it! Do you remember the——"

"Don't!" I said, remembering Willem's warning. "Don't tell me who. And don't tell me how. Just get the cards if you possibly can."

Fred stared at me a moment. "How many do you need?"

I opened my mouth to say, "Five." But the number that unexpectedly and astonishingly came out instead was, "One hundred."

When Fred opened the door to me just a week later, I gasped at the sight of him. Both eyes were a greenish purple, his lower lip cut and swollen.

"My friend took very naturally to the part," was all he would say.

But he had the cards. On the table in a brown manila envelope were one hundred passports to safety. Fred had already torn the "continuing coupon'' from each one. This final coupon was presented at the Food Office the last day of each month in exchange for the next month's card. With these coupons Fred could ''legally'' continue to issue us one hundred cards.

We agreed that it would be risky for me to keep coming to his house each month. What if he were to come to the Beje instead, dressed in his old meterman uniform?

The meter in the Beje was in the back hall at the foot of the stairs. When I got home that afternoon I pried up the tread of the bottom step, as Peter had done higher to hide the radio, and found a hollow space inside. Peter would be proud of me I thought as I worked—and was flooded by a wave of lonesomeness for that brave and cocksure boy. The hinge was hidden deep in the wood, the ancient riser undisturbed. I was ridiculously pleased with it.

We had our first test of the system on July 1. Fred was to come in through the shop as he always had, carrying the cards beneath his shirt. He would come at 5:30, when Betsie would have the back hall free of callers. To my horror at 5:25 the shop door opened and in stepped a policeman.

He was a tall man with close-cropped orange-red hair whom I knew by name—Rolf van Vliet—but little else. Rolf had brought in a watch that needed cleaning, and he seemed in a mood to talk. My throat had gone dry, but Father chatted cheerfully as he took off the back of Rolf's watch and examined it. What were we going to do? There was no way to warn Fred Koornstra. Promptly at 5:30 the door of the shop opened and in he walked, dressed in his blue workclothes. It seemed to me that his chest was too thick by a foot at least.

With magnificent aplomb Fred nodded to Father, the policeman, and me. ''Good evening.'' Courteous but a little bored.

He strode through the door at the rear of the shop and shut it behind him. My ears strained to hear him lift the secret lid. There! Surely Rolf must have heard it too.

The door behind us opened again. So great was Fred's control that he had not ducked out the alleyway exit, but came strolling back through the shop.

''Good evening,'' he said again.

''Evening.''

He reached the street door and was gone. We had got away with it this time, but somehow, some way, we were going to have to work out a warning system.

For meanwhile, in the weeks since Mrs. Kleermaker's unexpected visit, a great deal had happened at the Beje. Supplied with ration cards, Mrs. Kleermaker and the elderly couple and the next arrivals and the next had found homes in safer locations. But still the hunted people kept coming, and the needs were often more complicated than rations cards and addresses. If a Jewish woman became pregnant where could she go to have her baby? If a Jew in hiding died, how could he be buried?

''Develop your own sources,'' Willem had said. And from the moment Fred Koornstra's name had popped into my mind, an uncanny realization had been growing in me. We were friends with half of Haarlem! We knew nurses in the maternity hospital. We knew clerks in the Records Office. We knew someone in every business and service in the city.

We didn't know, of course, the political views of all these people. But—and here I felt a strange leaping of my heart—God did! I knew I was not clever or subtle or sophisticated; if the Beje was becoming a meeting place for need and supply, it was through some strategy far higher than mine.

A few nights after Fred's first ''meterman'' visit the alley bell rang long after curfew. I sped downstairs expecting another sad and stammering refugee. Betsie and I had already made up beds for four new overnight guests that evening: a Jewish woman and her three small children.

But to my surprise, close against the wall of the dark alley, stood Kik. ''Get your bicycle,'' he ordered with his usual young abruptness. "And put on a sweater. I have some people I want you to meet."

"Now? After curfew?" But I knew it was useless to ask questions. Kik's bicycle was tireless too, the wheel rims swathed in cloth. He wrapped mine also to keep down the clatter, and soon we were pedaling through the blacked-out streets of Haarlem at a speed that would have scared me even in daylight.

"Put a hand on my shoulder," Kik whispered. "I know the way."

We crossed dark side streets, crested bridges, wheeled round invisible corners. At last we crossed a broad canal and I knew we had reached the fashionable suburb of Aerdenhout.

We turned into a driveway beneath shadowy trees. To my astonishment Kik picked up my bicycle and carried both his and mine up the front steps. A serving girl with starched white apron and ruffled cap opened the door. The entrance hall was jammed with bicycles.

Then I saw him. One eye smiling at me, the other at the door, his vast stomach hastening ahead of him. Pickwick![6]

He led Kik and me into the drawing room where, sipping coffee and chatting in small groups, was the most distinguished-looking group of men and women I had ever seen. But all my attention, that first moment, was on the inexpressibly fragrant aroma in that room. Surely, was it possible, they were drinking real coffee?

Pickwick drew me a cup from the silver urn on the sideboard. It was coffee. After two years, rich, black, pungent Dutch coffee. He poured himself a cup too, dropping in his usual five lumps of sugar as though rationing had never been invented. Another starched and ruffled maid was passing a tray heaped high with cakes.

Gobbling and gulping I trailed about the room after Pickwick, shaking the hands of the people he singled out. They were strange introductions for no names were mentioned, only, occasionally, an address, and "Ask for Mrs. Smit."

When I had met my fourth Smit, Kik explained with a grin, "It's the only last name in the underground."

So this was really and truly the underground! But—where were these people from? I had never laid eyes on any of them. A second later I realized with a shiver down my spine that I was meeting the national group.

Their chief work, I gleaned from bits of conversation, was liaison with England and the Free Dutch forces fighting elsewhere on the continent. They also maintained the underground route through which downed Allied plane crews reached the North Sea coast.

But they were instantly sympathetic with my efforts to help Haarlem's Jews. I blushed to my hair roots to hear Pickwick describe me as "the head of an operation here in this city." A hollow space under the stairs and some haphazard friendships were not an operation. The others here were obviously competent, disciplined, and professional.

But they greeted me with grave courtesy, murmuring what they had to offer as we shook hands. False identity papers. The use of a car with official government plates. Signature forgery.

In a far corner of the room Pickwick introduced me to a frail-appearing little man with a wispy goatee. "Our host informs me," the little man began formally, "that your headquarters building lacks a secret room. This is a danger for all, those you are helping as well as yourselves and those who work with you. With your permission I will pay you a visit in the coming week. . . ."

Years later I learned that he was one of the most famous architects in Europe. I knew him only as Mr. Smit.

Just before Kik and I started our dash back to the Beje, Pickwick slipped an arm through mine. "My dear, I have good news. I understand that Peter is about to be released." . . .

So he was, three days later, thinner, paler,

---

6. **Pickwick.** The author recognizes one of her wealthy Dutch customers who looks like Pickwick, the Dickens character.

and not a whit daunted by his two months in a concrete cell. Nollie, Tine, and Betsie used up a month's sugar ration baking cakes for his welcome-home party.

And one morning soon afterward the first customer in the shop was a small thin-bearded man named Smit. Father took his jeweler's glass from his eye. If there was one thing he loved better than making a new acquaintance, it was discovering a link with an old one.

"Smit," he said eagerly. "I know several Smits in Amsterdam. Are you by any chance related to the family who——"

"Father," I interrupted, "this is the man I told you about. He's come to, ah, inspect the house."

"A building inspector? Then you must be the Smit with offices in the Grote Hout Straat. I wonder that I haven't——"

"Father!" I pleaded, "he's not a building inspector, and his name is not Smit."

"Not Smit?"

Together Mr. Smit and I attempted to explain, but Father simply could not understand a person's being called by a name not his own. As I led Mr. Smit into the back hall we heard him musing to himself, "I once knew a Smit on Koning Straat. . . ."

Mr. Smit examined and approved the hiding place for ration cards beneath the bottom step. He also pronounced acceptable the warning system we had worked out. This was a triangle-shaped wooden sign advertising "Alpina Watches" which I had placed in the dining room window. As long as the sign was in place, it was safe to enter.

But when I showed him a cubby hole behind the corner cupboard in the dining room, he shook his head. Some ancient redesigning of the house had left a crawl space in that corner and we'd been secreting jewelry, silver coins, and other valuables there since the start of the occupation. Not only the rabbi had brought us his library but other Jewish families had brought their treasures to the Beje for safekeeping. The space was large enough that we had believed a person could

crawl in there if necessary, but Mr. Smit dismissed it without a second glance.

"First place they'd look. Don't bother to change it though. It's only silver. We're interested in saving people, not things."

He started up the narrow corkscrew stairs, and as he mounted so did his spirits. He paused in delight at the odd-placed landings, pounded on the crooked walls, and laughed aloud as the floor levels of the two old houses continued out of phase.

"What an impossibility!" he said in an awe-struck voice. "What an improbable, unbelievable, unpredictable impossibility! Miss ten Boom, if all houses were constructed like this one, you would see before you a less worried man."

At last, at the very top of the stairs, he entered my room and gave a little cry of delight. "This is it!" he exclaimed.

"You want your hiding place as high as possible," he went on eagerly. "Gives you the best chance to reach it while the search is on below." He leaned out the window, craning his thin neck, the little faun's beard pointing this way and that.

"But . . . this is my bedroom. . . ."

Mr. Smit paid no attention. He was already measuring. He moved the heavy, wobbly old wardrobe away from the wall with surprising ease and pulled my bed into the center of the room. "This is where the false wall will go!" Excitedly he drew out a pencil and drew a line along the floor thirty inches from the back wall. He stood up and gazed at it moodily.

"That's as big as I dare," he said. "It will take a cot mattress, though. Oh yes. Easily!"

I tried again to protest, but Mr. Smit had forgotten I existed. Over the next few days he and his workmen were in and out of our house constantly. They never knocked. At each visit each man carried in something. Tools in a folded newspaper. A few bricks in a briefcase. "Wood!" he exclaimed when I ventured to wonder if a wooden wall would not be easier to build. "Wood sounds hollow. Hear it in a minute. No, no. Brick's the only thing for false walls."

After the wall was up, the plasterer came, then the carpenter, finally the painter. Six days after he had begun, Mr. Smit called Father, Betsie, and me to see.

We stood in the doorway and gaped. The smell of fresh paint was everywhere. But surely nothing in this room was newly painted! All four walls had that streaked and grimy look that old rooms got in coal-burning Haarlem. The ancient molding ran unbroken around the ceiling, chipped and peeling here and there, obviously undisturbed for a hundred and fifty years. Old water stains streaked the back wall, a wall that even I who had lived half a century in this room, could scarcely believe was not the original, but set back a precious two-and-a-half feet from the true wall of the building.

Built-in bookshelves ran along this false wall, old, sagging shelves whose blistered wood bore the same water stains as the wall behind them. Down in the far lefthand corner, beneath the bottom shelf, a sliding panel, two feet high and two wide, opened into the secret room.

Mr. Smit stooped and silently pulled this panel up. On hands and knees Betsie and I crawled into the narrow room behind it. Once inside we could stand up, sit, or even stretch out one at a time on the single mattress. A concealed vent, cunningly let into the real wall, allowed air to enter from outside.

"Keep a water jug there," said Mr. Smit, crawling in behind us. "Change the water once a week. Hardtack and vitamins keep indefinitely. Anytime there is anyone in the house whose presence is unofficial, all possessions except the clothes actually on his back must be stored in here."

Dropping to our knees again we crawled single file out into my bedroom. "Move back into this room," he told me. "Everything exactly as before."

With his fist he struck the wall above the bookshelves.

"The Gestapo could search for a year," he said. "They'll never find this one."

□□

Discussion

1. (a) Describe the various ways that people reacted to Peter's playing of the "Wilhelmus." (b) Why did Peter's action arouse such intense feelings in his countrymen? (c) Why did the Germans treat his action harshly?

2. (a) Why did Willem urge ten Boom to develop her own sources, and to have as few connections as possible with anyone? (b) How does Fred Koornstra's method of covering up the fake robbery of the Food Office illustrate the wisdom of Willem's advice?

3. Compare the way that ten Boom regards herself and her activities with the way that others regard her.

4. (a) Describe the hiding place. (b) Which details of its construction most surprised ten Boom?

Extension · Reading

To learn if the secret room was discovered and how ten Boom survived imprisonment and forced labor in a concentration camp, read *The Hiding Place* (Chosen Books), the book from which this selection was taken.

Corrie ten Boom 1892 ·

Corrie ten Boom was fifty-two years old when the Nazis, suspecting the family of hiding Jews, arrested them. Imprisoned, her father was the first to die; then Betsie, who along with Corrie had endured unspeakable torments in the concentration camp at Ravensbruck.

As the result of a clerical error, Corrie was released close to the end of the war instead of being sent to the gas chambers. When she returned to her home in Holland, her appearance was so changed that close friends did not recognize her.

Sustained by her deep religious faith, she achieved health and went on to establish a home for other victims of the Nazi purges—providing care not only for the tormented but also for some who had been their tormentors. She even set up a rehabilitation camp for Germans in Germany itself, at Dormstedt, in a former concentration camp.

As she walked into one of the barracks still surrounded by rolls of rusting barbed wire, she said, ''Window boxes . . . we'll have them at every window. The barbed wire must come down, of course, and then we'll need paint. Green paint. Bright yellow-green, the color of things coming up new in the Spring . . .''

By Courtesy of the Netherlands State Institute for War Documentation.

from Annapurna
The Summit

Maurice Herzog

When Maurice Herzog (her'tsōk) and Louis Lachenal (läsh näl') stood atop Annapurna on June 3, 1950, they were the first mountaineers to conquer so high a summit. Annapurna is one of fourteen peaks over 8,000 meters (26,000 feet) in the Himalaya Mountains. Often called "the roof of the world," the Himalayas stretch for sixteen hundred miles along the northern border of India, their major peaks being in Nepal.

The French Himalayan Expedition, led by Herzog, arrived in Nepal in April, 1950. The nine experienced members of the Expedition hoped to be the first mountaineers to reach the summit of an "eight thousander." Since the summer monsoon was predicted for early June, they had only two months to accomplish their task. The Expedition first attempted to surmount Dhaulagiri (dou'lu gi'rē), which is 26,795 feet high. After weeks of exploration, this peak proved to be unclimbable, and the mountaineers turned their efforts to Annapurna (26,493 feet). They had to find Annapurna, for its approaches had not been previously explored. By mid-May, they had located the peak and had decided that the most practical route to the summit lay along Annapurna's northwest flank. Racing against time—the monsoon was only three weeks away— the mountaineers began their laborious assault. They worked in two-man teams to establish a series of five camps between the mountain base and the summit. The highest of these camps, Camp V, was established by Herzog and Lachenal on the second of June.

Maurice Herzog and Louis "Biscante" Lachenal spent the night of June 2, 1950, at Camp V. Their tent was perched on a dangerously steep slope of Annapurna at 24,600 feet. The wind threatened to blow them off the mountain and heavy snows nearly crushed them where they lay.

On the third of June, 1950, the first light of dawn found us still clinging to the tent poles at Camp V. Gradually the wind abated and, with daylight, died away altogether. I made desperate attempts to push back the soft, icy stuff which stifled me, but every movement became an act of heroism. My mental powers were numbed: thinking was an effort, and we did not exchange a single word.

What a repellent place it was! To everyone who reached it, Camp V became one of the worst memories of their lives. We had only one thought—to get away. We should have waited for the first rays of the sun, but at half-past five we felt we couldn't stick it any longer.

"Let's go, Biscante," I muttered. "Can't stay here a minute longer."

"Yes, let's go," repeated Lachenal.

Which of us would have the energy to make tea? Although our minds worked slowly we were quite able to envisage all the movements that

From the book ANNAPURNA by Maurice Herzog. Translated by Nea Martin and Janet Adam Smith. Copyright, 1952, by E. P. Dutton & Co., Inc. Reprinted by permission of E. P. Dutton & Company and Jonathan Cape Ltd.

would be necessary—and neither of us could face up to it. It couldn't be helped—we would just have to go without. It was quite hard enough work to get ourselves and our boots out of our sleeping bags—and the boots were frozen stiff so that we got them on only with the greatest difficulty. Every movement made us terribly breathless. We felt as if we were being stifled. Our gaiters were stiff as a board, and I succeeded in lacing mine up; Lachenal couldn't manage his.

"No need for the rope, eh, Biscante?"

"No need," replied Lachenal laconically.

That was two pounds saved. I pushed a tube of condensed milk, some nougat, and a pair of socks into my sack; one never knew, the socks might come in useful—they might even do as balaclavas.[1] For the time being I stuffed them with first-aid equipment. The camera[2] was loaded with a black-and-white film; I had a color film in reserve. I pulled the movie camera out from the bottom of my sleeping bag, wound it up, and tried letting it run without film. There was a little click, then it stopped and jammed.

"Bad luck after bringing it so far," said Lachenal.

In spite of our photographer, Ichac's, precautions[3] taken to lubricate it with special grease, the intense cold, even inside the sleeping bag, had frozen it. I left it at the camp rather sadly: I had looked forward to taking it to the top. I had used it up to 24,600 feet.

We went outside and put on our crampons,[4] which we kept on all day. We wore as many clothes as possible; our sacks were very light. At six o'clock we started off. It was brilliantly fine, but also very cold. Our super lightweight crampons bit deep into the steep slopes of ice and hard snow up which lay the first stage of our climb.

Later the slope became slightly less steep and more uniform. Sometimes the hard crust bore our weight, but at others we broke through and sank into soft powder snow which made progress exhausting. We took turns in making the track and often stopped without any word having passed between us. Each of us lived in a closed and private world of his own. I was suspicious of my mental processes; my mind was working very slowly and I was perfectly aware of the low state of my intelligence. It was easiest just to stick to one thought at a time—safest, too. The cold was penetrating; for all our special eiderdown clothing we felt as if we'd nothing on. Whenever we halted, we stamped our feet hard. Lachenal went as far as to take off one boot which was a bit tight; he was in terror of frostbite.

"I don't want to be like Lambert," he said. Raymond Lambert, a Geneva guide, had to have all his toes amputated after an eventful climb during which he got his feet frostbitten.[5] While Lachenal rubbed himself hard, I looked at the summits all around us; already we overtopped them all except the distant Dhaulagiri. The complicated structure of these mountains, with which our many laborious explorations had made us familiar, was now spread out plainly at our feet.

The going was incredibly exhausting, and every step was a struggle of mind over matter. We came out into the sunlight, and by way of marking the occasion made yet another halt. Lachenal continued to complain of his feet. "I can't feel anything. I think I'm beginning to get frostbite." And once again he undid his boot.

I began to be seriously worried. I realized very well the risk we were running; I knew from experience how insidiously and quickly frostbite can set in if one is not extremely careful. Nor was Lachenal under any illusions. "We're in danger of having frozen feet. Do you think it's worth it?"

This was most disturbing. It was my responsibility as leader to think of the others.

---

1. **they might even do as balaclavas.** A balaclava (bä′ lə klä′ və) is a knitted cap which covers the head, neck, and shoulders.
2. **The camera,** the still camera. Herzog had carried a still camera and a movie camera to Camp V.
3. **our photographer, Ichac's, precautions.** Marcel Ichac (ē shak′) was the Expedition's cameraman.
4. **our crampons** (kram′pənz), spiked iron plates which mountaineers fasten to their boots to prevent slipping.
5. **Raymond Lambert** (läm bär′) . . . **feet frostbitten.** In May 1952, Lambert reached the highest point yet attained on Mount Everest.

There was no doubt about frostbite being a very real danger. Did Annapurna justify such risks? That was the question I asked myself; it continued to worry me.

Lachenal had laced his boots up again, and once more we continued to force our way through the exhausting snow. The whole of the Sickle Glacier[6] was now in view, bathed in light. We still had a long way to go to cross it, and then there was that rock band—would we find a gap in it?

My feet, like Lachenal's, were very cold and I continued to wriggle my toes, even when we were moving. I could not feel them, but that was nothing new in the mountains, and if I kept on moving them it would keep the circulation going.

Lachenal appeared to me as a sort of specter—he was alone in his world, I in mine. But—and this was odd enough—any effort was slightly *less* exhausting than lower down. Perhaps it was hope lending us wings. Even through dark glasses the snow was blinding—the sun beating straight down on the ice. We looked down upon precipitous ridges which dropped away into space, and upon tiny glaciers far, far below. Familiar peaks soared arrowlike into the sky. Suddenly Lachenal grabbed me:

"If I go back, what will you do?"

A whole sequence of pictures flashed through my head: the days of marching in sweltering heat, the hard pitches[7] we had overcome, the tremendous efforts we had all made to lay siege to the mountain, the daily heroism of all my friends in establishing the camps. Now we were nearing our goal. In an hour or two, perhaps, victory would be ours. Must we give up? Impossible! My whole being revolted against the idea. I had made up my mind, irrevocably. Today we were consecrating an ideal, and no sacrifice was too great. I heard my voice clearly:

"I should go on by myself."

I would go alone. If he wished to go down it was not for me to stop him. He must make his own choice freely.

"Then I'll follow you."

The die was cast. I was no longer anxious. Nothing could stop us now from getting to the top. The psychological atmosphere changed with these few words, and we went forward now as brothers.

I felt as though I were plunging into something new and quite abnormal. I had the strangest and most vivid impressions, such as I had never before known in the mountains. There was something unnatural in the way I saw Lachenal and everything around us.[8] I smiled to myself at the paltriness of our efforts, for I could stand apart and watch myself making these efforts. But all sense of exertion was gone, as though there were no longer any gravity. This diaphanous landscape, this quintessence of purity— these were not the mountains I knew: they were the mountains of my dreams.

The snow, sprinkled over every rock and gleaming in the sun, was of a radiant beauty that touched me to the heart. I had never seen such complete transparency, and I was living in a world of crystal. Sounds were indistinct, the atmosphere like cotton wool.

An astonishing happiness welled up in me, but I could not define it. Everything was so new, so utterly unprecedented. It was not in the least like anything I had known in the Alps, where one feels buoyed up by the presence of others—by people of whom one is vaguely aware, or even by the dwellings one can see in the far distance.

This was quite different. An enormous gulf was between me and the world. This was a different universe—withered, desert,[9] lifeless; a fantastic universe where the presence of man was not foreseen, perhaps not desired. We were braving an interdict, overstepping a boundary, and yet we had no fear as we continued upward.

---

6. *Sickle Glacier,* large mass of ice, shaped like a sickle, that lies near the summit of Annapurna.
7. *hard pitches,* difficult slopes.
8. *There was something unnatural . . . around us.* Herzog is feeling the effects of the altitude. At great heights, the low oxygen content of the air produces intense fatigue and grogginess.
9. *desert,* dry, barren.

I thought of the famous ladder of St. Teresa of Avila.[10] Something clutched at my heart.

Did Lachenal share these feelings? The summit ridge drew nearer, and we reached the foot of the ultimate rock band. The slope was very steep and the snow interspersed with rocks.

"Couloir!"[11]

A finger pointed. The whispered word from one to another indicated the key to the rocks—the last line of defense.

"What luck!"

The couloir up the rocks though steep was feasible.

The sky was a deep sapphire blue. With a great effort we edged over to the right, avoiding the rocks; we preferred to keep to the snow on account of our crampons and it was not long before we set foot in the couloir. It was fairly steep, and we had a minute's hesitation. Should we have enough strength left to overcome this final obstacle?

Fortunately the snow was hard, and by kicking steps we were able to manage, thanks to our crampons. A false move would have been fatal. There was no need to make handholds—our axes,[12] driven in as far as possible, served us for an anchor.

Lachenal went splendidly. What a wonderful contrast to the early days![13] It was a hard struggle here, but he kept going. Lifting our eyes occasionally from the slope, we saw the couloir opening out on to . . . well, we didn't quite know, probably a ridge. But where was the top—left or right? Stopping at every step, leaning on our axes, we tried to recover our breath and to calm down our racing hearts, which were thumping as though they would burst. We knew we were there now—that nothing could stop us. No need to exchange looks—each of us would have read the same determination in the other's eyes. A slight detour to the left, a few more steps—the summit ridge came gradually nearer—a few rocks to avoid. We dragged ourselves up. Could we possibly be there?

Yes!

A fierce and savage wind tore at us.

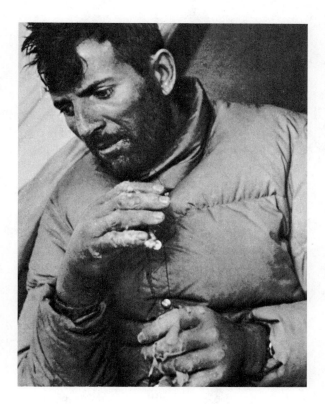

We were on top of Annapurna! 8,075 meters, 26,493 feet.

Our hearts overflowed with an unspeakable happiness.

"If only the others could know. . . ."

If only everyone could know!

The summit was a corniced crest of ice, and the precipices on the far side which plunged vertically down beneath us were terrifying, unfathomable. There could be few other mountains in the world like this. Clouds floated halfway down, concealing the gentle, fertile valley of Pokhara, 23,000 feet below. Above us there was nothing!

Our mission was accomplished. But at the

10. *the famous ladder of St. Teresa* (tə rā′sə) *of Avila.* St. Teresa was a 16th-century nun who established convents in Spain. At one time she envisioned a ladder leading to heaven.
11. *"Couloir!"* A couloir (kül wär′) is a gorge on a mountainside. It is more common to find couloirs in the European Alps than in the Himalayas.
12. *our axes,* ice axes.
13. *the early days!* Herzog is referring to the first days of high-altitude climbing when the members of the Expedition were still unaccustomed to the low oxygen content of the air.

Photographs from the book *Annapurna* by Marcel Ichac from the book *Annapurna* by Maurice Herzog: Copyright, 1952, by E. P. Dutton & Co., Inc. Diagram based upon a map by Marcel Ichac from the book *Annapurna* by Maurice Herzog: Copyright, 1952, by E. P. Dutton & Co., Inc., New York; Reproduced by permission of E. P. Dutton & Co., Inc., and Jonathan Cape Ltd., London.

same time we had accomplished something infinitely greater. How wonderful life would now become! What an inconceivable experience it is to attain one's ideal and, at the very same moment, to fulfill oneself. I was stirred to the depths of my being. Never had I felt happiness like this—so intense and yet so pure. That brown rock, the highest of them all, that ridge of ice— were these the goals of a lifetime? Or were they, rather, the limits of man's pride?

"Well, what about going down?"

Lachenal shook me. What were his own feelings? Did he simply think he had finished another climb, as in the Alps? Did he think one could just go down again like that, with nothing more to it?

"One minute, I must take some photographs."

"Hurry up!"

I fumbled feverishly in my sack, pulled out the camera, took out the little French flag which was right on the bottom, and the pennants. Useless gestures, no doubt, but something more than symbols—eloquent tokens of affection and good will. I tied the strips of material—stained by sweat and by the food in the sacks—to the shaft of my ice ax, the only flagstaff at hand. Then I focused my camera on Lachenal.

"Now, will you take me?"

"Hand it over—hurry up!" said Lachenal.

He took several pictures and then handed me back the camera. I loaded a color film and we repeated the process to be certain of bringing back records to be cherished in the future.

"Are you mad?" asked Lachenal. "We haven't a minute to lose: we must go down at once."

And in fact a glance round showed me that the weather was no longer gloriously fine as it had been in the morning. Lachenal was becoming impatient.

"We must go down!"

He was right. His was the reaction of the mountaineer who knows his own domain. But I just could not accustom myself to the idea that we had won our victory. It seemed inconceivable that we should have trodden those summit snows.

It was impossible to build a cairn; there were no stones; everything was frozen. Lachenal stamped his feet; he felt them freezing. I felt mine freezing too, but paid little attention. The highest mountain to be climbed by man lay under our feet! The names of our predecessors on these heights raced through my mind: Mummery, Mallory and Irvine, Bauer, Welzenbach, Tilman, Shipton.[14] How many of them were dead—how many had found on these mountains what, to them, was the finest end of all?

My joy was touched with humility. It was not just one party that had climbed Annapurna today, but a whole expedition. I thought of all the others in the camps perched on the slopes at our feet, and I knew it was because of their efforts and their sacrifices that we had succeeded. There are times when the most complicated actions are suddenly summed up, distilled, and strike you with illuminating clarity: so it was with this irresistible upward surge which had landed us two here.

Pictures passed through my mind—the Chamonix Valley,[15] where I had spent the most marvelous moments of my childhood; Mont Blanc, which so tremendously impressed me! I was a child when I first saw "the Mont Blanc people" coming home, and to me there was a queer look about them; a strange light shone in their eyes.

"Come on, straight down," called Lachenal.

He had already done up his sack and started going down. I took out my pocket aneroid: 8,500 meters.[16] I smiled. I swallowed a little condensed milk and left the tube behind—the only trace of our passage. I did up my sack, put on my gloves

---

14. **The names of our predecessors . . . Shipton.** Herzog names mountaineers who had previously assaulted Himalayan peaks.
15. **Chamonix** (shä′mô nē′) **Valley,** mountain valley in eastern France, north of Mont Blanc (môɴ bläɴk′). Mont Blanc, long familiar to Herzog, is the highest mountain in the Alps (15,781 feet).
16. **pocket aneroid** (an′ə roid): **8,500 meters.** An aneroid barometer indicates altitude by the pressure of air on the elastic lid of a box containing no air.

and my glasses, seized my ice ax; one look around and I, too, hurried down the slope. Before disappearing into the couloir I gave one last look at the summit which would henceforth be all our joy and all our consolation.

Lachenal was already far below; he had reached the foot of the couloir. I hurried down in his tracks. I went as fast as I could, but it was dangerous going. At every step one had to take care that the snow did not break away beneath one's weight. Lachenal, going faster than I thought he was capable of, was now on the long traverse. It was my turn to cross the area of mixed rock and snow. At last I reached the foot of the rock band. I had hurried and I was out of breath. I undid my sack. What had I been going to do? I couldn't say.

"My gloves!"

Before I had time to bend over, I saw them slide and roll. They went farther and farther straight down the slope. I remained where I was, quite stunned. I watched them rolling down slowly, with no appearance of stopping. The movement of those gloves was engraved in my sight as something irredeemable, against which I was powerless. The consequences might be most serious. What was I to do?

"Quickly, down to Camp V."

Rébuffat and Terray would be there.[17] My concern dissolved like magic. I now had a fixed objective again: to reach the camp. Never for a minute did it occur to me to use as gloves the socks which I always carry in reserve for just such a mishap as this.

On I went, trying to catch up with Lachenal. It had been two o'clock when we reached the summit; we had started out at six in the morning, but I had to admit I had lost all sense of time. I felt as if I were running, whereas in actual fact I was walking normally, perhaps rather slowly, and I had to keep stopping to get my breath. The sky was now covered with clouds, everything had become gray and dirty-looking. An icy wind sprang up, boding no good. We must push on! But where was Lachenal? I spotted him a couple of hundred yards away, looking as if he was never going to stop. And I had thought he was in indifferent form!

The clouds grew thicker and came right down over us; the wind blew stronger, but I did not suffer from the cold. Perhaps the descent had restored my circulation. Should I be able to find the tents in the mist? I watched the rib[18] ending in the beaklike point which overlooked the camp. It was gradually swallowed up by the clouds, but I was able to make out the spearhead rib lower down. If the mist should thicken I would make straight for that rib and follow it down, and in this way I should be bound to come upon the tent.

Lachenal disappeared from time to time, and then the mist was so thick that I lost sight of him altogether. I kept going at the same speed, as fast as my breathing would allow.

The slope was now steeper; a few patches of bare ice followed the smooth stretches of snow. A good sign—I was nearing the camp. How difficult to find one's way in thick mist! I kept the course which I had set by the steepest angle of the slope. The ground was broken; with my crampons I went straight down walls of bare ice. There were some patches ahead—a few more steps. It was the camp all right, but there were *two tents!*

So Rébuffat and Terray had come up. What a mercy! I should be able to tell them that we had been successful, that we were returning from the top. How thrilled they would be!

I got there, dropping down from above. The platform had been extended, and the two tents were facing each other. I tripped over one of the guy ropes of the first tent; there was movement inside, they had heard me. Rébuffat and Terray put their heads out.

"We've made it. We're back from Anna-purna!"

Rébuffat and Terray received the news with great excitement.

---

17. *Rébuffat* (rā bʏ'fä') *and* **Terray** (tə rā') *would be there.* Gaston Rébuffat and Lionel Terray were scheduled to advance from Camp IV to Camp V this same day.
18. *the rib,* a ridge.

"But what about Biscante?" asked Terray anxiously.

"He won't be long. He was just in front of me! What a day—started out at six this morning—didn't stop . . . got up at last."

Words failed me. I had so much to say. The sight of familiar faces dispelled the strange feeling that I had experienced since morning, and I became, once more, just a mountaineer.

Terray, who was speechless with delight, wrung my hands. Then the smile vanished from his face: "Maurice—your hands!" There was an uneasy silence. I had forgotten that I had lost my gloves; my fingers were violet and white and hard as wood. The other two stared at them in dismay—they realized the full seriousness of the injury. But, still blissfully floating on a sea of joy remote from reality, I leaned over toward Terray and said confidentially, "You're in such splendid form, and you've done so marvelously, it's absolutely tragic you didn't come up there with us!"

"What I did was for the Expedition, my dear Maurice, and anyway you've got up, and that's a victory for the whole lot of us."

I nearly burst with happiness. How could I tell him all that his answer meant to me? The rapture I had felt on the summit, which might have seemed a purely personal, egotistical emotion, had been transformed by his words into a complete and perfect joy with no shadow upon it. His answer proved that this victory was not just one man's achievement, a matter for personal pride; no—and Terray was the first to understand this—it was a victory for us all, a victory for mankind itself.

"Hi! Help! Help!"

"Biscante!" exclaimed the others.

Still half-intoxicated and remote from reality, I had heard nothing. Terray felt a chill at his heart, and his thoughts flew to his partner on so many unforgettable climbs; together they had so often skirted death, and won so many splendid victories. Putting his head out, and seeing Lachenal clinging to the slope a hundred yards lower down, he dressed in frantic haste.

Out he went. But the slope was bare now; Lachenal had disappeared. Terray was horribly frightened, and he could only utter unintelligible cries. It was a ghastly moment for him. A violent wind sent the mist tearing by. Under the stress of emotion Terray had not realized how it falsified distances.

"Biscante! Biscante!"

He had spotted him, through a rift in the mist, lying on the slope much lower down than he had thought. Terray set his teeth and glissaded down like a madman.[19] How would he be able to brake without crampons, on the wind-hardened snow? But Terray was a first-class skier, and with a jump turn he stopped beside Lachenal, who was suffering from concussion after his tremendous fall. In a state of collapse, with no ice ax, balaclava, or gloves, and only one crampon, he gazed vacantly around him.

"My feet are frostbitten. Take me down . . . take me down, so that Oudot[20] can see to me."

"It can't be done," said Terray sorrowfully. "Can't you see we're in the middle of a storm? . . . It'll be dark soon."

But Lachenal was obsessed by the fear of amputation. With a gesture of despair he tore the ax out of Terray's hands and tried to force his way down, but soon saw the futility of his action and resolved to climb up to the camp. While Terray cut steps without stopping, Lachenal, ravaged and exhausted as he was, dragged himself along on all fours.

Meanwhile I had gone into Rébuffat's tent. He was appalled at the sight of my hands and, as rather incoherently I told him what we had done, he took a piece of rope and began flicking my fingers. Then he took off my boots with great difficulty, for my feet were swollen, and beat my feet and rubbed me. We soon heard Terray giving Lachenal the same treatment in the other tent.

For our comrades it was a tragic moment: Annapurna was conquered, and the first eight-

19. **Terray . . . glissaded down like a madman.** Terray made a sliding descent of the snow slope while in a standing position.
20. **Oudot** (u dō'), Jacques Oudot, the Expedition's doctor.

thousander had been climbed. Every one of us had been ready to sacrifice everything for this. Yet, as they looked at our feet and hands, what can Terray and Rébuffat have felt?

Outside the storm howled and the snow was still falling. The mist grew thick and darkness came. As on the previous night we had to cling to the poles to prevent the tents being carried away by the wind. The only two air mattresses were given to Lachenal and myself while Terray and Rébuffat both sat on ropes, rucksacks, and provisions to keep themselves off the snow. They rubbed, slapped, and beat us with a rope. Sometimes the blows fell on living flesh, and howls arose from both tents. Rébuffat persevered; it was essential to continue, painful as it was. Gradually life returned to my feet as well as to my hands, and circulation started again. Lachenal, too, found that feeling was returning.

Now Terray summoned up the energy to prepare some hot drinks. He called to Rébuffat that he would pass him a mug, so two hands stretched out toward each other between the two tents and were instantly covered with snow. The liquid was boiling though scarcely more than 60 degrees centigrade[21] (140 degrees Fahrenheit). I swallowed it greedily and felt infinitely better.

The night was absolute hell. Frightful onslaughts of wind battered us incessantly, while the never-ceasing snow piled up on the tents.

Now and again I heard voices from next door—it was Terray massaging Lachenal with admirable perseverance, only stopping to ply him with hot drinks. In our tent Rébuffat was quite worn out, but satisfied that warmth was returning to my limbs.

Lying half-unconscious I was scarcely aware of the passage of time. There were moments when I was able to see our situation in its true dramatic light, but the rest of the time I was plunged in an inexplicable stupor with no thought for the consequences of our victory.

As the night wore on the snow lay heavier on the tent, and once again I had the frightful feeling of being slowly and silently asphyxiated. I tried,

with all the strength of which I was capable, to push off with both forearms the mass that was crushing me. These fearful exertions left me gasping for breath and I fell back into the same exhausted state. It was much worse than the previous night.

"Rébuffat! Gaston! Gaston!"

I recognized Terray's voice.

"Time to be off!"

I heard the sounds without grasping their meaning. Was it light already? I was not in the least surprised that the other two had given up all thought of going to the top, and I did not at all grasp the measure of their sacrifice.

Outside the storm redoubled in violence. The tent shook and the fabric flapped alarmingly. It had usually been fine in the mornings: did this mean the monsoon was upon us? We knew it was not far off—could this be its first onslaught?

"Gaston! Are you ready?" Terray called again.

"One minute," answered Rébuffat. He did not have an easy job: he had to put my boots on and do everything to get me ready. I let myself be handled like a baby. In the other tent Terray finished dressing Lachenal whose feet were still swollen and would not fit into his boots. So Terray gave him his own, which were bigger. To get Lachenal's on to his own feet he had to make slits in them. As a precaution he put a sleeping bag and some food into his sack and shouted to us to do the same. Were his words lost in the storm? Or were we too intent on leaving this hellish place to listen to his instructions?

Lachenal and Terray were already outside.

"We're going down!" they shouted.

Then Rébuffat tied me on the rope and we went out. There were only two ice axes for the four of us, so Rébuffat and Terray took them as a matter of course. For a moment as we left the two tents of Camp V, I felt childishly ashamed at leaving all this good equipment behind.

Already the first rope seemed a long way down below us. We were blinded by the squalls

---

21. **The liquid was boiling . . . centigrade.** At high altitudes the boiling point of liquids is lower than it is at sea level.

of snow and we could not hear each other a yard away. We had both put on our *cagoules*,[22] for it was very cold. The snow was apt to slide and the rope often came in useful.

Ahead of us the other two were losing no time. Lachenal went first and, safeguarded by Terray, he forced the pace in his anxiety to get down. There were no tracks to show us the way, but it was engraved on all our minds—straight down the slope for four hundred yards then traverse to the left for one hundred fifty to two hundred yards to get to Camp IV. The snow was thinning and the wind less violent. Was it going to clear? We hardly dared to hope so. A wall of seracs[23] brought us up short.

"It's to the left," I said, "I remember perfectly."

Somebody else thought it was to the right. We started going down again. The wind had dropped completely, but the snow fell in big flakes. The mist was thick, and, not to lose each other, we walked in line: I was third and I could barely see Lachenal, who was first. It was

impossible to recognize any of the pitches. We were all experienced enough mountaineers to know that even on familiar ground it is easy to make mistakes in such weather. Distances are deceptive, one cannot tell whether one is going up or down. We kept colliding with hummocks which we had taken for hollows. The mist, the falling snowflakes, the carpet of snow, all merged into the same whitish tone and confused our vision. The towering outlines of the seracs took on fantastic shapes and seemed to move slowly around us.

Our situation was not desperate, we were certainly not lost. We would have to go lower down; the traverse must begin further on—I remembered the serac which served as a milestone. The snow stuck to our *cagoules*, and turned us into white phantoms noiselessly flitting against a background equally white. We began to

---

22. *cagoules* (kä gül'), hoods. *[French]*
23. *A wall of seracs.* A serac (sə rak') is a pinnacle of ice among the crevices of a glacier.

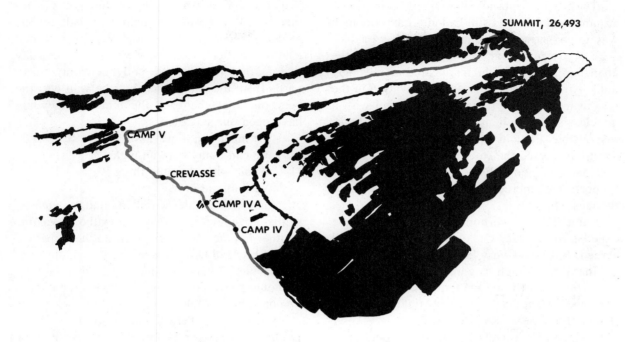

SUMMIT, 26,493

CAMP V

CREVASSE

CAMP IV A

CAMP IV

sink in dreadfully, and there is nothing worse for bodies already on the edge of exhaustion.

Were we too high or too low? No one could tell. Perhaps we had better try slanting over to the left! The snow was in a dangerous condition, but we did not seem to realize it. We were forced to admit that we were not on the right route, so we retraced our steps and climbed up above the serac which overhung us. No doubt, we decided, we should be on the right level now. With Rébuffat leading, we went back over the way which had cost us such an effort. I followed him jerkily, saying nothing, and determined to go on to the end. If Rébuffat had fallen I could never have held him.

We went doggedly on from one serac to another. Each time we thought we had recognized the right route, and each time there was a fresh disappointment. If only the mist would lift, if only the snow would stop for a second! On the slope it seemed to be growing deeper every minute. Only Terray and Rébuffat were capable of breaking the trail, and they relieved each other

at regular intervals without a word and without a second's hesitation.

I admired this determination of Rébuffat's for which he is so justly famed. He did not intend to die! With the strength of desperation and at the price of superhuman effort he forged ahead. The slowness of his progress would have dismayed even the most obstinate climber, but he would not give up, and in the end the mountain yielded in face of his perseverance.

Terray, when his turn came, charged madly ahead. He was like a force of nature: at all costs he would break down these prison walls that penned us in. His physical strength was exceptional, his will power no less remarkable. Lachenal gave him considerable trouble. Perhaps he was not quite in his right mind. He said it was no use going on; we must dig a hole in the snow and wait for fine weather. He swore at Terray and called him a madman. Nobody but Terray would have been capable of dealing with him—he just tugged sharply on the rope and Lachenal was forced to follow.

We were well and truly lost.

The weather did not seem likely to improve. A minute ago we had still had ideas about which way to go—now we had none. This way or that. . . . We went on at random to allow for the chance of a miracle which appeared increasingly unlikely. The instinct of self-preservation in the two fit members of the party alternated with a hopelessness which made them completely irresponsible. Each in turn did the maddest things: Terray traversed the steep and avalanchy slopes with one crampon badly adjusted. He and Rébuffat performed incredible feats of balance without the least slip.

Camp IV was certainly on the left, on the edge of the Sickle. On that point we were all agreed. But it was very hard to find. The wall of ice that gave it such magnificent protection was now ironical, for it hid the tents from us. In mist like this we should have to be right on top of them before we spotted them.

Perhaps if we called, someone would hear us? Lachenal gave the signal, but snow absorbs sound and his shout seemed to carry only a few yards. All four of us called out together: "One . . . two . . . three . . . *Help!*"

We got the impression that our united shout carried a long way, so we began again: "One . . . two . . . three . . . *Help!*" Not a sound in reply!

Now and again Terray took off his boots and rubbed his feet; the sight of our frostbitten limbs had made him aware of the danger and he had the strength of mind to do something about it. Like Lachenal, he was haunted by the idea of amputation. For me, it was too late: my feet and hands, already affected from yesterday, were beginning to freeze up again.

We had eaten nothing since the day before, and we had been on the go the whole time, but men's resources of energy in face of death are inexhaustible. When the end seems imminent, there still remain reserves, though it needs tremendous will power to call them up.

Time passed, but we had no idea how long. Night was approaching, and we were terrified, though none of us made any complaint. Rébuffat and I found a way that we thought we remembered, but were brought to a halt by the extreme steepness of the slope—the mist turned it into a vertical wall. We were to find next day that at that moment we had been only thirty yards from the camp, and that the wall was the very one that sheltered the tent which would have been our salvation.

"We must find a crevasse."[24]

"We can't stay here all night!"

"A hole—it's the only thing."

"We'll all die in it."

Night had suddenly fallen, and it was essential to come to a decision without wasting another minute; if we remained on the slope, we should be dead before morning. We would have to bivouac.[25] What the conditions would be like, we could guess, for we all knew what it meant to bivouac above 23,000 feet.

With his ax Terray began to dig a hole. Lachenal went over a snow-filled crevasse a few yards further on, then suddenly let out a yell and disappeared before our eyes. We stood helpless: should we, or rather would Terray and Rébuffat, have enough strength for all the maneuvers with the rope that would be needed to get him out? The crevasse was completely blocked up save for the one little hole which Lachenal had fallen through.

"Lachenal!" called Terray.

A voice, muffled by many thicknesses of ice and snow, came up to us. It was impossible to make out what it was saying.

"Lachenal!"

Terray jerked the rope violently; this time we could hear.

"I'm here!"

"Anything broken?"

"No! It'll do for the night! Come along."

This shelter was heaven-sent. None of us would have had the strength to dig a hole big enough to protect the lot of us from the wind.

---

24. *crevasse* (krə vas'), deep crack or crevice in the ice of a glacier.
25. *to bivouac* (biv'wak), to camp outdoors without tents.

Without hesitation Terray let himself drop into the crevasse, and a loud "Come on!" told us he had arrived safely. In my turn I let myself go; it was a regular toboggan slide. I shot down a sort of twisting tunnel, very steep, and about thirty feet long. I came out at great speed into the opening beyond and was literally hurled to the bottom of the crevasse. We let Rébuffat know he could come by giving a tug on the rope.

The intense cold of this minute grotto shriveled us up, the enclosing walls of ice were damp and the floor a carpet of fresh snow; by huddling together there was just room for the four of us. Icicles hung from the ceiling, and we broke some of them off to make more head room and kept little bits to suck—it was a long time since we had anything to drink.

That was our shelter for the night. At least we should be protected from the wind, and the temperature would remain fairly even, though the damp was extremely unpleasant. We settled ourselves in the dark as best we could. As always in a bivouac we took off our boots; without this precaution the constriction would cause immediate frostbite. Terray unrolled the sleeping bag which he had had the foresight to bring, and settled himself in relative comfort. We put on everything warm that we had, and to avoid contact with the snow I sat on the movie camera. We huddled close up to each other, in our search for a hypothetical position in which the warmth of our bodies could be combined without loss, but we couldn't keep still for a second.

We did not open our mouths—signs were less of an effort than words. Every man withdrew into himself and took refuge in his own inner world. Terray massaged Lachenal's feet; Rébuffat felt his feet freezing too, but he had sufficient strength to rub them himself. I remained motionless, unseeing. My feet and hands went on freezing, but what could be done? I attempted to forget suffering by withdrawing into myself; trying to forget the passing of time, trying not to feel the devouring and numbing cold which insidiously gained upon us.

Terray shared his sleeping bag with Lache-nal, putting his feet and hands inside the precious eiderdown. At the same time he went on rubbing.

Anyhow the frostbite won't spread further, he was thinking.

None of us could make any movement without upsetting the others, and the positions we had taken up with such care were continually being altered so that we had to start all over again. This kept us busy. Rébuffat persevered with his rubbing and complained of his feet; like Terray he was thinking: We mustn't look beyond tomorrow—afterward we'll see. But he was not blind to the fact that "afterward" was one big question mark.

Terray generously tried to give me part of his sleeping bag. He had understood the seriousness of my condition, and knew why it was that I said nothing and remained quite passive; he realized that I had abandoned all hope for myself. He massaged me for nearly two hours; his feet, too, might have frozen, but he didn't appear to give the matter a thought. I found new courage simply in contemplating his unselfishness; he was doing so much to help me that it would have been ungrateful of me not to go on struggling to live. Though my heart was like a lump of ice itself, I was astonished to feel no pain. Everything material about me seemed to have dropped away. I seemed to be quite clear in my thoughts and yet I floated in a kind of peaceful happiness. There was still a breath of life in me, but it dwindled steadily as the hours went by. Terray's massage no longer had any effect upon me. All was over, I thought. Wasn't this cavern the most beautiful grave I could hope for? Death caused me no grief, no regret—I smiled at the thought.

After hours of torpor a voice mumbled "Daylight!"

This made some impression on the others. I only felt surprised—I had not thought that daylight would penetrate so far down.

"Too early to start," said Rébuffat.

A ghastly light spread through our grotto and we could just vaguely make out the shapes of each other's heads. A queer noise from a long way off came down to us—a sort of prolonged hiss. The noise increased. Suddenly I was buried, blinded, smothered beneath an avalanche of new snow. The icy snow spread over the cavern, finding its way through every gap in our clothing. I ducked my head between my knees and covered myself with both arms. The snow flowed on and on. There was a terrible silence. We were not completely buried, but there was snow everywhere. We got up, taking care not to bang our heads against the ceiling of ice, and tried to shake ourselves. We were all in our stockinged feet in the snow. The first thing to do was to find our boots.

Rébuffat and Terray began to search and realized at once that they were blind. Yesterday they had taken off their glasses to lead us down and now they were paying for it. Lachenal was the first to lay hands upon a pair of boots. He tried to put them on, but they were Rébuffat's. Rébuffat attempted to climb up the chute down which we had come yesterday, and which the avalanche had followed in its turn.

"Hi, Gaston! What's the weather like?" called up Terray.

"Can't see a thing. It's blowing hard."

We were still groping for our things. Terray found his boots and put them on awkwardly, unable to see what he was doing. Lachenal helped him, but he was all on edge and fearfully impatient, in striking contrast to my immobility. Terray then went up the icy channel, puffing and blowing, and at last reached the outer world. He was met by terrible gusts of wind that cut right through him and lashed his face.

Bad weather, he said to himself, this time it's the end. We're lost . . . we'll never come through.

At the bottom of the crevasse there were still two of us looking for our boots. Lachenal poked fiercely with an ice ax. I was calmer and tried to proceed more rationally. We extracted crampons and an ax in turn from the snow, but still no boots.

Well—so this cavern was to be our last resting place! There was very little room—we were bent double and got in each other's way. Lachenal decided to go out without his boots. He called frantically, hauled himself up on the rope, trying to get a hold or to wiggle his way up, digging his toes into the snow walls. Terray from outside pulled as hard as he could. I watched him go; he gathered speed and disappeared.

When he emerged from the opening he saw the sky was clear and blue, and he began to run like a madman, shrieking, "It's fine, it's fine!"

I set to work again to search the cave. The boots *had* to be found, or Lachenal and I were done for. On all fours, with nothing on my hands or feet I raked the snow, stirring it around this way and that, hoping every second to come upon something hard. I was no longer capable of thinking—I reacted like an animal fighting for its life.

I found one boot! The other was tied to it—a pair! Having ransacked the whole cave I at last found the other pair. But in spite of all my efforts I could not find the movie camera, and gave up in despair. There was no question of putting my boots on—my hands were like lumps of wood and I could hold nothing in my fingers; my feet were very swollen—I should never be able to get boots on them. I twisted the rope around the boots as well as I could and called up the chute:

"Lionel. . . . Boots!"

There was no answer, but he must have heard, for with a jerk the precious boots shot up. Soon after the rope came down again. My turn. I wound the rope around me. I could not pull it tight so I made a whole series of little knots. Their combined strength, I hoped, would be enough to hold me. I had no strength to shout again; I gave a great tug on the rope, and Terray understood.

At the first step I had to kick a notch in the hard snow for my toes. Further on I expected to be able to get up more easily by wedging myself across the tunnel. I wriggled up a few yards like this and then I tried to dig my hands and my feet into the wall. My hands were stiff and hard right up to the wrists and my feet had no feeling up to the ankles; the joints were inflexible, and this hampered me greatly.

Somehow or other I succeeded in working my way up, while Terray pulled so hard he nearly choked me. I began to see more distinctly and so knew I must be nearing the opening. Often I fell back, but I clung on and wedged myself in again as best I could. My heart was bursting and I was forced to rest. A fresh wave of energy enabled me to crawl to the top. I pulled myself out by clutching Terray's legs; he was just about all in and I was in the last stages of exhaustion. Terray was close to me and I whispered:

"Lionel . . . I'm dying!"

He supported me and helped me away from the crevasse. Lachenal and Rébuffat were sitting in the snow a few yards away. The instant Lionel let go of me I sank down and dragged myself along on all fours.

The weather was perfect. Quantities of snow had fallen the day before and the mountains were resplendent. Never had I seen them look so beautiful—our last day would be magnificent.

Rébuffat and Terray were completely blind; as he came along with me Terray knocked into things and I had to direct him. Rébuffat, too, could not move a step without guidance. It was terrifying to be blind when there was danger all around. Lachenal's frozen feet affected his nervous system. His behavior was disquieting—he was possessed by the most fantastic ideas:

"I tell you we must go down . . . down there. . . ."

"You've nothing on your feet!"

"Don't worry about that."

"You're off your head. The way's not there . . . it's to the left!"

He was already standing up; he wanted to go straight down to the bottom of the glacier. Terray held him back, made him sit down, and though he couldn't see, helped Lachenal put his boots on.

Behind them I was living in my own private dream. I knew the end was near, but it was the end that all mountaineers wish for—an end in keeping with their ruling passion. I was con-

sciously grateful to the mountains for being so beautiful for me that day, and as awed by their silence as if I had been in church. I was in no pain, and had no worry. My utter calmness was alarming. Terray came staggering toward me, and I told him: "It's all over for me. Go on . . . you have a chance . . . you must take it . . . over to the left . . . that's the way."

I felt better after telling him that. But Terray would have none of it: "We'll help you. If we get away, so will you."

At this moment Lachenal shouted: "Help! Help!"

Obviously he didn't know what he was doing. . . . Or did he? He was the only one of the four of us who could see Camp II down below. Perhaps his calls would be heard. They were shrieks of despair, reminding me tragically of some climbers lost in the Mont Blanc massif[26] whom I had endeavored to save. Now it was our turn. The impression was vivid: we were lost.

I joined in with the others: "One . . . two . . . three . . . *Help!* One . . . two . . . three . . . *Help!*" We tried to shout together, but without much success; our voices could not have carried more than ten feet. The noise I made was more of a whisper than a shout. Terray insisted that I should put my boots on, but my hands were dead. Neither Rébuffat nor Terray, who were unable to see, could help much, so I said to Lachenal: "Come and help me to put my boots on."

"Don't be silly, we must go down!"

And off he went once again in the wrong direction, straight down. I was not in the least angry with him; he had been sorely tried by the altitude and by everything he had gone through.

Terray resolutely got out his knife, and with fumbling hands slit the uppers of my boots back and front. Split in two like this I could get them on, but it was not easy and I had to make several attempts. Soon I lost heart—what was the use of it all anyway since I was going to stay where I was? But Terray pulled violently and finally he

---

26. **massif** (ma sēf'), principal mountain mass.

succeeded. He laced up my now-gigantic boots, missing half the hooks. I was ready now. But how was I going to walk with my stiff joints?

"To the left, Lionel!"

"You're crazy, Maurice," said Lachenal, "it's to the right, straight down."

Terray did not know what to think of these conflicting views. He had not given up like me, he was going to fight; but what, at the moment, could he do? The three of them discussed which way to go.

I remained sitting in the snow. Gradually my mind lost grip—why should I struggle? I would just let myself drift. I saw pictures of shady slopes, peaceful paths, there was a scent of resin. It was pleasant—I was going to die in my own mountains. My body had no feeling—everything was frozen.

"Aah . . . aah!"

Was it a groan or a call? I gathered my strength for one cry: "They're coming!" The others heard me and shouted for joy. What a miraculous apparition! "Schatz[27] . . . it's Schatz!"

Barely two hundred yards away Marcel Schatz, waist-deep in snow, was coming slowly toward us like a boat on the surface of the slope. I found this vision of a strong and invincible deliverer inexpressibly moving. I expected everything of him. The shock was violent, and quite shattered me. Death clutched at me, and I gave myself up.

When I came to again the wish to live returned and I experienced a violent revulsion of feeling. All was not lost! As Schatz came nearer my eyes never left him for a second—twenty yards—ten yards—he came straight toward me. Why? Without a word he leaned over me, held me close, hugged me, and his warm breath revived me.

I could not make the slightest movement—I was like marble. My heart was overwhelmed by such tremendous feelings and yet my eyes remained dry.

"It is wonderful—what you have done!"

---

27. **Schatz** (shätz), Marcel Schatz, who had moved from Camp III to Camp IV the day before. On the third of June he unexpectedly decided to make a track between Camp IV and Camp V, which would guide Herzog and Lachenal on their descent. Thus he happened to be on the right spot at the right moment to rescue the lost party.

Discussion

1. Judging from this selection, explain the dangers mountaineers face in high-altitude climbing.

2. As Herzog and Lachenal move from Camp V toward the summit of Annapurna, Lachenal reveals his "terror of frostbite." What does this incident tell you about (a) Lachenal's character, and (b) Herzog's character?

3. In describing the ascent, Herzog comments: "I felt as though I were plunging into something new and quite abnormal" (382b,3). Why does he feel that Annapurna is a unique experience?

4. (a) What are Herzog's feelings when he stands on the summit? (b) Do you think Lachenal's impatience with Herzog is justified? Explain why or why not.

5. Terray tells Herzog that the conquest of Annapurna is "a victory for the whole lot of us" (386a,5). Why does Herzog react as he does to Terray's comment?

6. Cite at least four instances in which the behavior of Terray and Rébuffat illustrates the selfless teamwork of the expedition.

7. (a) Trace the shifts in Herzog's state of mind during the descent from Camp V. (b) What physical conditions contributed to these shifts? (c) What emotional factors were involved?

8. (a) Would you agree or disagree that Herzog regards the conquest of Annapurna as an act of heroism? (b) Would a more objective account support this view? Explain.

Vocabulary
Context and Dictionary

Look up the following words in your Glossary. Choose the correct word to complete each sentence. Be sure you can pronounce and spell the words.

domain   insidious
feasible   laconic
incessant   paltry
               perseverance

1. Within the _____ of criminal investigation, Manuela van Gliden is the best.

2. She is a hard worker and her _____ is almost legendary.

3. In spite of the _____ evidence found in the toughest cases, Manuela's insight leads her to the suspect.

4. Among reporters trying for a story, her _____ reserve is well known.

5. In one rare interview, Manuela stated, "I understand completely the _____ workings of the criminal mind, and I have no patience with misdirected intelligence."

6. When the interview was published, crooks from all over voluntarily turned themselves in because, with Manuela van Gliden after them, "it seemed the most _____ thing to do."

Maurice Herzog 1919 ·

Born in Lyons, France, as a boy Herzog spent his holidays on the dizzy heights of the Alps. His skill in rock, ice, and snow climbing earned him the leadership of the French Himalayan Expedition when he was thirty-one. An engineer by profession, Herzog also holds a law degree and a degree in business administration. He commanded mountain troops during World War II.

Herzog began writing *Annapurna* in 1951 while recovering from the severe injuries he incurred on the descent from the summit. The book had to be dictated, for Annapurna had cost Herzog his fingers and toes.

notes and comments

The Writer as Architect

Without a skeleton, your body would be a mass of uncontrolled muscles, nerves, and organs. Without some form of suspension, a bridge would not stand. Without structure, the goal of a writer— development of a mood, communication of facts, statement of an opinion, defense of a theory— would never be achieved.

Structure is the basic organizational framework of a piece of literature. The structure of a particular work may be *formal*— containing a clear beginning, end, and middle. Or it may be *infor-* mal—the organization developing as the writer proceeds, often rambling, sometimes digressing, occasionally losing the main direction of thought. More often than not, an essay is a combination of the two—the writer having a general organizational pattern in mind, yet breaking from that pattern at certain points because such a break "feels" right. When a writer's thoughts seem to flow from idea to idea, impression to impression, without a clear pattern, his method is termed *stream-of-consciousness*.

Be aware of additional organization structures: *order of importance, cause-effect,* and other logical patterns. Look for words and phrases such as *once, then, therefore, but, in addition, for me, for us,* and *at last* to give you clues to the organization.

The structure of an essay is like the framework of a house. Without doors, windows, siding, paint, or wiring, the framework is not much of a place to live in. But without a framework, the house would never be a house.

Back to Bachimba

Enrique Hank López

I am a *pocho* from Bachimba, a rather small Mexican village in the state of Chihuahua, where my father fought with the army of Pancho Villa.[1] He was, in fact, the only private in Villa's army.

Pocho is ordinarily a derogatory term in Mexico, but I use it in a very special sense. To me that word has come to mean "uprooted Mexican," and that's what I have been all my life. Though my entire upbringing and education took place in the United States, I have never felt completely American, and when I am in Mexico, I sometimes feel like a displaced gringo[2] with a curiously Mexican name—Enrique Preciliano López y Martinez de Sepulveda de Sapien de Quien-sabe-quien.[3] One might conclude that I'm either a schizo-cultural Mexican or a cultured schizoid American.

In any event, the schizo-ing began a long time ago, when my father and many of Pancho Villa's troops fled across the border to escape the oncoming *federales* who eventually defeated Villa. My mother and I, traveling across the hot desert plains in a buckboard wagon, joined my father in El Paso, Texas, a few days after his hurried departure. With more and more Villistas[4] swarming into El Paso every day, it was quickly apparent that jobs would be exceedingly scarce and insecure; so my parents packed our few belongings and we took the first available bus to Denver. My father had hoped to move to Chicago because the name sounded so Mexican, but my mother's meager savings were hardly enough to buy tickets for Colorado.

There we moved into a ghetto of Spanish-speaking residents who chose to call themselves Spanish Americans and resented the sudden migration of their brethren from Mexico, whom they sneeringly called *surumatos* (slang for "southerners"). These so-called Spanish Americans claimed direct descent from the original *conquistadores* of Spain. They also insisted that they had *never* been Mexicans, since their region of New Spain (later annexed to the United States) was never a part of Mexico. But what they claimed most vociferously—and errone-

ously—was an absence of Indian ancestry. Still, these *manitos*, as they were snidely labeled by the *surumatos*, stubbornly refused to be identified with Mexico, and would actually fight anyone who called them Mexican. So intense was this intergroup rivalry that the bitterest "race riots" I have ever witnessed—and engaged in—were between the look-alike, talk-alike *surumatos* and *manitos* who lived near Denver's Curtis Park. In retrospect the harsh conflicts between us were all the more silly and self-defeating when one recalls that we were all lumped together as "spiks" and "greasers" by the Anglo-Saxon community.

Predictably enough, we *surumatos* began huddling together in a subneighborhood within the larger ghetto, and it was there that I became painfully aware that my father had been the only private in Pancho Villa's army. Most of my friends were the sons of captains, colonels, majors, and even generals, though a few fathers were admittedly mere sergeants and corporals. My father alone had been a lowly private in that famous Division del Norte. Naturally, I developed a most painful complex, which led me to all sorts of compensatory fibs. During one brief spell I fancied my father as a member of the dreaded *los dorados*, the "golden ones," who were Villa's favorite henchmen. (Later I was to learn that my father's cousin, Martin López, was a genuine and quite notorious *dorado*.) But all my inventions were quickly un-invented by my very own father, who seemed to take a perverse delight in being Pancho's only private.

No doubt my chagrin was accentuated by the fact that Pancho Villa's exploits were a constant topic of conversation in our household. My

Adapted from an article in the Winter 1967 issue of HORIZON Magazine. Reprinted by permission. © 1967 American Heritage Publishing Co., Inc.

1. *Pancho Villa* (vē'yä), Francisco Villa (1877–1923), Mexican revolutionary leader.
2. *gringo,* a white foreigner, but especially an American.
3. *de Sapien de Quien-sabe-quien.* López's full name includes his mother's maiden name and father's surname. He adds a witty note by adding "de Sapien . . . quien" meaning "from who knows who or where."
4. *Villistas* (vē yē'stäs), followers of Villa, both men and women.

entire childhood seems to be shadowed by his presence. At our dinner table, almost every night, we would listen to endlessly repeated accounts of this battle, that stratagem, or some great act of Robin Hood kindness by *el centauro del norte*.[5] I remember how angry my parents were when they saw Wallace Beery in *Viva Villa!* "Garbage by stupid gringos," they called it. They were particularly offended by the sweaty, unshaven sloppiness of Beery's portrayal.

As if to deepen our sense of *Villismo*,[6] my parents also taught us "Adelita" and *"Se llevaron el cañon para Bachimba"* ("They took the cannons to Bachimba"), the two most famous songs of the Mexican revolution. Some twenty years later (during my stint at Harvard Law School), while strolling along the Charles River, I would find myself softly singing *"Se llevaron el cañon para Bachimba, para Bachimba, para Bachimba"* over and over again. That's all I could remember of that poignant rebel song. Though I had been born there, I had always regarded "Bachimba" as a fictitious, made-up, Lewis Carroll[7] kind of word. So that eight years ago, when I first returned to Mexico, I was literally stunned when I came to a crossroad south of Chihuahua and saw an old road marker: "Bachimba 18 km." Then it really exists—I shouted inwardly—Bachimba is a real town! Swinging onto the narrow, poorly paved road, I gunned the motor and sped toward the town I'd been singing about since infancy. It turned out to be a quiet, dusty village with a bleak worn-down plaza that was surrounded by nondescript buildings of uncertain vintage.

Aside from the songs about Bachimba and Adelita and all the folk tales about Villa's guerrilla fighters, my early years were strongly influenced by our neighborhood celebrations of Mexico's two most important patriotic events: Mexican Independence Day on September 16 and the anniversary of the battle of Puebla on May 5. On those two dates Mexicans all over the world are likely to become extremely chauvinistic. In Denver we would stage annual parades that included three or four floats skimpily decorated with crepe paper streamers, a small band, several adults in threadbare battle dress, and hundreds of kids marching in wild disorder. It was during one of these parades—I was ten years old then—that I was seized with acute appendicitis and had to be rushed to a hospital. The doctor subsequently told my mother that I had made a long, impassioned speech about the early revolutionist Miguel Hidalgo while the anesthetic was taking hold, and she explained with pardonable pride that it was the speech I was to make at Turner Hall that evening. Mine was one of the twenty-three *discursos* scheduled on the postparade program, a copy of which my mother still retains. My only regret was missing the annual *discurso* of Don Miguel Gómez, my godfather, a deep-throated orator who would always climax his speech by falling to his knees and dramatically kissing the floor, almost weeping as he loudly proclaimed: *"Ay, Mexico! Beso tu tierra, tu mero corazon."* ("Ah, Mexico! I kiss your sacred soil, the very heart of you.") He gave the same oration for seventeen years, word for word and gesture for gesture, and it never failed to bring tears to his eyes. But not once did he return to Chihuahua, even for a brief visit.

My personal Mexican-ness eventually produced serious problems for me. Upon entering grade school I learned English rapidly, and rather well, always ranking either first or second in my class; yet the hard core of me remained stubbornly Mexican. This chauvinism may have been a reaction to the constant racial prejudice we encountered on all sides. The neighborhood cops were always running us off the streets and calling us "dirty greasers," and most of our teachers frankly regarded us as totally inferior. I still remember the galling disdain of my sixth-

---

5. *el centauro del norte,* the centaur of the north. A centaur was a legendary half-man, half-horse. Villa was an excellent horseman.
6. *Villismo* (vē yēs'mō), the spirit of, and belief in Villa.
7. **Lewis Carroll,** pseudonym of Charles Dodgson (1832–1898), author of *Alice in Wonderland,* in which many strange made-up words are used.

grade teacher, whose constant mimicking of our heavily accented speech drove me to a desperate study of *Webster's Dictionary* in the hope of acquiring a vocabulary larger than hers. Sadly enough, I succeeded only too well, and for the next few years I spoke the most ridiculous high-flown rhetoric in the Denver public schools. One of my favorite words was "indubitably," and it must have driven everyone mad. I finally got rid of my accent by constantly reciting "Peter Piper picked a peck of pickled peppers" with little round pebbles in my mouth. Somewhere I had read about Demosthenes.[8]

During this phase of my childhood the cultural tug of war known as "Americanization" almost pulled me apart. There were moments when I would identify completely with the gringo world (what could have been more American than my earnest high-voiced portrayal of George Washington, however ridiculous the cotton wig my mother had fashioned for me?); then quite suddenly I would feel so acutely Mexican that I would stammer over the simplest English phrase. I was so ready to take offense at the slightest slur against Mexicans that I would imagine prejudice where none existed. But on other occasions, in full confidence of my belonging, I would venture forth into social areas that I should have realized were clearly forbidden to little chicanos from Curtis Park. The inevitable rebuffs would leave me floundering in self-pity; it was small comfort to know that other minority groups suffered even worse rebuffs than we did.

The only non-Mexican boy on our street was a black, named Leroy Logan, who was probably my closest childhood friend. Leroy was the best athlete, the best whistler, the best liar, the best horseshoe player, the best marble shooter and the best mumblety-pegger[9] in our neighborhood. Because he considered "Mexican" a derogatory word bordering on obscenity, Leroy would pronounce it "Mesican" so as to soften its harshness. I remember him with great affection and a touch of sadness. I say sadness because eventually Leroy was to suffer the misery of being an outsider in an already outside ghetto. As he grew older, it was apparent that he longed to be a Mexican, that he felt terribly dark and alone. "Sometimes," he would tell me, "I feel like my skin's too tight, like I'm gonna bust out of it. Man, you sure lucky to be a Mesican."

Later, Leroy moved out of Denver to live with relatives in Georgia. When I saw him off at the bus station, he grabbed my shoulder and whispered huskily, "You gonna miss me, man. You watch what I tellya." "Indubitably," I said. "Aw, man, cut that stuff. You the most fancy-pants Mesican I know." Those were his last words to me, and they caused a considerable dent in my ego. Not enough, however, to diminish my penchant for fancy language. The dictionary continued to be my comic book well into high school.

My own Mexican-ness, after years of decline at Harvard University, suddenly burst forth again when I returned to Chihuahua and stumbled on the town of Bachimba. I had long conversations with an uncle I'd never met before, my father's younger brother, Ramón. It was Tio Ramón who chilled my spine with eyewitness stories about Pancho Villa's legendary *dorados,* one of whom was Martin López. "He was your second cousin. The bravest young buck in Villa's army." Tio Ramón's eyes were wet with pride. "What is more important, he died with great valor."

As I listened to Tio Ramón's soft nostalgic voice that evening, there in the sputtering light of the kerosene lamp on his back patio, I felt as intensely Mexican as I shall ever feel.

But not for long. Within six weeks I was destined to feel *less* Mexican than I had ever felt. The scene of my trauma was the Centro Mexicano de Escritores,[10] where the finest young writers of Mexico met regularly to discuss works in progress and to engage in erudite literary and

---

8. *Demosthenes* (di·mos'thə·nēz'), a famous Greek orator (c.383–322 B.C), who had a speech impediment as a child but overcame it by talking with pebbles in his mouth.
9. *mumblety-pegger,* one who plays mumblety-peg, a game in which a pocketknife is flipped into the ground in various ways.
10. *Centro Mexicano de Escritores,* Mexican Writers' Center.

philosophical discussions. Week after week I sat among them, dumbstruck by my inadequacy in Spanish and my total ignorance of their whole frame of reference. How could I have possibly imagined that I was Mexican?

Can any of us really go home again? I, for one, am convinced that I have no true home, that I must reconcile myself to a schizo-cultural limbo, with a mere hyphen to provide some slight cohesion between my split selves. This inevitable splitting is a plague and a pleasure.

Recently, when I expressed these views to an old friend, he smiled quite knowingly: "Let's face it, Hank, you're not really a Mexican—despite that long, comical name of yours. You're an American through and through." But that, of course, is a minority view and almost totally devoid of realism. One could just as well say that Martin Luther King was not black, that he was merely an American. But the plain truth is that neither I nor the Martin Luther Kings of our land can escape the fact that we are Mexican and black with roots planted so deeply in the United States that we have grown those strong little hyphens that make us Mexican-American and black-American. This assertion may not please some idealists who would prefer to blind themselves to our obvious ethnic and racial differences, who are unwittingly patronizing when they insist that we are all alike and indistinguishable. But the politicians, undoubtedly the most pragmatic creatures in America, are completely aware that ethnic groups *do* exist and that they seem to huddle together, complain together, and sometimes vote together.

When all is said and done, we hyphenated Americans are here to stay, bubbling happily or unhappily in the great nonmelting pot. Much has been gained and will be gained from the multiethnic aspects of the United States, and there is no useful purpose in attempting to wish it away or to homogenize it out of existence.

And if there are those of us who may never feel completely at home, we can always make that brief visit to Bachimba.

□ □

Discussion

1. What major events during his childhood contributed to López's later feeling that he is neither completely American nor completely Mexican?

2. (a) How does López try to combat the sixth-grade teacher who mimics his accent? (b) Do you think that his efforts to enlarge his vocabulary and to eliminate his accent added to or diminished his feelings of security and self-esteem?

3. What does López mean when he asks, "Can any of us really go home again?"

Enrique Hank López

Besides his active career as a writer, López has been an actor, a practicing lawyer, and a politician. In 1958 he ran for Secretary of State in California, losing only by one percent of the cast votes.

He was born in Chihuahua (chi wä'wä), Mexico, and when he was still a child, his parents moved to the United States. He was raised in Denver, Colorado, and received his degree in law from Harvard University.

López has assisted several famous people in writing their autobiographies, including Lyndon Johnson and Katherine Anne Porter.

New York's My Home

Alice Childress

Paul Fusco, Magnum

Owen Franken; Stock, Boston

Marge, sometimes out of town visitors can be a real drag if you live in New York City . . . Well, you remember the time my friend Mamie visited me for two weeks? . . . Of course I enjoyed her company, but she almost gave me a nervous breakdown! . . . Yes girl, she came here with a list as long as your arm and had every minute of her time planned right down to the second . . . No, I didn't mind that at all, but what got me was the fact that my time had to go right along with it . . . Honey! She had to see *all* the museums, the Statue of Liberty, the Empire State Building, the United Nations, Radio City, Central Park, Bronx Park, Small's Paradise, Birdland, Randolph's, the theatres, the markets, and, of course, she never got her fill of bus and boat sight-seeing trips . . . My dear, I never did so much subway ridin' and transferrin' in my natural life . . . I can tell you that I was some worn out. About two

days before she left she decided to make the rounds of all the big department stores . . . Marge, we hit every floor in Macy's and then run over to Gimbel's and . . .

Girl! Are you out of your mind? Of course she didn't soak me for all the bills, in fact she made an announcement the first day she got here . . . "Mildred, I'm goin' to pay my own way everywhere I go" . . . That was great, Marge, but the fact remains that I had to pay *my* way and traipse along with her, and when she left I was two steps from the poor house and a nervous breakdown.

Wait a minute, I haven't told it all . . . Well, she also had to sample all the different foods in the different restaurants. We had Chinese din-

"New York's My Home" from LIKE ONE OF THE FAMILY.
Originally published by Independence Publishers. Copyright ©
1956 by Alice Childress. Reprinted by permission of the author's
agent, Flora Roberts, Inc., 65 East 55th St., New York, N.Y. 10022.

ners, French lunches, Italian suppers and so forth and so on, then to cap the climax she just *had* to ride one of those horse and buggy things through Central Park . . . Yes, we did that day before she left . . . There I was leaning back in this carriage, my arms full of packages and my blood pressure hittin' close to two hundred when out she comes with this remark: "New York is all right to visit but I could *never* live here. It's too much rush and hectic going all the time. The pace is too fast, the buildings are too close together, and I like peace and quiet."

My dear, you could have cut the silence with a knife because countin' to ten was not enough and I had to go past seventy-five before I dared answer her . . . But before I could open my mouth she adds, "How do you ever stand it?" I took ten more after that and mumbled something about, "Oh, I don't live this fast all the time." . . . Believe me when I say that the prettiest sight I ever saw in my life was that big train sittin' in the station waitin' to carry her away from here. That's a fact . . . and you know I'm fond of Mamie!

Today . . . listen close now . . . *today* I get a letter from her sister June sayin' that Mamie had such a good time while she was here that she . . . June . . . had decided to spend her vacation with me next summer. My ankles started to swell just sittin' there thinkin' about it, and I made up my mind then and there that I could not go through the business of bein' personal guide on a merry-go-round for another two-week stretch . . . Of course, she's welcome but no more of this jumpin' through hoops for yours truly, especially when half of the time the visitor goes back home without the least idea of what New York City is all about or why millions of people stay here and also like it . . . I know it! All these out-of-towners think we're a bunch of good-timers!

Marge, you know it is a rare thing for me to be runnin' different places . . . and even if my health could stand it, my pocketbook can't . . . That's right, there's hardly a small town in the land where you'll find people goin' less than your friend Mildred, but whenever I go away I soon find that I'm gettin' real homesick for this New York . . . because I like it!

When I'm here, I enjoy stayin' home with the thought that there is a million places for me to go if I wanted to, but when I'm away I hate stayin' home with the thought that I *have* to because nothin's goin' on . . . Yes, ma'am, that makes a real difference.

When I'm away I miss the subway . . . No, not the rush and crowd, but the people. I like ridin' with folks of every race, color and kind . . . They make stories go round in my head, and sometimes I go past my stop because I'm so busy imaginin' their children and homes and what kind of lives they live . . . One day I was in a supermarket and I saw this East Indian with a beautiful pink turban on his head . . . Oh, he was busy buyin' a box of Uneeda biscuits . . . That stayed on my mind for a long time because the turban made me think of pearls and palaces . . . but there he was big as life . . . with biscuits! . . . Yes, I miss these things when I'm away. I miss the people walkin' along with their little radios held up to their ear so's they can listen to the Dodgers,[1] the big ships standin' still and mighty in the harbor, the tough little tug boats huffin' and puffin' up the river, the fellas pushin' carts of suits and dresses in and out of downtown traffic, people readin' all manner of foreign newspapers and such, all the big sounds of swishin' automobiles, planes overhead and children shoutin' until it all comes together and turns into one big "New York-sound."

. . . Talk about missin' things! . . . I miss the friendliness of total strangers when they gather on a corner and try to direct somebody who doesn't speak English . . . Yes Marge, I bet many a soul has ended up on the west side of nowhere tryin' to follow the advice of New Yorkers who are always gettin' lost themselves, even though they have been here ever since the flood . . . Ain't it the truth? . . . I also miss the nice way your neighbors don't bother to keep up with what time you come and go or who visits your

---

1. **Dodgers.** At the time of this account, Brooklyn was still the home of this baseball team.

house and how long they stayed . . . That's true, too, them same neighbors will rallyround in case of sickness or death . . . I miss seein' the line in front of the Apollo waitin' to see all those fine stars like Nat King Cole and Sammy Davis and Eartha Kitt and Count Basie and everything . . . Tell it now!

Talk about things to miss! . . . I miss the way the workmen are always diggin' at the street pipes . . . It's kind of mystifying because you never know what's bein' dug, but you can stop and watch a little while anyway and think about nothin' in particular and then pass on . . . Oh honey! . . . I miss *life!*

But Marge, what I miss most is a feelin' in the air, a feelin' that hits you right in the railroad station . . . I can't describe it in words too well, but it seeps into you and it's real excitin'. I guess maybe you'd call it a "something's-gonna-happen-and-you-don't-know-what-it-is" kind of feelin' . . . You right . . . I get sick and tired of folks sayin' "I could never *live* here" . . . because even though I may not ever get hold of enough money to travel to far-off places, I can still say I've met some fine Puerto Ricans and Irish, and Italian, and French, and African and some of all kind of folk . . . This City is far from perfect, but it gets you to the place where you just want to try and *make* it perfect. Oh, sure, I don't mind June comin' to visit, but I'm gonna try and make her see my home the way I see it!

. . . Hold on, Marge! Now, I wouldn't go that far . . . I ain't sayin' that everything here is better than any place else and neither will I take any cracks at the South! Because home is where the heart is and everybody knows their own home the best.

All I'm sayin' is I wish people would stop tellin' us "I could *never* live here." ☐☐

Discussion

1. (a) What does Mildred's account of her friend Mamie's visit reveal about Mildred? **(b)** about Mamie? Describe each woman and explain what details lead you to describe them as you do.

2. (a) If New York is your home, with what details of Mildred's description do you agree or disagree? What would you change or add? **(b)** If you have visited New York, which of Mamie's activities were also on your list? **(c)** If you have never been in New York, does Mildred's description of why she likes it make you want to go there? Why or why not?

Extension
Writing and Speaking

1. Suppose that you are a director. Write a description of the way you would want an actress to present this dramatic monologue. What tone should she use at the start of the telephone call? At what points thereafter should she change her tone? Why and how?

2. Appoint a classmate to present the monologue orally, following a "director's" instructions.

Alice Childress 1920 ·

Childress is a playwright, a novelist, an editor, an actress, and a director. For twelve years she was director of American Negro Theatre in New York, and one of her plays *Trouble in Mind*, won the OBIE Award for the best original off-Broadway play in 1956. In 1971 she edited *Black Scenes: Collection of Scenes from Plays Written by Black People About Black Experience*, and in 1973 she published *A Hero Ain't Nothin' But a Sandwich*, a book for adolescent readers. Born in Charleston, South Carolina, Ms. Childress lives in New York City.

from The Woman Warrior

Maxine Hong Kingston

When I last visited my parents, I had trouble falling asleep, too big for the hills and valleys scooped in the mattress by child-bodies. I heard my mother come in. I stopped moving. What did she want? Eyes shut, I pictured my mother, her white hair frizzy in the dark-and-light doorway, my hair white now too, Mother. I could hear her move furniture about. Then she dragged a third quilt, the thick, homemade Chinese kind, across me. After that I lost track of her location. I spied from beneath my eyelids and had to hold back a jump. She had pulled up a chair and was sitting by the bed next to my head. I could see her strong hands in her lap, not working fourteen pairs of needles. She is very proud of her hands, which can make anything and stay pink and soft while my father's became like carved wood. Her palm lines do not branch into head, heart, and life lines like other people's but crease with just one atavistic fold. That night she was a sad bear; a great sheep in a wool shawl. She recently took to wearing shawls and granny glasses, American fashions. What did she want, sitting there so large next to my head? I could feel her stare—her eyes two lights warm on my graying hair, then on the creases at the sides of my mouth, my thin neck, my thin cheeks, my thin arms. I felt her sight warm each of my bony elbows, and I flopped about in my fake sleep to hide them from her criticism. She sent light at full brightness beaming through my eyelids, her eyes at my eyes, and I had to open them.

"What's the matter, Mama? Why are you sitting there?"

She reached over and switched on a lamp she had placed on the floor beside her. "I swallowed that LSD pill you left on the kitchen counter," she announced.

"That wasn't LSD, Mama. It was just a cold pill. I have a cold."

"You're always catching colds when you come home. You must be eating too much *yin.*[1] Let me get you another quilt."

"No, no more quilts. You shouldn't take pills that aren't prescribed for you. 'Don't eat pills you find on the curb,' you always told us."

"You children never tell me what you're really up to. How else am I going to find out what you're really up to?" As if her head hurt, she closed her eyes behind the gold wire rims. "Aiaa," she sighed, "how can I bear to have you leave me again?"

How can I bear to leave her again? She would close up this room, open temporarily for me, and wander about cleaning and cleaning the shrunken house, so tidy since our leaving. Each chair has its place now. And the sinks in the bedrooms work, their alcoves no longer stuffed with laundry right up to the ceiling. My mother has put the clothes and shoes into boxes, stored against hard times. The sinks had been built of gray marble for the old Chinese men who boarded here before we came. I used to picture modest little old men washing in the mornings and dressing before they shuffled out of these bedrooms. I would have to leave and go again into the world out there which has no marble ledges for my clothes, no quilts made from our own ducks and turkeys, no ghosts of neat little old men.

The lamp gave off the sort of light that comes from a television, which made the high ceiling disappear and then suddenly drop back into place. I could feel that clamping down and see how my mother had pulled the blinds down so low that the bare rollers were showing. No passer-by would detect a daughter in this house. My mother would sometimes be a large animal, barely real in the dark; then she would become a mother again. I could see the wrinkles around her big eyes, and I could see her cheeks sunken without her top teeth.

"I'll be back again soon," I said. "You know that I come back. I think of you when I'm not here."

"Yes, I know you. I know you now. I've

From THE WOMAN WARRIOR: MEMOIRS OF A GIRLHOOD AMONG GHOSTS, by Maxine Hong Kingston. Copyright © 1975, 1976 by Maxine Hong Kingston. Reprinted by permission of Alfred A. Knopf, Inc. and John Schaffner, Literary Agent.

1. *eating too much yin.* In Chinese philosophy and religion the universe has two great complementary forces: *yin* and *yang.* Illness is attributed to an overbalance of either *yin* or *yang* in the body. Some foods are hot or *yang,* others are cold or *yin.*

always known you. You're the one with the charming words. You have never come back. 'I'll be back on Turkeyday,' you said. Huh.''

I shut my teeth together, vocal cords cut, they hurt so. I would not speak words to give her pain. All her children gnash their teeth.

"The last time I saw you, you were still young,'' she said. "Now you're old.''

"It's only been a year since I visited you.''

"That's the year you turned old. Look at you, hair gone gray, and you haven't even fattened up yet. I know how the Chinese talk about us. 'They're so poor,' they say, 'they can't afford to fatten up any of their daughters.' 'Years in America,' they say, 'and they don't eat.' Oh, the shame of it—a whole family of skinny children. And your father—he's so skinny, he's disappearing.''

"Don't worry about him, Mama. Doctors are saying that skinny people live longer. Papa's going to live a long time.''

"So! I knew I didn't have too many years left. Do you know how I got all this fat? Eating your leftovers. Aiaa, I'm getting so old. Soon you will have no more mother.''

"Mama, you've been saying that all my life.''

"This time it's true. I'm almost eighty.''

"I thought you were only seventy-six.''

"My papers are wrong. I'm eighty.''

"But I thought your papers are wrong, and you're seventy-two, seventy-three in Chinese years.''

"My papers are wrong, and I'm eighty, eighty-one in Chinese years. Seventy. Eighty. What do numbers matter? I'm dropping dead any day now. The aunt down the street was resting on her porch steps, dinner all cooked, waiting for her husband and son to come home and eat it. She closed her eyes for a moment and died. Isn't that a wonderful way to go?''

"But our family lives to be ninety-nine.''

"That's your father's family. My mother and father died very young. My youngest sister was an orphan at ten. Our parents were not even fifty.''

"Then you should feel grateful you've lived so many extra years.''

"I was so sure you were going to be an orphan too. In fact, I'm amazed you've lived to have white hair. Why don't you dye it?''

"Hair color doesn't measure age, Mother. White is just another pigment, like black and brown.''

"You're always listening to Teacher Ghosts, those Scientist Ghosts, Doctor Ghosts.''[2]

"I have to make a living.''

"I never do call you Oldest Daughter. Have you noticed that? I always tell people, 'This is my Biggest Daughter.' ''

"Is it true then that Oldest Daughter and Oldest Son died in China? Didn't you tell me when I was ten that she'd have been twenty; when I was twenty, she'd be thirty?'' Is that why you've denied me my title?

"No, you must have been dreaming. You must have been making up stories. You are all the children there are.''

(Who was that story about—the one where the parents are throwing money at the children, but the children don't pick it up because they're crying too hard? They're writhing on the floor covered with coins. Their parents are going out the door for America, hurling handfuls of change behind them.)

She leaned forward, eyes brimming with what she was about to say: "I work so hard,'' she said. She was doing her stare—at what? My feet began rubbing together as if to tear each other's skin off. She started talking again, "The tomato vines prickle my hands; I can feel their little stubble hairs right through my gloves. My feet squish-squish in the rotten tomatoes, squish-squish in the tomato mud the feet ahead of me have sucked. And do you know the best way to stop the itch from the tomato hairs? You break open a fresh tomato and wash yourself with it. You cool your face in tomato juice. Oh, but it's the potatoes that will ruin my hands. I'll get

2. **Teacher Ghosts . . . Doctor Ghosts.** See the author's comments on page 410.

rheumatism washing potatoes, squatting over potatoes.''

She had taken off the Ace bandages around her legs for the night. The varicose veins stood out.

"Mama, why don't you stop working? You don't have to work anymore. Do you? Do you really have to work like that? Scabbing in the tomato fields?'' Her black hair seems filleted with the band of white at its roots. She dyed her hair so that the farmers would hire her. She would walk to Skid Row and stand in line with the hobos, the winos, and the junkies, . . . until the farm buses came and the farmers picked out the workers they wanted. "You have the house," I said. "For food you have Social Security. And urban renewal must have given you something. It was good in a way when they tore down the laundry. Really, Mama, it was. Otherwise Papa would never have retired. You ought to retire too."

"Do you think your father wanted to stop work? Look at his eyes; the brown is going out of his eyes. He has stopped talking. When I go to work, he eats leftovers. He doesn't cook new food," she said, confessing, me maddened at confessions. "Those Urban Renewal Ghosts gave us moving money. It took us seventeen years to get our customers. How could we start all over on moving money, as if we two old people had another seventeen years in us? Aa"—she flipped something aside with her hand—"White Ghosts can't tell Chinese age."

I closed my eyes and breathed evenly, but she could tell I wasn't asleep.

"This is terrible ghost country, where a human being works her life away," she said. "Even the ghosts work, no time for acrobatics. I have not stopped working since the day the ship landed. I was on my feet the moment the babies were out. In China I never even had to hang up my own clothes. I shouldn't have left, but your father couldn't have supported you without me. I'm the one with the big muscles."

"If you hadn't left, there wouldn't have been a me for you two to support. Mama, I'm really

sleepy. Do you mind letting me sleep?'' I do not believe in old age. I do not believe in getting tired.

"I didn't need muscles in China. I was small in China." She was. The silk dresses she gave me are tiny. You would not think the same person wore them. This mother can carry a hundred pounds of Texas rice up- and downstairs. She could work at the laundry from 6:30 A.M. until midnight, shifting a baby from an ironing table to a shelf between packages, to the display window, where the ghosts tapped on the glass. "I put you babies in the clean places at the laundry, as far away from the germs that fumed out of the ghosts' clothes as I could. Aa, their socks and handkerchiefs choked me. I cough now because of those seventeen years of breathing dust. Tubercular handkerchiefs. Lepers' socks." I thought she had wanted to show off my baby sister in the display window.

In the midnight unsteadiness we were back at the laundry, and my mother was sitting on an orange crate sorting dirty clothes into mountains—a sheet mountain, a white shirt mountain, a dark shirt mountain, a work-pants mountain, a long underwear mountain, a short underwear mountain, a little hill of socks pinned together in pairs, a little hill of handkerchiefs pinned to tags. Surrounding her were candles she burned in daylight, clean yellow diamonds, footlights that ringed her, mysterious masked mother, nose and mouth veiled with a cowboy handkerchief. Before undoing the bundles, my mother would light a tall new candle, which was a luxury, and the pie pans full of old wax and wicks that sometimes sputtered blue, a noise I thought was the germs getting seared.

"No tickee, no washee, mama-san?'' a ghost would say, so embarrassing.

"Noisy Red-Mouth Ghost," she'd write on its package, naming it, marking its clothes with its name.

Back in the bedroom I said, "The candles must have helped. It was a good idea of yours to use candles."

"They didn't do much good. All I have to do

is think about dust sifting out of clothes or peat dirt blowing across a field or chick mash falling from a scoop, and I start coughing." She coughed deeply. "See what I mean? I have worked too much. Human beings don't work like this in China. Time goes slower there. Here we have to hurry, feed the hungry children before we're too old to work. I feel like a mother cat hunting for its kittens. She has to find them fast because in a few hours she will forget how to count or that she had any kittens at all. I can't sleep in this country because it doesn't shut down for the night. Factories, canneries, restaurants—always somebody somewhere working through the night. It never gets done all at once here. Time was different in China. One year lasted as long as my total time here; one evening so long, you could visit your women friends, drink tea, and play cards at each house, and it would still be twilight. It even got boring, nothing to do but fan ourselves. Here midnight comes and the floor's not swept, the ironing's not ready, the money's not made. I would still be young if we lived in China."

"Time is the same from place to place," I said unfeelingly. "There is only the eternal present, and biology. The reason you feel time pushing is that you had six children after you were forty-five and you worried about raising us. You shouldn't worry anymore, though, Mama. You should feel good you had so many babies around you in middle age. Not many mothers have that. Wasn't it like prolonging youth? Now wasn't it? You mustn't worry now. All of us have grown up. And you can stop working."

"I can't stop working. When I stop working, I hurt. My head, my back, my legs hurt. I get dizzy. I can't stop."

"I'm like that too, Mama. I work all the time. Don't worry about me starving. I won't starve. I know how to work. I work all the time. I know how to kill food, how to skin and pluck it. I know how to keep warm by sweeping and mopping. I know how to work when things get bad."

"It's a good thing I taught you children to look after yourselves. We're not going back to China for sure now."

"You've been saying that since nineteen forty-nine."

"Now it's final. We got a letter from the villagers yesterday. They asked if it was all right with us that they took over the land. The last uncles have been killed so your father is the only person left to say it is all right, you see. He has written saying they can have it. So. We have no more China to go home to."

It must be all over then. My mother and father have stoked each other's indignation for almost forty years telling stories about land quarrels among the uncles, the inlaws, the grandparents. Episodes from their various points of view came weekly in the mail, until the uncles were executed kneeling on broken glass by people who had still other plans for the land. How simply it ended—my father writing his permission. Permission asked, permission given twenty-five years after the Revolution.

"We belong to the planet now, Mama. Does it make sense to you that if we're no longer attached to one piece of land, we belong to the planet? Wherever we happen to be standing, why, that spot belongs to us as much as any other spot." Can we spend the fare money on furniture and cars? Will American flowers smell good now?

"I don't want to go back anyway," she said. "I've gotten used to eating. And the Communists are much too mischievous. You should see the ones I meet in the fields. They bring sacks under their clothes to steal grapes and tomatoes from the growers. They come with trucks on Sundays. And they're killing each other in San Francisco." One of the old men caught his visitor, another old fellow, stealing his bantam; the owner spotted its black feet sticking out of his guest's sweater. We woke up one morning to find a hole in the ground where our loquat tree had stood. Later we saw a new loquat tree most similar to ours in a Chinese neighbor's yard. We knew a family who had a sign in their vegetable patch: "Since this is not a Communist garden but cabbages grown by private enterprise, please do not steal from my garden." It was dated and signed in good handwriting.

"The new immigrants aren't Communists, Mother. They're fugitives from the real Communists."

"They're Chinese, and Chinese are mischievous. No, I'm too old to keep up with them. They'd be too clever for me. I've lost my cunning, having grown accustomed to food, you see. There's only one thing that I really want anymore. I want you here, not wandering like a ghost from Romany. I want every one of you living here together. When you're all home, all six of you with your children and husbands and wives, there are twenty or thirty people in this house. Then I'm happy. And your father is happy. Whichever room I walk into overflows with my relatives, grandsons, sons-in-law. I can't turn around without touching somebody. That's the way a house should be." Her eyes are big, inconsolable. A spider headache spreads out in fine branches over my skull. She is etching spider legs into the icy bone. She pries open my head and my fists and crams into them responsibility for time, responsibility for intervening oceans.

The gods pay her and my father back for leaving their parents. My grandmother wrote letters pleading for them to come home, and they ignored her. Now they know how she felt.

"When I'm away from here," I had to tell her, "I don't get sick. I don't go to the hospital every holiday. I don't get pneumonia, no dark spots on my x-rays. My chest doesn't hurt when I breathe. I can breathe. And I don't get headaches at 3:00. I don't have to take medicines or go to doctors. Elsewhere I don't have to lock my doors and keep checking the locks. I don't stand at the windows and watch for movements and see them in the dark."

"What do you mean you don't lock your doors?"

"I do. I do. But not the way I do here. I don't hear ghost sounds. I don't stay awake listening to walking in the kitchen. I don't hear the doors and windows unhinging."

"It was probably just a Wino Ghost or a Hobo Ghost looking for a place to sleep."

"I don't want to hear Wino Ghosts and Hobo Ghosts. I've found some places in this country that are ghost-free. And I think I belong there, where I don't catch colds or use my hospitalization insurance. Here I'm sick so often, I can barely work. I can't help it, Mama."

She yawned. "It's better, then, for you to stay away. The weather in California must not agree with you. You can come for visits." She got up and turned off the light. "Of course, you must go, Little Dog."

A weight lifted from me. The quilts must be filling with air. The world is somehow lighter. She has not called me that endearment for years—a name to fool the gods. I am really a Dragon, as she is a Dragon, both of us born in dragon years. I am practically a first daughter of a first daughter.

"Good night, Little Dog."

"Good night, Mother."

She sends me on my way, working always and now old, dreaming the dreams about . . . a Chinatown bigger than the ones here.

□ □

From the Author

"Ghosts" is my translation of the Chinese word *Guai* (gwāy), which could be translated "demon," "devil," "monster." It is a word that is used very often in spoken Cantonese. I used "ghosts" because I liked the general quality of this word. I wanted an English word with as many uses as in Chinese. The Chinese call white people *bok guai*—*bok* means "white."

Guai is a common epithet. The Chinese language is very aggressive, and Chinese like to make up names for people. When we swear at each other, we call each other *guai*—as in "You crazy ghost," "You dead ghost," or "You dumb, stupid ghost." But *guai* has many other uses. In fairy tales there are beautiful women who are ghosts too; they do not necessarily look monstrous;

they are lovely. The English word *ghosts* can also refer to beautiful ladies. I did not choose to use "demon" or "devil" because I feel these words necessarily mean ugly creatures (as is the connotation in "bok guai"), and also because they are the translations used in movie stereotypes. . . .

Discussion

1. About what does the mother criticize her daughter?
2. What about her mother worries the daughter?
3. (a) To what extent do mother and daughter agree with each other? disagree? (b) How does the way that each responds to the other help to characterize their relationship?
4. Do you feel sorry for the daughter and/or her mother? Why or why not?

Maxine Hong Kingston
1940 ·

Kingston's parents emigrated from China separately: her father in 1924, her mother in 1939, after experiencing the invasion of China by Japan. Her mother, a doctor, had done much to ease the suffering of war refugees.

Born in Stockton, California, Kingston grew up there with the old legends, traditions, and folk beliefs her parents brought with them from China.

She graduated from the University of California at Berkeley, and now lives in Honolulu, where she teaches English and creative writing. "I cannot imagine living without writing," she says, "writing is like breathing."

Clean Your Room

Art Buchwald

You don't really feel the generation gap in this country until a son or daughter comes home from college for Christmas. Then it strikes you how out of it you really are.

This dialogue probably took place all over America last Christmas week:

"Nancy, you've been home from school for three days now. Why don't you clean up your room?"

"We don't have to clean up our rooms at college, Mother."

"That's very nice, Nancy, and I'm happy you're going to such a freewheeling institution. But while you're in the house, your father and I would like you to clean up your room."

"What difference does it make? It's *my* room."

"I know, dear, and it really doesn't mean that much to me. But your father has a great fear of the plague. He said this morning if it is going to start anywhere in this country, it's going to start in your room."

"Mother, you people aren't interested in anything that's relevant. Do you realize how the major corporations are polluting our environment?"

"Your father and I are very worried about it. But right now we're more concerned with the pollution in your bedroom. You haven't made your bed since you came home."

"I never make it up at the dorm."

"Of course you don't, and I'm sure the time you save goes toward your education. But we still have these old-fashioned ideas about making beds in the morning, and we can't shake them. Since you're home for such a short time, why don't you do it to humor us?"

"For heaven's sake, Mother, I'm grown up now. Why do you have to treat me like a child?"

"We're not treating you like a child. But it's

Reprinted by permission of G. P. Putnam's Sons from I NEVER DANCED AT THE WHITE HOUSE by Art Buchwald. Copyright © 1971, 1972, 1973 by Art Buchwald.

very hard for us to realize you're an adult when you throw all your clothes on the floor.''

"I haven't thrown all my clothes on the floor. Those are just the clothes I wore yesterday.''

"Forgive me. I exaggerated. Well, how about the dirty dishes and empty soft-drink cans on your desk? Are you collecting them for a science project?''

"Mother, you don't understand us. You people were brought up to have clean rooms. But our generation doesn't care about things like that. It's what you have in your head that counts.''

"No one respects education more than your father and I do, particularly at the prices they're charging. But we can't see how living in squalor can improve your mind.''

"That's because of your priorities. You would rather have me make up my bed and pick up my clothes than become a free spirit who thinks for myself.''

"We're not trying to stifle your free spirit. It's just that our Blue Cross has run out, and we have no protection in case anybody in the family catches typhoid.''

"All right, I'll clean up my room if it means that much to you. But I want you to know you've ruined my vacation.''

"It was a calculated risk I had to take. Oh, by the way, I know this is a terrible thing to ask of you, but would you mind helping me wash the dinner dishes?''

"Wash dishes? Nobody washes dishes at school.''

"Your father and I were afraid of that.'' □□

Discussion

1. One technique for winning an argument is to agree with your opponent's ideas in part or in whole, but then return to the point you want to make, and to keep making that same point no matter how often your opponent tries to change it or to divert you from it. **(a)** Select several lines showing the mother's skillful use of this technique. **(b)** Does Nancy realize how her arguments are being foiled? Explain.

2. (a) Look up the word *cliché* and cite as many examples from the selection as you can. **(b)** How are they relevant to the generation gap the narrator mentions in the first paragraph?

Extension · Speaking

Select one of the roles in this selection and find a classmate to take the other. Practice reading the selection aloud until you can read it loud enough to be heard at the back of a classroom, clearly enough to be understood by someone who hasn't read it, and with enough expression to convey its humor. When you think you have reached these goals, try performing it for students who haven't read it.

Art Buchwald 1925 ·

Only sixteen at the start of World War II, Buchwald quit high school to join the Marines. After serving in the Pacific, he attended the University of Southern California for three years, editing a college humor magazine and almost failing an English course in humor. He left in 1948 without finishing his degree requirements when a veteran's bonus bought him a one-way airline ticket to Paris. He wrote there a syndicated column through the Paris edition of the *New York Herald Tribune*. The column was translated into many foreign languages. In 1962, he moved his beat to Washington, D.C.

If I were to remember other things, I should be someone else.

from The Names

N. Scott Momaday

In my earliest years I traveled a number of times from Oklahoma to the Navajo reservation in New Mexico and Arizona and back again. The two landscapes are fixed in my mind. They are separate realities, but they are sometimes confused in my memory. I place my feet in the plain, but my prints are made on the mountain.

I was much alone. I had no brothers or sisters, and as it happened in my childhood, much of it, my peers were at removes from me, across cultures and languages. I had to create my society in my mind. And for a child this kind of creation is accomplished easily enough. I imagined much.

When I was three years old my head must have been full of Indian as well as English words. The sounds of both Kiowa and Navajo are quite natural and familiar to me, and even now I can make these sounds easily and accurately with my voice, so well established are they in my ear. I lived very close to these "foreign" languages, poised at a crucial time in the learning process to enter into either or both of them wholly. But my mother was concerned that I should learn English as my "native" language, and so English is first and foremost in my possession. My mother's love of books, and of English literature in particular, is intense, and naturally she wanted me to share in it. I have seen Grendel's[1] shadow on the walls of Canyon de Chelly, and once, having led the sun around Hoskinini Mesa, I saw Copperfield[2] at Oljeto Trading Post.

In 1936 Haske Noswood, a Navajo friend, invited my parents and me to come to Gallup, New Mexico, where my mother and father hoped to find work in the Indian Service. We arrived at the time of Naa'ahoohai, the old celebration of the Navajos which had by that time become the Intertribal Indian Ceremonial. The Navajos came from far and wide to Gallup, which is called in Navajo Na'nizhoozhi, the "place of the bridge" on the Rio Puerco. We lived in the Del Mar Hotel, across from the old Harvey House on the Santa Fe Railroad, and I slept in a bureau drawer. My father found a temporary job: he painted signs for the traders in the Ceremonial exhibit hall at fifty cents a sign. And later he got on as a truck dispatcher with the Roads Department, Indian Service, at Shiprock, which is called in Navajo Naat'aaniineez (literally "tall chief"; the town takes its name from the great monolith that stands nearby in an arid reach of the San Juan Basin). The name Shiprock, like other Anglicizations in this region, seems incongruous enough, but from certain points of view—and from the air, especially—the massive rock Naat'aaniineez resembles very closely a ship at sea. Soon thereafter my mother was offered the job of switchboard operator at Shiprock Agency, which she accepted, and we were a solvent and independent entity. My

From pp. 59-65 in THE NAMES: A MEMOIR by N. Scott Momaday. Copyright © 1976 by N. Scott Momaday. By permission of Harper & Row, Publishers, Inc.

1. **Grendel,** the monster in *Beowulf,* the English epic poem from the eighth century.
2. **Copperfield,** David Copperfield, a hero in the Charles Dickens novel of that name.

parents have told me time and again what an intoxication were those days, and I think back to them on that basis; they involve me in a tide of confidence and well-being. What on earth was not possible? I must have been carried along in the waves of hope and happiness that were gathered in the hearts of my young and free and beautiful parents.

In the years between 1936 and 1943 we lived on the Navajo reservation at Shiprock, New Mexico, and at Tuba City, then Chinle, Arizona. There were in that span of time a number of sojourns away from home—to Oklahoma, to Kentucky, even to Louisiana (where my aunt Ethel lived at the time), and for several months my mother and I, while my father waited in Oklahoma to be drafted into the army (it turned out that he wasn't drafted, though the war was raging then), lived on the San Carlos Apache reservation in the southeastern quadrant of Arizona—but "home" was particularly the Navajo country, Dine bikeyah. My earliest playmates and schoolmates were Navajo children and the children of Indian Service employees. Just at the time I was learning to talk, I heard the Navajo language spoken all around me. And just as I was coming alive to the wide world, the vast and beautiful landscape of Dine bikeyah *was* my world, all of it that I could perceive.

Memory begins to qualify the imagination, to give it another formation, one that is peculiar to the self. I remember isolated, yet fragmented and confused, images—and images, shifting, enlarging, is the word, rather than moments or events—which are mine alone and which are especially vivid to me. They involve me wholly and immediately, even though they are the disintegrated impressions of a young child. They call for a certain attitude of belief on my part now; that is, they must mean something, but their best reality does not consist in meaning. They are not stories in that sense, but they are storylike, mythic, never evolved but evolving ever. There are such things in the world: it is in

their nature to be believed; it is not necessarily in them to be understood. Of all that must have happened to and about me in those my earliest days, why should these odd particulars alone be fixed in my mind? If I were to remember other things, I should be someone else.

There is a room full of light and space. The walls are bare; there are no windows or doors of which I am aware. I am inside and alone. Then gradually I become aware of another presence in the room. There is an object, something not extraordinary at first, something of the room itself—but what I cannot tell. The object does not matter at first, but at some point—after a moment? an hour?—it moves, and I am unsettled. I am not yet frightened; rather I am somewhat surprised, vaguely anxious, fascinated, perhaps. The object grows; it expands farther and farther beyond definition. It is no longer an object but a mass. It is so large now that I am dwarfed by it, reduced almost to nothing. And *now* I am afraid, nearly terrified, and yet I have no will to resist; I remain attentive, strangely curious in proportion as I am afraid. The huge, shapeless mass is displacing all of the air, all of the space in the room. It swells against me. It is soft and supple and resilient, like a great bag of water. At last I am desperate, desperately afraid of being suffocated, lost in some dimple or fold of this vague, enormous thing. I try to cry out, but I have no voice.

Restore my voice for me.

How many times has this memory been nearly recovered, the definition almost realized! Again and again I have come to that awful edge, that one word, perhaps, that I cannot bring from my mouth. I sometimes think that it is surely a name, the name of someone or something, that if only I could utter it, the terrific mass would snap away into focus, and I should see and recognize what it is at once; I should have it then, once and for all, in my possession.

Five Generations of Momadays. Left to right: Great-grandmother Keahdinekeah, Grandfather Mammedaty, Aunt Clara, Cousin Marland, Great-great-grandmother Kau-au-ointy.

Photo on jacket of THE NAMES: A Memoir by N. Scott Momaday. Copyright © 1976 by N. Scott Momaday. By permission of Harper & Row, Publishers, Inc.

It is a bright, hot day, but the arbor is cool. The smooth gray wood of the benches is cool to the touch. The worn patchwork covers are cool and soft. The red, hard-packed earth of the floor is dark and cool. It is quiet and sleepy inside. I love this place. I love the cool well water that I bring in a dipper to my mouth.

> One time the creek was backed up, and my dad . . .
> Was it that time he saw the animal, the . . .
> Yes, that was it; that was the time.

We set out, my father and I, in the afternoon. We walk down the long grade to the ravine that runs diagonally below, up again and through the brambles. The sun burns my skin. I feel the stiff spines and furry burrs at my legs and hear the insects humming there all around. We walk down into the shadows of Rainy Mountain Creek. The banks are broad and the mud is dry and cracked, broken into innumerable large facets like shards of pottery, smooth, delicately curved, where the water has risen and then withdrawn and the sun has baked the bank. The water is brown and runs very slowly at the surface; here and there are glints of light and beams that strike through the trees and splash on the rocks and roots and underbrush. We cross the creek on a log and climb up the west bank where the woods are thicker. There is a small clearing, and inside the clearing is a single tree that was bent down to the ground and tied as a sapling; and so it remains curved, grown over in a long, graceful arc, its nimble new branches brushing whorls on the ground. It is one of my delights, for it is a wonderful, lively swing. My father lifts me up and I take hold of the slender, tapered trunk, and then he pulls me down and lets me go. I spring up, laughing, laughing, and bob up and down.

We continue on, through fields now, to "across the creek," as the house there was always called when I was a child. It is Keahdinekeah's house, built for her by my grandfather; but when you are a child you don't think of houses as possessions; it does not occur to you that anyone has ownership in them. "Across the creek" is where Justin Lee lives, a cousin not much older than I, with his sister, Lela, and his parents, Jim and Dorothy Ware, and his grandmother Keahdinekeah.

It seems reasonable to suppose that I visited my great-grandmother on other occasions, but I remember only this once, and I remember it very well. My father leads me into her room. It is dark and close inside, and I cannot see until my eyes become accustomed to the dim light. There is a certain odor in the room and not elsewhere in the house, the odor of my great-grandmother's old age. It is not unpleasant, but it is most particular and exclusive, as much hers as is her voice or her hair or the nails of her hands. Such a thing has not only the character of great age but something also of the deep self, of one's own dignity and well-being. Because of this, I believe, this old blind woman is like no one I have ever seen or shall ever see. To a child her presence is formidable. My father is talking to her in Kiowa, and I do not understand what is being said, only that the talk is of me. She is seated on the side of her bed, and my father brings me to stand directly in front of her. She reaches out for me and I place my hands in hers. *Eh neh neh neh neh.* She begins to weep very softly in a high, thin, hollow voice. Her hands are little and soft, so soft that they seem not to consist in flesh and bone, but in the softest fiber, cotton or fine wool. Her voice is so delicate, so surely expressive of her deep feelings. Long afterwards I think: That was a wonderful and beautiful thing that happened in my life. There, on that warm, distant afternoon: an old woman and a child, holding hands across the generations. There is great good in such a remembrance; I cannot imagine that it might have been lost upon me. □ □

Discussion

1. (a) Momaday reports three specific memories. Describe the content of these memories in your own words. (b) What aspects of his childhood or of his character do these memories reveal?

2. In the first four paragraphs describing his childhood, the author uses the past tense. When he describes his specific memories, he uses the present tense. How does his use of the present tense enhance or diminish the effect of his accounts?

3. Each of Momaday's memories focuses on sets of contrasts. For example, the first memory begins in "a room full of light and space" and ends with a "huge, shapeless mass . . . displacing all of the air, all of the space in the room." (a) Reread the other two memories and identify several contrasts within each segment. (b) Identify contrasts among the three memories. (c) How does this emphasis on contrasts in the memory section of this selection relate to the first four paragraphs?

Extension · Writing

Select one of the three memories in *The Names* as a model and write a description of one of your most vivid recollections.

N. Scott Momaday 1934 ·

Navarre Scott Momaday was born in Lawton, Oklahoma, the son of artists and educators who inspired him to seek a life in the arts, grounded in the Kiowa culture.

He lived on reservations as a boy, and later attended several universities. He now teaches English and comparative literature at the University of California at Berkeley.

His novel, *House Made of Dawn,* won the 1969 Pulitzer Prize.

In a prefatory note to *The Names,* the memoir from which this selection is taken, Momaday says that he was given his Indian first name *Tsoai-talee,* "Rock-Tree Boy," by a storyteller who believed that "a man's life proceeds from his name, in the way that a river proceeds from its source."

Car Sickness

Richard Selzer

I sing of cars and passengers.[1] Of those who suffer from car sickness. Would that mankind might earn the largeness of spirit to embrace these pitiful outscourings of the human race, who do but express in unequivocal terms their antipathy toward the automobile. Lacking perhaps the physiological restraint of astronauts, the decorum of hikers, and the delirium of jockeys, with all of whom they share this mutual contempt of cars, the victims of car sickness are shunned like lepers by a society that takes callous pride only in ac and de celeration.

For the greater part of my life I have been among those wretches with what I shall henceforth call *mal de voiture*,[2] in whom the mere slamming of a car door is enough to bring on the first wamblings of nausea.

Sunday in Troy was a day of retrenchment. About the only thing to do was to take a ride *en famille*[3] to the country. This was not mere custom; it was rite. Everyone did it, as though it were some elemental thread binding us to our forefathers and our descendants. A ride in the country was healthy; it was restorative; and, at least for me, it was dreadful. How I yearned to be left behind to wander alone the unmoving pavement, the changeless cobblestones of Troy until, come nightfall, I could welcome home the rustic riders serene of heart, steady of stomach.[4] Such a leaving was not meant to be. More, it was considered tantamount to disloyalty by my father and child abandonment by my mother, who, at the mere suggestion, would whiten at the imagined horrors that would surely befall me, left alone and palely loitering.[5] At the very least I would descend to solitary or group vice, touch the dark underside of Trojan[6] life, and be lost forever to the lists of decent people. Perhaps she was right at that. The propensity for such a fall has ever been just beneath my surface, and it is a wise mother who knows her own child.

Thus was all entreaty denied, all supplication ill-received. Fate had decreed that I was to celebrate the Sabbath in my own fashion all over Rensselaer and the adjacent counties of upstate New York. I have vomited in Saratoga, Glens Falls, and Speculator; in French Cohoes as in Dutch Albany; in the pastoral town of Melrose and all along the Mohawk Trail. In every country corner of our land I deposited my unparceled ejecta so that the callowest novice of a hunter could have traced the motorings of our family by my pathetic spoor. Would time stand still, I wondered, and Monday never come were I to fail to carry out this ritual? In the throes of *mal de voiture* I decided that I had been chosen to suffer for a higher purpose as yet unknown to me, and that when the true meaning of my affliction would be revealed, I would be venerated as, if not the patron saint, at least the martyr of the automobile.

"It's all in your head," said Father.

"Mind over matter," said Mother.

For a time I believed them, and would tell myself stories in a constant murmuring undertone to match the hums of the motor. In one I was a strange sinewy Tartar[7] who returned from riding his horse through fields of flowers, and the sweet smell of the hooves of my steed would cause to swoon the beautiful yellow princess who waited. This story merely hastened the inevitable gastric upheaval. In another I was the Royal Gardener of the Empress Wu of the T'ang dynasty who had petulantly ordered that all the flowers in the Imperial Garden were to bloom on the same day. By virtue of my horticultural genius I was able to bring this about, with the

---

From MORTAL LESSONS by Richard Selzer. Copyright © 1974, 1975, 1976 by Richard Selzer. Reprinted by permission of Simon & Schuster, a Division of Gulf & Western Corporation and Paul R. Reynolds, Inc.

1. I sing . . . passengers, an allusion to the first line of the *Aeneid,* "I sing of arms and the man." This epic poem by Virgil (70–19 B.C.) told about Aeneas, a warrior who fought in the Trojan War.

2. mal de voiture (mȧ də vwä tür'), car sickness. [French]

3. en famille, as a family. [French]

4. serene of heart, steady of stomach, phrases that imitate those used in epic poetry, like "breaker of horses," "brave in battle."

5. alone and palely loitering, line from the poem "La Belle Dame Sans Merci" (The Beautiful Lady Without Pity) by John Keats (1795–1821). The complete lines read, "O what can ail thee, Knight-at-arms,/Alone and palely loitering?"

6. Trojan, having to do with Troy or its people. The author lived in Troy, N.Y., named after ancient Troy, site of the Trojan War.

7. Tartar (tär'tər). The Tartars were tribes from mainly central Asia. Led by Genghis Khan, they invaded Europe and Asia in the Middle Ages.

sole exception of the sweet-smelling peony, which refused to bloom, for which revolutionary act I was beheaded. But first I threw up.

Later when I had reached the age of reason I came to know the feeble mutterings of my parents as airy persiflage. It had nothing to do with mind. Ever since, I have looked askance at the hypotheses of psychosomatic medicine.[8] Years later I learned, not without some bitter satisfaction, that my distress was due to the tilting of fluid in my middle ear, that this caused an alteration in my sense of position relative to things outside, leading to reflex nausea and its roadside consummation. The straight unemotional flavor of these scientific words was nothing short of a justification for my existence. With what untrammeled joy did I read that the doughty astronauts suffered motion sickness aboard their mooncraft, and were reduced to mouthing comfort bags. The suffering of our heroes has always made us happy. Alas, even these truths did not set me free.

You have not known true agony until you have struggled to contain an attack of *mal de voiture*. There is the first skidding shudder of the stomach, the telltale yawn, the gathering of saliva, the fullness of the abdomen that insists that belt and clothing be loosened and held free of the skin—even the slightest contact will speed the internal vortex—the clenching of the teeth, the grim efforts at distraction, the fixing of the gaze straight ahead, and finally the awful knowledge that nothing is going to help. There comes the moment when resolve snaps, and the sour belch of despair fills the car with its rank miasma. Now you grow cold, turn green. You sweat. Soon you will die. And all the while there is the guilt laced with shame that you have, with cank and with cark,[9] spoiled the ride. You are a killjoy, a blight.

Then comes the whispered command from your lips: "Stop the car." Who would think that such a phrase, barely audible, scarcely more than an exhalation, would bring the demon to an immediate halt? Wordless now you slip from the car to slump against the nearest tree, a rock, the ground, whilst the survivors, torn by their own violent emotions, alternately watch the drama unfold or turn aside to gaze in envy at the happy tourists whizzing by.

Only Father would dismount, heaving himself from behind the wheel to stand behind me, one hand supporting my forehead, the other arm looped about my pelvis, holding me upright. Little beads of disappointment, I supposed, formed and burst in his chest. What comfort could he take in this rancid geyser of a son whose well-being depended upon remaining motionless? O sharper than a serpent's tooth to have a car-sick child! At last, my heart all laden with rue, I was led back in disgrace to the Iron Maiden.[10]

"Have a good puke?" said my brother Billy. He had the stomach of a whirling dervish.[11]

"I do not like that word," said Mother.

"He's got throw-up on his sleeve," insisted Billy. "It stinks."

"I do not like that word either," said Mother.

At which point Father would reach one arm into the back seat and give Billy a wallop.

"I have to do it again," I would announce.

Even today I do not like riding in a car, would vastly prefer going on foot or taking the train. Actually, I would prefer to stay home while the rest of the family went out for a drive. But they won't let me. So it happened that while out for a Sunday ride not long ago, my second son grew quiet, still, and pale. Then came those words that drove a stake through my heart. "Stop the car." Quickly I pulled off to the side of the road, while the fleet and heartless world whooshed carelessly past. I held the wracked and wretching little boy over what I knew to be the first of countless road-shoulders and ditches all over America. Suddenly I felt a cold chill grip my flesh, and turned to see if someone, something were gaining on me. □□

---

8. the hypotheses of psychosomatic medicine, the idea that the cause of sickness is psychological rather than physiological.
9. with cank and with cark, with his sickness and the trouble it caused.
10. Iron Maiden, an ancient instrument of torture made in the shape of a human.
11. whirling dervish, member of a Muslim order which observes ecstatic dancing, chanting, etc., in their worship.

Discussion

1. (a) Select paragraph 3 or 4 and rephrase it in "plain English." (b) How do such changes affect the tone and humor of the passage? of the whole selection?

2. (a) Father, Mother, and Billy are quoted briefly (419b, 1,2) and 420b, 2-5). Change their statements so that they sound like the main speaker's statements. (b) How do such changes affect the tone and humor of these passages? of the whole selection?

3. Review *Allusion* in the Handbook of Literary Terms, and cite at least five examples from the selection. Then explain how these allusions contribute to the humor of the selection.

Vocabulary
Structure and Dictionary

The root *path* and the combining form *-pathy* are derived from Greek words meaning either "feeling" or "disease."

From the list of words below choose those that most correctly complete the following sentences. Be sure you can spell and pronounce each word. Use a dictionary for reference. You will not need all the words.

antipathy	pathogen
apathy	pathology
empathy	pathos
osteopathy	psychopathy
pathetic	sympathy

1. The _____ plight of stray cats and dogs led her to leave her estate to the humane society.

2. The scientist was able to isolate the _____ causing the epidemic.

3. Friends' expressions of _____ are a comfort when one is unhappy.

4. The _____ in our homeroom was such that we didn't even bother to nominate a representative to the governing board.

5. The jungle guide had no fear of lions or rhinos, but he had an _____ to spiders.

6. His brother specialized in surgery, but Pete is more interested in research and wants to study _____ .

7. _____ is still not fully recognized by the medical community, but many people would not be treated by any other method.

8. Marguerite is a fine art historian; she has such _____ for artists' works.

Richard Selzer 1928 ·

Selzer is a surgeon at the Yale-New Haven Hospital in Connecticut and a writer of essays and short stories. In 1975, a series of his essays about medical subjects earned him a National Magazine Award.

His ability to write in a way that appeals to people's feelings is evident in *Mortal Lessons,* his book about the art of surgery, his patients, and those closest to them. These moving vignettes show why he believes "that man is not ugly, but that he is Beauty itself."

See **STYLE** Handbook of Literary Terms

The Bird and the Machine

Loren Eiseley

I suppose their little bones have years ago been lost among the stones and winds of those high glacial pastures. I suppose their feathers blew eventually into the piles of tumbleweed beneath the straggling cattle fences and rotted there in the mountain snows, along with dead steers and all the other things that drift to an end in the corners of the wire. I do not quite know why I should be thinking of birds over the *New York Times* at breakfast, particularly the birds of my youth half a continent away. It is a funny thing what the brain will do with memories and how it will treasure them and finally bring them into odd juxtapositions with other things, as though it wanted to make a design, or get some meaning out of them, whether you want it or not, or even see it.

It used to seem marvelous to me, but I read now that there are machines that can do these things in a small way, machines that can crawl about like animals, and that it may not be long now until they do more things—maybe even make themselves—I saw that piece in the *Times* just now. And then they will, maybe—well, who knows—but you read about it more and more with no one making any protest, and already they can add better than we and reach up and hear things through the dark and finger the guns over the night sky.

This is the new world that I read about at breakfast. This is the world that confronts me in my biological books and journals, until there are times when I sit quietly in my chair and try to hear the little purr of the cogs in my head and the tubes flaring and dying as the messages go through them and the circuits snap shut or open. This is the great age, make no mistake about it; the robot has been born somewhat appropriately along with the atom bomb, and the brain they say now is just another type of more complicated feedback system. The engineers have its basic principles worked out; it's mechanical, you know; and humans can always improve on nature once they get the idea. Well, they've got it all right and that's why, I guess, that I sit here in my chair, with the article crunched in my hand, remembering those two birds and that blue mountain sunlight. There is another magazine article on my desk that reads "Machines Are Getting Smarter Every Day." I don't deny it, but I'll still stick with the birds. It's life I believe in, not machines.

I'll never forget those birds—I was young then and left alone in a great desert—part of an expedition that had scattered its men over several hundred miles in order to carry on research more effectively. There had been talk of birds in connection with my duties. Birds are intense, fast-living creatures—reptiles, I suppose one might say, that have escaped out of the heavy sleep of time, transformed fairy creatures dancing over sunlit meadows. It is a youthful fancy, no doubt, but because of something that happened up there among the escarpments of that range, it remains with me a lifelong impression. I can never bear to see a bird imprisoned.

We came into that valley through the trailing mists of a spring night. It was a place that looked as though it might never have known the foot of man, but our scouts had been ahead of us and we knew all about the abandoned cabin of stone that lay far up on one hillside. It had been built in the land rush of the last century and then lost to the cattlemen again as the marginal soils failed to take to the plow.

There were spots like this all over that country. Lost graves marked by unlettered stones and old corroding rim-fire cartridge cases

Copyright © 1955 by Loren Eiseley. Reprinted from THE IMMENSE JOURNEY, by Loren Eiseley, by permission of Random House, Inc.

lying where somebody had made a stand among the boulders that rimmed the valley. They are all that remain of the range wars; the men are under the stones now. I could see our cavalcade winding in and out through the mist below us: torches, the reflection of the truck lights on our collecting tins, and the far-off bumping of a loose dinosaur thigh bone in the bottom of a trailer. I stood on a rock a moment looking down and thinking what it cost in money and equipment to capture the past.

We had, in addition, instructions to lay hands on the present. The word had come through to get them alive—birds, reptiles, anything. A zoo somewhere abroad needed restocking. It was one of those reciprocal matters in which science involves itself. Maybe our museum needed a stray ostrich egg and this was the payoff. Anyhow, my job was to help capture some birds and that was why I was there before the trucks.

The cabin had not been occupied for years. We intended to clean it out and live in it, but there were holes in the roof and the birds had come in and were roosting in the rafters. You could depend on it in a place like this where everything blew away, and even a bird needed some place out of the weather and away from coyotes. A cabin going back to nature in a wild place draws them till they come in, listening at the eaves, I imagine, peeking softly among the shingles till they find a hole and then suddenly the place is theirs and man is forgotten.

Sometimes of late years I find myself thinking the most beautiful sight in the world might be the birds taking over New York after the last person has run away to the hills. I will never live to see it, of course, but I know just how it will sound because I've lived up high and I know the sort of watch birds keep on us. I've listened to sparrows tapping tentatively on the outside of air conditioners when they thought no one was listening, and I know how other birds test the vibrations that come up to them through the television aerials.

"Is he gone?" they ask, and the vibrations come up from below, "Not yet, not yet."

Well, to come back, I got the door open softly and I had the spotlight all ready to turn on and blind whatever birds there were so they couldn't see to get out through the roof. I had a short piece of ladder to put against the far wall where there was a shelf on which I expected to make the biggest haul. I had all the information I needed just like any skilled assassin. I pushed the door open, the hinges squeaking only a little. A bird or two stirred—I could hear them—but nothing flew and there was a faint starlight through the holes in the roof.

I padded across the floor, got the ladder up and the light ready, and slithered up the ladder till my head and arms were over the shelf. Everything was dark as pitch except for the starlight at the little place back of the shelf near the eaves. With the light to blind them, they'd never make it. I had them. I reached my arm carefully over in order to be ready to seize whatever was there and I put the flash on the edge of the shelf where it would stand by itself when I turned it on. That way I'd be able to use both hands.

Everything worked perfectly except for one detail—I didn't know what kind of birds were there. I never thought about it at all, and it wouldn't have mattered if I had. My orders were to get something interesting. I snapped on the flash and sure enough there was a great beating and feathers flying, but instead of my having them, they, or rather he, had me. He had my hand, that is, and for a small hawk not much bigger than my fist he was doing all right. I heard him give one short metallic cry when the light went on and my hand descended on the bird beside him; after that he was busy with his claws and his beak was sunk in my thumb. In the struggle I knocked the lamp over on the shelf, and his mate got her sight back and whisked neatly through the hole in the roof and off among the stars outside. It all happened in fifteen seconds and you might think I would have fallen down the ladder, but no, I had a professional assassin's reputation to keep up, and the bird, of course, made the mistake of thinking the hand was the enemy and not the eyes behind it. He chewed my thumb up pretty effectively and lacerated my hand with his claws, but in the end I got him, having two hands to work with.

He was a sparrow hawk and a fine young male in the prime of life. I was sorry not to catch the pair of them, but as I dripped blood and folded his wings carefully, holding him by the back so that he couldn't strike again, I had to admit the two of them might have been more than I could have handled under the circumstances. The little fellow had saved his mate by diverting me, and that was that. He was born to it, and made no outcry now, resting in my hand hopelessly, but peering toward me in the shadows behind the lamp with a fierce, almost indifferent glance. He neither gave nor expected mercy and something out of the high air passed from him to me, stirring a faint embarrassment.

I quit looking into that eye and managed to get my huge carcass with its fist full of prey back down the ladder. I put the bird in a box too small to allow him to injure himself by struggle and walked out to welcome the arriving trucks. It had been a long day, and camp still to make in the darkness. In the morning that bird would be just another episode. He would go back with the bones in the truck to a small cage in a city where he would spend the rest of his life. And a good thing, too. I sucked my aching thumb and spat out some blood. An assassin has to get used to these things. I had a professional reputation to keep up.

In the morning, with the change that comes on suddenly in that high country, the mist that had hovered below us in the valley was gone. The sky was a deep blue, and one could see for miles over the high outcroppings of stone. I was up early and brought the box in which the little hawk was imprisoned out onto the grass where I was building a cage. A wind as cool as a mountain spring ran over the grass and stirred my hair. It was a fine day to be alive. I looked up and all around and at the hole in the cabin roof out of which the other little hawk had fled. There was no sign of her anywhere that I could see.

"Probably in the next county by now," I thought cynically, but before beginning work I decided I'd have a look at my last night's capture.

Secretively, I looked again all around the camp and up and down and opened the box. I got him right out in my hand with his wings folded properly and I was careful not to startle him. He lay limp in my grasp and I could feel his heart pound under the feathers but he only looked beyond me and up.

I saw him look that last look away beyond me into a sky so full of light that I could not follow his gaze. The little breeze flowed over me again, and nearby a mountain aspen shook all its tiny leaves. I suppose I must have had an idea then of what I was going to do, but I never let it come up into consciousness. I just reached over and laid the hawk on the grass.

He lay there a long minute without hope, unmoving, his eyes still fixed on that blue vault above him. It must have been that he was already so far away in heart that he never felt the release from my hand. He never even stood. He just lay with his breast against the grass.

In the next second after that long minute he was gone. Like a flicker of light, he had vanished with my eyes full on him, but without actually seeing even a premonitory wing beat. He was gone straight into that towering emptiness of light and crystal that my eyes could scarcely bear to penetrate. For another long moment there was silence. I could not see him. The light was too intense. Then from far up somewhere a cry came ringing down.

I was young then and had seen little of the world, but when I heard that cry my heart turned over. It was not the cry of the hawk I had captured; for, by shifting my position against the sun, I was now seeing further up. Straight out of the sun's eye, where she must have been soaring restlessly above us for untold hours, hurtled his mate. And from far up, ringing from peak to peak of the summits over us, came a cry of such unutterable and ecstatic joy that it sounds down across the years and tingles among the cups on my quiet breakfast table.

I saw them both now. He was rising fast to meet her. They met in a great soaring gyre that turned to a whirling circle and a dance of wings. Once more, just once, their two voices, joined in a harsh wild medley of question and response, struck and echoed against the pinnacles of the valley. Then they were gone forever somewhere into those upper regions beyond the eyes of humans.

I am older now, and sleep less, and have seen most of what there is to see and am not very much impressed any more, I suppose, by anything. "What Next in the Attributes of Machines?" my morning headline runs. "It Might Be the Power to Reproduce Themselves."

I lay the paper down and across my mind a phrase floats insinuatingly: "It does not seem that there is anything in the construction, constituents, or behavior of the human being which it is essentially impossible for science to duplicate and synthesize. On the other hand . . ."

All over the city the cogs in the hard, bright mechanisms have begun to turn. Figures move through computers, names are spelled out, a thoughtful machine selects the fingerprints of a wanted criminal from an array of thousands. In the laboratory an electronic mouse runs swiftly through a maze toward the cheese it can neither taste nor enjoy. On the second run it does better than a living mouse.

"On the other hand . . ." Ah, my mind takes up, on the other hand the machine does not bleed, ache, hang for hours in the empty sky in a torment of hope to learn the fate of another machine, nor does it cry out with joy nor dance in the air with the fierce passion of a bird. Far off, over a distance greater than space, that remote cry from the heart of heaven makes a faint buzzing among my breakfast dishes and passes on and away. □□

Discussion

1. Reread the third paragraph. Does Loren Eiseley admire our age or not?

2. Three times, Loren Eiseley refers to himself as a professional assassin. What purpose does this exaggerated description of his role serve?

3. Find descriptions of the hawk in which the author uses human terms to describe the bird. What does this use of personification reveal about the author's attitude toward the bird?

Vocabulary
Context, Structure, and Dictionary

Answer the following questions about the italicized words by studying the sentences from "The Bird and the Machine" in which the words are found. Use your Glossary for reference.

1. "It is a funny thing what the brain will do with memories and how it will treasure them and finally bring them into odd *juxtapositions* with other things, as though it wanted to make a design, . . ."

What is the root word? If you know that *juxta-* means "beside," can you determine the meaning of the word?

2. [The abandoned cabin] "had been built in the land rush of the last century and then lost to the cattlemen again as the *marginal* soils failed to take to the plow."

Knowing the meaning of the word *margin* and considering the context of the sentence, what do you think is the meaning of *marginal*?

3. ". . . came a cry of such unutterable and *ecstatic* joy that it sounds down across the years. . ."

What does *ecstatic* mean? What part of speech is it?

4. "It does not seem there is anything in the construction, . . . of the human being which it is essentially impossible for science to duplicate and *synthesize.*"

You are probably familiar with the word *synthetic*. Does that knowledge aid in determining the meaning of *synthesize*? Which is the stressed syllable of the word?

Extension · Writing

Arrange the last paragraph to look like a poem. Be prepared to explain why you begin or end lines where you do, and why you arrange the lines in the shape you choose.

Loren Eiseley 1907 · 1977

Though better known to his colleagues as an outstanding anthropologist whose scientific books consistently won awards, Loren Eiseley also acquired renown as a poet and general writer.

He was born in Lincoln, Nebraska, and was a brilliant student of American ancient history. He served most of his academic years at the University of Pennsylvania in the Department of Anthropology. As well as writing for scientific journals, he contributed verse and prose to literary anthologies and edited a literary review, the *Prairie Schooner.*

Among his enduring qualities was a concern for human destiny. He regarded the mysteries of life and nature with wonder and reverence not to be understood by reason alone. People need time to dream, he believed: ". . . when the human mind exists in the light of reason and no more than reason, we may say with absolute certainty that man and all that made him will be in that instant gone."

6: Prose Forms

CONTENT REVIEW

1. A number of selections in the unit show how people think about or behave toward one another. What kind(s) of behavior nourishes a good relationship between younger and older persons? Give examples from three selections that support your opinion. What kind(s) of behavior prevents or withers good relationships between younger and older persons? Give examples from three selections that support your opinion.

2. In almost every family, adults pass on to children their favorite sayings about adversity and how to cope with it. For example: "Trouble tests character"; "Hardship builds character"; "Every cloud has a silver lining"; "Hard times strain love"; "Things look darkest before the dawn"; "Nothing is so bad that some good doesn't come from it." Choose a saying about adversity that your family commonly uses, or one of the sayings above, or the following one by the essayist Francis Bacon: "Adversity is not without comforts and hopes." Choose a selection in VICTORIES which illustrates the truth or falseness of the saying you have chosen. Share your choices with the class. Be prepared to support your opinions with evidence from the selection.

3. Choose the one work in each section of this unit which helped most to extend your understanding of what it means to be victorious—what constitutes loyalty. Then suppose that you have the opportunity to meet and speak with the authors of these two selections. Explain to each author what that particular selection meant to you.

Unit 6, Test I
INTERPRETATION: NEW MATERIAL

from Me and Mine

Helen Sekaquaptewa (sē′kə kwäp′tü ə), as told to
Louise Udall

In 1878 government boarding schools were established for the education of Indian children. Many children were taken great distances from their homes to remove them from the influence of the family and educate them to the ways of white people. The day school was less effective in stripping Indian children of their culture, but both schools were hated and resisted.

The author grew up in the Hopi village of Oraibi (ō rī′bē) in northeastern Arizona. This selection recalls some of her experiences with an Indian day school of the early 1900s.

After you have read the passage, answer the questions on a separate sheet of paper.

When we were five or six years of age, we, with our parents became involved with the school officials, assisted by the Navajo policemen, in a serious and rather desperate game of hide-and-seek, where little Hopi boys and girls were the forfeit in the game. Every day the school principal sent out a truant officer, and many times he himself went with the officer, going to Hopi homes to take the children to school. The Navajo policemen

By permission from ME AND MINE: *The Life Story of Helen Sekaquaptewa As Told to Louise Udall,* Louise Udall, Tucson: University of Arizona Press, copyright 1969.

who assisted in finding hidden children were dressed in old army uniforms, and they wore regular cavalry hats over their long hair, done up in a knot. This made quite a picture—especially the traditional hair style with a white man's hat. It had not been customary for Indians to wear hats up to that time.

When September came there was no peace for us. Early in the morning, from our houses on the mesa, we could see the principal and the officer start out from the school, walking up the trail to "get" the children. Hostile parents tried every day in different ways to hide us from them, for once you were caught, you had lost the game. You were discovered and listed and you had to go to school and not hide any more. I was finally caught and went to the Oraibi day school one session, when I was about six years old, but not before many times outwitting Mr. Schoolman.

Sometimes, after a very early breakfast, somebody's grandmother would take a lunch and go with a group of eight to twelve little girls and hide them in the cornfields away out from the village. On another day another grandmother would go in the other direction over the hills among the cedars where we would play in a ravine, have our lunch and come back home in the afternoon. Men would be out with little boys playing this game of hide-and-seek. One day I got left behind and was sent out with a group of boys. I didn't know the man, and the boys' games were not for me, and I cried all day.

A place where one or two small children could be stowed away on short notice was the rabbit blanket. A rabbit blanket is made by cutting dressed rabbit skins in two-inch strips and weaving them into a warp of wool thread. When not in use, in warm weather, this blanket is hung by the four corners from a hook in the rafter beam, to prevent it from being moth-eaten. But once discovered, this hiding place was out. The school officer would feel of the rabbit blanket first thing on coming into the room.

Most houses have a piki[1] storage cupboard in a partition wall. This would be the thickness of the wall and about two by three feet. A cloth covered the front, making a good place to keep the piki supply dry and clean. One day the officers were only two doors away when my mother was aware of their presence. She snatched her young son Henry and put him curled up in the piki cupboard just in time to win the game—that day.

Our houses were two and three stories high. When a lower room became old and unsafe, it was used as a dump place for ashes, peach stones, melon and squash seeds, and bits of dis-

---

1. *piki,* bread made of Indian corn, and baked in thin sheets.

carded corn; anything that could be eaten was preserved in the ashes, and the room was gradually filled. Then in time of famine these bits of food could be dug out and eaten. In the home of my childhood such a room was about three-fourths filled. One September morning my brother and I were hidden there. We lay on our stomachs in the dark, facing a small opening. We saw the feet of the principal and policeman as they walked by, and heard their big voices as they looked about wondering where the children were. They didn't find us that day.

One morning an older man took several boys out to hide. Emory, who later was my husband, was one of these boys. The man took them off the mesa where there was a big fissure in a sheer cliff with a bigger space behind it, away down in the rocks where no horse could go. The grandfather told the boys to stay there and be quiet. He then went a little way away and began hoeing in an orchard. The boys soon wanted to come out and play, but the grandfather said "no." Pretty soon they heard the sound of approaching horses' hoofs and looking up to the top of the cliff saw the Navajo policeman. He rode around out of sight, but pretty soon was seen coming up the valley toward the grandfather. The policeman couldn't get into the crack in the rock but he got off his horse looking for footprints. The boys had been careful to step on rocks and grass and left no footprints. After looking around a while the policeman got on his horse and rode away. After he left and they were sure he would not come back, then the boys came out to play, and later the grandfather brought out the lunch.

Some boys made trouble after they were enrolled in school. At recess they would run away. They could outrun the principal. One principal, in desperation, got himself a .22 rifle with blank bullets. When he shot at the boys they stopped running.

I don't remember for sure just how I came to be "caught." Maybe both my mother and myself got a little tired of getting up early every morning and running off to hide all day. She probably thought to herself, "Oh, let them get her. I am tired of this. It is wearing me down." The hide-and-seek game continued through September, but with October, the colder weather was on the schoolman's side.

So, one morning, I was "caught." Even then, it was the rule among mothers not to let the child go voluntarily. As the policeman reached to take me by the arm, my mother put her arm around me. Tradition required that it appear that I was forced into school. I was escorted down off the mesa to the schoolhouse, along with several other children. First, each was given a bath by one of the Indian women who worked at the school. Baths were given in the kitchen in a round, galvanized tub. Then

we were clothed in cotton underwear, cotton dresses, and long black stockings and heavy shoes, furnished by the government. Each week we had a bath and a complete change of clothing. We were permitted to wear the clothes home each day, but my mother took off the clothes of the detested white man as soon as I got home, until it was time to go to school the next day.

Names were given to each child by the school. Mine was "Helen." Each child had a name card pinned on, for as many days as it took for the teacher to learn and remember the name she had given us. Our teacher was Miss Stanley. She began by teaching us the names of objects about the room. We read a little from big charts on the wall later on, but I don't remember ever using any books. □□

A. Multiple Choice
Write the letter indicating the best answer.

1. Of the hiding places parents used to resist the school authorities, the least successful was the **(a)** rabbit blanket; **(b)** piki cupboard; **(c)** cornfield; **(d)** mesa.

2. Once the children were "caught," tradition required the mothers to **(a)** let the children go voluntarily; **(b)** resist the policeman; **(c)** instruct the children to run away; **(d)** none of these.

3. The hide-and-seek game the author writes of was **(a)** fun for everyone involved; **(b)** a traditional ceremony; **(c)** a serious concern for the children's parents; **(d)** the only opposition the parents showed to their children's education at the schools.

4. The refusal of Helen's mother to allow her daughter to wear school clothes at home is indicative of **(a)** the good sense of mothers everywhere; **(b)** the thrift of Helen's mother; **(c)** the conflict between the cultures; **(d)** a misunderstanding between Helen and her mother.

5. You might characterize the author's tone in this article as **(a)** bitter; **(b)** melancholy; **(c)** matter-of-fact; **(d)** ironic.

6. One factor that helped the school officials was **(a)** the fine school building; **(b)** the children's curiosity; **(c)** the grandparents' approval; **(d)** the weather.

7. Of the following types of nonfiction prose, which best describes this selection: **(a)** open letter; **(b)** informal essay; **(c)** formal essay; **(d)** autobiography.

8. Several selections in this unit are accounts of adults looking back on their childhood experiences. Of the following, Helen Sekaquaptewa would probably relate most closely to the experience of **(a)** Christy Brown; **(b)** Mary Hollingsworth; **(c)** Richard Selzer; **(d)** Enrique Hank López.

B. Short Answer

Write the word or phrase that best answers the questions on the same paper as **A.**

9. What indications are in the article that not all the Indians felt the same antipathy for the school?

10. One person who read this selection said, "I found this fascinating and chilling." Why do you think he used the word "chilling"?

11. From whose point of view is this story told? What is this point of view called?

12. How would this account have been different if it had been told from the point of view of the Navajo policemen?

Unit 6, Test II
COMPOSITION

From the assignments below choose one to write about.

1. Loren Eiseley expresses his thoughts regarding technology and living creatures in "The Bird and the Machine." Explain to your classmates how you feel about the same issues. Include any experiences that you feel are pertinent.

2. The articles in the VIC-TORIES section of the unit present different kinds of bravery. Choose any three characters from any of the articles in the section and compare and contrast their particular sorts of bravery. Whose bravery do you most admire and why?

3. Several of the articles in the LOYALTIES section deal with differences and conflicts between cultures. Discuss, compare, and contrast any two of the following articles: "Back to Bachimba," "from *The Woman Warrior*," "from *The Names*," and "from *Me and Mine*."

4. The writers of "Car Sickness" and "Clean Your Room" take commonplace events and, through their style of writing, create amusing articles. In the first instance, the author uses numerous literary allusions and a highly formal style in writing about the experience of car sickness. In the second, the author uses numerous clichés to make humorous a common confrontation between parents and children. Write an article that might be submitted to the school paper about some ordinary experience.

5. In "New York's My Home," Mildred does not think that her guest saw the "real" New York. Write a description for your area, town, or city's visitor center telling tourists about its various attractions—entertainment, sights, climate, recreation, or any combination of these. Include also any lesser-known events, characteristics of the natives, and so forth that the casual visitor would probably otherwise miss.

SHAKESPEAREAN DRAMA
Julius Caesar

I The Globe Announces Shakespeare's Play

London in the last decade of the sixteenth century was the largest and most exciting city in England. Among its many attractions were the numerous playhouses and inn-theaters, where Elizabethans gathered for an afternoon's entertainment. Shakespeare's playhouse, the Globe, first opened in 1599. Here Londoners watched the greatest actors of the time perform the greatest English drama of all time—the plays of Shakespeare.

On one September morning in 1599, freshly mounted playbills appeared in London's crowded and twisted streets. They announced, in bold black letters, that the afternoon performance at the Globe would be *"The Tragedy of Julius Caesar . . . a new play by William Shakespeare."* The playbills would draw over two thousand people—noblemen and apprentices, merchants and housewives, law students and sailors—to the Globe Playhouse at two o'clock.

In order to obtain standing room in the playhouse yard, an Elizabethan apprentice made an especially early start. In his dark-blue livery and jaunty flat cap, he hurried toward the Thames River while the city bells were tolling the noon hour. At the water's edge, one penny bought him a place in an already crowded boat that ferried playgoers to the opposite shore. Looking across the river, he could see the white silk flag floating above the playhouse turret. The flag continued to beckon as each stroke of the boatman's oars brought the apprentice closer; finally he stepped ashore. Dodging the other playgoers, he made his way down Maiden Lane to Globe Alley, across a footbridge, and then stood before the playhouse entrance.

II The Exterior of the Globe Playhouse

The Globe Playhouse was a *three-storied octagon.* In between sturdy oak timbers, the exterior walls were coated with sparkling white plaster. From a previous visit, the apprentice knew that the eight sides of the playhouse frame enclosed a brick-paved *yard* that was open to the skies. It was fortunate, he thought, that the day was warm and sunny, for he would be standing in the unroofed yard during this afternoon's performance. Without further delay, he dropped a penny into the doorkeeper's box and stepped within the Globe Playhouse.

III The Interior of the Globe Playhouse

If you were to join an Elizabethan apprentice as he steps into the playhouse yard, you would face the performing area of the Globe. This performing area fills one-fourth of the octagon. It consists of a *platform stage* and, behind the platform, a three-storied structure which is called the *tiring house.*

The most important stage in the performing area is the *platform* (1), which juts into the yard. Its two ornate pillars support a *canopy* (2) which, in turn, support the *huts* (3) and the playhouse *turret* (4). Elizabethans refer to the canopy, the huts, and the turret as the "Heavens." The area underneath the platform, where stage properties are stored, is known as "Hell" (5). In the center of the platform floor is the largest of five *trap doors* (6). The trap doors are not visible to the audience until they are opened from below.

The three-storied wall of the tiring house acts as a background for the platform. On its first level, the tiring house consists of a curtained *inner stage* (7), which is flanked at right and at left by doors (8). The inner stage has two trap doors—a floor trap and a

The physical features of Shakespeare's Globe Playhouse, as described in the text and as shown in the illustrations, are based upon the data assembled by Dr. John Cranford Adams in his *Globe Playhouse* (Barnes & Noble) and upon the model of the Globe constructed by Dr. Adams and Irwin Smith.

ceiling trap. On its second level, the tiring house consists of a curtained *balcony stage* (9). The balcony stage projects slightly over the platform and is flanked at right and left by *bay-window stages* (10). The curtained *music gallery* (11), on the third level, may also function as a stage.

The inner stage and the balcony stage are almost identical. When the front curtains of either stage are drawn apart, you can see that the stage suggests the interior of a room. The side walls are made of tapestry hangings, which can be changed between scenes, and the rear wall has a door and a window with similar tapestry hangings in between. By replacing the tapestry with hangings made of plain or painted cloth, it is possible for the inner stage to represent the interior of a tent or the corner of a garden. When plain or painted hangings are used at the rear, they cover the entire wall.

The backstage area of the tiring house with its dressing rooms, storage rooms, and connecting stairways is not visible to the audience.

Since the Globe Playhouse has several stages on different levels, you may wonder how each stage will be used in this afternoon's play. The platform will always be used when a scene takes place *outdoors*. At various times in *Julius Caesar*

the platform will represent a street, or a public place, or an army camp, or a battlefield. During these exterior scenes, the curtains of the inner and balcony stages are closed; actors enter and exit the platform through the doors at right and left or through the inner-stage curtains.

Scenes which take place *indoors* will use the inner stage or the balcony stage. Thus, the curtains of the inner stage will be drawn apart to reveal the interior of a tent or public building; the curtains of the balcony stage will be drawn apart to reveal the interior of a house. On one occasion, a bay-window stage will represent an interior. Actors enter and exit the inner and balcony stages through the rear door or through the side hangings.

In *Julius Caesar*, action on the inner stage is always combined with action on the platform. The platform, for example, will represent a garden and the inner stage a secluded corner of that garden. Or, the platform will represent an army camp and the inner stage a tent in that camp. Sometimes an outdoor scene on the platform requires the use of an elevated place, such as a raised pulpit or a hill. The narrow area between the closed balcony curtains and the balcony railing will represent these elevated places. In order to ascend the "pulpit" or

"hill," an actor exits the platform and, by means of the backstage stairs, reappears at the balcony railing within twenty seconds.

While you have been examining the performing area of the Globe, many more spectators have entered the playhouse. Five hundred Elizabethans now jam the unroofed yard; fifteen hundred people have paid additional pennies to sit in the galleries that fill three-fourths of the Globe octagon. The crowd is boisterous and impatient for the play to begin. Vendors hawking apples and books elbow their way across the yard. Some people pass the time playing cards or reading; others speculate loudly about Shakespeare's play. From overhearing snatches of their conversation, it is obvious that Elizabethans already know a great deal about Julius Caesar and the events that led to the collapse of the Roman republic. If you are not as well informed, you will find it helpful to read the following sketch of Julius Caesar before Shakespeare's play begins.

IV Julius Caesar and His Times

The short span of Caesar's life, 100–44 B.C., was an important period in the history of Rome. For centuries Romans had debated and even fought civil wars to decide whether a *monarchy,* a *republic,* or a *dictatorship* was the best form of government.

Before 509 B.C. Rome was a monarchy; but in that year a revolt, headed by the Brutus family, forced the cruel Tarquinius Superbus from the throne. The Romans established a republic, but the common people, or plebeians, soon found that they had merely exchanged the rule of a king for the rule of a group of wealthy, highborn citizens called patricians. The two consuls, chief magistrates of the republic, were patricians; the Senate, composed entirely of patricians, made the laws, while the popular assemblies, composed of plebeians, had no real power. Gradually the plebeians won the right to select tribunes—men who had the power to protect the lives and properties of plebeians and to intervene in any department of government. In time, the plebeians won the right to be elected as consuls or to hold seats in the Senate.

By Julius Caesar's time, Rome was a moderate democracy in form, but in practice was ruled by the Senate. The Senate, however, was disturbed by personal rivalries among its members. For the first time military leaders entered Rome with their legions to seize control of the government. Since it was possible to appoint a dictator during periods of emergency, an ambitious man could become an absolute ruler. Some Roman dictators championed the people's party; others belonged to the senatorial party.

Julius Caesar, a patrician, cast his lot with the people. Serving in various offices, he won their support by spending money for public entertainments and by establishing laws to free farmers and tradesmen from crushing taxes and debts. In 60 B.C. Caesar formed, with Crassus and Pompey, a triumvirate (a three-man rule) to govern Rome and its provinces. Two years later he was made governor of the part of Gaul (now southern France and northern Italy) which Rome then controlled. He conquered the rest of Gaul, and money from his conquests flowed into Rome. Much of it was used to provide bonuses for his soldiers and to relieve some of the burdens of the common people.

For a short time the triumvirate worked smoothly, but trouble was brewing. While conducting a campaign in Mesopotamia, Crassus was slain. Pompey, jealous of Caesar's popularity, turned more and more toward the senatorial party. The senators, alarmed by Caesar's advance toward unlimited power, issued a decree ordering him to disband his army or be considered an enemy of the state. Caesar accepted the challenge. He led his army across the Rubicon River, which separated his provinces in Gaul from Italy, invaded Rome, and gathered the reins of power into his own hands.

During the next four years Caesar made himself absolute ruler of the Roman world. After securing Spain and the West, Caesar followed Pompey to the East, where he had fled. In the decisive battle of Pharsalus, Pompey's forces were routed; Pompey himself fled to Egypt and was later killed. Three years after this battle, Caesar made his final campaign against Pompey's faction and defeated Pompey's two sons at Munda, Spain. In the meantime he had been voted extraordinary honors; in 48 B.C. he was named dictator; in 46 B.C. he was made dictator for ten years; and in 45 B.C. the term was extended to life. Thus Caesar was the undisputed master of the Roman world when he returned in triumph from Spain. It is at this point that Shakespeare begins his play.

Pages 434–437. Copyright © 1964 by Scott, Foresman and Company.

Cast of Characters

JULIUS CAESAR

OCTAVIUS CAESAR ⎫
MARCUS ANTONIUS ⎬ Triumvirs after the death of Julius Caesar
M. AEMILIUS LEPIDUS ⎭

CICERO ⎫
PUBLIUS ⎬ Senators
POPILIUS LENA ⎭

MARCUS BRUTUS ⎫
CASSIUS ⎪
CASCA ⎪
TREBONIUS ⎬ Conspirators against Julius Caesar
LIGARIUS ⎪
DECIUS BRUTUS ⎪
METELLUS CIMBER ⎪
CINNA ⎭

FLAVIUS and MARULLUS   Tribunes
ARTEMIDORUS OF CNIDOS   A teacher of rhetoric
A SOOTHSAYER   A poet

CINNA ⎫
LUCILIUS ⎪
TITINIUS ⎪
MESSALA ⎬ Friends to Brutus and Cassius
YOUNG CATO ⎪
VOLUMNIUS ⎭

VARRO ⎫
CLITUS ⎪
CLAUDIUS ⎪
STRATO ⎬ Servants to Brutus
LUCIUS ⎪
DARDANIUS ⎭

PINDARUS   Servant to Cassius
CALPURNIA   Wife to Caesar
PORTIA   Wife to Brutus

SENATORS,
CITIZENS,
GUARDS,
    ATTENDANTS, Etc.

Act One

Scene 1: Rome. A street.

It is February fifteenth. The people of Rome are gathering to welcome CAESAR *whose triumphant return from Spain coincides with the festival of Lupercalia* (lü′pər kā′li ə). *The* COMMONERS *are in a holiday mood, eager to celebrate* CAESAR's *victory over Pompey's sons. There are other Romans, however, who fear* CAESAR's *power and popularity. Like* FLAVIUS *and* MARULLUS, *they resent celebrating a victory over fellow Romans.*

A crowd of excited COMMONERS, *dressed in their holiday garments, rush onto the platform at left door. All talk at once and look expectantly toward the right, the direction in which* CAESAR's *procession will appear. Offstage shouts and cheers, an indication that* CAESAR *draws much closer, send the* COMMONERS *scurrying for vantage points.*

Meanwhile, the tribunes FLAVIUS *and* MARULLUS *have entered at inner-stage curtains. As they stride briskly forward, it is apparent that the tribunes disapprove of the general holiday mood.* FLAVIUS *addresses the* COMMONERS *angrily.*

FLAVIUS. Hence! Home, you idle creatures, get you home!
　Is this a holiday? What! Know you not,
　Being mechanical,¹ you ought not walk
　Upon a laboring day without the sign
5　Of your profession?² *(Singling one out.)* Speak, what trade art
　　thou?

FIRST COMMONER. Why, sir, a carpenter.

MARULLUS. Where is thy leather apron and thy rule?
　What dost thou with thy best apparel on?
　(To another.) You, sir, what trade are you?

10 SECOND COMMONER. Truly, sir, in respect of a fine workman, I am but,
　as you would say, a cobbler.³

MARULLUS *(impatiently).* But what trade art thou? Answer me di-
　rectly.

SECOND COMMONER. A trade, sir, that, I hope, I may use with a safe
15　conscience; which is, indeed, sir, a mender of soles.

(The COMMONERS *laugh at the pun.)*

FLAVIUS *(scowling).* Thou art a cobbler, art thou?

SECOND COMMONER. Truly, sir, all that I live by is with the awl; I
　meddle with no tradesman's matters nor women's matters, but
　with awl.⁴ I am, indeed, sir, a surgeon to old shoes; when they are
20　in great danger, I re-cover them.

FLAVIUS. But wherefore art not in thy shop today?
　Why dost thou lead these men about the sreets?

SECOND COMMONER *(grinning).* Truly, sir, to wear out their shoes, to
　get myself into more work. But, indeed, sir, we make holiday, to

1. *mechanical,* workingmen.

2. *you ought not . . . profession.* Shakespeare here refers to an English law of his own time, which required workingmen to wear their laboring clothes and carry the tools of their profession.

3. *cobbler.* In Shakespeare's time this word meant a clumsy workman and did not refer specifically to a mender of shoes. That explains Marullus' next question.

4. *I meddle . . . with awl.* How would spelling the last word *all* change the meaning? Elizabethan audiences delighted in such puns.

25 see Caesar and to rejoice in his triumph.

(The mob shouts its agreement.)

MARULLUS *(addressing the mob).* Wherefore rejoice? What conquest
  brings he home?
 What tributaries[5] follow him to Rome,
 To grace in captive bonds his chariot wheels?

(The shouting of the mob grows louder.)

 You blocks, you stones, you worse than senseless things!
30 O you hard hearts, you cruel men of Rome,
 Knew you not Pompey?[6] Many a time and oft
 Have you climbed up to walls and battlements,
 To towers and windows, yea, to chimney tops,[7]
 Your infants in your arms, and there have sat
35 The livelong day, with patient expectation
 To see great Pompey pass the streets of Rome:
 And when you saw his chariot but appear,
 Have you not made an universal shout,
 That Tiber[8] trembled underneath her banks,
40 To hear the replication of your sounds
 Made in her concave shores?
 And do you now put on your best attire?
 And do you now cull out a holiday?
 And do you now strew flowers in his way
45 That comes in triumph over Pompey's blood?[9]

(The mob, subdued by MARULLUS' *words, is silent now.)*

 Be gone!
 Run to your houses, fall upon your knees,
 Pray to the gods to intermit the plague
 That needs must light on this ingratitude.
50 FLAVIUS. Go, go good countrymen, and, for this fault,
 Assemble all the poor men of your sort;
 Draw them to Tiber banks, and weep your tears
 Into the channel, till the lowest stream
 Do kiss the most exalted shores of all.[10]

(The COMMONERS, *singly or in pairs, file off the platform at left.)*

55 *(To* MARULLUS.*)* See, whether their basest metal be not moved;
 They vanish tongue-tied in their guiltiness.

(There is a loud flourish of trumpets offstage.)

 Go you down that way toward the Capitol;
 This way will I: disrobe the images,[11]
 If you do find them decked with ceremonies.
60 MARULLUS *(cautiously).* May we do so?
 You know it is the feast of Lupercal.[12]
 FLAVIUS. It is no matter; let no images
 Be hung with Caesar's trophies. I'll about,
 And drive away the vulgar[13] from the streets:

5. tributaries, captives who must pay tribute to Rome for their freedom.

6. Knew you not Pompey? Only a short time before, the fickle mob had been cheering Caesar's enemy Pompey, champion of Rome's conservative party.

7. chimney tops. There were no chimneys in ancient Rome. Such a slip on the part of an author is called an anachronism (ə nak′rə-niz′ əm).

8. Tiber (tī′bər), a river flowing through Rome.

9. Pompey's blood. Caesar had slain Pompey's sons in Spain on March 17, 45 B.C. Marullus thinks Rome should have been horrified at the slaughter of two of its noblest sons.

10. weep your tears . . . of all, weep enough tears to bring the lowest waterline up to the highest. This type of exaggeration, used for effect, is called hyperbole (hī-pér′bə lē).

11. disrobe the images, take down the decorations and trophies that have been placed on Caesar's statues.

12. the feast of Lupercal (lü′pər kal). On February 15 of each year, the Romans celebrated in honor of Lupercus, god of fertility. The celebrants, young men who were priests of Lupercus, ran a specified course on the Palatine Hill, carrying thongs of goatskin with which they struck people who stood in their way. Women desiring children purposely sought to be struck by the runners, for they believed that the touch of the thongs would cure them of barrenness.

13. the vulgar, the common people.

65   So do you, too, where you perceive them thick.
     These growing feathers[14] plucked from Caesar's wing
     Will make him fly an ordinary pitch,
     Who else would soar above the view of men
     And keep us all in servile fearfulness.
     (The tribunes exit, going in different directions.)

Scene 2: Rome. A public place.
Groups of COMMONERS *run onto the platform, looking offstage at*
CAESAR's *approaching procession.* SOLDIERS *march on at right door*
and force the people back so that the procession can pass. There is a
loud flourish of trumpets; and CAESAR *appears at right, accompanied*
by ANTONY, CALPURNIA, PORTIA, DECIUS, CICERO, BRUTUS, CASSIUS, *and*
CASCA. *More* COMMONERS *follow; among them is a* SOOTHSAYER. *Amid*
shouts and cheers, CAESAR *leads the procession well onto the plat-*
form, then he stops. Everyone bows, rendering homage to CAESAR.

CAESAR. Calpurnia!

CASCA.   Peace, ho! Caesar speaks.

CAESAR.   Calpurnia!

CALPURNIA *(stepping forward)*. Here, my lord.

CAESAR. Stand you directly in Antonius' way
     When he doth run his course.[1] Antonius!

*(*ANTONY *hurries forward and stands before* CAESAR.*)*

5 ANTONY. Caesar, my lord?

CAESAR. Forget not, in your speed, Antonius,
     To touch Calpurnia; for our elders say
     The barren, touchèd in this holy chase,
     Shake off their sterile curse.[2]

ANTONY.   I shall remember:
10   When Caesar says, "Do this," it is performed. *(He steps back.)*

CAESAR. Set on; and leave no ceremony out.
(The trumpets flourish; the procession starts forward.)

SOOTHSAYER *(in awesome tones)*. Caesar!

CAESAR *(stopping)*. Ha![3] Who calls?
(The crowd murmurs, wondering who thus has accosted CAESAR.*)*

CASCA. Bid every noise be still: peace yet again!

15 CAESAR. Who is it in the press that calls on me?
     I hear a tongue, shriller than all the music,
     Cry, "Caesar!" Speak; Caesar is turned to hear.[4]

SOOTHSAYER *(ominously)*. Beware the ides of March.[5]

CAESAR *(looking to right and left)*.   What man is
       that?

BRUTUS. A soothsayer bids you beware the ides of March.

20 CAESAR. Set him before me; let me see his face.

CASSIUS *(stepping forward)*. Fellow, come from the throng; look upon
       Caesar.

14. *These growing feathers,* meaning Caesar's new followers. Falconers sometimes clip the wings of their birds to keep them from flying to too great a height, or pitch. So Caesar, without the help of the common people, would be checked in his ambition to rise to greater heights.

1. *When he doth run his course.* Antony, as head of the priests of Lupercus, is one of the young nobles who are to run through certain streets on the Palatine Hill, carrying goatskin thongs.

2. *Forget not . . . sterile curse.* This passage shows Caesar's desire for an heir. To Cassius this concern was indicative of Caesar's desire to be king.

3. *Ha!* This is an exclamation of surprise, rather than a word denoting laughter.

4. *Caesar is turned to hear.* In using his name when referring to himself, Caesar adopts a practice reserved only for royalty. The other patricians are quick to notice this assumption of undue authority on his part.

5. *the ides* (īdz) *of March,* the fifteenth day of the month of March.

(SOLDIERS *drag the* SOOTHSAYER *before* CAESAR.)

CAESAR. What sayest thou to me now? Speak once again.

SOOTHSAYER. Beware the ides of March.

(For a moment CAESAR, *looking disturbed, stares at the* SOOTHSAYER; *then he turns to* ANTONY, *who begins to laugh. When others join in* ANTONY's *derisive laughter,* CAESAR, *with a gesture, dismisses the* SOOTHSAYER.)

CAESAR. He is a dreamer; let us leave him: pass.

(The trumpets flourish; the procession and the crowd go out at left, BRUTUS *and* CASSIUS *remaining behind.* BRUTUS *stands at one side, lost in thought.* CASSIUS *approaches him.)*

25 CASSIUS. Will you go see the order of the course?

BRUTUS. Not I.

CASSIUS. I pray you, do.

BRUTUS. I am not gamesome; I do lack some part
    Of that quick spirit[6] that is in Antony.

30   Let me not hinder, Cassius, your desires;
    I'll leave you.

CASSIUS. Brutus, I do observe you now of late:
    I have not from your eyes that gentleness
    And show of love as I was wont to have:[7]

35   You bear too stubborn and too strange a hand
    Over your friend that loves you.

BRUTUS.   Cassius,
    Be not deceived: if I have veiled my look,
    I turn the trouble of my countenance
    Merely upon myself.[8] Vexed I am

40   Of late with passions of some difference,
    Conceptions only proper to myself,
    Which give some soil perhaps to my behaviors;
    But let not therefore my good friends be grieved—
    Among which number, Cassius, be you one—

45   Nor construe any further my neglect,
    Than that poor Brutus, with himself at war,
    Forgets the shows of love to other men.

CASSIUS. Then, Brutus, I have much mistook your passion;
    By means whereof this breast of mine hath buried

50   Thoughts of great value, worthy cogitations.[9]
    Tell me, good Brutus, can you see your face?

BRUTUS. No, Cassius; for the eye sees not itself, but by reflection, by
    some other things. *(He moves toward front platform;* CASSIUS
        follows.)

CASSIUS. 'Tis just:

55   And it is very much lamented, Brutus,
    That you have no such mirrors as will turn
    Your hidden worthiness into your eye,

6. *quick spirit,* lively disposition.

7. *as I was wont to have,* that I customarily had.

8. *I turn . . . upon myself.* Brutus is troubled by his own thoughts, not by anything that Cassius has done to him.

9. *Then, Brutus . . . worthy cogitations.* Here Cassius hints of the thoughts (cogitations) that lie locked in his own breast and begins sounding out Brutus to see whether he will join forces with the conspirators. Brutus is an idealistic, impractical sort of man; and Cassius wishes to open his eyes to the dangers that lie in Caesar's rising ambition.

That you might see your shadow. I have heard,
Where many of the best respect in Rome,
60 Except immortal Caesar, speaking of Brutus
And groaning underneath this age's yoke,
Have wished that noble Brutus had his eyes.
    BRUTUS *(facing* CASSIUS*).* Into what dangers would you lead me, Cassius,
That you would have me seek into myself
65 For that which is not in me?
    CASSIUS. Therefore, good Brutus, be prepared to hear:
And since you know you cannot see yourself
So well as by reflection, I, your glass,
Will modestly discover to yourself
70 That of yourself which you yet know not of.
And be not jealous on me, gentle Brutus;
Were I a common laugher,[10] or did use
To stale with ordinary oaths my love
To every new protester; if you know
75 That I do fawn on men and hug them hard
And after scandal them, or if you know
That I profess myself in banqueting
To all the rout,[11] then hold me dangerous.

(There is a flourish of trumpets offstage, then loud cheers. BRUTUS
and CASSIUS *look up.)*

    BRUTUS. What means this shouting? I do fear the people
80 Choose Caesar for their king.
    CASSIUS.   Aye, do you fear it?
Then must I think you would not have it so.
    BRUTUS. I would not, Cassius; yet I love him well.
But wherefore do you hold me here so long?
What is it that you would impart to me?
85 If it be aught toward the general good,
Set honor in one eye and death in the other,
And I will look on both indifferently,[12]
For let the gods so speed me as I love
The name of honor more than I fear death.
90 CASSIUS. I know that virtue to be in you, Brutus,
As well as I do know your outward favor.
Well, honor *is* the subject of my story.
I cannot tell what you and other men
Think of this life; but, for my single self,
95 I had as lief not be as live to be
In awe of such a thing as I myself.
I was born free as Caesar; so were you:
We both have fed as well, and we can both
Endure the winter's cold as well as he:

10. *a common laugher,* a buffoon laughed at or scorned by everybody.

11. *the rout,* the rabble; worthless people.

12. *If it be . . . indifferently.* If what Cassius has in mind is for the public welfare and is honorable, Brutus will do it even though it means death.

100   For once, upon a raw and gusty day,
The troubled Tiber chafing with her shores,
Caesar said to me, "Darest thou, Cassius, now
Leap in with me into this angry flood,
And swim to yonder point?" Upon the word,
105   Accoutered as I was,[13] I plungèd in
And bade him follow; so indeed he did.
The torrent roared, and we did buffet it,
With lusty sinews, throwing it aside
And stemming it with hearts of controversy.
110   But ere we could arrive the point proposed,
Caesar cried, "Help me, Cassius, or I sink!"
I, as Aeneas, our great ancestor,
Did from the flames of Troy upon his shoulder
The old Anchises bear,[14] so from the waves of Tiber
115   Did I the tired Caesar. *(Angrily.)* And this man
Is now become a god, and Cassius is
A wretched creature and must bend his body,
If Caesar carelessly but nod on him. *(He pauses.)*
He had a fever when he was in Spain,
120   And when the fit[15] was on him, I did mark
How he did shake: 'tis true, this god did shake;
His coward lips did from their color fly,[16]
And that same eye whose bend doth awe the world
Did lose his[17] luster: I did hear him groan:
125   Aye, and that tongue of his that bade the Romans
Mark him and write his speeches in their books,
Alas, it cried, "Give me some drink, Titinius,"
As a sick girl. Ye gods, it doth amaze me
A man of such a feeble temper[18] should
130   So get the start of the majestic world
And bear the palm[19] alone.
    (Loud shouts and the flourish of trumpets heard offstage.)
    BRUTUS *(crossing to right pillar).* Another general shout!
    I do believe that these applauses are
    For some new honors that are heaped on Caesar.
135 CASSIUS *(following).* Why, man, he doth bestride the narrow world
    Like a Colossus,[20] and we petty men
    Walk under his huge legs and peep about
    To find ourselves dishonorable graves.
    Men at some time are masters of their fates:
140   The fault, dear Brutus, is not in our stars,
    But in ourselves, that we are underlings.[21]
    Brutus and Caesar: what should be in that "Caesar"?
    Why should that name be sounded more than yours?
    Write them together, yours is as fair a name;

13. *Accoutered* (ə kü′tərd) *as I was.* Cassius was fully dressed.

14. *I, as Aeneas* (i nē′əs) . . . *Anchises* (an kī′sēz) *bear.* Aeneas, carrying his aged father Anchises and leading his little son, escaped from burning Troy. For years he wandered; then at last he reached the banks of the Tiber, where his descendants founded Rome.

15. *the fit.* Caesar was subject to epileptic seizures, then termed "the falling sickness."

16. *His coward lips . . . fly.* His lips became white.

17. *his,* modern usage, *its.* Its was just coming into use when the play was written.

18. *A man of such a feeble temper.* The Romans worshiped physical strength, and Cassius didn't see how a physical weakling could rule all the known world.
19. *the palm,* the symbol of victory and triumph.

20. *Like a Colossus* (kə los′əs). The Colossus was a huge statue of Apollo at Rhodes. This wonder of the ancient world was so enormous that according to legend, it bestrode the entrance to the harbor, and ships passed between its legs.
21. *Men at some time . . . underlings.* Cassius believes that the star a man is born under is not so important in determining his destiny as is his own character.

145   Sound them, it doth become the mouth as well;
    Weigh them, it is as heavy; conjure with 'em,
    "Brutus" will start a spirit[22] as soon as "Caesar."
    Now, in the names of all the gods at once,
    Upon what meat doth this our Caesar feed,
150   That he is grown so great?

(Loud shouts and the flourish of trumpets offstage.)

BRUTUS *(thoughtfully).*   What you have said
    I will consider; what you have to say
    I will with patience hear, and find a time
    Both meet to hear and answer such high things.
    Till then, my noble friend, chew upon this:
155   Brutus had rather be a villager
    Than to repute himself a son of Rome
    Under these hard conditions as this time
    Is like to lay upon us.

CASSIUS. I am glad that my weak words
160   Have struck but thus much show of fire from Brutus.

(The sounds of approaching people are heard from offstage.)

BRUTUS. The games are done and Caesar is returning.

CASSIUS. As they pass by, pluck Casca by the sleeve;
    And he will, after his sour fashion, tell you
    What hath proceeded worthy note today.

(CAESAR and his followers reenter at left and start across the platform. ANTONY is on CAESAR's left; CASCA is at the rear of the procession.)

165 BRUTUS. I will do so. But look you, Cassius,
    The angry spot doth glow on Caesar's brow,
    And all the rest look like a chidden train.[23]
    Calpurnia's cheek is pale; and Cicero
    Looks with such ferret and such fiery eyes[24]
170   As we have seen him in the Capitol,
    Being crossed in conference by some senators.

CASSIUS. Casca will tell us what the matter is.

(CAESAR stops before he reaches center platform and looks speculatively at CASSIUS.)

CAESAR. Antonius!

ANTONY. Caesar?

175 CAESAR. Let me have men about me that are fat;
    Sleek-headed men and such as sleep o' nights.
    Yond Cassius has a lean and hungry look;
    He thinks too much; such men are dangerous.

ANTONY. Fear him not, Caesar; he's not dangerous;
180   He is a noble Roman and well-given.

CAESAR. Would he were fatter! But I fear him not:
    Yet if my name were liable to fear,

22. *start a spirit,* call forth a ghost from the spirit world.

23. *like a chidden train,* like a group of people who have been harshly scolded.
24. *such ferret and such fiery eyes,* eyes that are red and angry looking, like the eyes of a weasel.

I do not know the man I should avoid
So soon as that spare Cassius. He reads much;
185 He is a great observer, and he looks
Quite through the deeds of men; he loves no plays,
As thou dost, Anthony; he hears no music;
Seldom he smiles, and smiles in such a sort
As if he mocked himself and scorned his spirit
190 That could be moved to smile at anything.
Such men as he be never at heart's ease
Whiles they behold a greater than themselves,
And therefore are they very dangerous.
I rather tell thee what is to be feared
195 Than what I fear; for always I am Caesar.
Come on my right hand, for this ear is deaf,
And tell me truly what thou think'st of him.

(ANTONY, *as bid, steps to* CAESAR's *right. The trumpets sound again and the procession, with* CASCA *still at its rear, moves slowly out at right door. When* CASCA *reaches center platform he is detained by* BRUTUS *and* CASSIUS.)

CASCA. You pulled me by the cloak; would you speak with me?

BRUTUS. Aye, Casca; tell us what hath chanced today,
200 That Caesar looks so sad.

CASCA. Why, you were with him, were you not?

BRUTUS. I should not then ask Casca what had chanced.

CASCA. Why, there was a crown offered him; and being offered him,
he put it by with the back of his hand, thus; and then the people
205 fell a-shouting.

BRUTUS. What was the second noise for?

CASCA. Why, for that, too.

CASSIUS. They shouted thrice; what was the last cry for?

CASCA. Why, for that, too.

210 BRUTUS (*incredulously*). Was the crown offered him thrice?

CASCA. Aye, marry,²⁵ was't, and he put it by thrice, every time gentler
than other.

CASSIUS. Who offered him the crown?

CASCA. Why, Antony.

215 BRUTUS. Tell us the manner of it, gentle Casca.

CASCA. I can as well be hanged as tell the manner of it: it was mere
foolery; I did not mark it. I saw Mark Antony offer him a crown—
yet 'twas not a crown neither, 'twas one of these coronets—and,
as I told you, he put it by once; but, for all that, to my thinking, he
220 would fain have had it. Then he offered it to him again; then he
put it by again; but, to my thinking, he was very loath to lay his
fingers off it. And then he offered it the third time; he put it the
third time by; and still as he refused it, the rabblement hooted and
clapped their chapped hands and threw up their sweaty nightcaps

25. *marry,* a mild oath. Its original
form was "by the Virgin Mary."
(Why is Shakespeare's use of it
here an anachronism?)

225 and uttered such a deal of stinking breath because Caesar refused the crown that it had almost choked Caesar; for he swounded[26] and fell down at it; and for mine own part, I durst not laugh, for fear of opening my lips and receiving the bad air.

CASSIUS. But, soft, I pray you; what, did Caesar swound?

230 CASCA. He fell down in the market place, and foamed at mouth, and was speechless.

BRUTUS. 'Tis very like; he hath the falling sickness.

CASSIUS. No, Caesar hath it not; but you and I
And honest Casca, we have the falling sickness.

235 CASCA. I know not what you mean by that; but I am sure Caesar fell down. If the tag-rag people did not clap him and hiss him, according as he pleased and displeased them, as they used to do the players in the theater, I am no true man.

BRUTUS. What said he when he came unto himself?

240 CASCA. When he came to himself again, he said if he had done or said anything amiss, he desired their worships to think it was his infirmity. Three or four wenches, where I stood, cried, ''Alas, good soul!'' and forgave him with all their hearts. But there's no heed to be taken of them; if Caesar had stabbed their mothers,
245 they would have done no less.

BRUTUS. And after that, he came, thus sad, away?

CASCA. Aye.

CASSIUS. Did Cicero say anything?

CASCA. Aye, he spoke Greek.

250 CASSIUS. To what effect?

CASCA. Nay, an[27] I tell you that, I'll ne'er look you i' th' face again; but those that understood him smiled at one another and shook their heads. But, for mine own part, it was Greek to me.[28] I could tell you more news, too: Marullus and Flavius, for pulling scarfs
255 off Caesar's images, are put to silence.[29] Fare you well. There was more foolery yet, if I could remember it.

CASSIUS. Will you sup with me tonight, Casca?

CASCA. No, I am promised forth.

CASSIUS. Will you dine with me tomorrow?

260 CASCA. Aye, if I be alive and your mind hold and your dinner worth the eating.

CASSIUS. Good; I will expect you.

CASCA. Do so. Farewell, both.

(He exits at inner-stage curtains.)

BRUTUS. What a blunt fellow is this grown to be!
265 He was quick mettle[30] when he went to school.

CASSIUS. So is he now in execution
Of any bold or noble enterprise,
However he puts on this tardy form.
This rudeness is a sauce to his good wit,

26. *swounded* (swound'əd), became faint.

27. *an,* if.

28. *it was Greek to me.* People still quote this expression to signify that something is too difficult to be understood.
29. *put to silence,* deprived of their rank as tribunes and banished.

30. *quick mettle,* easily stirred to action.

270 Which gives men stomach to digest his words
With better appetite.
BRUTUS. And so it is. For this time I will leave you;
Tomorrow, if you please to speak with me,
I will come home to you; or, if you will,
275 Come home to me, and I will wait for you.
CASSIUS. I will do so; till then, think of the world.
(BRUTUS *exits at left.*)
Well, Brutus, thou art noble;[31] yet, I see,
Thy honorable metal may be wrought
From that it is disposed. Therefore it is meet
280 That noble minds keep ever with their likes;
For who so firm that cannot be seduced?
Caesar doth bear me hard;[32] but he loves Brutus.
If I were Brutus now and he were Cassius,
He should not humor me.[33] I will this night,
285 In several hands,[34] in at his windows throw,
As if they came from several citizens,
Writings all tending to the great opinion
That Rome holds of his name; wherein obscurely
Caesar's ambition shall be glancèd at[35]:
290 And after this let Caesar seat him sure;
For we will shake him, or worse days endure.
(*He exits at inner-stage curtains.*)

Scene 3: Rome. A street.
It is the night before the ides of March. A month has gone by since
CASSIUS *first spoke to* BRUTUS *about the danger from* CAESAR.
Unperturbed by this wild and stormy night, CICERO *enters with a*
lantern at left. There is a flash of lightning, then a violent clap of
thunder just as CASCA, *his sword drawn, enters at right.*
CICERO (*calmly*). Good even,[1] Casca; brought you Caesar home?
Why are you breathless? And why stare you so?
CASCA. Are not you moved, when all the sway of earth
Shakes like a thing unfirm? O Cicero,
5 I have seen tempests, when the scolding winds
Have rived the knotty oaks, and I have seen
The ambitious ocean swell and rage and foam,
To be exalted with the threatening clouds;
But never till tonight, never till now,
10 Did I go through a tempest dropping fire.
(*Another crash of thunder, followed by a scream.* CASCA *darts to left*
pillar.)
Either there is a civil strife in heaven,
Or else the world, too saucy with the gods,
Incenses them to send destruction.

31. *Well, Brutus, thou art noble.*
Here Cassius begins the play's first soliloquy (sə lil'ə kwē), a speech made by an actor to himself. The speaker of a soliloquy is usually alone on the stage. If other characters are present, they do not hear the soliloquy.
32. *Caesar doth bear me hard.*
Caesar hates me.
33. *humor me,* win me over to his opinions.
34. *In several hands,* in different handwritings.

35. *glancèd at,* hinted at.

1. *even,* evening.

CICERO (*drawing closer*). Why, saw you anything more wonderful?

15 CASCA. A common slave—you know him well by sight—
Held up his left hand, which did flame and burn
Like twenty torches joined, and yet his hand,
Not sensible of fire,[2] remained unscorched.
And yesterday the bird of night did sit
20 Even at noon day upon the market place,
Hooting and shrieking. When these prodigies
Do so conjointly meet, let not men say,
"These are their reasons; they are natural";
For, I believe, they are portentous things
25 Unto the climate that they point upon.[3]

CICERO. Indeed, it is a strange-disposèd time:
But men may construe things after their fashion,
Clean from the purpose of the things themselves.[4]
Comes Caesar to the Capitol tomorrow?

30 CASCA. He doth; for he did bid Antonius
Send word to you he would be there tomorrow.

CICERO. Good night then, Casca: this disturbèd sky
Is not to walk in.

CASCA.   Farewell, Cicero.

(*Leaving his lantern behind,* CICERO *exits at right. There is another
flash of lightning and* CASCA *retreats to rear platform, where he takes
shelter under the projecting balcony.* CASSIUS *enters at left.*)

CASSIUS. Who's there?

CASCA.   A Roman.

CASSIUS.   Casca, by your voice.

(*He joins* CASCA *under the balcony.*)

35 CASCA. Your ear is good. Cassius, what night[5] is this!

CASSIUS. A very pleasing night to honest men.

CASCA. Who ever knew the heavens menace so?

CASSIUS. Those that have known the earth so full of faults.
For my part, I have walked about the streets,
40 Submitting me unto the perilous night,
And, thus unbracèd,[6] Casca, as you see,
Have bared my bosom to the thunder-stone.

CASCA. But wherefore did you so much tempt the heavens?
It is the part of men to fear and tremble
45 When the most mighty gods by tokens send
Such dreadful heralds to astonish us.

CASSIUS. Now could I, Casca, name to thee a man
Most like this dreadful night,
That thunders, lightens, opens graves, and roars,
50 A man no mightier than thyself or me
In personal action, yet prodigious grown
And fearful, as these strange eruptions are.

2. *Not sensible of fire,* not feeling the fire.

3. *When these prodigies . . . point upon.* Though some people may try to explain these marvels (prodigies) as natural things, Casca regards them as omens foretelling disaster for the Romans.

4. *But men may . . . themselves.* Cicero thinks men who are greatly troubled often read undue significance into such happenings as these.

5. *what night,* what a night.

6. *thus unbracèd.* Cassius opens his garment at the neck, exposing his chest to the thunderbolts.

CASCA. 'Tis Caesar that you mean; is it not, Cassius?

CASSIUS. Let it be who it is: for Romans now
55   Have thews and limbs like to their ancestors;
    But, woe the while! Our fathers' minds are dead,
    And we are governed with our mothers' spirits;
    Our yoke and sufferance show us womanish.

CASCA. Indeed, they say the senators tomorrow
60   Mean to establish Caesar as a king;
    And he shall wear his crown by sea and land,
    In every place, save here in Italy.

CASSIUS. I know where I will wear this dagger then;
    Cassius from bondage will deliver Cassius.[7]
65   That part of tyranny that I do bear
    I can shake off at pleasure.

(The thunder rumbles menacingly; the two men gradually move forward.)

CASCA.   So can I;
    So every bondman in his own hand bears
    The power to cancel his captivity.

CASSIUS. And why should Caesar be a tyrant then?
70   Poor man! I know he would not be a wolf,
    But that he sees the Romans are but sheep:
    He were no lion, were not Romans hinds.[8]
    Where hast thou led me? I perhaps speak this
    Before a willing bondman; then I know
75   My answer must be made. But I am armed,
    And dangers are to me indifferent.

CASCA. You speak to Casca, and to such a man
    That is no fleering[9] tell-tale. *(Offering his hand.)* Hold, my
      hand;
    Be factious for redress of all these griefs,[10]
80   And I will set this foot of mine as far
    As who goes farthest.

CASSIUS.   There's a bargain made.
    Now know you, Casca, I have moved already
    Some certain of the noblest-minded Romans
    To undergo with me an enterprise
85   Of honorable-dangerous consequence;
    And I do know, by this, they stay for me
    In Pompey's porch;[11] for now, this fearful night,
    There is no stir or walking in the streets;
    And the complexion of the element
90   In favor's like the work we have in hand,
    Most bloody, fiery, and most terrible.

(Hurrying footsteps are heard offstage at right.)

CASCA. Stand close awhile, for here comes one in haste.

7. Cassius from bondage . . . Cassius. Cassius will kill himself rather than live with Caesar as his acknowledged king.

8. He were no lion . . . hinds. Caesar's ambition would not be so great had he less chance of attaining it. The Romans are so weak that they make Caesar appear lionlike in contrast.

9. fleering, deceitful.

10. Be factious . . . griefs, be ready to join with Casca to right the grievances that the Romans have suffered at the hands of Caesar.

11. stay . . . porch, wait for me in the porch of Pompey's theater.

CASSIUS. 'Tis Cinna; I do know him by his gait;
    He is a friend.

(CINNA *enters in haste.*)

                    Cinna, where haste you so?

95 CINNA. To find out you. *(Moving forward.)* Who's that? Metellus
        Cimber?

CASSIUS. No, it is Casca; one incorporate
    To our attempts.¹² Am I not stayed for, Cinna?

CINNA. I am glad on't. What a fearful night is this!
    There's two or three of us have seen strange sights.

100 CASSIUS. Am I not stayed for? Tell me.

CINNA.   Yes, you are.
    O Cassius, if you could
    But win the noble Brutus to our party—

CASSIUS. Be you content. Good Cinna, take this paper,
    And look you lay it in the praetor's chair,¹³

105 Where Brutus may but find it; and throw this
    In at his window; set this up with wax
    Upon old Brutus' statue.¹⁴ All this done,
    Repair to Pompey's porch, where you shall find us.
    Is Decius Brutus and Trebonius there?

110 CINNA *(stopping).* All but Metellus Cimber; and he's gone
    To seek you at your house. Well, I will hie,
    And so bestow these papers as you bade me.

CASSIUS. That done, repair to Pompey's theater.

(CINNA *runs off at right as* CASSIUS *turns to* CASCA.)

    Come, Casca, you and I will yet ere day

115 See Brutus at his house: three parts of him
    Is ours already, and the man entire
    Upon the next encounter yields him ours.¹⁵

CASCA. Oh, he sits high in all the people's hearts;
    And that which would appear offense in us,

120 His countenance, like richest alchemy,
    Will change to virtue and to worthiness.¹⁶

CASSIUS. Him and his worth and our great need of him
    You have right well conceited.¹⁷ Let us go,
    For it is after midnight; and ere day

125 We will awake him and be sure of him.

(CASSIUS *and* CASCA *collect the lantern and then move off at right.*)

12. *one incorporate . . . attempts,* one who knows of our plans and is in sympathy with us.

13. *in the praetor's chair.* Brutus, at this time, was praetor (prē′tər), Roman judge or magistrate.

14. *Upon old Brutus' statue,* upon the statue of Lucius Junius Brutus, ancestor of the present Brutus. He had acted as leader in expelling Tarquinius Superbus, the last of the seven Roman kings.

15. *three parts of him . . . ours.* Brutus is almost persuaded to join the conspirators; when they next meet with him, they will undoubtedly win him over completely.

16. *His countenance . . . worthiness.* The high regard with which the Romans hold Brutus and his honorable family name is a great asset. Linking him to the plan will give it sanction and worth.

17. *conceited,* estimated.

Discussion

Scene 1

1. (a) What quality of the mob does Marullus satirize in his speech beginning "Wherefore rejoice" (440, line 26)? (b) Do you think that his opinion is true of mobs in general?

2. (a) In talking with the tribunes do the commoners show: (1) a cringing fear; (2) a scornful contempt; or (3) a good-natured desire to annoy the officials? (b) With which group of people do you sympathize—the commoners or the tribunes? Why?

3. Would you say Shakespeare's main purpose in this scene was: (a) to provide a touch of humor for the beginning of the play; (b) to foreshadow a serious conflict; (c) to introduce the main characters? After making your choice, explain how Shakespeare achieves that purpose.

Scene 2

1. (a) As the scene begins, what attitude do various characters seem to take toward Caesar? (b) What are your own first impressions of the man?

2. (a) What physical weaknesses of Caesar are revealed later in the scene? How is each one brought out? (b) Does Caesar show any signs of being superstitious? (c) How good is he at sizing up individuals (Cassius, for example)? (d) Of the men around him, which could he safely trust? (e) How do we know the common people of Rome loved and idolized him?

3. (a) What is Cassius leading up to in his long talk with Brutus? (b) Why doesn't he come to the point at once? (c) What ideas does he develop that would be most likely to influence Brutus?

4. Does Casca, later on, help or hinder Cassius in influencing Brutus? How?

5. (a) What fear does Brutus express to Cassius concerning Caesar? (b) Do you think Brutus is sincere in saying "yet I love him well"? (c) How are his feelings about Caesar related to his statement that lately he has been "at war" with himself?

6. (a) What is the conflict that was foreshadowed in Scene 1 and that is now taking more definite form? (b) On which side do you think Brutus will decide to be?

Scene 3

1. (a) What subject is bothering Casca when he first encounters Cassius? (b) How does Cassius cleverly turn the conversation to the subject that *he* considers most important?

2. (a) Why does Cassius think the Roman people themselves are largely responsible for Caesar's growing ambition? (b) Keeping in mind Casca's opinion of the "tag-rag people" as indicated in Scene 2, explain why Cassius' explanation of Caesar's tyranny would appeal to Casca. (c) What decision does Casca make regarding the conspirators?

3. (a) How does Cassius plan to use Cinna in advancing the conspirators' plan? (b) Why are he and the others so eager to have Brutus join them? (c) Quote at least three passages that show the conspirators' opinion of Brutus.

Vocabulary
Context and Dictionary

Reread the following words within their context in the play. When you have determined the meanings of the words, rewrite the following sentences to include the appropriate word. You will not need all the words.

conjure (446, line 146)
construe (442, line 45)
fawn (444, line 75)
loath (447, line 221)
prodigious (450, line 51)

1. While trying to set a new world record, the student swallowed an amazing number of goldfish.

2. During the reign of Louis XIV, many of the court nobles dabbled in black magic and tried to summon up spirits.

3. The members of the student council interpret the new regulation differently.

4. We were all extremely reluctant to ford the river, but there was no other way to get across.

Make a brief outline indicating what has happened in Act One. Use as the first statement in your outline: Caesar returns to Rome after defeating the last of his opposition.

Extension · Speaking

1. (a) Why do you think Elizabethans watching the play at the Globe Playhouse awaited Act Two with keen interest? (b) What questions would be uppermost in their minds?

2. You have undoubtedly encountered words in which a mark has been placed over or under one of the letters. In such words as *rôle* and *façade*, the *diacritical mark* indicates the sound of a particular letter.

The grave accent (ˋ) and the dieresis (¨) may indicate an *extra syllable.* In reading lines of poetry, it is important to observe these marks carefully. The word *disposed*, for example, is usually pronounced as two syllables. This pronunciation, however, could affect the iambic flow of a blank-verse line:

Indeed, it is a strange-disposed time.

If *disposed* were pronounced as three syllables, the iambic flow would be maintained. The addition of a grave accent accomplishes this: Indeed, it is a strange-disposèd time.

Assume for a moment that you are the actor who first created the role of Caesar on the Globe platform. Lines from five of your speeches are given below. Each passage contains an italicized word to which a diacritical mark has been added. Read each passage aloud, paying careful attention to the diacritical mark.

1. Forget not, in your speed, Antonius,
   To touch Calpurnia; for our elders say

   The barren *touchèd* in this holy chase
   Shake off their sterile curse.
2. Caesar shall forth; the things that threatened me
   Ne'er looked but on my back; when they shall see
   The face of Caesar, they are *vanishèd*,
3. She dreamt tonight she saw my *statuë*
   Which, like a fountain with an hundred spouts,
   Did run pure blood. . . .
4. How foolish do your fears seem now, Calpurnia!
   I am *ashamèd* I did yield to them.
5. Thy brother by decree is *banishèd*;
   If thou dost bend and pray and fawn for him,
   I spurn thee like a cur out of my way. . . .

notes and comments

Blank Verse As a Medium for Dialogue

" . . . *trippingly on the tongue"*
Hamlet, III, iii

A modern playgoer will usually say that he is going to *see* a play, but an Elizabethan usually said that he was going to *hear* one. An Elizabethan playgoer was an attentive listener because the actors of his time had to speak their lines as rapidly as possible. In order to take advantage of the daylight, performances began at two o'clock and ended at about four. Thus the actors had but two short hours in which to enact their play. One of

Shakespeare's problems as a dramatist was to create dialogue which could be delivered rapidly, yet clearly.

Shakespeare cast his plays in *blank verse*. In its rhythm and its flexibility, blank verse is ideal for dialogue; it duplicates the natural rhythm of English speech. As such, it falls easily upon a playgoer's ears and an actor can speak it "trippingly on the tongue."

As natural as blank verse may be to listener and speaker alike, it can be very stiff when one *end-stopped* line follows another, like this:

O, Heaven be judge how I love
    Valentine,
Whose life's as tender to me as my
    soul!
And full as much, for more there
    cannot be,
I do detest false perjured Proteus.
    Two Gentlemen of Verona

These four lines are end-stopped because sense suggests a pause at the end of each line. Shakespeare relied heavily upon end-stopped lines in his early plays; however, by the time he wrote *Julius Caesar*, he had mastered the more flexible *run-on* line:

Why, man he doth bestride the
    narrow world
Like a Colossus, and we petty men
Walk under his huge legs and peep
    about
To find ourselves dishonorable
    graves.

Lines 1, 2, and 3 of this passage are run-on lines because the sense runs on from one line to another. The sense of line 1 is completed in line 2 with the word *Colossus*. The sense of lines 2 and 3 is completed in line 4. A series of run-on lines (a verse paragraph) gives Shakespeare's blank verse the flexibility to express the complicated thoughts and emotions of his characters.

Shakespeare departed from blank verse occasionally. He often used *prose* speeches, for example, for the people of inferior birth. (See the cobbler's lines, p. 439, lines 17-20, 23-25.) He would also strike a note of finality by concluding some platform scenes with a *rhymed couplet*. (See Cassius' lines, p. 449, lines 290 and 291.)

Notes and Comments on pp. 454-457, 473-474, 494, 509-510, 521-522. Copyright © 1964 by Scott, Foresman and Company.

notes and comments

Henry V, I, i, "within this wooden O"

The Londoners who flocked to see *Julius Caesar* in September of 1599 were among the first to attend a performance at the new Globe Playhouse. The Globe was the newest theater in London, but its basic design was as old as England's first permanent playhouse.

James Burbage, who was both a carpenter and an actor, built the first public playhouse in London in 1576. In designing his building, he combined some features of an innyard with the shape of an arena. Like other Elizabethan actors, Burbage

Stratford Shakespearean Festival Foundation of Canada

The interior of the Stratford Festival Theatre, which duplicates the Elizabethan platform stage with its multiple acting levels.

had usually performed in the courtyards of various London inns. Most inns were three-storied structures that enclosed a rectangular and unroofed yard. The innyard was converted into a theater by placing a temporary platform at one side of the yard. The spectators stood in the yard or filled the tiers of balconies that overlooked the yard. Like other Londoners, Burbage was also familiar with the circular arenas or "gardens," where bullbaiting and bearbaiting contests were held. In these arenas, spectators stood on wooden scaffolds that surrounded the baiting ring. They were protected from the animals by a fence.

Burbage adapted the circular shape of the "gardens" for his playhouse. Then, in the three-storied frame of his building, he constructed spectator galleries similar to inn balconies. Because of his example, Elizabethans came to think of a playhouse as an arena with galleries surrounding (or almost surrounding) an open yard. It could hardly have been a surprise to Elizabethan playgoers that the new eight-sided Globe was, in effect, a "wooden O."

It was the size of the Globe platform, not the shape of the playhouse, that astonished Shakespeare's audience. Measuring about 942 square feet, the Globe platform was the largest of its time. Why did the Elizabethan platform stage disappear in later theaters?

About the same time that the Globe opened, playwrights began to write more and more scenes for the inner stage. As this stage became more important, it had to be enlarged. In theaters of the late seventeenth century, the inner stage was wider and deeper: all that remained of the Elizabethan platform was the narrow apron in front of the curtains. This is the stage you probably know the best—the picture-frame stage.

In a theater with a picture-frame stage, the audience sits in front at some distance from the actors. As a result, playgoers tend to be less actively involved in a performance than were the Elizabethans who had the platform thrust into their midst. Many modern theaters have recaptured the close relationship between actor and spectator by reviving the platform stage. In theaters such as these, it is more nearly possible to stage Shakespeare's plays as he intended them to be staged.

Courtesy: The Tyrone Guthrie Theatre

The platform stage of the Tyrone Guthrie Theatre in Minneapolis.

Act Two

Scene 1: Rome. Brutus' orchard.[1]
It is a few hours later. The scene opens as the curtains of the inner
stage are drawn apart to reveal BRUTUS *in a secluded corner of his*
garden. He is seated, deep in thought, on a small bench which is
flanked by a pair of trees. BRUTUS *has spent a wakeful night, and now*
he begins to walk restlessly back and forth. Suddenly he strides
forward, onto the platform, and calls to his serving boy, who lies
asleep just inside the window at upper right.

BRUTUS *(at the window).* What, Lucius, ho!

   (To himself.) I cannot by the progress of the stars,

   Give guess how near to day. *(Calling.)* Lucius, I say!

   I would it were my fault to sleep so soundly.

5   When, Lucius, when? Awake, I say! What, Lucius!

*(*LUCIUS *appears in the window; he opens the casement and leans*
out.)

LUCIUS *(sleepily).* Called you, my lord?

BRUTUS. Get me a taper in my study, Lucius;

   When it is lighted, come and call me here.

LUCIUS. I will, my lord.

(As LUCIUS *withdraws,* BRUTUS *resumes his restless pacing. He is*
alone with his thoughts, which he now speaks.)

10 BRUTUS. It must be by his[2] death; and for my part

   I know no personal cause to spurn at him,

   But for the general.[3] He would be crowned;

   How that might change his nature, there's the question.

   It is the bright day that brings forth the adder;

15   And that craves wary walking. Crown him?—that;—

   And then, I grant, we put a sting in him,

   That at his will he may do danger with.

   The abuse of greatness is, when it disjoins

   Remorse[4] from power: and, to speak truth of Caesar,

20   I have not known when his affections swayed

   More than his reason. But 'tis a common proof,

   That lowliness is young ambition's ladder,

   Whereto the climber-upward turns his face;

   But when he once attains the upmost round,

25   He then unto the ladder turns his back,

   Looks in the clouds, scorning the base degrees

   By which he did ascend. So Caesar may.

   Then, lest he may, prevent.[5] And, since the quarrel

   Will bear no color for the thing he is,

30   Fashion it thus; that what he is, augmented,

   Would run to these and these extremities:

   And therefore think him as a serpent's egg

1. **orchard,** garden.

2. **his,** Caesar's.

3. **I know no personal . . . general.**
Though Brutus has no personal
reason for striking at Caesar, he
nevertheless feels that he must do
so for the public (general) good.

4. **Remorse,** pity.

5. **prevent,** he must be prevented.

Which, hatched, would, as his kind, grow mischievous,
And kill him in the shell.

*(LUCIUS, yawning, enters the platform at right door. He carries a
letter—a small scroll.)*

35 LUCIUS. The taper burneth in your closet,[6] sir.
Searching the window for a flint, I found
This paper, thus sealed up; and I am sure
It did not lie there when I went to bed. *(He gives BRUTUS the
letter.)*

BRUTUS. Get you to bed again; it is not day.

(LUCIUS starts to leave.)

40 Is not tomorrow, boy, the ides of March?

LUCIUS. I know not, sir.

BRUTUS. Look in the calendar, and bring me word.

LUCIUS. I will, sir.

(He exits at right.)

BRUTUS. The exhalations whizzing in the air[7]
45 Give so much light that I may read by them. *(He opens the letter
and reads.)*

*Brutus, thou sleepest: awake, and see thyself.
Shall Rome, etc. Speak, strike, redress!*

"Brutus, thou sleepest: awake!"
Such instigations have been often dropped
50 Where I have took them up.
"Shall Rome, etc." Thus must I piece it out:
Shall Rome stand under one man's awe? What, Rome?
My ancestors did from the streets of Rome
The Tarquin[8] drive, when he was called a king.
55 "Speak, strike, redress!" Am I entreated
To speak and strike? *(He raises a clenched fist.)* O Rome, I make
thee promise;
If the redress will follow, thou receivest
Thy full petition at the hand of Brutus!

(LUCIUS reenters.)

LUCIUS. Sir, March is wasted fifteen days.

(There is a knock at left.)

60 BRUTUS. 'Tis good. Go to the gate; somebody knocks,

(LUCIUS hurries to open the door at left.)

Since Cassius first did whet me against Caesar,
I have not slept.
Between the acting of a dreadful thing
And the first motion, all the interim is
65 Like a phantasma, or a hideous dream:
The Genius and the mortal instruments[9]

6. **closet,** study; room.

7. **The exhalations . . . air,** the
falling stars.

8. **The Tarquin,** Tarquinius
Superbus, the last Roman king.

9. **The Genius and the mortal
instruments,** the soul and the body.

Are then in council; and the state of man,
Like to a little kingdom, suffers then
The nature of an insurrection.

70 LUCIUS *(rejoining* BRUTUS*).* Sir, 'tis your brother Cassius[10] at the
    door,
Who doth desire to see you.
BRUTUS.   Is he alone?
LUCIUS. No, sir, there are moe[11] with him.
BRUTUS.   Do you know them?
LUCIUS. No, sir; their hats are plucked about their ears,
And half their faces buried in their cloaks,
75 That by no means I may discover them
By any mark of favor.[12]
BRUTUS.   Let 'em enter.
They are the faction. O conspiracy,
Sham'st thou to show thy dangerous brow by night,
When evils are most free? Oh, then by day
80 Where wilt thou find a cavern dark enough
To mask thy monstrous visage? Seek none, conspiracy;
Hide it in smiles and affability;
For if thou path, thy native semblance on,
Not Erebus itself were dim enough
85 To hide thee from prevention.[13]

(LUCIUS *ushers in the* CONSPIRATORS—CASSIUS, CASCA, DECIUS, CINNA,
METELLUS CIMBER, LIGARIUS, *and* TREBONIUS. *While the* CONSPIRATORS
are approaching BRUTUS, LUCIUS *exits at right.)*

CASSIUS *(stepping forward).* I think we are too bold upon your rest;
Good morrow, Brutus; do we trouble you?
BRUTUS. I have been up this hour, awake all night.
Know I these men that come along with you?
90 CASSIUS. Yes, every man of them, and no man here
But honors you; and every one doth wish
You had but that opinion of yourself
Which every noble Roman bears of you.
This is Trebonius.
BRUTUS *(extending his hand).* He is welcome hither.
95 CASSIUS. This, Decius Brutus.
BRUTUS.   He is welcome, too.
CASSIUS. This, Casca; this, Cinna; and this, Metellus Cimber.
BRUTUS. They are all welcome.
What watchful cares do interpose themselves
Betwixt your eyes and night?
100 CASSIUS. Shall I entreat a word?
(BRUTUS *and* CASSIUS *step back a little to speak privately. The other*
CONSPIRATORS *talk idly.)*
DECIUS. Here lies the east; doth not the day break here?

10. *your brother Cassius.* We would
say brother-in-law. Cassius had
married Brutus' sister, Junia.

11. *moe,* more.

12. *any mark of favor,* any features
by which they can be recognized.

13. *For if thou path . . . prevention.*
If the conspirators walk about,
plotting openly, not even Erebus
(er'ə bəs) would be dim enough to
hide them. Erebus, according to
Greek and Roman mythology, was a
dark, gloomy place through which
the dead passed en route to Hades.

CASCA. No.

CINNA. Oh, pardon, sir, it doth; and yon gray lines
That fret the clouds are messengers of day.

105 CASCA. You shall confess that you are both deceived.
Here, as I point my sword, the sun arises.

(BRUTUS and CASSIUS *rejoin the group.*)

BRUTUS. Give me your hands all over, one by one.

CASSIUS. And let us swear our resolution.

BRUTUS. No, not an oath; if not the face of men,
110 The sufferance of our souls, the time's abuse—
If these be motives weak, break off betimes,
And every man hence to his idle bed;
So let high-sighted tyranny range on,
Till every man drop by lottery.[14] But if these,
115 As I am sure they do, bear fire enough
To kindle cowards and to steel with valor
The melting spirits of women, then, countrymen,
What need we any spur but our own cause? (*He clasps hands with all.*)

CASSIUS. But what of Cicero? Shall we sound him?
120 I think he will stand very strong with us.

CASCA. Let us not leave him out.

CINNA. No, by no means.

METELLUS CIMBER. Oh, let us have him, for his silver hairs
Will purchase us a good opinion
And buy men's voices to commend our deeds;
125 It shall be said, his judgment ruled our hands;
Our youths and wildness shall no whit appear,
But all be buried in his gravity.

BRUTUS. Oh, name him not; let us not break with him;[15]
For he will never follow anything
130 That other men begin.

CASSIUS. Then leave him out.

CASCA. Indeed he is not fit.

DECIUS. Shall no man else be touched but only Caesar?

CASSIUS. Decius, well urged. I think it is not meet[16]
Mark Antony, so well beloved of Caesar,
135 Should outlive Caesar; we shall find of him
A shrewd contriver; and, you know, his means,[17]
If he improve them, may well stretch so far
As to annoy[18] us all—which to prevent,
Let Antony and Caesar fall together.

140 BRUTUS. Our course will seem too bloody, Caius Cassius,
To cut the head off and then hack the limbs,
Like wrath in death and envy afterwards;
For Antony is but a limb of Caesar;

14. *if not the face . . . by lottery.* If the wrongs the conspirators see about them are not sufficient to bind them to firm purpose, then let each man go his own way, become a weakling, and die when it suits a tyrant's whims.

15. *break with him*, break the news of the conspiracy to him.

16. *meet*, fitting; suitable.

17. *his means*, Antony's influence.

18. *annoy*, harm.

Let us be sacrificers, but not butchers, Caius.
145 We all stand up against the spirit of Caesar;
And in the spirit of men there is no blood.
Oh, that we then could come by Caesar's spirit,
And not dismember Caesar! But, alas,
Caesar must bleed for it! And, gentle friends,
150 Let's kill him boldly, but not wrathfully;
Let's carve him as a dish fit for the gods,
Not hew him as a carcass fit for hounds.
And for Mark Antony, think not of him;
For he can do no more than Caesar's arm
155 When Caesar's head is off.
CASSIUS *(still unconvinced).* Yet I fear him;
For in the ingrafted love he bears to Caesar—
BRUTUS. Alas, good Cassius, do not think of him;
If he love Caesar, all that he can do
Is to himself, take thought and die for Caesar;
160 And that were much he should; for he is given
To sports, to wildness and much company.
TREBONIUS. There is no fear in him;[19] let him not die;
For he will live, and laugh at this hereafter.
(A clock offstage begins to strike.)
BRUTUS. Peace! Count the clock.[20]
CASSIUS. The clock hath stricken three.
165 TREBONIUS. 'Tis time to part.
CASSIUS. But it is doubtful yet,
Whether Caesar will come forth today, or no;
For he is superstitious grown of late,
Quite from the main opinion he held once
Of fantasy, of dreams, and ceremonies.
170 It may be, these apparent prodigies,
The unaccustomed terror of this night,
And the persuasion of his augurers[21]
May hold him from the Capitol today.
DECIUS. Never fear that: if he be so resolved,
175 I can o'ersway him; for he loves to hear
That unicorns may be betrayed with trees,
And bears with glasses, elephants with holes,
Lions with toils,[22] and men with flatterers;
But when I tell him he hates flatterers,
180 He says he does, being then most flattered.
Let me work;
For I can give his humor the true bent,[23]
And I will bring him to the Capitol.
CASSIUS. Nay, we will all of us be there to fetch him.
185 BRUTUS. By the eighth hour; is that the uttermost?

19. *There is no fear in him,* there is no reason to fear Antony.

20. *Count the clock.* This is a famous anachronism. There were, of course, no striking clocks in Caesar's day.

21. *his augurers* (ô'gər ərz), official interpreters who predicted the future by reading signs. They frequently were called *augurs.* In the next scene we hear of sacrificial animals being cut open; the way the inner parts (entrails) arranged themselves was considered significant in foretelling the future.

22. *That unicorns . . . toils,* methods thought effective for capturing wild beasts. The mythological unicorn was incited to charge; the hunter quickly stepped behind a nearby tree, and the unicorn, unable to stop, drove his horn firmly into the trunk. It was thought that a dangerous bear could be distracted by a mirror placed in its paws; it would be so fascinated by its reflection that a hunter could easily kill it. Elephants were captured in pits, and lions were sometimes rendered helpless by nets (toils).

23. *I can give his humor . . . bent.* Decius Brutus knows how to handle Caesar.

CINNA. Be that the uttermost, and fail not then.

CASSIUS. The morning comes upon 's; we'll leave you, Brutus.
    And friends, disperse yourselves; but all remember
    What you have said, and show yourselves true Romans.

190 BRUTUS. Good gentlemen, look fresh and merrily;
    Let not our looks put on[24] our purposes,
    But bear it as our Roman actors do,
    With untired spirits and formal constancy;
    And so good morrow to you every one.

(The CONSPIRATORS *move off at left. For a moment* BRUTUS *stands lost in thought; then he crosses to the window at upper right and calls.)*

195   Boy! Lucius! Fast asleep? It is no matter;
    Enjoy the honey-heavy dew of slumber;
    Thou hast no figures nor no fantasies,
    Which busy care draws in the brains of men.
    Therefore thou sleepest so sound.

*(*PORTIA, *wearing a night robe, enters at right. Her face is pale and worried as she follows* BRUTUS *to the inner stage.)*

PORTIA.   Brutus, my lord!

200 BRUTUS. Portia, what mean you? Wherefore rise you now?
    It is not for your health thus to commit
    Your weak condition to the raw cold morning.

PORTIA. Nor for yours neither. You've ungently, Brutus,
    Stole from my bed; and yesternight, at supper,
205   You suddenly arose, and walked about,
    Musing and sighing, with your arms across,
    And when I asked you what the matter was,
    You stared upon me with ungentle looks;
    I urged you further; then you scratched your head,
210   And too impatiently stamped with your foot;
    Yet I insisted; yet you answered not,
    But, with angry wafture of your hand,
    Gave sign for me to leave you; so I did,
    Fearing to strengthen that impatience
215   Which seemed too much enkindled, and withal[25]
    Hoping it was but an effect of humor,[26]
    Which sometime hath his hour with every man.
    It will not let you eat, nor talk, nor sleep,
    And could it work so much upon your shape
220   As it hath much prevailed on your condition,
    I should not know you, Brutus. *(Pleadingly.)* Dear my lord,
    Make me acquainted with your cause of grief.

BRUTUS. I am not well in health, and that is all.

PORTIA. Brutus is wise, and, were he not in health,
225   He would embrace the means to come by it.

24. *put on,* betray.

25. *withal,* in addition to this.
26. *an effect of humor,* a whim.

BRUTUS. Why, so I do. *(He seats himself wearily on the nearby bench.)*
　　Good Portia, go to bed.
　　PORTIA *(drawing closer).* Is Brutus sick? And is it physical
　　　To walk unbracèd and suck up the humors
　　　Of the dank morning? What, is Brutus sick,
230　　And will he steal out of his wholesome bed,
　　　To dare the vile contagion of the night
　　　And tempt the rheumy and unpurgèd air[27]
　　　To add unto his sickness? No, my Brutus;
　　　You have some sick offense within your mind,
235　　Which, by the right and virtue of my place,
　　　I ought to know of; and, upon my knees *(falling to her knees)*
　　　I charm you, by my once commended beauty,
　　　By all your vows of love and that great vow
　　　Which did incorporate and make us one,
240　　That you unfold to me, yourself, your half,
　　　Why you are heavy, and what men tonight
　　　Have had resort to you; for here have been
　　　Some six or seven, who did hide their faces
　　　Even from darkness.
　　BRUTUS.　　　　　　Kneel not, gentle Portia. *(He raises her.)*
245　PORTIA. I should not need, if you were gentle Brutus.
　　　Within the bond of marriage, tell me, Brutus,
　　　Is it excepted I should know no secrets
　　　That appertain to you?[28]
　　BRUTUS. You are my true and honorable wife,
250　　As dear to me as are the ruddy drops
　　　That visit my sad heart.
　　PORTIA. If this were true, then should I know this secret.
　　　I grant I am a woman, but withal
　　　A woman that Lord Brutus took to wife;
255　　I grant I am a woman, but withal
　　　A woman well-reputed, Cato's daughter.
　　　Think you I am no stronger than my sex,
　　　Being so fathered[29] and so husbanded?
　　　Tell me your counsels, I will not disclose 'em;
260　　I have made strong proof of my constancy,
　　　Giving myself a voluntary wound
　　　Here, in the thigh: can I bear that with patience,
　　　And not my husband's secrets?
　　BRUTUS *(to the heavens).*　　　　O ye gods,
　　　Render me worthy of this noble wife!
265　*(Turning to* PORTIA*)* Portia, go in awhile:
　　　And by and by thy bosom shall partake
　　　The secrets of my heart.
　　　All my engagements I will construe[30] to thee,

27. *the rheumy* (rü'mē) . . . *air,* the air that causes colds because it has not yet been purified (purged) by the sun.

28. *Is it excepted . . . you?* Portia is asking if an exception was made in the marriage vows so that she would have no legal right to inquire into Brutus' affairs.

29. *Being so fathered.* Portia's father, Cato the Younger, had killed himself rather than submit to tyranny.

30. *construe,* explain.

All the character[31] of my sad brows;

270   Leave me with haste.

(PORTIA *hastens to right door and exits.* BRUTUS *remains seated on the bench as the curtains of the inner stage are drawn closed.*)

Scene 2: Rome. Caesar's house.

It is early morning on the ides of March. Several hours have elapsed since the CONSPIRATORS *met in* BRUTUS' *garden. The curtains of the balcony stage (above) are drawn open just as* CAESAR *enters at right. Speaking to himself, he crosses to the left, where his street robe is draped across a high-backed chair.*

CAESAR. Nor heaven nor earth have been at peace tonight;
   Thrice hath Calpurnia in her sleep cried out,
   ''Help! Ho! They murder Caesar!'' Who's within? (*He claps his hands.*)

(*A* SERVANT *enters at left.*)

SERVANT. My lord?

5 CAESAR. Go bid the priests do present sacrifice
   And bring me their opinions of success.[1]

SERVANT. I will, my lord.

(*He exits at the door in the rear wall of the balcony stage as* CALPURNIA, *who is clad in her night robe, enters at right.*)

CALPURNIA. What mean you, Caesar? Think you to walk forth?
   You shall not stir out of your house today.

10 CAESAR. Caesar shall forth; the things that threatened me
   Ne'er looked but on my back; when they shall see
   The face of Caesar, they are vanishèd.

CALPURNIA. Caesar, I never stood on ceremonies,[2]
   Yet now they fright me. There is one within,[3]

15   Besides the things that we have heard and seen,
   Recounts most horrid sights seen by the watch.
   A lioness hath whelpèd in the streets;
   And graves have yawned, and yielded up their dead;
   Fierce fiery warriors fought upon the clouds,

20   In ranks and squadrons and right form of war,
   Which drizzled blood upon the Capitol;
   The noise of battle hurtled in the air,
   Horses did neigh, and dying men did groan,
   And ghosts did shriek and squeal about the streets.

25   O Caesar! These things are beyond all use,[4]
   And I do fear them.

CAESAR.   What can be avoided
   Whose end is purposed by the mighty gods?[5]
   Yet Caesar shall go forth; for these predictions
   Are to the world in general as to Caesar.

30 CALPURNIA. When beggars die, there are no comets seen;

31. *charactery,* lines of worry.

1. *Go bid the priests . . . success.* Caesar wishes to consult the augurers.

2. *I never stood on ceremonies.* Calpurnia had never been one to believe greatly in signs and portents.
3. *one within,* a servant.

4. *beyond all use,* not customary; supernatural.

5. *What can be avoided . . . gods?* Note Caesar's belief in fatalism.

The heavens themselves blaze forth the death of princes.

CAESAR. Cowards die many times before their deaths;
The valiant never taste of death but once.
Of all the wonders that I yet have heard,
35 It seems to me most strange that men should fear,
Seeing that death, a necessary end,
Will come when it will come.

(The SERVANT *reenters.)*

What say the augurers?

SERVANT. They would not have you to stir forth today.
Plucking the entrails of an offering forth,
40 They could not find a heart within the beast.

CAESAR. The gods do this in shame of cowardice;
Caesar should be a beast without a heart
If he should stay at home today for fear.
No, Caesar shall not; danger knows full well
45 That Caesar is more dangerous than he.
We[6] are two lions littered in one day,
And I the elder and more terrible;
And Caesar shall go forth.

6. We, Caesar and danger.

CALPURNIA *(going to him).*   Alas, my lord;
Your wisdom is consumed in confidence.
50 Do not go forth today; call it my fear
That keeps you in the house, and not your own.
We'll send Mark Antony to the Senate-house;
And he shall say you are not well today. *(She kneels.)*
Let me, upon my knee, prevail in this.

55 CAESAR *(raising her).* Mark Antony shall say I am not well;
And, for thy humor, I will stay at home.

*(*DECIUS *enters at rear door.)*

Here's Decius Brutus, he shall tell them so.

DECIUS *(bowing).* Caesar, all hail! Good morrow, worthy Caesar;
I come to fetch you to the Senate-house.

60 CAESAR. And you are come in very happy time,
To bear my greeting to the senators
And tell them that I will not come today—
Cannot is false, and that I *dare* not, falser;
I *will* not come today. Tell them so, Decius.

65 CALPURNIA. Say he is sick.

CAESAR *(loudly).*   Shall Caesar send a lie?
Have I in conquest stretched mine arm so far,
To be afeard to tell graybeards the truth?
Decius, go tell them Caesar will not come.

DECIUS. Most mighty Caesar, let me know some cause,
70 Lest I be laughed at when I tell them so.

CAESAR. The cause is in my will: I will not come;

That is enough to satisfy the Senate.
But for your private satisfaction,
Because I love you, I will let you know:
75 Calpurnia here, my wife, stays me at home;
She dreamt tonight she saw my statuë,[7]
Which, like a fountain with an hundred spouts,
Did run pure blood; and many lusty Romans
Came smiling, and did bathe their hands in it;
80 And these does she apply for warnings, and portents,
And evils imminent; and on her knee
Hath begged that I will stay at home today.

DECIUS. This dream is all amiss interpreted;
It was a vision fair and fortunate:
85 Your statue spouting blood in many pipes,
In which so many smiling Romans bathed,
Signifies that from you great Rome shall suck
Reviving blood.
This by Calpurnia's dream is signified.

90 CAESAR. And this way have you well expounded it.

DECIUS. I have, when you have heard what I can say;
And know it now: the Senate have concluded
To give this day a crown to mighty Caesar.
If you shall send them words you will not come,
95 Their minds may change. Besides, it were a mock
Apt to be rendered,[8] for someone to say,
"Break up the Senate till another time,
When Caesar's wife shall meet with better dreams."
If Caesar hide himself, shall they not whisper,
100 "Lo, Caesar is afraid"?
Pardon me, Caesar; for my dear, dear love
To your proceeding bids me tell you this;
And reason to my love is liable.

CAESAR. How foolish do your fears seem now, Calpurnia!
105 I am ashamèd I did yield to them.
Give me my robe, for I will go.

(While DECIUS is assisting CAESAR with his robe, PUBLIUS, BRUTUS,
LIGARIUS, METELLUS, CASCA, TREBONIUS, and CINNA enter at rear door.
Each man, in turn, bows to CAESAR.)
And look where Publius is come to fetch me.

PUBLIUS. Good morrow, Caesar.

CAESAR (in a dignified manner). Welcome, Publius.
What, Brutus, are you stirred so early, too?
110 Good morrow, Casca. Caius Ligarius,
Caesar was ne'er so much your enemy
As that same ague which hath made you lean.
What is 't o'clock.

7. *statuë* (stach'ü ə), pronounced in three syllables for the sake of the meter.

8. *it were a mock . . . rendered*, people would be likely to sneer at Caesar's excuse.

BRUTUS.   Caesar, 'tis strucken eight.

CAESAR. I thank you for your pains and courtesy.

(ANTONY *enters at rear door.*)

115   See! Antony, that revels long o' nights,

Is notwithstanding up. Good morrow, Antony.

ANTONY *(bowing).* So to most noble Caesar.

CAESAR.   Bid them prepare within;

I am to blame to be thus waited for.

Now, Cinna; now, Metellus; what, Trebonius!

120   I have an hour's talk in store for you.

Remember that you call on me today;

Be near me, that I may remember you.

TREBONIUS. Caesar, I will. *(Aside.)* And so near will I be

That your best friends shall wish I had been further.

(CAESAR, *followed by the others, leaves at rear door.* CALPURNIA *lingers a moment, then exits as the curtains of the balcony stage are drawn closed.*)

Scene 3: Rome. A street near the Capitol.

ARTEMIDORUS, *a teacher of rhetoric, enters at left. In his hands he carries a paper which he intends to present to* CAESAR. *Moving slowly across the platform, he begins to read to himself in a low tone.*

ARTEMIDORUS *(reading).* ''Caesar, beware of Brutus; take

heed of Cassius; come not near Casca; have an eye to

Cinna; trust not Trebonius; mark well Metellus Cimber;

Decius Brutus loves thee not; thou hast wronged Caius

5   Ligarius. There is but one mind in all these men, and it

is bent against Caesar. If thou beest not immortal, look

about you; security gives way to conspiracy.[1] The mighty

gods defend thee! Thy lover,[2]

                           ARTEMIDORUS.''

10   Here will I stand till Caesar pass along,

And as a suitor will I give him this.

If thou read this, O Caesar, thou mayst live;

If not, the Fates with traitors do contrive.

(*He exits.*)

Scene 4: Rome. Another part of the same street, before the house of Brutus.

It is now nearly nine o'clock on the morning of the ides of March. Though it is only a short time since BRUTUS *left for the Capitol,* PORTIA's *anxiety has become well-nigh unbearable. She enters the platform at inner-stage curtains, followed by* LUCIUS, *the serving boy.*

PORTIA. I prithee, boy, run to the Senate-house;

(LUCIUS *starts to speak, but* PORTIA *continues.*)

1. *security gives way to conspiracy.* False confidence makes things easy for conspirators.
2. *lover.* Shakespeare often used this word to mean ''friend.''

Stay not to answer me, but get thee gone.
(LUCIUS *looks at her questioningly as she talks on.*)
    Why dost thou stay?
LUCIUS *(in bewilderment).* To know my errand, madam.
PORTIA. I would have had thee there, and here again,
5   Ere I can tell thee what thou shouldst do there.
    O constancy,[1] be strong upon my side;
    Set a huge mountain 'tween my heart and tongue!
    I have a man's mind, but a woman's might.
    How hard it is for women to keep counsel![2]
10   Art thou here yet?
LUCIUS.   Madam, what should I do?
    Run to the Capitol, and nothing else?
PORTIA. Yes, bring me word, boy, if thy lord look well,
    For he went sickly forth; and take good note
    What Caesar doth, what suitors press to him.
15   Hark, boy! What noise is that?[3]
LUCIUS. I hear none, madam.
PORTIA.   Prithee, listen well;
    I heard a bustling rumor, like a fray,[4]
    And the wind brings it from the Capitol.
LUCIUS. Sooth,[5] madam, I hear nothing.
(The SOOTHSAYER *enters at left.*)
20 PORTIA *(eagerly).* Come hither, fellow; which way hast thou been?
SOOTHSAYER. At mine own house, good lady.
PORTIA. What is 't o'clock?
SOOTHSAYER.   About the ninth hour, lady.
PORTIA. Is Caesar yet gone to the Capitol?
SOOTHSAYER. Madam, not yet: I go to take my stand,
25   To see him pass on to the Capitol.
PORTIA. Thou hast some suit to Caesar, hast thou not?
SOOTHSAYER. That I have, lady; if it will please Caesar
    To be so good to Caesar as to hear me,
    I shall beseech him to befriend himself.
30 PORTIA. Why, know'st thou any harm's intended toward him?
SOOTHSAYER. None that I know will be, much that I fear may
      chance.
    Good morrow to you. Here the street is narrow;
    The throng that follows Caesar at the heels,
    Of senators, of praetors, common suitors,
35   Will crowd a feeble man almost to death.
    I'll get me to a place more void, and there
    Speak to great Caesar as he comes along.
(He crosses to right door and exits.)
PORTIA. I must go in. Aye me, how weak a thing
    The heart of woman is! O Brutus,

1. *O constancy,* O self-control.

2. *to keep counsel,* to keep a secret.

3. *Hark, boy! What noise is that?*
Note Portia's extreme nervousness.
What does this tell you about her
knowledge of Brutus' plans?
4. *like a fray,* like fighting.

5. *Sooth,* short for *in sooth,* or *in
truth.*

40   The heavens speed thee in thine enterprise!
   (Aside.) Sure the boy heard me.
   (Speaking breathlessly to LUCIUS.)   Brutus hath a suit
   That Caesar will not grant. Oh, I grow faint.
   Run, Lucius, and commend me to my lord;
   Say I am merry; come to me again,
45   And bring me word what he doth say to thee.
   *(*LUCIUS *runs off at right;* PORTIA *exits at inner-stage curtains.)*

Discussion

Scene 1

1. In this scene Brutus delivers several *soliloquies*; that is, he speaks aloud while on the stage alone. **(a)** What do you think is the purpose of his soliloquies? **(b)** Judging from them alone, would you say he has completely made up his mind regarding whether or not he will join the conspirators? **(c)** How does he justify the decision that he reaches?

2. **(a)** Why does Shakespeare have Brutus uncertain of the exact date? **(b)** What earlier incident has established this date as being of great importance?

3. The conspirators, while at Brutus' house, make various important decisions. **(a)** What is their decision concerning Cicero? **(b)** Concerning Mark Antony? **(c)** Explain the conspirators' final plan of action.

4. **(a)** How would you characterize Portia? **(b)** Do you consider her genuinely devoted to Brutus? Why or why not? **(c)** Do you blame Brutus for failing to confide in her? Explain your answer.

Scene 2

1. **(a)** What one question dominates this entire scene? **(b)** What traits does Caesar display as he wrestles with this problem?

2. **(a)** One of Caesar's speeches in this scene is very famous. Which one is it? **(b)** After explaining the meaning of the speech, comment on its truth.

3. **(a)** Keeping in mind what you learned in Act Two, Scene 1, explain why Decius is the first of the conspirators to arrive at Caesar's house. **(b)** In what way does Decius show his understanding of Caesar's personality during their conversation?

4. **(a)** How does Calpurnia compare with Portia as a "noble Roman matron"? **(b)** Trace her feelings as the argument with Caesar progresses. At what point does she realize that she has lost?

5. **(a)** Why would the audience be apprehensive about Caesar when, at the end of the scene, the famous Roman calls for his robe and plans to go to the Capitol? **(b)** What has the dramatist done to make the audience feel this way?

Scenes 3 and 4

1. How does Artemidorus' letter differ from the warnings in earlier scenes?

2. **(a)** How do you know that Portia now shares Brutus' secret? **(b)** Do you think she approves of the plot against Caesar? Give reasons for your answer.

3. **(a)** In what ways does Shakespeare bring out Portia's feverish anxiety? **(b)** How does she almost give away her secret thought to Lucius?

Vocabulary
Context and Dictionary

Each of the following words has more than one meaning. Reread each in its context in the play to be sure you understand its meaning there. Read the following sentences. Write *yes* on your paper if the sentence uses the word as it is used in the play; *no* if it does not.

   base (458, line 26)
   contrive (462, line 136)
   hew (463, line 153)

muse (465, line 206)

taper (458, line 7)

1. His *base* betrayal of his friends cannot be forgiven.

2. The new skyscraper is most controversial; it *tapers* toward the top.

3. My father is very conservative; he *hews* to the old-fashioned way of doing things.

4. The prisoners *contrived* a plot to escape from their captivity.

5. At the *base* of the tree they set a plaque to commemorate the battle.

6. Her *muse* is so fickle that Teresa often goes for days without writing a poem or even a line.

7. I fail to see how he'll *contrive* to get to work without a car.

8. The telephone company is coming this morning to *hew* some of the limbs off the old elm tree.

9. We're all set if the lights go out this winter; we've laid in a supply of *tapers* and oil lamps.

10. He claims to be *musing* on the problems of mankind, but he really just wants to stay sitting there under the tree.

1. Write a brief outline of the events in Act Two and add it to your outline of Act One.

2. What are the three most important things that have happened in this act? Explain.

3. (a) Why do you think Shakespeare introduces Portia and Calpurnia in Act Two? **(b)** How does each contribute to your interest in the play?

4. How does Shakespeare, in this act, build up an increasing sense of dread and foreboding?

5. Do you see any possible way left open for Caesar to escape death?

notes and comments

"Piece out our imperfections . . ."
Henry V, 1, i

The Globe Playhouse did not have realistic scenery to represent the various localities in *Julius Caesar.* Nor was it customary to provide the playgoers with printed programs outlining the time and place of each scene. It was Shakespeare's task to set his scene in his dialogue.

Assume for a moment that you are attending a performance of *Julius Caesar* at the Globe. You cannot rely upon realistic scenery, a printed program, or the stage directions in your textbook to tell you where and when a scene takes place. Discuss with other members of the class the *dialogue clues* that Shakespeare provides in Act One, Scene 1, to tell you that the scene takes place on a street in Rome. Which lines indicate that the scene occurs during the daytime? Cite lines from Act Two, Scene 1, which indicate that this scene takes place early in the morning of the ides of March.

In addition to such verbal clues, Shakespeare employed two *visual devices* to indicate a

Shakespearean Stagecraft

change of locality. The first visual device is used when one platform scene follows another as they do in Act One. It consists of *emptying* the platform at the conclusion of a scene. How many platform scenes are there in Act One? What different localities do they represent? Do any characters remain on the platform at the conclusion of these scenes? Are there any dead bodies which must be carried off in order to empty the stage? It was unnecessary for Shakespeare to empty the inner and balcony stages in this way, because their front curtains could be drawn closed at the end of a scene.

The second visual device for indicating a change of locality is to use a *different* stage. A shift from the platform (Act One, Scene 3) to the inner stage (Act Two, Scene 1) indicates a change of place. What change of locality takes place when the action shifts to the balcony stage in Act Two?

Shakespeare must have been aware of how much he depended upon the imagination of his audience. In another of his plays, *Henry V*, he asks the playgoers to "piece out our imperfections with your thoughts."

A Midsummer Night's Dream, I, ii "I will draw a bill of properties . . ."

Shakespeare does such a masterful job of setting his scenes in the dialogue of *Julius Caesar* that it would be possible to stage the play without special costumes or stage properties. The stage manager at the Globe, however, did have devices for heightening the illusion of reality. What kinds of stage properties did he have and how might they have been used in *Julius Caesar?*

Most of the properties used on the platform were light enough and small enough for the actors to carry on and off as part of their stage business. Backstage at the Globe could be found a large assortment of portable properties—swords and daggers, shields and scrolls, cushions, lutes, dishes, flagons. You have seen Cicero enter with a lantern and Casca with a sword in Act One, Scene 3. Both the sword and the lantern are carried off when Casca exits with Cassius.

Larger and heavier properties were stored in "Hell." Like the rock which will be used in Act Five, Scene 4, these properties were raised onto the platform through the large trap door.

It was possible to create greater scenic effects on the inner stage. Here the walls could be hung with cloth painted to suggest the garden of Act Two or with cloth drab enough to suggest the tent interior of Act Four. Several heavy properties could also be positioned on the inner stage before the curtains were drawn apart. Like the trees and bench of Act Two, Scene 1, these properties were stored backstage or in "Hell" until needed.

Any discussion of Elizabethan staging must take into consideration that Shakespeare's plays were performed in broad daylight. How, then, did the stage manager help Shakespeare create the illusion of night and darkness in *Julius Caesar?* This was done by indicating the need for light; that is, an actor would carry a torch or a lantern, or perhaps light a taper.

Act Three

Scene 1: Rome. Before the Capitol.

*Today—the ides of March—*CAESAR *is to meet with the Senators.* ARTEMIDORUS *and the* SOOTHSAYER *enter at left. They are among a crowd of people who are gathering to honor* CAESAR *upon his arrival at the Capitol. The crowd bursts into cheers as* CAESAR *enters at right, followed by* ANTONY, POPILIUS, PUBLIUS, *and the* CONSPIRATORS. CAESAR *advances until he faces the* SOOTHSAYER; *he speaks to him defiantly.*

CAESAR. The ides of March are come.

SOOTHSAYER. Aye, Caesar; but not gone.

*(*CAESAR, *waving the* SOOTHSAYER *aside, is approached by* ARTEMIDORUS, *who presents his paper.)*

ARTEMIDORUS. Hail, Caesar! Read this schedule.

*(*DECIUS *hurries forward and pushes* ARTEMIDORUS *aside.)*

DECIUS. Trebonius doth desire you to o'er-read,

5   At your best leisure, this his humble suit.

ARTEMIDORUS. O Caesar, read mine first; for mine's a suit

    That touches Caesar nearer: read it, great Caesar.

CAESAR. What touches us ourself shall be last served.

ARTEMIDORUS. Delay not, Caesar. *(He thrusts his paper in* CAESAR'*s face.)* Read it instantly.

10 CAESAR. What, is the fellow mad?

*(*PUBLIUS *and* CASSIUS *force* ARTEMIDORUS *aside.)*

PUBLIUS.   Sirrah, give place.

CASSIUS. What, urge you your petitions in the street?

    Come to the Capitol.

*(*CASSIUS *points toward the inner stage, where the curtains are slowly being drawn apart to reveal the interior of the Senate-house. Some Senators are already seated on the stage; a statue of Pompey stands well forward at left.* CAESAR *moves onto the inner stage. He is followed by* ANTONY, PUBLIUS, METELLUS, TREBONIUS, *and* CAIUS LIGARIUS.*)*

POPILIUS *(passing* CASSIUS*)*. I wish your enterprise today may thrive.

CASSIUS *(innocently)*. What enterprise, Popilius?

POPILIUS.   Fare you well. *(He joins* CAESAR.*)*

15 BRUTUS *(fearfully)*. What said Popilius Lena?

CASSIUS. He wished today our enterprise might thrive.

    I fear our purpose is discovered.

BRUTUS. Look, how he makes to Caesar;[1] mark him.

CASSIUS. Casca, be sudden, for we fear prevention.

20   Brutus, what shall be done? If this be known,

    Cassius or Caesar never shall turn back,

    For I will slay myself.

1. **makes to Caesar,** presses toward Caesar.

BRUTUS *(with relief)*.   Cassius, be constant;
 Popilius Lena speaks not of our purposes;
 For, look, he smiles, and Caesar doth not change.
(ANTONY and TREBONIUS leave the inner stage and move off the platform at right.)

25 CASSIUS. Trebonius knows his time; for, look you, Brutus,
 He draws Mark Antony out of the way.
DECIUS. Where is Metellus Cimber? Let him go,
 And presently prefer his suit[2] to Caesar.
BRUTUS. He is addressed;[3] press near and second him.

30 CINNA. Casca, you are the first that rears your hand.
(BRUTUS, CASSIUS, CASCA, DECIUS, and CINNA cross to the inner stage, where CAESAR is calling the group to order.)
CAESAR. Are we all ready? What is now amiss
 That Caesar and his Senate must redress?
METELLUS. Most high, most mighty, and most puissant Caesar,
 Metellus Cimber throws before thy seat
35 An humble heart——*(He falls on his knees.)*
CAESAR.   I must prevent thee, Cimber.
 These couchings[4] and these lowly courtesies
 Might fire the blood of ordinary men,
 And turn preordinance and first decree
 Into the law of children.[5] Be not fond,[6]
40 To think that Caesar bears such rebel blood
 That will be thawed from the true quality
 With that which melteth fools; I mean, sweet words,
 Low-crooked court'sies and base spaniel-fawning.
 Thy brother[7] by decree is banishèd;
45 If thou dost bend and pray and fawn for him,
 I spurn thee like a cur out of my way. *(He pushes METELLUS aside.)*
 Know, Caesar doth not wrong, nor without cause
 Will he be satisfied.
METELLUS. Is there no voice more worthy than my own,
50 To sound more sweetly in great Caesar's ear
 For the repealing of my banished brother?
BRUTUS *(kneeling)*. I kiss thy hand, but not in flattery, Caesar;
 Desiring thee that Publius Cimber may
 Have an immediate freedom of repeal.
55 CAESAR *(in surprise)*. What, Brutus!
CASSIUS *(kneeling also)*.   Pardon, Caesar; Caesar,
  pardon.
 As low as to thy foot doth Cassius fall,
 To beg enfranchisement for Publius Cimber.[8]
(One by one, the other CONSPIRATORS kneel.)
CAESAR. I could be well moved, if I were as you.

2. **prefer his suit,** present his petition.
3. **addressed,** ready.

4. **couchings,** kneelings.

5. **And turn preordinance . . . children,** and turn established laws and procedures into the whims of children. Note how Caesar, as he continues this speech, talks as if he were a crowned king.
6. **fond,** meaning here "foolish enough."
7. **Thy brother,** Publius Cimber, who had incurred Caesar's wrath.

8. **To beg enfranchisement** (en-fran'chīz mənt) . . . **Cimber,** to ask that Publius Cimber be allowed to return to Rome and be given again his full rights as a citizen.

If I could pray to move, prayers would move me;
60   But I am constant as the northern star,
Of whose true-fixed and resting quality
There is no fellow in the firmament.
The skies are painted with unnumbered sparks;
They are all fire and every one doth shine;
65   But there's but one in all doth hold his place.
So in the world: 'tis furnished well with men,
And men are flesh and blood, and apprehensive;[9]
Yet in the number I do know but one
That unassailable holds on his rank,
70   Unshaked of motion; and that I am he,
Let me a little show it, even in this;
That I was constant Cimber should be banished,
And constant do remain to keep him so.

CINNA. O Caesar,——

CAESAR.   Hence! Wilt thou lift up Olympus?

75 DECIUS. Great Caesar,——

CAESAR.   Doth not Brutus bootless[10] kneel?

CASCA (leaping to his feet). Speak, hands, for me! (He stabs
    CAESAR.)

(The other CONSPIRATORS, daggers in hand, spring to their feet. They
surge forward, and all but BRUTUS stab CAESAR. CAESAR, crying out,
tries to ward off the blows until he sees BRUTUS' uplifted dagger; then
he covers his face with his cloak and submits.)

CAESAR. Et tu, Brute![11] Then fall, Caesar!

(CAESAR staggers forward and dies at the foot of Pompey's statue.)

CINNA (shouting). Liberty! Freedom! Tyranny is dead!
    Run hence, proclaim, cry it about the streets.

80 CASSIUS. Some to the common pulpits,[12] and cry out,
    "Liberty, freedom, and enfranchisement."

(The CONSPIRATORS move onto the platform, where the people stand
stock still as if stunned by the sudden attack on CAESAR. Then the
crowd, including ARTEMIDORUS and the SOOTHSAYER, begins to flee in
panic.)

BRUTUS (calling out). People and senators, be not affrighted;
    Fly not; stand still; ambition's debt is paid.

CASCA. Go to the pulpit, Brutus.

DECIUS.   And Cassius, too.

85 BRUTUS. Where's Publius?

CINNA. Here, quite confounded with this mutiny.

METELLUS. Stand fast together, lest some friend of Caesar's
    Should chance——

BRUTUS. Talk not of standing. (Extending his hand.) Publius, good
    cheer;
90   There is no harm intended to your person,

9. **apprehensive,** aware of what is going on.

10. **bootless,** in vain.

11. **Et tu, Brute** (et tü, brü′tā), "you, too, Brutus!" [Latin] The betrayal completely overwhelms Caesar.

12. **the common pulpits,** the elevated areas in the Forum where public debates were held.

Nor to no Roman else; so tell them, Publius.

CASSIUS. And leave us, Publius; lest that the people,
Rushing on us, should do your age some mischief.

BRUTUS. Do so; and let no man abide this deed[13]
95 But we the doers.

(PUBLIUS, *accompanied by* POPILIUS, *moves off at left just as*
TREBONIUS *reenters at right.*)

CASSIUS.   Where is Antony?

TREBONIUS. Fled to his house amazed;
Men, wives, and children stare, cry out, and run
As it were doomsday.

BRUTUS *(resignedly).*   Fates,[14] we will know your pleasures;
That we shall die, we know; 'tis but the time
100 And drawing days out, that men stand upon.[15]

CASSIUS. Why, he that cuts off twenty years of life
Cuts off so many years of fearing death.

BRUTUS. Grant that, and then is death a benefit;
So are we Caesar's friends, that have abridged
105 His time of fearing death. Stoop, Romans, stoop,
And let us bathe our hands in Caesar's blood
Up to the elbows, and besmear our swords;
Then walk we forth, even to the market place,
And, waving our red weapons o'er our heads,
110 Let's all cry, "Peace, freedom, and liberty!"

(The CONSPIRATORS *kneel and begin to dip their hands in* CAESAR's
blood.)

CASSIUS. Stoop, then, and wash. How many ages hence
Shall this our lofty scene be acted over
In states unborn and accents yet unknown!

BRUTUS. How many times shall Caesar bleed in sport,
115 That now on Pompey's basis[16] lies along
No worthier than the dust!

CASSIUS.   So oft as that shall be,
So often shall the knot of us be called
The men that gave their country liberty.

(They rise.)

DECIUS. What, shall we forth?

CASSIUS.   Aye, every man away;
120 Brutus shall lead; and we will grace his heels
With the most boldest and best hearts of Rome.

(A SERVANT *of* ANTONY *enters at right.*)

BRUTUS. Soft! Who comes here? A friend of Antony's?

SERVANT *(kneeling).* Thus, Brutus, did my master bid me kneel.
Thus did Mark Antony bid me fall down;
125 And, being prostrate, thus he bade me say:
Brutus is noble, wise, valiant, and honest;

13. *abide this deed,* answer for this deed.

14. *Fates,* the three goddesses who were thought to control human destinies.
15. *stand upon,* are concerned with.

16. *on Pompey's basis,* at the foot of Pompey's statue.

Caesar was mighty, bold, royal, and loving.
Say I love Brutus, and I honor him;
Say I feared Caesar, honored him, and loved him.

130 If Brutus will vouchsafe that Antony
May safely come to him, and be resolved[17]
How Caesar hath deserved to lie in death,
Mark Antony shall not love Caesar dead
So well as Brutus living, but will follow

135 The fortunes and affairs of noble Brutus
Through the hazards of this untrod state[18]
With all true faith. So says my master Antony.

BRUTUS. Thy master is a wise and valiant Roman;
I never thought him worse.

140 Tell him, so please him come unto this place,
He shall be satisfied; and by my honor,
Depart untouched.

SERVANT.   I'll fetch him presently. (SERVANT *exits.*)

BRUTUS. I know that we shall have him well to friend.

CASSIUS. I wish we may; but yet have I a mind

145 That fears him much; and my misgiving still
Falls shrewdly to the purpose.[19]

(ANTONY, *reentering at right, strides toward* CAESAR's *body.*)

BRUTUS. But here comes Antony. Welcome, Mark Antony.

ANTONY (*ignoring* BRUTUS). O mighty Caesar! Dost thou lie so low?
Are all thy conquests, glories, triumphs, spoils,

150 Shrunk to this little measure? Fare thee well.
(*To the* CONSPIRATORS.) I know not, gentlemen, what you intend,
Who else must be let blood, who else is rank;[20]
If I myself, there is no hour so fit
As Caesar's death hour, nor no instrument

155 Of half that worth as those your swords, made rich
With the most noble blood of all this world.
I do beseech ye, if you bear me hard,
Now, whilst your purpled hands do reek and smoke,
Fulfill your pleasure. Live a thousand years,

160 I shall not find myself so apt[21] to die;
No place will please me so, no mean[22] of death,
As here by Caesar, and by you cut off,
The choice and master spirits of this age.

BRUTUS (*disturbed*). O Antony, beg not your death of us.

165 Though now we must appear bloody and cruel,
As, by our hands and this our present act,
You see we do, yet see you but our hands
And this the bleeding business they have done;
Our hearts you see not; they are pitiful;

170 And pity to the general wrong of Rome—

17. *be resolved,* have it explained to him.

18. *Through the hazards of this untrod state,* through all the uncertainties and dangers of this new and unfamiliar state of affairs.

19. *my misgiving . . . purpose.* Cassius' suspicions usually are justified.

20. *Who else must . . . rank,* who else must be destroyed.

21. *apt,* ready.
22. *mean,* method.

As fire drives out fire, so pity pity—[23]
Hath done this deed on Caesar. For your part,
To you our swords have leaden points, Mark Antony;
Our arms in strength of malice, and our hearts
175 Of brothers' temper, do receive you in
With all kind love, good thoughts, and reverence.

CASSIUS. Your voice shall be as strong as any man's
In the disposing of new dignities.

BRUTUS. Only be patient till we have appeased
180 The multitude, beside themselves with fear,
And then we will deliver you the cause,
Why I, that did love Caesar when I struck him,
Have thus proceeded.

ANTONY *(extending his hand).* I doubt not of your wisdom.
Let each man render me his bloody hand;
185 First, Marcus Brutus, will I shake with you;
Next, Caius Cassius, do I take your hand;
Now, Decius Brutus, yours; now, yours, Metellus;
Yours, Cinna; and, my valiant Casca, yours;
Though last, not least in love, yours, good Trebonius.
190 Gentlemen all—alas, what shall I say?
My credit now stands on such slippery ground
That one of two bad ways you must conceit[24] me,
Either a coward or a flatterer.
(Addressing CAESAR's *body.)* That I did love thee, Caesar, Oh, 'tis
        true;
195 If then thy spirit look upon us now,
Shall it not grieve thee dearer than thy death,
To see thy Antony making his peace,
Shaking the bloody fingers of thy foes,
Most noble! in the presence of thy corse?[25]
200 Had I as many eyes as thou hast wounds,
Weeping as fast as they stream forth thy blood,
It would become me better than to close
In terms of friendship with thine enemies.
Pardon me, Julius! Here wast thou bayed, brave hart;
205 Here didst thou fall; and here thy hunters stand,
Signed in thy spoil, and crimsoned in thy lethe.[26]
O world, thou wast the forest to this hart;
And this, indeed, O world, the heart of thee.
How like a deer, strucken by many princes,
210 Dost thou here lie!

CASSIUS *(sharply).* Mark Antony——

ANTONY.   Pardon me, Caius Cassius;
The enemies of Caesar shall say this;
Then, in a friend, it is cold modesty.

23. *so pity pity,* so pity for the wrongs Rome has endured from Caesar overshadows pity for Caesar's death.

24. *conceit,* consider.

25. *corse,* corpse.

26. *lethe* (lē'thē), death.

CASSIUS. I blame you not for praising Caesar so;
215 But what compact mean you to have with us?
Will you be pricked in number of our friends;[27]
Or shall we on, and not depend on you?
ANTONY. Therefore I took your hands, but was, indeed,
Swayed from the point, by looking down on Caesar.
220 Friends am I with you all and love you all,
Upon this hope, that you shall give me reasons
Why and wherein Caesar was dangerous.
BRUTUS. Or else were this a savage spectacle;
Our reasons are so full of good regard[28]
225 That were you, Antony, the son of Caesar,
You should be satisfied.
ANTONY.   That's all I seek;
And am moreover suitor that I may
Produce his body to the market place;
And in the pulpit, as becomes a friend,
230 Speak in the order of his funeral.
BRUTUS. You shall, Mark Antony.
CASSIUS (very much disturbed).   Brutus, a word with you.
(Taking BRUTUS aside.) You know not what you do; do not
      consent
That Antony speak in his funeral.
Know you how much the people may be moved
235 By that which he will utter?
BRUTUS.   By your pardon;
I will myself into the pulpit first,
And show the reason of our Caesar's death;
What Antony shall speak, I will protest
He speaks by leave and by permission,
240 And that we are contented Caesar shall
Have all true rites and lawful ceremonies.
It shall advantage more than do us wrong.
CASSIUS (dubiously). I know not what may fall; I like it not.
(BRUTUS and CASSIUS rejoin ANTONY and the others.)
BRUTUS. Mark Antony, here, take you Caesar's body.
245 You shall not in your funeral speech blame us,
But speak all good you can devise of Caesar,
And say you do 't by our permission;
Else shall you not have any hand at all
About his funeral; and you shall speak
250 In the same pulpit whereto I am going,
After my speech is ended.
ANTONY.   Be it so;
I do desire no more.
BRUTUS. Prepare the body then, and follow us.

27. pricked in number of our friends, numbered among our friends.

28. so full of good regard, so full of merit.

(The CONSPIRATORS *follow* BRUTUS *out at right.* ANTONY *stands looking at* CAESAR; *then he slowly covers the body with the dead man's cloak.)*

ANTONY. Oh, pardon me, thou bleeding piece of earth,
255   That I am meek and gentle with these butchers!
    Thou are the ruins of the noblest man
    That ever livèd in the tide of times.
    Woe to the hand that shed this costly blood!
    Over thy wounds now do I prophesy—
260   Which, like dumb mouths, do ope their ruby lips,
    To beg the voice and utterance of my tongue—
    A curse shall light upon the limbs of men;
    Domestic fury and fierce civil strife
    Shall cumber all the parts of Italy;
265   Blood and destruction shall be so in use
    And dreadful objects so familiar
    That mothers shall but smile when they behold
    Their infants quartered with the hands of war;
    All pity choked with custom of fell deeds;
270   And Caesar's spirit, ranging for revenge,
    With Ate[29] by his side come hot from hell,
    Shall in these confines with a monarch's voice
    Cry "Havoc,"[30] and let slip the dogs of war,[31]
    That this foul deed shall smell above the earth
275   With carrion men, groaning for burial.

(A SERVANT *enters at left.)*
    You serve Octavius Caesar, do you not?

SERVANT. I do, Mark Antony.

ANTONY. Caesar did write for him to come to Rome.

SERVANT. He did receive his letters, and is coming;
280   And bid me say to you by word of mouth——*(He sees the body.)*
    O Caesar!

ANTONY. Thy heart is big, get thee apart and weep.
    Passion, I see, is catching; for mine eyes,
    Seeing those beads of sorrow stand in thine,
285   Began to water. Is thy master coming?

SERVANT. He lies tonight within seven leagues[32] of Rome.

ANTONY. Post back with speed and tell him what hath chanced;
    Here is a mourning Rome, a dangerous Rome,
    No Rome of safety for Octavius yet;
290   Hie hence, and tell him so. *(The* SERVANT *starts to leave.)* Yet, stay awhile;
    Thou shalt not back till I have borne this corse
    Into the market place;[33] there shall I try,
    In my oration, how the people take

29. *Ate* (ā'tē), the Greek goddess of vengeance.

30. *Cry "Havoc."* This cry, which could be given only by a king, was a command which meant "Kill all! Take no prisoners."

31. *let slip the dogs of war,* let loose the dogs of war—fire, sword, and famine.

32. *within seven leagues,* within twenty-one miles.

33. *the market place,* meaning here the Forum.

The cruel issue of these bloody men;
295   According to the which, thou shalt discourse
      To young Octavius of the state of things.
      Lend me your hand.

(While ANTONY *and the* SERVANT *carry* CAESAR's *body off at right door, the curtains of the inner stage are drawn closed.)*

Scene 2: Rome. The Forum.

BRUTUS *and* CASSIUS, *with groups of indignant* CITIZENS *at their heels, enter at left. The* CITIZENS *are clamoring for an explanation of* CAESAR's *assassination. It is apparent from their threatening gestures and shouts that the people will become violent unless* BRUTUS *speaks to them. He does so from the balcony, which represents a raised pulpit in this scene.*

CITIZENS *(angrily).* We will be satisfied; let us be satisfied.

BRUTUS. Then follow me, and give me audience, friends.
      Cassius, go you into the other street,
      And part the numbers.[1]
5   *(Loudly.)* Those that will hear me speak, let 'em stay here;
      Those that will follow Cassius, go with him;
      And public reasons shall be rendered
      Of Caesar's death.

*(*BRUTUS *exits at inner-stage curtains in order to ascend the pulpit.)*

FIRST CITIZEN.   I will hear Brutus speak.

SECOND CITIZEN. I will hear Cassius; and compare their reasons,
10   When severally[2] we hear them rendered.

*(*CASSIUS *moves off at right, accompanied by various* CITIZENS *who clamor loudly.* BRUTUS *appears above at the balcony railing.)*

THIRD CITIZEN. The noble Brutus is ascended; silence!

BRUTUS *(speaking earnestly).* Be patient till the last. *(Pause.)*
      Romans, countrymen, and lovers!

(There are shouts from the mob.)

      Hear me for my cause, and be silent, that you may hear; believe
15   me for mine honor, and have respect to mine honor, that you may
      believe; censure me in your wisdom, and awake your senses, that
      you may the better judge. If there be any in this assembly, any
      dear friend of Caesar's, to him I say, that Brutus' love to Caesar
      was no less than his. If then that friend demand why Brutus rose
20   against Caesar, this is my answer: Not that I loved Caesar less,
      but that I loved Rome more. Had you rather Caesar were living
      and die all slaves, than that Caesar were dead, to live all free men?
      As Caesar loved me, I weep for him; as he was fortunate, I rejoice
      at it; as he was valiant, I honor him; but, as he was ambitious, I
25   slew him. There is tears for his love; joy for his fortune; honor for
      his valor; and death for his ambition. Who is here so base that
      would be a bondman? If any, speak; for him have I offended.

1. *part the numbers,* divide the crowd.

2. *severally,* separately.

484   JULIUS CAESAR

Who is here so rude that would not be a Roman? If any, speak; for him have I offended. Who is here so vile that will not love his

30 country? If any, speak; for him have I offended. I pause for a reply.

ALL *(shouting).* None, Brutus, none.

BRUTUS. Then none have I offended. I have done no more to Caesar than you shall do to Brutus. The question of his death is enrolled[3]

35 in the Capitol; his glory not extenuated,[4] wherein he was worthy, nor his offenses enforced, for which he suffered death.

*(*ANTONY *enters at left. Behind him come* ATTENDANTS *carrying* CAESAR'*s bier.)*

Here comes his body, mourned by Mark Antony; who, though he had no hand in his death, shall receive the benefit of his dying, a place in the commonwealth; as which of you shall not? With this I

40 depart—that, as I slew my best lover for the good of Rome, I have the same dagger for myself, when it shall please my country to need my death.

ALL *(shouting).* Live, Brutus! Live, live!

*(*BRUTUS *exits at balcony curtains in order to descend from the pulpit.)*

FIRST CITIZEN. Bring him with triumph home unto his house.

45 SECOND CITIZEN. Give him a statue with his ancestors.

THIRD CITIZEN. Let him be Caesar.

FOURTH CITIZEN.   Caesar's better parts
    Shall be crowned in Brutus.

FIRST CITIZEN.   We'll bring him to his house
    With shouts and clamors.

(The mob greets BRUTUS *with cheers as he reënters the platform at inner-stage curtains.)*

BRUTUS. My countrymen——
(The crowd cheers wildly.)

50 SECOND CITIZEN *(shouting).* Peace, silence! Brutus speaks.

FIRST CITIZEN.   Peace, ho!

BRUTUS. Good countrymen, let me depart alone.
    And, for my sake, stay here with Antony.
    Do grace to Caesar's corpse, and grace his speech
    Tending to Caesar's glories; which Mark Antony,

55 By our permission, is allowed to make.
    I do entreat you, not a man depart
    Save I alone, till Antony have spoke.

(He exits alone at right.)

FIRST CITIZEN. Stay, ho! And let us hear Mark Antony.

THIRD CITIZEN. Let him go up into the public chair;

60 We'll hear him. Noble Antony, go up.

(There are murmurs from the mob.)

ANTONY. For Brutus' sake, I am beholding to you.

3. The question of his death is enrolled, the reason for Caesar's death is recorded.
4. his glory not extenuated (ek-sten'yü āt əd), his fame has not been detracted from because of the manner of his dying.

(ANTONY *exits at inner-stage curtains in order to ascend the pulpit.*
His ANTENDANTS, *meanwhile, have placed* CAESAR'*s body well forward*
on platform.)

FOURTH CITIZEN. What does he say of Brutus?

THIRD CITIZEN.   He says for Brutus'
          sake,
     He finds himself beholding to us all.

FOURTH CITIZEN. 'Twere best he speak no harm of Brutus here.

65 FIRST CITIZEN. This Caesar was a tyrant.

THIRD CITIZEN.   Nay, that's certain;
     We are blest that Rome is rid of him.

(ANTONY *appears above at the balcony railing.*)

SECOND CITIZEN. Peace! Let us hear what Antony can say.

ANTONY. You gentle Romans——

(The crowd is not yet quiet.)

CITIZENS.   Peace, ho! Let us hear him.

ANTONY. Friends, Romans, countrymen, lend me your ears;
70   I come to bury Caesar, not to praise him.
     The evil that men do lives after them;
     The good is oft interrèd with their bones;
     So let it be with Caesar. The noble Brutus
     Hath told you Caesar was ambitious;
75   If it were so, it was a grievous fault,
     And grievously hath Caesar answered it.
     Here, under leave of Brutus and the rest——

(The mob murmurs angrily.)

     For Brutus is an honorable man;[5]
     So are they all, all honorable men—
80   Come I to speak in Caesar's funeral.
     He was my friend, faithful and just to me;
     But Brutus says he was ambitious;
     And Brutus is an honorable man.[6]
     He[7] hath brought many captives home to Rome,
85   Whose ransoms did the general coffers fill;[8]
     Did this in Caesar seem ambitious?
     When that the poor have cried, Caesar hath wept.
     Ambition should be made of sterner stuff;
     Yet Brutus said he was ambitious,
90   And Brutus is an honorable man.[9]
     You all did see that on the Lupercal
     I thrice presented him a kingly crown,
     Which he did thrice refuse; was this ambition?
     Yet Brutus says he was ambitious;
95   And, sure, he is an honorable man.
     I speak not to disprove what Brutus spoke,
     But here I am to speak what I do know.

5. **Brutus is an honorable man.** The crowd's anger at words against Brutus makes Antony quick to express his admiration for the absent Roman—and for the other conspirators.

6. **Brutus is an honorable man.** Note the tinge of irony. Remember Antony has promised to speak no harm of the conspirators. Is he really keeping his promise?
7. **He,** Caesar.
8. **the general coffers fill.** Caesar hadn't kept the ransom money for himself.

9. **Brutus is an honorable man.** Note how sarcasm begins to creep into the repetition of these words.

You all did love him once, not without cause;
What cause withholds you, then, to mourn for him?
100 O judgment! Thou art fled to brutish beasts,
And men have lost their reason.[10] (He pauses.) Bear with me;
My heart is in the coffin there[11] with Caesar,
And I must pause till it come back to me. (He weeps openly.)
FIRST CITIZEN (soberly). Methinks there is much reason in his
sayings.
105 SECOND CITIZEN. If thou consider rightly of the matter,
Caesar has had great wrong.
THIRD CITIZEN.   Has he, masters?
I fear there will a worse come in his place.
FOURTH CITIZEN. Marked ye his words? He would not take the
crown;
Therefore 'tis certain he was not ambitious.
110 FIRST CITIZEN. If it be found so, some will dear abide[12] it.
SECOND CITIZEN. Poor soul! His eyes are red as fire with weeping.
THIRD CITIZEN. There's not a nobler man in Rome than Antony.
FOURTH CITIZEN (pointing). Now mark him, he begins again to
speak.
ANTONY. But yesterday the word of Caesar might
115 Have stood against the world; now lies he there,
And none so poor to do him reverence.
O masters, if I were disposed to stir
Your hearts and minds to mutiny and rage,
I should do Brutus wrong, and Cassius wrong,
120 Who, you all know, are honorable men:[13]
(There is derisive laughter from the mob.)
I will not do them wrong; I rather choose
To wrong the dead, to wrong myself and you,
Than I will wrong such honorable men. (He pulls a scroll from his
garment.)
But here's a parchment with the seal of Caesar;
125 I found it in his closet, 'tis his will:
Let but the commons hear this testament—
Which, pardon me, I do not mean to read—
And they would go and kiss dead Caesar's wounds
And dip their napkins[14] in his sacred blood,
130 Yea, beg a hair of him for memory,
And, dying, mention it within their wills,
Bequeathing it as a rich legacy
Unto their issue.
FOURTH CITIZEN. We'll hear the will; read it, Mark Antony.
135 ALL (shouting). The will, the will! We will hear Caesar's will.
ANTONY. Have patience, gentle friends, I must not read it;
It is not meet you know how Caesar loved you. (He puts the will
away.)

10. *And men have lost their reason.* Here Antony is overcome with grief and finds himself unable to go on. Do you think he realizes the effectiveness of this pause? Are his tears genuine?
11. *in the coffin there.* Here is another anachronism. The Romans did not use coffins; they cremated their dead.

12. *abide,* pay for.

13. *honorable men.* Note Antony's mounting sarcasm.

14. *napkins,* handkerchiefs.

You are not wood, you are not stones, but men;
And, being men, hearing the will of Caesar,
140 It will inflame you, it will make you mad.
     (There are cries of "No! No!")
     'Tis good you know not that you are his heirs;
     For, if you should, Oh, what would come of it!
FOURTH CITIZEN. Read the will; we'll hear it, Antony.
     (There are cries of "Yes! Yes!")
     You shall read us the will, Caesar's will.
145 ANTONY. Will you be patient? Will you stay awhile?
     I have o'ershot myself[15] to tell you of it.
     I fear I wrong the honorable men
     Whose daggers have stabbed Caesar; I do fear it.
     (There are angry shouts from the mob.)
FOURTH CITIZEN. They were traitors; *(sarcastically)* honorable men!
150 ALL *(clamoring)*. The will! The testament!
SECOND CITIZEN. They were villains, murderers; the will!
     Read the will.
     (There are cries of "Read! Read!")
ANTONY. You will compel me, then, to read the will?
     Then make a ring about the corpse of Caesar,
155 And let me show you him that made the will.
     Shall I descend? And will you give me leave?
SEVERAL CITIZENS. Come down.
SECOND CITIZEN. Descend.
THIRD CITIZEN. You shall have leave.
     *(ANTONY exits at balcony curtains in order to descend from the pulpit;
     the crowd circles CAESAR's body.)*
160 FOURTH CITIZEN. A ring; stand round.
FIRST CITIZEN. Stand from the hearse,[16] stand from the body,
     *(The crowd moves back, opening the ring, when ANTONY reenters the
     platform.)*
SECOND CITIZEN. Room for Antony, most noble Antony.
ANTONY. Nay, press not so upon me; stand far off.
SEVERAL CITIZENS. Stand back; room; bear back!
165 ANTONY. If you have tears, prepare to shed them now.
     You all do know this mantle. *(Pointing to CAESAR's cloak.)* I
        remember
     The first time Caesar ever put it on;
     'Twas on a summer evening, in his tent,
     That day he overcame the Nervii;[17]
170 Look, in this place ran Cassius' dagger through;
     See what a rent the envious Casca made;
     Through this the well-beloved Brutus stabbed,[18]
     And as he plucked his cursèd steel away,
     Mark how the blood of Caesar followed it,
175 As rushing out of doors, to be resolved

15. *I have o'ershot myself.* Antony has said more than he intended, or pretends he has.

16. hearse, bier.

17. *Nervii* (nėr′vē ī), the most warlike of the tribes of Gaul. Caesar led the decisive charge against them in person.

18. *Through this . . . Brutus stabbed.* Could Antony possibly have known which cut Brutus made?

If Brutus so unkindly knocked, or no;
For Brutus, as you know, was Caesar's angel;
Judge, O you gods, how dearly Caesar loved him!
This was the most unkindest cut of all;
180 For when the noble Caesar saw him stab,
Ingratitude, more strong than traitor's arms,
Quite vanquished him; then burst his mighty heart;
And, in his mantle muffling up his face,
Even at the base of Pompey's statuë,
185 Which all the while ran blood, great Caesar fell.
Oh, what a fall was there, my countrymen!
Then I, and you, and all of us fell down,
Whilst bloody treason flourished over us.
Oh, now you weep; and, I perceive, you feel
190 The dint[19] of pity; these are gracious drops.
Kind souls, what, weep you when you but behold
Our Caesar's vesture wounded?[20] *(He flings* CAESAR's *cloak aside.)*
    Look you here!
Here is himself, marred as you see, with traitors.

19. *dint,* effect.

20. *Caesar's vesture wounded,* the rents in Caesar's clothing.

(The CITIZENS *cry out in horror.)*
    FIRST CITIZEN. O piteous spectacle!
195 SECOND CITIZEN. O noble Caesar!
    THIRD CITIZEN. O woeful day!
    FOURTH CITIZEN. O traitors, villains!
    FIRST CITIZEN. O most bloody sight!
    SECOND CITIZEN. We will be revenged.
200 ALL *(shouting).* Revenge! About! Seek! Burn! Fire! Kill! Slay!
    Let not a traitor live! *(They start to leave.)*
    ANTONY *(commandingly).* Stay, countrymen.
    FIRST CITIZEN. Peace there! Hear the noble Antony.
    SECOND CITIZEN. We'll hear him, we'll follow him, we'll die with
      him.
(The mob returns to ANTONY.)
205 ANTONY. Good friends, sweet friends, let me not stir you up
To such a sudden flood of mutiny.
They that have done this deed are honorable;
What private griefs[21] they have, alas, I know not,
That made them do it; they are wise and honorable,
210 And will, no doubt, with reasons answer you.
I come not, friends, to steal away your hearts;[22]
I am no orator, as Brutus is,
But, as you know me all, a plain, blunt man,
That love my friend; and that they know full well
215 That gave me public leave to speak of him;[23]
For I have neither wit, nor words, nor worth,
Action, nor utterance, nor the power of speech,

21. *private griefs,* personal reasons.

22. *I come not . . . hearts.* Is Antony sincere here?

23. *public leave to speak of him,* permission to speak of him in public.

To stir men's blood; I only speak right on;[24]
I tell you that which you yourselves do know;
220 Show you sweet Caesar's wounds, poor, poor, dumb mouths,
And bid them speak for me. But were I Brutus,
And Brutus Antony, there were an Antony
Would ruffle up your spirits and put a tongue
In every wound of Caesar that should move
225 The stones of Rome to rise and mutiny.

(The excitement of the mob is at fever pitch. They are nearly uncontrollable and shout wildly.)

ALL. We'll mutiny!

FIRST CITIZEN. We'll burn the house of Brutus!

THIRD CITIZEN. Away, then! Come, seek the conspirators!

(Again the mob starts to leave.)

ANTONY. Yet hear me, countrymen; yet hear me speak.

230 ALL *(turning).* Peace, ho! Hear Antony. Most noble Antony!

ANTONY. Why, friends, you go to do you know not what;
Wherein hath Caesar thus deserved your loves?
Alas, you know not; I must tell you then:
You have forgot the will I told you of. *(He takes the will from his garment.)*

235 ALL *(returning to him).* Most true. The will! Let's stay and hear the will.

ANTONY *(showing it).* Here is the will, and under Caesar's seal. *(He breaks the seal, unrolls the scroll, and reads.)*
To every Roman citizen he gives,
To every several[25] man, seventy-five drachmas.[26]

(The mob murmurs its approval.)

SECOND CITIZEN. Most noble Caesar! We'll revenge his death.

240 THIRD CITIZEN. O royal Caesar!

ANTONY. Hear me with patience.

ALL. Peace, ho!

ANTONY. Moreover, he hath left you all his walks,
His private arbors and new-planted orchards,
245 On this side Tiber; he hath left them you,
And to your heirs forever, common pleasures,
To walk abroad, and recreate yourselves.
Here was a Caesar! When comes such another?

FIRST CITIZEN. Never, never! Come, away, away!
250 We'll burn his body in the holy place,
And with the brands fire the traitors' houses!
Take up the body!

(A group of CITIZENS *take up* CAESAR's *bier.)*

SECOND CITIZEN. Go fetch fire!

THIRD CITIZEN. Pluck down benches!

255 FOURTH CITIZEN. Pluck down forms,[27] windows, anything!

24. *right on,* openly; frankly.

25. *several,* separate; individual.
26. *seventy-five drachmas* (drak′məz). Authorities disagree in estimating this amount; some say as little as $10 a person; others, as much as $100. Whatever the exact amount, the purchasing power of money was far greater in Caesar's time than today.

27. *forms,* public benches.

(The CITIZENS, *bearing* CAESAR's *body aloft, exit at right door.)*

ANTONY. Now let it work. Mischief, thou art afoot;

Take thou what course thou wilt!

(A SERVANT *of* OCTAVIUS CAESAR *enters at left.)*

How now, fellow!

SERVANT. Sir, Octavius is already come to Rome.

ANTONY. Where is he?

260 SERVANT. He and Lepidus are at Caesar's house.

ANTONY. And thither will I straight to visit him.

He comes upon a wish. Fortune is merry,

And in this mood will give us anything.

SERVANT. I heard him say, Brutus and Cassius

265 Are rid[28] like madmen through the gates of Rome.

ANTONY. Belike they had some notice of the people,

How I had moved them. Bring me to Octavius.

(ANTONY leads his ATTENDANTS and the SERVANT out at left door.)

28. Are rid, have ridden. Brutus and Cassius are fleeing before the wrath of the mob.

Discussion

Scene 1

1. (a) After Caesar appears at the Capitol, what incidents cause the conspirators to fear that their plans may go wrong? (b) How do they show alertness in warding off these dangers?

2. (a) What is your final opinion of Caesar in this scene? (b) Why are his dying words especially dramatic? (c) Do you think that he was afraid to die?

3. (a) What urgent problem do the assassins face immediately after stabbing Caesar? (b) Which of them assumes the leadership in attacking that problem? (c) State briefly his argument of justification for Caesar's murder.

4. Which of the following statements best sums up the impression that Antony wishes to make on the conspirators? And which of them represents his true feelings?

(a) Although I loved Caesar, I admire Brutus greatly and will follow him unquestioningly.

(b) I intend to arouse the fury of the people against the butcher of Caesar.

(c) I loved Caesar; I admire Brutus; I am willing to be friendly with the conspirators once I understand why they considered Caesar dangerous.

5. (a) Why is Cassius worried by Brutus' promise to allow Mark Antony to speak at Caesar's funeral? (b) Why is Brutus willing for Antony to do so?

6. What does Shakespeare foreshadow in the final speeches of this scene?

Scene 2

1. Because the crowd is so great, Brutus asks some of the people to go into "the other street" and hear Cassius speak there. Why do you think Shakespeare does not include Cassius' speech in this play?

2. (a) In his speech, does Brutus appeal principally to the people's intellect or emotions? **(b)** Quote the parts of his speech that you think best explain why the conspirators killed Caesar. **(c)** How do the citizens' comments show that they have missed the entire point of Brutus' speech?

3. As Mark Antony ascends the pulpit, the citizens are still shouting. **(a)** From their remarks what do you learn about their present feelings toward Brutus? **(b)** Toward the dead Caesar? **(c)** If Antony is to change those feelings, he must choose his words carefully. Cite what you consider the best examples of his skill in using words that play on the emotions of his audience.

4. (a) Why is Antony's pause where he stops to look at Caesar's body (page 488, line 101) effective? **(b)** Why doesn't he read Caesar's will when he first mentions it? **(c)** How does he almost miss the chance to read it at all? **(d)** In what way does he appeal to the morbid curiosity of the crowd? **(e)** Do you think crowds of today sometimes exhibit a similar morbid curiosity? If so, cite some examples.

Vocabulary
Context and Dictionary

On your paper write sentences using the words below. Compose the sentences so that one who was unfamiliar with the words would have a clue to their meaning from their context. Use your Glossary for reference.
Example: appease
Poor: He *appeased* the crowd.
Good: His quiet voice and calm manner *appeased* the restless crowd.

carrion
coffer
enfranchise
firmament
legacy

Extension · Writing

1. Continue your outline of the play, listing the most important events that take place in Act Three.

2. In Act Three we see Brutus assuming leadership of the anti-Caesar forces. Keeping in mind what you have learned about him in this act, answer the following questions. Explain why you decided as you did.

(a) Does Brutus really regard Caesar as being a dangerous man as far as Roman liberties are concerned?

(b) Is Brutus respected by both the pro-Caesar and the anti-Caesar forces?

(c) Does Brutus show self-confidence in his acts?

(d) Is he aware of the dangers of trusting men less sincere than himself?

(e) Is he capable of judging the common people accurately?

3. (a) What qualities of leadership does Mark Antony possess? **(b)** Which of them do you consider most important?

4. (a) What is Mark Antony's attitude toward the future as Act Three comes to an end? **(b)** Do you think his expectations will be met? Explain your answer.

Macbeth, V, v, "his hour upon the stage"

Shakespeare was an actor as well as a playwright. He must have been a competent performer, for in 1594 he was a member of the Lord Chamberlain's Company—one of the principal acting companies of the time.

The acting companies usually consisted of ten or twelve adult actors and six boy apprentices. All of the women's roles in Elizabethan plays were performed by the apprentices. The patronage of an important nobleman, like the Lord Chamberlain of England, protected the actors from London authorities who wished to suppress the playhouses. What particular abilities did an actor possess to qualify for membership in an Elizabethan acting company?

The prime requisite must have been a resonant speaking voice. From his personal experience, Shakespeare undoubtedly learned to value dialogue that could be spoken rapidly, yet clearly. In addition, an actor had to be a singer and musician. Since most Elizabethan plays featured songs, an actor was frequently assigned a role, like the role of Lucius in *Julius Caesar*, which required him to sing and play a musical instrument.

Plays of the period also featured numerous duels and mock battles. The daggers, swords, and rapiers used in these scenes were sharp, not blunted weapons. To avoid injury, an actor had to be a competent swordsman. Some plays demanded that he be an acrobat as well!

An Elizabethan actor also possessed an astonishing memory. As many as forty plays were given during a single season, but an actor might memorize eighty roles. The practice of *doubling*, that is, of performing two or more roles in a single play, was typical of the Elizabethan stage. Most acting companies had only eighteen people to enact, for example, the thirty or more speaking parts of *Julius Caesar*. Extra actors could be hired, but the problem was largely solved through doubling. Thus the actor who portrayed Flavius in Act One of *Julius Caesar* might also have portrayed Artemidorus in Acts Two and Three and Octavius in Acts Four and Five.

If an actor performed well, the audience applauded; if not, they pelted him with apple cores. An actor who strutted "his hour upon the stage" was paid out of the penny admissions which were charged to enter the playhouse. If he was a part-owner of the playhouse, as Shakespeare was, he also shared in the gallery admissions.

Act Four

Scene 1: A house in Rome.

For many months after Caesar's death in March, 44 B.C., chaos has reigned in Rome. The leading conspirators have fled eastward to Greece and Asia Minor. Mark Antony has attempted to make himself virtual dictator of Rome, but has been opposed by young Octavius Caesar, the grandnephew and political heir of Julius Caesar; and a devastating civil war has broken out. In October, 43 B.C., Antony and Octavius agree to combine forces, and invite M. Aemilius Lepidus, one of Julius Caesar's former lieutenants, to join them in forming the second triumvirate. Together they will control Rome—and rule the world.

The scene begins as the curtains of the balcony stage are drawn apart to reveal ANTONY, OCTAVIUS, *and* LEPIDUS *seated around a table. They are scrutinizing a wax tablet which lists the names of those Romans who might oppose them. The three men are making plans to crush all opposition to their scheme.*

ANTONY. These many, then, shall die; their names are pricked.[1]

OCTAVIUS. Your brother, too, must die; consent you, Lepidus?

LEPIDUS. I do consent——

OCTAVIUS.   Prick him down, Antony.

LEPIDUS. Upon condition Publius shall not live,

5   Who is your sister's son, Mark Antony.

ANTONY *(picking up the stylus)*. He shall not live; look, with a spot I
     damn him.[2]

   But, Lepidus, go you to Caesar's house;

   Fetch the will hither, and we shall determine

   How to cut off some charge in legacies.[3]

10 LEPIDUS. What, shall I find you here?

OCTAVIUS. Or here, or at the Capitol.

(LEDIDUS *leaves at the door in the rear wall of the balcony stage.*)

ANTONY. This is a slight, unmeritable man,

   Meet to be sent on errands; is it fit,

   The threefold world divided, he should stand

15   One of the three to share it?

OCTAVIUS.   So you thought him;

   And took his voice who should be pricked to die,

   In our black sentence and proscription.[4]

ANTONY. Octavius, I have seen more days than you;

   And though we lay these honors on this man,

20   To ease ourselves of divers sland'rous loads,

   He shall but bear them as the ass bears gold,

   To groan and sweat under the business,

   Either led or driven, as we point the way;

   And having brought our treasure where we will,

1. *These many . . . pricked.* With a needle, knife, or stylus the list of the names of many men has been marked.

2. *with a spot I damn him.* The puncture condemns him to death.

3. *we shall determine . . . legacies.* Antony wishes to find a way to reduce the amount Caesar has bequeathed each Roman. Here Antony reveals himself as a grafter.

4. *our black sentence and proscription,* the list indicating those condemned to death.

25 Then take we down his load, and turn him off,
Like to the empty ass, to shake his ears,
And graze in commons.[5]

OCTAVIUS.   You may do your will;
But he's a tried and valiant soldier.

ANTONY. So is my horse. And now, Octavius,
30 Listen great things: Brutus and Cassius
Are levying powers; we must straight make head;[6]
Therefore let our alliance be combined,
Our best friends made, our means stretched,
And let us presently go sit in council,
35 How covert matters may be best disclosed,
And open perils surest answered.[7]

OCTAVIUS. Let us do so; for we are at the stake,[8]
And bayed about with many enemies;
And some that smile have in their hearts, I fear,
40 Millions of mischiefs.

(As ANTONY and OCTAVIUS exit, the curtains of the balcony stage are
drawn closed.)

Scene 2: Brutus' camp at Sardis, a city in Asia Minor. Before
Brutus' tent.
Several months have passed since the members of the second
triumvirate made their plans. Far from Rome, BRUTUS awaits the
arrival of CASSIUS, whose actions have so troubled BRUTUS that he has
asked him here for a conference.

The scene begins as LUCIUS enters the platform at inner-stage
curtains. He then draws the curtains aside, revealing the interior of
BRUTUS' tent. The interior is sparsely furnished with a table, some low
stools, and a few cushions.

While LUCIUS busies himself within the tent, BRUTUS and a group of
his SOLDIERS enter the platform at left door. LUCILIUS and TITINIUS,
friends of BRUTUS, enter the platform at right. They have just returned
from CASSIUS' camp and are accompanied by his servant PINDARUS.

BRUTUS (raising his arm in salute). Stand, ho![1]

LUCILIUS. Give the word, ho![2] And stand.

BRUTUS. What now, Lucilius! Is Cassius near?

LUCILIUS. He is at hand; and Pindarus is come
5 To do you salutation[3] from his master.

BRUTUS. He greets me well. Your master, Pindarus,
In his own change, or by ill officers,[4]
Hath given me some worthy cause to wish
Things done, undone; but if he be at hand,
10 I shall be satisfied.[5]

PINDARUS.   I do not doubt
But that my noble master will appear
Such as he is, full of regard and honor.

5. commons, the public pasture lands. Here again we have an anachronism: the custom of having public pasture lands came about in the Middle Ages.

6. Brutus and Cassius . . . head. Brutus and Cassius were in Greece and Asia Minor, gathering forces and strengthening themselves; Antony knew that the triumvirate must do so also.

7. How covert matters . . . answered, how hidden (covert) dangers may be discovered, and dangers already known be met.
8. we are at the stake, an allusion to the English custom of tying a bear to a stake and setting dogs on it.

1. Stand, ho! Halt!

2. Give the word, ho! Pass the word Halt along to the soldiers.

3. To do you salutation, to bring you greeting.

4. In his own change, or by ill officers, by a change of heart himself or by bad advice from troublemakers.

5. be satisfied, find out.

BRUTUS. He is not doubted. *(Motioning* LUCILIUS *aside.)* A word,
　　Lucilius,
　　How he received you; let me be resolved.[6]

15 **LUCILIUS.** With courtesy and with respect enough;
　　But not with such familiar instances,[7]
　　Nor with such free and friendly conference,
　　As he hath used of old.

BRUTUS.　　　　　　　　　Thou hast described
　　A hot friend cooling; ever note, Lucilius,
20 　　When love begins to sicken and decay,
　　It useth an enforcèd ceremony.[8]
　　There are no tricks in plain and simple faith.
　　Comes his army on?

LUCILIUS. They mean this night in Sardis to be quartered;
25 　　The greater part, the horse in general,[9]
　　Are come with Cassius.

*(Martial music is heard offstage, followed by a sentry's ringing
challenge and the murmured answer.)*

BRUTUS.　　　　　　　　Hark! He is arrived.

*(*CASSIUS, *accompanied by a group of his* SOLDIERS, *enters at right.)*

CASSIUS *(saluting).* Stand, ho!

BRUTUS *(returning the salute).* Stand, ho! Speak the word along.

FIRST SOLDIER. Stand!

SECOND SOLDIER. Stand!

30 **THIRD SOLDIER.** Stand!

CASSIUS. Most noble brother, you have done me wrong.

BRUTUS. Judge me, you gods! Wrong I mine enemies?
　　And, if not so, how should I wrong a brother?

CASSIUS. Brutus, this sober form of yours hides wrongs;
35 　　And when you do them—

BRUTUS *(interrupting).*　　　Cassius, be content;
　　Speak your griefs softly; I do know you well.
　　Before the eyes of both our armies here,
　　Which should perceive nothing but love from us,
　　Let us not wrangle. Bid them move away;
40 　　Then in my tent, Cassius, enlarge your griefs,
　　And I will give you audience.

CASSIUS *(to his servant).*　　　Pindarus,
　　Bid our commanders lead their charges off
　　A little from this ground.

*(*PINDARUS, *followed by the* SOLDIERS *of* CASSIUS, *departs at right.)*

BRUTUS. Lucilius, do you the like; and let no man
45 　　Come to our tent till we have done our conference.
　　Let Lucius and Titinius guard our door.

*(*BRUTUS *watches as his* SOLDIERS *follow* LUCILIUS *off at left. Then he
and* CASSIUS *move to the inner stage.)*

6. *A word, Lucilius . . . resolved.*
Not content with Pindarus'
assurance of Cassius' loyalty,
Brutus wishes further report from
Lucilius.
7. *familiar instances,* marks of
friendship.

8. *an enforcèd ceremony,* forced
politeness.

9. *the horse in general,* the regular
cavalry.

Scene 3: Sardis. Within Brutus' tent.

Only a few seconds have elapsed since the preceding scene. LUCIUS
and TITINIUS *guard the entrance to* BRUTUS' *tent.* BRUTUS *and* CASSIUS
stand facing each other on the inner stage. CASSIUS' *anger is very
apparent.*

CASSIUS. That you have wronged me doth appear in this:
    You have condemned and noted[1] Lucius Pella
    For taking bribes here of the Sardians;[2]
    Wherein my letters, praying on his side
5   Because I knew the man, were slighted off.
BRUTUS. You wronged yourself to write in such a case.
CASSIUS. In such a time as this it is not meet
    That every nice offense should bear his comment.[3]
BRUTUS. Let me tell you, Cassius, you yourself
10   Are much condemned to have an itching palm;[4]
    To sell and mart[5] your offices for gold
    To undeservers.
CASSIUS *(hotly).*   I an itching palm!
    You know that you are Brutus that speaks this,
    Or, by the gods, this speech were else your last!
15 BRUTUS. The name of Cassius honors this corruption,
    And chastisement doth therefore hide his head.[6]
CASSIUS. Chastisement!
BRUTUS. Remember March, the ides of March remember;
    Did not great Julius bleed for justice' sake?
20   What villain touched his body, that did stab,
    And not for justice? What, shall one of us,
    That struck the foremost man of all this world
    But for supporting robbers,[7] shall we now
    Contaminate our fingers with base bribes,
25   And sell the mighty space of our large honors
    For so much trash as may be graspèd thus?
    I had rather be a dog, and bay the moon,
    Than such a Roman.
CASSIUS.   Brutus, bait not me;
    I'll not endure it; you forget yourself,
30   To hedge me in;[8] I am a soldier, I,
    Older in practice, abler than yourself
    To make conditions.[9]
BRUTUS.   Go to; you are not, Cassius.
CASSIUS. I am.
BRUTUS *(firmly).* I say you are not.
35 CASSIUS. Urge me no more, I shall forget myself;
    Have mind upon your health, tempt me no further.
BRUTUS *(unconcernedly).* Away, slight man!
CASSIUS *(in amazement).* Is 't possible?

1. *noted,* disgraced.

2. *For taking bribes . . . Sardians*
(sär′dē ənz). Brutus had, on the
complaints of the Sardians, publicly
accused Lucius Pella (pel′ə) of
embezzling public money and, upon
finding him guilty, had condemned
him. Cassius, on the other hand,
had acquitted two of his friends
similarly accused.

3. *That every nice offense . . .
comment,* that every minor offense
should be criticized.

4. *to have an itching palm,* to be
greedy for money.

5. *mart,* market.

6. *The name of Cassius . . . head.* If
anyone but Cassius had been guilty
of these deeds, he would have
received severe punishment.

7. *That struck . . . robbers,* who
killed Caesar for protecting grafters.

8. *hedge me in,* interfere with me.

9. *To make conditions,* to plan the
campaign and tend to its details.

BRUTUS. Hear me, for I will speak.
   Must I give way and room to your rash choler?[10]
40   Shall I be frighted when a madman stares?
CASSIUS. O ye gods, ye gods! Must I endure all this?
BRUTUS. All this! Aye, more. Fret till your proud heart break;
   Go show your slaves how choleric you are,
   And make your bondmen tremble. Must I budge?
45   Must I observe you? Must I stand and crouch
   Under your testy humor? By the gods,
   You shall digest the venom of your spleen,
   Though it do split you; for, from this day forth,
   I'll use you for my mirth, yea, for my laughter,
50   When you are waspish.
CASSIUS *(in disbelief).*   Is it come to this?
BRUTUS. You say you are a better soldier;
   Let it appear so; make your vaunting true,
   And it shall please me well; for mine own part,
   I shall be glad to learn of noble men.
55 CASSIUS *(pleading).* You wrong me every way; you wrong me,
      Brutus;
   I said an elder soldier, not a better;
   Did I say "better"?
BRUTUS *(indifferently).* If you did, I care not.
CASSIUS. When Caesar lived, he durst not thus have moved me.
BRUTUS. Peace, peace! You durst not so have tempted him.
60 CASSIUS. I durst not!
BRUTUS. No.
CASSIUS. What, durst not tempt him!
BRUTUS.   For your life you durst not.
CASSIUS *(hand on dagger).* Do not presume too much upon my
      love;
   I may do that I shall be sorry for.
65 BRUTUS. You have done that you should be sorry for.
   There is no terror, Cassius, in your threats,
   For I am armed so strong in honesty
   That they pass by me as the idle wind,
   Which I respect not. I did send to you
70   For certain sums of gold, which you denied me;
   For I can raise no money by vile means;
   By heaven, I had rather coin my heart,
   And drop my blood for drachmas than to wring
   From the hard hands of peasants their vile trash
75   By any indirection;[11] I did send
   To you for gold to pay my legions,
   Which you denied me; was that done like Cassius?
   Should I have answered Caius Cassius so?

10. *your rash choler* (kol'ər), your violent temper.

11. *I had rather . . . indirection.* Brutus seems rather unrealistic here. How was Cassius to get money except by taking from farmers their eggs and cattle and hoarded money? And wasn't Brutus as guilty as Cassius if he was willing to use the money thus secured?

When Marcus Brutus grows so covetous,
80 To lock such rascal counters[12] from his friends,
Be ready, gods, with all your thunderbolts;
Dash him to pieces!

CASSIUS.   I denied you not.

BRUTUS. You did.

CASSIUS. I did not; he was but a fool that brought
85 My answer back. Brutus hath rived[13] my heart;
A friend should bear his friend's infirmities,
But Brutus makes mine greater than they are.

BRUTUS. I do not, till you practice them on me.

CASSIUS. You love me not.

BRUTUS (coldly).   I do not like your faults.

90 CASSIUS. A friendly eye could never see such faults.

BRUTUS. A flatterer's would not, though they do appear
As huge as high Olympus.

CASSIUS (tragically). Come, Antony, and young Octavius, come,
Revenge yourselves alone on Cassius,
95 For Cassius is aweary of the world;
Hated by one he loves; braved by his brother;
Checked like a bondman; all his faults observed,
Set in a notebook, learned, and conned by rote,[14]
To cast into my teeth. Oh, I could weep
100 My spirit from mine eyes! (He unsheathes his dagger.) There is my
    dagger,
And here my naked breast; within, a heart
Dearer than Plutus' mine,[15] richer than gold;
If that thou be'st a Roman, take it forth,
I, that denied thee gold, will give my heart;
105 Strike, as thou didst at Caesar; for, I know
When thou didst hate him worst, thou lovedst him better
Than ever thou lovedst Cassius.

BRUTUS (his good humor returning). Sheathe your dagger.
Be angry when you will, it shall have scope;
110 Do what you will, dishonor shall be humor.[16]
O Cassius, you are yokèd with a lamb
That carries anger as the flint bears fire;
Who, much enforcèd, shows a hasty spark,
And straight is cold again.

CASSIUS (misunderstanding).   Hath Cassius lived
115 To be but mirth and laughter to his Brutus,
When grief and blood ill-tempered vexeth him?

BRUTUS. When I spoke that, I was ill-tempered, too.

CASSIUS. Do you confess so much? Give me your hand.

BRUTUS. And my heart, too.

CASSIUS (overcome with emotion). O Brutus!

12. *rascal counters,* worthless coins.

13. *rived,* broken.

14. *conned by rote,* memorized until letter-perfect.

15. *Plutus' mine.* Plutus (plü′təs), the Greek god of wealth, was believed to control all precious minerals.

16. *dishonor shall be humor,* when you dishonor me by insults, I shall consider it merely your whim.

BRUTUS.   What's the matter?

120 CASSIUS. Have not you love enough to bear with me,
When that rash humor which my mother gave me
Makes me forgetful?

BRUTUS.   Yes, Cassius; and, from henceforth,
When you are over-earnest with your Brutus,
He'll think your mother chides, and leave you so. *(Stepping
forward, he sees that* LUCILIUS *has rejoined* TITINIUS.*)*

125 Lucilius and Titinius, bid the commanders
Prepare to lodge their companies tonight.

CASSIUS. And come yourselves, and bring Messala with you
Immediately to us.

*(*LUCILIUS *and* TITINIUS *exit at left.)*

BRUTUS.   Lucius, a bowl of wine!

*(*LUCIUS *follows* BRUTUS *to the inner stage. He crosses to the table,
where he lights a taper and pours a bowl of wine for* BRUTUS.*)*

CASSIUS *(wryly).* I did not think you could have been so angry.

130 BRUTUS. O Cassius, I am sick of many griefs.

CASSIUS. Of your philosophy you make no use,[17]
If you give place to accidental evils.

BRUTUS. No man bears sorrow better. Portia is dead.

CASSIUS. Ha! Portia!

135 BRUTUS. She is dead.

CASSIUS. How 'scaped I killing when I crossed you so?
O insupportable and touching loss!
Upon what sickness?

BRUTUS.   Impatient of my absence,
And grief that young Octavius with Mark Antony

140 Have made themselves so strong—for with her death
That tidings came—with this she fell distract
And, her attendants absent, swallowed fire.[18]

CASSIUS. And died so?

BRUTUS *(nodding his head).* Even so.

CASSIUS.   O ye immortal gods!

BRUTUS. Speak no more of her. Give me a bowl of wine.

145 In this I bury all unkindness, Cassius. *(He drinks.)*

CASSIUS. My heart is thirsty for that noble pledge.
Fill, Lucius, till the wine o'erswell the cup;
I cannot drink too much of Brutus' love.

*(*LUCIUS *pours a bowl of wine for* CASSIUS. *As he does so,* BRUTUS
greets TITINIUS, *who has reentered the platform at left.* TITINIUS *is
accompanied by* MESSALA, *a friend of* BRUTUS.*)*

BRUTUS. Come in, Titinius!
Welcome, good Messala.

150 Now sit we close about this taper here,
And call in question our necessities,[19]

17. Of your philosophy . . . use.
Brutus was a Stoic (stō'ik).
Believers in this philosophy thought
that people should rise above
emotional upsets and be unmoved
by any of life's happenings.

18. swallowed fire. Portia reportedly
snatched some burning charcoal
from a fire, and holding it in her
closed mouth, stifled herself and
thus died.

19. call in question our necessities,
discuss our problems.

Messala, I have here receivèd letters,
That young Octavius and Mark Antony
Come down upon us with a mighty power,
155 Bending their expedition toward Philippi.
*(BRUTUS, CASSIUS, TITINIUS, and MESSALA seat themselves at the table.
BRUTUS unrolls a scroll.)*
MESSALA. Myself have letters of the selfsame tenor.[20]
BRUTUS. With what addition?
MESSALA. That by proscription and bills of outlawry,[21]
Octavius, Antony, and Lepidus
160 Have put to death an hundred senators.
BRUTUS. Therein our letters do not well agree;
Mine speaks of seventy senators that died
By their proscriptions, Cicero being one.
CASSIUS *(in disbelief).* Cicero one!
MESSALA.   Cicero is dead,
165 And by that order of proscription.
BRUTUS. Well, to our work alive.[22] What do you think
Of marching to Philippi presently?[23]
CASSIUS. I do not think it good.
BRUTUS.   Your reason?
CASSIUS.   This it is:
'Tis better that the enemy seek us;
170 So shall he waste his means, weary his soldiers,
Doing himself offense; whilst we, lying still,
Are full of rest, defense, and nimbleness.
BRUTUS. Good reasons must, of force, give place to better.
The people 'twixt Philippi and this ground
175 Do stand but in a forced affection;
For they have grudged us contribution;
The enemy, marching along by them,
By them shall make a fuller number up,
Come on refreshed, new-added, and encouraged;
180 From which advantage shall we cut him off,
If at Philippi we do face him there,
These people at our back.
CASSIUS *(pleading).*   Hear me, good brother.
BRUTUS. Under your pardon. You must note beside,
That we have tried the utmost of our friends,
185 Our legions are brimful, our cause is ripe;
The enemy increaseth every day;
We, at the height, are ready to decline.
There is a tide in the affairs of men,
Which, taken at the flood, leads on to fortune;
190 Omitted, all the voyage of their life
Is bound in shallows and in miseries.

20. *of the selfsame tenor,* bearing the same tidings.

21. *bills of outlawry,* public notices declaring certain persons no longer protected by Roman law. As enemies of the state they may be killed.

22. *to our work alive,* to work that concerns the living.
23. *presently,* immediately.

On such a full sea are we now afloat;
And we must take the current when it serves,
Or lose our ventures.

CASSIUS *(resignedly).*   Then, with your will, go on;
195   We'll along ourselves, and meet them at Philippi.

BRUTUS. The deep of night is crept upon our talk,
And nature must obey necessity;
Which we will niggard²⁴ with a little rest.
There is no more to say?

CASSIUS.   No more. Good night.
200   Early tomorrow will we rise, and hence.

BRUTUS *(standing).* Lucius! My gown. *(To the three others.)* Farewell,
    good Messala;
Good night, Titinius. Noble, noble Cassius,
Good night, and good repose.

CASSIUS.   O my dear brother!
This was an ill beginning of the night;
205   Never come such division 'tween our souls!
Let it not, Brutus.

BRUTUS.   Everything is well.

CASSIUS. Good night, my lord.

BRUTUS.   Good night, good brother.

TITINIUS *and* MESSALA. Good night, Lord Brutus.

BRUTUS.   Farewell, every one.

*(*CASSIUS, TITINIUS, *and* MESSALA *move from the inner stage to the
platform and exit at right.* LUCIUS *unfolds his master's night robe.)*
Give me the gown. Where is thy instrument?²⁵

210   LUCIUS. Here in the tent.

BRUTUS.   What, thou speak'st drowsily?
Poor knave,²⁶ I blame thee not; thou art o'er-watched.²⁷
Call Claudius and some other of my men;
I'll have them sleep on cushions in my tent.

LUCIUS *(moving onto platform).* Varro and Claudius!

*(*VARRO *and* CLAUDIUS, *entering the platform at left, cross to the inner
stage.)*

215   VARRO. Calls my lord?

BRUTUS. I pray you, sirs, lie in my tent and sleep;
It may be I shall raise you by and by
On business to my brother Cassius.

VARRO. So please you, we will stand and watch your pleasure.

220   BRUTUS. I will not have it so; lie down, good sirs;
It may be I shall otherwise bethink me.
Look, Lucius, here's the book I sought for so;
I put it in the pocket of my gown.

*(*VARRO *and* CLAUDIUS *lie down on the cushions.)*

LUCIUS. I was sure your lordship did not give it me.

24. *we will niggard,* we will satisfy somewhat.

25. *thy instrument,* thy lute.

26. *knave,* lad.
27. *thou art o'er-watched.* Lucius has been on sentry duty too long.

225 **BRUTUS.** Bear with me, good boy, I am much forgetful.
　　　Canst thou hold up thy heavy eyes awhile,
　　　And touch thy instrument a strain or two?
LUCIUS. Aye, my lord, an't[28] please you.
BRUTUS.　　　　　　　　　　　　It does, my boy;
　　　I trouble thee too much, but thou art willing.

230 **LUCIUS.** It is my duty, sir.
BRUTUS. I should not urge thy duty past thy might;
　　　I know young bloods look for a time of rest. *(He seats himself at*
　　　　　the table.)
LUCIUS. I have slept, my lord, already.
BRUTUS. It was well done; and thou shalt sleep again;
235　　I will not hold thee long; if I do live,
　　　I will be good to thee.
(LUCIUS sits on some cushions near the table and plays and sings,
gradually falling asleep.)
BRUTUS. This is a sleepy tune. O murderous slumber,
　　　Lay'st thou thy leaden mace[29] upon my boy,
　　　That plays thee music? Gentle knave, good night;

29. thy leaden mace. Morpheus
(môr'fē əs), the Greek god of
dreams, carried a leaden club with
which he cast the spell of slumber.

240　　I will not do thee so much wrong to wake thee;
　　　If thou dost nod, thou break'st thy instrument.
　　　I'll take it from thee; and, good boy, good night.
　　　Let me see, let me see; is not the leaf turned down[30]
　　　Where I left reading? Here it is, I think. *(He begins to read.)*
(The GHOST OF CAESAR slowly ascends through the trap door in the
floor of the inner stage.)

30. the leaf turned down. Here is
another anachronism. Roman books
were in the form of large scrolls.

245　　How ill this taper burns![31] Ha! Who comes here?
　　　I think it is the weakness of mine eyes
　　　That shapes this monstrous apparition.
　　　It comes upon me——Art thou anything?
　　　Art thou some god, some angel, or some devil,
250　　That mak'st my blood cold and my hair to stare?
　　　Speak to me what thou art.

31. How ill this taper burns!
According to a popular superstition
of the times, the presence of a
ghost made lights burn blue.

GHOST *(in sepulchral tones).*　Thy evil spirit, Brutus.
BRUTUS. Why com'st thou?
GHOST. To tell thee thou shalt see me at Philippi.
BRUTUS. Well; then I shall see thee again?
255 **GHOST.** Aye, at Philippi.
BRUTUS. Why, I will see thee at Philippi, then.
(The GHOST descends.)
　　　Now I have taken heart thou vanishest;
　　　Ill spirit, I would hold more talk with thee.
　　　Boy, Lucius! Varro! Claudius! Sirs, awake!
260　　Claudius!
LUCIUS *(still half-asleep).* The strings, my lord, are false.
BRUTUS. He thinks he still is at his instrument.

Lucius, awake!

LUCIUS. My lord?

BRUTUS. Didst thou dream, Lucius, that thou so criedst out?

265 LUCIUS. My lord, I do not know that I did cry.

BRUTUS. Yes, that thou didst; didst thou see anything?

LUCIUS. Nothing, my lord.

BRUTUS. Sleep again, Lucius. Sirrah Claudius! *(To* VARRO.*)* Fellow
    thou, awake!

VARRO. My lord?

270 CLAUDIUS. My lord?

BRUTUS. Why did you so cry out, sirs, in your sleep?

VARRO *and* CLAUDIUS. Did we, my lord?

BRUTUS.   Aye, saw you anything?

VARRO. No, my lord, I saw nothing.

CLAUDIUS.   Nor I, my lord.

BRUTUS. Go and commend me to my brother Cassius;

275   Bid him set on his powers betimes before,[32]
    And we will follow.

VARRO *and* CLAUDIUS.   It shall be done, my lord.

*(*VARRO *and* CLAUDIUS *move from the inner stage to the platform and
exit at right.* BRUTUS *and* LUCIUS *remain on the inner stage as the
curtains are drawn closed.)*

32. *set on . . . before,* start his
forces moving ahead.

Discussion

Scene 1

1. **(a)** What is the significance of the marked names on Antony's list? **(b)** What does the plan for dealing with the suspected Romans show about the character of each man in the second triumvirate? **(c)** What would the plan be called in a modern dictatorship?

2. When Antony characterizes Lepidus for Octavius (see Act Four, Scene 1, lines 12-15, 18-27), he also betrays his own traits. What does he reveal about himself?

3. **(a)** How had Antony used Caesar's will to his advantage when he swayed the commoners during the funeral oration? **(b)** How does he propose to use it now?

Scenes 2 and 3

1. **(a)** What is the state of affairs between Brutus and Cassius when Brutus sends for Cassius at the army camp near Sardis? **(b)** Keeping in mind what you have learned in the play up to this point, explain why a quarrel between the two men was inevitable. **(c)** With which of them are your sympathies? Why?

2. **(a)** Upon what plan of action do Brutus and Cassius decide after their quarrel? **(b)** What is your opinion of this plan?

3. Over two years have elapsed since Julius Caesar was killed. **(a)** Do you think that Brutus often thinks of him? **(b)** How does the dead man again become an important character as the play nears its end?

Vocabulary
Pronunciation and Dictionary

A. For each word in column I choose the word from column II that is most nearly its synonym. Write both words on a separate sheet of paper. You will not use all the words of column II.

I	II
apparition	vain
chastise	appearance
choleric	boast
covetous	selfish
sepulchral	merry
vaunt	irritable
	solemn
	envious
	punish
	praise
	gloomy
	ghost

B. Determine the accented syllable of each word in column I. On the same sheet of paper as **A,** write a word that *rhymes* with the accented syllable. Use your Glossary for reference.

Extension · Writing

1. Make a brief outline of the main events in Act Four, and add it to your outline for the first three acts.

2. As a dramatist advances the plot of his play, he must be very careful to keep the actions of each of his characters consistent with what has gone before. How have the actions of the leading characters in Act Four of *Julius Caesar* been consistent with their natures as portrayed earlier in the play?

Playwright

The first reference to William Shakespeare is a baptismal record for April 26, 1564, at Holy Trinity Church in Stratford-on-Avon. Since in that time it was customary for infants to be baptized when three days old, it is generally assumed that Shakespeare was born on April 23. His father was John Shakespeare, a glove-maker and a dealer in farm products. During William's boyhood his father was elected to one civic office after another, becoming in time high bailiff, or mayor. There is little doubt that once young William had learned to read and write English he was admitted to the free grammar school which had been the pride of Stratford since the Middle Ages. In a sixteenth-century grammar school the boys studied the classical languages—first Latin and then Greek.

When Will Shakespeare was about thirteen, his father suffered business reverses. The boy probably left school and became an apprentice at some trade. At eighteen he married Anne Hathaway, and in 1583 his daughter Susanna was born. Two years later, twins, Hamnet and Judith, were born.

About 1584 Shakespeare left Stratford. No one knows exactly the reasons for his going. By 1592 he was in London and was well enough known as a playwright to excite the jealousy of a fellow playwright, Robert Greene, who wrote a vicious attack on him. How he had spent the eight missing years is not known. It is not possible to determine with which acting company Shakespeare was first associated, but by 1594 he was both actor and playwright with the Lord Chamberlain's Company. (When James I became king in 1603, he took the members of the Lord Chamberlain's Company under his patronage and from that time on they were known as the King's Men.)

For fifteen years (1594-1609) Shakespeare was the principal playwright of this company and wrote an average of two plays a year. Among his first group of plays were light, gay comedies and historical plays about some of the past kings of England. The genius of Shakespeare began to show itself in his second group of plays—dramas like *A Midsummer Night's Dream, Romeo and Juliet,* and *The Merchant of Venice.* The plays of the third group sparkle with Elizabethan humor and vigor. Here are the comedies, *As You Like It* and *Twelfth Night,* and the great chronicle plays, *Henry IV* and *Henry V.*

By 1597 Shakespeare was a successful man, prosperous enough to purchase the house and gardens of New Place, one of the largest homes in Stratford. Two years later he purchased an interest in the Globe Playhouse. Although he now probably spent some time each year in Stratford, London remained his headquarters. It was at this time that he wrote his fourth group of plays. Most of these plays, beginning with *Julius Caesar*, are tragedies; among them are *Hamlet*, *Othello, King Lear*, and *Macbeth*.

About 1610 Shakespeare seems to have left London for Stratford to live the life of a retired gentleman. Probably the last few of his plays, including *The Winter's Tale* and *The Tempest*, were written there. On April 23, 1616, he died and was buried in the chancel of Holy Trinity Church at Stratford.

notes and comments

Character Foils

". . . the noblest Roman . . ."
Julius Caesar, V, iv

In his thirty-seven plays, Shakespeare created a vast array of realistic characters who are as fascinating to modern playgoers as they were to the patrons of the Globe. Brutus—"the noblest Roman of them all"—is one of Shakespeare's most memorable creations.

Shakespeare develops the character of Marcus Brutus through *contrast;* that is, he endows Brutus with a personality that contrasts sharply with the personalities of Cassius and Antony. Early in the play, Brutus emerges as an idealist willing to murder his friend only because he is convinced that Caesar's death will benefit the Roman people. Throughout the play, Brutus will act according to his ideals of what ought to be. In Brutus, idealism is both a strength and a weakness, for it prevents him from seeing people and events as they really are.

Acting as a *foil* to Brutus, is Cassius. Practical as well as ambitious, Cassius is willing to murder Caesar because he envies Caesar's power. He will always be more concerned with action than theory. Cassius, moreover, is a shrewd judge of character. In class discuss whether in persuading Brutus to join the conspiracy, Cassius appeals to Brutus' ambition or to his sense of honor.

During Act Two, Scene 1 (lines 107-161) and Act Three, Scene 1 (lines 231-243), Brutus' idealism overrides Cassius' practicality. Describe these two incidents. Does Cassius reveal a weakness in being too easily influenced by Brutus? Discuss your answer. Brutus overrides Cassius for a third time in Act Four, Scene 3 (lines 166-195). What decision does Brutus make? Do his reasons seem to be practical? Judging from the two previous incidents, do you think his decision will prove to be the right one? Why or why not?

Antony emerges as a *foil* to Brutus in Act Three, Scene 1. How does Antony's personality differ from Brutus'? What incident in this scene excites your admiration for Antony? How does Antony's funeral oration in Scene 2 show that he is a far more clever politician than Brutus could ever be? Would Brutus be capable of the actions that Antony takes in Act Four, Scene 1? Discuss your answer.

A lesser dramatist than Shakespeare would have drawn a superficial contrast, for example, between Brutus (the paragon of virtue) and Antony (the dastardly villain). By contrasting both the strength and the weakness he saw in Brutus, Cassius, and Antony, Shakespeare achieves the realism that makes his characters so memorable.

Julius Caesar, I, iii, "This dreadful night that thunders"

During a performance of *Julius Caesar*, the stagehands and musicians at the Globe were busy creating a variety of special effects.

Act One, Scene 3, for example, calls for a "dreadful night that thunders, lightens, opens graves, and roars." To simulate thunder, stagehands in the huts (above) rolled a cannonball back and forth or down a few stairs. Elizabethan stagehands could create lightning with a squib (a ball of shiny cloth filled with sulfur powder), which they had attached to the top of a long wire. They lowered the wire through the opening in the canopy and then ignited the squib. This small firework rolled down the wire with a fine hissing sound and exploded with a resounding "crack."

Since Elizabethan audiences delighted in the sight of blood and gore, the assassination

scene in Act Three must have pleased them mightily. The actor portraying Caesar probably wore (beneath his costume) a bladder filled with sheep's blood. When the moment for stabbing Caesar arrived, Casca punctured the bladder with his dagger. Later the conspirators "washed" their hands in this blood. It is likely that Antony delivered his funeral oration over a dummy corpse of Caesar. When Antony flung Caesar's cloak aside, the dummy's many gaping wounds undoubtedly horrified the Globe audience.

Stagehands operating the trap doors from "Hell" were responsible for the ghostly appearances. A ghost ascended through the floor traps in the platform or, like the Ghost of Caesar in Act Four, ascended through the floor trap in the inner stage.

If *Julius Caesar* had called

for angels and spirits, the actors portraying these beings would have been lowered and raised (by means of a pulley) through the trap door in the canopy.

The battle scenes in Act Five call for sound effects, such as the clash of arms offstage. The musicians created the alarums with their trumpets, drums, and cymbals. Sometimes real cannons were discharged to increase the realism of a battle scene. However, the use of explosives in a building made of wood and thatch was ill-advised, for it was the discharge of a backstage cannon that destroyed the Globe Playhouse in June of 1613. An eyewitness account describes the fire in this way: ". . . and certain chambers being shot off some of the paper or other stuff wherewith one of them was stopped, did light on the thatch, where being thought at first but an idle smoke . . . it kindled inwardly and ran around like a train, consuming within less than an hour the whole house to the very ground. . . . Nothing did perish but wood and straw, and a few forsaken cloaks. Only one man had his breeches set on fire, that would perhaps have broiled him, if he had not by the benefit of a provident wit put it out with bottle ale."

Act Five

Scene 1: The plains of Philippi.
The combined armies of BRUTUS *and* CASSIUS *have engaged the*
combined forces of ANTONY *and* OCTAVIUS. *Offstage can be heard*
occasional cries, the staccato clash of arms, and the sound of
soldiers fleeing to more distant points. For a moment there is silence;
then BRUTUS *enters at left, followed by* CASSIUS.

CASSIUS.   Now, most noble Brutus,
   The gods today stand friendly, that we may,
   Lovers in peace, lead on our days to age!¹
   But since the affairs of men rest still incertain,
5   Let's reason with the worst that may befall.
   If we do lose this battle, then is this
   The very last time we shall speak together;
   What are you then determined to do?
BRUTUS. Even by the rule of that philosophy²
10   By which I did blame Cato³ for the death
   Which he did give himself—I know not how,
   But I do find it cowardly and vile,
   For fear of what might fall, so to prevent
   The time of life⁴—arming myself with patience
15   To stay the providence of some high powers
   That govern us below.⁵
CASSIUS *(unbelievingly).*   Then if we lose this battle,
   You are contented to be led in triumph
   Through the streets of Rome?
BRUTUS. No, Cassius, no; think not, thou noble Roman,
20   That ever Brutus will go bound to Rome;
   He bears too great a mind. But this same day
   Must end that work the ides of March begun;
   And whether we shall meet again I know not.
   Therefore, our everlasting farewell take;
25   Forever, and forever, farewell, Cassius! *(He places his hand on*
      CASSIUS' *shoulder.)*
   If we do meet again, why, we shall smile;
   If not, why then, this parting was well made.
CASSIUS. Forever, and forever, farewell, Brutus!
   If we do meet again, we'll smile indeed;
30   If not, 'tis true this parting was well made.
BRUTUS. Why, then, lead on. Oh, that a man might know
   The end of this day's business ere it come!
   But it sufficeth that the day will end,
   And then the end is known. Come, ho! Away!
*(*BRUTUS *and* CASSIUS *move off at right.)*

1. *Now . . . lead on our days to age!*
Cassius hopes that the gods will be
on their side so that the two men
will end their days as friends in
peaceful times.

2. *that philosophy.* Stoicism (stō'ə-
siz'əm), which taught indifference
to pleasure or pain. The Stoics did
not believe in suicide.
3. *Cato,* Cato (kā'tō) the Younger,
the father-in-law of Brutus. He had
killed himself rather than submit to
Julius Caesar's tyranny.
4. *to prevent the time of life,* to cut
short one's own life by suicide.
5. *To stay . . . below.* As a Stoic,
Brutus regards suicide as cowardly,
and believes that a man should bear
his troubles with patience and await
(stay) a normal death to be sent
when the gods so decree.

Scene 2: The field of battle.

The battle is well under way. BRUTUS *and his followers form the left flank of the combined army and face the forces of* OCTAVIUS; CASSIUS *and his men form the right flank and are opposed to* ANTONY. BRUTUS, *with* MESSALA *following, enters at left. He has been observing the battle and has prepared various dispatches which he must send to* CASSIUS *and his legions.*

BRUTUS. Ride, ride, Messala, ride and give these bills
    Unto the legions on the other side.
(Loud alarums are heard offstage.)
    Let them set on at once; for I perceive
    But cold demeanor in Octavius' wing,
5   And sudden push gives them the overthrow.[1]
    Ride, ride, Messala; let them all come down.
*(*BRUTUS *and* MESSALA *exit, going in different directions.)*

Scene 3: A hill in another part of the battlefield.

It is now late afternoon. Several SOLDIERS, *disheveled and weary from the fighting, enter at right and group themselves near the left pillar. As offstage alarums sound,* CASSIUS *and* TITINIUS *enter at right.* CASSIUS *carries a broken standard in his left hand. He speaks with great anger.*

CASSIUS *(pointing to right).* Oh, look, Titinius, look, the villains fly!
    Myself have to mine own turned enemy;[1]
    This ensign here of mine was turning back;
    I slew the coward, and did take it[2] from him.
5 TITINIUS. O Cassius, Brutus gave the word too early;
    Who, having some advantage on Octavius,
    Took it too eagerly; his soldiers fell to spoil,
    Whilst we by Antony are all enclosed.[3]
*(*CASSIUS *tosses the broken standard to the* SOLDIERS. *As they move off at left,* PINDARUS, *the servant of* CASSIUS, *runs on at right.)*
PINDARUS. Fly further off, my lord, fly further off;
10 Mark Antony is in your tents, my lord;
    Fly, therefore, noble Cassius, fly far off.
CASSIUS. This hill is far enough. Look, look, Titinius;
    Are those my tents where I perceive the fire?
TITINIUS. They are, my lord.
CASSIUS.   Titinius, if thou lovest me,
15 Mount thou my horse, and hide thy spurs in him,
    Till he have brought thee up to yonder troops,
    And here again; that I may rest assured
    Whether yon troops are friend or enemy.[4]
TITINIUS. I will be here again, even with a thought.[5]
*(*TITINIUS *hurries off at right.)*
20 CASSIUS *(pointing to the balcony).* Go, Pindarus, get higher on that
    hill;

1. *I perceive . . . overthrow.* The signs of faltering (cold demeanor) that Brutus sees in Octavius' men lead him to hazard everything on one swift, punishing general attack.

1. *Myself have to . . . enemy.* Cassius has had to turn on some of his own men who were deserting. Even a standard bearer (ensign) was in headlong flight.
2. *it,* the standard.

3. *his soldiers fell . . . enclosed.* Brutus' soldiers, thinking Cassius' men had attacked at the same time and had been as successful as they, were plundering Octavius' camp. Actually Cassius' forces had been encircled by Antony's men. Their plight seemed doubly tragic to them because they knew it could have been avoided.

4. *that I may rest . . . enemy.* Since so many of his men have deserted, Cassius wonders if the horsemen he sees approaching are deserters from his army or are Antony's men. In reality, they are messengers from Brutus. They are led by Messala and bear tidings of Brutus' victory over Octavius.
5. *even with a thought,* quick as a thought.

My sight was ever thick; regard Titinius,
And tell me what thou not'st about the field.

(PINDARUS *exits at inner-stage curtains in order to ascend the hill.*)

This day I breathèd first; time is come round,
And where I did begin, there shall I end;[6]
25   My life is run his compass. Sirrah, what news?

PINDARUS (*appearing above*). O my lord!

CASSIUS. What news?

PINDARUS. Titinius is enclosèd round about
With horsemen, that make to him on the spur;
30   Yet he spurs on. Now they are almost on him.
Now, Titinius! Now some light. Oh, he lights, too.
He's ta'en.

(*There are shouts offstage*)

                    And, hark! They shout for joy.[7]

CASSIUS. Come down, behold no more.
Oh, coward that I am, to live so long,
35   To see my best friend ta'en before my face!

(PINDARUS *exits at balcony curtains in order to descend from the hill.
In a moment he rejoins* CASSIUS.)

Come hither, sirrah.
In Parthia[8] did I take thee prisoner;
And then I swore thee, saving of thy life,
That whatsoever I did bid thee do,
40   Thou shouldst attempt it.[9] Come now, keep thine oath;
Now be a freeman; and with this good sword,
That ran through Caesar's bowels, search this bosom.[10]
Stand not to answer; here, take thou the hilts;
And, when my face is covered, as 'tis now,
45   Guide thou the sword.

(PINDARUS *obeys and stabs* CASSIUS.)

                    Caesar, thou art revenged.
Even with the sword that killed thee. (CASSIUS *dies.*)

PINDARUS. So, I am free; yet would not so have been,
Durst I have done my will. O Cassius,
Far from this country Pindarus shall run,
50   Where never Roman shall take note of him.

(PINDARUS, *leaving* CASSIUS' *sword behind, hastens to left door and
exits. Then,* TITINIUS, *with* MESSALA, *reenters at right. On his head*
TITINIUS *wears a garland signifying victory.*)

MESSALA. It is but change,[11] Titinius; for Octavius
Is overthrown by noble Brutus' power,
As Cassius' legions are by Antony.

TITINIUS. These tidings will well comfort Cassius.

55   MESSALA. Where did you leave him?

TITINIUS.   All disconsolate,

6. *This day I breathèd . . . end.* This is Cassius' birthday.

7. *He's ta'en . . . shout for joy.* Pindarus misinterprets this meeting. Brutus' messengers are telling Titinius of their victory over Octavius and are giving him a victor's wreath to carry to Cassius.

8. *Parthia* (pär'thē ə), an ancient country in Asia southeast of the Caspian Sea.

9. *And then I swore . . . attempt it.* Pindarus, in return for his life, had had to swear to do whatever Cassius ordered.

10. *Now be a freeman . . . bosom.* Cassius will give Pindarus liberty if he (Pindarus) will kill Cassius.

11. *but change,* a fair exchange.

With Pindarus his bondman, on this hill.

MESSALA. Is not that he that lies upon the ground?

TITINIUS *(running forward).* He lies not like the living. O my heart!

MESSALA. Is not that he?

TITINIUS *(sadly).*   No, this was he, Messala,

60 But Cassius is no more. O setting sun,
    As in thy red rays thou dost sink tonight,
    So in his red blood Cassius' day is set;
    The sun of Rome is set! Our day is gone;
    Clouds, dews, and dangers come; our deeds are done!
65 Mistrust of my success hath done this deed.

MESSALA. Mistrust of good success hath done this deed.
    O hateful error, melancholy's child,
    Why dost thou show to the apt thoughts of men
    The things that are not?[12] O error, soon conceived,
70 Thou never com'st unto a happy birth,
    But kill'st the mother that engendered thee!

TITINIUS *(calling).* What, Pindarus! Where art thou, Pindarus?

MESSALA. Seek him, Titinius, whilst I go to meet
    The noble Brutus, thrusting this report
75 Into his ears; I may say thrusting it,
    For piercing steel and darts envenomed
    Shall be as welcome to the ears of Brutus
    As tidings of this sight.

TITINIUS.   Hie, you, Messala,
    And I will seek for Pindarus the while.

(As MESSALA *exits at left,* TITINIUS *falls to one knee beside* CASSIUS.)

80 Why didst thou send me forth, brave Cassius?
    Did I not meet thy friends? And did not they
    Put on my brows this wreath of victory,
    And bid me give it thee? Didst thou not hear their shouts?
    Alas, thou hast misconstrued everything![13]
85 But, hold thee, take this garland on thy brow;
    Thy Brutus bid me give it thee, and I
    Will do his bidding. *(He rises.)* Brutus, come apace,
    And see how I regarded Caius Cassius. *(He picks up* CASSIUS'
        sword.)
    By your leave, gods—this is a Roman's part;[14]
90 Come, Cassius' sword, and find Titinius' heart. *(He kills him-
        self.)*

(Alarums sound offstage. MESSALA *reenters at left. He is accompanied by* BRUTUS, *young* CATO, STRATO, VOLUMNIUS, LUCILIUS, *and
several* SOLDIERS.)

BRUTUS. Where, where, Messala, doth his body lie?

MESSALA. Lo, yonder, and Titinius mourning it.

BRUTUS. Titinius' face is upward.

12. *Why dost thou . . . not,* why do men so readily accept things as true when they really are not.

13. *Alas, thou hast misconstrued everything!* Titinius is appalled by the fact that Cassius' tragic death is due to a misinterpretation of the meeting between him (Titinius) and Messala's men. Had Cassius realized that the men were Brutus' and that they bore news of a victory, he would still be alive!

14. *this is a Roman's part.* The Romans prided themselves on being freemen, and traditionally preferred death at their own hands to acknowledging another man their master.

(Titinius kills himself
(guilt & grief).

CATO (*going to* TITINIUS). He is slain.

BRUTUS. O Julius Caesar, thou art mighty yet!

95   Thy spirit walks abroad, and turns our swords

    In our own proper entrails.

(*There are low alarums offstage.*)

CATO.   Brave Titinius!

    Look, whether he have not crowned dead Cassius!

BRUTUS. Are yet two Romans living such as these?

    The last of all the Romans, fare thee well!

100   It is impossible that ever Rome

    Should breed thy fellow. Friends, I owe more tears

    To this dead man that you shall see me pay.

    I shall find time, Cassius, I shall find time.

(*He motions to the* SOLDIERS, *who pick up the bodies of* CASSIUS *and*
TITINIUS.)

    Come, therefore, and to Thasos[15] send his body;

105   His funerals shall not be in our camp,

    Lest it discomfort us. Lucilius, come;

    And come, young Cato; let us to the field.

    We shall try fortune in a second fight.

(*All exit at left.*)

Scene 4: *Another part of the battlefield.*

*As the scene begins, a large rock is raised through the trap door in
the center of the platform. Then* VOLUMNIUS, *carrying a lighted torch,
enters at left. He is followed by* BRUTUS, CLITUS, DARDANIUS, *and*
STRATO. *All are overcome with fatigue and their sense of defeat.*

BRUTUS. Come, poor remains of friends, rest on this rock.

CLITUS. Statilius showed the torchlight, but, my lord,

    He came not back; he is or ta'en or slain.[1]

BRUTUS. Sit thee down, Clitus; slaying is the word;

5   It is a deed in fashion. Hark thee, Clitus. (*He whispers to*
        CLITUS.)

CLITUS. What, I, my lord? No, not for all the world.

BRUTUS. Peace, then! No words.

CLITUS (*with fervor*).   I'll rather kill myself.

BRUTUS. Hark thee, Dardanius. (*Again* BRUTUS *whispers his re-
    quest.*)

DARDANIUS (*aghast*).   Shall I do such a deed?

(BRUTUS *walks away from the men.*)

CLITUS. O Dardanius!

10 DARDANIUS. O Clitus!

CLITUS. What ill request did Brutus make to thee?

DARDANIUS. To kill him, Clitus. Look, he meditates.

CLITUS. Now is that noble vessel full of grief,

    That it runs over even at his eyes.

15. **Thasos** (thä'sôs), an island in
the Aegean Sea.

1. **Statilius** (stə til'ē əs) . . . **slain.**
Statilius had volunteered to slip
through the enemy's lines and
observe happenings in their camp;
later—if all was well with him—he
would signal with a torch. Although
his signal was seen, Statilius did not
return. It was thought he lost his
life shortly after he flashed the
signal.

15   **BRUTUS.** Come hither, good Volumnius; list a word.

    VOLUMNIUS *(going to him).* What says my lord?

    BRUTUS.   Why, this,

       Volumnius:

    The ghost of Caesar hath appeared to me

    Two several times by night; at Sardis once,

    And, this last night, here in Philippi fields;

20   I know my hour is come.

    VOLUMNIUS.   Not so, my lord.

    BRUTUS. Nay, I am sure it is, Volumnius.

    Thou seest the world, Volumnius, how it goes;

    Our enemies have beat us to the pit;[2]

(Low alarums sound offstage signaling the approach of ANTONY *and*
OCTAVIUS.*)*

    It is more worthy to leap in ourselves

25   Than tarry till they push us. Good Volumnius,

    Thou know'st that we two went to school together;

    Even for that our love of old, I prithee,[3]

    Hold thou my sword hilts, whilst I run on it.

    VOLUMNIUS. That's not an office for a friend, my lord.

(More alarums are sounded, this time louder.)

30   **CLITUS.** Fly, fly, my lord; there is no tarrying here.

    BRUTUS *(going to each in turn).* Farewell to you; and you; and you,

       Volumnius.

    Strato, thou hast been all this while asleep;

    Farewell to thee, too, Strato. Countrymen,

    My heart doth joy that yet in all my life

35   I found no man but he was true to me.

    I shall have glory by this losing day

    More than Octavius and Mark Antony

    By this vile conquest shall attain unto.

    So fare you well at once; for Brutus' tongue

40   Hath almost ended his life's history;

    Night hangs upon mine eyes; my bones would rest,

    That hath but labored to attain this hour.

*(The alarum grows urgent and is accompanied by cries of "Fly, fly,
fly!")*

    CLITUS. Fly, my lord, fly!

    BRUTUS.   Hence! I will follow.

*(*CLITUS, DARDANIUS, *and* VOLUMNIUS *hurry off at right.* STRATO, *awake
now, starts to follow them.)*

    I prithee, Strato, stay thou by thy lord.

45   Thou art a fellow of a good respect;

    Thy life hath had some smatch[4] of honor in it;

    Hold then my sword, and turn away thy face,

    While I do run upon it. Wilt thou, Strato?

2. *Our enemies have . . . pit,* an allusion to the method of forming a large circle around a wild animal (such as a tiger) and beating on drums to drive it into a pit, where it can be captured.

3. *prithee,* pray thee.

4. *smatch,* taste; touch.

STRATO. Give me your hand first. Fare you well, my lord.

50 BRUTUS. Farewell, good Strato.

(STRATO *takes the sword, and holds it firmly with the blade exposed. As* STRATO *turns his face aside,* BRUTUS *runs upon the naked blade.*)

Caesar, now be still.
I killed not thee with half so good a will. (BRUTUS *dies.*)

(*Offstage trumpets sound retreat as two* SOLDIERS, *bearing torches, enter at left. They light the way for* ANTONY *and* OCTAVIUS. *More* SOLDIERS *follow, among them are* MESSALA *and* LUCILIUS *who have been taken prisoner. All see* STRATO *standing over the dead* BRUTUS.)

OCTAVIUS. What man is that?

MESSALA. My master's man. Strato, where is thy master?

STRATO. Free from the bondage you are in, Messala;

55 The conquerors can but make a fire of him;⁵
For Brutus only overcame himself,
And no man else hath honor by his death.⁶

LUCILIUS. So Brutus should be found.

OCTAVIUS. All that served Brutus, I will entertain them.⁷

60 Fellow, wilt thou bestow thy time with me?

STRATO. Aye, if Messala will prefer⁸ me to you.

OCTAVIUS. Do so, good Messala.

MESSALA. How died my master, Strato?

STRATO. I held the sword, and he did run on it.

65 MESSALA. Octavius, then take him to follow thee,
That did the latest service to my master.

ANTONY (*looking at the body*). This was the noblest Roman of them all.
All the conspirators, save only he,
Did that they did in envy of great Caesar;

70 He only, in a general honest thought
And common good to all, made one of them.⁹
His life was gentle, and the elements
So mixed in him that nature might stand up
And say to all the world, "This was a man!"

(ANTONY *removes his cloak and covers* BRUTUS *with it. He then signals to the* SOLDIERS *who lift* BRUTUS' *body onto their shields.*)

75 OCTAVIUS. According to his virtue let us use him,
With all respect and rites of burial.
Within my tent his bones tonight shall lie,
Most like a soldier, ordered honorable.
So call the field to rest; and let's away

80 To part the glories¹⁰ of this happy day.

(*All exit at right to the solemn accompaniment of offstage drums beating a death march.*)

5. **The conquerors can but make . . . him,** a reference to the Roman custom of burning their dead.

6. **no man else . . . death.** No one can claim the honor of defeating Brutus in combat.

7. **I will entertain them.** Octavius means to take all of Brutus' servants and make them his own.

8. **prefer,** recommend.

9. **made one of them,** joined them.

10. **part the glories,** divide the honors.

Discussion

Scenes 1 and 2

1. As a Stoic, Brutus has not believed in allowing the fortunes or misfortunes of life to affect him and he has frowned on the idea of suicide. Do any of his beliefs seem to be changing? Explain.

2. **(a)** What is the attitude of Brutus and Cassius toward each other as they part before the battle? **(b)** In what mood do Brutus and Cassius say farewell?

3. **(a)** What is the plan of attack that Brutus wishes to put into action? **(b)** For what purpose do you think Scene 2, which is so very short, is included in Act Five?

Scene 3

1. **(a)** What is Cassius' mood as this scene opens? **(b)** What reasons does he have for feeling as he does? **(c)** Who is the person responsible for the existing state of affairs?

2. **(a)** What mistake do Pindarus and Cassius make concerning Titinius? **(b)** What misleads them?

3. **(a)** How are Cassius' decision to die and the manner of his death in keeping with his character? **(b)** How does Pindarus help him? **(c)** Why does the servant flee afterwards?

4. **(a)** What effect does the death of Cassius have on Brutus? **(b)** Why does he exclaim, "O Julius Caesar, thou are mighty yet!"? **(c)** Do you consider Brutus a quitter? Why or why not?

Scene 4

1. As Brutus bids his friends farewell, he says that in all his life he has found "no man but he was true to me." **(a)** Who did take unfair advantage of Brutus' trust? Under what circumstances? **(b)** What does the making of that remark—after all that has happened—show about Brutus' character?

2. What do you think is the significance of Brutus' words as he was about to die: "Caesar, now be still"?

3. **(a)** What was your reaction to Antony's estimate of Brutus? **(b)** Do you feel that Antony was sincere?

4. Decide what the word *tragedy* means to you. Then complete this sentence: The chief tragedy of Brutus' life was . . . .

5. As the play ends, Octavius and Antony speak of dividing the honors that have come from the victory. **(a)** What do you think Rome's future will be under these men? **(b)** From an encyclopedia or a history book find out what actually did happen after the battle at Philippi and see how accurately you prophesied the future.

Vocabulary
Context and Structure

The Latin prefix *en-* means "to cause to be" as in *enfeeble* or "to put in or on" as in *enthrone.* Form new words from the prefix *en-* and the following words. Then choose the correct new words to complete the sentences below. You may need to change the form or tense of the words.

circle   rich
large   shrine
live   venom
noble

1. The student council's treasury was greatly _____ with the profits from the car wash and bake sale.

2. This is such a good picture we want to have it _____ to hang on the living room wall.

3. The swimming pool at the new club is completely _____ with flowering bushes and shrubs.

4. The headhunters of Brazil used to _____ their darts with the juice of a local plant.

5. Roberto's presence always _____ a party.

[handwritten: Pits man against man and society against man]

Shakespearean Tragedy

". . . the death of princes"
Julius Caesar, II, ii

Now that you have read *Julius Caesar*, you can see that a Shakespearean tragedy is more than "a serious play having an unhappy ending." What aspects of *Julius Caesar* are typical of a Shakespearean tragedy?

(1) Shakespeare always develops a *tragic hero* as a focal point of his tragedy. His tragic hero is a nobleman and a leader whose death affects the course of empire. Moreover, Shakespeare endows his tragic hero with a character weakness, or *flaw*, that ultimately causes him to make a fatal mistake. Both Caesar and Brutus qualify as the tragic hero of *Julius Caesar*. What is Caesar's fatal mistake? What weaknesses in his character cause him to make this mistake? What errors in judgment does Brutus commit?

[handwritten: Ignoring signs / Pride Spared Antony, etc. / Naive trust]

What do you consider his tragic flaw to be? Discuss.

(2) Shakespeare builds a tragedy on external and internal *conflicts*. He uses the political controversy in Rome to create the external conflict in *Julius Caesar*. How does Shakespeare develop this external conflict in the play? What internal conflict does Caesar experience? What internal conflict does Brutus experience?

(3) Shakespeare uses *humor* to relieve the somber mood of a tragedy. Describe the two humorous incidents that occur in Act One of *Julius Caesar*. Why would comic relief be inappropriate to Act Three? *[handwritten: p 448 f.]*

(4) Shakespeare often includes a *supernatural* incident in a tragedy. What do the supernatural incidents in *Julius Caesar* reveal about Caesar and Brutus? *[handwritten: Ides of March (lack of regard) Caesar's ghost (can't rest until justice is done.)]*

(5) Major characters in Shakespeare's tragedies are often motivated by a desire for *revenge*. To what extent does revenge figure in *Julius Caesar*? *[handwritten: p 483 A.'s soliloquy]*

(6) Shakespeare introduces *chance happenings* that precipitate tragic catastrophes. In Act Five, Scene 3 of *Julius Caesar*, for example, Cassius and Pindarus misinterpret the meeting between Titinius and Brutus' men. How does this chance happening affect the fortunes of Cassius and Brutus?

A Shakespearean tragedy is a serious blank-verse play having an unhappy ending. In his *Tragedy of Julius Caesar*, Shakespeare combines the following dramatic elements: a tragic hero with a tragic flaw; external and internal conflicts; humorous relief; supernatural incidents; a revenge motive; and a chance happening.

The Taming of the Shrew, IV, iii, ". . . with silken coats and caps . . ."

Costuming on the Elizabethan stage was both lavish and colorful. Shakespeare's fellow actors— "with silken coats and caps and golden rings, with ruffs and cuffs and farthingales and things"—were a brilliant sight to behold.

The costumes worn by Elizabethan actors usually were so costly that it was necessary to protect them from soil or other damage during the course of a performance. For this reason, rushes were strewn on the inner stage, the rear platform, and the outer edges of the platform. When the moment came for an actor to fall down, for example, he would be careful to fall on one of these rush-strewn areas.

Costuming has always been an important visual device to help playgoers distinguish one character from another. Appropriate costuming may also reinforce characterization. In staging their plays, Elizabethan acting companies usually did not attempt to duplicate historical dress. Some of the characters in *Julius Caesar* may have worn Roman robes and cloaks as they do in the illustrations in your textbook. It is more likely, however, that Roman characters wore sixteenth-century dress. The Globe audience did not think it strange to see Brutus and Antony in Elizabethan doublet and hose! When Shakespeare's plays are staged today, some productions will adopt historical dress, while others will adopt modern dress.

Although Elizabethans probably did not duplicate Roman dress in *Julius Caesar*, the chances are that their costumes combined fabric and color in a symbolic way. Englishmen of Shakespeare's time were extremely class-conscious. One indication of a person's "high" or "low" estate was the fabric of his clothing. This was true of stage costumes as well. On the Globe platform, aristocratic Romans would be distinguished by their costumes of satin or taffeta, damask or velvet. The commoners would be identified by their coarse linsey-woolsey; workingmen by their canvas aprons. If the Ghost of Caesar did not wear the same costume as the living Caesar, he would be clad in leather.

Color also symbolized social status to Elizabethans. It was customary in those days to see apprentices, for example, in their liveries of dark blue, and to see Queen Elizabeth I in her state robes of scarlet. On the stage, dark blue was also reserved for one who served, just as scarlet was reserved for one who ruled. In addition to symbolizing social status, color symbolized such abstract qualities as love or courage. A costume with many touches of yellow would indicate that a character was jealous. Similarly, orange would represent pride; azure blue would convey honor; and rose would symbolize gallantry.

7: Julius Caesar

CONTENT REVIEW

1. The physical conditions of an Elizabethan playhouse, like the Globe, made specific demands upon Shakespeare's stagecraft. Reread "notes and comments" on pages 454–455 and pages 473–474; then, answer the following questions.

(a) Elizabethan actors usually spoke between twenty and twenty-five lines a minute. Why did they deliver their lines so rapidly? What problem did this situation create for Shakespeare?

(b) Why is blank verse an excellent medium for dialogue? How does Shakespeare make his blank verse flexible enough to express the complicated thoughts and emotions of his characters? Where in *Julius Caesar* does Shakespeare use prose?

(c) Part of Shakespeare's task was to set his own scenes in his dialogue. Why did he have to do this?

(d) Shakespeare empties the platform at the end of a platform scene. He also shifts the action of the play from one stage to another. Why did Shakespeare use these two visual devices?

2. Shakespeare's insight into the behavior of human beings was profound; no dramatist has ever surpassed him in creating characters that are true to life. Reread "notes and comments" on page 509 before answering the following questions.

(a) What is a character foil? How does Shakespeare use character foils in *Julius Caesar?*

(b) How does Shakespeare make his characters realistic? Cite the realistic qualities that you find in Caesar and Brutus, Antony and Cassius.

3. A *tragedy* may be defined as "a serious play having an unhappy ending." Why is this an inadequate definition of a Shakespearean tragedy? Rereading the first "notes and comments" on page 521 will help you answer this question.

4. Some scholars believe that Shakespeare was correct in titling his play *The Tragedy of Julius Caesar.* Other scholars argue that he should have titled his play *The Tragedy of Marcus Brutus.* Read the following two quotations and then explain which title you prefer and why.

"It is the spirit of Caesar which is the dominant power of the tragedy; against this—the spirit of Caesar—Brutus fought; but Brutus, who forever errs in practical politics, succeeded only in striking down Caesar's body; he who had been weak now rises pure in spirit, strong and terrible, and avenges himself upon the conspirators."

Edward Dowden,
Shakespeare, A Critical Study of His Mind and Heart (Routledge & Kegan Paul, Ltd., 1949).
page 287

"The true hero of the piece is Brutus . . . Shakespeare, having so arranged his drama that Brutus should be its tragic hero, had to concentrate his art on placing him in the foreground, and making him fill the scene. . . . He had to be the center and pivot of everything, and therefore Caesar was diminished and belittled to such a degree, unfortunately, that this matchless genius in war and statesmanship has become a miserable caricature."

Georg M. C. Brandes,
William Shakespeare: A Critical Study (Macmillan, 1936).
page 306

from *Henry the Fourth*, Part Two, Act IV, Scene 5
William Shakespeare

The scene you are about to read comes from one of Shakespeare's history plays which means the people in it actually lived, as did the characters of *Julius Caesar.* The scene concerns the death of King Henry the Fourth. His reign has been a troubled one. He was not born a king, but was crowned after a rebellion. His fellow nobles, dissatisfied with his rule, have constantly rebelled against his authority.

As he lies dying, Henry's hopes for the future of the country are bleak. He feels that his son, the Prince of Wales, is indifferent to the affairs of the crown, and that the boy's irresponsibility will lead to the eventual destruction of the kingdom.

Immediately prior to this scene, the prince, sitting alone at his father's bedside, thinks that the king has died. Deeply grieved, he takes up the crown pledging to defend the honor which has descended to him, and leaves the room. When the king awakens, he misses his son and crown and angrily asks for them. The prince reenters the room.

After you have read the passage, answer the questions on a separate sheet of paper.

CAST OF CHARACTERS
KING HENRY THE FOURTH, King of England
HENRY, PRINCE OF WALES, afterwards KING HENRY THE FIFTH

PRINCE. I never thought to hear you speak again.
KING HENRY. Thy wish was father, Harry, to that thought:
    I stay too long by thee,[1] I weary thee.
    Dost thou so hunger for my empty chair
5   That thou wilt needs invest thee with mine honours
    Before thy hour be ripe? O foolish youth!
    Thou seek'st the greatness that will overwhelm thee.
    Stay but a little; for my cloud of dignity
    Is held from falling with so weak a wind
10   That it will quickly drop: my day is dim.
    Thou hast stol'n that which after some few hours
    Were thine without offence; and at my death
    Thou hast seal'd up[2] my expectation:
    Thy life did manifest thou lov'dst me not,
15   And thou wilt have me die assur'd of it.
    Thou hid'st a thousand daggers in thy thoughts,

1. *by thee,* by your opinion.

2. *seal'd up,* finally confirmed.

Which thou hast whetted on thy stony heart,
To stab at half an hour of my life.
What! canst thou not forbear me half an hour?
20 Then get thee gone and dig my grave thyself,
And bid the merry bells ring to thine ear
That thou art crowned, not that I am dead. . . .
Pluck down my officers, break my decrees;
For now a time is come to mock at form.[3]
25 Harry the Fifth is crown'd! Up, vanity!
Down, royal state! all you sage counsellors, hence!
And to the English court assemble now,
From every region, apes of idleness! . . .
For the fifth Harry from curb'd licence[4] plucks
30 The muzzle of restraint, and the wild dog
Shall flesh[5] his tooth in every innocent.
O my poor kingdom! sick with civil blows.[6]
When that my care could not withhold thy riots,
What wilt thou do when riot is thy care?
35 O! thou wilt be a wilderness again,
Peopled with wolves, thy old inhabitants.
PRINCE. O! pardon me, my liege; but for many tears,
The moist impediments unto my speech,
I had forestall'd this dear[7] and deep rebuke
40 Ere you with grief had spoke and I had heard
The course of it so far. There is your crown;
And he that wears the crown immortally
Long guard it yours! If I affect[8] it more
Than as your honour and as your renown,
45 Let me no more from this obedience[9] rise,—
Which my most true and inward duteous spirit
Teacheth,—this prostrate and exterior bending.
God witness with me, when I here came in,
And found no course of breath within your majesty,
50 How cold it struck my heart! If I do feign,
O! let me in my present wildness die
And never live to show the incredulous world
The noble change that I have purposed.
Coming to look on you, thinking you dead,
55 And dead almost, my liege, to think you were,
I spake unto the crown as having sense,
And thus upbraided it: 'The care on thee depending
Hath fed upon the body of my father;
Therefore, thou best of gold art worst of gold:
60 Other, less fine in carat,[10] is more precious,
Preserving life in medicine potable:[11]
But thou most fine, most honour'd, most renown'd,

3. *form,* order.

4. *curb'd licence,* restrained vice.

5. *flesh,* imbed in flesh, bite.
6. *civil blows,* civil wars.

7. *dear,* earnest.

8. *affect,* desire.

9. *obedience,* act of obedience, i.e., kneeling.

10. *carat,* a measure of the purity of gold.
11. *medicine potable,* refers to *aurum potabile,* a liquid medicine containing gold, thought suitable for curing illness by primitive physicians.

Hast eat thy bearer up.' Thus, my most royal liege,
Accusing it, I put it on my head,
65 To try with it, as with an enemy
That had before my face murder'd my father,
The quarrel of a true inheritor.
But if it did infect my blood with joy,
Or swell my thoughts to any strain of pride; . . .
70 Let God forever keep it from my head,
And make me as the poorest vassal[12] is
That doth with awe and terror kneel to it!

KING HENRY. O my son
God put it in thy mind to take it hence,
75 That thou mightst win the more thy father's love,
Pleading so wisely in excuse of it.
Come hither, Harry: sit thou by my bed;
And hear, I think, the very latest[13] counsel
That ever I shall breathe. God knows, my son,
80 By what by-paths and indirect crook'd ways
I met[14] this crown; and I myself know well
How troublesome it sat upon my head:
To thee it shall descend with better quiet,
Better opinion, better confirmation;
85 For all the soil of the achievement[15] goes
With me into the earth. It seem'd in me
But as an honour snatch'd with boisterous hand,
And I had many living to upbraid
My gain of it by their assistances;
90 Which daily grew to quarrel and to bloodshed,
Wounding supposed[16] peace. All these bold fears
Thou seest with peril I have answered; . . .
Yet, though thou stand'st more sure than I could do,
Thou art not firm enough, since griefs are green;[17]
95 And all my friends, which thou must make thy friends,
Have but their stings and teeth newly ta'en out;
By whose fell working[18] I was first advanc'd,
And by whose power I well might lodge a fear
To be again displac'd: which to avoid
100 I cut them off; and had a purpose now
To lead out many to the Holy Land,
Lest rest and lying still might make them look
Too near unto my state.[19] Therefore, my Harry,
Be it thy course to busy giddy minds
105 With foreign quarrels; that action, hence borne out,
May waste the memory of the former days.
More would I, but my lungs are wasted so
That strength of speech is utterly denied me.

12. *vassal,* slave.

13. *latest,* last.

14. *met,* gained.

15. *soil . . . achievement,* the shame of the winning.

16. *supposed,* imaginary.

17. *griefs are green,* griefs are fresh.

18. *fell working,* fierce labors.

19. *look . . . state,* examine my claims to the throne too closely.

How I came by the crown, O God, forgive!
110 And grant it may with thee in true peace live.
PRINCE. My gracious liege,
You won it, wore it, kept it, gave it me;
Then plain and right must my possession be:
Which I with more than with a common pain
115 'Gainst all the world will rightfully maintain.

A. Multiple Choice

Write the letter indicating the best answer.

1. When Harry enters, his father accuses him of (a) wishing him dead; (b) plotting his death; (c) being indifferent to his death; (d) false grief over his death.

2. Lines 16–18 contain an example of (a) allusion; (b) alliteration; (c) extended metaphor; (d) irony.

3. In lines 23–26 the King predicts for Harry a reign that is (a) prosperous; (b) filled with foreign wars; (c) lawless and confused; (d) uneventful.

4. The Prince says (lines 56–63) the crown has "eaten up" the King. Here the crown is a symbol of (a) graft and corruption; (b) the demands of kingship; (c) Harry's indifference; (d) the senseless desire of Harry for more power.

5. The King thinks (lines 73–79) this quarrel has (a) severed them forever; (b) strained his wits; (c) brought them closer together; (d) wasted too much time.

6. In this scene the conflict is caused by (a) evil forces; (b) misunderstanding; (c) petty hatreds; (d) clever trickery.

7. The tone of the King's final speech (lines 73–110) is (a) light-hearted; (b) fatherly; (c) condescending; (d) desolate.

B. Short Answer

Write the word or phrase that best answers the question.

8. King Henry suggests that his son initiate some overseas wars. Why?

9. What is the turning point in the conflict of this scene? Cite the line numbers.

10. Does King Henry think the crown will "descend with better quiet" (line 83) to his son? Why or why not?

Unit 7, Test II
COMPOSITION

From the assignments below choose one to write about.

1. Discuss Shakespeare's use of the supernatural in *Julius Caesar* and the effect it has on character and events.

2. Assume that you are a journalist in Caesar's time. Compose an editorial that, according to your opinions, either defends Brutus' actions or denounces them.

3. Write a study of Antony's character as presented in *Julius Caesar*. Cite specific examples to back up your statements.

4. You are writing an address for a symposium on governmental power. Discuss various aspects of governmental authority as found in *Julius Caesar* and the scene from *Henry the Fourth*. In your address cover the following questions: How is governmental authority gained and transferred from one power to another? In which cases is power used for good? for bad? What effect does power have on those in authority? What effect does power have on those who are ruled?

THE NOVELLA
Neighbour Rosicky
WILLA CATHER

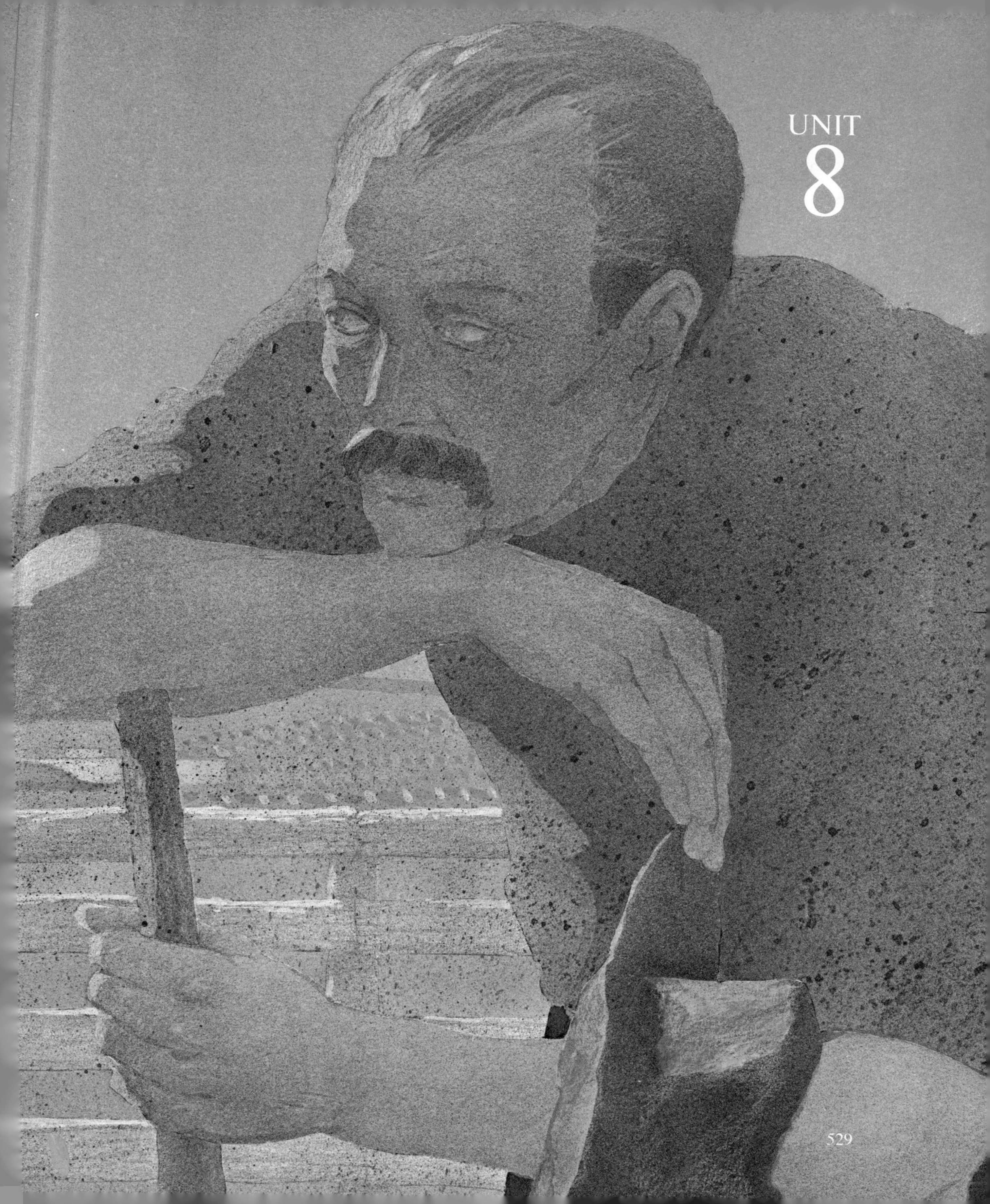

UNIT
8

I

When Doctor Burleigh told neighbour Rosicky he had a bad heart, Rosicky protested.

"So? No, I guess my heart was always pretty good. I got a little asthma, maybe. Just a awful short breath when I was pitchin' hay last summer, dat's all."

"Well now, Rosicky, if you know more about it than I do, what did you come to me for? It's your heart that makes you short of breath, I tell you. You're sixty-five years old, and you've always worked hard, and your heart's tired. You've got to be careful from now on, and you can't do heavy work any more. You've got five boys at home to do it for you."

The old farmer looked up at the Doctor with a gleam of amusement in his queer triangular-shaped eyes. His eyes were large and lively, but the lids were caught up in the middle in a curious way, so that they formed a triangle. He did not look like a sick man. His brown face was creased but not wrinkled, he had a ruddy colour in his smooth-shaven cheeks and in his lips, under his long brown moustache. His hair was thin and ragged around his ears, but very little grey. His forehead, naturally high and crossed by deep parallel lines, now ran all the way up to his pointed crown. Rosicky's face had the habit of looking interested,—suggested a contented disposition and a reflective quality that was gay rather than grave. This gave him a certain detachment, the easy manner of an onlooker and observer.

"Well, I guess you ain't got no pills fur a bad heart, Doctor Ed. I guess the only thing is fur me to git me a new one."

Doctor Burleigh swung round in his desk-chair and frowned at the old farmer. "I think if I were you I'd take a little care of the old one, Rosicky."

Rosicky shrugged. "Maybe I don't know how. I expect you mean fur me not to drink my coffee no more."

"I wouldn't, in your place. But you'll do as you choose about that. I've never yet been able to separate a Bohemian from his coffee or his pipe. I've quit trying. But the sure thing is you've got to cut out farm work. You can feed the stock and do chores about the barn, but you can't do anything in the fields that makes you short of breath."

"How about shelling corn?"

"Of course not!"

Rosicky considered with puckered brows.

"I can't make my heart go no longer'n it wants to, can I, Doctor Ed?"

"I think it's good for five or six years yet, maybe more, if you'll take the strain off it. Sit around the house and help Mary. If I had a good wife like yours, I'd want to stay around the house."

His patient chuckled. "It ain't no place fur a man. I don't like no old man hanging round the kitchen too much. An' my wife, she's a awful hard worker her own self."

"That's it; you can help her a little. My heavens, Rosicky, you are one of the few men I know who has a family he can get some comfort out of; happy dispositions, never quarrel among themselves, and they treat you right. I want to see you live a few years and enjoy them."

"Oh, they're good kids, all right," Rosicky assented.

The Doctor wrote him a prescription and asked him how his oldest son, Rudolph, who had married in the spring, was getting on. Rudolph had struck out for himself, on rented land. "And how's Polly? I was afraid Mary mightn't like an American daughter-in-law, but it seems to be working out all right."

"Yes, she's a fine girl. Dat widder woman bring her daughters up very nice. Polly got lots of spunk, an' she got some style, too. Da's nice, for young folks to have some style." Rosicky inclined his head gallantly. His voice and his

Copyright 1932 by Willa Cather and renewed 1960 by The Executors of the Estate of Willa Cather. Reprinted from OBSCURE DESTINIES, by Willa Cather, by permission of Alfred A. Knopf, Inc.

twinkly smile were an affectionate compliment to his daughter-in-law.

"It looks like a storm, and you'd better be getting home before it comes. In town in the car?" Doctor Burleigh rose.

"No, I'm in de wagon. When you got five boys, you ain't got much chance to ride round in de Ford. I ain't much for cars, noway."

"Well, it's a good road out to your place; but I don't want you bumping around in a wagon much. And never again on a hay-rake, remember!"

Rosicky placed the Doctor's fee delicately behind the desk-telephone, looking the other way, as if this were an absent-minded gesture. He put on his plush cap and his corduroy jacket with a sheepskin collar, and went out.

The Doctor picked up his stethoscope and frowned at it as if he were seriously annoyed with the instrument. He wished it had been telling tales about some other man's heart, some old man who didn't look the Doctor in the eye so knowingly, or hold out such a warm brown hand when he said good-bye. Doctor Burleigh had been a poor boy in the country before he went away to medical school; he had known Rosicky almost ever since he could remember, and he had a deep affection for Mrs. Rosicky.

Only last winter he had had such a good breakfast at Rosicky's, and that when he needed it. He had been out all night on a long, hard confinement case at Tom Marshall's,—a big rich farm where there was plenty of stock and plenty of feed and a great deal of expensive farm machinery of the newest model, and no comfort whatever. The woman had too many children and too much work, and she was no manager. When the baby was born at last, and handed over to the assisting neighbour woman, and the mother was properly attended to, Burleigh refused any breakfast in that slovenly house, and drove his buggy—the snow was too deep for a car—eight miles to Anton Rosicky's place. He didn't know another farm-house where a man could get such a warm welcome and such good strong coffee with rich cream. No won-

der the old chap didn't want to give up his coffee!

He had driven in just when the boys had come back from the barn and were washing up for breakfast. The long table, covered with a bright oilcloth, was set out with dishes waiting for them, and the warm kitchen was full of the smell of coffee and hot biscuit and sausage. Five big handsome boys, running from twenty to twelve, all with what Burleigh called natural good manners,—they hadn't a bit of the painful self-consciousness he himself had to struggle with when he was a lad. One ran to put his horse away, another helped him off with his fur coat and hung it up, and Josephine, the youngest child and the only daughter, quickly set another place under her mother's direction.

With Mary, to feed creatures was the natural expression of affection,—her chickens, the calves, her big hungry boys. It was a rare pleasure to feed a young man whom she seldom saw and of whom she was as proud as if he belonged to her. Some country housekeepers would have stopped to spread a white cloth over the oilcloth, to change the thick cups and plates for their best china, and the wooden-handled knives for plated ones. But not Mary.

"You must take us as you find us, Doctor Ed. I'd be glad to put out my good things for you if you was expected, but I'm glad to get you any way at all."

He knew she was glad,—she threw back her head and spoke out as if she were announcing him to the whole prairie. Rosicky hadn't said anything at all; he merely smiled his twinkling smile, put some more coal on the fire, and went into his own room to pour the Doctor a little drink in a medicine glass. When they were all seated, he watched his wife's face from his end of the table and spoke to her in Czech. Then, with the instinct of politeness which seldom failed him, he turned to the Doctor and said slyly, "I was just tellin' her not to ask you no questions about Mrs. Marshall till you eat some breakfast. My wife, she's terrible fur to ask questions."

The boys laughed, and so did Mary. She watched the Doctor devour her biscuit and sausage, too much excited to eat anything herself. She drank her coffee and sat taking in everything about her visitor. She had known him when he was a poor country boy, and was boastfully proud of his success, always saying: "What do people go to Omaha for, to see a doctor, when we got the best one in the State right here?" If Mary liked people at all, she felt physical pleasure in the sight of them, personal exultation in any good fortune that came to them. Burleigh didn't know many women like that, but he knew she was like that.

When his hunger was satisfied, he did, of course, have to tell them about Mrs. Marshall, and he noticed what a friendly interest the boys took in the matter.

Rudolph, the oldest one (he was still living at home then), said: "The last time I was over there, she was lifting them big heavy milk-cans, and I knew she oughtn't to be doing it."

"Yes, Rudolph told me about that when he come home, and I said it wasn't right," Mary put in warmly. "It was all right for me to do them things up to the last, for I was terrible strong, but that woman's weakly. And do you think she'll be able to nurse it, Ed?" She sometimes forgot to give him the title she was so proud of. "And to think of your being up all night and then not able to get a decent breakfast! I don't know what's the matter with such people."

"Why, Mother," said one of the boys, "if Doctor Ed had got breakfast there, we wouldn't have him here. So you ought to be glad."

"He knows I'm glad to have him, John, any time. But I'm sorry for that poor woman, how bad she'll feel the Doctor had to go away in the cold without his breakfast."

"I wish I'd been in practice when these were getting born." The doctor looked down the row of close-clipped heads. "I missed some good breakfasts by not being."

The boys began to laugh at their mother because she flushed so red, but she stood her ground and threw up her head. "I don't care, you wouldn't have got away from this house without breakfast. No doctor ever did. I'd have had something ready fixed that Anton could warm up for you."

The boys laughed harder than ever, and exclaimed at her: "I'll bet you would!" "She would, that!"

"Father, did you get breakfast for the doctor when we were born?"

"Yes, and he used to bring me my breakfast,

too, mighty nice. I was always awful hungry!'' Mary admitted with a guilty laugh.

While the boys were getting the Doctor's horse, he went to the window to examine the house plants. "What do you do to your geraniums to keep them blooming all winter, Mary? I never pass this house that from the road I don't see your windows full of flowers.''

She snapped off a dark red one, and a ruffled new green leaf, and put them in his buttonhole. "There, that looks better. You look too solemn for a young man, Ed. Why don't you git married? I'm worried about you. Settin' at breakfast, I looked at you real hard, and I seen you've got some grey hairs already.''

"Oh, yes! They're coming. Maybe they'd come faster if I married.''

"Don't talk so. You'll ruin your health eating at the hotel. I could send your wife a nice loaf of nut bread, if you only had one. I don't like to see a young man getting grey. I'll tell you something, Ed; you make some strong black tea and keep it handy in a bowl, and every morning just brush it into your hair, an' it'll keep the grey from showin' much. That's the way I do!''

Sometimes the Doctor heard the gossipers in the drug-store wondering why Rosicky didn't get on faster. He was industrious, and so were his boys, but they were rather free and easy, weren't pushers, and they didn't always show good judgment. They were comfortable, they were out of debt, but they didn't get much ahead. Maybe, Doctor Burleigh reflected, people as generous and warm-hearted and affectionate as the Rosickys never got ahead much; maybe you couldn't enjoy your life and put it into the bank, too.

II

When Rosicky left Doctor Burleigh's office he went into the farm-implement store to light his pipe and put on his glasses and read over the list Mary had given him. Then he went into the general merchandise place next door and stood about until the pretty girl with the plucked eyebrows, who always waited on him, was free. Those eyebrows, two thin India-ink strokes, amused him, because he remembered how they used to be. Rosicky always prolonged his shopping by a little joking; the girl knew the old fellow admired her, and she liked to chaff with him.

"Seems to me about every other week you buy ticking, Mr. Rosicky, and always the best quality,'' she remarked as she measured off the heavy bolt with red stripes.

"You see, my wife is always makin' goose-fedder pillows, an' de thin stuff don't hold in dem little down-fedders.''

"You must have lots of pillows at your house.''

"Sure. She makes quilts of dem, too. We sleeps easy. Now she's makin' a fedder quilt for my son's wife. You know Polly, that married my Rudolph. How much my bill, Miss Pearl?''

"Eight eighty-five.''

"Chust make it nine, and put in some candy fur de women.''

"As usual. I never did see a man buy so much candy for his wife. First thing you know, she'll be getting too fat.''

"I'd like dat. I ain't much fur all dem slim women like what de style is now.''

"That's one for me, I suppose, Mr. Bohunk!''[1] Pearl sniffed and elevated her India-ink strokes.

When Rosicky went out to his wagon, it was beginning to snow,—the first snow of the season, and he was glad to see it. He rattled out of town and along the highway through a wonderfully rich stretch of country, the finest farms in the county. He admired this High Prairie, as it was called, and always liked to drive through it. His own place lay in a rougher territory, where there was some clay in the soil and it was not so productive. When he bought his land, he hadn't the money to buy on High Prairie; so he told his

1. **Bohunk,** a derogatory term for someone from east central or southeastern Europe.

boys, when they grumbled, that if their land hadn't some clay in it, they wouldn't own it at all. All the same, he enjoyed looking at these fine farms, as he enjoyed looking at a prize bull.

After he had gone eight miles, he came to the graveyard, which lay just at the edge of his own hay-land. There he stopped his horses and sat still on his wagon seat, looking about at the snowfall. Over yonder on the hill he could see his own house, crouching low, with the clump of orchard behind and the windmill before, and all down the gentle hill-slope the rows of pale gold cornstalks stood out against the white field. The snow was falling over the cornfield and the pasture and the hay-land, steadily, with very little wind,—a nice dry snow. The graveyard had only a light wire fence about it and was all overgrown with long red grass. The fine snow, settling into this red grass and upon the few little evergreens and the headstones, looked very pretty.

It was a nice graveyard, Rosicky reflected, sort of snug and homelike, not cramped or mournful,—a big sweep all round it. A man could lie down in the long grass and see the complete arch of the sky over him, hear the wagons go by; in summer the mowing-machine rattled right up to the wire fence. And it was so near home. Over there across the cornstalks his own roof and windmill looked so good to him that he promised himself to mind the Doctor and take care of himself. He was awful fond of his place, he admitted. He wasn't anxious to leave it. And it was a comfort to think that he would never have to go farther than the edge of his own hayfield. The snow, falling over his barnyard and the graveyard, seemed to draw things together like. And they were all old neighbours in the grave-yard, most of them friends; there was nothing to feel awkward or embarrassed about. Embarrassment was the most disagreeable feeling Rosicky knew. He didn't often have it,—only with certain people whom he didn't understand at all.

Well, it was a nice snowstorm; a fine sight to see the snow falling so quietly and graciously over so much open country. On his cap and

shoulders, on the horses' backs and manes, light, delicate, mysterious it fell; and with it a dry cool fragrance was released into the air. It meant rest for vegetation and men and beasts, for the ground itself; a season of long nights for sleep, leisurely breakfasts, peace by the fire. This and much more went through Rosicky's mind, but he merely told himself that winter was coming, clucked to his horses, and drove on.

When he reached home, John, the youngest boy, ran out to put away his team for him, and he met Mary coming up from the outside cellar with her apron full of carrots. They went into the house together. On the table, covered with oilcloth figured with clusters of blue grapes, a place was set, and he smelled hot coffee-cake of some kind. Anton never lunched in town; he thought that extravagant, and anyhow he didn't like the food. So Mary always had something ready for him when he got home.

After he was settled in his chair, stirring his coffee in a big cup, Mary took out of the oven a pan of *kolache*[2] stuffed with apricots, examined them anxiously to see whether they had got too dry, put them beside his plate, and then sat down opposite him.

Rosicky asked her in Czech if she wasn't going to have any coffee.

She replied in English, as being somehow the right language for transacting business: "Now what did Doctor Ed say, Anton? You tell me just what."

"He said I was to tell you some compliments, but I forgot 'em." Rosicky's eyes twinkled.

"About you, I mean. What did he say about your asthma?"

"He says I ain't got no asthma." Rosicky took one of the little rolls in his broad brown fingers. The thickened nail of his right thumb told the story of his past.

"Well, what is the matter? And don't try to put me off."

"He don't say nothing much, only I'm a little

2. *kolache* (kə lä′chē), a rich pastry with fruit or poppyseed filling originating in eastern Europe. [Czech]

older, and my heart ain't so good like it used to be.''

Mary started and brushed her hair back from her temples with both hands as if she were a little out of her mind. From the way she glared, she might have been in a rage with him.

"He says there's something the matter with your heart? Doctor Ed says so?''

"Now don't yell at me like I was a hog in de garden, Mary. You know I always did like to hear a woman talk soft. He didn't say anything de matter wid my heart, only it ain't so young like it used to be, an' he tell me not to pitch hay or run de corn-sheller.''

Mary wanted to jump up, but she sat still. She admired the way he never under any circumstances raised his voice or spoke roughly. He was city-bred, and she was country-bred; she often said she wanted her boys to have their papa's nice ways.

"You never have no pain there, do you? It's your breathing and your stomach that's been wrong. I wouldn't believe nobody but Doctor Ed about it. I guess I'll go see him myself. Didn't he give you no advice?''

"Chust to take it easy like, an' stay round de house dis winter. I guess you got some carpenter work for me to do. I kin make some new shelves for you, and I want dis long time to build a closet in de boys' room and make dem two little fellers keep dere clo'es hung up.''

Rosicky drank his coffee from time to time, while he considered. His moustache was of the soft long variety and came down over his mouth like the teeth of a buggy-rake over a bundle of hay. Each time he put down his cup, he ran his blue handkerchief over his lips. When he took a drink of water, he managed very neatly with the back of his hand.

Mary sat watching him intently, trying to find any change in his face. It is hard to see anyone who has become like your own body to you. Yes, his hair had got thin, and his high forehead had deep lines running from left to right. But his neck, always clean shaved except in the busiest seasons, was not loose or baggy. It was burned a dark reddish brown, and there were deep creases in it, but it looked firm and full of blood. His cheeks had a good colour. On either side of his mouth there was a half-moon down the length of his cheek, not wrinkles, but two lines that had come there from his habitual expression. He was shorter and broader than when she married him; his back had grown broad and curved, a good deal like the shell of an old turtle, and his arms and legs were short.

He was fifteen years older than Mary, but she had hardly ever thought about it before. He was her man, and the kind of man she liked. She was rough, and he was gentle,—city-bred, as she always said. They had been shipmates on a rough voyage and had stood by each other in trying times. Life had gone well with them because, at bottom, they had the same ideas about life. They agreed, without discussion, as to what was most important and what was secondary. They didn't often exchange opinions, even in Czech,—it was as if they had thought the same thought together. A good deal had to be sacrificed and thrown overboard in a hard life like theirs, and they had never disagreed as to the things that could go. It had been a hard life, and a soft life, too. There wasn't anything brutal in the short, broad-backed man with the three-cornered eyes and the forehead that went on to the top of his skull. He was a city man, a gentle man, and though he had married a rough farm girl, he had never touched her without gentleness.

They had been at one accord not to hurry through life, not to be always skimping and saving. They saw their neighbours buy more land and feed more stock than they did, without discontent. Once when the creamery agent came to the Rosickys to persuade them to sell him their cream, he told them how much money the Fasslers, their nearest neighbours, had made on their cream last year.

"Yes," said Mary, "and look at them Fassler children! Pale, pinched little things, they look like skimmed milk. I'd rather put some colour into my children's faces than put money into the bank."

The agent shrugged and turned to Anton.

"I guess we'll do like she says," said Rosicky.

Discussion

1. Describe Anton Rosicky's reaction to Dr. Burleigh's news that his heart is weak and probably will be good for only five or six more years. What does his reaction tell us about his character?

2. After Rosicky leaves the doctor's office, Dr. Burleigh remembers having breakfast the past winter with the Rosickys. **(a)** How had Dr. Burleigh come to breakfast at the Rosickys'? **(b)** What does Dr. Burleigh's recollection reveal about the kind of family the Rosickys are?

3. At the end of Part I, Dr. Burleigh thinks about the Rosickys' life and concludes: " . . . maybe you couldn't enjoy your life and put it into the bank, too." Explain and discuss.

4. After leaving the doctor's office, Rosicky does some shopping for his wife Mary. At the store he chats with the clerk. What does this episode tell us about Rosicky's nature?

5. On the way home from town, Rosicky stops his wagon by the graveyard and looks on it with some pleasure. "The snow, falling over his barnyard and the graveyard, seemed to draw things together like." Why does this thought appear to give satisfaction to Rosicky? Discuss.

6. (a) What is Mary's reaction to Rosicky's news from the doctor? **(b)** How does her reaction bring out the differences between her nature and her husband's?

III

Mary very soon got into town to see Doctor Ed, and then she had a talk with her boys and set a guard over Rosicky. Even John, the youngest, had his father on his mind. If Rosicky went to throw hay down from the loft, one of the boys ran up the ladder and took the fork from him. He sometimes complained that though he was getting to be an old man, he wasn't an old woman yet.

That winter he stayed in the house in the afternoons and carpentered, or sat in the chair between the window full of plants and the wooden bench where the two pails of drinking-water stood. This spot was called "Father's corner," though it was not a corner at all. He had a shelf there, where he kept his Bohemian papers and his pipes and tobacco, and his shears and needles and thread and tailor's thimble. Having been a tailor in his youth, he couldn't bear to see a woman patching at his clothes, or at the boys'. He liked tailoring, and always patched all the overalls and jackets and work shirts. Occasionally he made over a pair of pants one of the older boys had outgrown, for the little fellow.

While he sewed, he let his mind run back over his life. He had a good deal to remember, really; life in three countries. The only part of his youth he didn't like to remember was the two years he had spent in London, in Cheapside, working for a German tailor who was wretchedly poor. Those days, when he was nearly always hungry, when his clothes were dropping off him for dirt, and the sound of a strange language kept him in continual bewilderment, had left a sore spot in his mind that wouldn't bear touching.

He was twenty when he landed at Castle Garden in New York, and he had a protector who got him work in a tailor shop in Vesey Street, down near the Washington Market. He looked upon that part of his life as very happy. He became a good workman, he was industrious, and his wages were increased from time to time. He minded his own business and envied no-

body's good fortune. He went to night school and learned to read English. He often did over-time work and was well paid for it, but somehow he never saved anything. He couldn't refuse a loan to a friend, and he was self-indulgent. He liked a good dinner, and a little went for beer, a little for tobacco; a good deal went to the girls. He often stood through an opera on Saturday nights; he could get standing-room for a dollar. Those were the great days of opera in New York, and it gave a fellow something to think about for the rest of the week. Rosicky had a quick ear, and a childish love of all the stage splendour; the scenery, the costumes, the ballet. He usually went with a chum, and after the performance they had beer and maybe some oysters somewhere. It was a fine life; for the first five years or so it satisfied him completely. He was never hungry or cold or dirty, and everything amused him: a fire, a dog fight, a parade, a storm, a ferry ride. He thought New York the finest, richest, friendliest city in the world.

Moreover, he had what he called a happy home life. Very near the tailor shop was a small furniture-factory, where an old Austrian, Loeffler, employed a few skilled men and made unusual furniture, most of it to order, for the rich

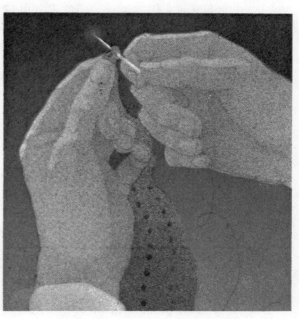

German housewives up-town. The top floor of Loeffler's five-storey factory was a loft, where he kept his choice lumber and stored the odd pieces of furniture left on his hands. One of the young workmen he employed was a Czech, and he and Rosicky became fast friends. They persuaded Loeffler to let them have a sleeping-room in one corner of the loft. They bought good beds and bedding and had their pick of the furniture kept up there. The loft was low-pitched, but light and airy, full of windows, and good-smelling by reason of the fine lumber put up there to season. Old Loeffler used to go down to the docks and buy wood from South America and the East from the sea captains. The young men were as foolish about their house as a bridal pair. Zichec, the young cabinet-maker, devised every sort of convenience, and Rosicky kept their clothes in order. At night and on Sundays, when the quiver of machinery underneath was still, it was the quietest place in the world, and on summer nights all the sea winds blew in. Zichec often practised on his flute in the evening. They were both fond of music and went to the opera together. Rosicky thought he wanted to live like that for ever.

But as the years passed, all alike, he began to get a little restless. When spring came round, he would begin to feel fretted, and he got to drinking. He was likely to drink too much of a Saturday night. On Sunday he was languid and heavy, getting over his spree. On Monday he plunged into work again. So he never had time to figure out what ailed him, though he knew something did. When the grass turned green in Park Place, and the lilac hedge at the back of Trinity churchyard put out its blossoms, he was tormented by a longing to run away. That was why he drank too much; to get a temporary illusion of freedom and wide horizons.

Rosicky, the old Rosicky, could remember as if it were yesterday the day when the young Rosicky found out what was the matter with him. It was on a Fourth of July afternoon, and he was sitting in Park Place in the sun. The lower part of New York was empty. Wall Street, Liberty Street, Broadway, all empty. So much stone and asphalt with nothing going on, so many empty windows. The emptiness was intense, like the stillness in a great factory when the machinery stops and the belts and bands cease running. It was too great a change, it took all the strength out of one. Those blank buildings, without the stream of life pouring through them, were like empty jails. It struck young Rosicky that this was the trouble with big cities; they built you in from the earth itself, cemented you away from any contact with the ground. You lived in an unnatural world, like the fish in an aquarium, who were probably much more comfortable than they ever were in the sea.

On that very day he began to think seriously about the articles he had read in the Bohemian papers, describing prosperous Czech farming communities in the West. He believed he would like to go out there as a farm hand; it was hardly possible that he could ever have land of his own. His people had always been workmen; his father and grandfather had worked in shops. His mother's parents had lived in the country, but they rented their farm and had a hard time to get along. Nobody in his family had ever owned any land,—that belonged to a different station of life altogether. Anton's mother died when he was little, and he was sent into the country to her parents. He stayed with them until he was twelve, and formed those ties with the earth and the farm animals and growing things which are never made at all unless they are made early. After his grandfather died, he went back to live with his father and stepmother, but she was very hard on him, and his father helped him to get passage to London.

After that Fourth of July day in Park Place, the desire to return to the country never left him. To work on another man's farm would be all he asked; to see the sun rise and set and to plant things and watch them grow. He was a very simple man. He was like a tree that has not many roots, but one tap-root that goes down deep. He subscribed for a Bohemian paper printed in Chicago, then for one printed in Omaha. His mind got farther and farther west. He began to save a little money to buy his liberty. When he was thirty-five, there was a great meeting in New York of Bohemian athletic societies, and Rosicky left the tailor shop and went home with the Omaha delegates to try his fortune in another part of the world.

IV

Perhaps the fact that his own youth was well over before he began to have a family was one reason why Rosicky was so fond of his boys. He had almost a grandfather's indulgence for them. He had never had to worry about any of them—except, just now, a little about Rudolph.

On Saturday night the boys always piled into the Ford, took little Josephine, and went to town to the moving-picture show. One Saturday morning they were talking at the breakfast table about starting early that evening, so that they would have an hour or so to see the Christmas things in the stores before the show began. Rosicky looked down the table.

"I hope you boys ain't disappointed, but I want you to let me have de car tonight. Maybe some of you can go in with de neighbours."

Their faces fell. They worked hard all week, and they were still like children. A new jack-knife or a box of candy pleased the older ones as much as the little fellow.

"If you and Mother are going to town," Frank said, "maybe you could take a couple of us along with you, anyway."

"No, I want to take de car down to Rudolph's, and let him an' Polly go in to de show. She don't git into town enough, an' I'm afraid she's gettin' lonesome, an' he can't afford no car yet."

That settled it. The boys were a good deal dashed. Their father took another piece of apple-cake and went on: "Maybe next Saturday night de two little fellers can go along wid dem."

"Oh, is Rudolph going to have the car every Saturday night?"

Rosicky did not reply at once; then he began to speak seriously: "Listen, boys; Polly ain't lookin' so good. I don't like to see nobody lookin' sad. It comes hard fur a town girl to be a farmer's wife. I don't want no trouble to start in Rudolph's family. When it starts, it ain't so easy to stop. An American girl don't git used to our

ways all at once. I like to tell Polly she and Rudolph can have the car every Saturday night till after New Year's, if it's all right with you boys.''

''Sure it's all right, Papa,'' Mary cut in. ''And it's good you thought about that. Town girls is used to more than country girls. I lay awake nights, scared she'll make Rudolph discontented with the farm.''

The boys put as good a face on it as they could. They surely looked forward to their Saturday nights in town. That evening Rosicky drove the car the half-mile down to Rudolph's new, bare little house.

Polly was in a short-sleeved gingham dress, clearing away the supper dishes. She was a trim, slim little thing, with blue eyes and shingled yellow hair, and her eyebrows were reduced to a mere brush-stroke, like Miss Pearl's.

''Good evening, Mr. Rosicky. Rudolph's at the barn, I guess.'' She never called him father or Mary mother. She was sensitive about having married a foreigner. She never in the world would have done it if Rudolph hadn't been such a handsome, persuasive fellow and such a gallant lover. He graduated in her class in the high school in town, and their friendship began in the ninth grade.

Rosicky went in, though he wasn't exactly asked. ''My boys ain't goin' to town tonight, an' I brought de car over fur you two to go in to de picture show.''

Polly, carrying dishes to the sink, looked over her shoulder at him. ''Thank you. But I'm late with my work tonight, and pretty tired. Maybe Rudolph would like to go in with you.''

''Oh, I don't go to de shows! I'm too old-fashioned. You won't feel so tired after you ride in de air a ways. It's a nice clear night, an' it ain't cold. You go an' fix yourself up, Polly, an' I'll wash de dishes an' leave everything nice fur you.''

Polly blushed and tossed her bob. ''I couldn't let you do that, Mr. Rosicky. I wouldn't think of it.''

Rosicky said nothing. He found a bib apron on a nail behind the kitchen door. He slipped it over his head and then took Polly by her two elbows and pushed her gently toward the door of her own room. ''I washed up de kitchen many times for my wife, when de babies was sick or somethin'. You go an' make yourself look nice. I like you to look prettier'n any of dem town girls when you go in. De young folks must have some fun, an' I'm goin' to look out fur you, Polly.''

That kind, reassuring grip on her elbows, the old man's funny bright eyes, made Polly want to drop her head on his shoulder for a second. She restrained herself, but she lingered in his grasp at the door of her room, murmuring tearfully: ''You always lived in the city when you were young, didn't you? Don't you ever get lonesome out here?''

As she turned round to him, her hand fell naturally into his, and he stood holding it and smiling into her face with his peculiar, knowing, indulgent smile without a shadow of reproach in it. ''Dem big cities is all right fur de rich, but dey is terrible hard fur de poor.''

''I don't know. Sometimes I think I'd like to take a chance. You lived in New York, didn't you?''

''An' London. Da's bigger still. I learned my trade dere. Here's Rudolph comin', you better hurry.''

''Will you tell me about London some time?''

''Maybe. Only I ain't no talker, Polly. Run an' dress yourself up.''

The bedroom door closed behind her, and Rudolph came in from the outside, looking anxious. He had seen the car and was sorry any of his family should come just then. Supper hadn't been a very pleasant occasion. Halting in the doorway, he saw his father in a kitchen apron, carrying dishes to the sink. He flushed crimson and something flashed in his eye. Rosicky held up a warning finger.

''I brought de car over fur you an' Polly to go to de picture show, an' I made her let me finish here so you won't be late. You go put on a clean shirt, quick!"

"But don't the boys want the car, Father?"

"Not tonight dey don't." Rosicky fumbled under his apron and found his pants pocket. He took out a silver dollar and said in hurried whisper: "You go an' buy dat girl some ice cream an' candy tonight, like you was courtin'. She's awful good friends wid me."

Rudolph was very short of cash, but he took the money as if it hurt him. There had been a crop failure all over the county. He had more than once been sorry he'd married this year.

In a few minutes the young people came out, looking clean and a little stiff. Rosicky hurried them off, and then he took his own time with the dishes. He scoured the pots and pans and put away the milk and swept the kitchen. He put some coal in the stove and shut off the draughts, so the place would be warm for them when they got home late at night. Then he sat down and had a pipe and listened to the clock tick.

Generally speaking, marrying an American girl was certainly a risk. A Czech should marry a Czech. It was lucky that Polly was the daughter of a poor widow woman; Rudolph was proud, and if she had a prosperous family to throw up at him, they could never make it go. Polly was one of four sisters, and they all worked; one was book-keeper in the bank, one taught music, and Polly and her younger sister had been clerks, like Miss Pearl. All four of them were musical, had pretty voices, and sang in the Methodist choir, which the eldest sister directed.

Polly missed the sociability of a store position. She missed the choir, and the company of her sisters. She didn't dislike housework, but she disliked so much of it. Rosicky was a little anxious about this pair. He was afraid Polly would grow so discontented that Rudy would quit the farm and take a factory job in Omaha. He had worked for a winter up there, two years ago, to get money to marry on. He had done very well, and they would always take him back at the stockyards. But to Rosicky that meant the end of

everything for his son. To be a landless man was to be a wage-earner, a slave, all your life; to have nothing, to be nothing.

Rosicky thought he would come over and do a little carpentering for Polly after the New Year. He guessed she needed jollying. Rudolph was a serious sort of chap, serious in love and serious about his work.

Rosicky shook out his pipe and walked home across the fields. Ahead of him the lamplight shone from his kitchen windows. Suppose he were still in a tailor shop on Vesey Street, with a bunch of pale, narrow-chested sons working on machines, all coming home tired and sullen to eat supper in a kitchen that was a parlour also; with another crowded, angry family quarrelling just across the dumb-waiter shaft, and squeaking pulleys at the windows where dirty washings hung on dirty lines above a court full of old brooms and mops and ash-cans. . . .

He stopped by the windmill to look up at the frosty winter stars and draw a long breath before he went inside. That kitchen with the shining windows was dear to him; but the sleeping fields and bright stars and the noble darkness were dearer still.

Discussion

1. That winter, forced by his family to take it easier, Rosicky's mind often goes back to his past life. He remembers his arrival at age twenty in New York, the kind of life he had there, and his decision finally to leave the city. What was his life in the city? What about it made him restless?

2. Rosicky recalls, too, particular details about his boyhood in Czechoslovakia. How is this recollection related to the discovery he remembers making in New York which finally made him decide to leave the city?

3. One Saturday Rosicky tells the boys that he is going to let their brother Rudolph have the car in order to take Polly to town and to the movies. What does the reaction of the boys tell us about them?

4. (a) Why is Rosicky so concerned about the young couple? **(b)** What is he afraid might happen? Why?

Willa Cather 1873 · 1947

In an essay entitled "My First Novels," Willa Cather describes her elation on discovering for her fiction the right material—the kind of material she was eventually to use in *Neighbour Rosicky:*
". . . I began to write a book *O Pioneers!* entirely for myself; a story about some Scandinavians and Bohemians who had been neighbours of ours when I lived on a ranch in Nebraska, when I was eight or nine years old. . . . This was like taking a ride through familiar country on a horse that knew the way, on a fine morning when you felt like riding. . . ." This discovery was important because in her first writing she attempted to work with sophisticated Eastern materials then popular in fiction but with which she was not familiar. She finally found her material at home, out of her own Nebraska experiences and observations.

Her most popular novel, *My Antonia*, appeared in 1918 and established her reputation as a leading American novelist. Like *Neighbour Rosicky,* it deals with hard life in the small towns and the great empty spaces of Nebraska, presenting as its heroine the energetic, vibrant daughter of a Bohemian immigrant. Her novel *One of Ours* (1922) portrays the death of a young Nebraskan in World War I and won for Cather a Pulitzer Prize. Her other novels include *Death Comes for the Archbishop* (1927), set in the past and the American Southwest, and *Shadows on the Rock* (1931), a historical novel set in Quebec. Although her fiction shows people's cruelty to one another, it tends to focus on such virtues as self-reliance and sensitivity to the feelings of others, and openness to the fullness of life's experiences.

V

On the day before Christmas the weather set in very cold; no snow, but a bitter, biting wind that whistled and sang over the flat land and lashed one's face like fine wires. There was baking going on in the Rosicky kitchen all day, and Rosicky sat inside, making over a coat that Albert had outgrown into an overcoat for John. Mary had a big red geranium in bloom for Christmas, and a row of Jerusalem cherry trees, full of berries. It was the first year she had ever grown these; Doctor Ed brought her the seeds from Omaha when he went to some medical convention. They reminded Rosicky of plants he had seen in England; and all afternoon, as he stitched, he sat thinking about those two years in London, which his mind usually shrank from even after all this while.

He was a lad of eighteen when he dropped down into London, with no money and no connexions except the address of a cousin who was supposed to be working at a confectioner's. When he went to the pastry shop, however, he found that the cousin had gone to America. Anton tramped the streets for several days, sleeping in doorways and on the Embankment,

until he was in utter despair. He knew no English, and the sound of the strange language all about him confused him. By chance he met a poor German tailor who had learned his trade in Vienna, and could speak a little Czech. This tailor, Lifschnitz, kept a repair shop in a Cheapside basement, underneath a cobbler. He didn't much need an apprentice, but he was sorry for the boy and took him in for no wages but his keep and what he could pick up. The pickings were supposed to be coppers given you when you took work home to a customer. But most of the customers called for their clothes themselves, and the coppers that came Anton's way were very few. He had, however, a place to sleep. The tailor's family lived upstairs in three rooms; a kitchen, a bedroom, where Lifschnitz and his wife and five children slept, and a living-room. Two corners of this living-room were curtained off for lodgers; in one Rosicky slept on an old horsehair sofa, with a feather quilt to wrap himself in. The other corner was rented to a wretched, dirty boy, who was studying the violin. He actually practised there. Rosicky was dirty, too. There was no way to be anything else. Mrs. Lifschnitz got the water she cooked and washed with from a pump in a brick court, four flights down. There were bugs in the place, and multitudes of fleas, though the poor woman did the best she could. Rosicky knew she often went empty to give another potato or a spoonful of dripping to the two hungry, sad-eyed boys who lodged with her. He used to think he would never get out of there, never get a clean shirt to his back again. What would he do, he wondered, when his clothes actually dropped to pieces and the worn cloth wouldn't hold patches any longer?

It was still early when the old farmer put aside his sewing and his recollections. The sky had been a dark grey all day, with not a gleam of sun, and the light failed at four o'clock. He went to shave and change his shirt while the turkey was roasting. Rudolph and Polly were coming over for supper.

After supper they sat round in the kitchen, and the younger boys were saying how sorry they were it hadn't snowed. Everybody was sorry. They wanted a deep snow that would lie long and keep the wheat warm, and leave the ground soaked when it melted.

"Yes, sir!" Rudolph broke out fiercely; "if we have another dry year like last year, there's going to be hard times in this country."

Rosicky filled his pipe. "You boys don't know what hard times is. You don't owe nobody, you got plenty to eat an' keep warm, an' plenty water to keep clean. When you got them, you can't have it very hard."

Rudolph frowned, opened and shut his big right hand, and dropped it clenched upon his knee. "I've got to have a good deal more than that, Father, or I'll quit this farming gamble. I can always make good wages railroading, or at the packing house, and be sure of my money."

"Maybe so," his father answered dryly.

Mary, who had just come in from the pantry and was wiping her hands on the roller towel, thought Rudy and his father were getting too serious. She brought her darning-basket and sat down in the middle of the group.

"I ain't much afraid of hard times, Rudy," she said heartily. "We've had a plenty, but we've always come through. Your father wouldn't never take nothing very hard, not even hard times. I got a mind to tell you a story on him. Maybe you boys can't hardly remember the year we had that terrible hot wind, that burned everything up on the Fourth of July? All the corn an' the gardens. An' that was in the days when we didn't have alfalfa yet,—I guess it wasn't invented.

"Well, that very day your father was out cultivatin' corn, and I was here in the kitchen makin' plum preserves. We had bushels of plums that year. I noticed it was terrible hot, but it's always hot in the kitchen when you're preservin', an' I was too busy with my plums to mind. Anton come in from the field about three o'clock, an' I asked him what was the matter.

" 'Nothin',' he says, 'but it's pretty hot, an' I think I won't work no more today.' He stood round for a few minutes, an' then he says: 'Ain't you near through? I want you should git up a nice supper for us tonight. It's Fourth of July.'

"I told him to git along, that I was right in the middle of preservin', but the plums would taste good on hot biscuit. 'I'm goin' to have fried chicken, too,' he says, and he went off an' killed a couple. You three oldest boys was little fellers, playin' round outside, real hot an' sweaty, an' your father took you to the horse tank down by the windmill an' took off your clothes an' put you in. Them two box-elder trees was little then, but they made shade over the tank. Then he took off all his own clothes, an' got in with you. While he was playin' in the water with you, the Methodist preacher drove into our place to say how all the neighbours was goin' to meet at the schoolhouse that night, to pray for rain. He drove right to the windmill, of course, and there was your father and you three with no clothes on. I was in the kitchen door, an' I had to laugh, for the preacher acted like he ain't never seen a naked man before. He surely was embarrassed, an' your father couldn't git to his clothes; they was all hangin' up on the windmill to let the sweat dry out of 'em. So he laid in the tank where he was, an' put one of you boys on top of him to cover him up a little, an' talked to the preacher.

"When you got through playin' in the water, he put clean clothes on you and a clean shirt on himself, an' by that time I'd begun to get supper. He says: 'It's too hot in here to eat comfortable. Let's have a picnic in the orchard. We'll eat our supper behind the mulberry hedge, under them linden trees.'

"So he carried our supper down, an' a bottle of my wild-grape wine, an' everything tasted good, I can tell you. The wind got cooler as the sun was goin' down, and it turned out pleasant, only I noticed how the leaves was curled up on the linden trees. That made me think, an' I asked your father if that hot wind all day hadn't been terrible hard on the gardens an' the corn.

" 'Corn,' he says, 'there ain't no corn.'

" 'What you talkin' about?' I said. 'Ain't we got forty acres?'

" 'We ain't got an ear,' he says, 'nor nobody else ain't got none. All the corn in this country was cooked by three o'clock today, like you'd roasted it in an oven.'

" 'You mean you won't get no crop at all?' I asked him. I couldn't believe it, after he'd worked so hard.

" 'No crop this year,' he says. 'That's why we're havin' a picnic. We might as well enjoy what we got.'

"An' that's how your father behaved, when all the neighbours was so discouraged they couldn't look you in the face. An' we enjoyed ourselves that year, poor as we was, an' our neighbours wasn't a bit better off for bein' miserable. Some of 'em grieved till they got poor digestions and couldn't relish what they did have.''

The younger boys said they thought their father had the best of it. But Rudolph was thinking that, all the same, the neighbours had managed to get ahead more, in the fifteen years since that time. There must be something wrong about his father's way of doing things. He wished he knew what was going on in the back of Polly's mind. He knew she liked his father, but he knew, too, that she was afraid of something. When his mother sent over coffee-cake or prune tarts or a loaf of fresh bread, Polly seemed to regard them with a certain suspicion. When she observed to him that his brothers had nice manners, her tone implied that it was remarkable they should have. With his mother she was stiff and on her guard. Mary's hearty frankness and gusts of good humour irritated her. Polly was afraid of being unusual or conspicuous in any way, of being ''ordinary,'' as she said!

When Mary had finished her story, Rosicky laid aside his pipe.

"You boys like me to tell you about some of dem hard times I been through in London?'' Warmly encouraged, he sat rubbing his forehead along the deep creases. It was bothersome to tell a long story in English (he nearly always talked to the boys in Czech), but he wanted Polly to hear this one.

"Well, you know about dat tailor shop I worked in in London? I had one Christmas dere I ain't never forgot. Times was awful bad before Christmas; de boss ain't got much work, an' have it awful hard to pay his rent. It ain't so much fun, bein' poor in a big city like London, I'll say! All de windows is full of good t'ings to eat, an' all de pushcarts in de streets is full, an' you smell 'em all de time, an' you ain't got no money,—not a bit. I didn't mind de cold so much, though I didn't have no overcoat, chust a short jacket I'd outgrowed so it wouldn't meet on me, an' my hands was chapped raw. But I always had a good appetite, like you all know, an' de sight of dem pork pies in de windows was awful fur me!

"Day before Christmas was terrible foggy dat year, an' dat fog gits into your bones and makes you all damp like. Mrs. Lifschnitz didn't give us nothin' but a little bread an' drippin' for supper, because she was savin' to try for to give us a good dinner on Christmas Day. After supper de boss say I can go an' enjoy myself, so I went into de streets to listen to de Christmas singers. Dey sing old songs an' make very nice music, an' I run round after dem a good ways, till I got awful hungry. I t'ink maybe if I go home, I can sleep till morning an' forgit my belly.

"I went into my corner real quiet, and roll up in my fedder quilt. But I ain't got my head down, till I smell somet'ing good. Seem like it git stronger an' stronger, an' I can't git to sleep noway. I can't understand dat smell. Dere was a gas light in a hall across de court, dat always shine in at my window a little. I got up an' look round. I got a little wooden box in my corner fur a stool, 'cause I ain't got no chair. I picks up dat box, and under it dere is a roast goose on a platter! I can't believe my eyes. I carry it to de window where de light comes in, an' touch it and smell it to find out, an' den I taste it to be sure. I say, I will eat chust one little bite of dat goose, so I can go to sleep, and tomorrow I won't eat none

at all. But I tell you, boys, when I stop, one half of dat goose was gone!''

The narrator bowed his head, and the boys shouted. But little Josephine slipped behind his chair and kissed him on the neck beneath his ear.

"Poor little Papa, I don't want him to be hungry!"

"Da's long ago, child. I ain't never been hungry since I had your mudder to cook fur me.''

"Go on and tell us the rest, please,'' said Polly.

"Well, when I come to realize what I done, of course, I felt terrible. I felt better in de stomach, but very bad in de heart. I set on my bed wid dat platter on my knees, an' it all come to me; how hard dat poor woman save to buy dat goose, and how she get some neighbour to cook it dat got more fire, an' how she put it in my corner to keep it away from dem hungry children. Dey was a old carpet hung up to shut my corner off, an' de children wasn't allowed to go in dere. An' I know she put it in my corner because she trust me more'n she did de violin boy. I can't stand it to face her after I spoil de Christmas. So I put on my shoes and go out into de city. I tell myself I

better throw myself in de river; but I guess I ain't dat kind of a boy.

"It was after twelve o'clock, an' terrible cold, an' I start out to walk about London all night. I walk along de river awhile, but dey was lots of drunks all along; men, and women too. I chust move along to keep away from de police. I git onto de Strand, an' den over to New Oxford Street, where dere was a big German restaurant on de ground floor, wid big windows all fixed up fine, an' I could see de people havin' parties inside. While I was lookin' in, two men and two ladies come out, laughin' and talkin' and feelin' happy about all dey been eatin' an' drinkin', and dey was speakin' Czech,—not like de Austrians, but like de home folks talk it.

"I guess I went crazy, an' I done what I ain't never done before nor since. I went right up to dem gay people an' begun to beg dem: 'Fellow-countrymen, *please* give me money enough to buy a goose!'

"Dey laugh, of course, but de ladies speak awful kind to me, an' dey take me back into de restaurant and give me hot coffee and cakes, an' make me tell all about how I happened to come to London, an' what I was doin' dere. Dey take my name and where I work down on paper, an' both of dem ladies give me ten shillings.

"De big market at Covent Garden ain't very far away, an' by dat time it was open. I go dere an' buy a big goose an' some pork pies, an' potatoes and onion, an' cakes an' oranges fur de children,—all I could carry! When I git home, everybody is still asleep. I pile all I bought on de kitchen table, an' go in an' lay down on my bed, an' I ain't waken up till I hear dat woman scream when she come out into her kitchen. My goodness, but she was surprise! She laugh an' cry at de same time, an' hug me and waken all de children. She ain't stop fur no breakfast; she git de Christmas dinner ready dat morning, and we all sit down an' eat all we can hold. I ain't never seen dat violin boy have all he can hold before.

"Two three days after dat, de two men come to hunt me up, an' dey ask my boss, and he give me a good report an' tell dem I was a steady boy all right. One of dem Bohemians was very smart an' run a Bohemian newspaper in New York, an' de odder was a rich man, in de importing business, an' dey been travelling togedder. Dey told me how t'ings was easier in New York, an' offered to pay my passage when dey was goin' home soon on a boat. My boss say to me: 'You go. You ain't got no chance here, an' I like to see you git ahead, fur you always been a good boy to my woman, and fur dat fine Christmas dinner you give us all.' An' da's how I got to New York.''

That night when Rudolph and Polly, arm in arm, were running home across the fields with the bitter wind at their backs, his heart leaped for joy when she said she thought they might have his family come over for supper on New Year's Eve. ''Let's get up a nice supper, and not let your mother help at all; make her be company for once.''

''That would be lovely of you, Polly,'' he said humbly. He was a very simple, modest boy, and he, too, felt vaguely that Polly and her sisters were more experienced and worldly than his people.

VI

The winter turned out badly for farmers. It was bitterly cold, and after the first light snows before Christmas there was no snow at all,—and no rain. March was as bitter as February. On those days when the wind fairly punished the country, Rosicky sat by his window. In the fall he and the boys had put in a big wheat planting, and now the seed had frozen in the ground. All that land would have to be ploughed up and planted over again, planted in corn. It had happened before, but he was younger then, and he never worried about what had to be. He was sure of himself and of Mary; he knew they could bear what they had to bear, that they would always pull through somehow. But he was not so sure about the young ones, and he felt troubled because Rudolph and Polly were having such a hard start.

Sitting beside his flowering window while the panes rattled and the wind blew in under the door, Rosicky gave himself to reflection as he had not done since those Sundays in the loft of the furniture-factory in New York, long ago. Then he was trying to find what he wanted in life for himself; now he was trying to find what he wanted for his boys, and why it was he so hungered to feel sure they would be here, working this very land, after he was gone.

They would have to work hard on the farm, and probably they would never do much more than make a living. But if he could think of them as staying here on the land, he wouldn't have to fear any great unkindness for them. Hardships, certainly; it was a hardship to have the wheat freeze in the ground when seed was so high; and to have to sell your stock because you had no feed. But there would be other years when everything came along right, and you caught up. And what you had was your own. You didn't have to choose between bosses and strikers, and go wrong either way. You didn't have to do with dishonest and cruel people. They were the only things in his experience he had found terrifying and horrible; the look in the eyes of a dishonest and crafty man, of a scheming and rapacious woman.

In the country, if you had a mean neighbour, you could keep off his land and make him keep off yours. But in the city, all the foulness and misery and brutality of your neighbours was part of your life. The worst things he had come upon in his journey through the world were human,— depraved and poisonous specimens of man. To this day he could recall certain terrible faces in the London streets. There were mean people everywhere, to be sure, even in their own country town here. But they weren't tempered, hardened, sharpened, like the treacherous people in cities who live by grinding or cheating or poisoning their fellow-men. He had helped to bury two of his fellow-workmen in the tailoring trade, and he was distrustful of the organized industries that see one out of the world in big cities. Here, if you were sick, you had Doctor Ed to look after you; and if you died, fat Mr. Haycock, the kindest man in the world, buried you.

It seemed to Rosicky that for good, honest boys like his, the worst they could do on the farm was better than the best they would be likely to do in the city. If he'd had a mean boy, now, one who was crooked and sharp and tried to put anything over on his brothers, then town would be the place for him. But he had no such boy. As for Rudolph, the discontented one, he would give the shirt off his back to anyone who touched his heart. What Rosicky really hoped for his boys was that they could get through the world without ever knowing much about the cruelty of human beings. "Their mother and me ain't prepared them for that," he sometimes said to himself.

These thoughts brought him back to a grateful consideration of his own case. What an escape he had had, to be sure! He, too, in his time, had had to take money for repair work from the hand of a hungry child who let it go so wistfully; because it was money due his boss. And now, in all these years, he had never had to take a cent from anyone in bitter need,—never had to look at the face of a woman become like a wolf's from struggle and famine. When he thought of these things, Rosicky would put on his cap and jacket and slip down to the barn and give his work-horses a little extra oats, letting them eat it out of his hand in their slobbery fashion. It was his way of expressing what he felt, and made him chuckle with pleasure.

The spring came warm, with blue skies,—but dry, dry as a bone. The boys began ploughing up the wheat-fields to plant them over in corn. Rosicky would stand at the fence corner and watch them, and the earth was so dry it blew up in clouds of brown dust that hid the horses and the sulky plough and the driver. It was a bad outlook.

The big alfalfa-field that lay between the home place and Rudolph's came up green, but Rosicky was worried because during that open windy winter a great many Russian thistle plants had blown in there and lodged. He kept asking the boys to rake them out; he was afraid their seed would root and "take the alfalfa." Rudolph said that was nonsense. The boys were working so hard planting corn, their father felt he couldn't insist about the thistles, but he set great store by that big alfalfa field. It was a feed you could depend on,—and there was some deeper reason, vague, but strong. The peculiar green of that clover woke early memories in old Rosicky, went back to something in his childhood in the old world. When he was a little boy, he had played in fields of that strong blue-green colour.

One morning, when Rudolph had gone to town in the car, leaving a work-team idle in his barn, Rosicky went over to his son's place, put the horses to the buggy-rake, and set about quietly raking up those thistles. He behaved with guilty caution, and rather enjoyed stealing a march on Doctor Ed, who was just then taking his first vacation in seven years of practice and was attending a clinic in Chicago. Rosicky got the thistles raked up, but did not stop to burn them. That would take some time, and his breath was pretty short, so he thought he had better get the horses back to the barn.

He got them into the barn and to their stalls, but the pain had come on so sharp in his chest that he didn't try to take the harness off. He started for the house, bending lower with every step. The cramp in his chest was shutting him up like a jack-knife. When he reached the windmill, he swayed and caught at the ladder. He saw Polly coming down the hill, running with the swiftness of a slim greyhound. In a flash she had her shoulder under his armpit.

"Lean on me, Father, hard! Don't be afraid. We can get to the house all right."

Somehow they did, though Rosicky became blind with pain; he could keep on his legs, but he couldn't steer his course. The next thing he was conscious of was lying on Polly's bed, and Polly bending over him wringing out bath towels in hot water and putting them on his chest. She stopped only to throw coal into the stove, and she kept the tea-kettle and the black pot going. She put these hot applications on him for nearly an hour, she told him afterwards, and all that time he was drawn up stiff and blue, with the sweat pouring off him.

As the pain gradually loosed its grip, the stiffness went out of his jaws, the black circles round his eyes disappeared, and a little of his natural colour came back. When his daughter-in-law buttoned his shirt over his chest at last, he sighed.

"Da's fine, de way I feel now, Polly. It was a awful bad spell, an' I was so sorry it all come on you like it did."

Polly was flushed and excited. "Is the pain really gone? Can I leave you long enough to telephone over to your place?"

Rosicky's eyelids fluttered. "Don't telephone, Polly. It ain't no use to scare my wife. It's nice and quiet here, an' if I ain't too much trouble to you, just let me lay still till I feel like myself. I ain't got no pain now. It's nice here."

Polly bent over him and wiped the moisture from his face. "Oh, I'm so glad it's over!" she broke out impulsively. "It just broke my heart to see you suffer so, Father."

Rosicky motioned her to sit down on the chair where the tea-kettle had been, and looked up at her with that lively affectionate gleam in his eyes. "You was awful good to me, I won't never forget dat. I hate it to be sick on you like dis. Down at de barn I say to myself, dat young girl ain't had much experience in sickness, I don't want to scare her, an' maybe she's got a baby comin' or somet'ing."

Polly took his hand. He was looking at her so intently and affectionately and confidingly; his eyes seemed to caress her face, to regard it with pleasure. She frowned with her funny streaks of eyebrows, and then smiled back at him.

"I guess maybe there is something of that kind going to happen. But I haven't told anyone yet, not my mother or Rudolph. You'll be the first to know."

His hand pressed hers. She noticed that it was warm again. The twinkle in his yellow-brown eyes seemed to come nearer.

"I like mighty well to see dat little child, Polly," was all he said. Then he closed his eyes and lay half-smiling. But Polly sat still, thinking hard. She had a sudden feeling that nobody in the world, not her mother, not Rudolph, or anyone, really loved her as much as old Rosicky did. It perplexed her. She sat frowning and trying to puzzle it out. It was as if Rosicky had a special gift for loving people, something that was like an ear for music or an eye for colour. It was quiet, unobtrusive; it was merely there. You saw it in his eyes,—perhaps that was why they were merry. You felt it in his hands, too. After he dropped off to sleep, she sat holding his warm, broad, flexible brown hand. She had never seen another in the least like it. She wondered if it wasn't a kind of gypsy hand, it was so alive and quick and light in its communications,—very strange in a farmer. Nearly all the farmers she knew had huge lumps of fists, like mauls, or they were knotty and bony and uncomfortable-looking, with stiff fingers. But Rosicky's was like quicksilver, flexible, muscular, about the colour of a pale cigar, with deep, deep creases across the palm. It wasn't nervous, it wasn't a

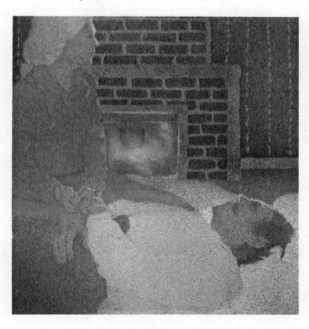

stupid lump; it was a warm brown human hand, with some cleverness in it, a great deal of generosity, and something else which Polly could only call "gypsy-like,"—something nimble and lively and sure, in the way that animals are.

Polly remembered that hour long afterwards; it had been like an awakening to her. It seemed to her that she had never learned so much about life from anything as from old Rosicky's hand. It brought her to herself; it communicated some direct and untranslatable message.

When she heard Rudolph coming in the car, she ran out to meet him.

"Oh, Rudy, your father's been awful sick! He raked up those thistles he's been worrying about, and afterwards he could hardly get to the house. He suffered so I was afraid he was going to die."

Rudolph jumped to the ground. "Where is he now?"

"On the bed. He's asleep. I was terribly scared, because, you know, I'm so fond of your father." She slipped her arm through his and they went into the house. That afternoon they took Rosicky home and put him to bed, though he protested that he was quite well again.

The next morning he got up and dressed and sat down to breakfast with his family. He told Mary that his coffee tasted better than usual to him, and he warned the boys not to bear any tales to Doctor Ed when he got home. After breakfast he sat down by his window to do some patching and asked Mary to thread several needles for him before she went to feed her chickens,—her eyes were better than his, and her hands steadier. He lit his pipe and took up John's overalls. Mary had been watching him anxiously all morning, and as she went out of the door with her bucket of scraps, she saw that he was smiling. He was thinking, indeed, about Polly, and how he might never have known what a tender heart she had if he hadn't got sick over there. Girls nowadays didn't wear their heart on their sleeve. But now he knew Polly would make a fine woman after the foolishness wore off. Either a woman had that sweetness at her heart or she hadn't. You couldn't always tell by the look of them; but if they had that, everything came out right in the end.

After he had taken a few stitches, the cramp began in his chest, like yesterday. He put his pipe cautiously down on the window-sill and bent over to ease the pull. No use,—he had better try to get to his bed if he could. He rose and groped his way across the familiar floor, which was rising and falling like the deck of a ship. At the door he fell. When Mary came in, she found him lying there, and the moment she touched him she knew that he was gone.

Doctor Ed was away when Rosicky died, and for the first few weeks after he got home he was hard driven. Every day he said to himself that he must get out to see that family that had lost their father. One soft, warm moonlight night in early summer he started for the farm. His mind was on other things, and not until his road ran by the graveyard did he realize that Rosicky wasn't over there on the hill where the red lamplight shone, but here, in the moonlight. He stopped his car, shut off the engine, and sat there for a while.

A sudden hush had fallen on his soul. Everything here seemed strangely moving and significant, though signifying what, he did not know. Close by the wire fence stood Rosicky's mowing-machine, where one of the boys had been cutting hay that afternoon; his own work-horses had been going up and down there. The new-cut hay perfumed all the night air. The moonlight silvered the long, billowy grass that grew over the graves and hid the fence; the few little evergreens stood out black in it, like shadows in a pool. The sky was very blue and soft, the stars rather faint because the moon was full.

For the first time it struck Doctor Ed that this was really a beautiful graveyard. He thought of city cemeteries, acres of shrubbery and heavy stone, so arranged and lonely and unlike anything in the living world. Cities of the dead, indeed; cities of the forgotten, of the "put away.'' But this was open and free, this little square of long grass which the wind forever stirred. Nothing but the sky overhead, and the many-coloured fields running on until they met that sky. The horses worked here in summer; the neighbours passed on their way to town; and over yonder, in the cornfield, Rosicky's own cattle would be eating fodder as winter came on.

Nothing could be more undeathlike than this place; nothing could be more right for a man who had helped to do the work of great cities and had always longed for the open country and had got to it at last. Rosicky's life seemed to him complete and beautiful.

New York, 1928

Discussion

1. On the day before Christmas, the Rosickys all gather for the holiday. The talk turns to hard times, and Rudolph says something about giving up farming. Mary tells her story of the great burning wind that destroyed the crops one Fourth of July. What is the point of her story and how does it affect Rudolph?

2. After Mary finishes her story, Rosicky tells his story about hard times in London, and he tells it in English because he "wanted Polly to hear this one." What is the main point of his story and why does he want Polly to hear it?

3. How do we find out the effect of these stories of Mary and Anton Rosicky on Polly? What is Rudolph's response to her reaction?

4. The hard winter had frozen the seed in the ground; the land would have to be replanted. Rosicky begins to reflect much as he had that Fourth of July long ago in New York. Then, he had figured out what he wanted for his life; now, he is discovering what he wants for his boys. What is it that he wants for them? Why? Discuss.

5. When Rosicky has his heart attack trying to remove the Russian thistles from the alfalfa fields, it is Polly who rescues him and sits by him holding his hand. Afterwards, we are told, Polly remembered that hour vividly. Why had it "been like an awakening to her"?

6. When Dr. Burleigh starts out to visit the Rosickys some weeks after the death of old Rosicky, he stops at the graveyard. What are his thoughts?

7. What role does Dr. Burleigh play in the story? Why does the work begin and end with his appearance?

Vocabulary
Context, Structure, Pronunciation, and Dictionary

A. Use your Glossary to answer the following questions. Be sure you know the meaning and pronunciation of each italicized word.

1. Is the *ch* in *chaff* pronounced like the *ch* in *chemistry, chair,* or *Chicago?*

2. Where is the accent in *implement?* What two Latin words form the basis for the word?

3. Is the *s* in *crimson* pronounced as the *s* in *crisp* or in *poison?* From what two languages is the word derived?

4. How many syllables are there in *rapacious?* Which syllable is accented?

5. Does the first syllable of *languid* rhyme with *fang* or with *fan?*

B. Use each of the following words in a sentence that shows you understand the meaning of the word.

nimble   unobtrusive
famine   impulsive
reproach

Extension · Writing

Neighbour Rosicky seems to show that people are full of stories, collecting many experiences during their lives. Notice how Mary and Anton Rosicky tell stories of past hard times. Talk with an older person you know (your mother, father, or a relative), and ask if that person remembers a particularly hard time in life. Or you might ask about some especially good time. If you can get the person to reminisce, there will probably be a story. Write a few paragraphs retelling the story, using the language of the teller if you can.

About Willa Cather *by Dorothy Van Ghent*

It is customary to speak of Willa Cather as an "elegist" of the American pioneer tradition. "Elegy" suggests celebration and lament for a lost and irrecoverable past; but the boldest and most beautiful of Willa Cather's fictions are characterized by a sense of the past not as an irrecoverable quality of events, wasted in history, but as persistent human truth repossessed—salvaged, redeemed—by virtue of memory and art.

She had been brought to Nebraska, from Virginia, when she was nine. This was in 1883, when Nebraska was still frontier territory, almost bare of human landmarks; the settlers lived in sod houses, scarcely distinguishable from the earth, or in caves in the clay bluffs; roads were faint wagon trails in a sea of red grass. The removal from an old, lush, settled country to a virtual wilderness was undoubtedly the determinative event of Willa Cather's life; the casting out upon a limitless wild prairie, opened her sensibility to primordial images and relationships that were to be the most powerful forces in her art.

Years later her friend Edith Lewis wrote of that Nebraska girlhood, which she too had known: "I remember . . . going back to that country after a number of years; as if the hot wind that so much of the time blew over it went on and left it behind, isolated, forgotten by the rest of the world . . . And I felt again that forlornness, that terrible restlessness that comes over young people born in small towns in the middle of the continent." That aridity and drabness formed another decisive pattern in the girl's [Cather's] emotional nature, a traumatic one that reappears in the stories and novels as a desperate impulse of "escape". . . .

Her "escape" was slow, uneven, costing years of drudgery. From 1891 to 1895, a period of crop failures and financial depression, she attended the state university at Lincoln, meeting many of her expenses by writing for the *State Journal*. For the next decade, from her twenty-third to her thirty-third year, she worked at various jobs in Pittsburgh: as a newspaperwoman, and as a teacher of English and Latin. In 1903 she published a book of poems, *April Twilights;* and in 1905 her first book of stories, *The Troll Garden*, was published by S. S. McClure—who immediately offered her a post in New York on his then brilliant magazine. In 1912, the year of the publication of her first novel, *Alexander's Bridge*, she resigned from McClure's, and from that time on was able to live the quiet and dedicated life of her craft.

Miss Cather said frequently that the only part of her life which made a lasting impression on her imagination and emotion was what happened before she was twenty. No doubt the remark overcondenses and oversimplifies, but one finds an impressive truth in it when one looks at those early years in the light of her mature work. It is as if the aridities of her girlhood, and the drudgery that followed, had left her with a haunting sense of a "self" that had been effaced and that tormented her for realization. She was to search for it in elusive ways all her life, and sometimes, in her greatest novels, when she left off searching for it she found it.

From WILLA CATHER by Dorothy Van Ghent. © Copyright 1964 by the University of Minnesota. University of Minnesota Press, Minneapolis.

8: Neighbour Rosicky

CONTENT REVIEW

1. Doctor Ed Burleigh is the only character outside the Rosicky family to play an important role in *Neighbour Rosicky.* Recall the scenes in which he appears. For what purpose does Cather use him in telling old Rosicky's story?

2. Using the breakfast episode with Dr. Burleigh and especially Mary's speech which begins "I don't care, you wouldn't have got away from this house . . ." (532b, 4) as a springboard, characterize Mary Rosicky and discuss her role in the story.

3. On the way home from the doctor's office, Rosicky stops by the graveyard. What might one expect his thoughts to have been? What does his affirmative vision of what the snow brings reveal about his personality?

4. After the young Rosicky discovers that he must leave the city for the country, Cather writes that he was "like a tree that has not many roots, but one tap-root that goes down deep." In what way is this true about the old farmer?

5. Rosicky is walking home from the evening he spent at his son's house after sending the young couple to town and the movies. He stops by the windmill and looks at his house. In what way do his thoughts suggest he does not find death horrifying?

What, besides his family, does his love encompass?

6. In the closing lines of the story, Dr. Burleigh sits thinking about Rosicky lying in the graveyard. "Rosicky's life seemed to him complete and beautiful." From what you know of Rosicky's life, are *complete* and *beautiful* the words you would select to apply to Rosicky's life? Give the reasons for your answer.

7. Select one of the following critical statements about *Neighbour Rosicky* that appears to you to be closest to the truth and defend your choice by referring to specific material in the story: **(a)** *Neighbour Rosicky* is too "romantic" because it portrays much too rosy a picture of Anton Rosicky. **(b)** *Neighbour Rosicky* is too "realistic" (or tries to be) because it portrays hard times too luridly, and in extremes. **(c)** *Neighbour Rosicky* is neither too romantic nor too realistic, but strikes about the right balance between the hardships and joys of living, the meanness of life and the wonder of life.

8. Despite the hardships of farm life, Rosicky believes that he and his family are better off than anyone in the city. The story of his last years seems to affirm this. However, readers may differ on this matter. Write a defense of the other side, the city side, using as a source some of the events in the story, as well as your own knowledge.

from A LANTERN IN HER HAND
Bess Streeter Aldrich

The granddaughter of a Scottish aristocrat, Abbie Deal dreamed as a child of the wonderful things she would do with her life. As a young woman, she would decide between the marriage proposals of two men: one offered her wealth; the other the life of a pioneer. Abbie chose to follow the covered-wagon trail to the Nebraska prairies with Will Deal, and the novel from which this selection is taken tells of their struggle to build a home and community on the unfriendly plains.

The following excerpt takes place in 1926, when Abbie is eighty. Her granddaughter, Laura, has just read a poem she has written that recalls to Abbie her life with Will and the experiences they shared as settlers.

After you have read the excerpt, answer the questions on a separate sheet of paper.

"What are you thinking about, Grandma?"

"That your life is like a field glass,¹ Laura. When you look into the one end, the landscape is dwarfed and far away,—when you look into the other, it looms large as though it were near at hand. Things that happened seventy years ago seem like yesterday. But, when I was a girl, eighty years seemed too remote to contemplate. And now, it has passed. The story is written."

"You sound as though you were sorry about something, Grandma."

"I didn't mean to, but I was thinking that when I was a little girl, my sister Belle used to tell me about our grandmother . . . that would be your great-great-grandmother. Her name was Isabelle Anders-Mackenzie. She was wealthy and beautiful and accomplished for her time. I used to think I would grow up to look just like her. I pictured her as an ideal and I would say to her in my mind, 'You'll be proud some day of the things I am going to accomplish.' All my girlhood I always planned to do something big . . . something constructive. It's queer what ambitious dreams a girl has when she is young. I thought I would sing before big audiences or paint lovely pictures or write a splendid book. I always had that feeling in me of wanting to do something worth while. And just think, Laura . . . now I am

A LANTERN IN HER HAND by Bess Streeter Aldrich, Nona Robinson, editor. Copyright, © 1956 by Mary Aldrich Beechner, Robert Streeter Aldrich, Charles S. Aldrich, James Whitson Aldrich, Renewed 1972. Abridged by permission of Prentice-Hall, Inc., Englewood Cliffs, New Jersey.

1. *field glass,* binoculars.

eighty and I have not painted nor written nor sung.''

''But you've done lots of things, Grandma. You've baked bread . . . and pieced quilts . . . and taken care of your children.''

Old Abbie Deal patted the young girl's hand. ''Well . . . well . . . out of the mouths of babes. That's just it, Laura, I've *only* baked bread and pieced quilts and taken care of children. But some women have to, don't they? . . . But I've dreamed dreams, Laura. All the time I was cooking and patching and washing, I dreamed dreams. And I think I dreamed them into the children . . . and the children are carrying them out . . . doing all the things I wanted to and couldn't. Margaret has painted for me and Isabelle has sung for me. Grace has taught for me . . . and you, Laura . . . you'll write my book for me I think. You'll have a fine education and you will probably travel. But I don't believe you can write a story because you have a fine education and have traveled. I think you must first have a seeing eye and an understanding heart and the knack of expressing what you see and feel. And you have them. So I think you, too, are going to do one of the things I wanted to do and never did.''

Abbie Deal thoroughly enjoyed talking to this grandchild. Any of the rest of the family would have been a little impatient with an old woman's musings. The others were always so alert, so active, so poised for flight. Of them all, only little Laura Deal wanted to sit and talk and dream. She told her that now.

''You are a great comfort to me, Laura. You are something like me . . . a part of me. We think alike . . . you and I. Between you and me, I think my reminiscences bore the others. Well, well . . . old people used to bore me when I was young.''

''They don't bore *me,* Grandma. They interest me.''

Abbie smiled across at her. No longer could she look down upon Laura. The twelve-year-old girl was larger than her little grandmother.

''And we old pioneers dreamed other things, too, Laura. We dreamed dreams into the country. We dreamed the towns and the cities, the homes and the factories, the churches and the schools. We dreamed the huge new capitol. When you walk under its wonderful tower, you say to yourself, 'My Grandfather and Grandmother Deal dreamed all this . . . they, and a thousand other young couples dreamed it all in the early days . . . and the architect had the imagination to catch the dream and materialize it. It is their vision solidified. They were like the foundation stones under the capitol . . . not decorative, but strong. They were not well-educated. They were not sophisticated. They were not cultured. But they had innate refinement and courage. And they could see visions and dream dreams.''

''How does it feel to be old, Grandma?''

Abbie laughed. ''Laura, it doesn't *feel* at all. People don't

understand about old age. I am an old woman . . . but *I* haven't changed. I'm still Abbie Deal. They think we're different . . . we old ones. The real Abbie Deal still has many of the old visions and longings. I'm fairly contented here in the old home. . . . There was a time when I thought I never could be . . . but . . . some way . . . we get adjusted. I've never grown tired of life as some old people do. I'm only tired of the aches and the pains and the inability to make my body do what I want it to do. I would like to live a long time yet . . . to see what can still be invented . . . to read the new things that will be written . . . to hear the new songs that will be sung . . . to see heavy foliage on all the new shrubbery . . . to see all the babies grow into men and women. But there comes an end . . ."

"Don't talk that way, Grandma. It makes me feel like crying."

"Why, it ought not, Laura . . . not when Grandma has happy memories to live over."

"What memories do you have, Grandma?"

"I have many . . . my little girlhood days when Chicago was a village . . . the three weeks' journey from Illinois into Iowa . . . the fun in the Big Woods behind my sister Janet's house. I can shut my eyes and smell the dampness and the Mayflowers there. The old log school and then the new white one with green shutters . . . my wedding . . . the trip from Iowa into Nebraska. . . . There are many memories. But I'll tell you the one I like to think of best of all. It's just a homely everyday thing, but to me it is the happiest of them all. It is evening time here in the old house and the supper is cooking and the table is set for the whole family. It hurts a mother, Laura, when the plates begin to be taken away one by one. First there are seven and then six and then five . . . and on down to a single plate. So I like to think of the table set for the whole family at supper time. The robins are singing in the cottonwoods and the late afternoon sun is shining across the floor. Will, your grandfather, is coming in to supper . . . and the children are all playing out in the yard. I can hear their voices and happy laughter. There isn't much to that memory is there? Out of a lifetime of experiences you would hardly expect that to be the one I would choose as the happiest, would you? But it is. The supper cooking . . . the table set for the whole family . . . the afternoon sun across the floor . . . the robins singing in the cottonwoods . . . the children's merry voices . . . Will coming in . . . eventide."

"I think it's a nice memory, Grandma, but something about the way you say it makes me sad."

"But it's not sad, Laura. My memories are not sad. They're pleasant. I'm happy when I'm living them over. You'll find out when you get old, Laura, that some of the realities seem dreams . . . but the dreams, Laura, . . . the dreams are all real." □□

A. Multiple Choice

On your paper write the letter of the best answer.

1. Life is like a field glass, according to Abbie, because (a) whoever holds it sees something different; (b) the longer one holds it, the more weary one becomes; (c) things advance or recede depending upon which end of the field glass one looks through; (d) everything seems close at hand and easy to reach.

2. Abbie tells Laura that to be a writer it is important to (a) travel extensively; (b) have a good education; (c) listen carefully to stories told by old people; (d) have a knack for expressing what one feels and sees.

3. Abbie Deal reminisces about all of the following except (a) Chicago as a village; (b) a log schoolhouse; (c) family suppertime; (d) singing around the campfire.

4. Abbie says that old people (a) feel basically the same as when they were younger; (b) change greatly as the years pass; (c) live only through their memories; (d) are happy to be relieved of their responsibilities.

5. Abbie's great accomplishment is (a) designing the state capitol; (b) living to be eighty; (c) transmitting her dreams to her talented children; (d) being a skilled storyteller.

6. From reading this excerpt you can infer that pioneers (a) thoroughly enjoyed their hard life; (b) sometimes had to set aside their individual ambitions; (c) had nothing but hard work and hardships their whole lives through; (d) had no other choice but to endure their bleak existence.

B. Short Answer

On the same paper as A, write the word or phrase that best answers the questions.

7. What three things did the young Abbie plan to do with her life?

8. Why didn't she accomplish the things she had hoped to?

9. What is Abbie's happiest memory? She doesn't say why this means so much to her. Why do you think it does?

10. Why do Laura and her grandmother get along so well?

11. How did the old pioneers help build the country, according to Abbie? To what does she compare the pioneers? Why is it an appropriate comparison?

12. Would you say that Abbie Deal or Neighbour Rosicky was more content with life? Why?

13. What do you think Abbie means by her last statement "that some of the realities seem dreams . . . but . . . the dreams are all real"?

From the following assignments choose one to write about.

1. Suppose you were Doctor Burleigh. Write a letter to be given, at a future date, to Rosicky's first grandchild, telling that child about the kind of man Grandfather Rosicky was.

2. Discuss the author's use of setting in *Neighbour Rosicky*. Include in your composition answers to the following questions: How does setting influence the life and death of Rosicky? What does setting reveal about Mary Rosicky? What effect does setting have on the relationship between Rudolph and Polly? What does setting reveal about the time in history the story takes place?

3. Suppose, like Abbie Deal, you were asked to tell your happiest memory. What would it be? Write a short composition telling your classmates about it. Make the reminiscence as vivid as possible through your use of imagery, setting, or characterization.

Handbook of Literary Terms: Acknowledgments

alliteration:

From "Alliteration, or The Siege of Belgrade," THE CHERRY TREE: A Collection of Poems chosen by Geoffrey Grigson. Published by The Vanguard Press, Inc. Copyright, © mcmlix, by Geoffrey Grigson. Reprinted by permission of the author.

From COLLECTED POEMS, Harper & Row. Copyright 1922, 1950 by Edna St. Vincent Millay. Reprinted by permission of Norma Millay Ellis.

From "The Hart Loves the High Wood," THE GAMBIT BOOK OF POPULAR VERSE, Edited with an Introduction by Geoffrey Grigson. Published by Gambit, Inc., 1971. Reprinted by permission of the author.

From BEOWULF, translated by Kevin Crossley-Holland. Reprinted with permission of Farrar, Straus & Giroux, Inc. and Macmillan, London and Basingstoke. Translation copyright © 1968 by Kevin Crossley-Holland.

From THE COMPLETE POEMS OF D. H. LAWRENCE edited by Vivian de Sola Pinto and F. Warren Roberts. Copyright © 1964, 1971 by Angelo Ravagli and C. M. Weekley, Executors of The Estate of Frieda Lawrence Ravagli. Reprinted by permission of The Viking Press and Laurence Pollinger Ltd.

analogy:

From POETRY VENTURED, Marjorie Schuck and George Garrott, Eds., Poetry Venture Publishers, 1972. Reprinted by permission.

"Our little kinsmen after rain" by Emily Dickinson from BOLTS OF MELODY, edited by Mabel Loomis Todd and Millicent Todd Bingham. Copyright 1945 by "The Trustees of Amherst College." Reprinted by permission of Harper & Row, Publishers, Inc.

assonance:

From "A Young Man's Song," MOUNTAINS BENEATH THE HORIZON by William Bell. Published by Faber and Faber Ltd., 1950.

From "The Compost Heap" by Vernon Watkins. © 1965 The New Yorker Magazine, Inc. Reprinted by permission.

cacophony/euphony:

From "Arctic Tern in a Museum" by Effie Lee Newsome, THE POETRY OF THE NEGRO, 1746-1949. Published by Doubleday & Company, 1970. Reprinted by permission of the author.

From BLOSSOMING ANTLERS by Winifred Welles. Copyright 1933 by Winifred Welles. Reprinted by permission of The Viking Press.

From "Cowboy Song" from SURVIVOR'S LEAVE by Charles Causeley. Published by The Hand and Flower Press. Reprinted by permission of David Higham Associates Limited.

"Pisces." From David Gascoyne COLLECTED POEMS, © Oxford University Press 1965. Reprinted by permission of Oxford University Press.

Copyright 1934 and renewed 1962 by Stephen Spender. Reprinted from COLLECTED POEMS 1928-1953, by permission of Random House, Inc. and Faber and Faber Ltd.

From "The Shell." Reprinted with permission of Macmillan Publishing Co., Inc., Mrs. Iris Wise, Macmillan London and Basingstoke, and The Macmillan Company of Canada Limited, from COLLECTED POEMS by James Stephens. Copyright 1916 by Macmillan Publishing Co., Inc., renewed 1944 by James Stephens.

characterization:

From EMMA by Jane Austen, 1816.

connotation/denotation:

"Four Glimpses of Night" by Frank Marshall Davis. From THE POETRY OF THE NEGRO 1746-1970. Published by Doubleday & Company, Inc. Reprinted by permission of the author.

consonance:

From "In Her Song She Is Alone" by Jon Swan. © 1957 The New Yorker Magazine, Inc. Reprinted by permission.

free verse:

From "XIV" by Alberto Caeiro (Fernando Pesson), translated by Jonathan Griffin, from Volume 1 of THE SELECTED POEMS OF FERNANDO PESSON. Carcanet Press. Reprinted by permission of Jonathan Griffin.

imagery:

From THE COMPLETE POETICAL WORKS OF AMY LOWELL. Copyright 1955 by Houghton Mifflin Company. Reprinted by permission of the publisher.

From CEREMONY by Leslie Marmon Silko. Published by The Viking Press, 1977.

lyric:

"Sent from the Capital to Her Elder Daughter" by Lady Ōtomo of Sakanoue (8th Century). Translated by Geoffrey Bownas and Anthony Thwaite. From ALONE AMID ALL THIS NOISE: A COLLECTION OF WOMEN'S POETRY selected by Ann Reit. Published by Four Winds Press, 1976.

From COLLECTED POEMS, Vol. III by Alfred Noyes. Copyright 1913, 1941 by Alfred Noyes. Reprinted by permission of J. B. Lippincott Company and Hugh Noyes.

metaphor:

From "Affinities" from HEROES, ADVISE US by Adrien Stoutenberg. Published by Charles Scribner's Sons. Copyright © 1964 by Adrien Stoutenberg. Reprinted by permission of Curtis Brown, Ltd.

From THE POETRY OF THE NEGRO 1746-1970, Edited by Langston Hughes and Arna Bontemps. Published by Doubleday & Company, Inc.

"Egg" is reprinted from THE FIVE STAGES OF GRIEF, Poems, by Linda Pastan, with the permission of the publisher, W. W. Norton & Company, Inc. and Manuscripts Unlimited. Copyright © 1978 by Linda Pastan. First appeared in POETRY, January 1977.

narrative poetry:

From LOSS OF THE MAGYAR by Patricia Beer. Published by Longman Group Ltd. Reprinted by permission of the author.

onomatopoeia:

Copyright © 1964 by Eve Merriam. From IT DOESN'T ALWAYS HAVE TO RHYME. Used by permission of Atheneum Publishers.

From SMOKE AND STEEL by Carl Sandburg, copyright, 1920, by Harcourt Brace Jovanovich, Inc.; copyright, 1948, by Carl Sandburg. Reprinted by permission of the publishers.

personification:

Copyright © 1971 by John Updike. Reprinted from TOSSING AND TURNING, by John Updike, by permission of Alfred A. Knopf, Inc. and Andre Deutsch Limited.

From "The Vikings," THE CHERRY TREE: A Collection of Poems chosen by Geoffrey Grigson. Published by The Vanguard Press, Inc. Copyright, © mcmlix, by Geoffrey Grigson. Reprinted by permission of the author.

From THE MYTH OF A WOMAN'S FIST by Ann Darr. Published by William Morrow & Company, Inc., 1973.

From "The Bird of Night" from THE BAT POET by Randall Jarrell. Copyright © Macmillan Publishing Company, Inc., 1963, 1964. Reprinted by permission of Macmillan Publishing Co., Inc. and Penguin Books Ltd.

From "Leaves," LEAVES DO NOT FALL, copyright © 1972 by Malka Heifetz Tussman. Translation copyright © 1976 by Marcia Falk. Reprinted by permission of Marcia Falk.

From "Hard Frost" from COLLECTED POEMS by Andrew Young. Reprinted by permission of Granada Publishing Limited.

plot:

"Grand Inquisitor" by G. B. Stern, THE LADIES' HOME JOURNAL, March 1931. Reprinted by permission of A. D. Peters & Co. Ltd.

rhyme:

From AESOP AND HYSSOP, translated by William Ellery Leonard. Reprinted by permission of Open Court Publishing Company, La Salle, Ill.

From THE POETRY OF THE NEGRO 1746-1970, Edited by Langston Hughes and Arna Bontemps. Published by Doubleday & Company, Inc.

"Midsummer Jingle" from GAY BUT WISTFUL by Newman Levy. Published by Alfred A. Knopf, Inc. Reprinted by permission of the estate of Newman Levy.

satire:

"The Rabbit" by Alan Brownjohn from THE RAILINGS (Digby Press, 1961). Reprinted by permission of the author.

setting:

Excerpt from REBECCA by Daphne du Maurier. Copyright 1938 by Daphne du Maurier Browning. Reprinted by permission of Doubleday & Company, Inc. and Curtis Brown, Ltd.

style:

From "That Was Paris" by Janet Flanner, THE NEW YORKER, March 11, 1972.

symbol:

From THE ONLY WORLD THERE IS by Miller Williams. Copyright © 1971, 1970, 1969, 1968 by Miller Williams. Reprinted by permission of the publishers, E. P. Dutton.

theme:

From COUNTRY SENTIMENT. Published by Alfred A. Knopf, Inc. Copyright 1920 by Robert Graves. Reprinted by permission of Curtis Brown, Ltd.

From SMOKE AND STEEL by Carl Sandburg, copyright, 1920, by Harcourt Brace Jovanovich, Inc.; copyright, 1948, by Carl Sandburg. Reprinted by permission of the publishers.

tone:

From TIMES THREE by Phyllis McGinley. Copyright 1954 by Phyllis McGinley. Reprinted by permission of The Viking Press and Martin Secker & Warburg Limited.

Handbook
of
Literary
Terms

alliteration

An Austrian army, awfully array'd,
Boldly by battery besiege Belgrade;

What is the recurring initial sound in each word of each of the above lines? These lines contain extreme examples of *alliteration*, the repetition of identical or similar sounds at the beginnings of words or within the words themselves, particularly at the beginning of accented syllables. You are probably already familiar with alliteration as it is used in advertising: "Quick Clean Car Care" or "Buy Big Broiled Burgers." Many ordinary expressions contain alliteration: *wild west; fair, fat, and forty; merry month of May; rough and ready.*

We like to use alliteration because it is pleasing to the ear and to the tongue, or as Charles Dickens once wrote:

Papa, potatoes, poultry, prunes and prism
are all very good words for the lips:
especially prunes and prism.

Alliteration can draw attention to certain words in a poem:

Safe upon the solid rock the
ugly houses stand:
Come and see my shining palace
built upon the sand!

Millay, *Figs from Thistles*

It can link together words that are similar in thought or feeling:

Cold are the crabs that crawl on yonder hills
Colder the cucumbers that grow beneath . . .

Lear, "Cold Are the Crabs"

It can point up contrasts:

The Hart loves the high wood,
the Hare loves the hill . . .

Alliteration in poetry gives pleasure, but a good poet may make the sound "an echo to the sense." How sound can echo sense or meaning is shown in the examples below:

When he saw Grendel's gruesome footprints,
that great man grieved for his retainers.

Beowulf (translated by Kevin Crossley-Holland)

Does the repeated *gr* sound help to make this line seem light or heavy?

Sea-Weed

Sea-weed sways and sways and swirls
as if swaying were its form of stillness;
and if it flushes against fierce rock
it slips over as shadows do, without hurting itself.

D. H. Lawrence

What effect does the repeated *s* sound have?

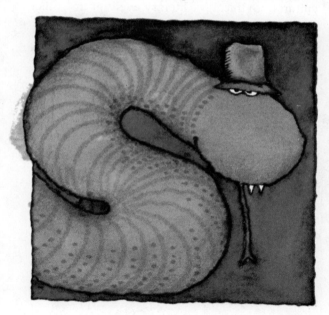

alliteration (ə lit'ə rā'shən)

The repetition of similar or identical sounds at the beginnings of words or in accented syllables. Alliteration is used to create melody, establish mood, call attention to certain words, and point up similarities and contrasts.

allusion

March 15 hit hard this year—grey, rainy, and a chill wind that bit right through my jacket. By the time I reached school, my shoes were soaked, my socks damp and itchy, and my homework soggy. As I sat down in my first-period class, world history, Mr. Brutto told us to take out a clean sheet of paper and clear our desks. It meant only one thing: a pop quiz. I guess that old bird was right when he said to beware the ides of March. I should've stayed in bed.

Who is the "old bird" referred to in the above paragraph? What does the writer of the paragraph mean by referring to the "ides of March?" How does the reference relate to the events in the paragraph? (For the source of the *allusion*, see *Julius Caesar*, act I, scene 2.)

An allusion is a reference to any historical, cultural, mythical, or literary event or any other aspect of ancient or modern culture. Some allusions are so familiar that you may not think of them as such. For example, the Biblical figures David and Goliath are commonly alluded to in any kind of match which involves opponents of apparently unequal size or strength. A fantastic young hitter on a baseball team might be called "the new Hank Aaron" by sportswriters.

Allusions in literature may be used to increase meaning, beauty, or mood, or to add depth to a work. They are a concise means of strengthening atmosphere or clarifying tone. Allusions may be incidental to a work, or they may be crucial to its understanding. Sometimes they require research on the part of the reader.

In order to understand the cartoon, the reader must be familiar with the German folk legend of the Pied Piper of Hamelin. In this story, the town of Hamelin is plagued by rats. While the town fathers are casting about for a solution to the problem, an oddly dressed man appears as if by magic. He claims he can rid the town of the rodents in return for one thousand gold pieces. The town fathers agree. The piper pipes a tune; all the rats of the town scurry out of their holes, follow him into the river, and drown. When the piper comes to collect his fee, however, the greedy aldermen refuse to pay. The piper pipes once again, and this time all the children of the town follow the piper. He leads them to a large hill which opens to allow them inside, and none are ever seen again. (Read Browning's "The Pied Piper of Hamelin" for the complete account.) The requirements for allusions are that they be accurate and appropriate to the subject at hand.

Unless one were being ironical or sarcastic, one would not describe routine tasks at home as the labors of Hercules, nor, when speaking of a beautiful woman would one allude to the head of Medusa who, in Greek myth, was beheaded. No one reads simply to fill his or her memory with sources of allusion, but the ability to recognize allusions is a satisfying and inevitable result of wide reading.

allusion (ə lü′zhən)

A reference to a historical or literary figure or event. It may allude to myth, religion, or to any other aspect of ancient or modern culture.

Aspirations
toward space
are not new.

5 Consider the worm
that becomes
a butterfly.

George Garrott

The poet is drawing an *analogy* between our comparatively recent desire to fly and explore space and the innate ability of the caterpillar to change into a butterfly. An analogy is a comparison drawn between two basically unlike things that nonetheless have points of similarity. Analogy is used particularly when one thing being compared is generally unknown or difficult to understand while the other is well known or easy to understand.

Our Little Kinsmen

Our little kinsmen after rain
In plenty may be seen,
A pink and pulpy multitude
The tepid ground upon.

5 A needless life it seemed to me
Until a little bird
As to a hospitality
Advanced and breakfasted.

As I of he, so God of me,
10 pondered, may have judged,
And left the little angleworm
With modesties enlarged.

Emily Dickinson

Who are "our little kinsmen"? Why are they not examples of "needless life"? If the "kinsmen" are half of the analogy, who is the other half? Why is this a humbling experience for the poet?

analogy (ə nal′ə jē)

An analogy is a comparison drawn between two basically different things that have some points in common. It is used particularly to explain a difficult idea or point in terms of a simpler one.

Maidens who this burning May
through the woods in quaint distress
wander til you find your way . . .

Bell, "A Young Man's Song"

What words and syllables are accented in the above lines? What vowel sound is often repeated in those accented words and syllables? The recurring *ā* sound is an example of *assonance:* identical or similar vowel sound followed by different consonant sounds. It occurs generally in accented words or syllables. Assonance differs from rhyme in that rhyme is a similarity of both vowel and consonant sounds. *Quaint* and *faint* are rhyming words; *quaint* and *maidens* illustrate assonance.

Point out the examples of assonance in the following lines.

Think from how many trees
Dead leaves are brought
To earth on seed or wing . . .

Watkins, "The Compost Heap"

Not only are the assonant words stressed rhythmically, assonance emphasizes words already associated in their meaning: *trees, leaves, seed*. Assonance can thus contribute not only to the sound or musical quality of a poem, but also to its meaning.

assonance (as′n əns)

The repetition of similar or identical vowel sounds followed by different consonant sounds in stressed words or syllables. Assonance can contribute to the meaning of a work, to its musical quality, and to its unity.

And at the threshold of her chamber door
The Carthage lords did there the queen await;
The trampling steed, with gold and purple decked,
Chawing the foamy bit, there fiercely stood.

Surrey, from *The Fourth Book of Virgil*

1. Do the above lines rhyme?
2. How many feet are there in each line?
3. What is the meter? (See RHYTHM for a discussion of meter and scansion.)

In the sixteenth century, English lyric poets discovered that the English language has a natural iambic beat. They also found that combinations of English words fall naturally into lines of five feet. Once the lyricists had recognized iambic pentameter as a natural English line, they used it extensively (though not exclusively) for rhymed verse.

Dramatists and narrative poets at first adopted the rhymed iambic pentameter line of the lyric poets, but they found it difficult to sustain the rhyme for five acts of a play or for several hundred or more lines of narrative poetry. They were forced to recognize that, although there is a great variety of final sounds in English, comparatively few words end with the same sound. Consequently, the narrative poets and dramatists began to write unrhymed iambic pentameter lines, or *blank verse.* Blank verse was later used in lyric poetry as well.

Read the following passages; explain whether or not each of them is in blank verse.

Come live with me and be my Love,
And we will all the pleasures prove
That hills and valleys, dales and fields,
Or woods or steepy mountain yields.

Marlowe,
"The Passionate Shepherd to His Love"

That time of year thou mayst in me behold
When yellow leaves, or none, or few, do hang
Upon those boughs which shake against the cold,
Bare ruined choirs where late the sweet birds sang.

Shakespeare, "Sonnet 73"

Alas! for this gray shadow, once a man—
So glorious in his beauty and thy choice,
Who madest him thy chosen, that he seemed
To his great heart none other than a god!

Tennyson, "Tithonus"

William Shakespeare was a master of both rhymed verse and blank verse. He cast his dramas in blank-verse lines.

Oh, he sits high in all the people's hearts;
And that which would appear offense in us,
His countenance, like richest alchemy,
Will change to virtue and to worthiness.

Shakespeare, *Julius Caesar,* act I, scene 3

Occasionally a line or lines of a blank-verse passage may depart from a regular iambic pattern. The following lines are spoken by one of the conspirators against Caesar. What line deviates from the iambic pentameter pattern?

Their minds may change. Besides, it were a mock
Apt to be rendered, for someone to say,
"Break up the Senate till another time,
When Caesar's wife shall meet with better dreams."
If Caesar hide himself, shall they not whisper,
"Lo, Caesar is afraid"?

Julius Caesar, act II, scene 2

Such shifts enabled Shakespeare to use blank verse to achieve a great variety of dramatic effects. Note how the last line of the passage above stands out because of its different line length. This dramatic line is the one which finally convinces Caesar to go to the Senate on the fateful ides of March, and so it is crucial to the play.

blank verse

Unrhymed poetry in iambic pentameter, ten-syllable lines with five unstressed syllables alternating with five stressed syllables. An unstressed syllable begins the line.

As you read the following lines, try to decide which words have harsh or jarring sounds and which words have gentle and soft sounds.

> Your pallid, still plumage
> In silver and white . . .
>
> Newsome, "Arctic Tern in a Museum"

> The broad sun above laughed a pitiless
>   laugh,
> 'Neath our feet broke the brittle bright
>   stubble like chaff . . .
>
> Robert Browning, "How They Brought
>   the Good News from Ghent to Aix"

> Bound to a boy's swift feet, hard blades of steel
> Ring out a brutal rhythm from black ice.
>
> Welles, "River Skater"

> I come from Salem County
>   Where the silver melons grow,
> Where the wheat is sweet as an angel's feet
>   And the zithering zephyrs blow.
>
> Causeley, "Cowboy Song"

List the words that contain a jolting sound and those that contain a harmonious sound. Is the meaning of the lines in which they are found reinforced by their sounds? A succession of discordants such as *brittle*, *hard*, and *brutal* is called *cacophony*. A succession of smooth, "rounded" sounds such as *plumage*, *silver*, *melons*, and *zephyrs* is called *euphony*. When used skillfully, cacophony and euphony result in sound echoing sense, thus heightening the effect of a poem.

Pisces[1]

> They glitter, but they sing
> Seldom: rather than swim
> They slide through that thick element the waves
> Roof in; swing the slow loop
> 5 Of a lassoo through which
> In reflex they can swoop
> And thus with cunning catch
> In their own track themselves. And then they
>   sweep
> Down sheerest slopes
> 10 And swerve
> Round sharpest curves
> And leap abruptly up, like swift sea-larks,
> To burst through their sky's rolling clouds of foam
> And briefly warble, before sinking home,
> 15 A stave of bubble-song; to which no sailor harks.
>
> David Gascoyne

Which particular sounds or words convey best the movement of the fish? Are the sounds cacophonous or euphonious? Note that there is a great deal of ALLITERATION in this poem. Alliteration may be either cacophonous or euphonious depending upon the repeated sound.

Read the following lines about a train.

> It is now she begins to sing—at first quite low
> Then loud, and at last with a jazzy madness—
> The song of her whistle screaming at curves,
> Of deafening tunnels, brakes, innumerable bolts.
>
> Spender, "The Express"

Which of the above lines is the least cacophonous? Which is the most cacophonous? What harsh sounds echo the progression of meaning of the lines? List some cacophonous

---

1. *Pisces* (pī'sēz), fish.

words that you might use in a poem about a factory. What sounds might be appropriate in a poem about bees?

> And then I pressed the shell
> Close to my ear,
> And listened well.
>
> And straightway, like a bell,
> 5 Came low and clear
> The slow, sad murmur of far distant seas,
> ....
>
> And in the hush of waters was the sound
> Of pebbles, rolling round;
> Forever rolling, with a hollow sound:
> ....
>
> 10 There was no day;
> Nor ever came a night
> Setting the stars alight
>
> To wonder at the moon:
> Was twilight only, and the frightened croon,
> 15 Smitten to whimpers, of the dreary wind
>
> And waves that journeyed blind . . .
> And then I loosed my ear.—Oh, it was sweet
> To hear a cart go jolting down the street!
>
> Stephens, "The Shell"

Where is the change of atmosphere in the above lines? How is that change reflected in the sound of the lines? Which lines or stanzas are euphonious? Which are cacophonous? What is the sense of the final two lines?

cacophony (kə kof′ə nē)

A succession of harsh, jolting sounds.

euphony (yü′ fə nē)

A succession of smooth, harmonious sounds.

People are interested in other people: how they act, where they go, what they think about in any number of situations. That interest is one of the reasons many people enjoy reading stories about imaginary people who seem real.

Characterization is the technique a writer uses to create lifelike characters. A writer may use any of various methods of characterization, but the most thorough depiction of a character will probably include all of the following. (The examples are from the novel *Emma* by Jane Austen, 1816.)

An author may simply describe a character:

Emma Woodhouse, handsome, clever, and rich, with a comfortable home and happy disposition, seemed to unite some of the best blessings of existence; and had lived nearly twenty-one years in the world with very little to distress or vex her.

With this method an author can tell the reader exactly what he or she wants the reader to know about a character's age, appearance, situation in life, or personality traits.

An author may choose to reveal a character's speech and behavior:

"And you have forgotten one matter of joy to me," said Emma, "and a very considerable one—that I made the match myself. I made the match, you know, four years ago; and to have it take place, and be proved in the right, when so many people said Mr. Weston would never marry again, may comfort me for anything."

This method makes demands on the reader's ability to make inferences about a character. On another occasion with two other friends, Harriet Smith and Mr. Elton, Emma again reveals her taste for matchmaking:

They now walked on together quietly, till within view of the vicarage pales, when a sudden resolution, of at least getting Harriet into the house, made her [Emma] again find something very much amiss about her boot, and fall behind to arrange it once more. She then broke the lace off short, and dexterously

throwing it into a ditch, was presently obliged to entreat them to stop, and acknowledge her inability to put herself to rights so as to be able to walk home in tolerable comfort.

"Part of my lace is gone," said she, "and I do not know how I am to contrive. I really am a most troublesome companion to you both, but I hope I am not often so ill-equipped. Mr. Elton, I must beg leave to stop at your house, and ask your house-keeper for a bit of ribband or string, or anything just to keep my boot on."

A writer may describe opinions and reactions of some characters to another character. In the next passage two of Emma's close acquaintances, Mrs. Weston and Mr. Knightley, speak together about Emma and her friendship with someone of whom they faintly disapprove, Harriet Smith:

". . . One hears sometimes of a child being 'the picture of health'; now Emma always gives me the idea of being the complete picture of grown-up health. She is loveliness itself. Mr. Knightley, is not she?"

"I have not a fault to find with her person," he replied. "I think her all you describe. I love to look at her; and I will add this praise, that I do not think her personally vain. Considering how very handsome she is, she appears to be little occupied with it; her vanity lies another way. Mrs. Weston, I am not to be talked out of my dislike of her intimacy with Harriet Smith, or my dread of its doing them both harm."

"And I, Mr. Knightley, am equally stout in my confidence of its not doing them any harm. With all dear Emma's little faults, she is an excellent creature. Where shall we see a better daughter, or a kinder sister, or a truer friend? No, no; she has qualities which may be trusted; she will never lead any one really wrong; she will make no lasting blunder; where Emma errs once, she is in the right a hundred times."

Again, the readers must draw their own conclusions about the personality of Emma by noting what is said about her.

Finally, a writer can reveal a character's personality by disclosing his or her thoughts and feelings. The following excerpt finds Emma contemplating her relationship with a young man, Frank Churchill, who has been visiting his relatives, the Westons, at their estate, Randalls, and who has now left for his own home.

Emma continued to entertain no doubt of her being in love. Her ideas only varied as to the how much. At first, she thought it was a good deal; and afterwards, but little. She had great pleasure in hearing Frank Churchill talked of; and, for his sake, greater pleasure than ever in seeing Mr. and Mrs. Weston; she was very often thinking of him, and quite impatient for a letter, that she might know how he was, how were his spirits, how was his aunt, and what was the chance of his coming to Randalls again this spring. But, on the other hand, she could not admit herself to be unhappy, nor, after the first morning, to be less disposed for employment than usual; she was still busy and cheerful; and, pleasing as he was, she could yet imagine him to have faults; and farther, though thinking of him so much, and, as she sat drawing or working, forming a thousand amusing schemes for the progress and close of their attachment, fancying interesting dialogues, and inventing elegant letters; the conclusion of every imaginary declaration on his side was that she *refused him*. Their affection was always to subside into friendship. Everything tender and charming was to mark their parting; but still they were to part. When she became sensible of this, it struck her that she could not be very much in love; for in spite of her previous and fixed determination never to quit her father, never to marry, a strong attachment certainly must produce more of a struggle than she could foresee in her own feelings.

These selections represent but a small part of Jane Austen's characterization of Emma, but having read them, you have an idea of the sort of person Emma is.

1. Is Emma plain featured?

2. Has she had a difficult life?

3. What is something she prides herself on doing?

4. Is Emma self-confident or hesitant in making decisions?

5. What is her relationship to her father?

6. Will she stoop to deception to bring about something she desires? Support your opinion.

7. Is she honest with herself?

Not all written works emphasize characterization. When plot or setting is emphasized over character the characters are apt to be stereotypes. (See STEREOTYPE.)

characterization

The technique a writer uses to create and reveal the personalities of the characters in a written work. A writer may describe a character's physical appearance and situation, reveal a character's thoughts, or show the reactions of other characters.

Below is a definition of the word *dentist* as it appears in a dictionary.

den·tist (den′tist), *n.* doctor whose work is the care of teeth. A dentist fills cavities in teeth, cleans, straightens, or extracts them, and supplies artificial teeth.

Does the word *dentist* have any personal meaning or association for you? How does your own meaning for *dentist* differ from the dictionary definition? What might the word mean to someone with a toothache? to someone whose parent is a dentist? to a dentist?

Many words in everyday use do double duty. On the one hand they have a dictionary meaning, or *denotation*. On the other, they have a *connotation*, or significance and association beyond the dictionary meaning. A connotative word gathers its associations from people's experiences, both personal and universal.

Because many experiences are personal, the significance of a word such as *home*, for example, is different to different people. It might mean untidiness, bickering, or a lack of privacy to some, while to others it might connote good food, love, or security. State possible connotations of the word *dog* to a (**a**) little child; (**b**) would-be thief; (**c**) person with allergies. State possible connotations of the word *food* to (**a**) an overweight person; (**b**) a grocery-store owner; (**c**) a hungry person. State possible connotations of the word *sky* to (**a**) a philosopher; (**b**) an airplane pilot; (**c**) an astronomer.

night (nīt), *n.* 1 the time between evening and morning; the time from sunset to sunrise, especially when it is dark. 2 the darkness of night; the dark. 3 the darkness of ignorance, sin, sorrow, old age, death, etc. 4 evening; nightfall.

What does the word *night* mean to you? Is it a time to go to sleep? a fearful time? a retreat from the day's work? Read the following poem to find the various ways the poet sees night.

Four Glimpses of Night

I. Eagerly
Like a woman hurrying to her lover
Night comes to the room of the world
And lies, yielding and content
Against the cool round face
Of the moon.

II. Night is a curious child, wandering
Between earth and sky, creeping
In windows and doors, daubing
The entire neighborhood
With purple paint.
Day
Is an apologetic mother
Cloth in hand
Following after.

III. Peddling
From door to door

Night sells
Black bags of peppermint stars
Heaping cones of vanilla moon
Until
His wares are gone
Then shuffles homeward
Jingling the grey coins
Of daybreak.

IV. Night's brittle song, sliver-thin
Shatters into a billion fragments
Of quiet shadows
At the blaring jazz
Of a morning sun.

Frank Marshall Davis

What are the different visions of night in each stanza? What characteristics does Davis give night which are not found in the dictionary definition?

connotation

The interpretations of a word beyond its literal definition.

denotation

The literal meaning of a word as found in a dictionary.

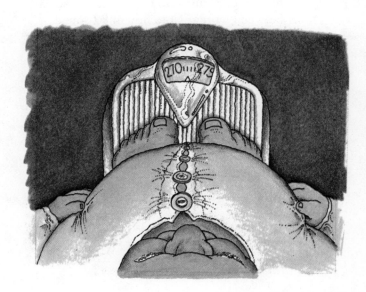

An old, mad, blind, despised, and dying king—

> Shelley, "England in 1819"

Read the above line softly to yourself. What sound is repeated several times? Where does the repeated sound most often appear? What effect does the repeated sound have on your reading of the line?

The repeated *d* sound at the end of words is an example of *consonance:* the repetition of the same consonant sound preceded by a different vowel sound. In the above line the repeated *d* sound has the effect of slowing the reading of the line, thus emphasizing the words in which it is found.

Consonance at the end of two or more lines of poetry is called *half rhyme* or *slant rhyme* because only the final consonant sounds are alike. (See RHYME.) Read the following stanza.

> Nothing lovelier than that lonely call,
> Bare and singular, like a gull,
> And three notes or four, then that was all.
> It drew up from the quiet like a well,
> Waited, sang, and vanishing, was still.
>
> Swan, "In Her Song She Was Alone"

Consonance is also used to suggest associations between words. Note how the *l* sound effectively unites key words of the stanza. What two pairs of words are particularly associated through consonance? The *l* sound has a lingering, almost echoing effect. How is that appropriate to the stanza's TONE?

---

consonance (kon′sə nəns)

The repetition of similar or identical consonant sounds preceded by different vowel sounds. It is often used instead of rhyme at the end of lines of poetry. Consonance can stress important words and strengthen meaning through word association. It may add to the unity of sound and sense in a poem.

Read each set of lines.

A. a. She has a pink-and-white complexion.
　　b. There is a garden in her face,
　　　　Where roses and lilies grow;

> Campion, "Cherry-Ripe"

B. a. When I am old, wrinkled, chilly, and
　　　　　　white-haired. . . .
　　b. When age hath made me what I am not
　　　　now;
　　　　And every wrinkle tells me where the
　　　　plough
　　　　Of time hath furrowed; when an ice
　　　　shall flow
　　　　Through every vein, and all my head
　　　　wear snow;

> Randolph, "Upon His Picture"

C. a. I forgot his answer.
　　b. And his answer trickled through my head,
　　　　Like water through a sieve.

> Dodgson, "The White Knight's Song"

Which lines are literal? Which lines suggest associations or comparisons? What things are being compared in each case? All of the **b** items contain examples of *figurative language.* Figurative language is the use of words outside their usual, or literal, meanings. By suggesting new associations or comparisons, they can add beauty and increase the impact or vitality of the lines and works in which they are found. Sometimes figurative language may seem even more direct than literal language because it enables the reader to grasp the idea quickly. The various elements of figurative language are called *figures of speech.* The most commonly used figures of speech are SIMILE (a comparison made explicit by the use of the word *like* or *as*), METAPHOR, PERSONIFICATION, and SYMBOL.

To be successful, figurative language must be appropriate. Although figurative language compares basically different things, there must be a point of similarity between the objects for the figure of speech to be effective. For ex-

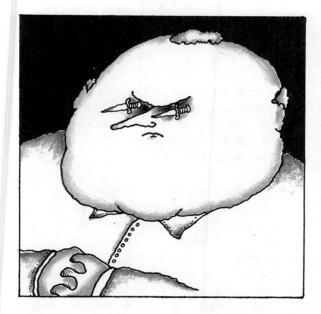

ample, a person might say, "I've been shoveling snow for an hour, and my hands are like blocks of ice." Most listeners would understand the speaker to mean that his or her hands are very cold and stiff because ice is cold and hard and hands can be cold and stiff. If, however, the person had compared his or her hands to lemons or tamales or rosebuds, the listener would very probably have no idea what was meant. There must be some recognizable point of similarity for the figure of speech to be appropriate. Read the following lines and decide (1) what things are being compared and (2) whether the figurative language is effective and appropriate.

A. The lion's roar rolled like thunder.

B. The frightened lost child cowered in the aisle
       like a golden eagle.

C. My love is like a red, red rose
    That's newly sprung in June:
  My love is like the melody
    That's sweetly played in tune.

      Burns, "A Red, Red Rose"

D. The tears on her cheeks were glistening rocks.

A figure of speech need not be limited to one phrase, line, sentence, or paragraph. It may often be extended to include any of these, or even the entire work. If a figure of speech extends through a paragraph, for instance, it should be consistent. That is, many different comparisons or associations should not be used to describe the same thing. For example, a lantern in the window may seem to a weary traveler to beam "a finger of light" that "points the way home," "beckons him in welcome," and "warmly strokes his cheek as he nears the house." It would be inconsistent then to change the image to compare the lantern to the sun or the moon.

Read the following lines. The main character, Macbeth, has just murdered his king while the king slept.

> Methought I heard a voice cry, "Sleep no more!
> Macbeth does murder sleep," the innocent sleep,
> Sleep that knits up the raveled sleave of care,
> The death of each day's life, sore labor's bath,
> Balm of hurt minds, great nature's second course,
> Chief nourisher in life's feast—
>
>   *Macbeth*, act II, scene 2

To what various things is sleep compared? What is Macbeth saying literally? How does the use of figurative language give the reader a clear idea about Macbeth's state of mind?

figurative language

The use of words outside their literal, or usual, meanings. Figurative language is used to add beauty, increase vitality and impact, suggest associations and comparisons, and develop conciseness.

Shortly after the opening of the story "The Monkey's Paw," the White family questions their guest, Sergeant-Major Morris, about the mummified monkey's paw he acquired in India. After telling them of the spell put on the paw that allows three men three wishes each, Morris is asked if he has had his three wishes.

" 'I have,' he said quietly, and his blotchy face whitened."

At this point the reader does not know what the monkey's paw can or cannot do, but does learn that the very thought of it frightens a professional soldier. This hint, clue, or indication of what is to come is called *foreshadowing.*

Foreshadowing serves two purposes: (1) It stimulates interest on the part of the reader, listener, or viewer to learn what happens next; and (2) it prepares the reader, listener, or viewer, in part at least, for the direction the plot will take, thus making it seem more real and less contrived.

In the first speech in *Medea* (page 302) the Nurse says of Medea,

. . . I fear she may be moving toward some dreadful plan; for her heart is violent. She will never submit to this cruel treatment. I know her well: her anger is great; and I know that any man who makes an enemy of her will have it hard.

Through this speech the reader or listener is alerted that the events to follow will probably be concerned with Medea's anger and a related violence.

As early as the second scene of Act I of *Julius Caesar* (page 441), the Soothsayer warns, "Beware the ides of March." Startled at first, Caesar laughs off the encounter. What is foreshadowed by this statement?

foreshadowing

The technique of giving the reader, listener, or viewer of a story or play hints of what is to come in that work.

I don't bother with rhymes. It is seldom
That there are two trees equal, side by side.

Alberto Caeiro, "XIV"
(translated by Jonathan Griffin)

Free verse, a form of unrhymed English poetry, has become a favorite form of many modern poets. (See also BLANK VERSE.) Free verse is called "free" because the poet does not follow set patterns of rhyme, meter, or line length.

Free-verse poets believe rhyme is an inadequate poetic device. They point out that rhyme may restrict, even dictate, the meaning of a poem. For example, imagine a poet who is composing a serious tercet, a stanza of three rhyming lines, about a dove he once held in his hand and touched gently. The word *dove* suggests that his three lines will rhyme the *-ove* sound. He begins:

A gray, white-throated dove
Lay quivering in my glove;

In the next line, he wants to say, "I gave it a gentle touch." *Touch* does not rhyme with *dove* or *glove* so he casts about for a word that does, with this result:

A gray, white-throated dove
Lay quivering in my glove;
I gave it a gentle shove.

The rhyme has drastically changed the poet's meaning. To avoid such a predicament, free-verse poets dispense with rhyme. If they regulate sound at all it is mainly through ALLITERATION and ASSONANCE.

Free-verse poets, unlike blank-verse poets, believe meter is an unnecessary poetic device since every word we use has a natural rhythm of its own. Depending upon the natural stress (or lack of stress) in words, free-verse lines such as these:

Beautiful evening
Calm, free

are just as rhythmical in their way as is this metrical version:

It is / a beau / teous eve / ning, calm / and free.

Wordsworth, "It Is a Beauteous Evening"

Often the free-verse poet gives his reader a clue to the movement of his poem by beginning each rhythmical unit on a new line.

When I Heard the Learn'd Astronomer

When I heard the learn'd astronomer,
When the proofs, the figures, were
    ranged in columns before me,
When I was shown the charts and
    diagrams, to add, divide, and
    measure them,
When I sitting heard the astronomer
    where he lectured with much
    applause in the lecture-room,
5 How soon unaccountable I became
    tired and sick,
Till rising and gliding out I wander'd
    off by myself,
In the mystical moist night air, and
    from time to time,
Look'd up in perfect silence at the
    stars.

Walt Whitman

free verse

Poetry that follows no set patterns of rhyme, meter, or line length.

The Pond

Cold, wet leaves
Floating on moss-coloured water,

And the croaking of frogs—
Cracked bell-notes in the twilight.

Amy Lowell

From the poem above, pick out the words or phrases that appeal to your sense of sight, sound, and touch. Sensory appeals made through descriptions and details are called *images.*

A skilled writer conveys to readers a sense of experiencing what they are reading about, and so involves them in the world of the written selection.

Read the passage below from Charles Dickens's *A Christmas Carol.*

It was his own room. There was no doubt about that. But it had undergone a surprising transformation. The walls and ceiling were so hung with living green, that it looked a perfect grove; from every part of which, bright gleaming berries glistened. The crisp leaves of holly, mistletoe, and ivy reflected back the light, as if so many little mirrors had been scattered there; and such a mighty blaze went roaring up the chimney, as that dull petrification of a hearth had never known in Scrooge's time, or Marley's, or for many and many a winter season gone. Heaped up on the floor, to form a kind of throne, were turkeys, geese, game, poultry, brawn, great joints of meat, suckling-pigs, long wreaths of sausages, mince-pies, plum-puddings, barrels of oysters, red-hot chestnuts, cherry-cheeked apples, juicy oranges, luscious pears, immense twelfth-cakes, and seething bowls of punch, that made the chamber dim with their delicious steam.

To which senses does the passage appeal? What details does Dickens add to the recital of food that make it more than a holiday grocery list? Which images appeal particularly to your sense of taste? of smell?

Read the following passage from *Ceremony,* a book by Leslie Silko, and try to imagine the

scene as you read. (Tayo is a young native American, home from the Korean War.)

Tayo stood near the horses, looking down the path over the way they had come. The plateaus and canyons spread out below him like clouds falling into each other past the horizon. The world below was distant and small; it was dwarfed by a sky so blue and vast the clouds were lost in it. Far into the south there were smoky blue ridges of the mountain haze at Zuni. He smoothed his hand over the top of his head and felt the sun. The mountain wind was cool; it smelled like springs hidden deep in mossy black stone. He could see no signs of what had been set loose upon the earth: the highways, the towns, even the fences were gone.

What images of sight, touch, and smell are depicted? In what part of the country would you say the story takes place? How is the sense of the vastness of the place communicated? What emotions or feelings does the description evoke?

The following passage is also from *Ceremony*. In it Tayo is hurt and losing consciousness.

Black pebbles and the ancient gray cinders the mountain had thrown poked into his backbone. He closed his eyes but did not sleep. He felt cold gusts of wind scattering dry oak leaves in the grass. He listened to the cowboy collect tobacco juice in his mouth and the squirting liquid sound when he spat. He was aware of the center beneath him; it soaked into his body from the ground through the torn skin on his hands, covered with powdery black dirt. The magnetism of the center spread over him smoothly like rainwater down his neck and shoulders: the vacant cool sensation glided over the pain like feather-down wings. It was pulling him back, close to the earth, where the core was cool and silent as mountain stone . . .

List examples of imagery that you find in the above passage. What is the most vivid image for you? How is the sensation of losing consciousness communicated to the reader?

imagery

The use of concrete details that appeal to the five senses. By appealing to a reader's senses, a writer can more easily communicate an experience.

irony

In the following excerpt from *The Sketch Book*, Washington Irving, an early nineteenth-century American author, explains his reasons for wanting to visit Europe and England: to see great men.

. . . for I had read in the works of various philosophers, that all animals degenerated in America, and man among the number. A great man of Europe, thought I, must therefore be as superior to a great man of America as a peak of the Alps to a highland of the Hudson; and in this idea I was confirmed by observing the comparative importance and swelling magnitude of many English travellers among us, who, I was assured, were very little people in their own country. I will visit this land of wonders, thought I, and see the gigantic race from which I am degenerated.

Does Irving really think the English are superior to Americans? What clues lead to your conclusions? Irving says one thing in this passage, but he means just the opposite. This is an example of *verbal irony*—the surface meaning of what one writes or says being the opposite of the intended meaning.

Verbal irony in everyday speech is easily recognized because the listener has the speaker's tone of voice and facial expression to aid him. For example, if you and a friend have planned a day picnicking and hiking, and when you step out the door it begins to rain, one of you might say, "Oh, good! I was hoping it would rain." This is actually just the opposite of what you were hoping and is an example of verbal irony. When reading, one must be alert to a writer's use of irony or the point may be missed entirely. Note Antony's use of *honorable* when speaking of Brutus in *Julius Caesar*, act III, scene 2 (486, lines 78-95). Verbal irony is frequently used as a device of SATIRE.

Irony of situation occurs when events turn out contrary to what is expected or what seems appropriate. "The Gift of the Magi," a short story by O. Henry, turns on irony of situation.

In it a penniless young couple want to buy each other special Christmas presents. The wife has her beautiful long hair cut off, sells it, and buys a chain worthy of her husband's prized gold pocket watch. The husband sells his watch to buy exquisite tortoise shell combs for his wife's beautiful long hair. What is the double irony of the story?

Irony may be gentle, sad, bitter, or, as in "The Gift of the Magi," bittersweet. The general TONE of the piece will indicate the author's intention.

The customer in the cartoon below is asking a reasonable question. What do you know that he does not which makes his question particularly humorous?

"You're sure I'll be able to swim with it?"

Copyright, 1977, Universal Press Syndicate.

lyric

Dramatic irony occurs when the reader or viewer knows more about the actual situation than the characters do. It is often found in drama; for example, an offhand remark is made or a seemingly unimportant action occurs which has significance hidden from the character involved, but revealed to the audience. Dramatic irony may be humorous, as in the cartoon; poignant, as in *Our Town* (page 184); or ominous, as in *Julius Caesar,* when the audience knows Brutus is plotting Caesar's death but Caesar does not.

Ironic is a word which may cause some confusion. According to the dictionary it means the same as *ironical:* "using or given to using or expressing irony." You may yourself have said "How ironic!" or have read of someone described as having an ironic smile. In the first instance, you simply mean that the situation being noted has taken a twist—the opposite of what might normally be expected (a championship skier slips and breaks a leg on a stairway), or that something has been expressed when the opposite was meant. An ironic smile may describe the expression of a character who may be fond of doing the opposite of what is anticipated or may be an appreciative observer of life's ironies. In any case, the word is usually a clue that the author expects the reader to infer that the character so described has a turn of mind or habit which employs or enjoys the unexpected ways things often work out.

irony

A contrast between what is said and what is actually meant is called *verbal irony; irony of situation* occurs when things turn out contrary to what is expected; *dramatic irony* occurs when the reader or viewer is aware of something about which the character involved knows nothing; *ironic* is an adjective which may be applied when any of the above situations are being described. Irony is a frequently used device of satire.

Sent from the Capital to Her Elder Daughter

More than the gems
Locked away and treasured
In his comb-box
By the God of the Sea,
5 I prize you, my daughter.
But we are of this world
And such is its way!
Summoned by your man,
Obedient, you journeyed
10 To the far-off land of Koshi.
Since we parted,
Like a spreading vine,
Your eyebrows, pencil-arched,
Like waves about to break,
15 Have flitted before my eyes,
Bobbing like tiny boats.
Such is my yearning for you
That this body, time-riddled,
May well not bear the strain.

Lady Ōtomo of Sakanoue (8th Century)
(translated by Geoffrey Bownas
and Anthony Thwaite)

What emotion is expressed in the poem? Is the poet's tone personal or impersonal? Do you think the poet is concerned primarily with telling a story or with expressing a feeling?

The poem above belongs to a category of poetry called *lyric* poetry. A lyric is a short poem expressing a personal, basic emotion such as love, sorrow, joy, patriotism, or religious feeling—anything that is deeply and sincerely felt by the poet.

The Rustling of Grass

I cannot tell why,
But the rustling of grass,
As the summer winds pass
Through the field where I lie,
5 Brings to life a lost day,
Long ago, far away,
When in childhood I lay
Looking up at the sky
And the white clouds that pass,
10 Trailing isles of grey shadow
Across the gold grass . . .
O, the dreams that drift by
With the slow flowing years,

metaphor

Hopes, Memories, tears,
15 In the rustling grass.

Alfred Noyes

What emotion is expressed in this poem?

lyric

A short poem expressing a basic, personal emotion such as grief, happiness, love, or melancholy.

metaphor

Read the following lines about a cat.

Thunder's loose guitar
is in him,
in miniature,
and the thistle's fire.

Stoutenberg, "Affinities"

Think about the characteristics of a thistle. How could a cat be like the "thistle's fire"? What, in a cat, is the "thunder's loose guitar"? Are the comparisons appropriate? The above lines are examples of *metaphor*, a figure of speech that implies comparison between two basically dissimilar things. The comparison is implied because no connective word such as *like* or *as* is used. (See FIGURATIVE LANGUAGE.)

We all use metaphors daily without giving them much thought. A student who is finally understanding chemistry might say he is beginning to see the light, or a teacher who is explaining the basics of trigonometry might say that the explanation was just the tip of the iceberg. In each case, qualities of one thing are being assigned to completely different things.

Writers use metaphors to expand meanings through surprising associations. A metaphor need not be limited to a single line or sentence. Sometimes a writer will continue a metaphor throughout a paragraph, stanza, or entire work. This is called an *extended metaphor*.

Forgotten Dreams

The soft gray hands of sleep
Toiled all night long
To spin a beautiful garment
Of dreams;
5 At dawn
The little task was done.
Awakening,
The garb so deftly spun
Was only a heap
10 Of ravelled thread—
A vague remembrance
In my head.

Edward Silvera

What things are being compared in the poem? Is the metaphor extended throughout the poem? Do you think the comparisons are appropriate? Are the metaphors used effective in describing dreams? For a metaphor to be effective, it must reveal or suggest a common quality between the things compared. For example, what if the poet had begun the poem with "The rough red hands of sleep"? Why would that not be as effective as "soft gray"?

Not only must a metaphor be appropriate, it must also be consistent. A metaphor that is not consistent is called a *mixed metaphor*. The commentator Edwin Newman calls a mixed metaphor "a figure of speech that is out of control." For example: "With feline grace, Alice stretched and strolled across the room, a great golden canary ready to pounce." What is inconsistent about this metaphor?

The following quote is from a newspaper article.

"I personally resent it: this commission being asked to draw a budget for a plan we had no part in developing," Frank said. "The rug was pulled out from under us, leaving us to hang in limbo and at the end of a primrose path," he said.

St. Louis Globe-Democrat.

What mixed metaphors do you find in this statement? What is Frank trying to say?

Egg

In this kingdom
the sun never sets;
under the pale oval
of the sky
5 there seems no way in
or out,
and though there is a sea here
there is no tide.

For the egg itself
10 is a moon
glowing faintly
in the galaxy of the barn,
safe but for the spoon's
ominous thunder,
15 the first delicate crack
of lightning.

Linda Pastan

What is the "sun"? the "pale oval of the sky"? the "sea"? What is meant by lines 15 and 16? Do you think the metaphors are appropriate? consistent?

metaphor

A figure of speech that implies comparison between two fundamentally different things. The qualities of one are ascribed to the other. An *extended metaphor* is a metaphor continued throughout a stanza, paragraph, or entire work. A *mixed metaphor* is an inconsistent comparison.

mood

Meeting at Night
I

The grey sea and the long black land;
And the yellow half-moon large and low;
And the startled little waves that leap
In fiery ringlets from their sleep,
5 As I gain the cove with pushing prow,
And quench its speed i' the slushy sand.

II

Then a mile of warm sea-scented beach;
Three fields to cross till a farm appears;
A tap at the pane, the quick sharp scratch
10 And blue spurt of a lighted match,
And a voice less loud, thro' its joys and
fears,
Than the two hearts beating each to each!

Robert Browning

narrative poetry

What time of day is it? Where is the narrator in the first stanza? in the second stanza? Who are meeting at night? Which words in the first stanza create an atmosphere of mystery? How is the sense of speed and urgency conveyed in the second stanza? To what senses does the author appeal? Would you characterize this poem as sad? cheerful? passionate?

Though the reader does not realize in the first stanza that the narrator is on his way to meet his beloved, the reader does note the details, such as "grey sea," "long black land," "yellow half-moon," that create a dim mysterious setting. A sense of speed is created through the description of "startled little waves," and the boat's "pushing prow."

The sense of urgency is reinforced in the second stanza by the recital of distances and events in quick succession: "a mile," "three fields," "a farm," "a tap."

Various details produce the IMAGERY that appeals to the reader's senses: the fragrance of the sea-scented beach, the sounds of the tap on the pane, the scratch of the match, and the hushed voice, the sights of the large low half-moon, and the blue spurt of flame. "Slushy sand" creates an image that appeals to both the senses of sound and touch.

All of these details, the descriptions, the imagery, the SETTING, and evocative words come together to create the *mood* of quiet, almost secret, eagerness that surrounds the poem.

mood

The atmosphere and feeling that a writer creates in a work through the choice of setting, imagery, details, descriptions, and other evocative words.

The Fifth Sense

A 65-year-old Cypriot Greek shepherd, Nicolis Loizou, was wounded by security forces early today. He was challenged twice; when he failed to answer, troops opened fire. A subsequent hospital examination showed that the man was deaf. NEWS ITEM, 30 December 1957.

Lamps burn all the night
Here, where people must be watched and seen,
And I, a shepherd, Nicolis Loizou,
Wish for the dark, for I have been
5 Sure-footed in the dark, but now my sight
Stumbles among these beds, scattered white boulders,
As I lean towards my far slumbering house
With the night lying upon my shoulders.

My sight was always good,
10 Better than others. I could taste wine and bread
And name the field they spattered when the harvest
Broke. I could coil in the red
Scent of the fox out of a maze of wood
And grass. I could touch mist, I could touch breath.
15 But of my sharp senses I had only four.
The fifth one pinned me to my death.

The soldiers must have called
The word they needed: Halt. Not hearing it,
I was their failure, relaxed against the winter
20 Sky, the flag of their defeat.
With their five senses they could not have told
That I lacked one, and so they had to shoot.
They would fire at a rainbow if it had
A colour less than they were taught.

25 Christ said that when one sheep
Was lost, the rest meant nothing any more.
Here in this hospital where others' breathing
Swings like a lantern in the polished floor
And squeezes those who cannot sleep,
30 I see how precious each thing is, how dear,
For I may never touch, smell, taste or see
Again, because I could not hear.

Patricia Beer

Who is the speaker in the above poem? Where is he as he speaks? Why is he there?

onomatopoeia

What details does the poem relate that are not found in the news item?

"The Fifth Sense" is a *narrative* poem, a poem that tells a story or relates a series of events, usually leading to a climax. What does the poem tell the reader about the kind of person Nicolis Loizou is? What does the reader learn about the soldiers?

Unlike a LYRIC poem, which is shorter and usually expresses one basic emotion, a narrative is both story and poem. A story is told, but in the compressed, dramatic, and FIGURATIVE LANGUAGE of poetry. Pick out some examples of figurative language from the poem.

narrative poetry

Poetry that relates a story or series of events.

onomatopoeia

Onomatopoeia

The rusty spigot
sputters,
utters
a splutter,
5 spatters a smattering of drops,
gashes wider;
slash,
splatters,
scatters,
10 spurts,
finally stops sputtering
and plash!
gushes rushes splashes
clear water dashes.

Eve Merriam

What action is the poet describing in the poem? What words does she use to create the effect of water coming from a rusty faucet? Words such as *sputters, spatters, gushes, plash* are examples of *onomatopoeia*, the use of words whose sounds suggest their sense. What are some onomatopoetic (on′ə mat′ə pō et′ik) words a poet might use to describe water bubbling in a brook? a river raging in a storm? Make a list of some of these words.

Read the following lines. Decide which words are examples of onomatopoeia.

Bang-whang-whang goes the drum, *tootle-te-tootle*
    the fife,
Oh, a day in the city-square, there is no such pleasure
    in life!

Robert Browning,
"Up at a Villa—Down in the City"

When blood is nipp'd and ways be foul,
Then nightly sings the staring owl,
    Tu-whit;
Tu-who, a merry note . . .

Shakespeare,
"Winter," from *Love's Labours Lost*

The wind blew east: we heard the roar
Of Ocean on his wintry shore,
And felt the strong pulse throbbing there
Beat with a low rhythm our inland air.

Whittier, "Snowbound"

Which words above strongly suggest their sense? Which words more subtly suggest their sense? Words such as *bam, pow,* and *clang,* and animal sounds such as *miaow, woof,* and *quack* are examples of onomatopoetic words used mainly when sound is the effect desired. Other words suggest their sense more subtly and may be used to create atmosphere, set the scene, or heighten IMAGERY. Examples of such words might be *slushing* through the melting snow, the *whistle* of the ball in the air, the *clatter* of horses' hooves on city streets.

paradox

Jazz Fantasia

Drum on your drums, batter on your banjoes,
sob on the long cool winding saxophones.
Go to it, O jazzmen.

Sling your knuckles on the bottoms of the happy
5 tin pans, let your trombones ooze, and go husha-
husha-hush with the slippery sand-paper.

Moan like an autumn wind high in the lonesome
      treetops, moan soft like
you wanted somebody terrible, cry like a racing
      car slipping away from a
motorcycle cop, bang-bang! you jazzmen, bang
      altogether drums, traps,
10 banjoes, horns, tin cans—make two people fight
      on the top of a stairway
and scratch each other's eyes in a clinch tumbling
      down the stairs.

Can the rough stuff . . . now a Mississippi
      steamboat pushes up the night
river with a hoo-hoo-hoo-oo . . . and the green
      lanterns calling to the high
soft stars . . . a red moon rides on the humps
      of the low river hills . . .
15 go to it, O jazzmen.

                  Carl Sandburg

What words in the first two stanzas of the
poem imitate the sounds of band instruments?
In the third stanza, with what natural sounds
does the poet compare the instrumental sounds?
In the last stanza, what picture is brought to
mind by the music? What mood is created?

onomatopoeia (on′ə mat′ə pē′ə)

The use of words whose sounds suggest their sense.

What is meant by the saying, "The more we
learn, the less we know"? It is a seemingly self-
contradictory statement, and yet there is sense
to be made of it. Such a statement that seems
to say two opposite things is called a *paradox.*
Writers employ paradoxical statements to concentrate the readers' attention or to emphasize
a point.

The term paradox also applies to people or
situations that seem to have two contradictory
elements: a wealthy person who chooses to live
in the conditions of severest poverty might be
considered a paradox. Something extremely out
of the ordinary such as a silent city street on a
weekday noon or (in the days before oil spills)
fire burning on water might be called paradoxes.
The English author G. K. Chesterton wrote a
collection of stories, *Tales of the Long Bow,*
each of which unfolds from a paradoxical situation. In this book and in others where paradoxes are found, their use is to make readers
stop and think about what they are reading and
about any possible symbolism developed or
emphasized by the use of apparent opposites.

paradox

A seemingly self-contradictory statement that is still
true. It is also said of a person or situation that seems
to incorporate two opposite elements.

personification

Sunday Rain

The window screen
is trying to do
its crossword puzzle
but appears to know
only vertical words.

John Updike

What is happening in this poem? Describe the action in literal terms. Obviously the screen cannot do crossword puzzles, but by relating the window screen's appearance to something human, the poet is able to condense his description and make it more vivid. We often give human characteristics to nonhuman things or events. If your car has a flat tire, you may say it "limped" into the nearest service station, or you may hear someone say that the television set sat staring into the living room. These figures of speech are called *personification*. Personification lets the reader see inanimate objects and abstract ideas in terms of familiar human qualities.

Personification is often contained in a line or two of poetry.

A. Bitter the storm tonight.
It hurls the white locks of the sea ...

from the Irish, "The Vikings"

B. Winter sat tight on
our shoulder blades,

Darr, "The Stone Under the Skin"

C. And the night holds its breath,

Jarrell, "The Bird of Night"

D. Leaves don't fall. They descend.
Longing for earth, they come winging.

Tussman, "Leaves"

What is being personified in the lines above? Point out the word or words the poet uses to personify the subject in each example.

A poet may use personification throughout a poem as in "Sunday Rain," or there may be personification in only one stanza within a poem.

But vainly the fierce frost
Interns poor fish, ranks trees in an armed host,
Hangs daggers from house eaves
And on the windows ferny ambush weaves;
In the long war grown warmer
The sun will strike him dead and strip his armor.

Young, "Hard Frost"

1. How is the frost made to seem like a person?

2. How is the sun made to seem human?

3. To what human event does the poet compare the actions described here?

Writers of prose use personification, too. Dickens employed it often, as illustrated in the following examples from "The Holly-Tree," a short story.

As we got into the country, everything seemed to have grown old and grey. The roads, the trees, the thatched roofs of cottages and homesteads, the ricks in farmers' yards.

...all the furniture, from the four posts of the bed to the two old silver candle-sticks, was tall, high-shouldered, and spindle-waisted.

...the midnight wind that rattled at my lattice windows came moaning at me from Stonehenge.

personification (pər son′ə fə kā′shən)

A figure of speech in which human characteristics are attributed to nonhuman things and events. Its use allows the writer to condense and make more vivid descriptions of impersonal subjects and abstract ideas.

plot

Grand Inquisitor

Haunted, sir? No, not what you'd call haunted. Of course, one of the gentlemen who lived here last was murdered but still . . . Haunted's a nasty thing to say about nice rooms like these, isn't it, sir? And so you're two brothers, as well as the Mr. Farmiloes. Funny how things do repeat themselves."

The resident housekeeper of No. 82, Regency Chambers, paused and eyed the prospective owners with a certain pleasant relish oozing through her habitual melancholy. It would be her task to cook for them and look after them. She was a crooked wisp of a woman, fading into the late sixties, with eyes like a jugged hare; narrow in the shoulders, she was yet broad in the beam, like an old ship; and her movements, too, were clumsy like those of an old-fashioned ship, of which her face, startled yet wooden, might have been the figurehead.

As the two gentlemen had already signed the contract for No. 82, she felt that they might be admitted at once to its privileges; so she told them the story of the bachelor brothers Farmiloe:

The elder, Roger, was big and handsome in a beefy sort of way. He had a self-confident chest and a beaming red face; and nearly everything he did, he did well. "Bet you can't do this!" he was often heard boasting to his pathetic little junior, and always he was right: Leslie couldn't do "this."

Leslie Farmiloe was not at all handsome. He was timid and had a sort of impediment in his speech, which sounded like the ghost of a chuckle. He was partially bald, too, though he was not yet forty, whereas Roger's hair was thick as a doormat.

Roger, retired from the army, worked in the City; and Leslie studied geology at home. He was supposed to be writing a tome on various minerals, their strata and sub-strata and was always surrounded by encyclopedias and dictionaries and maps. Endless notes he made on scraps of paper; but he never left these about, because Roger, his patron and hero, must not be annoyed by litter. At least, not by Leslie's litter; his own was different.

In the mornings, when they breakfasted together, Roger usually bullied him; but in the evenings he chaffed him. The two processes were very much alike. The legend stood that Leslie adored his bluff, genial brother, and would endure any amount of good-natured torment from him.

Sundays Roger spent in a knotted agony, sweating at every pore, over the *Weekly Scrutiny:* Leslie watching him with large mild blue eyes, the while thinking no doubt what a wonderful fellow this was, and what a shame that on every seventh day he should be so humiliated by the "Grand Inquisitor."

For this was Roger's one great weakness, and his only intellectual amusement—cross-word puzzles. And of all cross-word puzzles, the only ones he could not master with his usual swaggering facility were those set by Grand Inquisitor of the *Weekly Scrutiny.* They were devils, those Grand Inquisitor puzzles! Roger Farmiloe nearly burst his veins trying to solve them, but he had never yet succeeded in filling in the spaces of any one of them right up to the very end.

Occasionally he managed to wring out a quarter or even a third of the answers, and then he would sit for hours, staring and baffled; or else, in a boiling temper, flinging his dictionaries about; or resting his head helplessly against the cool varnished spaces of the Pacific Ocean on the old-fashioned globe of the world. Leslie was no help. Leslie would not even know that "yen" was a Japanese coin, or "emu" an Australian bird. Even the elementary mysteries of "eft" and "eli" were blank to Leslie. "To think," groaned Roger, "that my brother—my brother—should be a fool!"

Laboriously he set to work again, writhing a little in the ingenious web of clues, allusions, double meanings, anagrams, quotations, and beheaded syllables.

Leslie watched him with large mild blue eyes.

One Sunday afternoon Leslie Farmiloe was discovered lying dead on the carpet, his bald head and the globe of the world having come into too violent contact. The globe had hardly suffered at all.

There were three extraordinary things about the case. One was the expression on the face of the dead little man—sneering and triumphant. It was so unlike any that had ever been seen on him. The second thing that excited comment was the bits of paper strewn about the room, scrawled over and over—even the blotting paper; some crumpled up and hurled about, scribbled with amazing and incomprehensible messages, as though the unknown murderer had been surprised in the working out of some esoteric code: "Yolc" . . . "Cramoisy" . . . "Sckats" . . . "Ecaroh" . . . "Pachisi" . . . "Wolliw" . . .

And Roger Farmiloe had disappeared.

Eventually he was found and brought back, still apparently struggling under a terrific sense of grievance and anxious to tell the whole English-speaking world, his judge and his jury, the spectators at the trial, and the journalists who visited him eager for a good story, exactly what had led him to slay poor harmless Leslie.

For there the little brother had sat, Sunday after Sunday, meekly in his corner, his feet resting on the crossbar of the chair, so that his knees were almost level with his chin. Outwardly meek, but inwardly gloating, gloating with ruthless revengeful ferocity, remembering the humiliations he had suffered from Roger all through the past week; gloating over the full-blooded successful big brother helplessly caught in the toils of Grand Inquisitor's wheel and rack and thumbscrew. For instance: "In opposition to jug-jug." . . . "More than one eight gives the ear the second half of this cheers, two-thirds of eleven are the first half." . . . "The oat is heard above me in Calydon." . . . "The forge of the flea." . . . Until Roger, glancing up too suddenly, on that fatal afternoon when the tragedy had occurred, had surprised on little Leslie's face a fleeting grin of mockery. This week's was a particularly malevolent example of the Grand Inquisitor's most fiendish art, and Roger was frac-

tious. Immediately two dictionaries sped through the room and hit the wall, one on either side of the younger of the Farmiloe brothers.

"I suppose," bellowed Roger, "that you, being a half-wit and an imbecile and an idiot, imagine you can do this better than me?" and expected Leslie to shrink and cower, and to whisper his usual apologies after the usual challenge of "bet you can't do this."

But Leslie replied tranquilly, with that ghost of a chuckle bubbling through his speech: "Do you know—ch-ch—I rather think—ch-ch—I rather think I could."

"Come on, then," shouted Roger, marveling at the half-wit's effrontery. So little Leslie climbed down from his chair and tripped across the room, seized a pencil, bent over the folded page, the ruled squares of the cross-word blurred already and indented by poor Roger's attempts and crossings out.

And with swift neatness, still smiling in that odd triumphant way, he filled in the whole solution, first across and then down.

It was Roger's turn to watch, which he did in dumb, fishlike bewilderment.

This was outrageous! This was incredible! It couldn't be true, and yet—it was true. Three more words—two—one—and Leslie had finished. "You see," he said, kindly explaining, but not bothering to hide the fact that he was patronizing that poor burly oaf, Roger Farmiloe, "you see: 'Seat renowned for its association with Arachnida' must be 'tuffet.' Of course you know that Arachnida is the class name of spiders, scorpions and mites."

Either this was magic, or——

Suddenly Roger Farmiloe guessed.

With a roar like a bull, he flung down his accusation. "You! You're Grand Inquisitor!"

"Dear me, yes," replied little Leslie Farmiloe, sweetly and gently. "Fancy you only discovering that now! It's been such fun every Sunday, sitting here and watching you."

"Haunted, sir? No, not what you'd call haunted. Of course one of the gentlemen who lived here last was hanged. . . ."

Gladys Bronwyn Stern

The *plot* of a story is the series of related events that present a problem or *conflict*, lead to the *climax* or point at which the conflict must be resolved, and finally result in a *conclusion* of the conflict.

point of view

Who are the main characters of "Grand Inquisitor"? List some of the ways in which they differ. How have these differences affected their relationship?

In most stories there is a conflict of opposing forces that must be resolved. In "Grand Inquisitor" the conflict is between the two Farmiloe brothers: Roger, the bully, and Leslie, the bullied. Conflicts that pit character against character, character against nature (weather, animals), or character against the forces of society (opinion, convention) are called *external* conflicts.

Conflicts within the character such as between duty and desire, between opposing emotions, or between character and conscience are called *internal* conflicts. Conflict in a story is rarely entirely one or the other. Which sort of conflict do you find in "Grand Inquisitor"?

What is the conclusion of the conflict between Roger and Leslie? What brings it about? The climax of the story occurs when Roger realizes that Leslie is the author of the puzzles with which Roger wrestles each Sunday. At this point something has to happen. The conflict must be resolved. Why is Roger unable to accept his discovery about Leslie?

If, at the climax of the story, Roger had expressed his amazement and then gone on to admire Leslie's talent, how might the conclusion of the story have been different?

Roger cannot accept the knowledge that the brother he despises and bullies can best him at something and gloat over his victory. He murders Leslie. Given what you know of Roger, is this a logical conclusion to the story?

plot

A series of related events that present and resolve a conflict. The usual pattern of plot is conflict, climax, and conclusion.

Every literary work is told to the reader by a *speaker* or *voice*, commonly called the *narrator*. Though the author, of necessity, assumes the identity of the narrator while writing the work, it is important to recognize that in many cases, for the purposes of the story, the author and the narrator are not the same person.

The selection of the narrator by the author for his or her story is an important one because the narrator determines what kind of information, and how much, the reader will find. The relationship between the narrator and the story that he or she relates is called the *point of view*. There are basically two main *points of view: first person* and *third person.*

The following passage is from "Sorrow Rides a Fast Horse" (page 16).

Two weeks later Rufus and I came home from school to find mother standing in the hall with three suitcases on the floor. She was dressed in her good black coat and the plain blue dress that she wore to Sunday school.

..."You won't be going to school tomorrow," she told us. "We're going away."

The "I" in the passage refers to John, the narrator who tells the story about his mother and her journey with her two sons. As one of the sons, John is, in addition to being the story's narrator, also one of the main characters. The story is thus told from a *first-person point of view.* When John tells the story, however, he is an adult, and the events happened long before, so that he has had time to reflect on their meaning. The point of view is then called *first-person detached.*

A second kind of first-person point of view is found in this passage from "Philip Wedge" (page 145).

He was a nervous person, anyway. I recall (now that I'm thinking about these things) a day, probably three years ago, when he and I were walking together down Sixth Avenue. As we passed a letter-box, Wedge dropped a letter in—a slight incident which

I thought nothing of until, a block later, Wedge suddenly turned and darted back along the sidewalk, twisting and turning and looking from the rear very like a madman.

In the above paragraph the narrator is a minor character chiefly concerned with observing the main character and acting as his confidant. The narrator in this case reports on the behavior of the main character. This point of view is called *first-person observer.*

The third sort of first-person point of view is called *first-person subjective.* This occurs when the narrator is one of the characters in the work; he or she tells the story as though it were happening and as he or she sees the events unfolding. In this case the narrator has neither hindsight nor foresight. In this kind of narrative, the narrator seems to know no more than the reader, and may, in fact, not draw the inferences that the reader does.

The passage below is about Drake Forrester, the main character in "The Man Called Dead" (page 32).

. . . He might so welcome his freedom, he might do something entirely new, even take a new name and disappear from all he had known. He saw himself roaming about the world, a different person in one city or another. . . .

Forrester is alone in his room when this narrative takes place; no other character is with him to record his actions or speeches. Even if there had been, what is recorded in this passage is what is going on inside Forrester's mind. It could be known only by an all-knowing or *omniscient* (om nish′ənt) narrator. An omniscient narrator is anonymous himself, but is capable of relating what every character is saying, doing, and thinking. Sometimes, as in "The Man Called Dead," the narrator relates the thoughts of only one character. This is called the *limited omniscient* point of view.

The second kind of third-person point of view occurs when the narrator acts as an anonymous reporter, relating only what he sees and hears and drawing no conclusions of his own. This is called the *third-person objective* or *dramatic* point of view because the reader learns from the narrator only what he or she would learn from the characters in a play, as in *Twelve Angry Men;* that is, what they say and do, but not what they think (unless they say aloud what they are thinking).

The following passage is from "Emergency Society" (page 160).

Spinelli liked the news best on these occasions—better, if the truth be told, than the spectacle itself. He was looking forward to all the papers the next day; the heroes would be announced, the victims mourned. Even if there was grief and loss in some places, the following week would be celebrated by all the happy people who had truly emerged.

Is the above passage told in the first or third person? Does the narrator relate only what is happening or also what the character Spinelli is thinking? What point of view is represented in the passage?

point of view

The relationship between the narrator of a story and the story itself. The two most common points of view are first person and third person. Within these two wide categories, the following types of narration may be found:

First-Person Detached: The narrator is a major or minor character who tells the story from the vantage point of time and reflection.

First-Person Observer: The narrator is a minor character who reports what the main character says and does and who acts as a confidant to that main character.

First-Person Subjective: The narrator is a major or minor character who tells the story as though the events were in the process of unfolding and who has no special insight about the whys and wherefores of what is happening.

Third-Person Omniscient and *Limited Omniscient:* The narrator is anonymous and has insight into what characters think as well as what they say and do.

Third-Person Objective or *Dramatic Point of View:* The narrator acts as an anonymous reporter, relating only what can be seen and heard, drawing no conclusions.

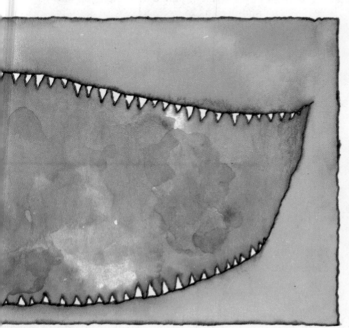

The leading character of a short story, play, or novel is called the *protagonist.* The work mainly concerns or is about the protagonist. Thus, the protagonist of "A Short Return" (page 108) is the young man who tells the story; the protagonist of "Average Waves in Unprotected Waters" (page 126) is Bet Blevins, the mother of Arnold.

In most stories the protagonist is opposed by an adversary called the *antagonist.* The antagonist may be a villainous character or he or she may simply be the source of conflict in the story. Edmond, the stepfather in "A Short Return" is the antagonist of that story. The antagonist need not be a character, however; "In Average Waves . . . ," for example, the antagonist is a combination of factors: Arnold's condition, Bet's poverty, and society's general lack of sympathy with people who are "different." In a well-known story by Jack London, "To Build a Fire," the sole character is the protagonist; the antagonist is the weather that surrounds him. Fate, chance, a set of events, a character, or any combination of these may be the antagonist of a work. Consider *Medea* (page 302). Is Jason the sole antagonist? What other factors create the conflict in the play? Who is the protagonist of "The Rocking-Horse Winner" (page 165)? the antagonist?

protagonist/antagonist (prō tag′ə nist); (an tag′ə nist)

The protagonist is the main character in a short story, play, or novel.
The adversary who opposes the protagonist is called the antagonist. The antagonist may be another character in the work, the forces of nature, fate, chance, or any combination of these.

The Swan and Goose

A rich man bought a Swan and Goose—	*a*
That for song and this for use.	*a*
It chanced his simple-minded cook	*b*
One night the Swan for Goose mistook.	*b*
5 But in the dark about to chop	*c*
The Swan in two above the crop,	*c*
He heard the lyric note, and stayed	*d*
The action of the fatal blade.	*d*
And thus we see a proper tune	*e*
10 Is sometimes very opportune.	*e*

Aesop
(translated by William Ellery Leonard)

*R*hyme is the repetition of similar or identical sounds. Where are the rhyming words in the lines above? How many different rhyming sounds are there in the poem? Which words that rhyme are not spelled similarly?

Rhyme is among the sound devices poets use. One of its chief uses is the pleasure it gives the reader. This fable might have been written in prose, but the use of rhyme adds to its amusing tone.

Rhyme found at the ends of lines is called *end rhyme.* When there is a definite pattern to the end rhyme, as in the poem, it is called *rhyme scheme.*

If one were to chart the rhyme scheme of a poem, one would represent the first rhyming sound as *a* and the second rhyming sound as *b.* Thus the rhyme scheme for ''The Swan and Goose'' would be: *a a b b c c d d, e e.* More intricate rhyme schemes are possible. Read the following poem. Chart the rhyme scheme.

The Craftsman

I ply with all the cunning of my art
This little thing, and with consummate care
I fashion it—so that when I depart,
Those who come after me shall find it fair
5 And beautiful. It must be free of flaws—
Pointing no laborings of weary hands;
And there must be no flouting of the laws
Of beauty—as the artist understands.

Through passion, yearnings infinite—yet dumb—
10 I lift you from the depths of my own mind
And gild you with my soul's white heat to plumb
The souls of future men. I leave behind
This thing that in return this solace gives:
"He who creates true beauty ever lives."

Marcus B. Christian

How does the rhyme scheme of the last two lines differ from that of the previous lines? Note how this difference emphasizes the last two lines and sets them apart from the rest of the poem. Notice also how the rhyme scheme divides the poem into four distinct parts. How many lines are there in the poem? The form of this poem and its rhyme is that of a Shakespearean sonnet.

Midsummer Jingle

I've an ingle, shady ingle, near a dusky bosky
    dingle
Where the sighing zephyrs mingle with the purling
    of the stream.
There I linger in the jungle, and it makes me thrill
    and tingle,
Far from city's strident jangle as I angle, smoke
    and dream.

5 Through the trees I'll hear a single ringing sound, a
    cowbell's jingle,
And its ting-a-ling'll mingle with the whispers of the
    breeze;
So, although I've not a single sou, no potentate or
    king'll
Make me jealous while I angle in my ingle 'neath
    the trees.

Newman Levy

Which words within the lines rhyme with the words at the ends of the lines? Rhyming sounds within lines are called *internal rhyme.*

Do *jingle, jangle,* and *jungle* rhyme? Words that sound similar but are not identical, are called *half rhymes* or *slant rhymes.* (See also CONSONANCE.)

Half rhyme adds variety to the sound of poems and is much used by more recent poets.

rhythm

Poets who use half rhyme have a much wider selection of words from which to choose since the number of identically rhyming words is actually rather limited.

> "And now there came both mist and snow,
> And it grew wondrous cold;
> And ice, mast-high, came floating by
> As green as emerald.
>
> 5 "And through the drifts the snowy clifts
> Did send a dismal sheen;
> Nor shapes of men nor beasts we ken——
> The ice was all between."
>
> Coleridge,
> "The Rime of the Ancient Mariner"

Point out examples of internal rhyme. What example of half rhyme is in the first stanza?

---

rhyme

The repetition of similar or identical sounds. Its use may give pleasure to the ear, emphasize important words or lines, and unify parts of the poem or the whole poem.

---

rhythm

Language has *rhythm* because we give words a certain stress, or accent, in pronouncing them. We say *beGIN* and *MERcy*, *interRUPT* and *BEAUtiful*. Both prose and poetry have rhythm, but in poetry the rhythm is regulated. What we call rhythm, or *meter*, in English poetry is the pattern of accented and unaccented syllables.

Rhythm alone does not make a poem, as these lines show:

> Birds GO rePAST the Ego YOU,
> DULL ROLLer SKATE sinCERE we DO.

Meter must echo sense. Poets who write solemnly of death do not want their lines to bounce along like a nursery jingle. They will use meter (in combination with other devices) to create a slow, solemn movement. The pace of a poem must be appropriate to the emotion.

The most common meter in English is *iambic,* an unaccented syllable followed by an accented syllable, ($\smile$ /). The English language has many words that consist of two syllables. Because most of these two-syllable words, like *beGIN,* are accented on the final syllable, English speech has a natural iambic beat. As a result, the rhythm of an iambic line moves smoothly:

> Her deck, / once red / with he / roes' blood.
> Holmes, "Old Ironsides"

Trochaic meter, an accented syllable followed by an unaccented syllable, (/$\smile$), as in *MERcy,* reverses the natural iambic beat. As such, a trochaic line seems to move roughly:

> Thou, when / thou re / turnst, wilt / tell me.
> Donne, "Song"

Anapestic meter ($\smile\smile$ /), as in *interRUPT,* lends itself effectively to the leaping action of Byron's narrative poem, "The Destruction of Sennacherib":

> The As syr / ian came down / like
> the wolf / on the fold.

Lord Tennyson found the thrust of *dactylic* meter (/$\smile\smile$), as in *BEAUtiful,* well suited to his "Charge of the Light Brigade":

> O the wild / charge they made!

Spondaic meter (˝) consists of two accented syllables. Poets can manipulate any one of the basic meters so that it moves quickly or slowly. They adjust the motion of a poem by occasionally substituting a different meter in a line. Identify the substitute meter in each example.

1. The shíp / wăs cheéred, / thĕ hár / bŏr cleáred,

   Mér rĭ / lў dĭd / wĕ dróp

   Coleridge, "The Rime of the Ancient Mariner"

2. Cán nŏn tŏ / rígh tŏf thĕm,

   Cán nŏn tŏ / léft of|thĕm,

   Cán nŏn bĕ / hínd thĕm

   Vól leўed and / thún deréd;

   Tennyson, "The Charge of the Light Brigade"

In the example from Coleridge, the pace quickens when the poet reverses the *accented* syllables. In the example from Tennyson the pace slows when the poet increases the *accented* syllables. This is *how* the movement changes, but it is even more important to recognize *why* the movement changes. Tennyson, for example, slows the line so that it echoes (and emphasizes) the mournful tone of the stanza. Rhythm is part of a poem's meaning.

Much modern poetry frequently departs from a regular meter or rhythm, but all poems have rhythm; that is, there are always some words or syllables that are stressed more than others.

Scansion (skan'shən)

When we scan a line of poetry, we determine the kind of meter it contains and then count the number of metrical units, or *feet*, in a line. A *foot* is a group of syllables constituting a metrical unit of a verse.

Thŭs Í

Păss bý

Ănd díe

Ăs óne

Ŭn knówn

Ănd góne.

Herrick, "Upon His Departure Hence"

Because each line of Herrick's poem is written in the *iambic* meter, and because each line contains *one* iambic foot, we say the lines of the poem are basically *iambic monometer*.

The English word *monometer* (mə nom'i tər) is derived from the Greek prefix *mono-* ("one") and the Greek word *metron* ("measure"). Other words that indicate the length of lines are:
dimeter (dim'i tər) (two feet)
trimeter (trim'i tər) (three feet)
tetrameter (te tram'ə tər) (four feet)
pentameter (pen tam'ə tər) (five feet)

Scan the following examples. On a separate sheet of paper, copy the defining sentence. Then fill in the name of the meter (*iambic, trochaic, anapestic,* or *dactylic*), number of feet in the lines (*1, 2, 3, 4,* or *5*), and the scansion pattern (the name of the meter plus *monometer, dimeter, trimeter, tetrameter,* or *pentameter*).

1. Mór tăl / mán and / wó măn,

   Gŏ úp / ŏn yŏur / trá vĕl!

   Elizabeth Barrett Browning,
   "A Drama of Exile"

Each of Browning's lines is written in the _____ meter. Because each line contains _____ feet, the lines are _____ _____ meter.

2. Hŏw líke / ă wín / tĕr háth / mў áb / sĕnce beén

   Frŏm theé, / thĕ pléa / sŭre óf / thĕ fleét / ĭng
   year! Shakespeare, "Sonnet 97"

THIS STRUCTURE WILL BE TORN DOWN AND REPLACED BY A NEW 44-STORY COOKIE

Each of Shakespeare's lines is written in the _____ meter. Because each line contains _____ feet, the lines are _____ _____ meter.

3. Cóld iñ hŭ / mán ĭ tў,

Bŭrn iñg iñ / sán ĭ tў.

Hood, "The Bridge of Sighs"

Each of Hood's lines is written in the _____ meter. Because each line contains _____ feet, the lines are _____ _____ meter.

4. 'Twas Jónes, / bráve Jónes / tŏ bát / tlĕ léd

Ăs bóld / ă créw / ăs év / ĕr bléd.

Freneau, "On the Memorable Victory"

Each of Freneau's lines is written in the _____ meter. Because each line contains _____ feet, the lines are _____ _____ meter.

rhythm

The arrangement of stressed and unstressed sounds in speech and writing.

Drawing by Lorenz; © 1977 The New Yorker Magazine, Inc.

1. What situation is the cartoonist making fun of?

2. Do you think the cartoonist is trying to correct the situation, or is he simply commenting on it?

3. Is the general tone of the cartoon humorous or critical? (See TONE.)

*S*atire is a device used by writers (and cartoonists) to ridicule people and their institutions, whether social, political, religious, or commercial, in order to reveal their foolishness or vice. The aim of satire is to comment on the situation, often with an eye toward correcting it by making society more aware of the problem.

Satire is frequently a more successful means of bringing a situation to the public's notice than plain criticism. While the subject and the writer's intent may well be serious, satire itself is entertaining, whether gently humorous or savagely witty. Irony, humor, sarcasm, and exaggeration are common devices of satire. (See IRONY.)

Read the following poem. Try to determine whether the poet is gently, or bitterly, humorous.

The Rabbit

We are going to see the rabbit.
We are going to see the rabbit.
Which rabbit, people say?
Which rabbit, ask the children?
5 Which rabbit?
The only rabbit,
The only rabbit in England,
Sitting behind a barbed-wire fence
Under the floodlights, neon lights,
10 Sodium lights,
Nibbling grass
On the only patch of grass
In England, in England
(Except the grass by the hoardings[1]
15 Which doesn't count.)
We are going to see the rabbit
And we must be there on time.

First we shall go by escalator,
Then we shall go by underground,
20 And then we shall go by motorway
And then by helicopterway,
And the last ten yards we shall have to go
On foot.

And now we are going
25 All the way to see the rabbit.
We are nearly there,
We are longing to see it,
And so is the crowd
Which is here in thousands
30 With mounted policemen
And big loudspeakers
And bands and banners,
And everyone has come a long way.
But soon we shall see it
35 Sitting and nibbling
The blades of grass
On the only patch of grass
In—but something has gone wrong!
Why is everyone so angry,
40 Why is everyone jostling
And slanging and complaining?

The rabbit has gone,
Yes, the rabbit has gone.
He has actually burrowed down into the earth
45 And made himself a warren,[2] under the earth,
Despite all these people.
And what shall we do?
What *can* we do?

It is all a pity, you must be disappointed,
50 Go home and do something else for today,
Go home again, go home for today.
For you cannot hear the rabbit, under the earth,
Remarking rather sadly to himself, by himself,
As he rests in his warren, under the earth:
55 "It won't be long, they are bound to come,
They are bound to come and find me, even here."

Alan Brownjohn

Why is the rabbit so special? What do you suppose has happened to the other rabbits? the grass? What is the poet commenting on in the second stanza? Is the poet optimistic or pessimistic about the future of wildlife? Do you think the poem is meant solely to entertain the reader or to stir a feeling that "something must be done"?

When people, actions, or literary works are satirized by ridiculous exaggeration, it is called *burlesque.* Comedians on television often perform burlesques of old movies and soap operas. In writing, burlesque may be characterized by a great discrepancy between the subject matter and the style: the struggle between a spider and a fly, for example, written in epic form.

Mimicking aimed at a particular writer or work is called *parody* (par′ə dē).

In parody the outstanding characteristics of a work or writer are so exaggerated that anyone in the least familiar with the original will recognize the parodied style. For example, as you read the following, determine which writer and work are being parodied.

---

1. *hoardings,* billboards.
2. *warren,* place underground where rabbits live.

setting

Wits, comics, funnymen, spare me your jeers;
I've come to help your humor, not to pan it.
Your skits are long, your repartee is dull;
Your jokes were old when Noah was a lad.

Do you recognize the original? If not, see page 486, lines 69-72. Try writing a parody of a well-known nursery rhyme.

satire

A technique that ridicules people and their institutions in an effort to expose their weaknesses and evils. The purpose of satire is often to bring about a change. Exaggeration and irony are frequent devices of satire. *Burlesque* is a means of making people, actions, or literary forms ridiculous through extreme exaggeration. *Parody* is mimicking aimed at making fun of a particular writer's style or work.

setting

The following passage is from the opening pages of *Rebecca* by Daphne du Maurier.

There was Manderley, our Manderley, secretive and silent as it had always been, the grey stone shining in the moonlight of my dream, the mullioned windows reflecting the green lawns and the terrace. Time could not wreck the perfect symmetry of those walls, nor the site itself, a jewel in the hollow of a hand. . . . When I thought of Manderley in my waking hours I would not be bitter. I should think of it as it might have been, could I have lived there without fear. I should remember the rose garden in summer, and the birds that sang at dawn. Tea under the chestnut tree, and the murmur of the sea coming up to us from the lawns below.

What is Manderley? Is the narrator still at Manderley? Is Manderley inland or on the coast? What do these lines tell the reader about the narrator?

The two paragraphs tell the observant reader a good deal about Manderley, the English country estate where most of *Rebecca* takes place. They describe the *setting* of the novel: an old, grand stone house in the midst of fine green lawns situated above the sea. The time is not specified, but the reader can infer that the narrator has lived at Manderley at some time in the past, and that the memories of having lived there are not all happy ones.

The setting is the time and place in which the action of a narrative occurs. Setting helps in the understanding of character and action. Later in the story, which is told in flashback, the narrator meets the owner of Manderley, Maximilian de Winter.

. . . I thought how unreal he would look against a Florida background. He belonged to a walled city of the fifteenth century, a city of narrow, cobbled streets, and thin spires, . . . a past of narrow stairways and dim dungeons, a past of whispers in the dark, of shimmering rapier blades, of silent, exquisite courtesy.

What does the narrator's imagined setting for Mr. de Winter tell you about him? Setting can help the reader understand character through association with familiar backgrounds.

A third function of setting is to help create the atmosphere and mood of the narrative. Consider the following paragraph from *Rebecca*, which describes the narrator's first ride up the drive to the great house.

This drive twisted and turned as a serpent, scarce wider in places than a path, and above our heads was a great colonnade of trees, whose branches nodded and intermingled with one another, making an archway for us, like the roof of a church. Even the midday sun would not penetrate the interlacing of those green leaves, they were too thickly entwined, one with another, and only little flickering patches of warm light would come in intermittent waves to dapple the drive with gold. It was very silent, very still. On the high-road there had been a gay west wind blowing in my face, making the grass on the hedges dance in unison, but here there was no wind. Even the engine of the car had taken a new note, throbbing low, quieter than before. As the drive descended to the valley so the trees came in upon us, great beeches with lovely smooth white stems, lifting their myriad branches to one another, and other trees, trees I could not name, coming close, so close that I could touch them with my hands. On we went, over a little bridge that spanned a narrow stream, and still this drive that was no drive twisted and turned like an enchanted ribbon through the dark and silent woods, penetrating even deeper to the very heart surely of the forest itself, and still there was no clearing, no space to hold a house.

Is the atmosphere created cheerful or subdued? What are the elements that add a slightly sinister quality to the description? How does the setting affect what you expect of the story?

Finally, setting may aid the development of the plot. When the narrator goes to Manderley, she goes as the second Mrs. de Winter. The reader is told that the first Mrs. de Winter, a beautiful and vivacious woman, was drowned in the bay below the grounds. Mrs. Danvers, the housekeeper, shows the narrator to her rooms in the east wing of the house overlooking the rose garden.

"You can't see the sea from here then," I said, turning to Mrs. Danvers.

"No, not from this wing," she answered, "you can't even hear it, either. You would not know the sea was anywhere near, not from this wing.

". . . the rooms in the west wing are very old. The bedroom in the big suite is twice as large as this, a very beautiful room too, with a scrolled ceiling."

. . . I did not know why she must speak with such an undercurrent of resentment, implying as she did at the same time that this room, where I found myself to be installed, was something inferior, not up to Manderley standard, a second-rate room, as it were, for a second-rate person.

. . . [Mrs. Danvers] paused an instant, feeling me with her eyes. "They used to live in the west wing and use those rooms when Mrs. de Winter was alive. That big room I was telling you about, that looked down to the sea, was Mrs. de Winter's bedroom."

The plot of *Rebecca* concerns the two wives, one dead and one the narrator. Do you see how the above passage foreshadows a rivalry between the women? Do you expect the sea to play an important role in the plot? One woman's room looks out over the sea and the rose garden; the other's room, only the rose garden. How do you think this might influence the plot?

setting

The time and place in which the action of a narrative occurs. The setting may be specifically described at the opening of a work, or it may be revealed gradually through dialogue and events. The setting may serve simply as a background for characters and events (thus making the story more believable to the reader) or it may help create the atmosphere from which the story evolves. Setting may directly affect the plot's development, and it may help in the understanding of character, or even be vital to that understanding.

stereotype

Read the following passages about different characters. Decide which person each passage is describing.

A. Jeffrey Lombard was tall and dark with just a tinge of silver at his temples. Always impeccably dressed, he wore his clothes with a kind of lazy grace that belied his athletic prowess. Well-read, witty, and assured of the best tables, Lombard was a sought-after escort, but, as yet, no woman had managed to hold him for long.

Lombard is probably a **(a)** coal miner; **(b)** truck driver; **(c)** secret agent; **(d)** jockey.

B. Grace Meadowes was smart, no doubt about that. When George had died, she'd invested wisely and was now nicely set up for life. If only her darling Billy hadn't married that silly Florence. What on earth had he seen in her anyway? Adjusting her best rose-trimmed hat, she resolutely set her shoulders as she glanced in the mirror. A plain face with a determined jaw gazed back at her.

Grace Meadowes is probably **(a)** a domineering mother-in-law; **(b)** a timid, retiring woman; **(c)** the heroine of a historical novel; **(d)** a duchess.

C. Herbie sweated profusely and seemed to shrink as he sagged against the wall. He was a weasel-faced little man with scanty hair and a pasty complexion. He was scared, but too out of breath to keep running. He hadn't worked these streets for all those years for nothing, though, so as they hovered close he blubbered out a deal.

Herbie is probably a **(a)** hardware salesman; **(b)** chef; **(c)** small-time crook; **(d)** veterinarian.

The above characters are examples of *stereotypes.* Stereotyped characters are those that embody a conventional idea about whatever character is being portrayed. Make a list of some other stereotyped characters.

Stereotypes in written works need to be recognized as stereotypes rather than as fully developed characters. Stereotypes are useful when the author wants to compare and contrast different reactions in a limited space or time as in "Twelve Angry Men," (page 44).

Secondary characters, too, are often presented as stereotypes; they are better foils if they remain one-dimensional.

Reading about stereotyped characters in popular fiction is often pleasurable because such characters are predictable, and the reader knows what to expect. Usually, however, a writer will try to develop characters more fully. (See CHARACTERIZATION.)

PLOTS and SETTINGS may be stereotyped also. Very likely as you have watched a program on television or read a book, you have suddenly realized that it is similar to something you have seen or read before. An example of a stereotyped plot might be one in which a doctor, a lawyer, or a policeman discovers that his best friend is taking drugs or bribes or kick-backs. Make a list of some other stereotyped plots you have seen on television or read.

Settings that for one reason or another are continually depicted in the same manner are stereotyped. Examples might be an idyllic farm, a wicked city, or the glamorous French Riviera. Anyone who lives in any of these places knows that such views are one-sided.

Stereotypes can be harmful if they lead a reader to accept certain standardized views about people, situations, or places. In real life they are all more complex.

---

stereotype (ster′ē ə tīp′)

Standardized, conventional ideas about characters, plots, and settings. An example of a stereotyped character might be an absent-minded professor; a stereotyped plot might be a story about a brave dog saving a small child; a stereotyped setting might be a smoke-filled newsroom.

---

style

As you read the following paragraphs, try to determine what makes them different.

A. At any time of year the view from the Paris bridges is very nice, especially in the evening. It is just like a picture postcard scene with the buildings on both sides of the river, and the big trees that come right down to the water. Behind them, in the west, you can see the large Louvre, the famous museum. It sort of glows when the sun goes down. Toward the other direction you can see the outline of the also famous Cathedral of Notre Dame.

B. At any season, and all year long, in the evening the view of the city from the bridges was always exquisitely pictorial. One's eyes became the eyes of a painter, because the sight itself approximated art, with the narrow, pallid façades of the buildings lining the river; with the tall trees growing down by the water's edge; with, behind them, the vast chiaroscuro[1] of the palatial Louvre, lightened by the luminous lemon color of the Paris sunset off toward the west; with the great square, pale stone silhouette of Notre Dame to the east.

Flanner, from "That Was Paris"

What do you think is the purpose of the paragraphs? to entertain? to inform? to create a scene? All of these things?

Which paragraph has more difficult words? Longer sentences? Which paragraph is more conversational? Does one paragraph give you a clearer picture of the scene than the other? If so, which? Are IMAGERY and FIGURATIVE LANGUAGE employed?

Two elements are necessary when writing: ideas (or a subject) and the words to express those ideas. The manner in which writers make words fit their ideas is called *style*. Style is a combination of the many techniques and devices of writing and the way they are used to express the writer's ideas.

Both paragraphs are about the view from the bridges of Paris, but the styles are vastly different. The first paragraph mainly informs the reader about the view. The writer uses simple, informal language. The tone might be described as conversational, much what one might write in a letter home. No particular mood is established, though it is plain the writer is enjoying the view.

In the second paragraph the style is much more complex. The writer attempts to make the scene as real for the reader as it is for the viewer. There is a faintly reminiscent tone, as though the writer were remembering how things looked rather than describing them as she now sees them. The language is more formal and ornate than that of the first paragraph, and the imagery and figurative language are more concrete: "narrow, pallid facades," "the palatial Louvre," "the luminous lemon color of the Paris sunset," and "the great square, pale stone silhouette of Notre Dame." A metaphor is found in the sentence: "One's eyes became the eyes of a painter." There is alliteration: "the palatial Louvre, lightened by the luminous lemon color. . . ." The mood created is quiet, almost dreamy.

Some authors so consistently write in a particular manner that their style is immediately distinguishable from other writers; hence, people speak of James Thurber's style or E. E. Cummings's style. All people who write, however, have their own individual ideas and use the language that they think best expresses those ideas. Thus, everyone has his or her own style of writing.

---

1. *chiaroscuro* (kē är'ə skyür'ō), pattern of light and shade.

---

style

The manner in which writers use words and sentences to fit their ideas. Style involves many choices on the part of the writer: types of words, placement of words in a sentence, the purpose of the written work, tone, mood, imagery, figurative language, sound devices, and rhythm.

---

symbol

"Judge not the play before the play be done."

The line above is literal advice that might be offered to any theatergoer. There is no reason to suppose "play" means or stands for anything except itself. Now read the line in the context of the poem.

> My soul, sit thou a patient looker on;
> Judge not the play before the play be done:
> Her plot has many changes; every day
> Speaks a new scene; the last act crowns the play.
>
> Quarles, from Emblems

1. What is the first indication that "play" now may mean more than just a theater production?

2. What might "play" refer to in this context?

3. What might the "plot" be?

4. What is the "last act"?

When read in context, "play" becomes a *symbol,* something that stands for or represents something else: in this case, a person's life.

Symbols are examples of FIGURATIVE LANGUAGE. Many literary symbols, such as "play" in the poem above, pertain only to the specific works in which they are found; "play" in another poem might have a literal and not a symbolic meaning.

Not all works employ symbolism. Readers should not try to force meaning that is not there, nor should they try to make symbols of things that have only literal meaning.

Are there any symbols in the following poem, in your opinion?

Plain

> Out of Mobile I saw a 60 Ford
> fingers wrapped like pieces of rope
> around the steering wheel
> foxtail flapping the head of the hood
> 5 of the first thing ever
> he has called his own.

> Between two Bardahls
> above the STP
> the flag flies backwards
> 10 Go To Church This Sunday
> Support Your Local Police
> Post 83
> They say the same thing
> They say
> 15 *I am not alone.*
>
> Miller Williams

1. Some of the stickers obviously "stand for" a product, but what more abstract idea does the poet say they also represent? In which lines of the poem does the poet tell the reader what he thinks the stickers "stand for"?

2. How do you think the stickers might make the owner feel less alone?

3. Of what might the car itself be a symbol?

---

symbol

Something concrete, such as an object, person, place, or happening, that stands for or represents something abstract, such as an idea, a quality, a concept, or a condition.

One Hard Look

Small gnats that fly
In hot July
And lodge in sleeping ears
Can rouse therein
5   A trumpet's din
With Day of Judgment fears.

Small mice at night
Can wake more fright
Than lions at midday;
10   A straw will crack
The camel's back—
There is no easier way.

One smile relieves
A heart that grieves
15   Though deadly sad it be,
And one hard look
Can close the book
That lovers love to see.

Robert Graves

How can small gnats create more noise than a trumpet, according to the first stanza of the poem above? How might mice rustling at night be more frightening than lions during the day? How might a sad person's smiling or being smiled at help lessen his or her grief? What is the poet saying in the last three lines of the third stanza? (Keep in mind the expression "face like an open book.")

Which of the following statements best reveals the main idea of the poem? (a) Small sounds at night seem noisier than loud ones during the day; (b) Things seem different by the light of day; (c) Small things in general can make big differences in the way one feels; (d) Don't despise the little things.

The main idea underlying a literary work is called the *theme*. The theme of the above poem is revealed in statement (c).

Statement (d) presents a moral: it tells the reader how to act. It is not the theme, because the poet does not tell the reader how to think or behave. He simply states various examples and leaves it up to the reader to infer the theme: seemingly insignificant things can make all the difference to the way one feels.

Statement (a) relates what plot there is in stanzas one and two. A PLOT is a pattern of events, things that happen in a narrative or poem. The theme is the central idea, what the work is about.

It is important to recognize the difference between the theme and the *subject* of a literary work. The subject is the topic about which the author has chosen to write. The theme, however, makes a statement about that topic or expresses an opinion about it. The subject of the above poem is suggested by the title, "One Hard Look"; the theme is the great effect small things can have.

Soup

I saw a famous man eating soup.
I say he was lifting a fat broth
Into his mouth with a spoon.
His name was in the newspapers that day
5   Spelled out in tall black headlines
And thousands of people were talking about him.

   When I saw him,
He sat bending his head over a plate
Putting soup in his mouth with a spoon.

Carl Sandburg

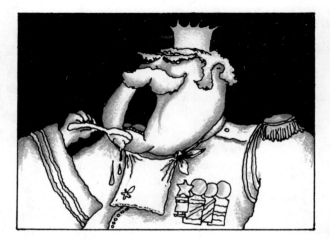

1. What sets the man in the poem apart from most other people?

2. What impression of him do you have from this poem?

3. What do you think is the theme of this poem?

Not every work has a theme. Works with no theme are most likely to be those written entirely for the entertainment of the reader. Examples might be mystery or adventure stories. Some literary works, *Julius Caesar*, for example, have more than one theme.

theme

The underlying main idea of a literary work. The theme may be stated or implied. Theme differs from the subject of a literary work in that it involves a statement or opinion about that subject. Not every literary work has a theme. Some literary works have more than one theme.

tone

The following passage is from the novel *Oliver Twist* by Charles Dickens. It concerns the members of the board who administer the affairs of the local workhouse where the paupers, or poor people of the area, may find employment, food, and lodging.

As you read, try to determine Dickens's attitude toward his subject.

The members of this board were very sage, deep, philosophical men; and when they came to turn their attention to the workhouse, they found out at once, what ordinary folks would never have discovered— the poor people liked it! It was a regular place of public entertainment for the poorer classes; a tavern where there was nothing to pay; a public breakfast, dinner, tea, and supper all the year round; a brick and mortar elysium,¹ where it was all play and no work. "Oho!" said the board, looking very knowing; "we are the fellows to set this to rights; we'll stop it all, in no time." So, they established the rule, that all poor people should have the alternative (for they would compel nobody, not they), of being starved by a gradual process in the house, or by a quick one out of it. With this view, they contracted with the water-works to lay on an unlimited supply of water; and with a corn-factor to supply periodically small quantities of oatmeal; and issued three meals of thin gruel a day, with an onion twice a week, and half a roll on Sundays. They made a great many other wise and humane regulations, having reference to the ladies, which it is not necessary to repeat; kindly undertook to divorce poor married people, in consequence of the great expense of a suit in Doctors' Commons; and, instead of compelling a man to support his family, as they had theretofore done, took his family away from him, and made him a bachelor! There is no saying how many applicants for relief, under these last two heads, might have started up in all classes of society, if it had not been coupled with the workhouse; but the board were long-headed men, and had provided for this difficulty. The relief was inseparable from the workhouse and the gruel; and that frightened people.

. . . It was rather expensive at first, in consequence of the increase in the undertaker's bill, and the necessity of taking in the clothes of all the paupers, which fluttered loosely on their wasted, shrunken forms, after a week or two's gruel. But the number of workhouse inmates got thin as well as the paupers; and the board were in ecstasies.

1. What do the board members discover about the workhouse that has apparently escaped everyone else's notice?

2. What changes do they institute?

3. What are the two choices left to the poor people?

4. Do you think Dickens admires the members of the board?

---

1. *elysium* (i lizh′əm, i liz′ē əm), paradise.

5. Do you think Dickens considers the poor people fortunate to have the workhouse to go to?

The attitude the writer expresses, whether stated or implied, toward his subject is called *tone*. In the passage above would you characterize the tone as *amused, indulgent, indignant, ironic, matter-of-fact,* or *self-righteous?*

A speaker may express his or her attitude toward something by the tone of voice—loud, soft, emphatic, sarcastic; any number of feelings may be revealed through the voice. Writers, however, must rely on their written words to convey tone in an article, poem, or story. Techniques used to express tone include word choice and arrangement, information given about events, ideas, and characters, and even rhythm, especially in poetry.

Reread the first sentence of the passage. There is a hint of Dickens's attitude in the words used to characterize the board members: *sage, deep, philosophical,* but the reference to "ordinary folks" and the exclamation point at the end of the phrase "the poor people liked it" are clear clues to the reader that he is assuming an ironic tone toward his subject.

Further on, Dickens explains parenthetically that the board would "compel" no one to adopt one manner of starvation over the other. What is the inference the reader may draw from this statement?

When relating the arrangements for food, Dickens points out that the board contracted for an "unlimited supply of water," and "small quantities of oatmeal" with an onion "twice a week" and "half a roll on Sundays." He then notes that the board made "a great many other wise and humane regulations" implying that the aforementioned are wise and humane also. Is that the actual case?

Noting that relief from family responsibilities might have proved too popular with "all classes of society," Dickens refers to the board members as "long-headed" men who had foreseen and provided for that event; that is, "The relief was inseparable from the workhouse and gruel; and that frightened people." What is the tone here?

The tone of the passage is continued in the second paragraph. Dickens points out that the new system was "rather expensive at first," but that soon there were fewer inmates to feed,

clothe, and bury. Why were the board in ecstasies?

Through his choice of words and the jux-
taposition of the cruelties inflicted on poor
people with the wisdom of the board in inflicting
them, Dickens has created a passage that is
ironic in tone with both humorous and serious
overtones to it.

Determine the tone of the following poem.

Daniel at Breakfast

His paper propped against the electric toaster
    (Nicely adjusted to his morning use),
Daniel at breakfast studies world disaster
    And sips his orange juice.

5 The words dismay him. Headlines shrilly chatter
    Of famine, storm, death, pestilence, decay.
Daniel is gloomy, reaching for the butter.
    He shudders at the way

War stalks the planet still, and men know hunger,
10   Go shelterless, betrayed, may perish soon.
The coffee's weak again. In sudden anger
    Daniel throws down his spoon

And broods a moment on the kitchen faucet
    The plumber mended, but has mended ill;

15 Recalls tomorrow means a dental visit,
    Laments the grocery bill.

Then, having shifted from his human shoulder
    The universal woe, he drains his cup,
Rebukes the weather (surely turning colder),
20   Crumples his napkin up
And, kissing his wife abruptly at the door,
Stamps fiercely off to catch the 8:04.

Phyllis McGinley

1. What terrible things are happening in the
world?

2. What "terrible" things are happening at
home to Daniel?

3. Which do you think upsets him more?
Do you think the narrator is sympathetic to
Daniel's trials?

4. What are some clues in the poem as to
the way the narrator views Daniel's situation?

tone

The attitude of the writer toward his or her subject.
Tone may be stated or implied. Tone may be revealed
by the author's word choice and arrangement of
ideas, events, and descriptions.

Glossary

The pronunciation of each word is shown just after the word, in this way: **ab bre vi ate** (ə brē′vē āt). The letters and signs used are pronounced as in the words below. The mark ′ is placed after a syllable with primary or heavy accent, as in the example above. The mark ′ after a syllable shows a secondary or lighter accent, as in **ab bre vi a tion** (ə brē′vē ā′shən).

Some words, taken from foreign languages, are spoken with sounds that do not otherwise occur in English. Symbols for these sounds are given in the key as "foreign sounds."

a	hat, cap	j	jam, enjoy	u	cup, butter
ā	age, face	k	kind, seek	ù	full, put
ä	father, far	l	land, coal	ü	rule, move
		m	me, am		
b	bad, rob	n	no, in	v	very, save
ch	child, much	ng	long, bring	w	will, woman
d	did, red			y	young, yet
		o	hot, rock	z	zero, breeze
e	let, best	ō	open, go	zh	measure, seizure
ē	equal, be	ô	order, all		
ėr	term, learn	oi	oil, voice	ə	represents:
		ou	house, out		a in about
f	fat, if				e in taken
g	go, bag	p	paper, cup		i in pencil
h	he, how	r	run, try		o in lemon
		s	say, yes		u in circus
i	it, pin	sh	she, rush		
ī	ice, five	t	tell, it		
		th	thin, both		
		ᴛʜ	then, smooth		

foreign sounds

Y as in French *du*.
Pronounce (ē) with the lips rounded as for (ü).

à as in French *ami*.
Pronounce (ä) with the lips spread and held tense.

œ as in French *peu*.
Pronounce (ā) with the lips rounded as for (ō).

N as in French *bon*.
The N is not pronounced, but shows that the vowel before it is nasal.

H as in German *ach*.
Pronounce (k) without closing the breath passage.

adj.	adjective	*prep.*	preposition
adv.	adverb	*pron.*	pronoun
conj.	conjunction	*v.*	verb
interj.	interjection	*v.i.*	intransitive verb
n.	noun	*v.t.*	transitive verb
sing.	singular	*pl.*	plural

From *Thorndike-Barnhart Advanced Dictionary*, Second Edition. Copyright © 1974 Scott, Foresman and Company.

a bate (ə bāt′), *v.*, **a bat ed, a bat ing.**
—*v.t.* 1 lessen in force or intensity; reduce or decrease: *Soft words did not abate her fury.* 2 put an end to; stop: *abate a nuisance.* —*v.i.* become less in force or intensity; diminish: *The storm has abated.* [< Old French *abatre* beat down < *a-* to + *batre* to beat] —**a bat′a ble,** *adj.* —**a bat′er,** *n.*

ab ject (ab′jekt, ab jekt′), *adj.* 1 so low or degraded as to be hopeless; wretched; miserable: *to live in abject poverty.* 2 deserving contempt; despicable: *the most abject flattery.* 3 slavish: *abject submission.* [< Latin *abjectum* cast down < *ab-* down + *jacere* to throw] —**ab ject′ly,** *adv.* —**ab ject′ness,** *n.*

-able, *suffix forming adjectives from verbs and nouns.* 1 that can be ____ed: *Enjoyable = that can be enjoyed.* 2 giving ____; suitable for ____: *Comfortable = giving comfort.* 3 inclined to ____: *Peaceable = inclined to peace.* 4 deserving to be ____ed: *Lovable = deserving to be loved.* 5 liable to be ____: *Breakable = liable to be broken.* [< Old French < Latin *-abilem*]

a brupt (ə brupt′), *adj.* 1 characterized by sudden change; unexpected: *an abrupt turn.* 2 very steep. 3 short or sudden in speech or manner; blunt. 4 disconnected: *an abrupt style of writing.* [< Latin *abruptum* broken off < *ab-* off + *rumpere* to break] —**a brupt′ly,** *adv.* —**a brupt′ness,** *n.*

a buse (ə byüz′), *v.t.*, **a bused, a bus ing.** 1 use wrongly; make improper use of; misuse: *to abuse a privilege.* 2 treat roughly or cruelly; mistreat: *to abuse a dog by beating it.* 3 use harsh and insulting language about or to; revile: *The candidates abused each other.* [< Old French *abuser* < Latin *abusum* misused < *ab-* away + *uti* to use] —**a bus′er,** *n.*

ac cen tu ate (ak sen′chü āt), *v.t.*, **-at ed, -at ing.** 1 call special attention to; emphasize: *Her white dress accentuated her sunburn.* 2 pronounce with an accent. 3 mark with an accent. —**ac cen′tu a′tion,** *n.*

ac qui esce (ak′wē es′), *v.i.*, **-esced, -esc ing.** give consent by keeping silent or by not making objections; accept (the conclusions or arrangements of others); accede: *acquiesce in a decision.* [< Latin *acquiescere* < *ad-* to + *quies* rest, quiet]

ac quit (ə kwit′), *v.t.*, **-quit ted, -quit ting.** 1 declare not guilty; set free after considering evidence; exonerate: *The jury acquitted the accused man.* 2 release from (a duty, obligation, etc.) [< Old French *aquiter* < *a-* to + *quite* free] —**ac quit′ter,** *n.*

ac quit tal (ə kwit′l), *n.* an acquitting; discharge; release.

a gent (ā′jənt), *n.* 1 person or company that has the authority to act for or in place of another; representative: *a business agent, an insurance agent.* 2 any power or cause that produces an effect by its action: *Yeast is an important agent in causing bread to rise.* 3 means; instrument. [< Latin *agentem* doing < *agere* do]

a gue (ā′gyü), *n.* 1 a malarial fever with chills and sweating that alternate at regular intervals. 2 any fit of shaking or shivering; chill. [< Middle French *aguë* < Latin *(febris) acuta* severe (fever)]

a lac ri ty (ə lak′rə tē), *n.* 1 brisk and eager action; liveliness: *move with alacrity.* 2 cheerful willingness. [< Latin *alacritatem* < *alacer* brisk]

al che my (al′kə mē), *n.* 1 the chemistry of the Middle Ages, which combined science, magic, and philosophy. Alchemy tried to find

a means of transmuting cheaper metals into gold and silver and to discover a universal solvent, a universal remedy for disease, and an elixir for prolonging life. 2 any miraculous power of transformation. [< Old French *alkemie* < Medieval Latin *alchimia* < Arabic *al-kīmiyā′* the art of alloying metals]

al le giance (ə lē′jəns), *n.* 1 the loyalty owed by a citizen to his country; obligation of a subject to his ruler or government. 2 faithfulness to a person, cause, etc.; loyalty; fidelity. [Middle English *alegeaunce* < Old French *ligeance* < *lige* liege]

am bi tion (am bish′ən), *n.* 1 the desire to distinguish oneself from other people; a strong desire to rise to high position or to attain rank, influence, or distinction. 2 thing strongly desired or sought after: *Her ambition is to be an oceanographer.* [< Latin *ambitionem* a canvassing for votes < *ambire* go around < *ambi-* around + *ire* go] —**am bi′tion less,** *adj.*

am bi tious (am bish′əs), *adj.* 1 full of or guided by ambition. 2 strongly desirous; eager: *ambitious for money, ambitious of power, ambitious to succeed.* 3 arising from or showing ambition: *an ambitious plan.* —**am bi′tious ly,** *adv.* —**am bi′tious ness,** *n.*

a mend (ə mend′), *v.t.* 1 make a change or changes in the form of (a law, bill, or motion) by addition, omission, or alteration of language. 2 change for the better; improve. 3 free from faults; make right; correct; emend. —*v.i.* reform oneself: *After he criticized me, I took pains to amend.* [< Old French *amender* < Latin *emendare* < *ex-* out of + *menda* fault.] —**a mend′a ble,** *adj.* —**a mend′er,** *n.*

a mi a bil i ty (ā′mē ə bil′ə tē), *n.* a being amiable; good nature.

a mi a ble (ā′mē ə bəl), *adj.* having a good-natured and friendly disposition; pleasant and agreeable. [< Old French < Late Latin *amicabilis* < Latin *amicus* friend.] —**a′mi a ble ness,** *n.* —**a′mi a bly,** *adv.*

am u let (am′yə lit), *n.* locket, carved image, or some other small object worn as a magic charm against evil, disease, etc. [< Latin *amuletum*]

an guish (ang′gwish), *n.* 1 severe physical pain; great suffering: *the anguish of unrelieved toothache.* 2 extreme mental pain or suffering: *the anguish of despair.* [< Old French *anguisse* < Latin *angustia* tightness < *angustus* narrow]

an guished (ang′gwisht), *adj.* full of anguish; distressed with severe pain; tormented.

an nex (*v.* ə neks′, an′eks; *n.* an′eks), *v.t.* 1 join or add to a larger or more important thing: *The United States annexed Texas in 1845.* 2 attach as a qualification, etc.: *annex a clause to a contract.* 3 add to a book or other writing; append: *a reader with a glossary annexed.* 4 INFORMAL. take as one's own; appropriate. —*n.* 1 an addition to an existing building; extension; wing. 2 appendage to a document, book, etc. 3 anything annexed; an added part. [< Latin *annexum* bound to < *ad-* to + *nectere* to bind] —**an nex′a ble,** *adj.* —**an nex′ment,** *n.*

an ti ma cas sar (an′ti mə kas′ər), *n.* a small covering to protect the back or arms of a chair, sofa, etc., against soiling. [< *anti-* against + *Macassar*, a hair oil]

an tip a thy (an tip′ə thē), *n.*, *pl.* **-thies.** 1 a strong or fixed dislike; feeling against; aversion: *an antipathy to snakes.* 2 object of

hat, āge, fär; let, ēqual, tèrm;
it, īce; hot, ōpen, ôrder;
oil, out; cup, put, rüle;
ch, child; ng, long; sh, she;
th, thin; ᴛʜ, then; zh, measure;

ə represents *a* in about, *e* in taken,
i in pencil, *o* in lemon, *u* in circus.

< = from, derived from, taken from.

aversion or dislike. [< Greek *antipatheia* < *anti-*against + *pathos* feeling]

an ti quat ed (an′tə kwā′tid), *adj.* 1 old-fashioned; out-of-date. 2 too old for work or service.

ap a thy (ap′ə thē), *n.*, *pl.* **-thies.** 1 lack of interest in or desire for activity; indifference. 2 lack of feeling. [< Greek *apatheia* < *a-* without + *pathos* feeling]

ap er ture (ap′ər chür, ap′ər chər), *n.* an opening; hole. A shutter regulates the size of the aperture through which light passes into a camera. [< Latin *apertura* < *aperire* to open.]

a plomb (ə plom′), *n.* self-possession springing from perfect confidence in oneself; assurance; poise. [< French < *à plomb* according to the plummet]

ap pall or **ap pal** (ə pôl′), *v.t.*, **-palled, -pall ing.** fill with consternation and horror; dismay; terrify: *The thought of another war appalled us.* [< Old French *apallir* make pale < *a-* to + *pale* pale]

ap pa ri tion (ap′ə rish′ən), *n.* 1 a supernatural sight or thing; ghost or phantom. 2 the appearance of something strange, remarkable, or unexpected. [< Late Latin *apparitionem*]

ap pease (ə pēz′), *v.t.*, **-peased, -peas ing.** 1 put an end to by satisfying (an appetite or desire): *A good dinner will appease your hunger.* 2 make calm or quiet; pacify. 3 give in to the demands of (especially those of a potential enemy): *Chamberlain appeased Hitler at Munich.* [< Old French *apaisier* < *a-* to + *pais* peace] —**ap peas′er,** *n.* —**ap peas′ing ly,** *adv.*

ar bi trar y (är′bə trer′ē), *adj.* 1 based on one's own wishes, notions, or will; not going by rule or law: *The judge tried to be fair and did not make arbitrary decisions.* 2 fixed or determined by chance: *an arbitrary serial number.* 3 using or abusing unlimited power; tyrannical; despotic: *an arbitrary king.* —**ar′bi trar′i ly,** *adv.* —**ar′bi trar′i ness,** *n.*

a skance (ə skans′), *adv.* 1 with suspicion or disapproval: *The students looked askance at the suggestion for having classes on Saturday.* 2 to one side; sideways. [origin uncertain]

a skew (ə skyü′), *adv.*, *adj.* out of the proper position; turned or twisted the wrong way; awry.

as per i ty (a sper′ə tē), *n.*, *pl.* **-ties.** 1 harshness or sharpness of temper, especially as shown in tone or manner. 2 severity; rigor: *The settlers suffered the asperities of a very cold winter.* [< Latin *asperitatem* < *asper* rough]

a sphyx i ate (a sfik′sē āt), *v.t.*, *v.i.*, **-at ed, -at ing.** suffocate.

as pi ra tion (as′pə rā′shən), *n.* 1 earnest desire; longing; ambition: *She had aspirations to be a doctor.* 2 an aspirating (of

603

sounds). **3** an aspirated sound. **4** act of drawing air into the lungs; breathing.

as pire (ə spīr′), *v.i.*, **-pired, -pir ing.** **1** have an ambition for something; desire earnestly; seek: *Scholars aspire after knowledge. I aspired to be captain of the team.* **2** rise high. [< Latin *aspirare* breathe toward, aspire < *ad-* toward + *spirare* breathe]

at a vism (at′ə viz′əm), *n.* **1** (in biology) the reappearance in an animal or plant of characteristics of a remote ancestor not found in its immediate ancestors, generally as a result of a recombination of genes. **2** reversion to a primitive type. [< Latin *atavus* ancestor]

at a vis tic (at′ə vis′tik), *adj.* **1** having to do with atavism. **2** having a tendency to atavism. **—at′a vis′ti cal ly,** *adv.*

-ate, *suffix forming adjectives, verbs, and nouns.* **1** of or having to do with ____: *Collegiate = having to do with college.* **2** having or containing ____: *Compassionate = having compassion.* **3** having the form of ____; like ____: *Stellate = having the form of a star.* **4** become ____: *Maturate = become mature.* **5** cause to be ____: *Alienate = cause to be alien.* **6** produce ____: *Ulcerate = produce ulcers.* **7** supply or treat with ____: *Aerate = treat with air.* **8** combine with ____: *Oxygenate = combine with oxygen.* [< Latin *-atus, -atum,* past participle endings]

au di ble (ô′də bəl), *adj.* that can be heard; loud enough to be heard. [< Latin *audire* hear] **—au′di bly,** *adv.*

aught (ôt), *n.* anything: *Has he done aught to help you?* **—***adv.* in any way; to any degree; at all: *Help came too late to avail aught.* Also, **ought.** [Old English *āwiht* < *ā-* ever + *wiht* thing]

aug ment (ôg ment′), *v.t., v.i.* make or become greater in size, number, amount, or degree; increase or enlarge. [< Late Latin *augmentare* < *augmentum* an increase < Latin *augere* to increase] **—aug ment′a ble,** *adj.* **—aug ment′er,** *n.*

aus tere (ô stir′), *adj.* **1** stern in manner or appearance; harsh: *a silent, austere man.* **2** severe in self-discipline; strict in morals: *The Puritans were austere.* **3** severely simple: *The tall, plain columns stood against the sky in austere beauty.* **4** grave; somber; serious.[< Greek *austēros < auos* dry] **—austere′ly,** *adv.* **—aus tere′ness,** *n.*

au to mat (ô′tə mat), *n.* restaurant in which food is obtained from compartments that can be opened after coins are inserted in slots.

aux il iar y (ôg zil′yər ē, ôg zil′ər ē), *adj., n., pl.* **-iar ies.** **—***adj.* **1** giving help or support; assisting: *The army was sent auxiliary troops.* **2** additional; subsidiary: *The main library has several auxiliary branches.* **3** kept in reserve or as a substitute; supplementary: *Some sailboats have auxiliary engines.* **—***n.* **1** person or thing that helps; aid. **2** a subsidiary group: *a men's club with a women's auxiliary.* **3** auxiliary verb. [< Latin *auxilium* aid]

av ar ice (av′ər is), *n.* too great a desire for money or property; greed for wealth. [< Old French < Latin *avaritia < avarus* greedy]

av a ri cious (av′ə rish′əs), *adj.* greatly desiring money or property; greedy for wealth. **—av′a ri′cious ly,** *adv.* **—av′a ri′cious ness,** *n.*

a venge (ə venj′), *v.,* **a venged, a veng ing. —***v.t.* take revenge for or on behalf of:

avenge an insult. **—***v.i.* get revenge. [< Old French *avengier < a-* to + *vengier* avenge < Latin *vindicare*] **—a veng′er,** *n.*

a vert (ə vėrt′), *v.t.* **1** keep (a disaster, misfortune, etc.) from happening; prevent; avoid: *She averted the accident by a quick turn of her car.* **2** turn away or turn aside (the face, eyes, mind, etc.). [< Latin *avertere < ab-* from + *vertere* to turn]

awe (ô), *n., v.,* **awed, aw ing. —***n.* **1 a** feeling of wonder and reverence inspired by anything of great beauty, sublimity, majesty, or power: *The sight of the great waterfall filled us with awe. The young girl stood in awe before the queen.* **2** dread mingled with reverence. **—***v.t.* **1** cause to feel awe; fill with awe: *The majesty of the mountains awed us.* **2** influence or restrain by awe. [< Scandinavian (Old Icelandic) *agi*]

ban ish (ban′ish), *v.t.* **1** compel (a person) to leave a country by order of political or judicial authority; exile. **2** force to go away; drive away; dismiss; expel: *banish all cares.* [< Old French *baniss-,* a form of *banir* < Germanic.] **—ban′ish er,** *n.* **—ban′ish ment,** *n.*

ban tam (ban′təm), *n.* **1** Often, **Bantam. a** small variety of domestic fowl. The roosters are often spirited fighters. **2 a** small person who is fond of fighting. **—***adj.* **1** light in weight; small. **2** laughably aggressive.[< *Bantam,* town in Java, where the fowl are imported from]

bar bar ic (bär bar′ik), *adj.* **1** like barbarians; suited to an uncivilized people; rough and rude. **2** crudely rich or splendid; flamboyant. **—bar bar′i cal ly,** *adv.*

bar rage (bə räzh′), *n., v.,* **-raged, -rag ing. —***n.* **1** barrier of artillery fire to check the enemy or to protect one's own soldiers when advancing or retreating. **2** a large number of words, blows, etc., coming quickly one after the other: *The reporters kept up a barrage of questions for an hour.* **—***v.t., v.i.* fire at with artillery; subject to a barrage. [< French < *barrer* to bar]

bar ren (bar′ən), *adj.* **1** not producing anything; unproductive: *A sandy desert is barren.* **2** not able to produce offspring or yield fruit; not fertile; sterile. **3** without interest; unattractive; dull. **4** of no advantage; fruitless; unprofitable. [< Old French *baraine*] **—bar′ren ly,** *adv.* **—bar′ren ness,** *n.*

base (bās), *adj.,* **bas er, bas est. 1** morally low or mean; selfish and cowardly: *Betraying a friend is a base action.* **2** fit for an inferior person or thing; menial; unworthy. **3** ARCHAIC. of humble birth or origin. **4** having little comparative value; inferior: *Iron and lead are base metals; gold and silver are precious metals.* **5** debased; counterfeit: *base coin.* [< Old French *bas* < Medieval Latin *bassus* low.] **—base′ly,** *adv.* **—base′ness,** *n.*

bay (bā), *n.* **1 a** deep, prolonged barking of a dog when pursuing or attacking. **2** position of a hunted animal that turns to face its pursuers when further flight is impossible: *The stag stood at bay on the edge of the cliff.* **3 a** stand by a person forced to face a foe, difficulty, persecution, etc. **4** position of an enemy or pursuers thus faced or kept off: *The stag held the hounds at bay.* **5 bring to bay,** put in a position from which escape is impossible. **—***v.i.* bark with long, deep sounds. **—***v.t.*

1 bark at; assail with barking. **2** utter or express by baying. **3** bring to bay. [< Old French *abai* a barking]

ben e fac tor (ben′ə fak′tər, ben′ə fak′tər), *n.* person who has helped others, either by gifts of money or by some kind act. [< Late Latin < Latin *benefactum* befitted < *bene* well + *facere* do]

be reave (bi rēv′), *v.t.,* **-reaved** or **-reft, -reav ing. 1** leave desolate and alone: *The family was bereaved by the death of the father.* **2** deprive ruthlessly; rob: *bereaved of hope.* [Old English *berēafian < be-* away + *rēafian* rob]

be seech (bi sēch′), *v.t.,* **-sought** or **-seeched, -seech ing.** ask earnestly; beg; implore. [Middle English *bisechen < be-* thoroughly + *sechen* seek] **—be seech′er,** *n.* **—be seech′ing ly,** *adv.*

be stride (bi strīd′), *v.t.,* **-strode, -strid den, -strid ing. 1** get on, sit on, or stand over (something) with one leg on each side. **2** straddle over. **3** stride across; step over.

be to ken (bi tō′kən), *v.t.* be a sign or token of; indicate; show.

be wil der (bi wil′dər), *v.t.* confuse completely; perplex: *The child was bewildered by the crowds.* **—be wil′der ing ly,** *adv.* **—be wild′er ment,** *n.*

bib u lous (bib′yə ləs), *adj.* **1** fond of drinking alcoholic liquor. **2** showing the effects of drinking alcoholic liquor; drunk. **3** absorbent of moisture. [< Latin *bibulus < bibere* to drink] **—bib′u lous ly,** *adv.* **—bib′u lous ness,** *n.*

big ot (big′ət), *n.* person who is bigoted; intolerant person. [< Middle French]

big ot ed (big′ə tid), *adj.* obstinately and unreasonably attached to a particular opinion, belief, party, etc., and intolerant of all who have different views; intolerant. **—big′-ot ed ly,** *adv.*

bil low (bil′ō), *n.* **1** a great, swelling wave or surge of the sea. **2** a great rolling or swelling mass of smoke, flame, air, etc. **—***v.i.* **1** rise or roll in big waves; surge. **2** swell out; bulge: *The sheets on the clothesline billowed in the wind.* [< Scandinavian (Old Icelandic) *bylgja*]

blun der (blun′dər), *n.* a stupid or careless mistake; bungle. **—***v.i.* **1** make a stupid or careless mistake. **2** move clumsily or thoughtlessly; stumble. **—***v.t.* **1** do clumsily or wrongly; bungle. **2** say or reveal clumsily, stupidly, or thoughtlessly; blurt out. [Middle English *blonderen* mix up] **—blun′der er,** *n.*

bog (bog, bôg), *n., v.,* **bogged, bog ging. —***n.* piece of wet, spongy ground, consisting chiefly of decayed or decaying moss and other vegetable matter, too soft to bear the weight of any heavy body on its surface; marsh; swamp. **—***v.t., v.i.* **1** sink or get stuck in a bog. **2 bog down,** sink in or get stuck so that one cannot get out without help: *She is bogged down with problems.* [< Irish or Scottish Gaelic, soft]

bois ter ous (boi′stər əs), *adj.* **1** noisily cheerful; exuberant: *a boisterous game.* **2** rough and stormy; turbulent: *a boisterous wind.* **3** rough and noisy; clamorous: *a boisterous child.* [Middle English *boistrous*] **—bois′ter ous ly,** *adv.* **—bois′ter ous ness,** *n.*

bond man (bond′mən), *n., pl.* **-men.** **1** slave. **2** (in the Middle Ages) a serf.

bon ny or **bon nie** (bon′ē), *adj.,* **-ni er, -ni est. 1** fair to see; rosy and pretty: *a bonny baby.* **2** cheerful. [Middle English

604

bonne, apparently < Old French *bone* good < Latin *bonus*] **—bon′ni ly,** *adv.* **—bon′ni ness,** *n.*

bough (bou), *n.* one of the branches of a tree, particularly one laden with blossoms or fruit. [Old English *bōg* bough, shoulder]

bowl er (bō′lər), *n.* 1 person who bowls. 2 BRITISH. a derby hat.

brach i o ce phal ic (brak′ē ə sə fal′ik), *adj.* having a short, broad skull. Also, **brachycephalic.** [< Greek *brachys* short + *kephalē* head]

brash (brash), *adj.* 1 showing lack of respect; impudent; saucy. 2 hasty; rash: *a brash act.* [origin uncertain] **—brash′ly,** *adv.* **—brash′ness,** *n.*

bra zen (brā′zn), *adj.* 1 having no shame; shameless; impudent. 2 loud and harsh; brassy. 3 made of brass. 4 like brass in color or strength. **—v.t.** 1 make shameless or impudent. 2 **brazen it out** or **brazen it through,** act as if one did not feel ashamed of it: *Although he was caught lying, he tried to brazen it out by telling another lie.* [Old English *bræsen* < *bræs* brass] **—bra′zen ly,** *adv.* **—bra′zen ness,** *n.*

breach (brēch), *n.* 1 an opening made by breaking down something solid, as a gap made in a wall or fortification. 2 a breaking or neglect (of a law, a trust, etc.); infraction; infringement: *For the guard to leave now would be a breach of duty.* 3 a breaking of friendly relations; quarrel. **—v.t.** break through; make an opening in: *The wall had been breached in several places.* [Old English *bræc* a break]

broach (brōch), *v.t.* 1 begin conversation or discussion about; introduce: *broach a subject.* 2 open by making a hole: *broach a barrel of cider.* 3 enlarge and finish (a drilled hole) with a broach. [< Old French *broche* < Latin *broccus* projecting] **—broach′er,** *n.*

brood (brüd), *v.i.* 1 (of birds) sit on eggs so as to hatch them; incubate. 2 cover or protect young with or as if with the wings. 3 think or worry a long time about some one thing. **—v.t.** 1 sit on (eggs) in order to hatch. 2 dwell on in thought: *For years he brooded vengeance.* 3 **brood on** or **brood over, a** keep thinking about. **b** hover over; hang close over. **—adj.** kept for breeding: *a brood mare.* [Old English *brōd*] **—brood′ing ly,** *adv.*

buf fet (buf′it), *n.* 1 a blow of the hand or fist. 2 a knock, stroke, or hurt. **—v.t.** 1 strike with the hand or fist. 2 knock about; strike repeatedly; beat back: *The waves buffeted me.* 3 fight or struggle against: *The boat buffeted the heavy waves caused by the storm.* **—v.i.** deal blows; struggle; contend. [< Old French, diminutive of *buffe* blow]

bun ga low (bung′gə lō), *n.* a small house, usually of one story or a story and a half, with low, sweeping lines. [< Hindustani *banglā* of Bengal]

buoy (boi, bü′ē), *n.* 1 a floating object anchored on the water to warn against hidden rocks or shallows or to indicate the safe part of a channel. 2 life buoy. **—v.t.** 1 furnish with buoys; mark with a buoy. 2 **buoy up, a** hold up; keep from sinking. **b** support or encourage. [< Old French *boie* chain, fetter < Latin *boiae*]

bur dock (bėr′dok′), *n.* a coarse weed of the composite family, with burs and broad leaves. [< *bur* + *dock*]

bur geon (bėr′jən), *v.i.* 1 grow or shoot forth; bud; sprout. 2 grow or develop rapidly; flourish: *New suburbs had burgeoned all*

around the city. **—n.** a bud; sprout. [< Old French *burjon* a bud]

bur ly (bėr′lē), *adj.,* **-li er, -li est.** great in bodily size; big and strong; sturdy: *a burly wrestler.* [Middle English *burli,* earlier *burlich, borlich,* Old English *borlice* nobly] **—bur′li ly,** *adv.* **—bur′li ness,** *n.*

cairn (kern, karn), *n.* 1 pile of stones heaped up as a memorial, tomb, or landmark. 2 cairn terrier. [< Scottish Gaelic *carn* heap of stones]

cal lous (kal′əs), *adj.* 1 hard or hardened, as parts of the skin that are exposed to constant pressure and friction. 2 unfeeling; insensitive: *Only a callous person can see suffering without trying to relieve it.* **—cal′lous ly,** *adv.* **—cal′lous ness,** *n.*

cal low (kal′ō), *adj.* 1 young and inexperienced: *a callow youth.* 2 not fully developed. 3 (of birds) without feathers sufficiently developed for flight. [Old English *calu* bald] **—cal′low ness,** *n.*

can non ade (kan′ə nād′), *n., v.,* **-ad ed, -ad ing. —n.** a continued firing of cannons; barrage. **—v.t.** attack with or as if with cannons.

can ny (kan′ē), *adj.,* **-ni er, -ni est.** 1 shrewd and cautious in dealing with others. 2 thrifty. **—can′ni ly,** *adv.* **—can′ni ness,** *n.*

ca reen (kə rēn′), *v.i.* lean to one side or sway sharply; tilt; tip: *The ship careened in the strong wind.* **—v.t.** 1 lay (a ship) over on one side for cleaning, painting, repairing, etc. 2 cause to lean to one side or sway sharply: *The gale careened the sailboat.* [< Middle French *carène* keel < Latin *carina*]

ca reer (kə rir′), *n.* 1 a general course of action or progress through life. 2 way of living; occupation; profession: *She planned to make law her career.* 3 a run at full speed; going with force; speed: *We were in full career when we struck the post.* **—v.i.** rush along wildly; dash: *The runaway horse careered through the streets.* [< Middle French *carrière* race course < Latin *carrus* wagon]

car riage (kar′ij), *n.* 1 vehicle that moves on wheels. Some carriages are pulled by horses and are used to carry people. 2 frame on wheels that supports a gun. 3 a moving part of a machine that supports some other part or object: *a typewriter carriage.* 4 manner of holding the head and body; bearing: *She has a queenly carriage.* [< Old French *cariage* < *carier*]

car ri on (kar′ē ən), *n.* 1 dead and decaying flesh. 2 rottenness; filth. **—adj.** 1 dead and decaying. 2 feeding on dead and decaying flesh. 3 rotten; filthy. [< Old French *caroine, carcass* < Popular Latin *caronia* < Latin *carnem* flesh]

cas cade (ka skād′), *n., v.,* **-cad ed, -cad ing. —n.** 1 a small waterfall. 2 anything like this: *Her dress had a cascade of ruffles down the front.* 3 series of pieces of apparatus serving to continue or develop a process. 4 series of reactions in which one causes or produces another. **—v.i.** fall, pour, or flow in a cascade. [< French < Italian *cascata* < Latin *casus* a falling]

cav al cade (kav′əl kād′, kav′əl kād′), *n.* 1 procession of persons riding on horses, in carriages, or in automobiles. 2 series of scenes or events: *a cavalcade of sports.* [< Middle French < Italian *cavalcata* <

hat, āge, fär; let, ēqual, tėrm;
it, īce; hot, ōpen, ôrder;
oil, out; cup, put, rüle;
ch, child; ng, long; sh, she;
th, thin; ᴛʜ, then; zh, measure;

ə represents *a* in about, *e* in taken, *i* in pencil, *o* in lemon, *u* in circus.

< = from, derived from, taken from.

cavalcare ride horseback < Late Latin *caballicare* < Latin *caballus* horse]

chaff (chaf), *v.t., v.i.* make fun of in a good-natured way to one's face; banter. **—n.** good-natured joking about a person to his face. [origin uncertain]

cha grin (shə grin′), *n.* a feeling of disappointment, failure, or humiliation. **—v.t.** cause to feel chagrin. [< French, apparently < *chat* cat + *grigner* to purse (the lips)]

chase[1] (chās), *v.,* **chased, chas ing,** *n.* **—v.t.** 1 run or follow after to catch or kill. 2 drive away. 3 run after; follow; pursue: *chase a ball.* 4 hunt. **—v.i.** INFORMAL. rush; hurry. **—n.** 1 act of chasing. 2 **give chase,** run after; pursue. 3 hunting as a sport; hunt: *We watched the chase.* 4 a hunted animal: *The chase escaped the hunter.* [< Old French *chacier* < Latin *captare*]

chase[2] (chās), *v.,* **chased, chas ing,** *n.* **—v.t.** decorate (metal, etc.) with embossed or engraved work. **—n.** a rectangular metal frame to hold type that is ready to print or make plates from. [< French *châsse* a frame, case]

chas tise (cha stīz′), *v.t.,* **-tised, -tis ing.** 1 inflict punishment or suffering on to improve; punish. 2 criticize severely; rebuke. [variant of *chasten*] **—chas tis′er,** *n.*

chau vin ism (shō′və niz′əm), *n.* 1 boastful, warlike patriotism; unreasoning enthusiasm for the military glory of one's country. 2 an excessive enthusiasm for one's sex, race, or group: *no lack of female chauvinism.* [< French *chauvinisme* < Nicolas Chauvin, an old soldier and enthusiastic admirer of Napoleon I]

chau vin is tic (shō′və nis′tik), *adj.* of chauvinism or chauvinists. **—chau′vin is′ti cal ly,** *adv.*

che nille (shə nēl′), *n.* 1 a soft, velvety cord of cotton, silk, or wool, used in embroidery, fringe, etc. 2 fabric woven from this cord, used for rugs, bedspreads, housecoats, etc. [< French, literally, caterpillar; from its furry look]

chiv al ry (shiv′əl rē), *n.* 1 qualities of an ideal knight in the Middle Ages; bravery, honor, courtesy, protection of the weak, respect for women, generosity, and fairness to enemies. 2 rules and customs of knights in the Middle Ages; system of knighthood. 3 knights as a group. 4 gallant warriors or gentlemen. [< Old French *chevalerie* < *chevalier*]

chol er ic (kol′ər ik), *adj.* 1 having an irritable disposition; easily made angry. 2 enraged; angry; wrathful: *a choleric outburst of temper.*

chor tle (chôr′tl), *v.,* **-tled, -tling,** *n.* **—v.i., v.t.** chuckle or snort with glee. **—n.** a gleeful chuckle or snort. [blend of *chuckle* and *snort;* coined by Lewis Carroll] **—chor′tler,** *n.*

chron ic (kron′ik), *adj.* 1 lasting a long time: *Rheumatism is often a chronic disease.* 2 suffering long from an illness: *a chronic* *invalid.* **3** never stopping; constant; habitual: *a chronic liar.* [< Greek *chronikos* of time < *chronos* time] —**chron′i cal ly,** *adv.*

cir cum stan tial (sėr′kəm stan′shəl), *adj.* **1** depending on or based on circumstances: *Stolen jewels found in a person's possession are circumstantial evidence that he stole them.* **2** not essential; not important; incidental: *Minor details are circumstantial compared with the main fact.* **3** giving full and exact details; complete: *a circumstantial report of an accident.* —**cir′cum stan′tial ly,** *adv.*

ci vil i ty (sə vil′ə tē), *n., pl.* **-ties. 1** polite behavior; courtesy. **2** act or expression of politeness or courtesy.

clam ber (klam′bər), *v.i., v.t.* climb, using both hands and feet; climb awkwardly or with difficulty; scramble. —*n.* an awkward or difficult climb. [Middle English *clambren*] —**clam′ber er,** *n.*

clar i fi ca tion (klar′ə fə kā′shən), *n.* **1** act or process of clarifying. **2** state of being clarified.

clar i fy (klar′ə fī), *v.,* **-fied, -fy ing.** —*v.t.* **1** make clearer; explain: *The teacher's explanation clarified the difficult instructions.* **2** make clear; purify. —*v.i.* become clear: *My mind suddenly clarified.* [< Old French *clarifier* < Late Latin *clarificare* < Latin *clarus* clear + *facere* make]

clench (klench), *v.t.* **1** close tightly together: *clench one's fists.* **2** grasp firmly; grip tightly: *The player clenched the bat to swing at the ball.* **3** clinch (a nail, staple, etc.). —*n.* **1** a firm grasp; tight grip. **2** clinch of a nail, staple, etc. [Old English *(be)clencan* hold fast] —**clench′er,** *n.*

cli ché (klē shā′), *n.* **1** a timeworn expression or idea. "Father Time," "white as snow," and "cheeks like roses" are clichés. **2** a trite or overused plot, scene, effect, etc. [< French, past participle of *clicher* to stereotype]

coax (kōks), *v.t.* **1** persuade by soft words; influence by pleasant ways; cajole: *We coaxed our parents into letting us go to the movies.* **2** get by coaxing: *The baby-sitter coaxed a smile from the baby.* [< obsolete *cokes* a fool] —**coax′er,** *n.* —**coax′ing ly,** *adv.*

cof fer (kô′fər, kof′ər), *n.* **1** box, chest, or trunk, especially one used to hold money or other valuable things. **2** an ornamental panel in a ceiling, etc. **3** cofferdam. **4 coffers,** *pl.* treasury; funds. [< Old French *cofre* < Latin *cophinum* basket]

co he sion (kō hē′zhən), *n.* **1** a sticking together; tendency to hold together. **2** (in physics) the attraction between molecules of the same kind: *Drops of water are a result of cohesion.* **3** (in botany) the union of one part with another. [< Latin *cohaesum* pressed together]

col lat er al (kə lat′ər əl), *adj.* **1** related but less important; secondary; indirect. **2** side by side; parallel. **3** in a parallel line of descent; descended from the same ancestors, but in a different line. Cousins are collateral relatives. **4** additional. **5** secured by stocks, bonds, etc. —*n.* **1** stocks, bonds, etc., pledged as security for a loan. **2** a collateral relative. [< Medieval Latin *collateralem* < Latin *com-* + *lateralem* lateral] —**col lat′er al ly,** *adv.*

com pel (kəm pel′), *v.t.,* **-pelled, -pel ling.**

1 drive or urge with force; force: *Rain compelled them to stop.* **2** cause or get by force: *A policeman can compel obedience to the law.* [< Latin *compellere* < *com-* + *pellere* to drive] —**com pel′ling ly,** *adv.*

com pen sa tion (kom′pən sā′shən), *n.* **1** something given as an equivalent; something given to make up for a loss, injury, etc. **2** pay: *He said that equal compensation should be given to men and women for equal work.* **3** a balancing by equal power, weight, etc. **4** means for doing this.

com pen sa to ry (kəm pen′sə tôr′ē, kəmpen′sə tōr′ē), *adj.* compensating.

con ci erge (kon′sē èrzh′; *French* kôn syerzh′), *n.* **1** doorkeeper. **2** janitor. [< French]

con cil i a to ry (kən sil′ē ə tôr′ē, kənsil′ē ə tōr′ē), *adj.* tending to win over, soothe, or reconcile.

con dole (kən dōl′), *v.i.,* **-doled, -dol ing.** express sympathy; grieve; sympathize: *Their friends condoled with them at the funeral.* [< Latin *condolere* < *com-* with + *dolere* grieve, suffer]

con fec tion er (kən fek′shə nər), *n.* person whose business is making or selling candies, ice cream, cakes, etc.

con fi dant (kon′fə dant′, kon′fə dant), *n.* person trusted with one's secrets, private affairs, etc.; close friend.

con fi dante (kon′fə dant′, kon′fə dant), *n.* a confidant.

con fine ment (kən fīn′mənt), *n.* **1** a confining. **2** a being confined. **3** imprisonment. **4** period a mother is confined to bed during and after childbirth.

con jure (kon′jər, kun′jər *for v.t. 1-3, v.i.;* kən jür′ *for v.t. 4*), *v.,* **-jured, -jur ing.** —*v.t.* **1** compel (a spirit, devil, etc.) to appear or disappear by a set form of words. **2** cause to appear or happen as if by magic: *conjure up a whole meal in a jiffy.* **3** cause to appear in the mind: *conjure a vision.* **4** make a solemn appeal; request earnestly; entreat. —*v.i.* **1** summon a devil, spirit, etc. **2** practice magic. **3** perform tricks by skill and quickness in moving the hands. [< Old French *conjurer* < Latin *conjurare* make a compact < *com-* together + *jurare* swear]

con spic u ous (kən spik′yü əs), *adj.* **1** easily seen; clearly visible: *A traffic sign should be conspicuous.* **2** worthy of notice; remarkable: *Lincoln is a conspicuous example of a poor boy who succeeded.* [< Latin *conspicuus* visible < *conspicere* look at < *com-* + *specere* look] —**con spic′u ous ly,** *adv.* —**con spic′u ous ness,** *n.*

con stit u ent (kən stich′ü ənt), *adj.* **1** forming a necessary part; that composes: *Flour, liquid, salt, and yeast are constituent parts of bread.* **2** appointing; electing. **3** having the power to make or change a political constitution: *a constituent assembly.* —*n.* **1** part of a whole; necessary part; component. **2** voter: *The congresswoman received many letters from her constituents.*

con straint (kən strānt′), *n.* **1** a holding back of natural feelings; forced or unnatural manner; embarrassed awkwardness. **2** force; compulsion. **3** confinement. **4** restraint.

con strue (kən strü′), *v.t.,* **-strued, -stru ing. 1** show the meaning of; explain; interpret: *Different judges may construe the same law differently.* **2** analyze the arrangement and connection of words in (a sentence, clause, phrase, etc.). [< Latin *construere* construct] —**con stru′a ble,** *adj.*

con sume (kən süm′), *v.,* **-sumed, -sum-**

ing. —*v.t.* **1** use up; spend; expend: *A student consumes much of his time in studying.* **2** eat or drink up. **3** destroy; burn up: *A huge fire consumed the entire forest.* **4** waste (time, money, etc.); exhaust; squander. **5 consumed with,** absorbed by (curiosity, envy, etc.). —*v.i.* waste away; be destroyed. [< Latin *consumere* < *com-* + *sumere* take up] —**con sum′a ble,** *adj.*

con tempt (kən tempt′), *n.* **1** the feeling that a person, act, or thing is mean, low, or worthless; scorn; despising; disdain: *We feel contempt for a cheat.* **2** a being scorned; disgrace: *A traitor is held in contempt by his countrymen.* **3** disobedience to or open disrespect for the rules or decisions of a court of law, a lawmaking body, etc. A person can be fined or put in jail for **contempt of court.**

con tempt i ble (kən temp′tə bəl), *adj.* deserving contempt or scorn; held in contempt; mean; low; worthless: *a contemptible lie.* —**con tempt′i ble ness,** *n.* —**con tempt′-i bly,** *adv.*

con temp tu ous (kən temp′chü əs), *adj.* showing contempt; scornful: *a contemptuous look.* —**con temp′tu ous ly,** *adv.* —**con temp′tu ous ness,** *n.*

con tend (kən tend′), *v.i.* **1** work hard against difficulties; fight; struggle: *The first settlers in America had to contend with sickness and lack of food.* **2** take part in a contest; compete: *Five runners were contending in the first race.* **3** argue; dispute. —*v.t.* declare to be a fact; maintain as true; assert: *Columbus contended that the earth was round.* [< Latin *contendere* strain, strive < *com-* + *tendere* stretch] —**con tend′er,** *n.*

contra-, *prefix.* in opposition; against: *Contradistinction = distinction by opposition or contrast.* [< Latin < *contra* against]

con tra dict (kon′trə dikt′), *v.t.* **1** say that (a statement, rumor, etc.) is not true; deny. **2** deny the words of (a person); say the opposite of what (a person) has said. **3** be contrary to; disagree with. [< Latin *contradictum* spoken against < *contra-* + *dicere* say] —**con′tra dict′a ble,** *adj.*

con tri tion (kən trish′ən), *n.* **1** sorrow for one's sins or guilt; being contrite; penitence. **2** deep regret.

con trive (kən trīv′), *v.t.,* **-trived, -triv ing. 1** plan with cleverness or skill; invent; design: *contrive a new kind of engine.* **2** plan; scheme; plot: *contrive a robbery.* **3** manage: *I will contrive to be there by ten o'clock.* **4** bring about. [< Old French *controver* < Late Latin *contropare* compare] —**con triv′er,** *n.*

con vulse (kən vuls′), *v.t.,* **-vulsed, -vulsing. 1** shake violently: *An earthquake convulsed the island.* **2** cause violent disturbance in; disturb violently: *His face was convulsed with rage.* **3** throw into convulsions; shake with muscular spasms: *The sick child was convulsed before the doctor came.* **4** throw into fits of laughter; cause to shake with laughter: *The clown convulsed the audience with his funny acts.* [< Latin *convulsum* torn away < *com-* + *vellere* to tear]

co quette (kō ket′), *n.* woman who tries to attract men merely to please her vanity; flirt.

co quet tish (kō ket′ish), *adj.* **1** of a coquette. **2** like a coquette. —**co quet′tish ly,** *adv.* —**co quet′tish ness,** *n.*

co ro net (kôr′ə net′, kor′ə net′), *n.* **1** a small crown, especially one indicating a rank of nobility below that of the sovereign. **2** a circle of gold, jewels, or flowers worn around the head as an ornament.

cor rode (kə rōd′), v., **-rod ed, -rod ing.**
—v.t. eat away gradually, especially by or as if by chemical action: *Moist air corrodes iron.* —v.i. become corroded. [< Latin *corrodere* < *com-* + *rodere* gnaw]

co ro na tion (kôr′ə nā′shən, kor′ə nā′shən), n. ceremony of crowning a king, queen, emperor, etc.

cov et ous (kuv′ə təs), adj. desiring things that belong to others. —**cov′et ous ly,** adv. —**cov′et ous ness,** n.

cra ven (krā′vən), adj. cowardly. —n. 1 coward. 2 **cry craven,** surrender; admit defeat. [< Old French *cravente* overcome < Popular Latin *crepantare* < Latin *crepare* crush; burst] —**cra′ven ly,** adv. —**cra′ven ness,** n.

cre dence (krēd′ns), n. belief; credit: *Never give credence to gossip.* [< Medieval Latin *credentia* < Latin *credere* believe]

cred i tor (kred′ə tər), n. person to whom money or goods are due; one to whom a debt is owed.

cre du li ty (krə dü′lə tē, krə dyü′lə tē), n. a too great readiness to believe.

cres cent (kres′nt), n. 1 shape of the moon in its first or last quarter. 2 anything that curves in a similar way. A curved street or row of houses is sometimes called a crescent. —adj. 1 shaped like the moon in its first or last quarter. 2 growing; increasing. [< Latin *crescentem* growing, increasing] —**cres′cent like′,** adj.

crest fall en (krest′fô′lən), adj. dejected; discouraged. —**crest′fall′en ly,** adv. — **crest′ fall′en ness,** n.

crim son (krim′zən), n. a deep red. —adj. deep-red. —v.t., v.i. make or become deep-red. [< Italian *cremesino* < *cremisi, chermisi* the color crimson < Arabic *qirmizī* < *qirmiz* kermes]

cull (kul), v.t. 1 pick out; select: *The lawyer culled important facts from the mass of evidence.* 2 pick over; make selections from. —n. something picked out as inferior or worthless. [< Old French *coillir* < Latin *colligere* collect] —**cull′er,** n.

cul ti vate (kul′tə vāt), v.t., **-vat ed, -vat ing.** 1 prepare and use (land) to raise crops by plowing it, planting seeds, and taking care of the growing plants; till. 2 help (plants) grow by labor and care. 3 loosen the ground around (growing plants) to kill weeds, etc. 4 improve or develop (the body, mind, or manners) by education or training. 5 give time, thought, and effort to; practice: *An artist cultivates his craft.* 6 seek the friendship of: *She cultivated people who could help her.* [< Medieval Latin *cultivatum* cultivated < *cultivus* under cultivation < Latin *colere* to till, cherish]

cul vert (kul′vərt), n. a small channel for water to run under a road, railroad, canal, etc. [origin uncertain]

cun ning (kun′ing), adj. 1 clever in deceiving; sly; *a cunning fox, a cunning thief.* 2 skillful; clever: *The old watch was a fine example of cunning workmanship.* 3 INFORMAL. pretty and dear; cute: *a cunning baby.* —n. 1 slyness in getting what one wants; cleverness in deceiving one's enemies: *The fox has a great deal of cunning.* 2 skill; cleverness. [Old English *cunnung* < *cunnan* know (how)] —**cun′ning ly,** adv. —**cun′ning ness,** n.

cy clone (sī′klōn), n. 1 storm moving around and toward a calm center of low pressure, which also moves. The motion of a cyclone is counterclockwise in the Northern

Hemisphere and clockwise in the Southern Hemisphere. 2 a very violent windstorm; tornado. [< Greek *kyklōn* moving around in a circle < *kyklos* wheel, circle]

cyn i cal (sin′ə kəl), adj. 1 doubting the sincerity and goodness of others. 2 sneering; sarcastic. —**cyn′i cal ly,** adv. —**cyn′i cal ness,** n.

cyn i cism (sin′ə siz′əm), n. 1 cynical quality or disposition. 2 a cynical remark.

das tard ly (das′tərd lē), adj. like a dastard; mean and cowardly; sneaking. —**das′tard li ness,** n.

deb o nair or **deb o naire** (deb′ə ner′, deb′ə när′), adj. pleasant, courteous, and gay. [< Old French *debonaire* < *de bon aire* of good disposition] —**deb′o nair′ly,** adv. —**deb′o nair′ness,** n.

de ci sive (di sī′siv), adj. 1 having or giving a clear result; settling something beyond question or doubt: *The Battle of Saratoga was a decisive victory for the Americans.* 2 having or showing decision; resolute: *a decisive answer.* —**de ci′sive ly,** adv. —**de ci′sive ness,** n.

de co rum (di kôr′əm, di kōr′əm), n. 1 proper behavior; good taste in conduct, speech, dress, etc.: *act with decorum.* 2 observance or requirement of polite society: *a meeting completely lacking in decorum.* [< Latin, (that which is) seemly < *decor* seemliness]

de cree (di krē′), n., v., **-creed, -cree ing.** —n. 1 something ordered or settled by authority; official decision. 2 a decision or order of a court or judge. 3 law of a church council, especially one settling a disputed point of doctrine. —v.t. 1 order or settle by authority: *Fate decreed that Ulysses should travel long and far.* 2 decide; determine. —v.i. decide; determine. [< Old French *decre* < Latin *decretum* < *de-* + *cernere* distinguish, separate]

de fend ant (di fen′dənt), n. person accused or sued in a court of law.

de fense (di fens′), n. 1 something that defends; means of guarding against attack or harm. 2 a guarding against attack or harm; defending or protecting. 3 action, speech, or writing in favor of something. 4 team or players defending a goal in a game. 5 a defendant and his lawyers. 6 answer of a defendant to an accusation or lawsuit against him. Also, BRITISH **defence.** [< Latin *defensa* < *defendere* defend]

de fer (di fėr′), v.t., v.i., **-ferred, -fer ring.** put off to some later time; delay; postpone: *defer an exam.* [< Latin *differe*] —**de fer′ra ble,** adj. —**de fer′rer,** n.

de lib e ra tion (di lib′ə rā′shən), n. 1 careful thought: *After long deliberation, I decided not to go.* 2 discussion of reasons for and against something; debate: *the deliberations of Congress.* 3 slowness and care: *The hunter aimed his gun with great deliberation.*

de mo ni ac (di mō′nē ak), adj. 1 of or like demons. 2 devilish; fiendish. 3 raging; frantic. 4 possessed by an evil spirit. —n. person supposed to be possessed by an evil spirit.

de ploy (di ploi′), v.t., v.i. 1 spread out (troops, military units, etc.) from a column into a long battle line. 2 spread out or extend (anything). [< French *déployer* < *dé-* de- + *ployer* to fold] —**de ploy′ment,** n.

de ride (di rīd′), v.t., **-rid ed, -rid ing.** make fun of; laugh at in scorn. [< Latin

hat, āge, fär; let, ēqual, tėrm; it, īce; hot, ōpen, ôrder; oil, out; cup, pu̇t, rüle; ch, child; ng, long; sh, she; th, thin; ᴛʜ, then; zh, measure;

ə represents *a* in about, *e* in taken, *i* in pencil, *o* in lemon, *u* in circus.

< = from, derived from, taken from.

deridere < *de-* + *ridere* to laugh] —**de rid′er,** n. —**de rid′ing ly,** adv.

de ri sion (di rizh′ən), n. 1 scornful laughter; ridicule. 2 object of ridicule. [< Latin *derisionem* < *deridere*. See DERIDE.]

de rog a to ry (di rog′ə tôr′ē, di rog′ə tōr′ē), adj. having the effect of lowering in honor or estimation; disparaging: *a derogatory remark.* —**de rog′a to′ri ly,** adv.

des cant (des′kant), n. 1 part music. 2 melody to be played or sung with another melody. 3 an extended comment; discourse. [< Old French *deschanter* <Medieval Latin *discantare* < Latin *dis-* + *cantus* song]

des o late (adj. des′ə lit; v. des′ə lāt), adj., v., **-lat ed, -lat ing.** —adj. 1 laid waste; devastated; barren: *desolate land.* 2 not lived in; deserted: *a desolate house.* 3 unhappy; forlorn; wretched. 4 left alone; solitary; lonely. 5 dreary; dismal: *a desolate life.* —v.t. 1 make unfit to live in; lay waste. 2 make unhappy: *We are desolated to hear that you are going away.* 3 deprive of inhabitants. [< Latin *desolatum* < *de-* + *solus* alone] —**des′o late ly,** adv. —**des′o late ness,** n.

des per ate (des′pər it), adj. 1 not caring what happens because hope is gone; reckless because of despair: *Suicide is a desperate act.* 2 ready to run any risk: *a desperate robber.* 3 having little chance for hope or cure; very dangerous or serious: *a desperate illness.* 4 hopelessly bad: *desperate circumstances.* 5 hopeless. [< Latin *desperatum* despaired, hopeless] —**des′per ate ly,** adv. —**des′per ate ness,** n.

des ti na tion (des′tə nā′shən), n. 1 place to which a person or thing is going or is being sent. 2 a setting apart for a particular purpose or use; intention.

de tach ment (di tach′mənt), n. 1 a taking apart; separation. 2 a standing apart; lack of interest; aloofness. 3 freedom from prejudice or bias; impartial attitude.

de ter (di tėr′), v.t., **-terred, -ter ring.** discourage or prevent from acting or proceeding by fear or consideration of danger or trouble; hinder: *The extreme heat deterred us from going downtown.* [< Latin *deterrere* < *de-* from + *terrere* frighten] —**de ter′ment,** n.

di aph a nous (dī af′ə nəs), adj. transparent: *Gauze is a diaphanous fabric.* < Greek *diaphanes* < *dia-* through + *phainein* to show] —**di aph′a nous ly,** adv. —**di aph′a nous ness,** n.

dil i gent (dil′ə jənt), adj. 1 hard-working; industrious. 2 careful and steady: *a diligent search.* [< Latin *diligentem* < *dis-* apart + *legere* choose] —**dil′i gent ly,** adv.

dint (dint), n. 1 force: *By dint of hard work the job was completed on schedule.* 2 dent. —v.t. make a dent in. [Old English *dynt*]

dis-, prefix. 1 opposite of; lack of; not: *Dishonest = not honest; opposite of honest. Discomfort = lack of comfort.* 2 do the

607

opposite of: *Disentangle* = *do the opposite of entangle.* **3** apart; away, as in *dispel.* [< Latin]

dis con so late (dis kon′sə lit), *adj.* **1** without hope; forlorn; unhappy: *disconsolate over the death of a friend.* **2** causing discomfort; cheerless: *a long, disconsolate day.* [< Medieval Latin *disconsolatus* < Latin *dis-* + *consolari* to console] —**dis con′-so late ly,** *adv.* —**dis con′so late ness,** *n.*

dis creet (dis krēt′), *adj.* very careful and sensible in speech and action; having or showing good judgment; wisely cautious. [< Old French *discret* < Late Latin *discretus* discerning < Latin *discernere* discern] —**dis creet′ly,** *adv.* —**dis creet′ness,** *n.*

dis crim i nate (*v.* dis krim′ə nāt; *adj.* dis-krim′ə nit), *v.,* **-nat ed, -nat ing.** —*v.i.* **1** make or see a difference; make a distinction: *discriminate between a mere exaggeration and a deliberate falsehood.* **2** accord a particular person, class, etc., distinctive (and usually unfair) treatment: *discriminate against people because of their race or beliefs.* —*v.t.* make or see a difference between; distinguish; differentiate: *discriminate good books from poor ones.* —*adj.* having discrimination; making careful distinctions. [< Latin *discriminatum* separated < *discrimen* separation < *discernere*] —**dis crim′i nate ly,** *adv.* —**dis crim′i na′tor,** *n.*

dis crim i nat ing (dis krim′ə nā′ting), *adj.* **1** able to discriminate well; discerning. **2** that discriminates. —**dis crim′i nat′ing ly,** *adv.*

dis dain (dis dān′), *v.t.* think unworthy of oneself or one's notice; regard or treat with contempt; scorn. —*n.* a disdaining; feeling of scorn. [< Old French *desdeignier* < *des-* dis- + *deignier* deign]

di shev eled or **di shev elled** (də shev′-əld), *adj.* **1** not neat; rumpled; mussed; untidy. **2** hanging loosely or in disorder: *disheveled hair.*

dis in te grate (dis in′tə grāt), *v.,* **-grat ed, -grat ing.** —*v.t.* break up; separate into small parts or bits. —*v.i.* **1** become disintegrated; break up. **2** (of atomic nuclei) undergo disintegration. —**dis in′te gra′tor,** *n.*

dis mem ber (dis mem′bər), *v.t.* **1** separate or divide into parts: *After the war the defeated country was dismembered.* **2** cut or tear the limbs from; divide limb from limb. —**dis mem′ber ment,** *n.*

dis perse (dis pèrs′), *v.,* **-persed, -pers ing.** —*v.t.* **1** send or drive off in different directions; scatter. **2** divide (light) into rays of different colors. —*v.i.* spread in different directions; scatter: *The crowd dispersed when it began raining.* [< Latin *dispersum* dispersed < *dis-* apart + *spargere* to scatter]

dis po si tion (dis′pə zish′ən), *n.* **1** one's habitual ways of acting toward others or of thinking about things; nature: *a cheerful disposition.* **2** tendency; inclination: *a disposition to argue.* **3** a putting in a proper or desired order or position; arrangement: *the disposition of soldiers in battle.*

dis sem ble (di sem′bəl), *v.,* **-bled, -bling.** —*v.t.* **1** hide (one's real feelings, thoughts, plans, etc.); disguise: *She dissembled her anger with a smile.* **2** pretend; feign: *The bored listener dissembled an interest he didn't feel.* —*v.i.* conceal one's opinions, motives, etc. [alteration (patterned after *resemble*) of obsolete *dissimule* dissimulate] —**dis-sem′bler,** *n.*

dis tract (dis trakt′), *v.t.* **1** turn aside or draw away (the mind, attention, etc.): *Noise distracts my attention from study.* **2** confuse; disturb. **3** make insane. [< Latin *distractum* drawn away < *dis-* + *trahere* to draw] —**dis tract′ed ly,** *adv.* —**dis tract′ing ly,** *adv.*

dis traught (dis trôt′), *adj.* **1** in a state of mental conflict and confusion; distracted. **2** crazed. [variant of obsolete *distract,* adjective, distracted]

di verge (də vėrj′, dī vėrj′), *v.,* **-verged, -verg ing.** —*v.i.* **1** move or lie in different directions from the same point; branch off: *Their paths diverged at the fork in the road.* **2** differ; vary. —*v.t.* cause to diverge. [< Late Latin *divergere* < Latin *dis-* off + *vergere* to slope]

div i na tion (div′ə nā′shən), *n.* **1** act of foreseeing the future or discovering what is hidden or obscure by supernatural or magical means. **2** augury; prophecy. **3** a skillful guess.

dog ged (dô′gid, dog′id), *adj.* not giving up; stubborn; persistent: *dogged determination.* [< *dog*] —**dog′ged ly,** *adv.* —**dog′ged-ness,** *n.*

do lor (dō′lər), *n.* sorrow; grief. [< Latin < *dolere* grieve]

do main (dō mān′), *n.* **1** territory under the control of one ruler or government. **2** land owned by one person; estate. **3** (in law) the absolute ownership of land. **4** field of thought, action, etc.; sphere of activity: *the domain of science, the domain of religion.* [< Middle French *domaine* < Latin *dominium* < *dominus* lord, master]

dom i nant (dom′ə nənt), *adj.* **1** most powerful or influential; controlling; ruling; governing. **2** rising high above its surroundings; towering over: *Dominant hills sheltered the bay.* **3** (in music) based on or having to do with the dominant. **4** (in biology) of, having to do with, or designating a dominant character. —*n.* **1** (in music) the fifth tone of the diatonic scale; fifth. G is the dominant in the key of C. **2** dominant character. **3** the most extensive and characteristic species in a plant community, determining the type and abundance of other species in the community. —**dom′i nant ly,** *adv.*

dom i na tion (dom′ə nā′shən), *n.* act of dominating; the exercise of ruling power; control; rule.

do min ion (də min′yən), *n.* **1** power or right of governing and controlling; rule; control. **2** territory under the control of one ruler or government. **3** a self-governing territory. **4** Dominion, name formerly used for a self-governing country within the British Commonwealth. —*adj.* Often, **Dominion.** (in Canada) relating to the country as a whole; national in scope. [< Medieval Latin, alteration of Latin *dominium* ownership < *dominum* lord, master]

dough ty (dou′tē), *adj.,* **-ti er, -ti est.** strong and bold; stout; brave; hearty. [Old English *dohtig* < *dugan* be of use] —**dough′ti ly,** *adv.* —**dough′ti ness,** *n.*

drear y (drir′ē), *adj.,* **drear i er, drear i-est.** **1** without cheer; dull; gloomy: *a cold, dreary day.* **2** ARCHAIC. sad; sorrowful. [Old English *drēorig*] —**drear′i ly,** *adv.* —**drear′i ness,** *n.*

dross (drôs, dros), *n.* **1** waste or scum that comes to the surface of melting metals. **2** waste material; rubbish. [Old English *drōs*]

du bi ous (dü′bē əs, dyü′bē əs), *adj.* **1** filled with or being in doubt; doubtful; uncertain: *a dubious compliment.* **2** feeling doubt; wavering or hesitating. **3** of questionable character; probably bad: *a dubious scheme for making money.* [< Latin *dubiosus* < *dubius* doubtful] —**du′bi ous ly,** *adv.* —**du′bi ous ness,** *n.*

du en na (dü en′ə, dyü en′ə), *n.* **1** an elderly woman who is the governess and chaperon of young girls in a Spanish or Portuguese family. **2** governess or chaperon. [< earlier Spanish, married woman < Latin *domina* mistress]

ec sta sy (ek′stə sē), *n., pl.* **-sies.** **1** condition of very great joy; thrilling or overwhelming delight: *The little girl was speechless with ecstasy over her new puppy.* **2** any strong feeling that completely absorbs the mind; uncontrollable emotion. **3** trance. [< Greek *ekstasis* distraction, trance < *existanai* put out of place < *ex-* out + *histanai* to place]

ec stat ic (ek stat′ik), *adj.* **1** full of ecstasy: *an ecstatic look of pleasure.* **2** caused by ecstasy: *an ecstatic mood.* —**ec stat′-i cal ly,** *adv.*

ed i fy (ed′ə fī), *v.t.,* **-fied, -fy ing.** improve morally; benefit spiritually; instruct and uplift. [< Old French *edifier* < Latin *aedificare* build] —**ed′i fi′er,** *n.*

e gress (ē′gres), *n.* **1** a going out: *The door was locked and no other egress was possible.* **2** a way out; exit; outlet: *The egress was plainly marked.* **3** right to go out. [< Latin *egressus* < *egredi* step out < *ex-* out + *gradi* to step, go]

e jac u la tion (i jak′yə lā′shən), *n.* **1** something said suddenly and briefly; exclamation. **2** ejection; discharge.

eld er (el′dər), *n.* **1** Usually, **elders,** *pl.* person who is older than oneself; one's senior. **2** person of advanced years. **3** one of the older men of a tribe or community to whom age and experience have brought wisdom and judgment. **4** any of various officers in certain churches. **5** presbyter. **6** pastor or minister. **7** member of a higher priesthood in the Mormon church. [Old English *eldra,* comparative of *eald* old]

el e gy (el′ə jē), *n., pl.* **-gies.** **1** a mournful or melancholy poem, usually a lament for the dead. Milton's *Lycidas* and Shelley's *Adonais* are elegies. **2** poem written in elegiac meter. [< Greek *elegeia* < *elegos* mournful poem]

e ma ci ate (i mā′shē āt), *v.t.,* **-at ed, -at-ing.** make unnaturally thin; cause to lose flesh or waste away: *A long illness had emaciated the patient.* [< Latin *emaciatum* made lean < *ex-* + *macies* leanness] —**e ma′ci a′tion,** *n.*

em a nate (em′ə nāt), *v.,* **-nat ed, -nat ing.** —*v.i.* originate from a person or thing as a source; come forth; spread out: *The rumor emanated from Chicago.* —*v.t.* send out; emit. [< Latin *emanatum* flowed out < *ex-* out + *manare* to flow]

em pha sis (em′fə sis), *n., pl.* **-ses** (-sēz′). **1** special force; stress; importance: *My high school puts much emphasis on studies that prepare its students for college.* **2** special force put on particular syllables, words, or phrases: *A speaker puts emphasis on important words by stressing them.* [< Latin < Greek < *emphainein* indicate < *en-* in + *phainein* to show]

en-, *prefix.* 1 cause to be ___; make ___: *Enfeeble = make feeble.* 2 put in ___; put on ___: *Enthrone = put on a throne.* 3 other meanings, as in *enact, encourage, entwine.* The addition of *en-* rarely changes the meaning of a verb except to make it more emphatic. [< Old French < Latin *in-*]

en fran chise (en fran′chīz), *v.t.,* **-chised, -chis ing.** 1 give the rights of citizenship to, especially the right to vote: *The 19th amendment to the Constitution enfranchised American women.* 2 set free. **—en fran′-chise ment,** *n.*

en gen der (en jen′dər), *v.t.* 1 bring into existence; produce; cause: *Filth engenders disease.* 2 beget: *Violence engenders violence.* [< Old French *engendrer* < Latin *ingenerare* < *in-* in + *generare* create]

en hance (en hans′), *v.t.,* **-hanced, -hanc ing.** make greater in quality, value, or importance; add to; heighten: *The gardens enhanced the beauty of the house.* [< Anglo-French *enhauncer,* variant of Old French *enhaucier* < *en-* on, up + *haucier* raise] **—en hance′ment,** *n.*

en tan gle (en tang′gəl), *v.t.,* **-gled, -gling.** 1 get twisted up and caught; tangle: *I entangled my feet in the coil of rope and fell down.* 2 get into difficulty; involve: *The villain tried to entangle the hero in an evil scheme.* 3 perplex; confuse. **—en tan′gle ment,** *n.*

en thrall or **en thral** (en thrôl′), *v.t.,* **-thralled, -thrall ing.** 1 hold captive by beauty or interest; fascinate; charm. 2 make a slave of; enslave. **—en thrall′ment,** *n.*

en ti ty (en′tə tē), *n., pl.* **-ties.** 1 something that has a real and separate existence either actually or in the mind. Persons, mountains, languages, and beliefs are distinct entities. 2 being; existence. [< Medieval Latin *entitatem* < Latin *enti-,* a form of *ens* thing, being]

en trails (en′trālz, en′trəlz), *n.pl.* 1 the inner parts of the body of a man or animal. 2 the intestines; bowels. [< Old French *entrailles* < Medieval Latin *intralia,* alteration of Latin *interanea* things inside < *inter* within]

e nu me rate (i nü′mə rāt′, i nyü′mə rāt′), *v.t.,* **-rat ed, -rat ing.** 1 name one by one; list: *He enumerated the capitals of the 50 states.* 2 find out the number of; count. [< Latin *enumeratum* counted < *ex-* out + *numerus* number] **—e nu′me ra′tion,** *n.* **—e nu′me ra′tor,** *n.*

en ven om (en ven′əm), *v.t.* 1 make poisonous. 2 fill with bitterness, hate, etc.

en vi a ble (en′vē ə bəl), *adj.* to be envied; worth having; desirable: *an enviable school record.* **—en′vi a ble ness,** *n.* **—en′-vi a bly,** *adv.*

en vis age (en viz′ij), *v.t.,* **-aged, -ag ing.** form a mental picture of; visualize: *The architect envisaged the finished house from the plans.*

ep i taph (ep′ə taf), *n.* a short statement in memory of a dead person, usually put on a gravestone or tombstone. [< Greek *epitaphion* funeral oration < *epi-* upon + *taphos* tomb]

e qui nox (ē′kwə noks), *n.* 1 either of the two times in the year when the center of the sun crosses the celestial equator, and day and night are of equal length in all parts of the earth, occurring about March 21 (**vernal equinox**) and about September 22 (**autumnal equinox**). 2 either of the two imaginary points in the sky at which the sun's path crosses the equator. [< Medieval Latin

equinoxium < Latin *aequinoctium* < *aequus* equal + *nox, noctem* night]

er ro ne ous (ə rō′nē əs), *adj.* containing error; wrong; mistaken; incorrect: *the erroneous belief that the earth is flat.* **—er ro′ne ous ly,** *adv.* **—er ro′ne ous ness,** *n.*

er u dite (er′ù dīt, er′yə dīt), *adj.* having much knowledge; scholarly; learned. [< Latin *eruditus* instructed < *ex-* + *rudis* rude] **—er′u dite′ly,** *adv.*

es carp ment (e skärp′mənt), *n.* 1 a steep slope; cliff. 2 ground made into a steep slope as part of a fortification. [< French]

eu lo gy (yü′lə jē), *n., pl.* **-gies.** 1 speech or writing in praise of a person or thing, especially a set oration in honor of a deceased person. 2 high praise. [< Greek *eulogia* < *eu-* well + *legein* speak]

ev i dence (ev′ə dəns), *n., v.,* **-denced, -denc ing.** **—n.** 1 anything that shows what is true and what is not; facts; proof: *The evidence showed that he had not been near the place.* 2 facts established and accepted in a court of law. Before deciding a case, the judge or jury hears all the evidence given by both sides. 3 indication; sign: *A smile gives evidence of pleasure.* 4 **in evidence,** easily seen or noticed: *Poverty is much in evidence in the city slums.* **—v.t.** make easy to see or understand; show clearly; prove: *His smiles evidenced his pleasure.*

e voc a tive (i vok′ə tiv, i vō′kə tiv), *adj.* tending to evoke. **—e voc′a tive ness,** *n.*

e voke (i vōk′), *v.t.,* **e voked, e vok ing.** call forth; bring out; elicit: *A good joke evokes a laugh.* [< Latin *evocare* < *ex-* out + *vocare* to call]

ex-¹, *prefix.* 1 former; formerly: *Ex-president = former president.* 2 out of; from; out: *Express = press out.* 3 thoroughly; utterly: *Exterminate = terminate (finish or destroy) thoroughly.* [< Latin < *ex* out of, without]

ex-², *prefix.* from; out of, as in *exodus.* Also, **ec-** before consonants. [< Greek]

ex as pe rate (eg zas′pə rāt′), *v.t.,* **-rat ed, -rat ing.** irritate very much; annoy extremely; make angry: *The little boy's constant noise exasperated his father.* [< Latin *exasperatum* irritated < *ex-* completely + *asper* rough] **—ex as′pe rat′ing ly,** *adv.*

ex as pe ra tion (eg zas′pə rā′shən), *n.* extreme annoyance; irritation; anger.

ex cep tion (ek sep′shən), *n.* 1 a leaving out; excepting: *I like all my studies, with the exception of German.* 2 person or thing left out: *She praised the pictures, with two exceptions.* 3 an unusual instance; case that does not follow the rule. 4 objection: *a statement liable to exception.* 5 **take exception,** a object. b be offended.

ex er tion (eg zėr′shən), *n.* 1 strenuous action; effort: *The exertions of the firemen kept the fire from spreading.* 2 a putting into action, active use; use: *exertion of authority.*

ex hil a rate (eg zil′ə rāt′), *v.t.,* **-rat ed, -rat ing.** make merry or lively; put into high spirits; cheer: *The joy of the holiday season exhilarates us all.* [< Latin *exhilaratum* made merry < *ex-* thoroughly + *hilaris* merry]

ex ile (eg′zīl, ek′sīl), *v.,* **-iled, -il ing,** *n.* **—v.t.** 1 force (a person) to leave his country or home, often by law as a punishment; banish. 2 remove (oneself) from one's country or home for a long time. **—n.** 1 person who is exiled. 2 condition of being exiled; banishment. 3 any prolonged absence from one's own country. [< Old French *exilier* < Latin *exiliare* < *exilium* period or place of exile]

famish

it, īce; hot, ōpen, ôrder;
oil, out; cup, pùt, rüle;
ch, child; ng, long; sh, she;
th, thin; ᴛʜ, then; zh, measure;

ə represents *a* in about, *e* in taken, *i* in pencil, *o* in lemon, *u* in circus.

< = from, derived from, taken from.

ex ot ic (eg zot′ik), *adj.* 1 from a foreign country; not native: *We saw many exotic plants at the flower show.* 2 fascinating or interesting because strange or different: *an exotic tropical island.* **—n.** an exotic person or thing. [< Greek *exōtikos* < *exō* outside < *ex* out of] **—ex ot′i cal ly,** *adv.*

ex pe di en cy (ek spē′dē ən sē), *n., pl.* **-cies.** 1 a helping to bring about a desired result; desirability or fitness under the circumstances; usefulness. 2 personal advantage; self-interest: *The salesman was influenced more by the expediency of making a sale than by the needs of the buyer.*

ex pe di ent (ek spē′dē ənt), *adj.* 1 very helping to bring about a desired result; desirable or suitable under the circumstances; useful; advantageous. 2 giving or seeking personal advantage; based on self-interest. **—n.** means of bringing about a desired result: *Having no packaged mix, I made a cake by the expedient of mixing my own ingredients.* **—ex pe′di ent ly,** *adv.*

ex u ber ant (eg zü′bər ənt), *adj.* 1 very abundant; overflowing; lavish: *exuberant joy, an exuberant welcome.* 2 profuse in growth; luxuriant: *the exuberant vegetation of the jungle.* 3 abounding in health and spirits; overflowing with good cheer: *an exuberant young man.* [< Latin *exuberantem* growing luxuriantly < *ex-* thoroughly + *uber* fertile] **—ex u′ber ant ly,** *adv.*

ex ul ta tion (eg′zul tā′shən, ek′sul tā′shən), *n.* an exulting; great rejoicing; triumph.

fac et (fas′it), *n., v.,* **-et ed, -et ing** or **-et ted, -et ting.** **—n.** 1 any one of the small, polished, flat surfaces of a cut gem. 2 any one of several sides or views. 3 one of the individual external visual units of a compound eye. **—v.t.** cut facets on. [< French *facette*]

fa kir (fa kir′, fā′kər), *n.* 1 a Moslem holy man who lives by begging. 2 dervish. 3 a Hindu ascetic. Fakirs sometimes do extraordinary things, such as lying upon sharp knives. [< Arabic *faqir* poor (man)]

fal li ble (fal′ə bəl), *adj.* 1 liable to be deceived or mistaken; liable to err. 2 liable to be erroneous, inaccurate, or false: *Strong emotion can make human judgment fallible.* [< Medieval Latin *fallibilis* < Latin *fallere* deceive] **—fal′li bly,** *adv.*

fam ine (fam′ən), *n.* 1 lack of food in a place; time of starving: *Many people died during the famine in India.* 2 starvation. 3 a great lack; scarcity; shortage: *a coal famine.* [< Old French < *faim* hunger < Latin *fames*]

fam ish (fam′ish), *v.i., v.t.* 1 be or make extremely hungry; starve. 2 starve to death.

farce (färs), *n.* 1 a play full of ridiculous happenings, absurd actions, and unreal situations, meant to be very funny. 2 kind of humor found in such plays; broad humor. 3 a ridiculous mockery; absurd pretense; sham: *The trial was a mere farce.* [< French, literally, stuffing < Old French *farcir* to stuff < Latin *farcire*]

fath om (faᴛʜ/əm), *n., pl.* **fath oms** or **fath om,** *v.* —*n.* unit of measure equal to 6 feet, used mostly in measuring the depth of water and the length of ships' ropes, cables, etc. —*v.t.* 1 measure the depth of (water); sound. 2 get to the bottom of; understand fully. [Old English *fæthm* width of the outstretched arms]

fath om a ble (faᴛʜ/ə mə bəl), *adj.* 1 that can be fathomed. 2 understandable.

fa tigue (fə tēg/), *n., v.,* **-tigued, -ti guing,** *adj.* —*n.* 1 weariness caused by hard work or effort. 2 task or exertion producing weariness. 3 a weakening (of metal) caused by long-continued use or strain. 4 a temporary decrease in the capacity of an organ or cell to function after excessive activity. —*v.t.* 1 make weary or tired; cause fatigue in; tire. 2 weaken (metal) by much use or strain. —*v.i.* become fatigued. —*adj.* having to do with fatigue. [< Middle French < *fatiguer* to tire < Latin *fatigare*]

fawn (fôn), *v.i.* 1 try to get favor or notice by slavish acts: *Many flattering relatives fawned on the rich old man.* 2 (of dogs, etc.) show fondness by crouching, wagging the tail, licking the hand, etc. [Old English *fagnian* < *fægen* fain] —**fawn/er,** *n.* —**fawn/ing ly,** *adv.*

fea si ble (fē/zə bəl), *adj.* 1 that can be done or carried out easily; possible without difficulty or damage; practicable: *The committee selected the plan that seemed most feasible.* 2 likely; probable: *The witness's explanation of the accident sounded feasible.* 3 suitable; convenient: *The road was too rough to be feasible for travel by automobile.* [< Old French *faisable,* ultimately < Latin *facere* do] —**fea/si ble ness,** *n.* —**fea/si bly,** *adv.*

fell (fel), *adj.* 1 fierce; savage; ruthless: *a fell blow.* 2 deadly; destructive. [< Old French *fel* < *felon* felon]

fes ter (fes/tər), *v.i.* 1 form pus: *The neglected wound festered and became very painful.* 2 cause soreness or pain; rankle: *Resentment festered in his mind.* 3 decay; rot. —*v.t.* 1 cause pus to form in. 2 cause to rankle: *Time festered the insult to his pride.* [< Old French *festre* < Latin *fistula* ulcer]

fil a ment (fil/ə mənt), *n.* 1 a very fine thread; very slender, threadlike part. 2 the threadlike wire that becomes incandescent by the passage of a current in an electric light bulb. 3 the heated wire that acts as the negative electrode in a vacuum tube. [< Late Latin *filamentum* < Latin *filum* thread]

fil i gree (fil/ə grē), *n.* 1 very delicate, lacelike, ornamental work of gold or silver wire. 2 any similar ornamental openwork. 3 anything very lacy, delicate, or fanciful. —*adj.* 1 ornamented with filigree. 2 delicate. [< French *filigrane* < Italian *filigrana* < Latin *filum* thread + *granum* grain]

fil let (fil/it; *usually* fi lā/, fil/ā *for n. 1 and v.t. 1*), *n.* 1 slice of fish or meat without bones or fat; filet. 2 a narrow band, ribbon, etc., worn around the head to hold the hair in place or as an ornament. 3 a narrow band or strip of any material. Fillets are often used between moldings, the flutes of a column, etc. —*v.t.* 1 cut (fish or meat) into fillets. When a fish is filleted, the flesh is cut away from the skeleton. Also, **filet.** 2 bind or decorate with a narrow band, ribbon, strip, etc. [< Old French *filet,* diminutive of *fil* thread < Latin *filum*]

fir ma ment (fėr/mə mənt), *n.* arch of the heavens; sky. [< Latin *firmamentum,* ultimately < *firmus* firm]

flair (fler, flar), *n.* 1 natural talent: *a flair for making clever rhymes.* 2 keen perception: *That trader has a flair for bargains.* [< Old French, scent < *flairer* to smell < Latin *fragrare*]

flit (flit), *v.,* **flit ted, flit ting,** *n.* —*v.i.* 1 fly lightly and quickly; flutter: *Birds flitted from tree to tree.* 2 pass lightly and quickly; dart: *Thoughts flitted through his head.* —*n.* a light, quick movement; flutter. [perhaps < Scandinavian (Old Icelandic) *flytja*]

floun der (floun/dər), *v.i.* 1 struggle awkwardly without making much progress; plunge about: *The horses were floundering in the deep snowdrifts.* 2 be clumsy or confused and make mistakes: *The frightened girl could only flounder through her song.* —*n.* a floundering. [perhaps blend of *founder* and *blunder*]

flut ed (flü/tid), *adj.* having long, round grooves.

fod der (fod/ər), *n.* coarse food for horses, cattle, etc. Hay and cornstalks with their leaves are fodder. —*v.t.* give fodder to. [Old English *fōdor* < *fōda* food]

fore bod ing (fôr bō/ding, fōr bō/ding), *n.* 1 prediction; warning. 2 a feeling that something bad is going to happen; presentiment.

fore sight (fôr/sīt, fōr/sīt/). *n.* 1 power to see or know beforehand what is likely to happen. 2 careful thought for the future; prudence. 3 a looking ahead; view into the future.

fort night (fôrt/nīt, fôrt/nit), *n.* two weeks. [Middle English *fourtenight* fourteen nights]

fra ter nal (frə tėr/nl), *adj.* 1 of or having to do with brothers or a brother; brotherly. 2 having to do with a fraternal order. 3 having to do with fraternal twins. [< Medieval Latin *fraternalis* < Latin *fraternus* brotherly < *frater* brother] —**fra ter/nal ly,** *adv.*

free wheel ing (frē/hwē/ling), *adj.* 1 (of a car, bicycle, etc.) coasting freely. 2 acting freely or without restraint.

fris son (frē/sōN), FRENCH. a shudder, a quiver; an agreeable feeling of fright.

fri vol i ty (fri vol/ə tē), *n., pl.* **-ties.** 1 a being frivolous; silly behavior; trifling. 2 a frivolous act or thing.

friv o lous (friv/ə ləs), *adj.* 1 lacking in seriousness or sense; silly: *Frivolous behavior is out of place in church.* 2 of little worth or importance; trivial. [< Latin *frivolus*] —**friv/o lous ly,** *adv.* —**friv/o lous ness,** *n.*

frond (frond), *n.* 1 the leaf of a fern, palm, or cycad. 2 a leaflike part which includes both stem and foliage, as the thallus of a lichen. [< Latin *frondem* leaf]

fur tive (fėr/tiv), *adj.* 1 done quickly and with stealth to avoid being noticed; secret: *a furtive glance into the forbidden room.* 2 sly; stealthy: *She had a furtive manner.* [< Latin *furtivus* < *furtum* theft < *fur* thief] —**fur/tive ly,** *adv.* —**fur/tive ness,** *n.*

fu sil lade (fyü/zə lād/), *n., v.,* **-lad ed, -lad ing.** —*n.* 1 a rapid or continuous discharge of many firearms at the same time. 2 something that resembles a fusillade: *The reporters greeted the mayor with a fusillade of questions.* —*v.t.* attack or shoot down by a fusillade. [< French]

gai ter (gā/tər), *n.* 1 an outer covering for the lower leg or ankle, made of cloth, leather, etc., for outdoor wear. 2 shoe with an elastic strip in each side. [< French *guêtre* < Germanic]

gall (gôl), *v.t.* 1 make sore by rubbing: *The rough strap galled the horse's skin.* 2 annoy; irritate. —*v.i.* become sore by rubbing. —*n.* 1 a sore spot on the skin caused by rubbing, especially one on a horse's back. 2 cause of annoyance or irritation.

gal lant (*adj.* gal/ənt *for 1-3;* gə lant/, gal/ənt *for 4*), *adj.* 1 noble in spirit or in conduct: *King Arthur was a gallant knight.* 2 brave and high-spirited; heroic: *a gallant antagonist.* 3 grand; splendid; stately: *a gallant ship with sails spread.* 4 very polite and attentive to women. [< Old French *galant,* present participle of *galer* make merry < *gale* merriment] —**gal/lant ly,** *adv.* —**gal/lant ness,** *n.*

gan gling (gang/gling), *adj.* awkwardly tall and slender; lank and loosely built.

gas tric (gas/trik), *adj.* 1 of or having to do with the stomach. 2 near the stomach. [< Greek *gastros* stomach]

gaunt (gônt, gänt), *adj.* 1 very thin and bony; with hollow eyes and a starved look: *Hunger and suffering had made him gaunt.* 2 looking bare and gloomy; desolate. [origin uncertain] —**gaunt/ly,** *adv.* —**gaunt/ness,** *n.*

gauze (gôz), *n.* 1 a very thin, light cloth, easily seen through. Gauze is often used for bandages. 2 a thinly woven open material resembling this fabric: *Wire gauze is used for screens.* [< Middle French *gaze*] —**gauze/like,** *adj.*

ge ne a lo gist (jē/nē al/ə jist, jē/nē ol/ə jist; jen/ē al/ə jist, jen/ē ol/ə jist), *n.* person who makes a study of or traces genealogies.

ge ne al o gy (jē/nē al/ə jē, jē/nē ol/ə jē; jen/ē al/ə jē, jen/ē ol/ə jē), *n., pl.* **-gies.** 1 account of the descent of a person or family from an ancestor or ancestors. 2 descent of a person or family from an ancestor; pedigree; lineage. 3 the making or investigation of accounts of descent; study of pedigrees. [< Greek *genealogia* < *genea* breed, generation + *-logos* treating of]

ges tic u late (je stik/yə lāt), *v.i.,* **-lat ed, -lat ing.** make or use gestures to show ideas or feelings. [< Latin *gesticulatum* gesticulated, ultimately < *gestus* gesture] —**ges tic/u la/tion,** *n.*

gey ser (gī/zər), *n.* 1 spring that spouts a column of hot water and steam into the air at frequent intervals. 2 anything that spurts or gushes like a geyser. [< Icelandic *Geysir,* name of such a spring in Iceland < *geysa* to gush]

gig (gig), *n.* a light, open, two-wheeled carriage drawn by one horse.

ging ham (ging/əm), *n.* a cotton cloth made from colored threads. Its patterns are usually in stripes, plaids, or checks. [< French *guingan* < Malay *ginggang* striped]

gnarled (närld), *adj.* containing gnarls; knotted; twisted: *The farmer's gnarled hands grasped the plow firmly.* [variant of *knurled*]

gnash (nash), *v.t.* 1 strike or grind together: *gnash one's teeth.* 2 bite by gnashing the teeth; bite upon. [Middle English *gnasten*]

grad u al (graj′ü əl), *adj.* happening by small steps or degrees; changing step by step; moving little by little: *a gradual slope. A child's growth into an adult is gradual.* [< Medieval Latin *gradualis* < Latin *gradus* step, degree] —**grad′u al ly**, *adv.* —**grad′-u al ness**, *n.*

gra tu i tous (grə tü′ə təs, grə tyü′ə təs), *adj.* 1 freely given or obtained; free. 2 without reason or cause; unnecessary; uncalled-for: *a gratuitous insult.* —**gra-tu′i tous ly**, *adv.* —**gra-tu′i tous ness**, *n.*

gri mace (grə mās′, grim′is), *n., v.,* -**maced**, -**mac ing.** —*n.* a twisting of the face; ugly or funny smile: *a grimace caused by pain.* —*v.i.* make grimaces. [< Middle French] —**gri-mac′er**, *n.*

grope (grōp), *v.,* **groped, grop ing.** —*v.i.* 1 feel about with the hands: *I groped for a flashlight when the lights went out.* 2 search blindly and uncertainly: *The detectives groped for some clue to the mysterious crime.* —*v.t.* find by feeling about with the hands; feel (one's way) slowly: *The blind man groped his way to the door.* [Old English *grāpian*] —**grop′ing ly**, *adv.*

grot to (grot′ō), *n., pl.* -**toes** or -**tos.** 1 cave or cavern. 2 an artificial cave made for coolness and pleasure. [< Italian *grotto, grotta* < Latin *crypta* < Greek *krypte* vault.]

grov el (gruv′əl, grov′əl), *v.i.,* -**eled, -el ing** or -**elled, -el ling.** 1 lie face downward; crawl at someone's feet; cringe: *When the dog saw the whip, he groveled before his master.* 2 abase or humble oneself: *I will apologize when I am wrong, but I will grovel before no one.* 3 enjoy low, mean, or contemptible things. [Middle English *groveling,* originally an adverb, in a prone position] —**grov′el er, grov′el ler,** *n.*

gru el ing or **gru el ling** (grü′ə ling), *adj.* very tiring; exhausting: *The marathon is a grueling contest.* —*n.* an exhausting or very tiring experience.

guf faw (gu fô′), *n.* burst of loud, coarse laughter. —*v.i.* laugh loudly and coarsely. [imitative]

gul let (gul′it), *n.* 1 esophagus. 2 throat. [< Old French *goulet,* ultimately < Latin *gula* throat]

gyre (jīr), *n.* circular or spiral motion, or a circle or a spiral outlined by a moving mass.

hag gard (hag′ərd), *adj.* looking worn from pain, fatigue, worry, hunger, etc.; careworn; gaunt. [perhaps < Old French *hagard*] —**hag′gard ly**, *adv.* —**hag′gard ness**, *n.*

hart (härt), *n., pl.* **harts** or **hart.** a male deer, especially the male European red deer after its fifth year; stag. [Old English *heorot*]

ha ven (hā′vən), *n.* 1 harbor or port. 2 place of shelter and safety. [Old English *hæfen*]

head y (hed′ē), *adj.,* **head i er, head i est.** 1 hasty; rash; headlong. 2 apt to affect the head and make one dizzy; intoxicating. —**head′i ly**, *adv.* —**head′i ness**, *n.*

he li o trope (hē′lē ə trōp, hē′lyə trōp), *n.* 1 any of a genus of plants of the same family as borage, having clusters of small, fragrant purple or white flowers. 2 a pinkish purple. 3 bloodstone. —*adj.* pinkish-purple. [< Greek *hēliotropion* < *hēlios* sun + *-tropos* turning]

hem or rhage (hem′ər ij), *n., v.,* -**rhaged, -rhag ing.** —*n.* discharge of blood, especially a heavy discharge from a damaged blood vessel. A nosebleed is a mild hemorrhage. —*v.i.* have a hemorrhage; lose much blood. [< Greek *haimorrhagia* < *haima* blood + *rhegnynai* to break, burst]

hench man (hench′mən), *n., pl.* -**men.** 1 a trusted attendant or follower. 2 an obedient, unscrupulous follower. [Middle English *henxstman,* originally, a groom < Old English *hengest* horse + *man* man]

hew (hyü), *v.,* **hewed, hewed** or **hewn, hew ing.** —*v.t.* 1 cut with an ax, sword, etc.; chop: *He hewed down the tree.* 2 cut into shape; form by cutting with an ax, etc.: *hew stone for building, hew logs into beams.* —*v.i.* hold firmly *(to);* stick fast or cling *(to): hew to the rules.* [Old English *hēawan*] —**hew′er**, *n.*

hie (hī), *v.,* **hied, hie ing** or **hy ing.** —*v.i.* go quickly; hasten; hurry. —*v.t.* cause to hasten. [Old English *hīgian*]

hom i cide (hom′ə sīd, hō′mə sīd), *n.* 1 a killing of one human being by another. Intentional homicide is murder. 2 person who kills another human being. [< Old French, ultimately < Latin *homo* man + *-cidium* act of killing or *-cida* killer]

ho mo ge ne ous (hō′mə jē′nē əs, hō′mə-jē′nyəs; hom′ə jē′ne əs, hom′ə jē′nyəs), *adj.* 1 of the same kind, nature, or character; similar. 2 made up of similar elements or parts; of uniform nature or character throughout: *The population of the island was homogeneous because there were no foreigners there.* 3 (in mathematics) of the same degree or dimensions. [< Medieval Latin *homogeneus* < Greek *homogenēs* < *homos* same + *genos* kind] —**ho′mo ge′ne ous ly,** *adv.* —**ho′mo ge′ne ous ness**, *n.*

ho mog e nize (hə moj′ə nīz), *v.t.,* -**nized, -niz ing.** make homogeneous. In **homogenized milk** the fat is distributed evenly throughout the milk and does not rise to the top in the form of cream. —**ho mog′-e ni za′tion**, *n.* —**ho mog′e niz′er**, *n.*

hov er (huv′ər, hov′ər), *v.i.* 1 hang fluttering or suspended in air: *The wren hovered over their nest.* 2 stay in or near one place; wait nearby: *The dogs hovered around the kitchen door at mealtime.* 3 be in an uncertain condition: *The patient hovered between life and death.* [Middle English *hoveren*] —**hov′er er**, *n.*

hu mi dor (hyü′mə dôr), *n.* 1 box, jar, etc., fitted with the means for keeping tobacco properly moist. 2 any similar device.

hum mock (hum′ək), *n.* 1 a very small, rounded hill; knoll; hillock. 2 a bump or ridge in a field of ice. [origin unknown]

hurl (hèrl), *v.t.* 1 throw with much force; fling: *The man hurled his spear at one bear, and the dogs hurled themselves at the other.* 2 throw forth (words, cries, etc.) violently; utter with vehemence: *He hurled insults at me.* —*n.* a forcible or violent throw. [Middle English *hurlen*] —**hurl′er**, *n.*

hur tle (hèr′tl), *v.,* -**tled, -tling**, *n.* —*v.i.* 1 dash or drive violently; come with a crash: *The car hurtled across the road into a fence.* 2 move with a clatter; rush noisily: *The old subway train hurtled past.* —*v.t.* dash or drive violently; fling: *The impact of the crash hurtled the driver against the windshield of the car.* —*n.* act or fact of hurtling; clash. [Middle English *hurtelen* < *hurten* to hurt, in early sense "dash against"]

hy dro plane (hī′drə plān), *n., v.,* -**planed,**

hat, āge, fär; let, ēqual, tèrm;
it, īce; hot, ōpen, ôrder;
oil, out; cup, put, rüle;
ch, child; ng, long; sh, she;
th, thin; ᴛʜ, then; zh, measure;

ə represents *a* in about, *e* in taken,
i in pencil, *o* in lemon, *u* in circus.

< = from, derived from, taken from.

-**plan ing.** —*n.* 1 motorboat that glides on the surface of water. 2 seaplane. —*v.i.* 1 glide on the surface of water. 2 use or ride in a hydroplane. 3 (of a vehicle) undergo hydroplaning.

hy poth e sis (hī poth′ə sis), *n., pl.* -**ses** (-sēz′). 1 something assumed because it seems likely to be a true explanation. 2 proposition assumed as a basis for reasoning. [< Greek < *hypo-* under + *thesis* a placing]

hy po thet i cal (hī′pə thet′ə kəl), *adj.* of or based on a hypothesis; assumed; supposed. —**hy′po thet′i cal ly**, *adv.*

id i om (id′ē əm), *n.* 1 phrase or expression whose meaning cannot be understood from the ordinary meanings of the words in it: *"Give in" is an English idiom meaning "yield."* 2 the language or dialect of a particular area or group: *the idiom of the French Canadians.* 3 a people's way of expressing themselves: *It is often hard to translate English into the French idiom.* 4 individual manner of expression in music, art, etc. [< Greek *idiōma* one's own manner of speaking < *idios* one's own]

id i o syn cra sy (id′ē ō sing′krə sē), *n., pl.* -**sies.** 1 a personal peculiarity of taste, behavior, opinion, etc. 2 (in medicine) a constitutional peculiarity that causes an unusual reaction to a drug, treatment, etc. [< Greek *idiosynkrasia* < *idios* one's own + *synkrasis* temperament]

il lit er ate (i lit′ər it), *adj.* 1 unable to read and write: *People who have never gone to school are usually illiterate.* 2 showing a lack of education; not cultured: *He writes in a very illiterate way.* —*n.* 1 person who is unable to read and write. 2 an uneducated person. —**il lit′er ate ly**, *adv.* —**il lit′er ate ness**, *n.*

il lu sion (i lü′zhən), *n.* 1 appearance or feeling that misleads because it is not real; thing that deceives by giving a false idea. 2 a false impression or perception: *an optical illusion.* 3 a false notion or belief: *Many people have the illusion that wealth is the chief cause of happiness.* 4 a delicate silk net or gauze, often used for veils and over wedding gowns. [< Latin *illusionem* < *illudere* mock < *in-* at + *ludere* play]

im be cile (im′bə səl), *n.* 1 person born with such limited mental capacities that he can be trained to do only very simple tasks and will probably never learn to read; person who does not develop beyond a mental age of three to eight years. 2 a very stupid or foolish person. —*adj.* 1 weak in the mind; lacking normal intelligence. 2 very stupid or foolish. [< Latin *imbecillus* weak < *in-* without + *bacillus* staff] —**im′be cile ly**, *adv.*

im me mo ri al (im/ə môr/ē əl, im/ə mōr/-ē əl), *adj.* extending back beyond the bounds of memory; ancient beyond record or knowledge; extremely old. —**im/me mo/-ri al ly,** *adv.*

im mi nent (im/ə nənt), *adj.* likely to happen soon; about to occur: *The black clouds showed that a storm was imminent.* [< Latin *imminentem* overhanging, threatening] —**im/mi nent ly,** *adv.*

im pen e tra ble (im pen/ə trə bəl), *adj.* 1 that cannot be penetrated, pierced, or passed: *A thick sheet of steel is impenetrable by an ordinary bullet.* 2 impossible to explain or understand; inscrutable: *an impenetrable mystery.* 3 not open to ideas, influences, etc.: *an impenetrable mind.* —**im pen/e tra ble ness,** *n.* —**im pen/e tra bly,** *adv.*

im per ti nence (im pèrt/n əns), *n.* 1 a being impertinent; impudence; insolence. 2 an impertinent act or speech. 3 lack of pertinence; irrelevance.

im per turb a ble (im/pər tèr/bə bəl), *adj.* not easily excited or disturbed; calm. —**im/per turb/a bly,** *adv.*

im ple ment (*n.* im/plə mənt; *v.* im/plə ment), *n.* a useful article of equipment; tool; instrument; utensil. A plow, an ax, a shovel, and a broom are implements. —*v.t.* 1 provide with implements or other means. 2 provide the power and authority necessary to accomplish or put (something) into effect: *implement an order.* 3 carry out; get done: *Do not undertake a project unless you can implement it.* [< Late Latin *implementum* that which fills a need < Latin *implere* to fill < *in-* in + *plere* to fill] —**im/ple men ta/tion,** *n.*

im pul sive (im pul/siv), *adj.* 1 acting or done upon impulse; with a sudden inclination or tendency to act: *The impulsive child gave all his money to the beggar.* 2 driving with sudden force; impelling. —**im pul/sive ly,** *adv.* —**im pul/sive ness,** *n.*

in an i mate (in an/ə mit), *adj.* 1 not living or alive; lifeless: *Stones are inanimate objects.* 2 without liveliness or spirit; dull. —**in an/i mate ly,** *adv.* —**in an/i mate ness,** *n.*

in au di ble (in ô/də bəl), *adj.* that cannot be heard. —**in au/di bly,** *adv.*

in can des cent (in/kən des/nt), *adj.* 1 heated to such a high temperature that it gives out light; glowing with heat; red-hot or white-hot. 2 shining brightly; brilliant. 3 having to do with or containing a material that gives light by incandescence. —**in/can des/cent ly,** *adv.*

in ces sant (in ses/nt), *adj.* never stopping; continued or repeated without interruption; continual: *the incessant noise from the factory.* [< Late Latin *incessantem* < Latin *in-* not + *cessare* cease] —**in ces/sant ly,** *adv.*

in cin e rate (in sin/ə rāt/), *v.t.,* **-rat ed, -rat ing.** burn to ashes. [< Medieval Latin *incineratum* burnt to ashes < Latin *in-* into + *cinis* ashes] —**in cin/e ra/tion,** *n.*

in cite (in sīt/), *v.t.,* **-cit ed, -cit ing.** stimulate to action; urge on; stir up; rouse. [< Latin *incitare* < *in-* on + *citare* arouse] —**in cit/er,** *n.*

in co her ent (in/kō hir/ənt), *adj.* 1 having or showing no logical connection of ideas; not coherent; disconnected; confused. 2 not sticking together; loose. —**in/co her/ent ly,** *adv.*

in con gru ous (in kong/grü əs), *adj.* 1 out of keeping; not appropriate; out of place: *A fur coat is incongruous with a bathing suit.* 2 lacking in agreement or harmony; not consistent. —**in con/gru ous ly,** *adv.* —**in con/gru ous ness,** *n.*

in cor rupt i bil i ty (in/kə rup/tə bil/ə tē), *n.* a being incorruptible.

in cor rupt i ble (in/kə rup/tə bəl), *adj.* 1 not to be corrupted; honest: *The incorruptible judge could not be bribed.* 2 not subject to decay; lasting forever: *Diamonds are incorruptible.* —**in/cor rupt/i bly,** *adv.*

in cu ba tor (ing/kyə bā/tər, in/kyə bā/tər), *n.* 1 box or chamber for hatching eggs by keeping them warm and properly supplied with moisture and oxygen. 2 any similar box or chamber. Very small babies and premature babies are sometimes kept for a time in incubators.

in cur (in kèr/), *v.t.,* **-curred, -cur ring.** run or fall into (something unpleasant or inconvenient); bring on oneself: *incur many expenses.* [< Latin *incurrere* < *in-* upon + *currere* to run]

in dig nant (in dig/nənt), *adj.* angry at something unworthy, unjust, unfair, or mean. [< Latin *indignantem* < *indignus* unworthy < *in-* not + *dignus* worthy] —**in dig/-nant ly,** *adv.*

in du bi ta ble (in dü/bə tə bəl, in dyü/bə-tə bəl), *adj.* too evident to be doubted; certain; unquestionable. —**in du/bi ta ble ness,** *n.* —**in du/bi ta bly,** *adv.*

in ert (in èrt/), *adj.* 1 having no power to move or act; lifeless: *A stone is an inert mass of matter.* 2 inactive; slow; sluggish. 3 with few or no active chemical, physiological, or other properties: *Helium and neon are inert gases.* [< Latin *inertem* idle, unskilled < *in-* without + *artem* art, skill] —**in ert/ly,** *adv.* —**in ert/ness,** *n.*

in er tia (in èr/shə), *n.* 1 tendency to remain in the state one is in, and not start changes. 2 tendency of all objects and matter in the universe to stay still if still, or if moving, to go on moving in the same direction, unless acted on by some outside force. [< Latin, inactivity < *inertem* idle. See INERT.]

in ev i ta ble (in ev/ə tə bəl), *adj.* not to be avoided; sure to happen; certain to come: *Death is inevitable.* [< Latin *inevitabilis* < *in-* not + *evitare* avoid < *ex-* out + *vitare* shun] —**in ev/i ta ble ness,** *n.* —**in ev/i ta bly,** *adv.*

in ex o ra ble (in ek/sər ə bəl), *adj.* not influenced by pleading or entreaties; relentless; unyielding: *The forces of nature are inexorable.* [< Latin *inexorabilis* < *in-* not + *exorare* prevail upon, pray earnestly < *ex-* out + *orare* pray, entreat] —**in ex/o ra ble ness,** *n.* —**in ex/o ra bly,** *adv.*

in ex tri ca ble (in ek/strə kə bəl), *adj.* 1 that one cannot get out of. 2 that cannot be disentangled or solved. —**in ex/tri ca bly,** *adv.*

in fal li bil i ty (in fal/ə bil/ə tē), *n.* 1 freedom from error; inability to be mistaken. 2 absolute reliability; sureness.

in fal li ble (in fal/ə bəl), *adj.* 1 free from error; that cannot be mistaken: *an infallible rule.* 2 absolutely reliable; sure: *infallible obedience, an infallible remedy.* —**in fal/li bly,** *adv.*

in fi ni tes i mal (in/fi nə tes/ə məl), *adj.* so small as to be almost nothing; extremely minute or insignificant. —**in/fi ni tes/-i mal ly,** *adv.*

in fir mi ty (in fèr/mə tē), *n., pl.* **-ties.**

1 weakness; feebleness. 2 sickness; illness. 3 weakness, flaw, or defect in a person's character.

in ge nu i ty (in/jə nü/ə tē, in/jə nyü/ə tē), *n., pl.* **-ties.** 1 skill in planning or making something; cleverness. 2 skillfulness of contrivance or design: *the ingenuity of a puzzle.* 3 an ingenious device or contrivance. [< Latin *ingenuitatem* frankness < *ingenuus* ingenuous; influenced by *ingenious*]

in gress (in/gres), *n.* 1 a going in or entering: *A high fence prevented ingress to the field.* 2 way of going in; entrance. 3 right to go in: *have free ingress to the public library.* [< Latin *ingressus* < *ingredi* go into < *in-* in + *gradi* go]

in sa tia ble (in sā/shə bəl), *adj.* that cannot be satisfied; extremely greedy: *an insatiable appetite.* —**in sa/tia ble ness,** *n.* —**in sa/tia bly,** *adv.*

in scru ta ble (in skrü/tə bəl), *adj.* that cannot be understood; so mysterious or obscure that one cannot make out its meaning; incomprehensible. [< Late Latin *inscrutabilis* < Latin *in-* not + *scrutari* examine, ransack < *scruta* trash] —**in scru/ta ble ness,** *n.* —**in scru/ta bly,** *adv.*

in sid i ous (in sid/ē əs), *adj.* 1 seeking to entrap or ensnare; wily or sly; crafty; tricky. 2 working secretly or subtly; developing without attracting attention: *an insidious disease.* [< Latin *insidiosus* < *insidiae* ambush < *insidere* sit in < *in-* in + *sedere* sit] —**in sid/i ous ly,** *adv.* —**in sid/i ous ness,** *n.*

in sig nif i cant (in/sig nif/ə kənt), *adj.* 1 of no consequence, influence, or distinction: *an insignificant position, an insignificant person.* 2 too small to be important; unimportant; trivial; petty: *an insignificant detail, an insignificant amount of money.* 3 having little or no meaning; meaningless: *an insignificant gesture.* —**in/sig nif/i cant ly,** *adv.*

in sin u ate (in sin/yü āt), *v.,* **-at ed, -at ing.** —*v.t.* 1 suggest in an indirect way; hint: *To say "That man can't do it; no coward can" is to insinuate that the man is a coward.* 2 push in or get in by an indirect, subtle way: *The stray cat insinuated itself into our kitchen. The spy insinuated himself into the confidence of important army officers.* —*v.i.* make insinuations. [< Latin *insinuatum* wound or twisted into < *in-* in + *sinus* a curve, winding] —**in sin/u at/ing ly,** *adv.* —**in sin/-u a/tor,** *n.*

in sti gate (in/stə gāt), *v.t.,* **-gat ed, -gat ing.** urge on; stir up: *instigate a quarrel.* [< Latin *instigatum* incited, urged on] —**in/sti ga/tion,** *n.* —**in/sti ga/tor,** *n.*

in teg u ment (in teg/yə mənt), *n.* 1 a natural outer covering; skin, shell, rind, etc.; tegument. 2 any covering or coating. [< Latin *integumentum* < *integere* enclose < *in-* on + *tegere* to cover]

in tel li gi ble (in tel/ə jə bəl), *adj.* capable of being understood; clear; comprehensible. [< Latin *intelligibilis* < *intelligere*] —**in tel/li gi bly,** *adv.*

in ter im (in/tər im), *n.* time between; the meantime. —*adj.* for the meantime; temporary. [< Latin, in the meantime < *inter* between]

in ter lop er (in/tər lō/pər), *n.* person who thrusts himself in where he is not wanted or has no right; intruder.

in ter mi na ble (in tèr/mə nə bəl), *adj.* 1 never stopping; unceasing; endless. 2 so long as to seem endless; very long and tiring. —**in ter/mi na bly,** *adv.*

in ter mit (in′tər mit′), *v.t., v.i.,* **-mit ted, -mit ting.** stop for a time; discontinue; suspend. [< Latin *intermittere* < *inter-* between + *mittere* to leave]

in ter pose (in′tər pōz′), *v.,* **-posed, -pos ing.** —*v.t.* 1 put between; insert. 2 put forward; break in with: *She interposed an objection at this point.* —*v.i.* 1 come or be between other things. 2 interrupt. 3 interfere in order to help; intervene; intercede. [< Middle French *interposer* < *inter-* between + *poser* to place] —**in′ter pos′er,** *n.*

in ter sperse (in′tər spèrs′), *v.t.,* **-spersed, -spers ing.** 1 vary with something put here and there: *The grass was interspersed with beds of flowers.* 2 scatter or place here and there among other things: *Bushes were interspersed among the trees.* [< Latin *interspersum* scattered < *inter-* between + *spargere* to scatter]

in tim i date (in tim′ə dāt), *v.t.,* **-dat ed, -dat ing.** 1 make afraid; frighten: *intimidate one's opponents with threats.* 2 influence or force by fear: *intimidate a witness.* [< Medieval Latin *intimidatum* frightened < Latin *in-* + *timidus* fearful] —**in tim′i da′tion,** *n.* —**in tim′i da′tor,** *n.*

in tru sion (in trü′zhən), *n.* act of intruding; coming unasked and unwanted.

in tu i tion (in′tü ish′ən, in′tyü ish′ən), *n.* 1 immediate perception or understanding of truths, facts, etc., without reasoning: *By experience with many kinds of people the doctor had developed great powers of intuition.* 2 truth, fact, etc., so perceived or understood. [< Late Latin *intuitionem* a gazing at < Latin *intueri* consider, look upon < *in-* + *tueri* to look]

in vin ci ble (in vin′sə bəl), *adj.* unable to be conquered; impossible to overcome; unconquerable: *an invincible fighter.* [< Latin *invincibilis* < *in-* not + *vincere* conquer] —**in vin′ci ble ness,** *n.* —**in vin′ci bly,** *adv.*

ir i des cent (ir′ə des′nt), *adj.* displaying changing colors; changing color when moved or turned. [< Latin *iris, iridis* rainbow] —**ir′i des′cent ly,** *adv.*

irk (ėrk), *v.t.* cause to feel disgusted, annoyed, or troubled; weary by being tedious or disagreeable: *It irks us to wait for people who are late.* [< Middle English *irken*]

ir re deem a ble (ir′i dē′mə bəl), *adj.* 1 that cannot be redeemed or bought back. 2 that cannot be exchanged for coin: *irredeemable paper money.* 3 impossible to change; beyond remedy; hopeless: *an irredeemable mistake.* —**ir′re deem′a bly,** *adv.*

ir res o lute (i rez′ə lüt), *adj.* not resolute; unable to make up one's mind; not sure of what one wants; hesitating; vacillating. —**ir res′o lute ly,** *adv.* —**ir res′o lute ness,** *n.*

i tin e rar y (ī tin′ə rer′ē, i tin′ə rer′ē), *n., pl.* **-rar ies,** *adj.* —*n.* 1 route of travel; plan of travel. 2 record of travel. 3 guidebook for travelers. —*adj.* 1 of traveling or routes of travel. 2 itinerant.

-ive, *suffix forming adjectives from nouns.* 1 of or having to do with, as in *interrogative, inductive.* 2 tending to; likely to, as in *active, appreciative.* [< French *-ive* (feminine of *-if* < Latin *-ivus*) or directly < Latin]

-ize, *suffix forming verbs from adjectives and nouns.* 1 make _____: *Legalize = make legal.* 2 become _____: *Crystallize = become crystal.* 3 engage in or use _____: *Criticize = engage in criticism.* 4 treat or combine with _____:

Oxidize = combine with oxygen. 5 other meanings, as in *alphabetize, colonize, memorize.* Also, **-ise.** [< French *-iser* or Latin *-izare* < Greek *-izein,* or directly < Greek]

jab ber (jab′ər), *v.i., v.t.* talk or speak rapidly and indistinctly; chatter. —*n.* very fast, confused, or senseless talk; chatter. [probably imitative] —**jab′ber er,** *n.*

jo cose (jō kōs′), *adj.* full of jokes; given to joking; jesting; humorous. [< Latin *jocosus* < *jocus* jest] —**jo cose′ly,** *adv.* —**jo cose′ness,** *n.*

jos tle (jos′əl), *v.,* **-tled, -tling,** *n.* —*v.t.* shove, push, or crowd against; elbow roughly. —*v.i.* crowd, strike, or push. —*n.* a jostling; push; knock. Also, **justle.** [< *joust*] —**jos′tler,** *n.*

ju di cious (jü dish′əs), *adj.* having, using, or showing good judgment; wise; sensible: *A judicious historian selects and weighs facts carefully and critically.* —**ju di′cious ly,** *adv.* —**ju di′cious ness,** *n.*

jur y (jur′ē), *n., pl.* **jur ies.** 1 group of persons selected to hear evidence in a court of law and sworn to give a decision in accordance with the evidence presented to them. 2 group of persons chosen to give a judgment or to decide who is the winner in a contest and award prizes. [< Anglo-French *jurie* < Old French *jurer* swear < Latin *jurare* < *jus, juris* law]

jut (jut), *v.,* **jut ted, jut ting,** *n.* —*v.i.* stick out; stand out; project: *The pier juts out from the shore into the water.* —*n.* part that sticks out; projection. [variant of *jet*]

jux ta po si tion (juk′stə pə zish′ən), *n.* 1 a putting close together; a placing side by side. 2 position close together or side by side.

Ker man shah (ker′mən shä), *n.* city in Iran.

kins man (kinz′mən), *n., pl.* **-men.** a male relative.

kit tle (kit′l), *v.t.* **kit tled, kit tling.** to give birth to a litter of rabbits, kittens, etc.

lac e rate (*v.* las′ə rāt′; *adj.* las′ər it), *v.,* **-rat ed, -rat ing,** *adj.* —*v.t.* 1 tear roughly; mangle: *The bear's claws lacerated the hunter's arm.* 2 wound; hurt (the feelings, etc.). —*adj.* deeply or irregularly indented as if torn: *lacerate leaves.* [< Latin *laceratum* torn, mangled]

la con ic (lə kon′ik), *adj.* using few words; brief in speech or expression; concise; terse. [< Latin *Laconicus* Spartan < Greek *Lakōnikos;* Spartans were noted for pithy speech] —**la con′i cal ly,** *adv.*

la ment (lə ment′), *v.t.* 1 express grief for; mourn for: *lament the dead.* 2 regret: *We lamented his absence.* —*v.i.* express grief; mourn; weep: *Why does she lament?* —*n.* 1 expression of grief or sorrow; wail. 2 poem, song, or tune that expresses grief. [< Latin *lamentari* < *lamentum* a wailing] —**la ment′er,** *n.* —**la ment′ing ly,** *adv.*

lan guid (lang′gwid), *adj.* 1 without energy;

hat, āge, fär; let, ēqual, tèrm;
it, īce; hot, ōpen, ôrder;
oil, out; cup, pút, rüle;
ch, child; ng, long; sh, she;
th, thin; ᴛʜ, then; zh, measure;

ə represents *a* in about, *e* in taken, *i* in pencil, *o* in lemon, *u* in circus.

< = from, derived from, taken from.

drooping; weak; weary: *A hot, sticky day makes a person feel languid.* 2 without interest or enthusiasm; indifferent; listless. 3 not brisk or lively; sluggish; dull. [< Latin *languidus* < *languere* be faint] —**lan′guid ly,** *adv.* —**lan′guid ness,** *n.*

lan guor (lang′gər), *n.* 1 lack of energy; weakness; weariness: *A long illness causes languor.* 2 lack of interest or enthusiasm; indifference. 3 softness or tenderness of mood. 4 quietness; stillness: *the languor of a summer afternoon.* 5 lack of activity; sluggishness. [< Latin < *languere* be faint]

last (last), *n.* 1 block of wood or metal shaped like a person's foot, on which shoes and boots are formed or repaired. 2 **stick to one's last,** pay attention to one's own work; mind one's own business. —*v.t.* form (shoes and boots) on a last. [Old English *lǣste* footprint < *lǣst* track] —**last′er,** *n.*

lave (lāv), *v.,* **laved, lav ing.** —*v.t.* 1 wash; bathe. 2 wash or flow against: *The stream laves its banks.* —*v.i.* ARCHAIC. bathe. [Old English *lafian* < Latin *lavare*]

leg a cy (leg′ə sē), *n., pl.* **-cies.** 1 money or other property left to a person by the will of someone who has died; bequest. 2 something that has been handed down from an ancestor or predecessor: *the legacy of freedom.* [< Medieval Latin *legatia* < Latin *legatum* bequest < *legare* bequeath.]

li a bil i ty (lī′ə bil′ə tē), *n., pl.* **-ties.** 1 state of being susceptible: *liability to disease.* 2 state of being under obligation: *liability for a debt.* 3 **liabilities,** *pl.* debts or other financial obligations of a business. 4 something that is to one's disadvantage: *Poor handwriting is a liability for a teacher.*

li ba tion (lī bā′shən), *n.* 1 a pouring out of wine, water, etc., as an offering to a god. 2 the wine, water, etc., offered in this way. 3 INFORMAL. liquid poured out to be drunk; drink. [< Latin *libationem* < *libare* pour out]

lief (lēf), *adv.* willingly. [Old English *lēof* dear]

lin e age (lin′ē ij), *n.* 1 descent in a direct line from a common ancestor. 2 the descendants of a common ancestor. 3 family or race.

list (list), *n.* a tipping to one side; tilt: *the list of a ship.* —*v.i.* tip to one side; tilt. —*v.t.* cause a tipping or list in (a ship).

loath (lōth, lōᴛʜ), *adj.* unwilling or reluctant; averse: *The little girl was loath to leave her mother.* Also, **loth.** [Old English *lāth* hostile]

loathe (lōᴛʜ), *v.t.,* **loathed, loath ing.** feel strong dislike and disgust for; abhor; hate; detest: *loathe cockroaches.* [Old English *lāthian* to hate < *lāth* hostile]

log (lôg, log), *n.* 1 section of the trunk of a tree that has not been shaped or made into boards; a length of wood just as it comes from the tree. 2 the daily record of a ship's voyage. 3 a similar record of an airplane trip. 4 record of the operation or performance of an engine, etc. [Middle English *logge*]

loi ter (loi′tər), *v.i.* 1 linger idly or aimlessly on one's way; move or go in a slow or lagging manner. 2 waste time in idleness; idle; loaf. —*v.t.* spend (time) idly: *loiter the hours away.* [< Middle Dutch *loteren* be loose] — **loi′ter er,** *n.*

lo quat (lō′kwot, lō′kwät), *n.* 1 a small evergreen tree of the rose family with small, orange-yellow, edible, plumlike fruit, native to Asia, but grown in North America since the 1700's. 2 its fruit. [< Chinese (Canton) *lō-kwat*]

lu di crous (lü′də krəs), *adj.* causing derisive laughter; amusingly absurd; ridiculous. [< Latin *ludicrus* < *ludus* sport] —**lu′di crous ly,** *adv.* —**lu′di crous ness,** *n.*

lu gu bri ous (lü gü′brē əs, lü gyü′brē əs), *adj.* too sad; overly mournful: *the lugubrious howl of a dog.* [< Latin *lugubris* < *lugere* mourn] —**lu gu′bri ous ly,** *adv.* —**lu gu′bri ous ness,** *n.*

lum ba go (lum bā′gō), *n.* form of rheumatism characterized by pain in the muscles of the small of the back and in the loins. [< Late Latin < Latin *lumbus* loin]

lu mi nous (lü′mə nəs), *adj.* 1 shining by its own light: *The sun and stars are luminous bodies.* 2 full of light; shining; bright. 3 easily understood; clear; enlightening. —**lu′mi nous ly,** *adv.* —**lu′mi nous ness,** *n.*

lurch (lėrch), *n.* 1 a sudden leaning or roll to one side, like that of a ship, a car, or a staggering person. 2 a swaying motion or gait; stagger. —*v.i.* lean or roll suddenly to one side; make a lurch; stagger: *The injured man lurched forward.* [origin uncertain]

lux ur i ate (lug zhùr′ē āt, luk shùr′ē āt), *v.i.,* **-at ed, -at ing.** 1 indulge in luxury. 2 take great delight; revel: *luxuriate in a hot bath.* 3 grow very abundantly.

mack i naw (mak′ə nô), *n.* 1 kind of short coat made of heavy woolen cloth, often in a plaid pattern. 2 kind of thick woolen blanket, often with bars of color, used in the northern and western United States by Indians, lumbermen, etc. [< *Mackinaw* City, town in northern Michigan]

ma lign (mə līn′), *v.t.* speak evil of; slander: *You malign a generous person when you call him stingy.* —*adj.* 1 evil; injurious: *Gambling often has a malign influence.* 2 hateful; malicious. [< Late Latin *malignare* < Latin *malignus* disposed to evil < *malus* evil + *-gnus* born] —**ma lign′er,** *n.* —**ma lign′ly,** *adv.*

ma raud (mə rôd′), *v.i.* go about in search of plunder. —*v.t.* plunder. [< French *marauder*] —**ma raud′er,** *n.*

mar gin al (mär′jə nəl), *adj.* 1 written or printed in a margin: *a marginal comment.* 2 of a margin. 3 on or near the margin. 4 barely capable of producing goods, crops, etc., at a profitable rate: *marginal land.* 5 of, having to do with, or obtained from goods that are so produced and marketed: *marginal income.* —**mar′gin al ly,** *adv.*

maul (môl), *n.* a very heavy hammer or malle′ for driving stakes, piles, or wedges. —*v.t.* beat and pull about; handle roughly: *The lion mauled its keeper badly.* [variant of *mall*] —**maul′er,** *n.*

mea ger or **mea gre** (mē′gər), *adj.* 1 lacking fullness or richness; poor or scanty; sparse: *a meager meal.* 2 thin; lean: *a meager face.* [< Old French *maigre* < Latin *macer*] —**mea′ger ly, mea′gre ly,** *adv.* —**mea′ger ness, mea′gre ness,** *n.*

med ley (med′lē), *n., pl.* **-leys,** *adj.* —*n.* 1 mixture of things that ordinarily do not belong together. 2 piece of music made up of parts from other pieces. —*adj.* made up of parts that are not alike; mixed. [< Old French *medlee, meslee* < *mesler* to mix, ultimately < Latin *miscere*]

me squite (me skēt′), *n.* a deep-rooted tree or shrub of the pea family, common in the southwestern United States and in Mexico, that often grows in dense clumps or thickets and bears pods that are used as livestock fodder. [< Mexican Spanish *mezquite* < Nahuatl *mizquitl*]

me tic u lous (mə tik′yə ləs), *adj.* extremely or excessively careful about small details. [< Latin *meticulosus* fearful, timid < *metus* fear] —**me tic′u lous ly,** *adv.*

mi as ma (mī az′mə, mē az′mə), *n., pl.* **-mas, -ma ta** (-mə tə). 1 a bad-smelling vapor rising from decaying matter on the earth. The miasma of swamps was formerly thought to cause disease. 2 anything considered to resemble this in its ability to spread and poison: *a miasma of fear.* [< Greek, pollution < *miainein* pollute]

min a ret (min′ə ret′), *n.* a slender, high tower of a Moslem mosque with one or more projecting balconies, from which a muezzin, or crier, calls the people to prayer. [< French or Spanish < Arabic *manārah* lighthouse]

mi ser (mī′zər), *n.* person who loves money for its own sake; one who lives poorly in order to save money and keep it. [< Latin, wretched]

mol ten (mōlt′n), *adj.* 1 made liquid by heat; melted: *molten steel.* 2 made by melting and casting: *a molten image.*

mo men tous (mō men′təs), *adj.* very important; of great consequence; weighty. —**mo men′tous ly,** *adv.* —**mo men′tous ness,** *n.*

mon o lith (mon′l ith), *n.* 1 a single large block of stone. 2 monument, column, statue, etc., formed of a single large block of stone. [< Greek *monolithos* < *mono-* + *lithos* stone]

mo ri bund (môr′ə bund, mor′ə bund), *adj.* at the point of death or extinction; dying. [< Latin *moribundus* < *mori* die]

mo rose (mə rōs′), *adj.* gloomy; sullen; ill-humored: *a morose scowl, a morose person.* [< Latin *morosus,* originally, set in one's ways < *morem* custom, habit] —**mo rose′ly,** *adv.* —**mo rose′ness,** *n.*

mu ci lage (myü′sə lij), *n.* 1 a sticky substance, especially a solution of gum, glue, etc., in water, used as an adhesive. 2 any of various sticky, gelatinous secretions present in various plants such as seaweeds. [< Late Latin *mucilago* musty juice < Latin *mucus* mucus]

murk y (mėr′kē), *adj.,* **murk i er, murk i est.** 1 dark; gloomy: *a murky prison.* 2 very thick and dark; misty; hazy: *murky smoke.* 3 hard to understand; obscure: *a murky argument.* Also, **mirky.** —**murk′i ly,** *adv.* —**murk′i ness,** *n.*

muse (myüz), *v.,* **mused, mus ing.** —*v.i.* 1 be completely absorbed in thought; ponder; meditate. 2 look thoughtfully. —*v.t.* say thoughtfully. [< Old French *muser,* apparently (originally) put one's nose in the air < *muse* muzzle]

mus ter (mus′tər), *v.t.* 1 gather together; assemble; collect: *muster financial resources, muster soldiers.* 2 summon: *muster up courage.* 3 number; comprise: *The garrison musters eighty men.* [< Old French *mostrer* < Latin *monstrare* to show < *monstrum* portent]

mute (myüt), *adj., v.,* **mut ed, mut ing.** —*adj.* 1 not making any sound; silent: *The little girl stood mute with embarrassment.* 2 unable to speak; dumb. 3 not pronounced; silent: *The "e" in "mute" is mute.* 4 without speech or sound: *a mute refusal of an offer, mute astonishment.* —*v.t.* deaden or soften the sound of (a tone, voice, a musical instrument, etc.) with or as if with a mute: *He played the violin with muted strings.* [< Latin *mutus*] —**mute′ly,** *adv.* —**mute′ness,** *n.*

myr i ad (mir′ē əd), *n.* 1 ten thousand. 2 a very great number: *There are myriads of stars.* —*adj.* 1 ten thousand. 2 countless; innumerable. [< Greek *myriados* ten thousand, countless]

mys ti fy (mis′tə fī), *v.t.,* **-fied, -fy ing.** 1 bewilder purposely; puzzle; perplex: *The magician's tricks mystified the audience.* 2 make mysterious; involve in mystery.

na sal (nā′zəl), *adj.* 1 of, in, or from the nose: *nasal bones, a nasal voice.* 2 (in phonetics) requiring the nose passage to be open; spoken through the nose. M, n, and ng represent nasal sounds. —*n.* 1 a nasal bone or part. 2 (in phonetics) a nasal sound. [< Latin *nasus* nose] —**na′sal ly,** *adv.*

nec tar (nek′tər), *n.* 1 (in Greek and Roman myths) the drink of the gods. 2 any delicious drink. 3 a sweet liquid found in many flowers. [< Latin < Greek *nektar*] —**nec′tar like′,** *adj.*

ne ga tion (ni gā′shən), *n.* 1 a denying; denial: *Shaking the head is a sign of negation.* 2 absence or opposite of some positive thing or quality: *Darkness is the negation of light.* 3 a negative statement, doctrine, etc.

nim ble (nim′bəl), *adj.,* **-bler, -blest.** 1 active and sure-footed; light and quick; agile: *Goats are nimble in climbing among the rocks.* 2 quick to understand and to reply; clever: *a nimble mind.* [Old English *numol* quick to grasp] —**nim′ble ness,** *n.* —**nim′bly,** *adv.*

non de script (non′də skript), *adj.* not easily classified; not of any one particular kind: *She had nondescript eyes, neither brown, blue, nor gray.* [< *non-* + Latin *descriptum* (to be) described]

no pal (nō′pəl), *n.* prickly pear cactus.

nul li fy (nul′ə fī), *v.t.,* **-fied, -fy ing.** 1 make not binding; render void: *nullify a treaty.* 2 make of no effect; make unimportant, useless, or meaningless; destroy; cancel; wipe out: *The difficulties of the plan nullify its advantages.*

nur ture (nėr′chər), *v.,* **-tured, -tur ing,** *n.* —*v.t.* 1 bring up; care for; foster; rear; train. 2 nourish. —*n.* 1 a bringing up; rearing; training; education: *The two sisters had received very different nurture.* 2 nourishment. [< Old French *nourture* < Late Latin *nutritura* a nursing, suckling < Latin *nutrire* to feed] —**nur′tur er,** *n.*

o bit u ar y (ō bich′ü er′ē), *n., pl.* **-ar ies,** *adj.* —*n.* a notice of death, often with a brief account of the person's life. —*adj.* of a death; recording a death or deaths. [< Medieval Latin *obituarius* < Latin *obitus* death < *obire (mortem)* meet (death) < *ob-* away + *ire* go]

ob scure (əb skyůr′), *adj.*, **-scur er, -scur est,** *v.*, **-scured, -scur ing.** —*adj.* 1 not clearly expressed; hard to understand: *an obscure passage in a book.* 2 not expressing meaning clearly: *an obscure style of writing.* 3 not well known; attracting no notice: *an obscure little village, an obscure poet, an obscure position in the government.* 4 not easily discovered; hidden: *an obscure path, an obscure meaning.* 5 not distinct; not clear: *an obscure form, obscure sounds, an obscure view.* 6 dark; dim: *an obscure corner.* —*v.t.* 1 hide from view; make obscure; dim; darken: *Clouds obscure the sun.* 2 make dim or vague to the understanding. [< Latin *obscurus*] **—ob′scu ra′tion,** *n.* **—ob scure′ly,** *adv.* **—ob scure′ness,** *n.* **—ob scur′er,** *n.*

ob sti nate (ob′stə nit), *adj.* 1 not giving in; stubborn. 2 hard to control, treat, or remove; persistent: *an obstinate cough.* [< Latin *obstinatum* determined < *ob-* by + *stare* to stand] **—ob′sti nate ly,** *adv.* **—ob′sti nate ness,** *n.*

ob trude (əb trüd′), *v.*, **-trud ed, -trud ing.** —*v.t.* 1 put forward unasked and unwanted; force: *Don't obtrude your opinions on others.* 2 push out; thrust forward: *A turtle obtrudes its head from its shell.* —*v.i.* come unasked and unwanted; force oneself; intrude. [< Latin *obtrudere* < *ob-* toward + *trudere* to thrust] **—ob trud′er,** *n.*

ob tru sive (əb trü′siv), *adj.* inclined to obtrude; intrusive. **—ob tru′sive ly,** *adv.* **—ob tru′sive ness,** *n.*

Oc ci dent (ok′sə dənt), *n.* 1 countries in Europe and America as distinguished from those in Asia; the West. 2 **occident,** the west. [< Latin *occidentem* falling toward, going down < *ob-* toward + *cadere* to fall (with reference to the setting sun)]

Oc ci den tal (ok′sə den′tl), *adj.* 1 Western; of the Occident. 2 **occidental,** western. —*n.* native of the West. Europeans and Americans are Occidentals.

oc clude (o klüd′), *v.*, **-clud ed, -clud ing.** —*v.t.* 1 stop up (a passage, pores, etc.); close. 2 shut in, out, or off. —*v.i.* (in dentistry) meet closely in proper position. [< Latin *occludere* < *ob-* up + *claudere* to close]

of fice (ô′fis, of′is), *n.* 1 duty of one's position; task; job; work: *A teacher's office is teaching.* 2 act of kindness or unkindness; attention; service: *Through the good offices of a friend, I was able to get a job.* 3 a religious ceremony or prayer: *the communion office, last offices.* [< Latin *officium* service < *opus* work + *facere* do]

om i nous (om′ə nəs), *adj.* of bad omen; unfavorable; threatening: *ominous clouds.* **—om′i nous ly,** *adv.* **—om′i nous ness,** *n.*

om niv or ous (om niv′ər əs), *adj.* 1 eating every kind of food. 2 eating both animal and vegetable food: *Man is an omnivorous animal.* 3 taking in everything; fond of all kinds: *An omnivorous reader reads all kinds of books.* [< Latin *omnivorus* < *omnis* all + *vorare* eat greedily] **—om niv′or ous ly,** *adv.* **—om niv′or ous ness,** *n.*

on slaught (ôn′slôt′, on′slôt′), *n.* a vigorous attack: *The pirates made an onslaught on the ship.* [probably < Dutch *aanslag* an attempt, stroke]

o ra cle (ôr′ə kəl, or′ə kəl), *n.* 1 (in ancient Greece and Rome) an answer believed to be given by a god through a priest or priestess to some question. It often had a hidden meaning that was ambiguous or hard to understand. 2 place where the god was believed to give such answers. A famous oracle was at Delphi. 3 the priest, priestess, or other means by which the god's answer was believed to be given. 4 a very wise person. 5 something regarded as a very reliable and sure guide. 6 a very wise answer. [< Latin *oraculum* < *orare* speak formally]

or gan dy or **or gan die** (ôr′gən dē′), *n.*, *pl.* **-dies.** a fine, thin, stiff, transparent muslin, used for dresses, curtains, etc. [< French *organdi*]

-ous, *suffix forming adjectives from nouns.* 1 full of; having much; having: *Joyous = full of joy.* 2 characterized by: *Zealous = characterized by zeal.* 3 having the nature of: *Idolatrous = having the nature of an idolater.* 4 of or having to do with: *Monogamous = having to do with monogamy.* 5 like: *Thunderous = like thunder.* 6 committing or practicing: *Bigamous = practicing bigamy.* 7 inclined to: *Blasphemous = inclined to blasphemy.* 8 (in chemistry) indicating the presence in a compound of the designated element in a lower valence than indicated by the suffix *-ic,* as in *stannous, ferrous, sulfurous.* [< Old French *-os, -us* < Latin *-osum*]

out scour ings (out′skour ingz), *n.* that which is washed or scoured out.

o ver wrought (ō′vər rôt′), *adj.* 1 wearied or exhausted by too much work or excitement; greatly excited: *overwrought nerves.* 2 too elaborate.

pal lid (pal′id), *adj.* lacking normal color; wan; pale: *a pallid complexion.* [< Latin *pallidum*] **—pal′lid ly,** *adv.* **—pal′lid ness,** *n.*

pal try (pôl′trē), *adj.*, **-tri er, -tri est.** 1 almost worthless; trifling; petty; mean. 2 of no worth; despicable; contemptible. [probably related to Low German *paltrig* ragged, torn] **—pal′tri ly,** *adv.* **—pal′tri ness,** *n.*

pan-, *combining form.* all; of all; entirely: *Pan-American = of all Americans. Panchromatic = entirely chromatic.* [< Greek < *pan,* neuter of *pas* all]

pan de mo ni um (pan′də mō′nē əm), *n.* 1 place of wild disorder or lawless confusion. 2 wild uproar or lawlessness. [< Greek *pan-* + *daimōn* demon]

pan o plied (pan′ə plēd), *adj.* completely armed, equipped, covered, or arrayed. [< Greek *panoplia* < *pan-* + *hopla* arms]

pan to mime (pan′tə mīm), *n.*, *v.*, **-mimed, -mim ing.** —*n.* 1 a play without words, in which the actors express themselves by gestures. 2 gestures without words; dumb show. 3 mime or mimic, especially in the ancient Roman theater. —*v.t.* express by gestures. [< Greek *pantomimos* < *pantos* all + *mimos* mimic]

par a pher nal ia (par′ə fər nā′lyə), *n.*, *pl. or sing.* 1 personal belongings. 2 equipment; outfit. [< Medieval Latin < Greek *parapherna* a woman's personal property besides her dowry < *para-* + *phernē* dowry]

par ry (par′ē), *v.*, **-ried, -ry ing,** *n.*, *pl.* **-ries.** —*v.t.* 1 ward off or block (a thrust, stroke, weapon, etc.) in fencing, boxing, etc. 2 meet and turn aside (an awkward question, a threat, etc.); avoid; evade. —*n.* act of parrying; avoiding. [< French *parez,* imperative of *parer* ward off < Italian *parare* < Latin, prepare]

hat, āge, fär; let, ēqual, tėrm;
it, īce; hot, ōpen, ôrder;
oil, out; cup, pu̇t, rüle;
ch, child; ng, long; sh, she;
th, thin; ᴛʜ, then; zh, measure;

ə represents *a* in about, *e* in taken, *i* in pencil, *o* in lemon, *u* in circus.

< = from, derived from, taken from.

par son (pär′sən), *n.* 1 minister in charge of a parish. 2 any clergyman; minister. [< Medieval Latin *persona* < Latin, person]

pa thos (pā′thos), *n.* 1 quality in speech, writing, music, events, or a scene that arouses a feeling of pity or sadness; power of evoking tender or melancholy emotion. 2 a pathetic expression or utterance. [< Greek, suffering, feeling < *path-,* stem of *paschein* suffer]

pa tron ize (pā′trə nīz, pat′rə nīz), *v.t.*, **-ized, -iz ing.** 1 be a regular customer of; give regular business to: *We patronize our neighborhood stores.* 2 act as a patron toward; support or protect: *patronize the ballet.* 3 treat in a haughty, condescending way.

peer (pir), *n.* 1 person of the same rank, ability, etc., as another; equal. 2 man belonging to the nobility, especially a British nobleman having the rank of duke, marquis, earl, count, viscount, or baron. [< Old French *per* < Latin *par* equal.]

pel let (pel′it), *n.* a little ball of mud, paper, food, medicine, etc.; pill. [< Old French *pelote* < Popular Latin *pilotta* < Latin *pila* ball]

pen chant (pen′chənt), *n.* a strong taste or liking; inclination: *a penchant for taking long walks.* [< French, present participle of *pencher* to incline]

per am bu late (pə ram′byə lāt), *v.*, **-lat ed, -lat ing.** —*v.t.* 1 walk through. 2 walk through and examine. —*v.i.* walk or travel about; stroll. [< Latin *perambulatum* walked through < *per-* through + *ambulare* to walk] **—per am′bu la′tion,** *n.*

per dó na me (per ᴛʜó nä mā), SPANISH. forgive me; pardon me.

per func tor y (pər fungk′tər ē), *adj.* done merely for the sake of getting rid of the duty: *The little boy gave his face a perfunctory washing.* [< Late Latin *perfunctorius* < Latin *per-* through + *fungi* execute] **—per func′tor i ly,** *adv.* **—per func′tor iness,** *n.*

per plex (pər pleks′), *v.t.* 1 trouble with doubt; puzzle; bewilder. 2 make difficult to understand or settle; confuse. [< Latin *perplexus* confused < *per-* thoroughly + *plectere* intertwine] **—per plex′ed ly,** *adv.* **—per plex′ing ly,** *adv.*

per se ver ance (pėr′sə vir′əns), *n.* a sticking to a purpose or an aim; tenacity.

per si flage (pėr′sə fläzh), *n.* light, joking talk or writing. [< French < *persifler* to banter]

per sist (pər sist′, pər zist′), *v.i.* 1 continue firmly; refuse to stop or be changed; persevere. 2 remain in existence; last; stay: *On the tops of very high mountains snow persists throughout the year.* 3 say again and again; maintain. [< Latin *persistere* < *per-* to the end + *sistere* to stand]

persistence

per sist ence (pər sis′təns, pər zis′təns), n. 1 a persisting. 2 a being persistent; doggedness. 3 a continuing existence: *the persistence of a cough.*

per spec tive (pər spek′tiv), n. 1 art of picturing objects on a flat surface so as to give the appearance of distance or depth. 2 the effect of distance or depth on the appearance of objects: *Railroad tracks seem to meet at the horizon because of perspective.* 3 the effect of the distance of events upon the mind: *Perspective makes happenings of last year seem less important.* 4 view of things or facts in which they are in the right relations: *a lack of perspective.* 5 view in front; distant view: *a perspective of lakes and hills.* 6 a mental view, outlook, or prospect. [< Medieval Latin *perspectiva (ars)* (science of) optics < Latin *perspicere* look through < *per-* through + *specere* to look] —**per spec′tive ly**, adv.

per vert (pər vėrt′), v.t. 1 lead or turn from what is true, desirable, good, or morally right; corrupt. 2 give a wrong meaning to; distort: *His enemies perverted his friendly remark and made it into an insult.* 3 use for wrong purposes or in a wrong way: *A clever criminal perverts his talents.* 4 change from what is natural or normal. [< Latin *pervertere* < *per-* to destruction + *vertere* to turn] —**pervert′ed ly**, adv. —**per vert′er**, n.

pet ri fy (pet′rə fī), v., **-fied, -fy ing.** —v.t. 1 turn into stone; change (plant or animal matter) into a substance like stone. 2 make hard as stone; stiffen; deaden. 3 paralyze with fear, horror, or surprise: *The bird was petrified as the snake came near.* —v.i. 1 become stone or a substance like stone. 2 become rigid like stone; harden. [< French *pétrifier* < Latin *petra* stone]

pet ty (pet′ē), adj., **-ti er, -ti est.** 1 having little importance or value; small: *petty troubles.* 2 mean; narrow-minded. 3 lower in rank or importance; subordinate. [< Old French *petit* little, small.] —**pet′ti ly**, adv. —**pet′ti ness**, n.

pet u lance (pech′ə ləns), n. a being petulant; peevishness.

pet u lant (pech′ə lənt), adj. likely to have little fits of bad temper; irritable over trifles; peevish. [< Latin *petulantem*] —**pet′u lant ly**, adv.

pho bi a (fō′bē ə), n. a persistent, abnormal, or irrational fear of a certain thing or group of things. [< Greek *-phobia* < *phobos* fear]

phos phate (fos′fāt), n. 1 salt or ester of phosphoric acid. Bread contains phosphates. 2 fertilizer containing such salts. 3 drink of carbonated water flavored with fruit syrup, and containing a little phosphoric acid.

pig ment (pig′mənt), n. 1 a coloring matter, especially a powder or some easily pulverized dry substance that constitutes a paint or dye when mixed with oil, water, or some other liquid. 2 the natural substance occurring in and coloring the tissues of an animal or plant. [< Latin *pigmentum* < *pingere* to paint]

pince-nez (pans′nā′, pins′nā′), n., pl. **pince-nez** (pans′nāz′, pins′nāz′). eyeglasses kept in place by a spring that clips onto the bridge of the nose. [< French, pinch-nose]

pin ion (pin′yən), n. 1 the last joint of a bird's wing. 2 wing. 3 any one of the stiff flying feathers of the wing; quill. —v.t. 1 cut off or tie the pinions of (a bird) to prevent flying. 2 bind; bind the arms of; bind (to something): *pinion a man's arms.* [< Middle French *pignon* < Popular Latin *pinnionem* < Latin *penna* feather and *pinna* wing]

pin na cle (pin′ə kəl), n. 1 a high peak or point of rock. 2 the highest point: *at the pinnacle of one's fame.* 3 a slender turret or spire. [< Old French *pinacle* < Latin *pinnaculum,* diminutive of *pinna* wing, point]

pir ou ette (pir′ü et′), n., v., **-et ted, -et ting.** —n. a whirling about on one foot or on the toes, as in dancing. —v.i. whirl in this way. [< Middle French, spinning top]

piv ot (piv′ət), n. 1 shaft, pin, or point on which something turns. 2 a turn on a pivot. 3 that on which something turns, hinges, or depends; central point. —v.t. mount on, attach by, or provide with a pivot. —v.i. turn on or as if on a pivot. [< French]

plac id (plas′id), adj. pleasantly calm or peaceful; quiet: *a placid lake.* [< Latin *placidus* < *placere* to please] —**plac′id ly**, adv. —**plac′id ness**, n.

plau si ble (plô′zə bəl), adj. 1 appearing true, reasonable, or fair. 2 apparently worthy of confidence but often not really so: *a plausible liar.* [< Latin *plausibilis* deserving applause, pleasing < *plaudere* applaud] —**plau′si bly**, adv.

poign ant (poi′nyənt), adj. 1 very painful; piercing: *poignant suffering.* 2 stimulating to the mind, feelings, or passions; keen; intense: *a subject of poignant interest.* 3 sharp, pungent, or piquant to the taste or smell: *poignant sauces.* [< Old French, present participle of *poindre* to prick < Latin *pungere*] —**poign′ant ly**, adv.

pom pa dour (pom′pə dôr, pom′pə dōr), n. 1 arrangement of a woman's hair in which it is puffed high over the forehead or brushed straight up and back from the forehead. 2 hair so arranged. [< the Marquise de *Pompadour*]

pon toon (pon tün′), n. 1 a low, flat-bottomed boat. 2 such a boat, or some other floating structure, used as one of the supports of a temporary bridge. 3 either of two air-filled, watertight, boat-shaped parts of an aircraft for landing, floating on, or taking off from water; float. [< French *ponton* < Latin *pontonem* < *pons* bridge]

port a ble (pôr′tə bəl, pōr′tə bəl), adj. capable of being carried; easily carried: *a portable typewriter.* [< Late Latin *portabilis* < Latin *portare* carry]

por tent (pôr′tent, pōr′tent), n. 1 a warning of coming evil; sign; omen. 2 ominous significance. [< Latin *portentum* indicated beforehand]

por ten tous (pôr ten′təs, pōr ten′təs), adj. 1 indicating evil to come; ominous; threatening. 2 amazing; extraordinary. —**por ten′-tous ly**, adv. —**por ten′tous ness**, n.

pos ture (pos′chər), v.i., **-tured, -tur ing.** 1 take a certain posture: *The dancer postured before the mirror, bending and twisting her body.* 2 pose for effect. [< French *posture* < Latin *positura* < *ponere* to place] —**pos′tur er**, n.

po ten tial (pə ten′shəl), adj. possible as opposed to actual; capable of coming into being or action: *There is a potential danger of being bitten when one plays with a strange dog.* —n. something potential; possibility. —**po ten′tial ly**, adv.

prag mat ic (prag mat′ik), adj. 1 concerned with practical results or values; viewing things in a matter-of-fact way. 2 of or having to do with pragmatism: *a pragmatic philoso-*phy. [< Latin *pragmaticus* < Greek *pragmatikos* efficient, ultimately < *prassein* do] —**prag mat′i cal ly**, adv.

pre-, prefix. 1 before in time, rank, etc.: *Precambrian = before the Cambrian.* 2 before in position, space, etc.; in front of: *Premolar = in front of the molars.* [< Latin *prae-, pre-*]

pre am ble (prē′am′bəl), n. 1 a preliminary statement; introduction to a speech or a writing. The reasons for a law and its general purpose are often stated in a preamble. 2 a preliminary or introductory fact or circumstance, especially one showing what is to follow. [< Medieval Latin *praeambulum* < Late Latin, walking before < Latin *prae-* pre- + *ambulare* to walk]

pre car i ous (pri ker′ē əs, pri kar′ē əs), adj. 1 not safe or secure; uncertain; dangerous; risky. 2 dependent on chance or circumstance. 3 poorly founded; doubtful. [< Latin *precarius* obtainable by prayer, uncertain < *precem* prayer] —**pre car′i ous ly**, adv. —**pre car′i ous ness**, n.

pre cau tion (pri kô′shən), n. 1 care taken beforehand; thing done beforehand to ward off evil or secure good results: *Locking doors is a precaution against thieves.* 2 a taking care beforehand; prudent foresight.

prec i pice (pres′ə pis), n. 1 a very steep or almost vertical face of a rock, etc.; cliff, crag, or steep mountainside. 2 situation of great peril; critical position. [< Latin *praecipitium* < *praecipitem* steep, literally, headlong < *prae-* pre- + *caput* head]

pre cip i tous (pri sip′ə təs), adj. 1 like a precipice; very steep: *precipitous cliffs.* 2 hasty; rash. 3 rushing headlong; very rapid. —**pre cip′i tous ly**, adv. —**pre cip′-i tous ness**, n.

pre co cious (pri kō′shəs), adj. 1 developed earlier than usual in knowledge, skill, etc.: *This very precocious child could read well at the age of four.* 2 developed too early; occurring before the natural time. [< Latin *praecocem* < *praecoquere* to mature or ripen early < *prae-* pre- + *coquere* ripen] —**pre co′cious ly**, adv. —**pre co′cious-ness**, n.

pre dic a ment (pri dik′ə mənt), n. an unpleasant, difficult, or dangerous situation. [< Late Latin *praedicamentum* quality, category < Latin *praedicare* to predicate]

pre med i tate (prē med′ə tāt), v.t., **-tat ed, -tat ing.** consider or plan beforehand: *The murder was premeditated.*

pre mo ni tion (prē′mə nish′ən, prem′ə-nish′ən), n. notification or warning of what is to come; forewarning: *a vague premonition of disaster.* [< Latin *praemonitionem* < *praemonere* warn beforehand < *prae-* pre- + *monere* warn]

pre mon i to ry (pri mon′ə tôr′ē, pri-mon′ə tōr′ē), adj. giving warning beforehand.

pre pos ter ous (pri pos′tər əs), adj. contrary to nature, reason, or common sense; absurd; senseless: *It would be preposterous to shovel snow with a teaspoon.* [< Latin *praeposterus* with the posterior in front < *prae-* pre- + *posterus* coming after, behind] —**pre pos′ter ous ly**, adv. —**pre pos′-ter ous ness**, n.

pre sump tu ous (pri zump′chü əs), adj. acting without permission or right; too bold; forward. —**pre sump′tu ous ly**, adv. —**pre sump′tu ous ness**, n.

pri va tion (prī vā′shən), n. 1 lack of the comforts or of the necessities of life: *Many* *children were hungry and homeless because of privation during the war.* 2 a being deprived; loss; absence. [< Latin *privationem* < *privatum* deprived]

prod (prod), *v.t.*, **prod ded, prod ding.** 1 poke or jab with something pointed: *prod an animal with a stick.* 2 stir up; urge on: *The lateness of the hour prodded me to finish quickly.* [origin uncertain] **—prod′der,** *n.*

pro di gious (prə dij′əs), *adj.* 1 very great; huge; vast: *The ocean contains a prodigious amount of water.* 2 wonderful; marvelous. [< Latin *prodigiosus* < *prodigium* prodigy, omen] **—pro di′gious ly,** *adv.* **—pro di′gious ness,** *n.*

prod i gy (prod′ə jē), *n., pl.* **-gies.** 1 person endowed with amazing brilliance, talent, etc., especially a remarkably talented child: *a musical prodigy.* 2 a marvelous example: *Samson performed prodigies of strength.* 3 a wonderful sign or omen: *An eclipse of the sun seemed a prodigy to early man.* [< Latin *prodigium* omen]

prof fer (prof′ər), *v.t.* offer for acceptance; present; tender: *We proffered regrets at having to leave so early.* [< Anglo-French *proffrir* < Old French *pro-* forth + *offrir* to offer]

pro fuse (prə fyüs′), *adj.* 1 very abundant: *profuse thanks.* 2 spending or giving freely; lavish; extravagant. [< Latin *profusum* poured forth < *pro-* forth + *fundere* pour] **—pro fuse′ly,** *adv.* **—pro fuse′ness,** *n.*

pro long (prə lông′, prə long′), *v.t.* make longer; extend in time or space; stretch, lengthen, or protract: *The author cleverly prolonged the suspense in his mystery novel.* [< Late Latin *prolongare* < *pro-* forth + *longus* long]

prom on to ry (prom′ən tôr′ē, prom′əntōr′ē), *n., pl.* **-ries.** 1 a high point of land extending from the coast into the water; headland. 2 (in anatomy) part that bulges out. [< Latin *promonturium* < *pro-* forward + *montem* mountain]

proof (prüf), *n.* 1 way or means of showing beyond doubt the truth of something: *Is what you say a guess or have you proof?* 2 establishment of the truth of anything. 3 act of testing; trial: *That box looks big enough; but let us put it to the proof.* 4 a trial impression from type. A book is first printed in proof so that errors can be corrected. [< Old French *prouve* < Late Latin *proba* < Latin *probare* prove]

pro pen si ty (prə pen′sə tē), *n., pl.* **-ties.** a natural inclination or bent; leaning: *a propensity for athletics.* [< Latin *propensum* inclined < *pro-* forward + *pendere* hang]

pro sa ic (prō zā′ik), *adj.* like prose; matter-of-fact; ordinary; not exciting. **—pro sa′i cal ly,** *adv.*

pro sce ni um (prō sē′nē əm), *n., pl.* **-ni a** (-nē ə). 1 the part of the stage in front of the curtain. 2 curtain and the framework that holds it. 3 stage of an ancient theater. [< Latin < Greek *proskēnion* < *pro-* in front of + *skēnē* stage, scene]

pro scribe (prō skrīb′), *v.t.,* **-scribed, -scrib ing.** 1 prohibit as wrong or dangerous; condemn: *In earlier days, the church proscribed dancing and card playing.* 2 put outside of the protection of the law; outlaw. 3 forbid to come into a certain place; banish. [< Latin *proscribere* < *pro-* forth + *scribere* write] **—pro scrib′er,** *n.*

pros e cu tion (pros′ə kyü′shən), *n.* 1 the carrying on of a lawsuit: *The prosecution will be abandoned if the stolen money is returned.* 2 side that starts action against another in a

court of law. The prosecution makes certain charges against the defense. 3 a carrying out; following up: *the prosecution of a plan.*

pros trate (pros′trāt), *v.,* **-trat ed, -trat ing,** *adj.* **—v.t.** 1 lay down flat; cast down: *The captives prostrated themselves before the conqueror.* 2 make very weak or helpless; exhaust: *Sickness often prostrates people.* **—adj.** 1 lying flat with face downward: *She was humbly prostrate in prayer.* 2 lying flat: *I stumbled and fell prostrate on the floor.* 3 overcome; helpless: *a prostrate enemy.* [< Latin *prostratum* thrown down flat < *pro-* forth + *sternere* spread out]

pro vi sion (prə vizh′ən), *n.* 1 statement making a condition; stipulation: *A provision of the lease is that the rent must be paid promptly.* 2 act of providing; preparation: *They have made provision for their children's education.* 3 care taken for the future; arrangement made beforehand: *There is a provision for making the building larger if necessary.* **—v.t.** supply with provisions. [< Latin *provisionem* < *providere*]

prov o ca tion (prov′ə kā′shən), *n.* 1 act of provoking. 2 something that stirs up or provokes.

pru dence (prüd′ns), *n.* 1 wise thought before acting; good judgment. 2 good management; economy.

puck er (puk′ər), *v.t., v.i.* draw into wrinkles or irregular folds: *pucker one's brow, pucker cloth in sewing. The baby's lips puckered just before he began to cry.* **—n.** an irregular fold; wrinkle. [apparently < *poke*]

pu is sant (pyü′ə sənt, pyü is′nt, pwis′nt), *adj.* having great power or strength; powerful; mighty. [< Old French < Popular Latin *possentem* < Latin *potentem* potent] **—pu′is sant ly,** *adv.*

pul sate (pul′sāt), *v.i.,* **-sat ed, -sat ing.** 1 expand and contract rhythmically, as the heart or an artery; beat; throb. 2 vibrate; quiver. [< Latin *pulsatum* beaten, pushed < *pulsus* a beating, pulse]

punc tu al (pungk′chü əl), *adj.* on time; prompt: *be punctual to the minute.* [< Latin *punctum* point] **—punc′tu al ly,** *adv.* **—punc′ tu al ness,** *n.*

pun gent (pun′jənt), *adj.* 1 sharply affecting the organs of taste and smell: *a pungent pickle, the pungent smell of burning leaves.* 2 sharp; biting: *pungent criticism.* 3 stimulating to the mind; keen; lively: *a pungent wit.* [< Latin *pungentem* piercing, pricking < *punctum* point] **—pun′gent ly,** *adv.*

pur ga to ry (pėr′gə tôr′ē, pėr′gə tōr′ē), *n., pl.* **-ries.** 1 (in Roman Catholic belief) a temporary condition or place in which the souls of those who have died penitent are purified from venial sin or the effects of sin by punishment. 2 any condition or place of temporary suffering or punishment. [< Medieval Latin *purgatorium,* originally, purging < Latin *purgare*]

quad rant (kwod′rənt), *n.* 1 thing or part shaped like a quarter circle. 2 instrument with a scale of 90 degrees, used in astronomy, surveying, and navigation for measuring altitudes. 3 (in geometry) one of the four parts into which a plane is divided by two straight lines crossing at right angles. The upper right-hand section is the first quadrant, and, in a counterclockwise direction, the others are the second, third, and fourth quad-

hat, āge, fär; let, ēqual, tėrm;
it, īce; hot, ōpen, ôrder;
oil, out; cup, pút, rüle;
ch, child; ng, long; sh, she;
th, thin; ᴛʜ, then; zh, measure;

ə represents *a* in about, *e* in taken,
i in pencil, *o* in lemon, *u* in circus.

< = from, derived from, taken from.

rants respectively. [< Latin *quadrantem* a fourth]

quar ry (kwôr′ē, kwor′ē), *n., pl.* **-ries.** 1 animal chased in a hunt; game; prey. 2 anything hunted or eagerly pursued. [< Middle French *cuiree* < *cuir* skin, hide < Latin *corium*]

qua ver (kwā′vər), *v.i.* 1 shake tremulously; tremble: *The old man's voice quavered.* 2 (in music) to trill in singing or in playing on an instrument. **—n.** 1 a shaking or trembling, especially of the voice. 2 in music: **a** a trill in singing or in playing on an instrument. [frequentative form of earlier *quave* to shake] **—qua′ver ing ly,** *adv.*

quest (kwest), *n.* 1 a search or hunt: *She went to the library in quest of something to read.* 2 expedition of knights: *There are many stories about the quests of King Arthur's knights.* **—v.t.** search or seek for; hunt. **—v.i.** go about in search of something; search or seek. [< Old French *queste* < Popular Latin *quaesita* < Latin *quaerere* seek]

queue (kyü), *v.,* **queued, queu ing.** *v.i.* 1 form or stand in a long line. 2 **queue up,** line up. **—v.t.** arrange (persons) in a queue. Also, **cue. —queu′er,** *n.* [< French Latin *coda, cauda* tail]

quin tes sence (kwin tes′ns), *n.* 1 the purest form of some quality; pure essence. 2 the most perfect example of something: *Her dress was the quintessence of good taste and style.* [< Medieval Latin *quinta essentia* fifth essence; with reference to a fifth element supposed by medieval philosophers to be more pervasive than the four elements (earth, water, fire, and air)]

ra di ant (rā′dē ənt), *adj.* 1 shining; bright; beaming: *a radiant smile.* 2 sending out rays of light or heat: *The sun is a radiant body.* 3 sent off in rays from some source; radiated: *radiant heat.* **—ra′di ant ly,** *adv.*

rad i cal (rad′ə kəl), *adj.* 1 going to the root; fundamental: *If she wants to reduce, she must make a radical change in her diet.* 2 favoring extreme changes or reforms; extreme. 3 having to do with or forming the root of a number or quantity. [< Late Latin *radicalis* < Latin *radix* root] **—rad′i cal ly,** *adv.* **—rad′i cal ness,** *n.*

rak ish (rā′kish), *adj.* 1 smart; jaunty; dashing: *a hat set at a rakish angle.* 2 suggesting dash and speed: *He owns a rakish boat.* **—rak′ish ly,** *adv.* **—rak′ish ness,** *n.*

ral ly (ral′ē), *v.,* **-lied, -ly ing,** *n., pl.* **-lies.** **—v.t.** 1 bring together, especially to get in order again: *The commander was able to rally the fleeing troops.* 2 pull together; revive: *We rallied all our energy for one last effort.* **—v.i.** 1 come together in a body for a common purpose or action. 2 come to help a person,

ramification

party, or cause: *She rallied to the side of her injured friend.* [< Middle French *rallier* < *re-* again + *allier* to ally]

ram i fi ca tion (ram/ə fə kā/shən), n. 1 a dividing or spreading out into branches or parts. 2 manner or result of branching; branch; part; subdivision.

ram i fy (ram/ə fī), v.i., **-fied, -fy ing.** divide for spread out into branchlike parts. [< Middle French *ramifier* < Medieval Latin *ramificare* < Latin *ramus* branch + *facere* to make]

ran cid (ran/sid), adj. 1 stale; spoiled: *rancid butter.* 2 tasting or smelling like stale fat or butter: *rancid odor.* [< Latin *rancidus* < *rancere* be rank] **—ran/cid ly,** adv. **—ran/cid ness,** n.

rank (rangk), adj. 1 large and coarse: *rank grass.* 2 growing thickly in a coarse way: *a rank growth of weeds.* 3 producing a dense but coarse growth: *rank swampland.* 4 having a strong, bad smell or taste: *rank meat, rank tobacco.* 5 strongly marked; extreme: *rank ingratitude, rank nonsense.* [Old English *ranc* proud] **—rank/ly,** adv. **—rank/ness,** n.

ran kle (rang/kəl), v., **-kled, -kling. —v.i.** be sore; cause soreness; continue to give pain: *The memory of the insult rankled in her mind.* **—v.t.** cause pain or soreness in or to. [< Old French *rancler, draoncler* < Medieval Latin *dracunculus* sore]

ra pa cious (rə pā/shəs), adj. 1 seizing by force; plundering. 2 grasping; greedy. 3 living by the capture of prey; predatory. [< Latin *rapacem* grasping < *rapere* seize] **ra pa/cious ly,** adv. **—ra pa/cious ness,** n.

ra tion ale (rash/ə nal/, rash/ə nä/lē), n. the fundamental reason. [< Latin, neuter of *rationalis* rational]

rat tle (rat/l), v., **-tled, -tling. —v.i.** 1 make a number of short, sharp sounds: *The window rattled in the wind.* 2 move with short, sharp sounds: *The old car rattled down the street.* 3 talk in a quick, lively, and rather pointless manner. **—v.t.** 1 cause to rattle. 2 say or do quickly: *rattle off a series of numbers.* 3 INFORMAL. confuse; upset: *He is not very easily rattled.* [Middle English *ratelen*]

rat tling (rat/ling), adj. 1 that rattles. 2 lively; very fast. 3 INFORMAL. great; important. **—adv.** INFORMAL. extremely; especially: *a rattling good time.* **—rat/tling ly,** adv.

rav age (rav/ij), v., **-aged, -ag ing,** n. **—v.t.** damage greatly; lay waste; destroy: *The forest fire ravaged many miles of country.* **—n.** violence; destruction; great damage. [< French *ravager* < *ravir* ravish] **—rav/ag er,** n.

rav en ous (rav/ə nəs), adj. 1 very hungry. 2 greedy. 3 rapacious. **—rav/en ous ly,** adv. **—rav/en ous ness,** n.

re-, prefix. 1 again; anew; once more: *Reappear = appear again.* 2 back: *Repay = pay back.* Also, sometimes before vowels, **red-.** [< Latin]

rea son a ble (rē/zn ə bəl), adj. 1 according to reason; sensible; not foolish. 2 not asking too much; fair; just. 3 not high in price; inexpensive. 4 able to reason. **—rea/son a ble ness,** n. **—rea/son a bly,** adv.

re cip ro cal (ri sip/rə kəl), adj. 1 in return: *Although she gave me many presents, she expected no reciprocal gifts from me.* 2 mutual: *reciprocal distrust.* [< Latin *reciprocus* returning] **—re cip/ro cal ly,** adv.

re claim (ri klām/), v.t. 1 bring back to a useful, good condition: *The farmer reclaimed the swamp by draining it.* 2 get from discarded things: *reclaim metal from old tin cans.* 3 demand or ask for the return of. [< Old French *reclamer* call back < Latin *reclamare* < *re-* back + *clamare* cry out] **—re claim/a ble,** adj. **—re claim/er,** n.

re clu sion (ri klü/zhən), n. state of being shut up or withdrawn from the world. [< Late Latin *reclusum* shut up, enclosed < Latin *re-* back + *claudere* to shut]

rec on cil i a tion (rek/ən sil/ē ā/shən), n. 1 a reconciling; bringing together again in friendship. 2 a being reconciled; settlement or adjustment of disagreements or differences.

re cu pe rate (ri kyü/pə rāt/, ri kü/pə rāt/), v., **-rat ed, -rat ing. —v.i.** recover from sickness, exhaustion, loss, etc. **—v.t.** 1 restore to health, strength, etc. 2 get back; regain. [< Latin *recuperatum* recovered] **—re cu/pe ra/tion,** n.

re dress (v. ri dres/; n. rē/dres, ri dres/), v.t. set right; repair; remedy. **—n.** 1 a setting right; reparation; relief. 2 the means of a remedy. [< Middle French *redresser* < *re-* again + *dresser* straighten, arrange]

re flec tive (ri flek/tiv), adj. 1 that reflects; reflecting: *the reflective surface of polished metal.* 2 thoughtful: *a reflective look.* **—re flec/tive ly,** adv. **—re flec/tive ness,** n.

ref uge (ref/yüj), n. 1 shelter or protection from danger, trouble, etc.; safety; security. 2 place of safety or security. [< Latin *refugium* < *re-* back + *fugere* flee]

re fute (ri fyüt/), v.t., **-fut ed, -fut ing.** show (a claim, opinion, or argument) to be false or incorrect; prove wrong; disprove. [< Latin *refutare* cause to fall back] **—re fut/er,** n.

rem nant (rem/nənt), n. 1 a small part left; fragment. 2 piece of cloth, ribbon, lace, etc., left after the rest has been used or sold. [< Old French *remenant* < *remenoir* remain < Latin *remanere*]

re mon strate (ri mon/strāt), v.i., **-strat ed, -strat ing.** speak, reason, or plead in complaint or protest: *Mother remonstrated with us about our unruly behavior.* [< Medieval Latin *remonstratum* pointed out, ultimately < Latin *re-* back + *monstrum* sign] **—re/mon stra/tion,** n. **—re mon/stra tor,** n.

re nounce (ri nouns/), v.t., **-nounced, -nounc ing.** 1 declare that one gives up; give up entirely; give up: *He renounces his claim to the money.* 2 cast off; refuse to recognize as one's own; repudiate; disown. [< Middle French *renoncer* < Latin *renuntiare* < *re-* back + *nuntius* message] **—re nounce/ment,** n.

rent (rent), n. a torn place; tear; split. **—adj.** torn; split.

re pel lent (ri pel/ənt), adj. 1 disagreeable or distasteful; repugnant. 2 driving back; repelling. **—n.** anything that repels: *an insect repellent.* **—re pel/lent ly,** adv.

rep er to ry (rep/ər tôr/ē, rep/ər tōr/ē), n., pl. **-ries.** 1 repertoire. 2 store or stock of things ready for use. 3 storehouse. [< Late Latin *repertorium* inventory < *reperire* to find, get < *re-* again + *parere* beget]

re pos i to ry (ri poz/ə tôr/ē, ri poz/ə tōr/ē), n., pl. **-ries.** 1 place or container where things are stored or kept: *The box was the repository for old magazines.* 2 person to whom something is confided or entrusted.

re prieve (ri prēv/), v., **-prieved, -priev ing,** n. **—v.t.** 1 postpone the punishment of (a person), especially the execution of (a person condemned to death). 2 give relief from any evil or trouble. **—n.** 1 delay in carrying out a punishment, especially of the death penalty. 2 the order giving authority for such delay. 3 temporary relief from any evil or trouble. [< Old French *repris,* past participle of *reprendre* take back < Latin *reprehendere*]

rep ri mand (rep/rə mand), n. a severe or formal reproof. **—v.t.** reprove severely or formally; censure. [< French *réprimande* < Latin *reprimenda* to be repressed < *reprimere* < *re-* back + *premere* to press]

re proach (ri prōch/), n. 1 blame or censure. 2 a cause of blame or disgrace; discredit. 3 object of blame, censure, or disapproval. 4 expression of blame, censure, or disapproval. [< Middle French *reprocher* < Popular Latin *repropiare* lay at the door of, ultimately < Latin *re-* again + *prope* near] **—re proach/a ble,** adj. **—re proach/er,** n. **—re proach/ing ly,** adv. **—re proach/less,** adj.

re prove (ri prüv/), v.t., **-proved, -prov ing.** show disapproval of; find fault with; blame. [< Old French *reprover* < Late Latin *reprobare* < Latin *re-* + *probare* to test] **—re prov/er,** n. **—re prov/ing ly,** adv.

re pute (ri pyüt/), n., v., **-put ed, -put ing. —n.** 1 reputation: *a generous man by repute.* 2 good reputation. **—v.t.** suppose to be; consider; suppose: *He is reputed the richest man in the state.* [< Latin *reputare* consider < *re-* over + *putare* think]

re sil i ent (ri zil/ē ənt, ri zil/yənt), adj. 1 springing back; returning to the original form or position after being bent, compressed, or stretched: *resilient steel.* 2 readily recovering; buoyant; cheerful: *a resilient nature that throws off trouble.* [< Latin *resilientem* < *re-* back + *salire* to jump] **—re sil/i ent ly,** adv.

res o lute (rez/ə lüt), adj. 1 having a fixed resolve; determined; firm. 2 constant in pursuing a purpose; bold. [< Latin *resolutum* resolved] **—res/o lute/ly,** adv. **—res/o lute/ness,** n.

re solve (ri zolv/), v., **-solved, -solv ing,** n. **—v.t.** 1 make up one's mind; determine; decide: *resolve to do better work in the future.* 2 decide formally by vote; adopt or pass as a resolution: *It was resolved that our school should have a picnic.* 3 clear away; dispel: *The letter resolved all our doubts.* 4 clear up; explain; solve: *resolve a mystery.* **—v.i.** 1 come to a decision; decide. 2 break into parts or components. 3 (in music) progress from a dissonance to a consonance. **—n.** 1 thing determined on. 2 firmness in carrying out a purpose; determination. [< Latin *resolvere* < *re-un-* + *solvere* to loosen] **—re solv/a ble,** adj. **—re solv/er,** n.

re splend ent (ri splen/dənt), adj. very bright; shining; splendid: *a face resplendent with joy.* [< Latin *resplendentem* < *re-* back + *splendere* to shine] **—re splend/ent ly,** adv.

res ur rec tion (rez/ə rek/shən), n. 1 a coming to life again; rising from the dead. 2 **Resurrection,** the rising again of Christ after His death and burial. 3 a being alive again after death. 4 restoration from decay, disuse, etc.; revival. [< Latin *resurrectionem* < *resurgere* rise again < *re-* + *surgere* to rise]

re trench (ri trench/), v.t. cut down or reduce (expenses, etc.). **—v.i.** reduce ex-

618

penses. [< Middle French *retrencher* < *re-* back + *trencher* to cut] —**re trench′ment,** *n.*

ret ro spect (ret′rə spekt), *n.* 1 survey of past time, events, etc.; thinking about the past. 2 **in retrospect,** when looking back. —*v.t.* think of (something past). [< Latin *retro-* back + *specere* to look]

rev e la tion (rev′ə lā′shən), *n.* 1 act of making known. 2 the thing made known: *Her true nature was a revelation to me.* [< Latin *revelationem* < *revelare* reveal]

re vere (ri vir′), *v.t.,* **-vered, -ver ing.** love and respect deeply; honor greatly; show reverence for. [< Latin *revereri* < *re-* back + *vereri* stand in awe of, fear]

re vile (ri vīl′), *v.,* **-viled, -vil ing.** —*v.t.* call bad names; abuse with words. —*v.i.* speak abusively. [< Old French *reviler* despise < *re-* again + *vil* vile] —**re vile′ment,** *n.* —**re vil′er,** *n.*

rhet or ic (ret′ər ik), *n.* 1 art of using words effectively in speaking or writing. 2 book about this art. 3 mere display in language. [< Latin *rhetorica* < Greek *rhētorikē (technē)* (art) of an orator < *rhētōr* orator]

rife (rīf), *adj.* 1 happening often; common; numerous; widespread. 2 full; abounding: *The city was rife with rumors of political corruption.* [Old English *rīfe*] —**rife′ly,** *adv.*

rif fle (rif′əl), *v.t., v.i.,* **-fled, -fling.** 1 shuffle (cards) by placing the two halves of the deck close together, bending the edges slightly, and permitting the cards to fall so that they overlap alternately and can be slid together. 2 leaf through the pages of (a book, magazine, etc.) quickly. 3 make (water) flow in riffles; form a riffle. [origin uncertain]

rive (rīv), *v.t., v.i.,* **rived, rived** or **riv en, riv ing.** tear apart; split; cleave. [< Scandinavian (Old Icelandic) *rīfa*]

rough (ruf), *adj.* not smooth; not level; not even: *rough boards, rough bark.*

ru bi cund (rü′bə kund), *adj.* reddish; ruddy. [< Latin *rubicundus* < *rubere* be red]

rud dy (rud′ē), *adj.,* **-di er, -di est.** 1 red or reddish. 2 having a fresh, healthy, red look: *ruddy cheeks.* [Old English *rudig*] —**rud′di ly,** *adv.* —**rud′di ness,** *n.*

ru di ment (rü′də mənt), *n.* 1 part to be learned first; beginning: *the rudiments of grammar.* 2 something in an early stage; undeveloped or imperfect form. 3 an organ or part incompletely developed in size or structure: *the rudiments of wings on a baby chick.* [< Latin *rudimentum* < *rudis* rude, ignorant]

ru di men tar y (rü′də men′tər ē), *adj.* 1 to be learned or studied first; elementary. 2 in an early stage of development; undeveloped. —**ru′di men′tar i ly,** *adv.* —**ru′di men′tar i ness,** *n.*

rue¹ (rü), *v.,* **rued, ru ing,** *n.* —*v.t.* be sorry for; regret. —*n.* sorrow; regret. [Old English *hrēowan*]

rue² (rü), *n.* a strong-smelling, woody herb of the same family as the citrus, with yellow flowers, and bitter leaves that were formerly much used in medicine. [< Old French < Latin *ruta*]

sac ra ment (sak′rə mənt), *n.* 1 any of certain religious ceremonies of the Christian church, considered especially sacred, such as baptism. 2 Often, **Sacrament, a** the Eucharist or Holy Communion. **b** the consecrated bread and wine or the bread alone.

3 something especially sacred. [< Latin *sacramentum,* ultimately < *sacer* holy]

sa dism (sā′diz′əm, sad′iz′əm), *n.* 1 perversion marked by a love of cruelty. 2 an unnatural love of cruelty. [< French *sadisme* < Marquis de *Sade,* 1740-1814, who wrote about it]

saf fron (saf′rən), *n.* 1 an autumn crocus with purple flowers having orange-yellow stigmas. 2 an orange-yellow coloring matter obtained from the dried stigmas of this crocus. Saffron is used to color and flavor candy, drinks, etc. 3 an orange yellow. —*adj.* orange-yellow. [< Old French *safran,* ultimately < Arabic *za′farān*]

sa lute (sə lüt′), *v.,* **-lut ed, -lut ing,** *n.* —*v.t.* 1 honor in a formal manner by raising the hand to the head, by firing guns, by dipping flags, etc.: *The soldier saluted the officer.* 2 meet with kind words, a bow, a kiss, etc.; greet. 3 make a bow, gesture, or the like, to. 4 come to; meet: *Shouts of welcome saluted their ears.* —*v.i.* make a salute. —*n.* 1 act of saluting; expression of welcome, farewell, or honor. 2 position of the hand, rifle, etc., assumed in saluting. [< Latin *salutare* greet < *salus* good health] —**sa lut′er,** *n.*

sal vage (sal′vij), *n., v.,* **-vaged, -vag ing.** —*n.* 1 act of saving a ship or its cargo from wreck, capture, etc. 2 payment for saving it. 3 rescue of property from fire, flood, shipwreck, etc. 4 property salvaged: *the salvage from a shipwreck.* —*v.t.* save from fire, flood, shipwreck, etc. [< French, ultimately < Latin *salvus* safe] —**sal′vag er,** *n.*

sam u rai (sam′ù rī′), *n., pl.* **-rai.** 1 the military class in feudal Japan, consisting of the retainers of the great nobles. 2 member of this class. [< Japanese]

sas sy (sas′ē), *adj.,* **-si er, -si est.** saucy. —**sas′si ly,** *adv.* —**sas′si ness,** *n.*

sau cy (sô′sē), *adj.,* **-ci er, -ci est.** 1 showing lack of respect; impudent; rude. 2 pert; smart: *a saucy hat.* [< *sauce*] —**sau′ci ly,** *adv.* —**sau′ci ness,** *n.*

saun ter (sôn′tər, sän′tər), *v.i.* walk along slowly and happily; stroll: *saunter in the park.* —*n.* 1 a leisurely or careless gait. 2 a stroll. [origin uncertain] —**saun′ter er,** *n.*

sa vant (sə vänt′, sav′ənt), *n.* man of learning; sage; scholar. [< French, present participle of *savoir* know < Latin *sapere* be wise]

sa vor (sā′vər), *n.* 1 a taste or smell; flavor: *The soup has a savor of onion.* 2 a distinctive quality; noticeable trace: *There is a savor of conceit in what she says.* —*v.t.* 1 enjoy the savor of; perceive or appreciate by taste or smell: *We savored the soup.* 2 give flavor to; season. 3 show traces of the presence or influence of: *Bad manners savor a bad education.* —*v.i.* 1 taste or smell (*of*): *That sauce savors of lemon.* 2 have the quality or nature (*of*): *a request that savors of a command.* Also, BRITISH **savour.** [< Old French < Latin *sapor,* related to *sapere* to taste, be wise] —**sa′vor er,** *n.* —**sa′vor less,** *adj.*

scab (skab), *n., v.,* **scabbed, scab bing.** —*n.* 1 crust that forms over a sore or wound as it heals. 2 INFORMAL. workman who will not join a labor union or who takes a striker's job. 3 SLANG. rascal; scoundrel. —*v.i.* 1 become covered with a scab. 2 INFORMAL. act or work as a scab. [< Scandinavian (Danish) *skab*]

scan dal (skan′dl), *n.* 1 a shameful action, condition, or event that brings disgrace or shocks public opinion: *unearth a scandal in the government.* 2 damage to reputation;

hat, āge, fär; let, ēqual, tėrm;
it, īce; hot, ōpen, ôrder;
oil, out; cup, pùt, rüle;
ch, child; ng, long; sh, she;
th, thin; ᴛʜ, then; zh, measure;

ə represents *a* in about, *e* in taken,
i in pencil, *o* in lemon, *u* in circus.

< = from, derived from, taken from.

disgrace. 3 public talk about a person that will hurt his reputation; evil gossip; slander. 4 **be the scandal of,** scandalize. [< Latin *scandalum* < Greek *skandalon* trap]

scav enge (skav′ənj), *v.,* **-enged, -eng ing.** —*v.t.* 1 remove dirt and rubbish from. 2 pick over (discarded objects) for things to use or sell. —*v.i.* 1 be a scavenger. 2 undergo scavenging. [< *scavenger*]

schiz oid (skit′soid, skiz′oid), *adj.* having or tending toward schizophrenia. —*n.* person who has, or tends toward, schizophrenia.

schiz o phre ni a (skit′sə frē′nē ə, skit′-sə frē′nyə; skiz′ə frē′nē ə, skiz′ə frē′nyə), *n.* form of psychosis characterized by dissociation from the environment and deterioration of personality. [< New Latin < Greek *schizein* to split + *phrēn* mind]

scorch (skôrch), *v.t.* 1 burn slightly; burn on the outside of: *The cake tastes scorched.* 2 dry up; wither: *grass scorched by the sun.* 3 criticize with burning words. —*v.i.* 1 be or become scorched. 2 INFORMAL. drive or ride very fast. —*n.* a slight burn. [origin uncertain]

scorn (skôrn), *v.t.* 1 look down upon; think of as mean or low; despise: *scorn sneaks and liars.* 2 reject or refuse as low or wrong: *The judge scorned to take a bribe.* —*n.* 1 a feeling that a person, animal, or act is mean or low; contempt. 2 person, animal, or thing that is scorned or despised. [< Old French *escarnir;* of Germanic origin] —**scorn′er,** *n.*

scourge (skėrj), *n., v.,* **scourged, scourg ing.** —*n.* 1 a whip; lash. 2 any means of punishment. 3 some thing or person that causes great trouble or misfortune. Formerly, an outbreak of disease was called a scourge. —*v.t.* 1 whip; flog; punish severely. 2 trouble very much; afflict; torment. [< Old French *escorge,* ultimately < Latin *ex-* out + *corium* a hide] —**scourg′er,** *n.*

scowl (skoul), *v.i.* 1 look angry or sullen by lowering the eyebrows; frown. 2 have a gloomy or threatening aspect. —*v.t.* 1 affect by scowling. 2 express with a scowl. —*n.* an angry, sullen look; frown. [Middle English *skoulen*] —**scowl′er,** *n.*

scru ti nize (skrüt′n īz), *v.t.,* **-nized, -niz ing.** examine closely; inspect carefully: *The jeweler scrutinized the diamond for flaws.* —**scru′ti niz′er,** *n.* —**scru′ti niz′ing ly,** *adv.*

seep (sēp), *v.i.* leak slowly; trickle; ooze. [Old English *sipian*]

sen su al i ty (sen′shü al′ə tē), *n., pl.* **-ties.** 1 sensual nature. 2 a liking for the pleasures of the senses.

sen ti ment (sen′tə mənt), *n.* 1 mixture of thought and feeling. Admiration, patriotism, and loyalty are sentiments. 2 feeling, especially refined or tender feeling. 3 thought or saying that expresses feeling. 4 a mental attitude. 5 personal opinion. [< Late Latin *sentimentum* < Latin *sentire* to feel]

sen ti men tal i ty (sen′tə men tal′ə tē), *n.,*

pl. **-ties.** 1 tendency to be influenced by sentiment rather than reason. 2 excessive indulgence in sentiment. 3 feeling expressed too openly or sentimentally.

se pul chral (sə pul′krəl), *adj.* 1 of sepulchers or tombs. 2 of burial: *sepulchral ceremonies.* 3 deep and gloomy; dismal; suggesting a tomb: *sepulchral darkness.* —**se pul′chral ly,** *adv.*

serge (sėrj), *n.* kind of fabric having diagonal lines or ridges on its surface. [< Old French *sarge* < Latin *serica (vestis)* silken (garment) < Greek *sērikē* < *Sēres* the Chinese]

shab by (shab′ē), *adj.,* **-bi er, -bi est.** 1 much worn: *This old suit looks shabby.* 2 wearing old or much worn clothes. 3 poor or neglected; run-down: *a shabby old house.* 4 not generous; mean; unfair: *a shabby way to treat an old friend.* [< obsolete *shab* scab, Old English *sceabb*] —**shab′bi ly,** *adv.* —**shab′bi ness,** *n.*

shal low (shal′ō), *adj.* 1 not deep: *shallow water, a shallow dish.* 2 lacking depth of thought, knowledge, feeling, etc.: *a shallow mind, a shallow person.* [Middle English *shalowe*] —**shal′low ly,** *adv.* —**shal′low ness,** *n.*

sham ble (sham′bəl), *v.,* **-bled, -bling,** *n.* —*v.i.* walk awkwardly or unsteadily: *shamble across the room.* —*n.* a shambling walk. [probably special use of *shamble,* singular of obsolete *shambles* benches; with reference to the straddling legs of a bench]

shard (shärd), *n.* 1 piece of broken earthenware or pottery. 2 a broken piece; fragment. Also, **sherd.** [Old English *sceard*]

shoat (shōt), *n.* a young pig that no longer suckles. Also, **shote.** [origin uncertain]

shrewd (shrüd), *adj.* 1 having a sharp mind; showing a keen wit; clever. 2 keen; sharp. 3 mean; mischievous: *a shrewd turn.* [earlier *shrewed* bad-tempered, shrewish; wicked < *shrew*] —**shrewd′ly,** *adv.* —**shrewd′ness,** *n.*

shud der (shud′ər), *v.i.* tremble with horror, fear, cold, etc.: *shudder at the sight of a snake.* —*n.* a trembling; quivering. [Middle English *shodderen*] —**shud′der ing ly,** *adv.*

siege (sēj), *n., v.,* **sieged, sieg ing.** —*n.* 1 the surrounding of a fortified place by enemy forces trying to capture it; a besieging or a being besieged. 2 any long or persistent effort to overcome resistance; any long-continued attack: *a siege of illness.* 3 **lay siege to,** **a** besiege. **b** attempt to win or get by long and persistent effort. —*v.t.* besiege. [< Old French, seat, siege, ultimately < Latin *sedere* sit]

sil i ca (sil′ə kə), *n.* a common hard, white or colorless compound, silicon dioxide. Flint, opal, and sand are forms of silica. *Formula:* SiO_2 [< New Latin < Latin *silex* flint]

sin ew y (sin′yü ē), *adj.* 1 having strong sinews; strong; powerful: *sinewy arms.* 2 vigorous; forcible. 3 like sinews; having sinews; tough; stringy. —**sin′ew i ness,** *n.*

skein (skān), *n.* 1 a small, coiled bundle of yarn or thread. There are 120 yards in a skein of cotton yarn. 2 a confused tangle. [< Old French *escaigne*]

skimp (skimp), *v.t.* 1 supply in too small an amount: *Don't skimp the butter in making a cake.* 2 do imperfectly. —*v.i.* 1 be very saving or economical: *She had to skimp to send her daughter to college.* 2 do something imperfectly. [origin uncertain]

slan der (slan′dər), *n.* 1 a false statement spoken with intent to harm the reputation of another. 2 the spreading of false reports. —*v.t.* talk falsely about. —*v.i.* speak or spread slander. [< Old French *esclandre* scandal < Latin *scandalum*] —**slan′der er,** *n.*

smelt er (smel′tər), *n.* 1 person whose work or business is smelting ores or metals. 2 place where ores or metals are smelted. 3 furnace for smelting ores.

smirk (smėrk), *v.i.* smile in an affected, silly, or self-satisfied way; simper. —*n.* an affected, silly, or self-satisfied smile. [Old English *smearcian* smile]

smol der (smōl′dər), *v.i.* 1 burn and smoke without flame. 2 exist or continue in a suppressed condition. 3 show suppressed feeling. —*n.* 1 a slow, smoky burning without flame; smoldering fire. 2 a feeling of heated emotion: *a smolder of indignation.* Also, **smoulder.** [Middle English]

so journ (*v.* sō′jėrn′, sō jėrn′; *n.* sō′jėrn), *v.i.* stay for a time: *The Israelites sojourned in the land of Egypt.* —*n.* a brief stay. [< Old French *sojorner,* ultimately < Latin *sub* under + *diurnus* of the day] —**so′journ′er,** *n.*

sol ace (sol′is), *n., v.,* **-aced, -ac ing.** —*n.* 1 comfort or relief: *She found solace from her troubles in music.* 2 that which gives comfort or consolation. —*v.t.* comfort or relieve; cheer: *He solaced himself with a book.* [< Latin *solacium* < *solari* to console] —**sol′ac er,** *n.*

so phis ti cat ed (sə fis′tə kā′tid), *adj.* 1 experienced in worldly ways; lacking in natural simplicity or frankness. 2 appealing to the tastes of sophisticated people: *sophisticated humor.*

sough (suf, sou), *v.i.* make a rustling or murmuring sound. —*n.* a rustling or murmuring sound. [Old English *swōgan*]

sov er eign (sov′rən), *n.* 1 supreme ruler; king or queen; monarch. 2 person, group, or nation having supreme control or dominion; master: *sovereign of the seas.* —*adj.* 1 having the rank or power of a sovereign. 2 greatest in rank or power. 3 independent of the control of other governments. 4 above all others; supreme; greatest: *Character is of sovereign importance.* 5 very excellent or powerful. [< Old French *soverain,* ultimately < Latin *super* over] —**sov′er eign ly,** *adv.*

span ner (span′ər), *n.* BRITISH. tool for holding and turning a nut, bolt, etc.; wrench. [< German *Spanner*]

spasm (spaz′əm), *n.* 1 a sudden, abnormal, involuntary contraction of a muscle or muscles. 2 any sudden, brief fit or spell of unusual energy or activity. [< Greek *spasmos* < *span* draw up]

spas mod ic (spaz mod′ik), *adj.* 1 having to do with, like, or characterized by a spasm or spasms: *a spasmodic cough.* 2 occurring very irregularly; intermittent: *a spasmodic interest in reading.* 3 having or showing bursts of excitement. [< Greek *spasmodes* < *spasmos*] —**spas mod′i cal ly,** *adv.*

spat u la (spach′ə lə), *n.* tool with a broad, flat, flexible blade, used for mixing drugs, spreading paints or frostings, etc. [< Late Latin, diminutive of Latin *spatha* flat blade < Greek *spathē*]

spe cious (spē′shəs), *adj.* 1 seeming desirable, reasonable, or probable, but not really so; apparently good or right, but without real merit: *The teacher saw through that specious excuse.* 2 making a good outward appearance

in order to deceive: *a specious friendship, a specious flatterer.* [< Latin *speciosus* < *species* appearance, sort] —**spe′cious ly,** *adv.* —**spe′cious ness,** *n.*

spoor (spür), *n.* trail of a wild animal; track. —*v.t., v.i.* track by or follow a spoor. [< Afrikaans ≤ Middle Dutch]

spright ly (sprīt′lē), *adj.,* **-li er, -li est,** *adv.* —*adj.* lively. —*adv.* in a sprightly manner. Also, **spritely.** [< *spright,* variant of *sprite*] —**spright′li ness,** *n.*

spur (spėr), *n., v.,* **spurred, spur ring.** —*n.* 1 ridge sticking out from or smaller than the main body of a mountain or mountain range. 2 any short branch: *a spur of a railroad.* 3 brace, especially one strengthening a post. 4 **on the spur of the moment,** on a sudden impulse. [Old English *spura*] —**spur′like′,** *adj.*

squall (skwôl), *n.* 1 a sudden, violent gust of wind, often with rain, snow, or sleet. 2 INFORMAL. disturbance or commotion; trouble. —*v.i.* undergo or give rise to a squall. [apparently related to Swedish *skval* sudden rush of water]

squal or (skwol′ər), *n.* 1 misery and dirt; filth. 2 quality or condition of being morally squalid. [< Latin]

stac ca to (stə kä′tō), *adj.* 1 (in music) with breaks between the successive tones; disconnected; detached. 2 abrupt: *a staccato manner.* —*adv.* in a staccato manner. [< Italian, literally, detached]

stag nant (stag′nənt), *adj.* 1 not running or flowing: *stagnant air, stagnant water.* 2 foul from standing still: *a stagnant pool of water.* 3 not active; sluggish; dull: *During the summer, business is often stagnant.* [< Latin *stagnantem*] —**stag′nant ly,** *adv.*

stal wart (stôl′wərt), *adj.* 1 strongly built; sturdy; robust. 2 strong and brave; valiant. 3 firm; steadfast. —*n.* 1 a stalwart person. 2 a loyal supporter of a political party. [Old English *stælwierthe* serviceable < *stathol* position + *wierthe* worthy] —**stal′wart ly,** *adv.* —**stal′wart ness,** *n.*

staunch (stônch, stänch), *adj.* 1 strong or firm: *a staunch defense.* 2 loyal; steadfast: *a staunch supporter of the law.* [< Middle French *estanche* < *estanchier* to stop, hinder] —**staunch′ly,** *adv.* —**staunch′ness,** *n.*

sten to ri an (sten tôr′ē ən, sten tōr′ē ən), *adj.* very loud or powerful in sound: *a stentorian voice.*

stint (stint), *v.t.* keep on short allowance; be saving or careful in using or spending; limit: *The parents stinted themselves of food to give it to their children.* —*v.i.* be saving; get along on very little. —*n.* 1 limit; limitation: *give without stint.* 2 amount or share set aside. 3 task assigned: *Washing the breakfast dishes was her daily stint.* [Old English *styntan* to blunt] —**stint′er,** *n.* —**stint′ing ly,** *adv.*

stoke (stōk), *v.,* **stoked, stok ing.** —*v.t.* 1 poke, stir up, and feed (a fire). 2 tend the fire of (a furnace or boiler). —*v.i.* tend a fire. **stoke up,** **a** get or supply with fuel: *Stoke up the furnace.* **b** stir up: *stoke up hate.* **c** prepare. [< *stoker*]

strait (strāt), *n.* 1 a narrow channel connecting two larger bodies of water. 2 **straits,** *pl.* difficulty; need; distress: *be in desperate straits for money.* [< Old French *estreit* < Latin *strictum* drawn tight] —**strait′ly,** *adv.* —**strait′ness,** *n.*

strat a gem (strat′ə jəm), *n.* scheme or trick for deceiving an enemy; trickery. [< Greek *stratēgēma* < *stratēgein* be a general < *stratēgos* general]

strip ling (strip′ling), *n.* boy just coming into manhood; youth; lad. [< *strip* + *-ling*]

stroll (strōl), *v.i.* 1 take a quiet walk for pleasure; walk. 2 go from place to place: *strolling gypsies.* —*v.t.* stroll along or through. —*n.* a leisurely walk. [origin uncertain]

strop (strop), *n., v.,* **stropped, strop ping.** —*n.* a leather strap used for sharpening razors. —*v.t.* sharpen on a strop. [Old English < Latin *stroppus* band < Greek *strophos*]

stunt (stunt), *v.t.* check in growth or development: *Lack of proper food stunts a child.* [earlier sense "to confound" < Middle English and Old English *stunt* foolish]

sub-, *prefix.* 1 under; below: *Subnormal = below normal.* 2 down; further; again: *Subdivide = divide again.* 3 near; nearly: *Subtropical = nearly tropical.* 4 lower; subordinate: *Subcommittee = a lower or subordinate committee.* 5 resulting from further division: *Subsection = section resulting from further division of something.* 6 slightly; somewhat: *Subacid = slightly acid.* [< Latin *sub* under, beneath]

sub ser vi ent (səb sėr′vē ənt), *adj.* slavishly polite and obedient; tamely submissive; servile. —**sub ser′vi ent ly,** *adv.*

sub side (səb sīd′), *v.i.,* **-sid ed, -sid ing.** 1 grow less; die down; become less active; abate: *The storm finally subsided.* 2 sink to a lower level: *After the rain stopped, the flood waters subsided.* [< Latin *subsidere* < *sub-* down + *sidere* settle]

suc cor (suk′ər), *n.* person or thing that helps or assists; help; aid. —*v.t.* help, assist, or aid (a person, etc.). Also, BRITISH **succour.** [< Old French *sucurs,* ultimately < Latin *succurrere* run to help < *sub-* up to + *currere* to run] —**suc′cor er,** *n.*

sulk y (sul′kē), *adj.,* **sulk i er, sulk i est,** *n., pl.* **sulk ies.** —*adj.* silent and bad-humored because of resentment; sullen. —*n.* a light one-horse carriage with two wheels, for one person, now commonly used in trotting races. [origin uncertain] —**sulk′i ly,** *adv.* —**sulk′i ness,** *n.*

super-, *prefix.* 1 over; above: *Superimpose = impose over or above.* 2 besides; further: *Superadd = add besides or further.* 3 in high proportion; to excess; exceedingly: *Superabundant = abundant to excess.* 4 surpassing: *Supernatural = surpassing the natural.* [< Latin *super* over, above]

su per fi cial (sü′pər fish′əl), *adj.* 1 of the surface: *superficial measurement.* 2 on the surface; at the surface: *His burns were superficial and soon healed.* 3 concerned with or understanding only what is on the surface; not thorough; shallow: *superficial knowledge.* 4 not real or genuine: *superficial friendship.* [< Latin *superficialis* < *superficies* surface < *super-* above + *facies* form] —**su′per fi′cial ly,** *adv.* —**su′per fi′cial ness,** *n.*

su per sti tion (sü′pər stish′ən), *n.* 1 an unreasoning fear of what is unknown or mysterious; unreasoning expectation. 2 belief or practice founded on ignorant fear or mistaken reverence: *A common superstition considers 13 an unlucky number.* [< Latin *superstitionem,* originally, a standing over, as in wonder or awe < *super-* above + *stare* to stand]

su per vise (sü′pər vīz), *v.t.,* **-vised, -vising.** look after and direct (work or workers, a process, etc.); superintend; manage: *Study halls are supervised by teachers.* [< Medieval Latin *supervisum* overseen < Latin *super-* over + *videre* to see]

---

sup ple (sup′əl), *adj.,* **-pler, -plest,** *v.,* **-pled, -pling.** —*adj.* 1 bending or folding easily: *supple leather.* 2 moving easily or nimbly: *a supple dancer.* 3 readily adaptable to different ideas, circumstances, people, etc.; yielding: *a supple mind.* —*v.t., v.i.* make or grow supple. [< Old French *souple* < Latin *supplex* submissive < *supplicare* bend down, supplicate] —**sup′ple ly,** *adv.* —**sup′ple ness,** *n.*

sup pli cate (sup′lə kāt), *v.,* **-cat ed, -cat ing.** —*v.t.* beg humbly and earnestly: *supplicate a judge to pardon someone.* —*v.i.* pray humbly. [< Latin *supplicatum* bent down, suppliant < *sub-* down + *plicare* to bend] —**sup′pli cat′ing ly,** *adv.* —**sup′plica′tor,** *n.*

sup pli ca tion (sup′lə kā′shən), *n.* 1 a supplicating. 2 Usually, **supplications,** *pl.* a humble prayer addressed to God or a deity.

surge (sėrj), *v.,* **surged, surg ing,** *n.* —*v.i.* 1 rise and fall; move like waves: *A great wave surged over us. The crowd surged through the streets.* 2 rise or swell (up) violently or excitedly, as feelings, thoughts, etc. —*n.* 1 a swelling wave; sweep or rush of waves. 2 something like a wave: *A surge of anger swept over him.* [ultimately < Latin *surgere* rise < *sub-* up + *regere* to reach]

sur ly (sėr′lē), *adj.,* **-li er, -li est.** bad-tempered and unfriendly; rude; gruff: *They got a surly answer from the grouchy old man.* [Middle English *sirly,* perhaps < *sir* lord] —**sur′li ness,** *n.*

sur veil lance (sər vā′ləns, sər vā′lyəns), *n.* 1 watch kept over a person: *keep a suspected criminal under close surveillance.* 2 supervision. [< French < *sur-* over + *veiller* to watch]

sus cep ti ble (sə sep′tə bəl), *adj.* 1 easily influenced by feelings or emotions; very sensitive: *Poetry appealed to his susceptible nature.* 2 **susceptible to,** easily affected by; liable to; open to: *Vain people are susceptible to flattery.* [< Late Latin *susceptibilis,* ultimately < Latin *sub-* up + *capere* to take] —**sus cep′ti ble ness,** *n.* —**sus cep′ti bly,** *adv.*

swale (swāl), *n.* a low, wet piece of land; low place. [Middle English]

swathe (swāʁH), *v.,* **swathed, swath ing,** *n.* —*v.t.* 1 wrap up closely or fully: *swathed in a blanket.* 2 bind, wrap, or bandage. 3 envelop or surround like a wrapping: *White clouds swathed the mountain.* —*n.* a wrapping; bandage. [Old English *swathian*]

syn the size (sin′thə sīz), *v.t.,* **-sized, -sizing.** 1 combine into a complex whole. 2 make up by combining parts or elements. 3 treat synthetically. —**syn′the siz′er,** *n.*

tab leau (tab′lō), *n., pl.* **-leaux** (-lōz), **-leaus.** 1 a striking scene; picture. 2 representation of a picture, statue, scene, etc., by a person c group posing in appropriate costume. [< French, diminutive of *table* table]

ta bor, also **ta bour** (tā′bər), *n.* a small drum, used especially by persons playing a pipe or fife to accompany themselves. —*v.i.* beat or play on a tabor. [< Old French *tabour* < Persian *tabir*] —**ta′bor er,** *n.*

tac it (tas′it), *adj.* 1 implied or understood without being openly expressed; implicit: *His eating the food was a tacit confession that he liked it.* 2 unspoken; silent: *a tacit prayer.* [< Latin *tacitum* < *tacere* be silent] —**tac′it ly,** *adv.* —**tac′it ness,** *n.*

---

hat, āge, fär; let, ēqual, term; it, īce; hot, ōpen, ôrder; oil, out; cup, put, rüle; ch, child; ng, long; sh, she; th, thin; ʁH, then; zh, measure;

ə represents *a* in about, *e* in taken, *i* in pencil, *o* in lemon, *u* in circus.

< = from, derived from, taken from.

---

taint (tānt), *n.* 1 a stain or spot; trace of decay, corruption, or disgrace. 2 a cause of any such condition; contaminating or corrupting influence. —*v.t.* give a taint to; spoil, corrupt, or contaminate. —*v.i.* become tainted; decay. [< Old French *teint,* past participle of *teindre* to dye < Latin *tingere*] —**taint′less,** *adj.*

tal is man (tal′i smən, tal′iz mən), *n., pl.* **-mans.** 1 stone, ring, etc., engraved with figures or characters supposed to have magic power; charm. 2 anything that acts as a charm. [< French < Arabic *tilsam* < Greek *telesma* initiation into the mysteries < *telein* perform]

ta ma le (tə mä′lē), *n.* a Mexican food made of corn meal and minced meat. [< Mexican Spanish < Nahuatl *tamalli*]

tam bour (tam′bür), *n.* drum. [< French < Arabic *tanbūr*]

tan ta mount (tan′tə mount), *adj.* equivalent: *The withdrawal of his statement is tantamount to an apology.* [< Anglo-French *tant amunter* amount to as much]

ta per (tā′pər), *v.i.* 1 become gradually narrower toward one end: *The church spire tapers off to a point.* 2 grow less gradually; diminish. —*v.t.* make gradually narrower toward one end. —*adj.* becoming smaller toward one end. —*n.* 1 a gradual narrowing in width or girth. 2 a gradual decrease of force, capacity, etc. 3 figure that tapers to a point; slender cone or pyramid; spire. 4 a very slender candle. 5 a long wick coated with wax, for lighting a candle, cigarette, etc., from an open fire. [Old English *tapor*] —**ta′per ing ly,** *adv.*

taut (tôt), *adj.* 1 tightly drawn; tense: *a taut rope.* 2 in neat condition; tidy: *a taut ship.* [Middle English *tought*] —**taut′ly,** *adv.* —**taut′ness,** *n.*

ten dril (ten′drəl), *n.* 1 a threadlike part of a climbing plant that attaches itself to something and helps support the plant. 2 something similar: *curly tendrils of hair.* [< Middle French *tendrillon*]

ten ta tive (ten′tə tiv), *adj.* 1 done as a trial or experiment; experimental: *a tentative plan.* 2 hesitating: *a tentative laugh.* [< Medieval Latin *tentativus* < Latin *tentare* to try] —**ten′ta tive ly,** *adv.* —**ten′ta tive ness,** *n.*

tes ti mo ny (tes′tə mō′nē), *n., pl.* **-nies.** 1 statement used for evidence or proof: *A witness gave testimony that the defendant was at home all day Sunday.* 2 evidence: *The pupils presented their teacher with a watch in testimony of their respect and affection.* 3 an open declaration or profession of one's faith. [< Latin *testimonium* < *testis* witness]

teth er (teʁH′ər), *n.* rope or chain for fastening an animal so that it can graze or move only within a certain limit. —*v.t.* fasten or confine with or as with a tether. [< Scandinavian (Old Icelandic) *tjothr*]

621

thews (thüz), *n.pl.* 1 muscles. 2 sinews. 3 bodily force; might; strength. [Old English *thēaw* habit]

throe (thrō), *n.* 1 a violent pang; great pain. 2 **throes,** *pl.* **a** anguish; agony. **b** a desperate struggle; violent disturbance. [Middle English *throwe*]

tick ing (tik′ing), *n.* a strong cotton or linen fabric, used to cover mattresses and pillows and to make tents and awnings.

tol er ant (tol′ər ənt), *adj.* 1 willing to let other people do as they think best; willing to endure beliefs and actions of which one does not approve. 2 able to endure or resist the action of a drug, poison, etc. —**tol′- er ant ly,** *adv.*

tor por (tôr′pər), *n.* 1 torpid condition or quality; apathy; lethargy. 2 absence or suspension of movement or feeling, as of a hibernating animal. [< Latin < *torpere* be numb]

tor rent (tôr′ənt, tor′ənt), *n.* 1 a violent, rushing stream of water. 2 a heavy downpour: *The rain came down in torrents.* 3 any violent, rushing stream; flood: *a torrent of abuse.* [< Latin *torrentem* boiling, parching]

traipse (trāps), *v.i.,* **traipsed, traips ing,** *n.* INFORMAL. walk about aimlessly, carelessly, or needlessly. [origin unknown]

tram ple (tram′pəl), *v.,* **-pled, -pling,** *n.* —*v.t.* 1 tread heavily on; crush: *The herd of wild cattle trampled the farmer's crops.* 2 treat cruelly, harshly, or scornfully. 3 **trample on** or **trample upon,** treat cruelly, harshly, or scornfully: *The dictator trampled on the rights of his people.* —*v.i.* tread or walk heavily; stamp. —**tram′pler,** *n.*

trans act (tran zakt′, tran sakt′), *v.t.* attend to; manage; do; carry on (business): *transact business with stores all over the country.* —*v.i.* carry on business; deal. [< Latin *transactum* driven through, accomplished < *trans-* through + *agere* to drive]

trans it (tran′sit, tran′zit), *n.* 1 a passing across or through. 2 a carrying or a being carried across or through: *The goods were damaged in transit.* 3 transportation by trains, buses, etc.: *All systems of transit are crowded during the rush hour.* 4 transition or change. [< Latin *transitus* < *transire* pass through < *trans-* + *ire* go]

trans lu cent (tran slü′snt, tranz lü′snt), *adj.* letting light through without being transparent: *Frosted glass is translucent.* [< Latin *translucentem* < *trans-* through + *lucere* to shine] —**trans lu′cent ly,** *adv.*

trau ma (trô′mə, trou′mə), *n., pl.* **-mas, -ma ta** (-mə tə). 1 a wound or other external body injury. 2 an emotional shock which has a lasting effect on the mind. 3 an abnormal physical or mental condition produced by a wound, injury, or shock. [< Greek, wound]

trav erse (trav′ərs, trə vėrs′), *v.,* **-ersed, -ers ing.** —*v.t.* 1 pass across, over, or through: *We traversed the desert.* 2 go to and fro over or along (a place, etc.); cross. 3 ski or climb diagonally across. 4 read, examine, or consider carefully. 5 move sideways; turn from side to side. 6 turn (a cannon, etc.) to the right or left. 7 oppose; hinder; thwart. —*v.i.* 1 move back and forth: *That horse traverses.* 2 turn on or as if on a pivot; swivel. 3 ski in a diagonal course. [< Old French *traverser* < Late Latin *transversare* < Latin *transversum* transverse.] —**trav′ers a ble,** *adj.* —**trav′ers er,** *n.*

treach er ous (trech′ər əs), *adj.* 1 not to be trusted; not faithful; disloyal: *The treacherous soldier carried reports to the enemy.* 2 having a false appearance of strength, security, etc.; not reliable; deceiving: *This ice is treacherous.* —**treach′er ous ly,** *adv.* —**treach′er ous ness,** *n.*

trel lis (trel′is), *n.* frame of light strips of wood or metal crossing one another with open spaces in between; lattice, especially one supporting growing vines. [< Old French *trelis,* ultimately < Latin *trilix* triple-twilled < *tri-* three + *licium* thread]

trib une (trib′yün), *n.* 1 in ancient Rome: an official chosen by the plebeians to protect their rights and interests from arbitrary action by the patricians. 2 any defender of the rights and interests of the people. [< Latin *tribunus* < *tribus* tribe]

tri um vir ate (trī um′vər it, trī um′və rāt′), *n.* 1 government by three men together. 2 any association of three in office or authority. 3 position or term of office of a Roman triumvir. 4 any group of three.

tur ban (tėr′bən), *n.* 1 scarf wound around the head or around a cap, worn by men in parts of India and in some other countries of Asia. 2 any headdress like this, such as a big handkerchief tied around the head. 3 a small hat with little or no brim, worn by women and children. [< Middle French *turbant* < Turkish *tülbend*]

tur ret (tėr′it), *n.* 1 a small tower, often on the corner of a building. 2 any of various low, rotating, armored structures within which guns are mounted, as in a warship or tank. [< Old French *touret,* ultimately < Latin *turris* tower]

twine (twīn), *n., v.,* **twined, twin ing.** —*n.* 1 a strong thread or string made of two or more strands twisted together. 2 a twisting; twisting together. 3 a twisted thing; twist; tangle. —*v.i.* 1 wind or wrap around: *The vine twines around the tree.* 2 extend or proceed in a winding manner; meander. [Old English *twīn*]

tym pa num (tim′pə nəm), *n., pl.* **-nums, -na** (-nə). 1 eardrum. 2 middle ear. [< Latin, drum < Greek *tympanon*]

ty rant (tī′rənt), *n.* 1 person who uses his power cruelly or unjustly. 2 a cruel or unjust ruler; cruel master. 3 an absolute ruler, as in ancient Greece, owing his office to usurpation. [< Old French < Latin *tyrannus* < Greek *tyrannos*]

un-[1], *prefix.* not ____; the opposite of ____: *Unequal = not equal; the opposite of equal. Unchanged = not changed. Unjust = not just.* [Old English]

un-[2], *prefix.* do the opposite of ____; do what will reverse the act: *Unfasten = do the opposite of fasten. Uncover = do the opposite of cover.* [Old English *un-, on-*]

u nan i mous (yü nan′ə məs), *adj.* 1 in complete accord or agreement; agreed: *They were unanimous in their wish to go home.* 2 characterized by or showing complete accord: *She was elected president of her class by a unanimous vote.* [< Latin *unanimus* < *unus* one + *animus* mind] —**u nan′- i mous ly,** *adv.* —**u nan′i mous ness,** *n.*

un can ny (un kan′ē), *adj.* 1 strange and mysterious; weird: *The trees took uncanny shapes in the darkness.* 2 so far beyond what is normal or expected as to have some special power: *an uncanny knack for solving riddles.* —**un can′ni ly,** *adv.* —**un can′ni ness,** *n.*

un e quiv o cal (un′i kwiv′ə kəl), *adj.* clear; plain: *an unequivocal refusal.* —**un′- e quiv′o cal ly,** *adv.* —**un′e quiv′- o cal ness,** *n.*

un in tel li gi ble (un′in tel′ə jə bəl), *adj.* not intelligible; not able to be understood. —**un′in tel′li gi ble ness,** *n.* —**un′in tel′- li gi bly,** *adv.*

un ob tru sive (un′əb trü′siv), *adj.* not obtrusive; modest; inconspicuous. —**un′- ob tru′sive ly,** *adv.* —**un′ob tru′- sive ness,** *n.*

un scathed (un skāᵺd′), *adj.* not harmed; uninjured.

un tram meled or **un tram melled** (un tram′əld), *adj.* not hindered; not restrained; free.

u to pi a or **U to pi a** (yü tō′pē ə), *n.* 1 an ideal place or state with perfect laws. 2 a visionary, impractical system of political or social perfection. [< *Utopia,* an ideal commonwealth described by Sir Thomas More < Greek *ou* not + *topos* place]

va grant (vā′grənt), *n.* 1 an idle wanderer; tramp. 2 wanderer. —*adj.* 1 moving in no definite direction or course; wandering: *vagrant thoughts.* 2 wandering without proper means of earning a living. 3 of or having to do with a vagrant. [origin uncertain] —**va′grant ly,** *adv.*

vague (vāg), *adj.,* **va guer, va guest.** 1 not definitely or precisely expressed: *a vague statement.* 2 indefinite; indistinct: *a vague feeling.* 3 indistinctly seen or perceived; obscure; hazy: *In a fog everything looks vague.* 4 lacking clarity or precision: *a vague personality.* [< Old French < Latin *vagus* wandering] —**vague′ly,** *adv.* —**vague′ness,** *n.*

van quish (vang′kwish, van′kwish), *v.t.* 1 conquer, defeat, or overcome in battle or conflict. 2 overcome or subdue by other than physical means: *vanquish fear.* [< Old French *vainquiss-,* a form of *vainquir* vanquish < Latin *vincere*] —**van′quish a ble,** *adj.* —**van′quish er,** *n.*

vaunt (vônt, vänt), *v.t.* boast of. —*v.i.* brag or boast. —*n.* a boasting assertion or speech; brag. [< Old French *vanter* < Late Latin *vanitare* be vain, boast < *vanus* vain] —**vaunt′er,** *n.* —**vaunt′ing ly,** *adv.*

ven e rate (ven′ə rāt′), *v.t.,* **-rat ed, -rat ing.** regard with deep respect; revere: *He venerates his father's memory.* [< Latin *veneratum* revered < *Venus* Venus, originally, love] —**ven′e ı a′tor,** *n.*

venge ance (ven′jəns), *n.* 1 punishment in return for a wrong; revenge: *swear vengeance against an enemy.* 2 **with a vengeance, a** with great force or violence. **b** extremely. **c** much more than expected. [< Old French < *vengier* avenge < Latin *vindicare* < *vindex* avenger]

ven i son (ven′ə sən, ven′ə zən), *n.* 1 the flesh of a deer, used for food; deer meat. 2 (formerly) the flesh of any animal killed by hunting. [< Old French *venesoun* < Latin *venationem* a hunting < *venari* to hunt]

ver dict (vėr′dikt), *n.* 1 the decision of a jury: *The jury returned a verdict of "Not guilty."* 2 any decision or judgment. [< Anglo-French *verdit* < Old French *ver* true + *dit* spoken]

ver dure (vėr′jər), *n.* 1 fresh greenness. 2 a fresh growth of green grass, plants, or leaves. [< Old French *verd* green < Latin *viridis* < *virere* be green]

ver i fy (ver′ə fī), *v.t.,* **-fied, -fy ing.** 1 prove to be true; confirm: *The driver's report of the accident was verified by eyewitnesses.* 2 test the correctness of; check for accuracy: *You can verify the spelling of a word by looking in a dictionary.* [< Old French *verifier* < Medieval Latin *verificare* < Latin *verus* true + *facere* to make] —**ver′i fi′er,** *n.*

ves ti bule (ves′tə byül), *n.* 1 passage or hall between the outer door and the inside of a building. 2 the enclosed platform and entrance at the end of a railroad passenger car. [< Latin *vestibulum*]

vest ment (vest′mənt), *n.* 1 garment worn by a clergyman in performing sacred duties. 2 garment, especially a robe or gown, worn by an official on a ceremonial occasion. 3 something that covers as a garment; covering: *the green vestment of the meadow.* [< Latin *vestis* garment]

vi brate (vī′brāt), *v.,* **-brat ed, -brat ing.** —*v.i.* 1 move rapidly to and fro: *A piano string vibrates and makes a sound when a key is struck.* 2 be moved; quiver. 3 vacillate. 4 thrill: *Their hearts vibrated to the speaker's stirring appeal.* 5 resound: *The clanging vibrated in my ears.* —*v.t.* 1 cause to move to and fro, especially with a quick motion; set in vibration. 2 measure by moving to and fro: *A pendulum vibrates seconds.* [< Latin *vibratum* shaken]

vi cious (vish′əs), *adj.* 1 evil; wicked: *The criminal led a vicious life.* 2 having bad habits or a bad disposition; fierce; savage: *a vicious horse.* 3 spiteful; malicious: *vicious words.* 4 INFORMAL. unpleasantly severe: *a vicious headache.* 5 not correct; having faults: *This argument contains vicious reasoning.* [< Old French *vicieux* < Latin *vitiosus* < *vitium* vice] —**vi′cious ly,** *adv.* —**vi′cious ness,** *n.*

vis age (viz′ij), *n.* 1 face. 2 appearance or aspect. [< Old French < *vis* face < Latin *visus* sight < *videre* to see]

vo cif er ous (vō sif′ər əs), *adj.* loud and noisy; shouting; clamoring: *vociferous cheers.* —**vo cif′er ous ly,** *adv.* —**vo cif′er ous ness,** *n.*

voile (voil), *n.* a very thin cloth of silk, wool, cotton, etc., with an open weave, used for dresses. [< French, originally, veil < Latin *vela,* plural of *velum* covering]

vo li tion (vō lish′ən), *n.* 1 act of willing; decision or choice: *She went away of her own volition.* 2 power of willing: *The use of drugs has weakened his volition.* [< Medieval Latin *volitionem* < Latin *volo* I wish]

vol ley (vol′ē), *n., pl.* **-leys,** *v.* —*n.* 1 shower of stones, bullets, arrows, etc. 2 the discharge of a number of guns or other weapons firing missiles at once. 3 a rapid outpouring or burst of words, oaths, shouts, cheers, etc. [< Middle French *volée* flight < *voler* to fly < Latin *volare*]

vor tex (vôr′teks), *n., pl.* **-tex es** or **-ti ces.** 1 a whirling mass of water, etc., that sucks everything near it toward its center; whirlpool. 2 a violent whirl of air; cyclone; whirlwind. 3 whirl of activity or other situation from which it is hard to escape: *The two nations were unwillingly drawn into the vortex of war.* [< Latin, variant of *vertex*]

vouch safe (vouch sāf′), *v.t.,* **-safed, -safing.** be willing to grant or give; deign (to do or give): *The proud man vouchsafed no reply when we spoke to him.*

vul ner a ble (vul′nər ə bəl), *adj.* 1 that can be wounded or injured; open to attack: *Achilles was vulnerable only in his heel.* 2 sensitive to criticism, temptations, influences, etc.: *Most people are vulnerable to ridicule.* [< Late Latin *vulnerabilis* < Latin *vulnerare* to wound < *vulnus* wound] —**vul′ner a bly,** *adv.*

wam ble (wom′əl, wam′əl), *v.i.,* **-bled, -bling.** 1 feel nausea. 2 move unsteadily; stagger; totter; reel. [Middle English *wamelen*]

wasp ish (wos′pish, wôs′pish), *adj.* 1 like a wasp; like that of a wasp. 2 bad-tempered; irritable. —**wasp′ish ly,** *adv.* —**wasp′ish ness,** *n.*

wa ver (wā′vər), *v.i.* 1 move to and fro; flutter: *a wavering voice.* 2 vary in intensity; flicker: *a wavering light.* 3 be undecided; hesitate: *My choice wavered between the blue sweater and the green one.* [ultimately < *wave*] —**wa′ver er,** *n.* —**wa′ver ing ly,** *adv.*

wean (wēn), *v.t.* 1 accustom (a child or young animal) to food other than its mother's milk. 2 accustom (a person) to do without something; cause to turn away: *wean someone from a bad habit.* [Old English *wenian*]

weir (wir), *n.* 1 dam erected across a river to stop and raise the water, as for conveying a stream to a mill. 2 fence of stakes or broken branches put in a stream or channel to catch fish. 3 obstruction erected across a channel or stream to divert the water through a special opening to measure the quantity flowing. [Old English *wer*]

whelp (hwelp), *n.* 1 puppy or cub; young dog, wolf, bear, lion, tiger, etc. 2 an impudent boy or young man. —*v.i., v.t.* give birth to (whelps). [Old English *hwelp*]

hat, āge, fär; let, ēqual, tėrm;
it, īce; hot, ōpen, ôrder;
oil, out; cup, pút, rüle;
ch, child; ng, long; sh, she;
th, thin; ŦH, then; zh, measure;

ə represents *a* in about, *e* in taken,
i in pencil, *o* in lemon, *u* in circus.

< = from, derived from, taken from.

whet (hwet), *v.,* **whet ted, whet ting.** *n.* —*v.t.* 1 sharpen by rubbing: *whet a knife.* 2 make keen or eager; stimulate: *The smell of food whetted my appetite.* [Old English *hwettan*]

whorl (hwėrl, hwôrl), *n.* 1 circle of leaves or flowers round a single node or point on the stem of a plant. 2 one of the turns of a spiral shell. 3 anything that circles or turns on or around something else. A person can be identified by the whorls of his fingerprints. [Middle English *whorle,* apparently variant of *whirl*]

woe be gone (wō′bi gôn′, wō′bi gon′), *adj.* looking sad, sorrowful, or wretched. Also, **wobegone.**

worm (wėrm), *v.t.* 1 make (one's way, etc.) by creeping or crawling like a worm: *The soldier wormed his way toward the enemy's lines.* 2 work or get by persistent and secret means: *try to worm a secret out of someone, worm the truth from a person.* —*v.i.* 1 move like a worm; crawl or creep like a worm. 2 make one's way insidiously *(into).* [Old English *wyrm*]

wrack (rak), *n.* 1 wreckage; wreck. 2 ruin; destruction. 3 seaweed cast ashore by the waves or growing on the tidal seashore. 4 any of several species of brown algae. —*v.t., v.i.* wreck or be wrecked. [< Middle Dutch and Middle Low German *wrak* wreck]

wraith (rāth), *n.* 1 ghost of a person seen before or soon after his death. 2 specter; ghost. [origin uncertain]

wrest (rest), *v.t.* 1 twist, pull, or tear away with force; wrench away: *He bravely wrested the knife from his attacker.* 2 take by force: *The usurper wrested the power from the king.* 3 twist or turn from the proper meaning, use, etc. 4 obtain by persistence or persuasion; wring: *wrest a secret from someone.* [Old English *wrǣstan*] —**wrest′er,** *n.*

wrought (rôt), *adj.* 1 made: *The gate was wrought with great skill.* 2 formed with care; not rough or crude. 3 manufactured or treated; not in a raw state. 4 (of metals or metalwork) formed by hammering.

623

Index of Authors and Titles